ICONIC PLANNED COMMUNITIES
AND THE CHALLENGE OF CHANGE

THE CITY IN THE TWENTY-FIRST CENTURY

Eugenie L. Birch and Susan M. Wachter, Series Editors

A complete list of books in the series is available from the publisher.

ICONIC PLANNED COMMUNITIES AND THE CHALLENGE OF CHANGE

EDITED BY

Mary Corbin Sies

Isabelle Gournay

Robert Freestone

PENN

UNIVERSITY OF PENNSYLVANIA PRESS

Philadelphia

Published by

University of Pennsylvania Press

Philadelphia, Pennsylvania 19104-4112

www.upenn.edu/pennpress

Printed in the United States of America on acid-free paper

10 9 8 7 6 5 4 3 2 1

Library of Congress Cataloging-in-Publication Data

ISBN 978-0-8122-5114-2

CONTENTS

Plates follow page 232

INTRODUCTION

TOWARD CRITICAL RESILIENCE
IN ICONIC PLANNED COMMUNITIES

Mary Corbin Sies, Isabelle Gournay, and Robert Freestone

What happens to iconic planned communities once their glory days are over? How have they fared in navigating the inevitable challenges of growth and development, economic changes, and shifting demographics? What impact does their planning pedigree have on their viability? And what solutions or responses have stakeholders devised to preserve the key features and ideals of their purposeful designs while adapting to changing circumstances? *Iconic Planned Communities and the Challenge of Change* offers the first thoroughgoing attempt to address these questions by presenting nineteen international case studies examining the challenges that diverse iconic planned communities have faced in the decades following their initial heydays.

We conceived this collection in order to begin an international conversation on *whether* to conserve these iconic places as they evolve through time, and *how* to preserve the spirit and practical value of their innovative planning. A worldwide group of scholars brings the histories of these places up to date, reporting the ideas and strategies for preserving and building resilience in iconic planned communities in the recent past and present. By including a range of case studies on six continents, our volume encourages comparative analysis and cross-fertilization of the strategies that communities have deployed to sustain their planning legacies. Our aim is to bring prominence to these issues and to share knowledge among planners, planning historians, architects, preservationists, and local stakeholders around the globe.

We focus on some of the most iconic examples of planned residential greenfield communities constructed around the world from the early nineteenth to the late twentieth centuries. They include a spectrum of types: low-density garden suburbs, middle- to upper-middle-class enclaves and working-class communities, company towns, medium-density mixed-use developments, comprehensively planned suburbs, New Towns, and modern master-planned developments. The communities vary in terms of scale, function, private or public sponsorship, natural assets, densities, proximity to metropolitan centers, housing styles, affordability, range of amenities, governance, design philosophies, and heritage recognition and protection. They collectively illustrate an instructive set of conservation challenges, responses, and outcomes.

All of these places, when conceived, represented new departures in physical planning and in social and often political thought in their countries. Their subsequent development has tended to combine master planning that sets an overall vision with everyday efforts to change, maintain, improve, or adapt the community's distinctive features. Each community's planners designed the landscape and the built environment holistically, harnessing design to advance social goals (Gibson and Pendlebury 2009). We thus emphasize both dimensions in the phrase "planned community" to capture the physical and social plan contributing the broad framework that serves the residents. Our central proposition emerges with this understanding: both top-down (planned) and bottom-up (community) initiatives must contribute in dynamic combination to achieve ongoing livability and resilience.

Frequently planners, scholars, and tourists come to know the kinds of planned communities we feature through their iconic imagery. Such powerful and resonant representations—think of the languid sense of space conveyed in the design for Riverside, the artfully rendered Welwyn Garden City plan, or the pristine sunbelt neo-traditionalism of the Seaside streetscape—can focus attention on an idealization of planning and architecture, as if they were frozen in time. In our collection, however, the authors reveal iconic planned communities as messier, inhabited places.

Two of the editors, Mary Corbin Sies and Isabelle Gournay, reside in Greenbelt. When they began studying how this historic New Deal community near Washington, DC, had preserved the key features of its original planning, they discovered a complicated and potentially vulnerable situation (Gournay and Sies 2010). Although Greenbelt currently enjoys robust zoning protection, the city does not control its statutory or regulatory fate; the county does. Efforts to designate Greenbelt as a historic district on the United States National Register of Historic Places have not yet succeeded. The city, which has blocked the historic district nomination, has acted nonetheless to protect Greenbelt's assets. It has purchased and renovated several key properties, spruced up the landscaping of the town center, and reacquired portions of the original greenbelt. Citizens, however, have mustered the most effective form of protection to date; they have fought diligently across the decades to help shape Greenbelt's growth and preserve its key environmental and social features. An ongoing tradition of civic activism, which takes the form of steadfast loyalty to what some residents call their "Greenbelt principles," has shaped the town's enduring respect for its original planning ideas (Gournay and Sies 2010; Knepper 2001).

This is not a unique story. All the contributors to this volume report on how iconic planned communities experience and negotiate the challenges of change on the ground. If some iconic places seem timelessly two-dimensional because we have learned about them chiefly through imagery, this volume will bring readers up to date on how such communities have changed, sustained, and survived, despite threats such as burgeoning development on the one hand or damaging decline on the other, changing economic fortunes and drivers, evolving social relations, and, common to each, the passage of time. The key contribution is to assess these places created by planning from the past as they are lived now.

We present a philosophy toward conserving iconic planned communities that emphasizes the complexities of lived places undergoing change: changes in economy, society, population, culture, politics, regional context, and the built environment itself. In his study of Seaside, Steven Hurtt restates founder Robert Davis's articulation of a key dilemma that planned communities face: "How do we preserve the physical representations of our culture, place, and history, hold onto the material culture of the past, while the culture itself evolves—an evolution that inevitably changes the material culture?" (Hurtt, in this volume). Davis takes the view that most neighborhoods naturally undergo a process of "successional urbanism" (Davis 2013, 603). It is not a new concept. In 1949 the pioneering planner and preservationist Carl Feiss observed that a preservation plan "cannot survive in conflict with the growth of the place in which it is to be found nor can its development ignore the basic drives behind our dynamic society" (Feiss 1956, 4). More recently, Dennis Domer argued that freezing buildings or districts at a moment in history "misrepresents the basis of their history, which is adaptation and change over time" (2009, 95). In this collection, the contributors grapple with how to conserve the intrinsically special qualities of physical and social planning in a way that also serves the changing needs and circumstances of the people who live in iconic planned communities now (Isenstadt 2001, 41).

Resilience

We have carefully considered whether and how to characterize our preservation goals for iconic planned communities with the term *resilience*. A contested concept, resilience has a range of definitions,[1] but for our purposes, we define it in two ways: (1) the capacity of a community to experience stress or acute trauma while retaining function, structure, communal activity, and identity and/or (2) the capacity to change and adapt in order to maintain signature planning features and, therefore, identity and sense of place (McPhearson 2014, 3). Recurring stresses in the context of iconic planned communities include rising housing costs, inadequate transportation links, loss of open space, deteriorating infrastructure, development pressures, crime, adaptation to changing fashion, and community conflict. Acute traumas encompass infrastructure failures, loss of symbolic landscapes or structures, planning violations (such as highways bisecting communities), dramatic changes in political structure, and economic collapses caused by recessions or deindustrialization.[2] Resilience is a process that happens in context, where, as our case studies will show, the devil is in the details and no single formula can foster resilience in every location.

The constant contextual factor for iconic planned communities is their distinctive planning legacy, environmental and social, which effective resilience planning has to acknowledge. For that reason, we insist that preservation must become a central component of how we think about resilience,[3] despite the fact that heritage considerations are frequently omitted from discussions about planning for resilience or sustainability[4] (Kroessler 2014). In iconic planned communities, protecting heritage promotes resilience by contributing to cultural identity, social cohesion, stakeholders' sense of place, and, in some communities, economic vitality, as long as the original planning features continue to enhance livability and the needs and well-being of community members (Jigyasu 2013).

Heritage also expresses *culture*'s important role in ensuring the effectiveness and inclusiveness of resilience planning because cultural action is required to lay the groundwork for a resilient *and* sustainable community. Timon McPhearson (2014) advocates that planners link resilience to sustainability, so that the former helps communities move toward the latter aim of securing a world that can continue to provide future generations with a satisfactory quality of life. Jon Hawkes goes so far as to embrace *culture* as the "fourth pillar" of sustainability alongside economic development, ecological responsibility, and social equity. He argues that "a sustainable society depends upon a sustainable culture" with a shared sense of meaning and purpose (Hawkes 2001, 12). Cultural values and practices give a community identity, cohesiveness, and meaning; thus, the cultural pillar plays a vital role in activating a community's will to achieve sustainability. Heritage has a strong role to play in that process. According to Rohit Jigyasu, UNESCO Chair Professor at Ritsumeikan University, Kyoto, cultural heritage is increasingly instrumental in influencing the resilience and well-being of communities: "The acknowledgement and conservation of the diversity of cultural heritage, fair access to it and equitable sharing of the benefits deriving from its use enhance the feeling of place and belonging, mutual respect and sense of collective purpose, and ability to maintain a common good, which has the potential to contribute to the social cohesion of a community and reduce inequalities" (2013, 15). Many, though by no means all, iconic planned communities articulated social compacts like these in their original planning, and many scholars have pointed out how important the maintenance of cultural diversity and genuine civic engagement are for any strategy to build resilience (Jigyasu 2013; Vale 2016). With appropriate understanding and encouragement, each iconic community's planning heritage should feature prominently in its ability to mobilize action and improve the structures and functions that make it vital, livable, and adaptable to change (Jigyasu 2013).

Thus, the concept we expound here is a *critical resilience*, as Larry Vale defines the term: an approach that addresses contested questions in our communities. Who decides how to deal with stresses and traumas? Who controls the funding? Who benefits from those decisions? Which places and people suffer or get overlooked? (2016, 15). For Tom Slater, a British urban geographer, resilience and sustainability, for that matter, are pernicious buzzwords, veiling neoliberal policies that return cities to "the desired status quo of capital accumulation and elite wealth capture" while dispossessing the middle class and dislocating the poor (2014, 3). Critiques of neoliberal urban policies have relevance for iconic planned communities, some of which have seen the social equity of their original planning ethos eroded by gentrification or economic restructuring. Several contributors in this book raise troubling questions about equity, diversity, and runaway consumerism as they ponder questions such as the following: Who are the stewards overseeing heritage preservation and in whose interests are they acting? How are multiple heritages—either endemic to the design of iconic planned communities or introduced by demographic changes—preserved and interpreted? Do garden city forms, which guided many twentieth-century planned communities, still provide for equitable and livable places?

In connecting the importance of heritage preservation to contemporary well-being, social cohesion, and sustainable development, we advocate a critical resilience that provides an equitable sharing of the benefits of living. The critical resilience we envision is flexible and adaptable, and it has several components, beginning with the study and adjustment of the essential structure of the planning so that it can function accountably and continue to meet the needs of the stakeholder community today and in the future. Achieving resilience in these communities requires robust participation from stakeholder groups living or doing business there. The kind of grassroots planning needed is not tokenism toward different segments of the community but an inclusive effective engagement that mines cultural perspectives and knowledge bases as vital resources for achieving resilience. As Michele Grossman has argued, "ethnocultural diversity," and we would add class diversity, "needs to be understood and incorporated into resilience planning as an asset to be built upon or a resource to be valued and mobilized, rather than a problem to be surmounted or redressed" (2013, 9). This grassroots planning process has to grapple with assessing and adapting the community's distinctive physical and social design features inherited from the past to its present context and needs. It has to determine whether and how to embrace or adapt the cultural values and heritage of the place.

Effective critical resilience planning strives to be inclusive regarding who decides these matters and draws on community building and place-specific identity resources inherent to the original planning. Where appropriate, communities may debate how to acknowledge and provide for multiple kinds of uses, understandings of identity, and interpretations of cultural meaning and heritage. Readers will discover a range of efforts, with differing rates of success, for how communities address these components of critical resilience in the following chapters.

Idealism, Heritage, and Economic Revitalization

Besides resilience, three other lines of scholarly inquiry are relevant to this project, each with its own literature. The first is the history of the planned community as a fundamental touchstone of modern city planning's idealism. This particular genealogy (Daniels 2009; Reiner 1963) encompasses the continuous reinvention and refinement of planners' belief in the efficacy of the well-designed place through various socio-spatial expressions: from utopian communities and garden cities or suburbs to workers' towns, master-planned communities, New Towns, eco-villages, and the like. Apart from general place histories, many examples of which are cited in the case studies, scholars have analyzed the origins of these different community types, dissected their built forms, investigated their social and power structures, and assessed their livability in diverse post-occupancy studies (Grant 2006; Hall 2014; Mandelker 2010; Ward 2002). How planned places have accommodated processes of social, economic, and physical change and how these processes affected their distinctiveness as recognizably designed environments have already attracted some interest (Bartling 2007; Department for Communities and Local Government 2006; Forsyth 2005; Larkham 2004; Lee and Stabin-Nesmith 2001; Nyström and Lundström 2006; Pacione 2011; Whitehand and Carr 2001) and will be the primary focus of our collection.

A second thread centers on environmental heritage and concern with the conservation of the built environment, encompassing a range of practices such as preservation, restoration, reconstruction, and adaptation (Domer 2009; Marquis-Kyle and Walker 2004). The importance of recognizing the heritage of planned communities was identified in a seminal contribution by Carl Feiss in the 1940s. Feiss shifted preservationists' attention toward entire planned communities rather than individual buildings but lamented that "few of those communities, designed and built as complete units, have come down to us unmutilated" (Feiss 1941, 28). Another strand of this literature explores how the conservation, improvement, and utilization of existing built resources make crucial contributions to sustainable urban development in the broadest sense (Allison and Peters 2011; Gause and Franko 2007). Beyond the resilience literature, the connections among the history of planning, heritage conservation, livability, and sustainability turn out to be richly multifaceted (Avrami 2016; Longstreth 2011a; Rodwell 2007). Cultural issues remain something of a lacuna, a situation that this volume tries to remedy.

An important observation made by Feiss that has held up over time and across national borders is that few jurisdictions have effective mechanisms for preserving the key features of the master planning of *entire* communities. Part of the novelty of our book lies in a global comparative examination of how diverse places unified only by their significance in planning history have adapted to changing circumstances shaped by evolving social, political, and economic climates. The challenges they have faced are myriad: physical obsolescence for some communities and population growth pressures for others; threats to the environment; socioeconomic and demographic upheavals; declining or surging economic bases; destructive effects of infrastructure improvements, especially transportation; changes in local, regional, and national governance; and changing attitudes to conservation and protective statutes. The purity of the iconic communities celebrated in planning history textbooks has been buffeted relentlessly by broader forces of change.

Inevitably, some communities have survived and prospered, others have faltered and lost the mantle that once made them special, and most will boast a mixed conservation history. Because we are concerned with stimulating discussion and action regarding the challenges and opportunities for preservation, we have generally selected success stories, avoiding all-too-familiar worst-case scenarios and topocide (Porteous 1988). We are interested in recording constructive strategies—no matter what form they take—for the preservation of a planned community's most significant features, including their adaptation to meet the livability needs of present generations. Our intention is to inspire diverse stakeholders to inform themselves how best to harness their communities' distinctive heritage toward achieving resilience in environments of growth and change.

A third body of literature probes the relationship between preservation and economic revitalization. Preservation scholars often assume that one produces the other; the American real estate consultant Donovan D. Rypkema's *The Economics of Historic Preservation: A Community Leader's Guide* (1994) argues this close connection. More recently, however, scholars charge that little data exists to justify preservation on economic grounds. Erica Avrami (2016, 108) points out that little research has been conducted to assess "designation's impact on places and people, and on the local economy." The American urban studies scholars Stephanie Ryberg-Webster and Kelly L. Kinahan's review of this issue in 2014 turns up a range of ideas for how preservation can contribute to economic revitalization but concludes there is insufficient empirical testing of impact to date. *Iconic Planned Communities and the Challenge of Change* will not provide a definitive answer, but it joins the call that more research needs to be done to test this relationship; we insist that heritage conservation and economic strategies should be considered in relation to one another.

Planning, Architecture, and Community Building

The afterlives of iconic planned communities raise questions resonant for all communities attempting to define and maintain their connections to place and heritage and ultimately to achieve resilience in contemporary contexts fraught by economic decline, growth, changing demographics, and redevelopment. In his afterword, Bruce Stephenson suggests that "the prescience of this book was to document how residents translated their sacredness of place into a set of principles to navigate the future." Given the differences between the iconic places in this book, the varied regulatory environments and cultural traditions of their nations, and the range of challenges they face, we cannot logically present a "one-size-fits-all" set of principles to guide their planning and preservation. We aim, instead, to begin a cross-cultural conversation that draws insights from our authors about the key qualities, practices, and principles that make iconic planned communities as livable and resilient as possible for today's and tomorrow's generations.

The strongest conclusion that we derive from our chapters is our authors' observation that the quality of original planning is the single most important factor that ensures that an iconic planned community's distinctive features and livability will remain viable. Important factors for what enhances resilience, in other words, are effective planning vision, quality of design, and attention to both the social and physical fabric of the place. How has this worked? Stakeholders often say that remaining true to their community's plan and original vision makes the place livable over the long term and correlates with a well-functioning social fabric. These qualities inspire stewards to fight for their communities by supporting protective and revitalization measures to address disruptive challenges, as readers will see when perusing the case studies. Resilient iconic planned communities are more successful in managing even major changes—such as political transformations, economic distress, and population shifts—when the core features that make these locales desirable places to live stay mostly intact.

The key feature of nearly all of these places is their integration of planning, architecture, and community building. Such holistic planning poses challenges for stakeholders, especially as time goes on. How can iconic planned communities maintain their interrelated systems of place-making? To be effective, preservation and resilience strategies must be unsiloed so that they address the physical and environmental needs of a changing community along with its social, economic, cultural, and political facets (Ryberg-Webster and Kinahan 2014). In New Lanark, the Uplands, Colonel Light Gardens, Greenbelt, Tapiola, and Seaside, among other examples discussed in this book, residents, governing bodies, and local associations interweave community protections, activities to promote consciousness of heritage, civic pride and engagement, regulations such as zoning and design review, and designation, sometimes over a long period of time, in response to threats and changes. The following chapters reveal the different multiplicities of formal and informal protections that iconic planned communities produce to preserve the legacy and spirit of their holistic design. They also demonstrate the admirable interdisciplinary reach of scholarship that enables stakeholders to appreciate the complex balance of protection and revitalization that safeguards these planning legacies and makes them workable for those who inhabit them today.

Iconic planned communities, as Bruce Stephenson observes, "nurture our elemental instinct for communal life." We learn that the places most successful in fostering vital community life and civic engagement are most proactive in generating effective responses to the challenges of change. The most resilient communities link stakeholders to one another to create "more healthy and vital neighborhoods" (Gause and Franko 2007, 7). But how is that accomplished? As our authors reveal, our case studies have a mixed record on engaging residents and other stakeholders to build a resilient community capable of withstanding threats. The most successful create both the precedent and the capacity to involve local people in preservation planning and ascertain what stakeholders value in their cultural and physical environments and let that guide their heritage protection efforts (King 2011, 24). In addition, they unpack the differential impact of policies and protections on the range of income and cultural groups in the community (Vale 2016, 18). One of the most prominent patterns that our book uncovers is that once residents determine the tangible or intangible heritage they most value in their communities, they find ways to sustain it, frequently for decades.

Where community engagement is most robust, strong stewardship emerges to demand conservation of valued features in planning and architecture and to help manage the community's heritage. Stewardship can take different forms and manifest at different intensities. In Riverside, the original design and livability conferred have inspired multiple generations of residents to cherish and fight for maintenance of its iconic features. The same might be said for Colonel Light Gardens. In Japan, where mainstream culture does not highly regard preservation or provide a regulatory framework for the protection of houses, residents living in Den-en Chôfu have fostered a consensus that values the community's lush gardenlike landscaping and have maintained it over time. In Sunnyside Gardens, stewardship takes the form of democratic governance with strong citizen and municipal participation. In the garden communities of Letchworth, Hampstead Garden Suburb, and Welwyn, which benefit from designated conservation areas, private organizations are the primary stewards; they exercise planning authority and design review as they administer the respective schemes of management in place. In Greenbelt, multiple stewards—the municipality, its Department of Planning and Community Development, citizen volunteers, citizen activists, and the local newspaper—look after the town's tangible and intangible heritage. In iconic planned communities lacking local stewardship, planning can suffer and conservation can be harder to achieve.

Because our volume focuses on how iconic planned communities negotiate the challenges of change, one of our strongest contributions is a detailed comparative portrait of how this is done. As the heritage scholar Laurajane Smith argues, "Heritage is not only about the mediation of cultural and social conflicts, but is ultimately about the mediation of cultural change" (2006, 82). Our chapters should enable readers to build their knowledge about the strategies, practices, and mechanisms that places deploy to achieve their own balance between preservation and change and with what results. For example, some of our case studies depict communities that demonstrate the "capacity to change in order to maintain the same identity" (McPhearson 2014, 3). This is most dramatically the case in New Lanark where World Heritage Site designation and creative public-private partnerships have enabled the town to restore and adaptively reuse decommissioned mill buildings without sacrificing its historic legacy of labor history and social reform. Menteng's comprehensive planning, amenities, and status inspired aggressive stewardship and resourceful protection of the exclusive lifestyle the enclave was intended to provide, despite Indonesia's decolonization, Jakarta's transition to megacity status, and the suburb's racial shift in population. At the Cité Frugès, Le Corbusier's response to garden city housing, the original residents objected to the design of their units, adapting them in inharmonious ways. Over time, though, a flexible regulatory system has persuaded residents to reappropriate the radical modernist architecture, and the development is gradually returning to its original design heritage.

The details of how our case studies have accommodated change provide a range of creative strategies and resources for stakeholders in other communities. On the other hand, our collection also contains examples of excessive change, when alterations to the iconic built environment compromise the spirit of the original planning. In Römerstadt, for example, the U-bahn has bisected the community, interrupting the plan's integrity, vistas, and pedestrian mobility. In Sabaudia, the monumental city center and much of the original architecture are intact, but inadequate infrastructure and lack of growth controls over new development have stressed the town as it has transitioned from an agricultural to a more diverse economic center. These, among other, chapters analyze the lessons learned from planning failures and provide astute suggestions for accommodating their evolving circumstances while revitalizing key features of their iconic or social landscapes.

There are many preservation success stories among the garden cities and suburbs included in our chapters; the regulatory practices and mechanisms protecting these places are multilayered, resourceful, and worth studying in detail. Some communities inspired by the garden city movement raise troubling questions, however, about how we understand conservation, who it benefits, and at what point a garden city is no longer ideologically a garden city. Hampstead Garden Suburb, for example, cannot expand its territory or its density, so real estate values and gentrification have risen to the stratosphere. Wythenshawe has experienced the opposite problem as a result of multiple violations of the intended spirit of its planning: higher-density housing to accommodate people displaced by slum clearance in Manchester, highways routed through the garden city, lack of access to mass transportation, and a plague of crime, drug use, and poverty. At present, however, an infusion of resources into transportation, education, public health, housing, and policing is aimed at returning Wythenshawe to its original philosophy and architecture. Time will tell whether this community can restore the livability and communal social fabric associated with its origins. Tapiola applied the garden city idea to house a mix of Finnish citizens and housing types set in an idyllic and healthful site of field and forest. With increased urban development and departure from its original spirit, the town strives to maintain key features establishing its claim to identify as a garden city. With its transformation, Tapiola has moved from its original philosophy of anti-urbanism and anti-consumerism to a vibrant urban consumerist environment. These case studies raise questions about where one draws the line in determining whether the spirit of the original planning has been violated or sustained and whether the garden city form can provide livable towns in an era of late capitalism.

Affordability, Equity, and Rebuilding Social Fabric

Regardless of how seamless or difficult any town's adaptation to changing circumstances has become, our chapters clearly acknowledge the relentless pace and variety of challenges and opportunities that change brings in the decades after an iconic planned community's glory days. Since the Greenbelt chapter was completed in 2015, for example, five new threats or opportunities related to the city's preservation have surfaced. First, alterations have violated the design integrity of some of the iconic garden apartments. Second, the county's rewriting of its zoning code will eliminate Residential Planned Community (RPC) districts and substitute a yet unknown status, which may or may not afford the ongoing protection for Greenbelt's built environment.[5] Third, the Greenbelt Museum has acquired an adjacent unit, allowing the museum to expand its heritage presence in the community. Fourth, state officials have proposed routing a high-speed magnetic levitation train through the edge of Greenbelt. Fifth, a new voluntary preservation association is forming in response to these threats and opportunities. Greenbelt is hardly exceptional regarding the changes it is experiencing. Thus, we conclude this introduction with a call for ongoing dedication to the hard work of building resilient communities that take advantage of their heritage.

Iconic places experiencing the gravest challenges are most in need of community building and revitalization, but nearly all of our case studies could benefit from revisiting and enhancing their planning and social ideals as they engage the challenges of change. How to safeguard housing and communities earmarked for lower-income households is an important agenda item. Can iconic working-class or company towns be conserved without gentrification and displacement of residents? Measures to maintain or build affordable housing and to include industrial or service economy workers in local communal life are critical objectives and an acknowledgment that resilience requires a livable environment for all community dwellers.

Equity is a vital component of resilient communities, and it was an important premise of the social idealism that inspired many iconic planned communities. Does equity remain an important principle as these places have evolved over time and, if so, how does it manifest? There are three facets of equity important to think about. First, as Rohit Jigyasu (2013, 14) has asserted, "Cultural heritage continues to perform its irreplaceable role as a source of meaning and identity for communities and individuals. . . . Heritage is not a relic of the past, but is increasingly instrumental in steering sustainable development and the wellbeing of communities." To perform equitably, heritage conservation needs to represent and to engage all segments of the community. Second, maintaining cultural diversity into the future guarantees that communities can draw from a diverse set of cultural traditions and resources as they confront emerging challenges. This diversity principle is basic to cultural philosophies of sustainability and critical resilience; how to practice it in iconic planned communities today is one of the challenges these places face. Consequently, the third facet concerns how to engage the full range of constituents necessary to build a resilient community.

Thus, (re)establishing a robust communal social life is vital to the well-being of iconic planned communities. As we have suggested here, highly functioning social fabric helps galvanize residents to advocate for their cultural heritage and for policies that build resilience and represent everyone's interests. The Massachusetts Heritage Landscapes Inventory incorporates a participatory process of five goals that models a grassroots-driven procedure for bringing residents into important community conversations and integrating their needs and interests into any policy or political deliberations about revitalization or heritage conservation (Berg 2011, 30). We recommend it as a means of discovering what constituents value and of building community engagement from the ground up. Larry Vale's formula for cultivating critical resilience could be adapted to iconic planned communities as follows: (1) conservation of the planning and built environment; (2) restoration of a vital economy; (3) securing livability and well-being for all stakeholders, including the most vulnerable residents; and (4) making sure that governance or other community mechanisms are in place so that all categories of stakeholders can participate and be heard (2016, 19). This line of inquiry addresses the need to strengthen social fabric and generate new social ideals to safeguard and revitalize the communal life of iconic planned communities moving forward.

Our objective is to inform not only scholars but also decision makers, concerned citizens, and community advocates with findings to better frame an appreciation of both the challenges and opportunities presented for planned communities in dynamic twenty-first-century environments. We hope our book will stimulate scholars and stakeholders to recover many untold stories to engage in interdisciplinary conversations that generate ideas for addressing the challenges of affordability, equity, and rebuilding social fabric as well as many others. As advocates for critical resilience and preservation, we would also like to build greater capacity and infrastructure for international collaboration and research to address the challenges that iconic planned communities face. That might take the form of a task force to establish an international protocol for documenting the social, architectural, and planning features of these special places, for example, or convening international conferences to share research and strategies for building resilience that addresses heritage and social equity.[6] The following chapters begin this process by analyzing how twenty-three iconic planned communities are addressing the challenge of change. We hope they will build knowledge about and cross-fertilize strategies for judiciously conserving their legacies and considering how to build critical resilience.

Note on Methodology

Most of our contributors have based their observations on fieldwork and extensive, even intimate, familiarity with the built and social environment and legacy issues in their planned communities, as well as wider research across a range of primary and secondary sources. Because iconic planned communities are complex and their designers conceived them holistically—thinking through the interrelationships between so many phenomena—the analyses reported here are necessarily nuanced and inclined toward reflection on how the whole system works (or falters). Our authors variously apply the benefits of their disciplinary and multidisciplinary training to make legible distinctively different perspectives on the locales they study. This volume brings together leading scholars in architectural, art, and planning history; landscape architecture; geography; city planning and urban studies; architecture and urban design; community development; historic preservation and heritage conservation; American and Africana studies; and housing policy. The cumulative effect of their observations about how iconic planned communities make use of their planning heritage as they negotiate the challenges of change should enhance readers' grasp of the holistic thinking needed to understand how planned communities fare over time (Longstreth 2011b, 113–14).

The holism of planned communities is important to emphasize because historic preservation, at least as it is practiced in the United States, can impose a false separation between design excellence and the historic significance of places. The approach in this book tries to expunge any artificial barrier between built environments and the social, political, economic, and cultural forces through which planned communities derive much of their meaning (Longstreth 1991; Striner 1995, 28). This inevitably leads to a diverse range of considerations, including ecosystems, site planning, infrastructure, housing and landscape design, public spaces, community engagement, governance, transportation connections, responsiveness to demographic diversity, power relations, political economy, access to services, and local culture (Gause and Franko 2007). In other words, our contributors aspire to understand the important relationships between relevant components of planned communities over time—at the levels of both formal and informal planning—and be proactive in recommending priorities that enable both the character-defining features of distinctive planning and the needs and wishes of contemporary users to flourish. The complexity and interdisciplinary thinking required may be one reason heritage fields and enterprises have not yet adequately tackled the challenge of preserving and ensuring resilient holistically planned communities. That is a conversation we hope this project will animate.

A Guide for Readers

When we invited contributors to submit case studies, we asked them to address a common set of questions to facilitate learning from comparative analysis of the strengths, weaknesses, threats, and opportunities that iconic planned communities are experiencing and the strategies they are or could be forging to deal with those issues. These questions included the following:

- What are the strengths of the original physical/social planning, and how has the planning changed through time as the community has evolved physically, socially, and economically?
- What is the status of the community today?
- Which recent and current heritage issues have they faced?
- What is the nature of the regulatory environment for managing heritage-related growth and change and at what jurisdictional level (local, state, regional, national) does this occur?
- What means have these places used to maintain the key features of planning that made them special? Is it through official instruments, such as zoning, historic preservation mechanisms, and fine-grained development and environment control or by unofficial means such as grassroots community activism or resistance? What has and has not worked?
- How are special features being threatened, compromised, adapted, or conserved as the community evolves to be workable for current and future residents?
- What qualities of iconic planned communities make a place more successful in withstanding the challenges of change and growth?
- Does official designation as a landmark or historic town help or hinder the preservation of an iconic planned community and how?

In our nineteen case study chapters, leading scholars analyze twenty-three planned communities with reference to these questions (Table I.1). In determining what constitutes an iconic place, we have prized communities recognized or marketed with widely circulated visual representations encapsulating their social and design tenets. Isabelle Gournay analyzes our understanding of iconicity in detail in Chapter 20. We do not claim that our selection comprises the only or the best set

Table I.1
The Iconic Planned Communities

Community	City/Region	Country	Foundational Era	Key Designers/ Instigators	Type
New Lanark	Lanarkshire	Scotland	1780s	David Dale, Robert Owen	Company town
Riverside	Chicago	USA	1860s	Frederick Law Olmsted, William Le Baron Jenney	Elite railway suburban community
Hampstead Garden Suburb	London	England	1900s	Raymond Unwin, Barry Parker, Edwin Lutyens	Garden suburb
Letchworth Garden City	Southeast England	England	1900s	Raymond Unwin, Barry Parker	Garden city
The Uplands	Victoria, British Columbia	Canada	1900s	John C. Olmsted	Elite residential park
Menteng	Jakarta	Indonesia	1910s	Peter Adriaan, Jacobus Mooijen	Elite garden community
Den-en Chôfu	Tokyo	Japan	1910s	Kintaro Yabe, Shibusawa Eiichi	Railway garden suburb
Jardim América	São Paulo	Brazil	1910s	Barry Parker	Elite garden suburb
Pacaembu	São Paulo	Brazil	1910s	Barry Parker	Elite garden suburb
Welwyn Garden City	Southeast England	England	1920s	Louis de Soissons	Garden city
Colonel Light Gardens	Adelaide	Australia	1920s	Charles Reade	Garden suburb
Sunnyside Gardens	Queens, New York City	USA	1920s	Clarence Stein, Henry Wright	Affordable medium-density housing
Radburn	Fairlawn, New Jersey	USA	1920s	Clarence Stein, Henry Wright	Garden suburb "for the motor age"
Garbatella	Rome	Italy	1920s	Gustavo Giovannoni	Working-class public planned municipality
Römerstadt	Frankfurt	Germany	1920s	Ernst May	Housing settlement
Cité Frugès	Pessac, Bordeaux	France	1920s	Le Corbusier, Pierre Jeanneret	Experimental housing subdivision
Wythenshawe	Manchester	England	1930s	Barry Parker, Ernest Simon	Municipal garden city
Greenbelt	Washington, DC; Maryland	USA	1930s	Hale Walker, Douglas Ellington, Reginald Wadsworth	New Town
Baťovany-Partizánske	Trenčín region	Slovakia	1930s	Jiří Voženílek, Vladimir Karfik, Tomáš Baťa	Company town
Sabaudia	Pontine region	Italy	1930s	Luigi Piccinato	New rural service center
Soweto	Johannesburg	South Africa	1930s	Government committee	Black metropolitan township
Tapiola	Helsinki	Finland	1950s	Heikki von Hertzen	Garden city/New Town
Seaside	Florida Panhandle	USA	1980s	Andrés Duany, Elizabeth Plater-Zyberk, Robert Davis	New Urbanist community

of iconic planned community types. We clearly could not include every important planned community in this collection, but we hope that our book will inspire a diverse range of stakeholders to think about the conservation issues of these and other iconic towns, suburbs, or villages and how to best preserve the spirit and practical value of their plans and ideals.

We asked contributors to address the most important events related to the conservation and legacy of their communities. Some of these are quite complicated histories and regulatory circumstances, so we have inserted tables that contain brief chronological overviews of conservation-related developments for each place. These summaries will enable easier comparative analysis and may help readers identify case studies containing issues or circumstances similar to planned communities in which they have an interest. The tables follow the text in each case study chapter.

Finally, although the number of illustrations for each chapter has been capped, we included a small section of color plates. One or more color images has been selected for each chapter because they fulfill one of the following criteria: (1) they are classic iconic images of the planned community, (2) they are prominent marketing or propaganda images, or (3) they capture important planning or preservation issues or developments that the community is facing at present.

NOTES

1. *Merriam-Webster* defines "resilience" as "the ability to become strong, healthy, or successful again after something bad happens," or "an ability to recover from or adjust easily to misfortune or change." Probably the most widely used definition of resilience in urban and planning literature comes from the Rockefeller Foundation's 100 Resilient Cities project. The Foundation defined urban resilience as "the capacity of individuals, communities, institutions, businesses, and systems within a city to survive, adapt, and grow no matter what kinds of chronic stresses and acute shocks they experience." See Rockefeller Foundation 2013; Jigyasu 2013; McPhearson 2014; Spector 2016; Vale 2016. For a scathing critique of the concept, see Slater 2014.

2. Readers will find examples of each of these chronic stresses or acute traumas in the case study chapters.

3. We note that the Anglo-American concepts of heritage or preservation do not fully reflect preservation or conservation concepts associated with these words' translations into other languages and cultures, such as "patrimoine" in French. For convenience's sake, we will use the terms "heritage" or "legacy" as shorthand to describe these features, but we mean to use a generous umbrella here, one that includes both tangible and intangible heritage.

4. Perusing the rubrics developed by 100 Resilient Cities.org turns up few direct references to heritage. See the detailed set of rubrics at http://www.100resilientcities.org/resilience#/-_/. The resilience plan for Melbourne, Australia, is touted as an excellent example of a resilience plan, but it does not include direct reference to heritage preservation in its scope or approach to resilience planning. See *Resilient Melbourne* 2015 and *Resilient Melbourne* 2016.

5. The significance of Greenbelt's RPC zoning is discussed in Chapter 16.

6. The authors welcome additional ideas regarding the forms that international collaboration and research could take.

REFERENCES

Allison, Eric, and Lauren Peters. 2011. *Historic Preservation and the Livable City*. Hoboken, NJ: John Wiley and Sons.

Avrami, Erica. 2016. "Making Historic Preservation Sustainable." *Journal of the American Planning Association* 82(2): 104–12.

Bartling, Hugh. 2007. "The Persistence of the Planned Landscape: The Case of Winter Park, Florida." *Planning Perspectives* 22(3): 352–72.

Berg, Shary Page. 2011. "The Massachusetts Heritage Landscape Inventory: A Community-Based Approach to Identifying and Protecting Special Places." In *Sustainability and Historic Preservation: Toward a Holistic View*, edited by Richard Longstreth, 29–42. Newark: University of Delaware Press.

Daniels, Thomas L. 2009. "A Trail Across Time: American Environmental Planning from City Beautiful to Sustainability." *Journal of the American Planning Association* 75(2): 178–92.

Davis, Robert Smolian. 2013. "Epilogue." In *Visions of Seaside: Foundation/Evolution/Imagination: Built and Unbuilt Architecture*, edited by Dhiru Thadani et al. New York: Rizzoli.

Department for Communities and Local Government. 2006. "Housing: Transferable Lessons from the New Towns." London: DCLG Publications. http://www.futurecommunities.net /files/images/1_4_CLG_New_Towns_review_0.pdf.

Domer, Dennis. 2009. "Old but Not Good Old History: Prospects and Problems of Freezing Time in Old Buildings." *Journal of Architectural and Planning Research* 26(2): 95–110.

Feiss, Carl. 1941. "The Heritage of Our Planned Communities." *Journal of the American Society of Architectural Historians* 1(3/4): 27–32.

———. 1956. "Historic Town Keeping." *Journal of the Society of Architectural Historians* 15(4): 2–6.

Forsyth, Ann. 2005. *Reforming Suburbia: The Planned Communities of Irvine, Columbia and the Woodlands*. Berkeley: University of California Press.

Gause, Jo Ellen, and Richard Franko, eds. 2007. *Developing Sustainable Planned Communities*. Washington, DC: Urban Land Institute.

Gibson, Lisanne, and John Pendlebury, eds. 2009. *Valuing Historic Environments*. Farnham, Surrey: Ashgate.

Gournay, Isabelle, and Mary Corbin Sies. 2010. "Greenbelt, Maryland: Beyond the Iconic Legacy." In *Housing Washington: Two Centuries of Tradition and Innovation in the Nation's Capital and Surrounding Counties,* edited by Richard Longstreth, 203–28. Chicago: Center for American Places.

Grant, Jill. 2006. *Planning the Good Community: New Urbanism in Theory and Practice*. New York: Routledge.

Grossman, Michele. 2013. "Prognosis Critical: Resilience and Multiculturalism in Contemporary Australia." *M/C Journal* 16(5). http://journal.media-culture.org.au/index.php/mcjour nal/article/view/699.

Hall, Peter. 2014. *Cities of Tomorrow: An Intellectual History of Urban Planning and Design in the Twentieth Century*. 4th ed. Oxford: Wiley-Blackwell.

Hawkes, Jon. 2001. *The Fourth Pillar of Sustainability: Culture's Essential Role in Public Planning*. Melbourne, Australia: Cultural Development Network Victoria in association with Common Ground Publishing.

Isenstadt, Sandy. 2001. "Three Problems in Preserving the Postwar Landscape." *Forum Journal* 15(Spring): 35–42.

Jigyasu, Rohit. 2013. *Heritage and Resilience: Issues and Opportunities for Reducing Disaster Risks*. Paper prepared for Fourth Session of the Global Platform for Disaster Risk Reduction, May 19–23, in Geneva, Switzerland. http://nrl.northumbria.ac.uk/17231/1/Heritage _and_Resilience_Report_for_UNISDR_2013.pdf.

King, Thomas F. 2011. "Preservation, Sustainability, and Environmental Impact Assessment in Post-Colonial Developing Nations." In *Sustainability and Historic Preservation: Toward a Holistic View*, edited by Richard Longstreth, 17–28. Newark: University of Delaware Press.

Knepper, Cathy D. 2001. *Greenbelt, MD: A Living Legacy of the New Deal*. Baltimore: Johns Hopkins University Press.

Kroessler, Jeffrey A. 2014. "Preserving the Historic Garden Suburb: Case Studies from London and New York." *Suburban Sustainability* 2(1): 1–14.

Larkham, Peter. 2004. "Conserving the Suburb: Mechanisms. Tensions and Results." In *Suburban Form: An International Perspective*, edited by Kiril Stanilov and Brenda Case Scheer, 241–62. London: Routledge.

Lee, Chang-Moo, and Barbara Stabin-Nesmith. 2001. "The Continuing Value of a Planned Community: Radburn in the Evolution of Suburban Development." *Journal of Urban Design* 6(2): 151–84.

Longstreth, Richard. 1991. "The Significance of the Recent Past." *APT Bulletin* 23(2): 12–24.

———, ed. 2011a. *Sustainability and Historic Preservation: Toward a Holistic View*. Newark: University of Delaware Press.

———. 2011b. "On the Road Again: Preservation's Urgent Future." In *Sustainability and Historic Preservation: Toward a Holistic View*, edited by Richard Longstreth, 107–22. Newark: University of Delaware Press.

Mandelker, Daniel R. 2010. *Designing Planned Communities*. Bloomington, IN: Universe.

Marquis-Kyle, Peter, and Meredith Walker. 2004. *The Illustrated Burra Charter: Good Practices for Heritage Places*. Melbourne, Australia: Australia ICOMOS.

McPhearson, Timon. 2014. "The Rise of Resilience: Linking Resilience and Sustainability in City Planning." http://www.thenatureofcities.com/2014/06/08/the-rise-of-resilience-link ing-resilience-and-sustainability-in-city-planning/.

Nyström, Louise, and Mats Johan Lundström. 2006. "Sweden: The Life and Death and Life of Great Neighbourhood Centres." *Built Environment* 32(1): 32–52.

Pacione, Michael. 2011. "Continuity and Change in Scotland's First Garden Suburb: The Genesis and Development of Pollokshields, Glasgow." *Urban Geography* 32(1): 23–49.

Porteous, J. Douglas. 1988. "Topocide: The Annihilation of Place." In *Qualitative Methods in Human Geography*, edited by John Eyles and David Smith, 75–93. Cambridge, UK: Polity Press.

Reiner, Thomas L. 1963. *The Place of the Ideal Community in Urban Planning*. Philadelphia: University of Pennsylvania Press.

Resilient Melbourne: Preliminary Resilience Assessment: Identifying the Focus Areas for Melbourne's Resilience Strategy. 2015. City of Melbourne. (June.) http://resilientmelbourne.com .au/wp-content/uploads/2016/01/Endorsed_Resilient_Melbourne_Preliminary_Resil ience_Assessment_090615.pdf.

Resilient Melbourne: Viable Sustainable Livable Prosperous. 2016. City of Melbourne. http:// resilientmelbourne.com.au/wp-content/uploads/2016/05/COM_SERVICE_PROD-9860726-v1-Final_Resilient_Melbourne_strategy_for_web_180516.pdf.

Rockefeller Foundation. 2013. *100 Resilient Cities*. http://www.100resilientcities.org/#/-_/.

Rodwell, Dennis. 2007. *Conservation and Sustainability in Historic Cities*. Oxford: Blackwell.

Ryberg-Webster, Stephanie, and Kelly L. Kinahan. 2014. "Historic Preservation and Urban Revitalization in the Twenty-first Century." *Journal of Planning Literature* 29(2): 119–39.

Rypkema, Donovan D. 1994. *The Economics of Historic Preservation: A Community Leader's Guide.* Washington, DC: National Trust for Historic Preservation.

Slater, Tom. 2014. "The Resilience of Neoliberal Urbanism. Open Security: Conflict and Peace-building" (January 28). https://www.opendemocracy.net/opensecurity/tom-slater/resilience-of-neoliberal-urbanism.

Smith, Laurajane. 2006. *Uses of Heritage.* London: Routledge.

Spector, Julian. 2016. "The Rise of Resilience Planning" (May 31). CityLab. https://www.citylab.com/design/2016/05/100-resilient-cities-michael-berkowitz-rockefeller-foundation-projects/484400/.

Striner, Richard. 1995. "Scholarship, Strategy, and Activism in Preserving the Recent Past." *Preservation Forum* 19(Fall): 26–33.

Vale, Lawrence J. 2016. "Towards Critical Resilience: Learning from the History of Post-Trauma Urbanism." *Proceedings, 17th IPHS Conference, Delft* 2: 13–24. https://books.bk.tudelft.nl/index.php/press/catalog/view/501/512/128-1.

Ward, Stephen V. 2002. *Planning the Twentieth-Century City: The Advanced Capitalist World.* Chichester, UK: John Wiley and Sons.

Whitehand, J. W. R., and Christine M. H. Carr. 2001. *Twentieth-Century Suburbs: A Morphological Approach.* London: Routledge.

CHAPTER 1

NEW LANARK

Sustaining Robert Owen's Legacy in Scotland

John Minnery

New Lanark is a small industrial settlement, physically isolated from the mainstream of urban history, yet it holds a special place in the narratives of urban planning, industrial innovation, and social reform. It is some forty kilometers (twenty-four miles) southeast of Glasgow in Scotland.

New Lanark was started in 1785 by David Dale, who was a Scottish textile merchant, banker, and entrepreneur, in a brief partnership with Richard Arkwright, an English inventor and businessman. The site was chosen in part because of the steady flow of the River Clyde just below the Falls of Clyde. Today, New Lanark is still a lively village where people live and work. It retains the essential elements of its early physical structure, but today's activities are completely different to those of the town's early years. Along the way many of the eighteenth-century advantages of its location created difficulties for its various later owners.

Iconic Status and Challenges

New Lanark has three sources of special historical significance. First, it is a classic early example of a planned industrial settlement where a manufacturer provided jobs but also convenient, good-quality housing and supporting services for his workers. Colin Bell and Rose Bell (1972, 241) emphasize this combination: "There is nothing in the history of town planning, or industrialization, which makes any one of New Lanark's policies or artefacts stand out as unique, only their combination." In fact, Gordon Cherry (1974, 17, 18) argues that it "set the scene" as a stimulus for the town planning movement. Graham U'ren (who held various important town planning positions in Clydesdale District Council, South Lanarkshire Council, and the Royal Town Planning Institute in Scotland between 1975 and 2007), in email correspondence (January 21, 2013), argues that even modern urban-design visitors to the town recognize its overall qualities as a livable place.

Its second claim to iconic status is from the cotton-spinning mills around which the town was built. These provide an outstanding example of early industrialized production methods, housing several newly invented machines and at a scale bigger than anything seen before. The New Lanark mills were at one stage the "largest and most successful" of the cotton manufacturing enterprises in Scotland (Donnachie and Hewitt 1993, 16). In G. D. H. Cole's (1927 [1813–20], ix) estimation, they were "the largest and best equipped spinning mills in Scotland" in 1800. The mills in New Lanark were "amongst the most important of the Arkwright mills" as examples of industrial innovation (Pierson 1949, 11).

New Lanark's third source of iconicity is its intimate association with the social and educational reformer Robert Owen. Owen was for a critical period the manager and part owner of the town and its mills; in the period from 1800 to 1825 he put into practice many of his theories while his experience at New Lanark became the basis for many of his later reformist ideas—or at least was used in his effective and widespread self-publicity about them (Donnachie 2000; Holloway 1966, 105). Owen's social reforms resonate with the reforming utopianism that is one of the threads underpinning early British town planning (Cherry 1969, 49). Gerald Burke (1971, 136) even breathlessly claims that New Lanark "stimulated a long succession of schemes for the ideal community from a wide variety of sources including Quakers, Moravians, Unitarians, Anglicans, industrialists, social reformers and cranks."

Rather than being known for its size or any grand designs, New Lanark became an icon due to these three threads: early town planning, industrial innovation, and Owenism. At the peak of its population in the early nineteenth century, it housed only about 2,300 people (Donnachie and Hewitt 1993, 94).

The features that lie at the heart of its iconicity are also the causes of the challenges it has had to face. First, because the town was based on a single manufacturing activity, it was vulnerable to the fluctuating fortunes of that industry. From the mid-nineteenth century until the 1960s, the Scottish (and world) cotton manufacturing industry gradually declined. The New Lanark mills managed to avoid for a time the problems facing the industry because they had ready access to cheap water power and offered low wages (compensated for by low rents), but they were not able to avoid the industry's overall collapse. Second, although the location provided cheap power, it has poor road access. The town was started before working railways were invented but even today there is no direct rail line due to the inaccessibility of its river gorge location. Poor access created huge difficulties for later owners. The third great challenge was the single combined ownership of the mills and town. While for Dale and Owen the coupling was advantageous, to later manufacturers who bought the mills the management of the associated housing, school, and facilities was far outside their industrial expertise. Fourth, social and governance structures are radically different to those in the late eighteenth century. For example, today's housing standards bear almost no resemblance to expectations in

Dale and Owen's time, and many of Owen's radical innovations are now main-streamed into social and educational policy. Today these challenges have been confronted and partially overcome but many of the problems remain. The continuing story of New Lanark has many lessons for other iconic planned settlements.

A Brief History

The reliable source of water power adjacent to a flat site below the Falls of Clyde was the principal attraction for Richard Arkwright when he was taken to see it by David Dale in 1784 (New Lanark Trust n.d.). Access from Glasgow to Lanark had also been recently improved with the building of road bridges over the Clyde. Dale and Arkwright formed a partnership that obtained the land "for a feu duty," or for an annual rent, from Lord Justice Braxfield to build mills housing Arkwright's recently invented water-powered cotton-spinning machinery (Donnachie and Hewitt 1993, 25). Building of the mills started in 1785. After the partnership was dissolved in 1786, Dale continued as sole proprietor (New Lanark Trust n.d., 4). Because of the relative isolation, and because there was no easy source of labor, Dale needed to "scavenge for labour, and to keep it there, had to provide a town" (Bell and Bell 1972, 242). The town's physical shape was dictated by the limited building land available between the river and the steep-sided gorge (see Plates 1 and 2 for a modern and a historical perspective).

Some skilled labor was available in the nearby town of Lanark, including mechanics and watchmakers who were able to make and maintain the machinery in the mills. But the majority of the laboring workforce was made up of children, many of whom came from orphanages in Edinburgh and Glasgow. Dale also attracted reluctant adult workers who were forced by changes in agricultural methods and tenure to move from the land, including a group who were diverted from immigrating to America by Dale's offer of immediate employment and low-rent housing. By 1796 Dale had "four mills in operation, employing 1,340 hands, 750 of them children and half of those under nine years old. By the standards of the time, Dale was a model master—but the standards were quite plainly appalling" (Bell and Bell 1972, 244). Dale provided schooling for the children, including a day-school for under sixes, so that mothers were free to work in the mills during the day (New Lanark Trust n.d., 8).

Robert Owen, with whom New Lanark is more famously associated, was a successful Welsh industrialist who married Dale's eldest daughter, and set up a consortium from among his industrial associates in Manchester. The consortium bought the mills and town, and Owen took over as general manager in 1800. He had gained substantial experience in the textile industry while working in Lancashire. His extensive writings, dating mainly from his time at New Lanark and later in New Harmony in Indiana, give a self-aggrandizing view of the importance of his contribution, as well as setting out his philosophies on cooperation, education, and working conditions. Basically he held that a person's character is shaped by their environment and that a fundamental component of that shaping was the education of the child. It followed that "the governing powers of all countries should establish rational plans for the education and general formation of the characters of their subjects" (Owen 1927 [1813]-a, 20). This education should "train children from their earliest infancy in good habits of every description. . . . They must afterwards be rationally educated, and their labour be usefully directed" (Owen 1927 [1813]-a, 20). Owen felt that children could not be trained in good habits if they were forced to work in factories, so he abolished child labor at New Lanark. His *Second Essay* claimed to show how this new way of forming character worked in practice in New Lanark (Owen 1927 [1813]-b, 33). In his *Third Essay* (Owen 1927 [1813]-c, 43) he also made a strong case for the provision of "rooms for innocent amusements and rational recreation."

Owen used surplus profits voted by his various controlling boards to expand Dale's original town, adding further housing as well as many other facilities. These included a new school, a bakery, a communal wash-house and a cooperative store, as well as an Institute for the Formation of Character (opened in 1816). Although he was a successful entrepreneur and manufacturer, he fell out with his financial backers over the degree of investment he proposed in community facilities, so New Lanark was run, over the years, by a number of successive boards; but each time that it was necessary to get new backers the purchase price increased—from £60,000 in 1799 to £114,100 in 1813, for example (Donnachie and Hewitt 1993). A forced auction in 1813, brought about by internal politicking within the board, saw Owen outwit his opponents to retain ownership with a new board (including the economist Jeremy Bentham) sympathetic to his reforming ideals. He also took care to publicize widely these ideas and to identify New Lanark as an exemplar of successful practice. Some fifteen thousand visitors flocked to New Lanark during Owen's management: "they came not just to see an ideal community, but an efficient enterprise" (Bell and Bell 1972, 246). "For some time 2,000 visitors went annually to New Lanark, many of them eminent people, the Tsar of Russia included" (Cherry 1974, 18). In fact, "commercial success at New Lanark . . . was the vital ingredient in providing credibility for Owen's principles" (New Lanark Trust n.d., 14). "His great achievement," says William Ashworth (1954, 120), "was to transform the character of his village without injury to the business on which it depended. In the first thirteen years of his management the proprietors received over £50,000 in addition to 5 per cent on their capital . . . [and] . . . the output capacity was in-creased more than five-fold."

But having "run through three boards, [Owen] finally sold out his share to the only director of the last board he found at all acceptable, John Walker" (Bell and Bell 1972, 248). Walker, a Quaker, and his family thus obtained a controlling inter-est in the town and mills in 1825. Owen then left for the United States, where with William MacLure, the geologist and educationalist, he bought the 121-square-kilometer (30,000-acre) site of Harmonie, Indiana, renamed New Harmony, from the founder of the Harmony Society, George Rapp. He maintained an interest in New Lanark, continuing to use the town to publicize his ideals. Owen's aspirations for a new model community at New Harmony proved unattainable and after only three years he returned to the United Kingdom, having lost most of his personal fortune. He continued to proselytize on the national and international stage, but died in 1858.

By the 1830s the Scottish cotton industry faced fierce competition. Walker's sons had taken over from their father and tried, unsuccessfully, to sell the mills and the houses in 1851. They modernized some of the machinery and maintained Ow-en's innovations in the village, although obviously not with his fervor. By 1881, when New Lanark was sold to Henry Birkmyre and his brother-in-law, Robert Somerville, the town's population had decreased to a mere 706 people (Donnachie and Hewitt 1993, 144). Birkmyre was the principal partner in the Gourock Rope-work Company, which was expanding globally as a result of its successful associa-tion with the huge shipbuilding industry on the Lower Clyde. The Lanark Spin-ning Company continued to trade under that name until it merged with Gourock in 1903. Birkmyre and Gourock sought to maintain some of the social patterns that underpinned the town's success. They also diversified the factory activities. As well as cotton being spun, it was also woven on site (UNESCO 2001, 41), and output now included ship sails and fishing nets manufactured with looms brought in from other company mills, as well as the spinning of synthetic fibers (Donnachie and Hewitt 1993, 167, 188). The face of New Lanark was changed in other ways under the management of Gourock as well. In 1883 Mill Four burned down and was never rebuilt. In 1884 a water turbine was introduced "to power machinery . . . and ulti-mately make possible electricity generation to provide lighting to the mills and the village" (Donnachie and Hewitt 1993, 169). In the 1940s the top two stories of Mill Number One were removed due to instability from machines shaking (Figure 1.1).

Manufacturing production and profits fell considerably during the late nine-teenth century and into the twentieth century. By 1951 the town's population had declined further to only 550 (Donnachie and Hewitt 1993, 186). Although the company continued to support various social activities, "it was the village housing

Figure 1.1. Mill Number One in 1979, with its top stories removed and a copy of the repairs notice served on Metal Extractions Limited. (Courtesy New Lanark Trust; www.newlanark.org)

that presented the company with its biggest headache" (Donnachie and Hewitt 1993, 193). The increased standards required under a series of national Housing Acts were a continuing challenge. Although the housing provided by Dale and Owen was exemplary by eighteenth- and nineteenth-century standards, it failed miserably to meet mid-twentieth-century regulations. For example, the houses were not provided with piped water until 1933. The town was incorporated into the Royal Burgh of Lanark in 1951. If the council had enforced rigorously the relevant housing standards the whole village would have been demolished. The company offered the village (as an entity separate from the mills) to the Lanark Town Council for a nominal sum in 1962, but the council declined the offer because of the potential maintenance costs involved (Donnachie and Hewitt 1993, 193). Gourock was clearly recognizing the difficulties it faced in terms of the maintenance of housing that was almost two hundred years old and keeping alive the inheritance of a long-dead social reformer.

The New Lanark Association (NLA) was formed as a housing association in 1963 by an Edinburgh housing professional who remains associated with the village today, partly as a result of the failed effort of the company to sell to the council.

Jim Arnold, the former director of the New Lanark Trust, in an interview in late 2010, said that it was formed by a group of interested people concerned about heritage conservation issues as well as the deterioration of the housing in which a number of Gourock workers lived, in the light of an apparent lack of government interest in preserving the settlement. The NLA had very few resources, though later in 1963 it bought the housing stock, some of the other minor buildings, and extensive land holdings around the village from Gourock for a nominal amount. Jim Arnold gave the value as £250. Graham U'ren (in an email on January 21, 2013) pointed out that the only way for the new charitable housing association with no resources of its own to finance potentially costly improvements was for it to borrow from the town council. It was able to do so, despite the earlier decision of the council not to take over the village. Success in renovation of the housing was necessary to increase confidence in the future of the village. As the years progressed, various models for funding housing improvement were used. Central government took over the lending to fund social housing for rent; some houses were renovated and sold with covenants attached; some were sold without any repairs carried out but with accompanying grant packages set up. Jim Arnold and Graham U'ren (when interviewed in late 2010) pointed out that the NLA also used a national employment program (the Manpower Services Commission scheme) to employ the workforce to restore the shells of the terraces of housing while effectively gutting the interiors ready for redevelopment.

It was becoming increasingly clear that "New Lanark had become a millstone round 'the Gourock's' neck and it would be only time before the company unburdened itself" (Donnachie and Hewitt 1993, 198). In a major restructuring of its activities across Scotland in 1968, Gourock announced the closure of the mills and the loss of the final 350 jobs, "after which the village's population decline continued and its physical decay advanced" (Anonymous 1988, iv). The period has been described as the "end of manufacturing and the rapid slide into decay" (UNESCO 2001, 8).

It is important to note that from 1963 onward the village and the mills were under different ownerships. The original vision of a combined factory and supporting town had fractured, although their physical proximity meant that they were still mutually dependent. By this time, "the advantages that had proved attractive to late 18th century and early 19th century businessmen had little real relevance to the mid-20th century" in terms of both manufacturing and housing (Donnachie and Hewitt 1993, 199).

In 1970 the mill site was sold to Metal Extractions Limited, which extracted aluminum from scrap metal, but only a few jobs were created and the mills area

Figure 1.2. Robert Owen's school building with a collapsed roof in the mid-1970s. (Courtesy New Lanark Trust; www.new lanark.org)

rapidly came to resemble a scrap yard (Figure 1.1). "Many of the mill buildings began to deteriorate and the roof of the nearby Old School collapsed" (Donnachie and Hewitt 1993, 200) (Figure 1.2). Meantime the resident population had shrunk to eighty (Undiscovered Scotland n.d.).

Concerns about the future of the town and mills continued. A meeting of interested parties was convened in 1972 under the auspices of the Scottish Civic Trust, Lanarkshire County Council, and the Lanark Town Council, which led to a feasibility report on the future of the town and mills in 1973 (Feasibility Study Team 1973).

As a result of this, in 1974 the New Lanark Conservation Trust (NLCT) was founded to prevent demolition of the village and to "preserve New Lanark as a sustainable community, with a resident population and opportunities for employment" (NLWHS n.d.-b). Graham U'ren (in an email, January 21, 2013) noted that the Scottish Civic Trust and a number of eminent citizens supported the NLCT's formation. At this stage it was an unincorporated membership society, primarily engaged in advocating for the village's restoration.

In 1984 the NLCT was reconstituted as the New Lanark Trust (NLT), an incorporated body, when the mills were acquired and a voluntary support group called the Friends of New Lanark was started. The Friends also sponsor an annual Robert Owen Commemoration Lecture (NLWHS n.d.-a). As explained below, New Lanark was inscribed on the World Heritage List in 2001 after an unsuccessful attempt at listing in 1986.

In 2009 the NLA had wound down, and responsibility for the village's tenanted properties passed to the NLT under its wholly owned management company, New Lanark Homes, because as a registered housing association the NLA had been required to fulfill a number of onerous regulatory tasks that applied to all housing associations across Scotland, even though it supervised only forty-five tenants (Jim Arnold interview, 2010). The mills, the hotel, other nonresidential buildings, and the houses in the village that have not been sold are owned and operated by the NLT through three wholly owned companies: New Lanark Trading Ltd., New Lanark Hotels Ltd., and New Lanark Homes (NLWHS n.d.-b).

The main historical events relevant to New Lanark are summarized in Table 1.1.

The Heritage Framework

As noted in the documentation for the 2001 UNESCO World Heritage listing (UNESCO 2001, 37), "the integrity of the site is protected through a range of national designations: all but one building in the village is listed." Mills One, Two, and Three, and Owen's Institute for the Formation of Character were given a Grade A listing in January 1971 (Historic Scotland n.d.). The rest of the buildings were also subsequently listed and included within a statutory conservation area.

A critical and unusual step in the conservation of New Lanark occurred in 1979. As Graham U'ren explained (via email, January 21, 2013), there was increasing concern over the state of the mills and institutional buildings. In fact, villagers had to act to prevent the destruction of the original cast-iron plates from the loft of Mill Three. These events led to the local authority, Clydesdale District Council (which succeeded Lanark Town Council in the Scottish local government reorganization in 1975), taking action on the basis of the heritage designation. A statutory repairs notice was served on the scrap company in 1979, requiring extensive but still basic repair and weather-protection work to be carried out (Figure 1.1). In default of these repairs, a compulsory purchase order was made in 1980 to recover the mills and related industrial buildings from the company but it took three years for the Scottish Secretary to confirm this, even though the owner had not objected.

Figure 1.3. Mill Number One restored and converted into the New Lanark Mill Hotel. (Photo by John Minnery)

The delay was because of the sensitivity of government to imposing the liability for the buildings on a local authority but it also related to the question of who would pay the costs of compensation. Graham U'ren (via email, January 21, 2013) notes that the use of such a compulsory purchase order is rare.

The repairs notice included a professional estimate of the cost of repairs. In 1980 this was some £10 million, according to Graham U'ren when interviewed in 2010. There was considerable debate about the value of the compensation due to the mill owner—the cost of necessary repairs could even lead to a negative valuation. The owner was reluctant to provide the information needed to calculate business loss and relocation compensation but instead retrieved some value for himself by splitting two relatively sound buildings off into a separate company and receiving a positive valuation of some £60,000 for these. Jim Arnold and Graham U'ren confirmed that the compensation costs were met from a grant by the National Heritage Memorial Fund (NHMF) to the District Council as the acquiring authority. The funding for the acquisition of New Lanark's mills was one of the NHMF's early grants (NHMF n.d.). The mill and related buildings were then transferred at no cost to the New Lanark Trust, which now owns them and most of the rest of the village. Most of the buildings have been restored, although not all to their original use and the village has become a major tourist attraction (Beeho and Prentice 1997). Mill Number One has had its upper floors restored and is now the New Lanark Mill Hotel (Figure 1.3). In 2001 the mills and village were jointly inscribed as a UNESCO World Heritage Site (South Lanarkshire Council 2009a; Ward 2001). An earlier attempt (in 1986) to gain the World Heritage listing was not successful. The lack of success may have related to heritage values of the time: Arnold (2005, 18) claims that "industrial sites in Scotland had proved difficult to conserve. . . . Funding support has generally been allocated to country houses and palaces, art galleries and museums." When interviewed in 2010, Arnold felt that by 2001 attitudes had changed, and even UNESCO was more enthusiastic about conserving examples of Europe's industrial heritage. In addition, Margaret Thatcher's (Prime Minister, 1979–90) withdrawal of the United Kingdom from UNESCO held up the process.

The Issues Facing New Lanark

From this brief history it can be seen that the fundamental issue facing New Lanark is that its iconicity dates from events and innovations from the late eighteenth and early nineteenth centuries that do not easily fit with the present day. Some of the elements of the problems are discussed below, but in essence the location, activities, housing, and structures that benefited a settlement early in the Industrial Revolution—using water-powered machinery to run mills producing goods for which there was a strong demand, providing accommodation and services in an isolated site for an underprivileged working class, and demonstrating innovations at the leading edge of nineteenth-century social reform—are clearly from another time. Standards in housing and manufacturing have changed, transport networks matter in different ways, and social reforms have become mainstreamed.

Funding and Management

The mills at New Lanark were built for a particular industry and the village of New Lanark was created specifically to serve them. Then the industry declined and the mills ceased production in 1968. The village could no longer serve its original purpose. Like a number of other well-known industrial settlements (such as Saltaire in the United Kingdom, and Pullman near Chicago), its economic base has disap-

Figure 1.4. Repair work to a retaining wall. (Photo by John Minnery)

peared. The fundamental question then is where does the financial support for the village and the mills come from?

According to the NLT's website the New Lanark site is partly funded by the European Union, UNESCO, and the Heritage Lottery Fund (NLWHS n.d.-c). This short statement plays down the serious issues that face the trust in terms of funding. It is unusual for a World Heritage Site to be privately owned; most others are under public ownership and are funded through the public purse. Historically, much of the work of the NLT has been in sourcing funds for restoration (some very extensive), repairs, and maintenance from whatever granting agencies can be tapped. A variety of sources have been used over the years, with only a small continuous contribution from the local authority and national heritage organizations. Graham U'ren (via email, December 2014) listed the main sources as including the Manpower Services Commission, European Structural Funds, Scottish Enterprise, the Heritage Lottery Fund, and the Rural Development Fund.

Nowadays a place like New Lanark, which is almost completely restored, needs two main kinds of funding. One of these is the ongoing revenue needed for visitor management, school visits, administration, small-scale maintenance, advertising, and so on. About 95 percent of this revenue funding is generated by the commercial activities of the trust (U'ren email, December 2014). The trust is in fact diversifying its activities. These now include the visitor center (including interpretive displays, temporary exhibitions, and retail and catering operations), the New Lanark Mill Hotel, property letting, wool manufacture (using the demonstration spinning machines), ice cream manufacture, and hydro electricity from the turbine in one of the former water-wheel pits. These produce a financial surplus. About 5 percent of the revenue income comes from an annual Scottish government grant, used for repairs only. The other main form of required funding is for major building maintenance and repairs and for educational purposes (Figure 1.4). The trust sources these funds from the various granting bodies already noted. There was some core grant funding from South Lanarkshire Council but this was terminated in 2011.

The World Heritage inscription has added to New Lanark's attraction as a tourist location (Landorf 2009), which is an important source of funding. However, the site faces difficulties in providing the necessary infrastructure. For example, a car park has been built above the town to help keep tourists' cars out of the physically restricted site while still allowing access for tourist buses and employees' and residents' vehicles.

Heritage Protection

South Lanarkshire Council, within which New Lanark is now located, explains that "World Heritage Site status does not confer any additional statutory controls in Scotland. However, local authorities should develop planning policies to protect World Heritage Sites and their buffer zones and the significance of a World Heritage Site is a 'key material consideration' when making planning decisions" (South Lanarkshire Council 2009a, n.p.). UNESCO requires a management plan for each listed site and its designated buffer zone. The management plan for New Lanark was developed by the South Lanarkshire Council, the New Lanark Trust, and Historic Scotland, as well as a number of wider stakeholders such as Scottish Natural Heritage and Scottish Power (South Lanarkshire Council 2009a). The local authority's development assessment policy for the World Heritage Site and its buffer zone stipulates that the council will not permit "development that adversely affects the historical and topographical character and landscape quality" of both the "World Heritage Site and its setting (buffer zone)" (South Lanarkshire Council 2009c, n.p.). The council also lists a number of criteria that are used to assess development applications (South Lanarkshire Council 2009a, 2009b, 2009c), including that "development must preserve, protect and enhance the character, integrity and quality of the New Lanark World Heritage Site and its setting (buffer zone)" (South Lanarkshire Council 2011b, n.p.). There has since emerged a debate about whether the buffer zone represents the correct definition of the setting for the protection of the Outstanding Universal Value as recognized by UNESCO for the site. The South Lanarkshire Council recently decided to review the protection to New Lanark and the Falls of Clyde Conservation Area (which includes New Lanark, although it predates the World Heritage listing and has different boundaries to the World Heritage area and buffer zone but has greater standing in Scottish development control legislation). The council undertook a conservation area appraisal and put this analysis out for public consultation in 2011. While the result has been confirmation of needing to restrict building and development activities in the conservation area (South Lanarkshire Council 2011a), there remains uncertainty over parts of the buffer zone that are outside the conservation area. An important question that is illustrated from the experience of New Lanark regards the legal instruments available when the built environment has been damaged. In this case there were several aspects that caused concern. In the 1940s Gourock removed the top two stories from Mill Number One. Then in the 1970s the activities of the mill owner at the time damaged the historic fabric. The result was the unusual use of compulsory acquisition powers but this was supported by the earlier Scottish listing as heritage buildings. Even then there was a difficult legal procedure to go through as well as negotiations about the compensation to be paid and who would pay it.

The question of heritage protection has a number of additional dimensions in New Lanark. Perhaps unlike other planned settlements, where the plan or built environment itself is the source of iconicity, the very sources of the town's historical significance can cause difficulties. There are no grand buildings or any spectacular architecture in New Lanark, and industrial heritage may not be seen as important when compared with grand houses. And how does one conserve the physical symbols of Owen's workplace and educational reform? Owen's Institute for the Formation of Character is important because of what it stands for, for example, rather than because of its inherent architectural merit.

Changing Standards

New Lanark could not function merely as an outdoor museum. But the standards used for housing in the late eighteenth century and early nineteenth century do not match up to twenty-first-century expectations, even when the houses were exemplary for their time. Modern expectations have been codified into enforceable regulations, and noncompliance can lead to demolition, a threat that has faced

New Lanark in the past. The solution chosen for the village housing was a mixture of sale to private owners (with attached covenants) and rental of renovated dwellings, in each case preserving the external fabric but bringing the interiors up to modern living standards.

Ownership

Underpinning the way that threats have been faced and overcome is the fact that the village and the mills are not owned by the government. Even World Heritage inscription, although it must be supported by the relevant national government, does not lead to public ownership. In the case of New Lanark it does not lead directly to financial support from the government either. The situation in Scotland is complicated by the fact that the U.K. government is subject to the member-state obligations to UNESCO but it delegates management to the devolved Scottish government. The single ownership of the mills and town also created difficulties for owners whose business was solely manufacturing. By the mid-twentieth century the "solution" was to separate the ownership of the two, but this led to further problems. The separate ownerships have now been recombined (with the exception of a few private housing units) so that the village and the mills are now administered together.

Community Support

The population of New Lanark has never been substantial. Even today there is thus no large vociferous residential community. Rather there is a small dedicated group of people, some of whom are part of the NLT or the Friends of New Lanark. The interest extends to include people who support social and labor reform, because of Robert Owen's role in shaping the town. For example, New Lanark was chosen for a meeting in 1988 of the International Communal Studies Association and the National Historic Communal Societies Association that led to the founding of the Utopian Studies Society (Arnold 2005, 20). But a truly powerful local community voice is missing. There is a Village Group, to which over 90 percent of the residents belong, but in 1985 there were only 185 people living in 65 households in the village (Arnold 2005, 19). In 2014, according to the NLT, there were only 140 residents.

Conclusions

New Lanark's challenges provide a number of lessons for other historic planned settlements facing change. New Lanark is iconic because of its place in history rather than because of its designed form. Its place in history derives from the combination of housing, employment, and services; from its association with the reforming ideals of David Dale and Robert Owen; and because it serves as an example of early innovations in manufacturing technology. Its built environment is important insofar as it reflects its political, economic, and cultural history. Although it is a real place with real residents, there are far fewer now than in the town's heyday, although some of these residents have moved there because of their support for its conservation (Andreae 1984). It has lost its industrial base. Its very existence has been threatened in the past through changing housing standards (with their enforceable regulatory regimes) and through the redundancy of its industrial activities.

Protection of the UNESCO World Heritage–inscribed built environment of New Lanark is a "material consideration" in the local council's development plan but the council has some discretion in how it interprets "material consideration." Sanctions against abusing the World Heritage listing are basically threats to de-list. The current council has chosen to give the listing a strong emphasis but this policy position could change. U'ren (via email, January 21, 2015) notes that the system of protection of World Heritage sites is currently under review by the Built Environment Forum Scotland, of which the New Lanark Trust is a member, as part of a review of Scottish government planning and historic environment policy review. The town and the mills owe their continued existence to the exemplary work of the NLT and its ingenuity in sourcing funds. At times, the work of the trust has involved encouraging innovative use of local authority powers designed for other purposes. New Lanark is now a tourist attraction of some note rather than an industrial settlement, but it is arguable that the real passion for conserving it builds on its association with Robert Owen rather than deriving from its role as an industrial town.

The world has changed in many ways since 1785 and New Lanark has had to change as well. Iconicity provides a basis for arguing for continuing protection but does not provide protection in itself. Neither, in fact, does World Heritage inscription. New Lanark has shown how existing town planning and other legislative mechanisms, while not perfect, can be used with ingenuity and care to help protect iconic heritage. Funding for renovation and maintenance is difficult to obtain but can be gained from innovative sources. Uses can be changed while protecting the essence of the built form. These all need to be driven by the passionate commitment of dedicated people. In New Lanark's case, this is the trust rather than a vociferous local population. The town's future is hopeful but not certain.

Table 1.1
Summary of Historical Events and Heritage Benchmarks for New Lanark

Year	Event
1784	David Dale obtains land "for a feu duty."
1785	Dale starts building four water-powered mills and a village in partnership with Richard Arkwright. He dissolves the partnership in 1786.
1799	Robert Owen marries Dale's daughter and forms a partnership with his father-in-law.
1800	Owen and others buy the town and mills; he is made manager and starts implementing his reform ideas.
1813	The board forces an auction but Owen reacquires ownership with new partners.
1825	Owen sells the mills and village to the Walkers and leaves the United Kingdom for New Harmony in the United States. He returns to the U.K. in 1828 and dies in 1858.
1851	An unsuccessful attempt by the Walkers to sell the town and mills.
1881	Mills and town are sold to Birkmyre and Somerville, owners of the Gourock Ropework Company, as part of a worldwide expansion.
1903	Lanark Spinning Company merges with Gourock.
1962	The Lanark Town Council refuses an offer to purchase the village for a nominal sum, because of the potential repair costs.
1963	Creation of the New Lanark (Housing) Association, which purchases village houses for a nominal sum. The village and mills are under separate ownership for the first time. Housing refurbishment begins.
1968	Gourock closes the mills.
1970	Metal Extractions Limited purchases the mills.
1971	Historic Scotland lists Mills One, Two, and Three, as well as the Institute for the Formation of Character.
1974	The New Lanark Conservation Trust (now the New Lanark Trust) is created.
1983	The Lanark Town Council acquires mills following the 1979 listed building repairs notice and under the compulsory purchase procedure of U.K. planning law. Ownership transferred to the NLT (underwritten by the National Heritage Memorial Fund).
1986	A failed attempt at UNESCO World Heritage inscription.
1988	The visitor center opens in Mill Three and in the Institute building.
1998	The New Lanark Mill Hotel opens in Mill One.
2001	The New Lanark village and mills gain UNESCO World Heritage inscription.
2009	The New Lanark Housing Association winds down. New Lanark Homes (part of New Lanark Trust) manages housing.
2013	Publication of the mandatory World Heritage Site Management Plan.
2014	Successful stage 1 funding application is submitted to the Heritage Lottery Fund for a project that includes the last unrestored building in the village (Double Row).
	Population, 140; World Heritage Site, 360 acres [146 ha]; buffer zone, 1,648 acres [667 ha]; 65 dwelling units (45 rented, 20 owned).

REFERENCES

Andreae, Christopher. 1984. "The Rebirth of New Lanark." *Christian Science Monitor Special Feature* (February 7).

Anonymous. 1988. "Editorial Note: Model Industrial Settlements: The Continuing Stewardship." *Town Planning Review* 59(3): iii–vi.

Arnold, James E. 2005. "Utopia Matters: A Personal Testimony." In *Utopia Matters: Theory, Politics, Literature and the Arts*, edited by Fatima Vieira and Marinela Freitas, 17–21. Porto, Portugal: Universidade do Porto.

Ashworth, William. 1954. *The Genesis of Modern British Town Planning: A Study in Economics and Social History of the Nineteenth and Twentieth Centuries*. London: Routledge and Kegan Paul.

Beeho, A. J., and R. C. Prentice. 1997. "Conceptualising the Experiences of Heritage Tourists: A Case Study of New Lanark World Heritage Village." *Tourism Management* 18(2): 75–87.

Bell, Colin, and Rose Bell. 1972. *City Fathers: The Early History of Town Planning in Britain*. Harmondsworth: Penguin.

Burke, Gerald. 1971. *Towns in the Making*. London: Edward Arnold.

Cherry, Gordon. 1969. "Influences on the Development of Town Planning in Britain." *Journal of Contemporary History* 4(3): 43–58.

———. 1974. *The Evolution of British Town Planning: A History of Town Planning in the United Kingdom During the 20th Century and of the Royal Town Planning Institute, 1914–74*. Leighton Buzzard: Leonard Hill Books.

Cole, G. D. H. 1927 (1813–20). "Introduction." In *A New View of Society and Other Writings*, by Robert Owen, vii–xix. London: J. M. Dent and Sons Everyman's Library.

Donnachie, Ian. 2000. *Robert Owen: Owen of New Lanark and New Harmony*. East Linton: Tuckwell Press.

Donnachie, Ian, and George Hewitt. 1993. *Historic New Lanark: The Dale and Owen Industrial Community Since 1785*. Edinburgh: Edinburgh University Press.

Feasibility Study Team. 1973. *A Future for New Lanark: A Report to the New Lanark Working Party*. County Council of the County of Lanarkshire (unpublished mimeo).

Historic Scotland. n.d. *Listing of Historical Buildings*. http://www.historic-scotland.gov.uk.

Holloway, Mark. 1966. *Utopian Communities in America, 1680–1880*. 2nd ed. Mineola, NY: Dover.

Landorf, Christine, 2009. "Managing for Sustainable Tourism: A Review of Six Cultural World Heritage Sites." *Journal of Sustainable Tourism* 17(1): 53–70.

National Heritage Memorial Fund (NHMF). n.d. *National Heritage Memorial Fund*. http://www.nhmf.org.uk/Pages/home.aspx.

New Lanark Trust. n.d. *The Story of New Lanark*. Lanark: New Lanark Trust.

New Lanark World Heritage Site (NLWHS). n.d.-a. *Be a Friend of New Lanark*. http://www.newlanark.org/trust-friend.shtml.

———. n.d.-b. *The Trust*. http://www.newlanark.org/thetrust.shtml.

———. n.d.-c. *World Heritage Site*. http://www.newlanark.org/worldheritagesite.shtml.

Owen, Robert. 1927 (1813)-a. "Essays on the Formation of Character: First Essay." In *A New View of Society and Other Writings*, 14–21. London: J. M. Dent and Sons Everyman's Library.

———. 1927 (1813)-b. "Essays on the Formation of Character: Second Essay." In *A New View of Society and Other Writings*, 22–38. London: J. M. Dent and Sons Everyman's Library.

———. 1927 (1813)-c. "Essays on the Formation of Character: Third Essay." In *A New View of Society and Other Writings*, 39–62. London: J. M. Dent and Sons Everyman's Library.

Pierson, William Harvey, Jr. 1949. "Notes on Early Industrial Architecture in England." *Journal of the Society of Architectural Historians* 8(1–2): 1–32.

South Lanarkshire Council. 2009a. *South Lanarkshire Council Local Plan Policy ENV 21.* http://www.southlanarkshire.gov.uk.

———. 2009b. *South Lanarkshire Local Plan Volume 1: Development Strategy.* South Lanarkshire: South Lanarkshire Council (adopted March 23, 2009).

———. 2009c. *South Lanarkshire Local Plan Volume II: Development Policies Guidance and Appendices ENV 21 New Lanark Development Assessment Policy* (adopted March 23, 2009).

———. 2011a. *New Lanark to Get More Protection.* http://www.southlanarkshire.gov.uk/press /article/321/new_lanark_to_get_more_protection.

———. 2011b. *New Lanark World Heritage Site: Modification 82 'To ENV 21 New Lanark Development Assessment.* http://consult.southlanarkshire.gov.uk/portal/planning/lpms/ms?point Id= section_36.

Undiscovered Scotland. n.d. http://www.undiscoveredscotland.co.uk/lanark/newlanark/his tory2.html.

UNESCO World Heritage Committee Nomination Documentation. 2001. "New Lanark." File 429rev.pdf (December 16). http://whc.unesco.org/en/list/429/documents/.

Ward, D. 2001. "World Heritage Honour for Revolutionary Mills." *Guardian* (December 15).

CHAPTER 2

RIVERSIDE

The First Comprehensively Designed Suburban

Community in the United States

David Schuyler

Riverside, Illinois, is arguably the iconic American railroad suburb. Later communities boast more wealth, open space, or exclusiveness, but Riverside established the template that shaped suburbanization in the United States for decades to follow. Although many other individuals were involved in designing its buildings and infrastructure, Riverside in its conceptualization is the singular work of Frederick Law Olmsted. That its design and the fabric of its buildings retain such a remarkable degree of integrity today is a testament to the efforts of many residents who have cherished and protected their community over almost a century and a half.

When Olmsted first visited Chicago in the spring of 1863, he was surprised by the "[Aladdin's] lamp character" of the city. "Driven rapidly through a broad street to my hotel," he wrote, "a street lined with grand houses of marble or a stone of greater beauty and equal splendor—in gaslight, I had a sensation when I first entered the town almost like that of first passing at night through the boulevard l'Italien." The town was growing exponentially, doubling in population within ten years, seemingly reinventing itself almost overnight. Nevertheless, Olmsted expressed sadness upon observing "with how little forethought the town . . . is suffered to enlarge. It is only a multiplication of parallelograms upon a flat surface." Schools, parks, cultural institutions, and other attributes of an energetic civic culture were lacking or underfunded, even as labor commanded high wages and individuals who had invested in real estate reaped spectacular profits. The fault, he concluded, was privatism, the pursuit of individual gain rather than public good (Olmsted 1986, 590–98).

Five years later, in August 1868, Olmsted returned to Chicago. Together with John Bogart, a Prospect Park engineer, Olmsted traveled to Riverside to assess the suitability of a tract of land for development as a planned suburban community. The property in question was 1,600 acres in extent, most of which had been known as "Riverside Farm," which straddled the Des Plaines River about nine miles west of Chicago. In July 1868 Emery E. Childs had purchased the land, presumably on behalf of a group of investors, though the Riverside Improvement Company was not incorporated until March 11, 1869. The act of incorporation created a stock-holding company and gave it authority to lay out and develop the Riverside property and to build a parkway between Riverside and Chicago (Olmsted 1992, 289n, 266–68, 289n1).

Designing Riverside

Olmsted and Bogart toured the Riverside property on or about August 20, 1868. Olmsted's first impression of the land was guardedly optimistic. "The motive is like this," he informed his wife, Mary Perkins Olmsted,

> Chic. is on a dead flat. The nearest point having the slightest natural attractions is one about 9 miles straight back—West. It is a river (Aux Plaines) or creek 200 ft wide, flowing slowly on limestone bottom, banks generally sandy & somewhat elevated above the prairie level & about 10 ft above low water with sandy slopes & under water a little limestone debris. As a river not very attractive, but clean water 2 or 3 ft deep, banks & slopes rather ruggard & forlorn in minor detail but bearing tolerable trees—some very nice elms but generally oaks mostly dwarf. The sandy, tree-bearing land extends back irregularly, so that there is a good deal of rough grove land—very beautiful in contrast with the prairie and attractive. 1600 acres of land including a fair amount of this grove but yet mainly rich flat prairie have been secured, & the proprietors are now secretly securing land in a strip all the way to Chicago—for a continuous street approach—park-way. I propose to make the groves & river bank mainly public ground, by carrying a road with walks along it & to plan village streets with "parks" & little openings to include the few scattered motes on the open ground. An excellent R.R. passes through it & a street R.R. parallel with the park way is projected.

Olmsted wrote these words while traveling by train from Chicago to Buffalo, New York, where he would address citizens about the need for a park and parkway system in that city. Upon his return to New York, Olmsted must have worked furiously to prepare the firm's *Preliminary Report upon the Proposed Suburban Village at Riverside, Near Chicago*, which bears the date September 1, 1868 (Olmsted 1992, 266–68).

It is important to emphasize Olmsted's singular role in the design of Riverside: his partner, Calvert Vaux, had sailed for Europe on August 5, about two weeks before Olmsted first visited the site, and did not return until November 16. During

Vaux's absence Olmsted wrote the *Preliminary Report* and also prepared the site plan: in a letter to the attorney Edwin C. Larned of November 10, 1868, Olmsted claimed to have delivered a plat for more than three hundred Riverside lots before October 20, as well as another large plat early in November. Vaux may have participated in preparing the final Riverside plan, which was completed after his return, but it is unlikely that he could have changed the basic scheme Olmsted had determined and which conforms to the ideas contained in Olmsted's August 1868 letter to his wife. Childs wanted the plats quickly so that the company could begin selling lots, which would have made major alterations in the design virtually impossible. Thus the Riverside report and plan, which arguably codified the suburban ideal in the second half of the nineteenth century, were Olmsted's creation, not, as historians traditionally have asserted, the work of Olmsted & Vaux (Olmsted 1992, 266–72, 289n, 291–93; Schuyler 1986, 162–65; Withers 1868).

Olmsted's design for Riverside (Plate 3) was determined in part by topography and the location of such features as the river and the railroad. It also incorporated ideas he had formulated in his two prior ventures in community design. In 1860 he and Vaux were appointed as "landscape architects & designers" to a commission appointed to determine the location of streets and roads in northern Manhattan, the part of the island above 155th Street, the northernmost reach of the rectangular street system adopted in 1811. In the fragmentary documents that survive from this project, Olmsted articulated the importance of transportation routes as a means of directing and controlling an area's development. The second source of some of the ideas he incorporated at Riverside was Olmsted's planning of a residential subdivision as part of the grounds of the College of California at Berkeley. In the report he signed on behalf of the firm, Olmsted articulated a theory of landscape design appropriate to regional climate as well as to physical characteristics such as topography. Moreover, for Berkeley Neighborhood he also established a clear line of demarcation between public spaces within the community—roadsides, parks, and communal facilities—and the private, domestic landscape. Both of these earlier designs influenced the shape of Riverside (Olmsted 1983, 259–69; Olmsted 1990, 449–73, 546–73).

A third element of the Riverside plan that drew on Olmsted's previous work in landscape design was the parkway. Olmsted had first suggested a suburban road linking Berkeley Neighborhood to Oakland and, by ferry, to San Francisco in 1866. In the same year he and Vaux recommended the creation of a series of boulevards linking Prospect Park with other neighborhoods in Brooklyn and extending, by a bridge across the East River, to Central Park in Manhattan. Two years later, in urging the Brooklyn Park Commission once again to establish a parkway system, Olmsted and

Vaux argued that a system of broad, tree-lined roads would extend the benefits of parks throughout the city. Equally important, the parkways would become a spine around which a new urban form would take shape: they would "constitute the centre of a continuous neighborhood of residences of a more than usually open, elegant and healthy character" (Olmsted 1992, 26–27; Schuyler 1986, 126–28).

Although these earlier experiences contributed to the design of Riverside, Olmsted's report to the Riverside Improvement Company was his first comprehensive statement about the modern suburb, a carefully designed space in which "urban and rural advantages are agreeably combined." Like the parkways he envisioned for Brooklyn and Buffalo, the suburb was part of the evolving metropolitan landscape, another element in the "counter-tide of migration" from city to the urban periphery. Olmsted eagerly greeted the technological advances in transportation that made possible the separation of workplace and residence and thus promoted a more openly built city. He predicted that a suburb such as Riverside, if properly constructed, would exemplify "the most attractive, the most refined and the most soundly wholesome forms of domestic life, and the best application of the arts of civilization to which mankind has yet attained" (Olmsted 1992, 273–75).

Olmsted's Riverside report, like that for Berkeley Neighborhood, emphasized the importance of developing a modern infrastructure, or what he termed the creation of "abundant artificial conveniences." He deemed the construction of well-engineered roads most vital. Even with efficient rail transportation to Chicago, excellent (and expensive) roads would be essential to the success both of the Riverside Improvement Company and of the community itself. Infrastructure development also included the drilling of wells to provide a supply of clean water, as well as William Le Baron Jenney's water tower (Figure 2.1) to provide the pressure needed to deliver the water to houses. Equally important were thoroughly drained walks and the construction of such communal facilities as a nondenominational chapel and a business block, the Arcade Building, both designed by Olmsted's partner, the architect Frederick C. Withers, as well as a system of parks (Olmsted 1992, 273, 280–86; Riverside Improvement Company 1871, 13–17) (Figure 2.2). The cost of developing this infrastructure led the historian Carl Abbott to describe Riverside as the "most ambitious" of Chicago's early suburbs (1980, 121).

The streets and roads that Olmsted designed at Riverside defined and structured the community, just as he had suggested to the commissioners who were platting streets in northern Manhattan eight years earlier. First, he proposed an approach road, a parkway extending from Chicago to the suburb. He urged the promoters to acquire a strip of land ranging in width from two hundred to six hundred feet. This parkway would be an invaluable second link to the city, but

Figure 2.1. William Le Baron Jenney's water tower, from Riverside Improvement Company, *Riverside in 1871, with a Description of Its Improvements. Together with Some Engravings of Views and Buildings.* (Courtesy LuEsther T. Mertz Library of the New York Botanical Garden)

Opposite

Figure 2.2. Frederick Clarke Withers's Arcade Building (1870) as it appears today. (Photo by Isabelle Gournay)

Olmsted realized that such an approach road could confer other benefits as well. Like the parkways he proposed for Brooklyn and Buffalo, the approach road to Riverside would help separate commercial and carriage traffic as well as include paths for equestrians and pedestrians. The carriage road would be suitable for pleasure driving: along its route Olmsted proposed to set aside places for "sheltered seats and watering places." As a promenade, the parkway would also serve communal needs: it would function as an "open-air gathering for the purpose of easy, friendly, unceremonious greetings, for the enjoyment of change of scene, of cheerful and exhilarating sights and sounds, and of various good cheer, to which the people of a town, of all classes, harmoniously resort on equal terms, as to a common property." Together with the railroad, the proposed parkway would provide convenient access to the city and enable residents of Riverside to enjoy the "essential, intellectual, artistic, and social privileges which specially pertain to a metropolitan condition of society" (Olmsted 1992, 277–78). By 1871, the Riverside Improvement Company claimed that seven miles of parkway, with dimensions somewhat narrower than those Olmsted proposed, were being constructed (Riverside Improvement Company 1871, 19–20; see also Andreas 1884, 877).

Within the suburb, the streets would be characterized by spaciousness and gentle curves, thus differing with those of the city, where rectangular uniformity sym-

bolized an "eagerness to press forward." Olmsted believed that the roads of a suburb such as Riverside should "suggest and imply leisure, contemplativeness and happy tranquility" (Figure 2.3). Like the parkways, the street system within the suburb would also contribute to the residents' sense of community. Between the roads Olmsted placed a series of open public spaces having the "character of informal village-greens, commons and play-grounds," with fountains, sheltered seats, and facilities for active recreation. In urging yet another provision for neighborly recreation, Olmsted suggested that land adjacent to the Des Plaines River be set aside as a park (Figure 2.4), and that a series of rustic shelters, boat landings, pavilions, and terraces be built to enhance the attractiveness of the riverfront. The park space Olmsted provided accounted for a significant part of Riverside's land, and it occupies more than 40 percent of the village today (Olmsted 1992, 280, 288).

Important as these communal spaces were, Olmsted also believed that the "essential qualification of a suburb is domesticity," and he clearly established a distinction between park and home grounds. In their design for the Long Meadow at Prospect Park, for example, Olmsted and Vaux had created a sweeping lawn, visually endless in extent and surrounded by trees and a pool of water. The function of park space was to convey to visitors a sense of spaciousness, of range, of rural tranquility not otherwise obtainable in a large city. By contrast, a suburb such as Riverside

View of Long Common and Junction of Roads.

WALKS.

REFECTORY VERANDAH AND VIEW OF RIVER.

should provide for domestic seclusion. Families, Olmsted asserted, should be able to enjoy privacy both indoors and out (Schuyler 1986, 162–63). Shortly after reading Edward Everett Hale's *Sybaris and Other Homes* (1869), a series of fictional stories that idealized the communal aspects of suburban life, Olmsted gently protested that the author's ideas went so far as to place neighborliness above domesticity: "no house is [a] fit place for a family," he informed Hale, "that has not both public & *private outside apartments*," the latter defined by a fence, which Olmsted considered a "sort of outer wall of the house." This balancing of communal and familial interests was also evident in Olmsted's stricture that houses be set back from the road and that the intervening space contain several trees. These trees and lawns, together with the landscaped common spaces throughout Riverside, would create "an aspect of secluded peacefulness and tranquility" (Olmsted 1992, 287, 346–49, 286).

A final element of the Riverside plan, evident on the plat but not mentioned in the *Preliminary Report*, was the provision of very small house lots adjacent to the train station. In an 1871 report he prepared for a company developing a suburb at Tarrytown Heights, New York, Olmsted termed similar spaces as sites for "village houses." These he intended for homes for people of modest means who wanted to live in a suburban environment but who could not afford the expense of a large lot or keeping a carriage. In both designs Olmsted located small parks near the village lots (Olmsted 1992, 503–22).

Providing smaller lots within Riverside and Tarrytown Heights was important to Olmsted. He was acutely aware that most of the people who would benefit from suburban amenities would be the wealthy, who could afford both the cost of transportation to and from the city as well as the purchase of a spacious lot and house. Even though his professional obligations led him to work principally for the rich, he hoped to be able to extend the benefits of a suburban way of life to all classes. For example, at about the time he was formulating his ideas on Riverside, he tried to gain support for suburban subdivisions for families of the working class. Both his writings and his designs, Olmsted informed Edward Everett Hale in 1869, "urge principles, plans & measures tending to the ruralizing of *all* our urban population." His ultimate goal was the "suburbanizing of the residence parts of large towns, elbow room about a house without going into the country, without sacrifice of butchers, bakers

Figure 2.3. "View of Long Common and Junction of Roads," from Riverside Improvement Company, *Riverside in 1871, with a Description of Its Improvements. Together with Some Engravings of Views and Buildings.* (Courtesy LuEsther T. Mertz Library of the New York Botanical Garden)

Figure 2.4. "Refectory Verandah and View of River," from Riverside Improvement Company, *Riverside in 1871, with a Description of Its Improvements. Together with Some Engravings of Views and Buildings.* (Courtesy LuEsther T. Mertz Library of the New York Botanical Garden)

Figure 2.5. William Le Baron Jenney's L. Y. Schermerhorn House (1869), on Scottswood Road. (Photo by Isabelle Gournay)

& theatres" (Olmsted 1992, 346–49). Thus Olmsted's prototype for the suburban community envisioned the same degree of inclusiveness he hoped his parks would provide for the people of the city. At Central and Prospect Parks, in "Public Parks and the Enlargement of Towns," Olmsted wrote that "all classes [are] largely represented, with a common purpose, not at all intellectual, competitive with none, disposing to jealousy and spiritual or intellectual pride toward none, each individual adding by his mere presence to the pleasure of all others, all helping to the greater happiness of each. You may thus often see vast numbers of persons brought closely together, poor and rich, young and old, Jew and Gentile" (Olmsted 1871, 18).

Olmsted's plan for Riverside sketched an idealized community, a handsome landscape with public spaces yet also with secluded lots for dwellings. But the transition from plan to construction proved fraught with problems: although Riverside eventually would attain the serene beauty that Olmsted envisioned, his relationship with its developers was far from peaceful. At first glance, the Riverside commission promised to be enormously profitable. In the agreement Olmsted signed with the Riverside Improvement Company in the fall of 1868, Olmsted, Vaux & Company would receive lots in the community valued at $15,000 as compensation for completing the *Preliminary Report* and maps. Moreover, as payment for superintendence the firm would receive 7 1/2 percent of the money the company spent on construction. If the Riverside Improvement Company raised the $1.5 million it anticipated spending on improvements, Olmsted, Vaux & Company would earn more than $100,000 from superintendence. Olmsted also expected that the suburb would generate numerous commissions for his partners, architects Vaux and Withers, in preparing designs for cottages, villas, and other structures (Olmsted 1992, 31–32, 291–93, 343–46, 350).

Olmsted's initial reservations about being paid in lots, which could not be sold immediately (even as the firm was incurring substantial debts while preparing the plan and report and maintaining an office in Chicago), soon grew into outright alarm. Within a month of signing a contract with the Riverside Improvement Company, Olmsted realized that its president, Emery E. Childs, had grossly misrepresented the value of the lots. Because the prices actually paid for the first lots sold by the company were far below the value assigned to similar lots in the contract, early in November 1868 Olmsted feared that his already overextended firm had accepted payment for its services at less than market value. Within a year Olmsted, Vaux & Company twice initiated lawsuits to prevent Childs from terminating the firm's superintendence of construction. In October 1869 Childs even planned to erect his house in the middle of the Long Common, one of the most important public spaces in Riverside. When Olmsted protested, it was built across the street instead (Olmsted 1992, 350). Still, by that time Olmsted had to admit to himself that Childs, and undoubtedly other directors as well, had never accepted—or even understood—the principles of suburban design he had outlined in the *Preliminary Report*. As if adding insult to injury, the Riverside Improvement Company then asked Olmsted to explain in writing why trees in the suburb should not be planted in the same manner in which they would be placed along the street of a major city (Olmsted 1992, 31–32, 303–4).

By the fall of 1869 Olmsted concluded that Riverside was indeed a "regular flyaway speculation," managed with the same unethical behavior he attributed to the Wall Street financier Jay Gould. The warning signs quickly became more ominous. Withers, who was the firm's representative in Chicago, informed his partners that mismanagement and a lack of progress on the ground at Riverside were injuring the firm's reputation and causing it to lose potential business in the Midwest.

As their disagreements with the speculative developers intensified, the designers were left with little recourse: on October 30, 1870, Olmsted, Vaux & Company negotiated a release from its agreement with the Riverside Improvement Company (Olmsted 1992, 346–49; Vaux 1870).

Olmsted's hopes for Riverside suffered other setbacks. The great Chicago fire of 1871 destroyed the Riverside Improvement Company's records, and the economic panic of 1873 struck with such severity that the developers defaulted on their obligations. Recovery was long delayed because capital previously available for suburban development instead was needed to finance the rebuilding of Chicago. But as city and region recovered, so did Riverside, even after the improvement company's failure. Following the Riverside Company's demise, the village was incorporated in 1875 (Abbott 1980, 119; Sacchi and Guardi 2012, 27).

Developing the Community

If in conception Riverside was the singular achievement of Frederick Law Olmsted, the construction of the community and its evolution over time have been the result of the efforts of many individuals, most of them unidentified, who built the roads and parks, the houses and public buildings, and of residents who have cherished the village over generations. On the eve of the great fire, the Riverside Improvement Company reported that more than fifty homes had been built, along with several impressive public structures, including the water tower, the church, the business block, and a hotel. The rambling, Swiss-style structure (demolished), designed by Jenney, the engineer-architect who was one of the village's earliest residents, overlooked the Des Plaines River and attracted visitors from Chicago and elsewhere, while the business block provided goods and services to residents. In constructing the landscape, workers planted 47,000 shrubs and 39,000 trees, which, as they matured, would shroud the prairie landscape in shade. As Riverside grew in the aftermath of the fire and the financial crisis, the first generation of cottages and villas, many designed by Jenney, took shape along its curving roads (see Figure 2.5).

Even after the Olmsted firm withdrew from its involvement with the community, the building pattern conformed to the street plan and other aspects of the *Preliminary Report*, including setbacks from the public ways and construction of the park system. This was largely the result of Jenney's efforts, as he became the effective steward of Olmsted's 1869 plan. Most of the first generation of houses were cottages and modest villas (see Figure 2.6), though several dwellings were erected in village lots, just as Olmsted hoped, and were located at the southern end of the village, near the railroad sta-

Figure 2.6. Calvert Vaux's John Clarke Dore Cottage (1869), on Fairbank Road. (Photo by Isabelle Gournay)

tion, the business block, and the park along the Des Plaines River. Still, ambitious and attractive though it was, Riverside grew slowly throughout the last decades of the nineteenth century, as the North Shore suburbs attracted more of the wealthy seeking an alternative to the city. In 1900 the village's population was 1,551 (Grossman et al. 2004b; Riverside 1871, 17–19, 23).

Around the turn of the century several of Riverside's most iconic buildings were erected, including the village hall, designed by George Ashby and constructed 1893–95, Louis Sullivan's house for Henry B. Babson (1907; demolished 1960), and Frank Lloyd Wright's houses for Ferdinand Franklin Tomek (1907) and Avery Coonley (1908), the latter two early examples of the Prairie style that are now designated National Historic Landmarks. Riverside experienced a building boom in the 1920s, when much of the land in the northern part of the village was finally developed. The streets in the newly developing area conformed to the 1869 plan, though many of the lots were smaller than those originally platted. Bungalows and modest houses lined the streets at the northern end of the village, home to a rapidly increasing population of residents new to suburbia. Still, the village leaders, aware of their history, included in the 1922 zoning ordinance the setbacks established in Olmsted's *Preliminary Report* and the 1869 plan. The publication of *Frederick Law Olmsted: Landscape Architect* (2 vols., 1922, 1928), edited by Frederick Law Olmsted Jr. and Theodora Kimball, surely helped raise awareness of the community's principal designer (Grossman et al. 2004a, 712; Sacchi and Guardi 2012, 19, 33).

Despite continuing development, Riverside has successfully maintained its historic fabric. The new construction undertaken during the 1920s swelled its population to 6,770 in 1930, an increase of more than 150 percent in the decade, almost all of whom were white and the overwhelming majority relatively new to the community. According to the 1930 decennial census, 2,404 residents were of foreign or mixed parentage, and 941 were foreign-born whites (16 were African American and 2 were of other races). Almost half of all residents were immigrants or the children of at least one immigrant parent. These numbers are comparable to and in several cases lower than the percentages of residents of foreign or mixed parentage or foreign-born residents of several of the more prosperous North Shore suburbs Michael Ebner has studied. Even in 1930, however, there were still early residents living in the village, as well as children of the initial settlers who cherished a sense of place. When a group of citizens organized politically and proposed developing the Long Common into sites for houses and apartments in the 1920s or early 1930s, residents soundly defeated those plans. Villagers celebrated the national sesquicentennial in 1926 and organized a pageant to mark the centennial of the first white settlement of the area in 1932 (Grossman et al. 2004b; Sacchi and Guardi 2012, 111, 115, 117–18; U.S. Bureau of the Census 1931). The publication of Lewis Mumford's *Brown Decades* in 1931 brought Olmsted's career to greater prominence. Although he did not mention Riverside in his discussion of Olmsted in "The Renewal of Landscape" chapter, Mumford praised him as the individual "who almost single-handedly laid the foundations for a better order in city building" (Mumford 1955 [1931], 82). Residents of Riverside might only have added that what Olmsted accomplished in the design of their community was commensurate in importance to the design of public parks as a response to metropolitan development. In the same year as *Brown Decades*, Theodora Kimball Hubbard published Olmsted's Riverside report and related documents in the professional journal *Landscape Architecture*. In her introduction Hubbard observed that "the village is reported to be beloved by its inhabitants," who cherished Olmsted's design (Hubbard 1931, 257). The following year Howard K. Menhinick published "Riverside Sixty Years Later" in the same journal. Menhinick, who likened Riverside to a New England village, compared the original plan with the streets of the village at the time and was struck by how intact the community plan was more than six decades after completion of the *Preliminary Report* and the 1869 plan. "How many of our present-day developments," he wondered, referring obliquely to the forces of metropolitan expansion that were promoting rampant suburbanization, "are so planned that they can maintain their original character and identity for sixty years?" (Menhinick 1932, 109, 116, 117).

Preserving Riverside

At the depth of the Great Depression, Dr. S. S. Fuller headed the organization of a celebration marking one hundred years of development since the first whites settled within the boundaries of the village. One product of Fuller's effort was the publication of *Riverside Then and Now* (Bassman 1936), a history of the community from the days of the Native Americans through the dawn of the twentieth century, itself a testament to the strong sense that Riverside was a special place to which residents were deeply attached. In the chapter "A Model Suburb Is Born," Mrs. E. O. C. Hoefer recounted the names and houses of many of the early settlers of the village as well as patterns of social life in its first three decades. (She did, however, misspell Olmsted's name throughout.) The year after the publication of *Riverside Then and Now*, residents organized the Riverside Historical Society to preserve documents and artifacts relating to the community's history. These publications, commemorations, and awareness of history surely conveyed to residents that Riverside was distinctive. More than zoning or planning or preservation restrictions, this sense of the community's history, this sense of place, has been essential to Riverside's continuing adherence to much of the original Olmsted plan (Bassman 1936, 75–88; Sacchi and Guardi 2012, 111).

Riverside continued to increase in population during the post–World War II years, as a new wave of construction, again, of modest houses, built out the community (31 percent of all structures in the village were erected between 1940 and 1970). Population reached 9,750 residents in 1960 and 10,357 a decade later, at which time the community was still overwhelmingly white (Grossman et al. 2004b). The village did experience some demolition in those years, most notably that of the Babson house, but James and Carolyn Howlett, together with other citizens, worked effectively to save the Coonley house in the 1950s. To a remarkable degree Riverside retains its significance as a planned community that has evolved within the framework of its original plan. Formation of the Frederick Law Olmsted Society in the late 1960s has been important to this. Its founding president, Robert W. Heidrich, compiled and

Figure 2.7. William Le Baron Jenney's water tower, rebuilt to a greater height around 1914 and recently restored. (Photo by Isabelle Gournay)

submitted the Riverside Landscape Architectural District nomination, which was approved and entered in the National Register of Historic Places in August 1970 (at that time it was possible to nominate a district without municipal approval; the village formally adopted the National Register designation on March 20, 1972). The district is bounded by Ogden Avenue and the Des Plaines River to the south, 26th Street to the north, Harlem Avenue to the east, and Forbes Road to the west, thus embracing all of the area north of the river included in the 1869 plan. The American Planning Association designated the village a National Planning Landmark in 1991. Jenney's water tower, which was partly consumed by fire in 1913 and rebuilt to a greater height immediately thereafter, was landmarked by the American Water Works Association in 1970.

Although these designations do not provide strong legal protections against change, they are cherished by many residents as proof that theirs is a special place. In succeeding years the Riverside Historical Commission completed a study of *The*

Riverside Landscape (1981), and Malcolm D. Cairns and Gary B. Kesler prepared a *Historic Landscape Evaluation and Conservation Plan of Riverside* (1985), both of which have been adopted by the village, while the Olmsted Society has published *Landscaping in a Landmark Village*, a guide to help residents better understand, manage, and protect "the unique landscape of a historic landmark village" (Frederick Law Olmsted Society of Riverside n.d.; Grossman et al. 2004a, 712; Sacchi and Guardi 2012, 111).

In 1991 Riverside adopted a planning ordinance that strengthened regulatory protections over the physical fabric of the village. Included are appointed citizen commissions that oversee planning, the village landscape, and historic buildings. Each of the citizen commissions is empowered to review any changes that might affect the integrity of the historic district, and they can make recommendations to the village board, which has ultimate authority. The Riverside Village Code specifically charges the Landscape Advisory Commission to prepare and evaluate plans "in accordance with the landscape planting theories, concepts and principles of Frederick Law Olmsted." A village forester maintains trees on public property and advises residents of the care and, when necessary, replacement of trees on their lots (Riverside Village Code 1991, Title 2, chaps. 14–4 and 15, Title 11-1-14[B]).

Over time, virtually all the residential streets in Olmsted's plan for the Riverside property north of the Des Plaines River were laid out according to plan. Only a small part of the considerable section south of the Des Plaines River remains visually part of Riverside's tree-shrouded landscape and is a forest preserve. The remainder was developed as the site of the Brookfield Zoo in the 1930s and later by construction of the Brookfield-Riverside High School. But the land north of the river, the historic district, became and has remained the successful suburb Olmsted envisioned. That Riverside has retained its iconic form has been the result of the efforts of residents who have long appreciated their community more than regulations, which only recently acquired effective power. Riverside never had "the advantages of stringent private-deed restrictions and architectural control," Menhinick observed in 1932, "yet the provision of adequate open spaces, the setting of houses well back from the streets among trees and shrubs, and the consequent attraction of people with good taste and community pride, have accomplished nearly the same result." Community triumphed over the privatism Olmsted had decried in his 1863 description of Chicago, which enabled Riverside to remain an exception to the historic suburbs buffeted by change, the phenomenon that Menhinick referred to on page 117 of his 1932 article. And what residents accomplished is impressive: today, long since engulfed by the expanding metropolis, Riverside's tree-lined, curvilinear streets stand amid a sprawling gridiron—the relentless "multiplication of parallelograms" Olmsted lamented—its physical form a testament to the nineteenth-century suburban ideal and to generations of residents who have cherished their community (Olmsted 1986, 591).

Riverside retains much of the physical fabric Olmsted designed almost a century and a half ago, even as it has experienced an influx of newcomers over that time. Despite demographic renewals, in terms of its buildings and landscape Riverside is an aging community, with much of its housing stock erected more than a century ago (more than 61 percent before 1939). While many buildings have been restored recently, including Withers's business block (Figure 2.2) and Jenney's water tower (Figure 2.7), and many residences are well maintained, the landscape has suffered losses, especially in the number of trees and shrubs, which Olmsted had intended to separate the private realm of the family from the public arena of the street. Riverside's population in 2010 was 8,875 (a significant decline from the peak in 1970, but this appears to be more the result of the end of the baby boom generation than a significant aging of the village's population, as the median age was 42.6 years in 2010). Of residents, 91.3 percent were white; the Hispanic population (some of whom the Census Bureau classifies as white) was 10.5 percent; Asians represented 2.1 percent of residents; and African Americans accounted for 1.3 percent of the total. Riverside is still an affluent community, as the median value of a house was an estimated $397,200, and more than 60 percent of adult residents have a baccalaureate or advanced degree. Seventy percent of residential units are single-family detached, although the remainder, forty-four attached units and approximately one thousand apartments, represents a significant development of recent years that challenges the stereotype of suburbia in the United States (U.S. Bureau of the Census 2010).

Riverside has worked hard to maintain its history even as it entered a new millennium. A new, appropriately scaled but unimaginatively designed business block has been constructed opposite Withers's Arcade Building. In 1997 DLK/LDR/ Charles Beveridge completed a comprehensive plan, "Conserving the Olmsted Legacy," while in 2006 URS submitted a draft "Downtown Riverside Transit-Oriented Development Plan." The URS plan defines downtown as extending a quarter of a mile from the railroad station. Its premise is that Riverside needs a significant expansion of retail at its historic core, which is centered on Burlington and Quincy streets, which flank the railroad tracks. It advocates construction of a boutique hotel on the site of the former Riverside Hotel, now occupied by the Public Works Building; design enhancements to create a pedestrian-friendly downtown; new space for commercial development; and increased parking places. It also calls for the village to take a more active role in promoting and facilitating the development of a more vibrant downtown. On April 15, 2013, the village adopted the "Village of Riverside Central Business District Plan," prepared by the Chicago Metropolitan Agency for Planning (CMAP). This too is premised on surveys that reveal that residents want more retail and dining options downtown, and it calls for new, context-sensitive design to provide opportunities for economic development in the downtown. The CMAP plan advocates more effective signage to promote easier access to downtown, a more attractive rail corridor, and enhancing the downtown streetscape through landscaping, furniture, lighting, and sidewalk cafés. The plan supports history, especially strengthening the Riverside Historical Museum, and emphasizes the importance of the village's reconnecting with the riverfront (it calls for construction of a recreation and community center, not a hotel, on the Public Works Building site, shoreline restoration, the reintroduction of walking paths along the river, and greater use of the river as a recreational resource) (CMAP 2013; URS 2006).

Creating a vibrant downtown is a challenge that many historic suburbs face. Riverside's task is especially difficult because of its small population, the historic fabric of the community, the limited space available for redevelopment, and the lack of direct access from major roads outside the village. But it is important, both to meet the desire of residents for a more attractive and enticing downtown and to generate additional tax revenue. How well the village accomplishes this may well determine how appealing the community will remain in the future.

Residents of Riverside will celebrate the sesquicentennial of Olmsted's report in 2018 and the village's comprehensive plan the following year. They can be proud that they are part of the history of one of the oldest and most successful of iconic planned communities in the United States. To be sure, Riverside never achieved the degree of economic diversity Olmsted hoped for, and, despite recent gains in the Hispanic population, racial inclusiveness remains elusive, but the village has survived growth and change, the ordeal of economic depressions, and the transformation of metropolitan life in the years since World War II, yet it has retained the qualities that have made it a desirable place in which to live. The regulations in place promise to maintain those qualities, but the village government could, of course, eliminate those protections in the future. Moreover, balancing economic development while preserving the community's history in its landscape and architecture will require enlightened civic leadership and the full participation of the community. Only the ongoing commitment of residents to their collective heritage will ensure that Riverside will continue to exemplify the best of the nineteenth-century suburban ideal in the twenty-first century.

Table 2.1
Summary of Historical Events and Heritage Benchmarks for Riverside

Year	Event
1868	Emery E. Childs purchases 1,600 acres straddling the Des Plaines River. Frederick Law Olmsted writes his *Preliminary Report upon the Proposed Suburban Village at Riverside, Near Chicago.*
1869	Incorporation of the Riverside Improvement Company. Olmsted, Vaux & Company produces the village's General Plan.
1870	Olmsted, Vaux & Company negotiates a release from its agreement with the Riverside Improvement Company.
1875	The Riverside Improvement Company declares bankruptcy. Riverside is incorporated as a village.
1895	Construction of the Town Hall.
1908	Construction begins on Frank Lloyd Wright's Avery Coonley House.
1922	A zoning ordinance confirms the setbacks established in Olmsted's *Preliminary Report* and his 1869 plan.
1920s	Riverside experiences a building boom, its population increasing to 6,770. A garden apartment replaces William Le Baron Jenney's original hotel.
1931-32	The journal *Landscape Architecture* issues two studies of Riverside on the village's sixtieth anniversary.
1936	Herbert J. Bassman edits *Riverside Then and Now: A History of Riverside, Illinois.*
1960	Demolition of Louis Sullivan's Babson House of 1907.
Late 1960s	Creation of the Frederick Law Olmsted Society to sustain Olmsted's vision for Riverside for generations to come.
1970	Placement of the Riverside Landscape Architectural District on the National Register of Historic Places (formally adopted by the municipality in 1972).
1972	Designation of Jenney's water tower as an American Water Landmark.
1976	Opening of the Riverside Historical Commission Museum.
1985	The municipality adopts a *Historic Landscape Evaluation and Conservation Plan.*
1991	While Riverside receives National Planning Landmark designation; a new local planning ordinance strengthens regulatory protections of its plan, buildings, and landscape.
2005	Restoration of the recently decommissioned water tower to its 1913 appearance.
2010	Construction of a historically compatible mixed-use structure across the railroad tracks from F. C. Withers's restored 1870 business block.
	Population (as of 2010), 8,875; 1,260 acres [510 ha]; 3,680 dwelling units.

REFERENCES

Abbott, Carl. 1980. "'Necessary Adjuncts to Growth': The Railroad Suburbs of Chicago, 1854–1875." *Journal of the Illinois State Historical Society* 73(2): 117–23, 125–31.

Andreas, Alfred T. 1884. *History of Cook County, Illinois. From the Earliest Period to the Present Time.* Chicago: A. T. Andreas.

Bassman, Herbert C., ed. 1936. *Riverside Then and Now.* Riverside, IL: Riverside Historical Commission.

Chicago Metropolitan Agency for Planning (CMAP). 2013. "Village of Riverside Central Business District Plan." https://www.riverside.il.us/DocumentCenter/View/891/CMAP-Plan-for-Riversides-Central-Business-District-PDF.

Frederick Law Olmsted Society of Riverside. n.d. *Landscaping in a Landmark Village.* http://www.olmstedsociety.org/resources/landscape-resources.

Grossman, James R., Ann Durkin Keating, and Janice L. Reiff, eds. 2004. *Encyclopedia of Chicago.* Chicago: University of Chicago Press. http://www.encyclopedia.chicagohistory.org.

Hubbard, Theodora Kimball. 1931. "Riverside, Illinois: A Residential Neighborhood Designed over Sixty Years Ago." *Landscape Architecture* 21(4): 257–91.

Menhinick, Howard K. 1932. "Riverside Sixty Years Later." *Landscape Architecture* 22(2): 109–17.

Mumford, Lewis. 1955 (1931). *The Brown Decades: A Study of the Arts in America.* New York: Dover.

Olmsted, Frederick Law. 1871. "Public Parks and the Enlargement of Towns." *Journal of Social Science* 3: 1–36.

———. 1983. *The Papers of Frederick Law Olmsted, vol. 3, Creating Central Park, 1857–1861*, edited by Charles E. Beveridge and David Schuyler. Baltimore: Johns Hopkins University Press.

———. 1986. *The Papers of Frederick Law Olmsted, vol. 4, The Civil War and the U.S. Sanitary Commission, 1861–1863*, edited by Jane Turner Censer. Baltimore: Johns Hopkins University Press.

———. 1990. *The Papers of Frederick Law Olmsted, vol. 5, The California Frontier, 1863–1865*, edited by Victoria Post Ranney et al. Baltimore: Johns Hopkins University Press.

———. 1992. *The Papers of Frederick Law Olmsted, vol. 6, The Years of Olmsted, Vaux & Company, 1865–1874*, edited by David Schuyler and Jane Turner Censer. Baltimore: Johns Hopkins University Press.

Riverside Improvement Company. 1871. *Riverside in 1871, with a Description of Its Improvements. Together with Some Engravings of Views and Buildings.* Chicago: Riverside Improvement Company.

Riverside Village Code. 1991. http://www.sterlingcodifiers.com/codebook/index.php?book_id=610.

Sacchi, Lonnie, and Constance Guardi. 2012. *Riverside.* Charleston, SC: Arcadia Publishing.

Schuyler, David. 1986. *The New Urban Landscape: The Redefinition of City Form in Nineteenth-Century America.* Baltimore: Johns Hopkins University Press.

URS. 2006. "Downtown Riverside Transit-Oriented Development Plan." http://www.rtams.org/rtams/planningStudy.jsp?id=49.

U.S. Bureau of the Census. 1931. *Census of Population, vol. 3, Report by States Showing Composition and Characteristics of the Population for Counties, Cities, Townships or Other Minor Subdivisions.* Washington, DC: Government Printing Office. http://www.census.gov/www.abs/decennial/1930.html.

U.S. Bureau of the Census. 2010. http://www.factfinder2.census.gov.

Vaux, Calvert. 1870. Letter to Frederick Law Olmsted, April 11, 1870. Frederick Law Olmsted Papers, Manuscript Division, Library of Congress, Washington, DC.

Withers, Frederick C. 1868. Letter to Frederick Law Olmsted, November 16, 1868. Frederick Law Olmsted Papers, Manuscript Division, Library of Congress, Washington, DC.

CHAPTER 3

ENGLISH GARDEN CITIES

Challenges of Conservation and Change

Mervyn Miller

Letchworth Garden City (1903), Hampstead Garden Suburb (1907), and Welwyn Garden City (1920) are world renowned as iconic planned communities.[1] Their master planning by Barry Parker and Raymond Unwin (for the first two) and by Louis de Soissons (for the third) still influences community planning (Figures 3.1–3.3). In each, innovative housing design and sensitive landscaping and green reserves encapsulated Ebenezer Howard's "joyous union" of town and country (Beevers 1988). Enlightened private-sector real estate developments, they became outstandingly successful models for design and density standards imposed by United Kingdom governments as statutory town planning evolved from 1909. The 1919 Housing and Town Planning Act municipalized garden city standards for public housing and was emulated in private-sector suburban estates (Ward 1994, 30–34, 40–42). Informed by progressive American practice, the model was updated for Wythenshawe, Manchester's garden city satellite planned by Barry Parker (Deakin 1989; Miller 2010, 80–86; Hopkins and Hebbert, this volume). The New Towns Act of 1946 financed state development of new settlements under a program that ran from Stevenage (1946) through Milton Keynes (1967). The partly completed Welwyn Garden City was taken into the program in 1948 (Osborn and Whittick 1977, 180–91).

This chapter outlines the origins of the three exemplars and reviews how they fared post–World War II when the garden city environment appeared as an outdated middle-class concept compared to dynamic, state-promoted New Town development. Yet it survived to be cherished under heritage conservation, as the concern to protect historic areas rather than isolated buildings and ancient monuments emerged during the 1960s. Conservation areas were designated in all three exemplars between 1968 and 1974 ("designated heritage assets of national significance," to use current English Heritage terminology). Before the end of the twentieth century, pressure mounted for radical change and regeneration, potentially conflicting with their iconic spacious character and verdant landscaping. The rural reserves or greenbelts were already modified post-1945 by extensions of the town area at Letchworth and by the area added to Welwyn Garden City under its New Town designation. They came under renewed pressure at Letchworth with the delayed

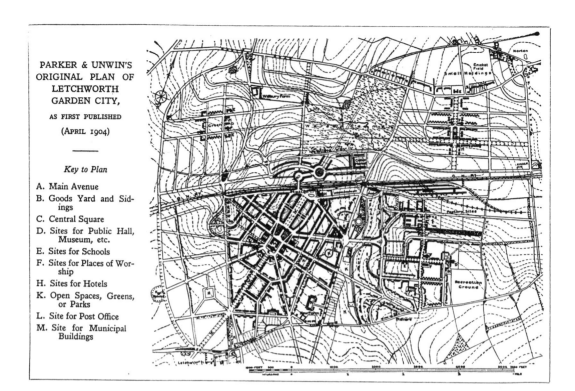

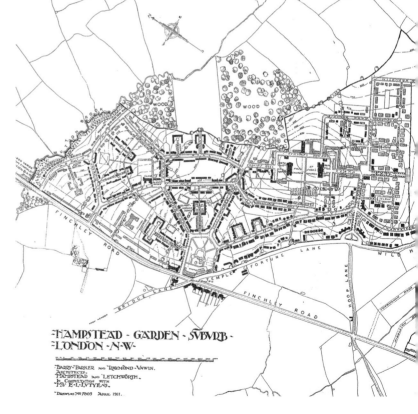

Figure 3.1. The original plan for Letchworth Garden City by Barry Parker and Raymond Unwin, as first published in 1904. Although details changed through the years, particularly in the outlying neighborhoods, the plan recognizably projects the bold axial line of Broadway and the landscaped valley on the east, which became Howard Park, both key elements of the layout. (C. B. Purdom, *The Garden City* [J. M. Dent & Sons Ltd., 1913])

updating of the Local Plan and the controversy over a large development proposed north of the Grange estate in 2016–18. At Welwyn Garden City the proposals for the "Shredded Wheat site" raised fundamental concern about the compatibility of higher density redevelopment with the adjacent historic original town center.

Although set against the historical backdrop of the garden city, I also need to consider the ongoing debate between government, communities, and professionals about the purpose of planning, initiated by the Conservative-led coalition government in 2011. This created uncertainty about the robustness of heritage protection under the National Planning Policy Framework (NPPF), operational from March 2012 (Department for Communities and Local Government [DCLG] 2012). This introduced a presumption for approval of sustainable development, although heritage conservation appears to have held up well so far. The Department of Communities and Local Government has also championed "localism" (DCLG 2012, paras. 183–85), with communities encouraged to engage in their own "development planning," hitherto the preserve of county and district councils. It remains to be seen whether such energy can be harnessed to agree to positive change, through neighborhood plans, particularly when heritage issues are involved, and which may initiate conflict with "official" local planning policies.

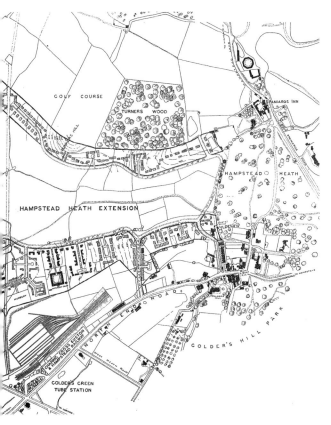

Figure 3.2. Unwin's plan for Hampstead Garden Suburb, shown in its 1911 version, which includes the completed artisans' quarter; at bottom left are the near-definitive layout of the Central Squares by Edwin Lutyens, and the Hampstead Heath extension, with its associated housing closes and culs-de-sac. (Courtesy Hampstead Garden Suburb Trust)

ROAD · & · RAIL · COMMUNICATIONS ·

DIAGRAM · OF · TOWN · PLAN · SHEWING · ZONES ·

SHOPS · PUBLIC · BUILDINGS · OPEN · SPACES · ETC ·

SCALE OF FEET

TO · LUTON ·

TO · THE NORTH

N

RIVER · MIMRAM

AGRICULTURAL · BELT

HERTFORD · ROAD

GREAT · NORTH · ROAD

AGRICULTURAL · BELT

AGRICULTURAL BELT

TO · HERTFORD ·

AGRICULTURAL · BELT ·

RIVER · LEA ·

G · N · R · MAIN · LINE

LONDON

AGRICULTURAL · BELT ·

LOUIS · DE · SOISSONS · F · RIBA · SADG · ARCHITECT ·

THIS · DIAGRAM · MUST · NOT · BE · TAKEN · AS · THE · BASIS · OF · ANY · TRANSACTIONS

WELWYN · GARDEN · CITY ·

Scale of Chains.

Scale of Feet

Residential Areas   Factory Areas

Open Spaces   Shopping Areas.

64

Evolution of Conservation Practice:
Listed Buildings and Conservation Areas

Statutory preservation of historic artifacts in Britain originated 130 years ago with the first of the Ancient Monuments Acts, which "scheduled" archaeological sites, castles, and ruined abbeys. Comprehensive "listing" of buildings begun during World War II has evolved to include buildings from the medieval period to thirty years from the present day. English Heritage estimates that there are 373,000 listed building entries in England, but these include tombs, gravestones, and group entries composing multiple buildings (English Heritage n.d.). Buildings are graded I, II*, or II, according to the degree of architectural or historic significance or quality; the top two grades ("designated heritage assets of the highest significance") account for about 6 percent and the remainder are graded II. Listing designations are currently made by the Secretary of State for Digital, Culture, Media and Sport, on advice from Historic England, formerly English Heritage. This organization has a national responsibility to investigate the historic environment. Listed building consent for alteration and extension is administered by district councils, which must consult Historic England about the wholesale demolition of all grades and about all work to grade I and II* buildings.

Conservation areas, introduced in 1967, have proved popular with communities and local governments: there are now about 9,300, of widely varied special interest, designated and administered by local councils (the local planning authorities [LPAs]) (Historic England 2016). The inventory includes historic cities, towns, and villages, including the two garden cities, many garden suburbs, and a few New

Figure 3.3. Master plan for Welwyn Garden City (1920) by Louis de Soissons. This is one of the most iconic of all new community plans, meticulously presented. The mainline east coast railway from London to Scotland more emphatically divided the community into two parts than had been the case at Letchworth. (C. B. Purdom, *The Building of Satellite Towns* [J. M. Dent & Sons Ltd., 1925])

Town neighborhoods. There is a requirement for community consultation before formal designation. Detailed character appraisals follow, which form the basis for ongoing management of change.

Government policy defines conservation as "the process of maintaining and managing change to a heritage asset in a way that sustains and where appropriate preserves its significance" (DCLG 2012, 51). How do we define heritage assets? They may be broad and general such as conservation areas, or the criterion of special architectural or historic interest may be applied more specifically to list individual buildings (English Heritage 2010; Historic England n.d.), which each of the three exemplars include. For example, the iconic twin churches designed by Edwin Lutyens in Central Square, Hampstead, are grade I; the Spirella Factory at Letchworth is grade II*; and the distinctive Shredded Wheat Factory at Welwyn is grade II. At Letchworth and Hampstead, much early artisan cottage housing and a representative selection of individual houses and public buildings have been listed. While this has ensured preservation of their physical form, it may have inhibited their original purpose as artisan housing through gentrification. The few listed buildings at Welwyn include the grade II* Templewood School (1949) by the Hertfordshire County Architect and the elegant grade II Knightsfield Flats (1955) by Louis de Soissons. Surprisingly, listing has not included the Georgian-style interwar housing neighborhoods from de Soissons's office, which defined the image of the place. Listing housing at Welwyn, particularly from its New Town era, might not be the most appropriate way of conserving the generic character, which stems from the relationship between buildings, the road layout, and associated landscaping, which are key matters addressed in conservation areas.

Conservation areas have long existed in all three exemplars. On the Letchworth Garden City Estate, Hertfordshire County Council (HCC) designated the historic villages of Norton and Willian in the late 1960s. Letchworth Garden City Conservation Area, designated by North Hertfordshire District Council (NHDC) in 1974, concentrated on the town center and major pre-1914 residential areas, but later extensions added important housing estates from the early 1920s (NHDC 2001). At Hampstead, they include the entire area developed under the Hampstead Garden Suburb Trust from 1907 ("Old Suburb") and the 1911 extension ("New Suburb") largely developed by the Co-partnership Tenants in the interwar period, as well as the contiguous The Bishop's Avenue, with its opulent individual houses, which was designated as Hampstead Garden Suburb Conservation Area by Barnet London Borough Council (BLBC) in 1968, with the later addition of Golders Green Crematorium. HCC designated the Welwyn Garden City Conservation Area in 1968, west of the railway, reinforcing a long-standing impression that the industrial east and its housing were on the wrong side of the tracks (Welwyn Hatfield Borough Council [WHBC] 2008), although WHBC later designated part of the 1930s Woodhall neighborhood on the east.

All LPAs are required to provide a full range of heritage policies in their Local Plans. At Hampstead, additional detailed control by BLBC is provided by an "Article 4 Direction," approved by the Secretary of State for the Environment in 1971, and subsequently strengthened (Miller 2006, 235). This overrides "permitted development" under the main planning legislation, which allows householders to erect small extensions and replace windows or roof tiles—work that has had a cumulative corrosive impact on the visual integrity of the overall character elsewhere.

Schemes of Management

All three exemplars possess additional regulation outside planning legislation. This derives from the powers of the original freehold landowner developers, exercised through leases under the long-standing dual layers of property ownership in the United Kingdom. Originally, individual housing plots were leased, not sold freehold, typically for 99 years at Letchworth and 999 years at Hampstead Garden Suburb and Welwyn Garden City. In 1967, the government passed a Leasehold Reform Act, enabling house owners to buy their freeholds, canceling leasehold control. However, under Section 19 of the Act, ground landlords could apply for a Scheme of Management (SoM), which was applicable to "well managed estates," subject to High Court approval. At Letchworth, the SoM is now administered by Letchworth Garden City Heritage Foundation (LGCHF). The original freehold estate owner-developer, First Garden City Limited, was taken over in the late 1950s, and, following local activism the Letchworth Garden City Corporation was formed in 1963, under private legislation in Parliament (Miller 2002). Its successor, LGCHF, created by further legislation, took control in 1995 (Miller 2002).

At Hampstead, the Hampstead Garden Suburb Trust (HGST) was reorganized in 1968, and its SoM was approved in 1974 (Miller 2006, 225–27). At Welwyn, the original landlord powers of Second Garden City Ltd. were established in 1948 and passed the following year to the Welwyn Garden City New Town Development Corporation with the SoM approved in 1973 (de Soissons 1988, 187–90). In 1978, the Commission for the New Towns (to which the assets of the Development Corporation were transferred in 1966) passed the SoM and administration of 5,800 social housing units to the planning authority WHBC (formed in 1974) (de Soissons 1988, 190–91). SoMs, although criticized as an additional layer of bureaucracy, have in the long term proved effective in reinforcing planning authority control over conservation areas, and they also reined in insensitive changes to individual houses. The HGST has been notably effective at achieving this. The LGCHF has also strengthened its procedures with beneficial effect. At Welwyn, the dual role of the council, as planning authority and ground landlord, has sometimes brought internal conflict, where development, otherwise permitted under planning legislation, has been contrary to the SoM. From 1980 the right to buy for tenants of local authority housing created further potential for uncontrolled change.

Shaping Change

The typology of garden city housing, which arose from the social reform ethic of the original developers, remains one of the most potent aspects of its iconicity. In the early 1990s, design guidance emerged as a means of encouraging sensitive change in all three exemplars. The Letchworth Design Guidance prepared by the LGCHF was strengthened in 2008–9 (LGCHF 2008), with the most detailed control applicable to pre-1930 properties, when garden city characteristics were strongest. An intensive survey to identify buildings of local significance provided an inventory against which to assess proposals to alter or extend houses.[2] Historic England has been proactive in encouraging conservation area appraisals (English Heritage 2008, 2010, 2012; Historic England 2016), itemizing strengths and weaknesses, designating buildings that make a positive contribution to the area, and fine-tuning conservation policies to specific locations. Both garden cities' local authorities have also produced appraisals (NHDC 2001; WHBC 2008), following community consultation, that were adopted officially as supplementary planning guidance.

The Welwyn Garden City appraisal includes a detailed history with archival illustrations. At Hampstead, BLBC and HGST collaborated, with the latter organizing community workshops to research and draft the appraisal, under the editorial guidance of the Trust's architectural advisor, David Davidson (BLBC 2010). The appraisal was simultaneously adopted by both bodies in October 2010. The HGST has become increasingly vigilant to ensure adherence to consents and only signing off their compliance after inspection of the completed work. Rectification of past infringements is often required when properties change hands, bringing an environmental improvement for the character of the suburb.

There has also been recognition of the benefit of promoting work well done. At Letchworth, modest grants to householders were introduced to assist bridging the cost gap between plastic-framed windows and concrete roof tiles (both widely used in housing modernization) and the more authentic timber windows and clay plain tiles.[3] The Letchworth Garden City Corporation and its successor initiated an award scheme to publicize good practice. While not bringing wholesale improvement, the awards have fostered greater respect for heritage values (assisted by the popularity of television programs on house restoration), which is also reflected in enhanced sale prices of well-conserved houses. The LGCHF assisted formation of an owners' group for the famous Cheap Cottages Exhibition of 1905 and Urban Cottages Exhibition of 1907, with attractive centennial plaques for each property (Letchworth's Exhibition Cottages). Some remarkable restoration has been recognized by awards, including prefabricated timber cottages, and a unique heavy concrete-panel cottage, No. 158 Wilbury Road (designed by the Liverpool City Engineer for the 1905 Exhibition), which is a grade II* listed building. Meticulous restoration has enhanced larger Arts and Crafts cottages, for example, No. 7 Willian Way, designed in 1909 by the local architect Wilson Bidwell as his family home.

Hampstead has introduced the Stuart Gray Award, commemorating the architect resident who did much in the early 1970s to raise consciousness of what architectural historian Nikolaus Pevsner aptly termed "the most nearly perfect example of the unique English invention and speciality—the Garden Suburb."[4] This award is administered by the HGS Residents' Association (HGSRA), who also maintain a website with a photograph of each house in the suburb (accessed through HGST 2002).

Regeneration

Conservation controls can only be a partial response to the challenge of change. A few years ago the Town and Country Planning Association (TCPA) examined the future of garden city communities, recording and analyzing change during the late twentieth century, looking toward management of innovation without compromising architectural and historic significance. The smaller, predominantly residential communities (which include Hampstead Garden Suburb) appeared less susceptible to harmful change, while the two garden cities, with extensive commercial and manufacturing areas, were influenced by national trends through the late twentieth century. The original objective of self-contained garden cities with a full range of employment, leisure, and shopping facilities changed swiftly after World War II. With its closer proximity to central London, Welwyn Garden City always had middle-class commuters, but the post-1946 interpolation of Stevenage New Town between it and Letchworth further altered regional dynamics, while railway electrification in the 1970s increased regional and metropolitan commuting, duly increasing the pressure for change. The dominance of national supermarket chains and a decline in manufacturing were reflected in the pattern of development opportunities. Recycling of industrial land for housing at Letchworth was ongoing from the 1980s (see below), but has only recently begun at Welwyn. The spectacular rise in house prices has fueled pressure for changes to (and redevelopment of) the existing housing stock.

Hampstead Garden Suburb

Unlike the two garden cities, there has been no scope for adding new neighborhoods since World War II, as the suburb boundaries were hemmed in by the outer London suburban spread during the 1930s. Rising affluence begetting unrealistic expectations has been exacerbated by what has been permitted beyond the suburb boundary. Within, there is the impossibility of creating off-street parking without the unacceptable sacrifice of front gardens and degradation of the street picture. There has also been growing pressure for demolition and replacement by "super-houses," unsuccessfully attempting to incorporate characteristics of suburb architecture, inflated in size, and including underground leisure suites and garaging, lately spreading to applications for basements beneath modest-sized existing houses (Miller 2006, 239–40). This phenomenon originated in The Bishop's Avenue, outside control by the HGST (although within the HGS Conservation Area). In 2010–11 the HGST received five applications for demolition and thirteen involving the addition of or extension to a basement under an existing house, out of 281 applications for HGST consent.[5]

The suburb has suffered traffic noise and severance since the 1920s on the controversial A1 link that cut through the northeast of the "new suburb" (Miller 2006, 150–51, 229–33). This has made regeneration of the Market Place shopping parades along that route very difficult. The Finchley Road has suffered heavy traffic and control over curbside parking. During the 1980s demolition of the Odeon Cinema released land for the Birnbeck Court sheltered housing for the elderly, visually successful, with a landmark tower memento of the Club House on Willifield Green (one of Henrietta Barnett's "social condensers"), which had been fatally damaged in a 1940 air raid (Miller 2006, 217) (Figure 3.4). Further south, a builders' depot was refurbished as a local Marks and Spencer store, now a commercial anchor of Finchley Road shopping (only its eastern side falls within the suburb).

Landscape restoration of Central Square was funded by a triumvirate of the HGST, BLBC, and the HGSRA in 2016–17, preceded by HGST-financed repairs at Sunshine Corner, where the vista from St. Jude's meets the Hampstead Heath Extension. But the most controversial new development in this precinct and in the suburb since 2000 has been extensions to the Henrietta Barnett School facing the square, exemplifying the clash of historic and contemporary design values that occur in iconic communities. The main building had originated as The Institute, a

bastion for education and enlightenment on Barnett's social agenda (Barnett 1928), designed by Lutyens in 1909 and developed in phases until 1930 (Miller 2006, 132–34). This was one element of his layout for the heart of the suburb, which included two churches, St. Jude's and The Free Church, both dominant buildings, capped by a tower and spire on the former, and a low dome and cupola on the latter. These framed The Institute, with residential squares to the north and south, all in Queen Anne style (Miller 2006, 117–23). It was Lutyens's most ambitious civic ensemble prior to New Delhi, and he made the most of it. The Henrietta Barnett School occupied classrooms in The Institute, and in the 1930s a Junior School was built to the north. Pressure for further expansion led to temporary buildings near the Central Square frontage. Lutyens had approved a composite drawing for completion of the frontage, but lack of funds and World War II prevented construction (Miller 2006).

Figure 3.4. Cricket on Willifield Green, Hampstead Garden Suburb, c. 1914, with the Club House by Parker and Unwin (destroyed by a German aerial landmine in 1940), one of Henrietta Barnett's "social condensers," and with the fringe of the artisans' quarter in the background. (Copyright of the University of Manchester)

Figure 3.5. One of the newly completed
(2010) wings of the Henrietta Barnett
School for Girls, Hampstead Garden
Suburb, with the silhouette of Lutyens's
Middlesex Building (1930) for the
former institute rising behind. Hopkins
Architects' use of high-quality materials
in a contextual modern design raised
extreme controversy among members
of the Residents' Association but
garnered architectural awards. (Hopkins
Architects; photographer Richard Brine)

The School and Institute parted company in the 1990s, and the latter left the site. The UK Department for Education offered a time-limited grant, paid out in March 2008 to fund improvements to eliminate the squalid huts. The design, by Hopkins Architects, approved by BLBC and HGST in autumn 2008,[6] featured low-key wings in high-quality traditional materials, not reproducing Lutyens's pomp and circumstance but concentrating on form and proportions, with minimal historical detailing, to produce outliers, closing off the voids on the Central Square frontage and enhancing its townscape. Slender timber canopies linked the classrooms and walkways (Figure 3.5). The HGSRA, claiming inadequate consultation, were (and remain) fiercely critical, particularly over omission of traditional sash windows. They have waged a war of attrition, passing a resolution at their 2010 annual general meeting for the buildings to be demolished without delay. In April 2012 the buildings won the London Region Award of the Royal Institute of British Architects and two British Council for School Environment Awards, vindicating the boldness of the concept (Hopkins Architects 2010).

Overall the suburb has fared well in care and appreciation of its historic built and natural environment, despite the pressures of the aspirational affluence of residents. Well-conserved houses of all sizes attract a premium in resale prices. However, as several speakers at the Trust's recent annual meetings have affirmed, there is a realization that this is increasingly at the expense of the social inclusion that had fired the reformist zeal of Henrietta Barnett in 1907 (Barnett 1928).

The Garden Cities

The two garden cities founded by Ebenezer Howard pursued the integration of town and country, implemented by dividend-limited private companies (Beevers 1988). The fundamental principle of defined town areas, protected by "agricultural belts," was achieved through land ownership and voluntary altruistic development limitation. These were precursors of the modern greenbelts, which were born out of post-1947 planning legislation. Both were originally designed for a maximum population of 32,000—though this was increased to 50,000 at Welwyn Garden City in 1954 after its inclusion in the postwar New Towns program. The aspirational balance between population and employment was diluted as they became commuter settlements. Redevelopment of industrial land for housing mirrored the decline of manufacturing in the United Kingdom since the 1980s. A decade earlier, reassessment of their original design characteristics had brought designation as conservation areas. Since then increasing pressure for change has heightened concern for conservation of their heritage and identity, summarized below.

Letchworth Garden City

Although Letchworth avoided a state takeover into the New Towns program, its postwar development was influenced by desire for modernization, following trends at nearby Stevenage New Town. This was reflected in public housing estates from the late 1940s to the 1970s—the Grange on the north and Jackmans on the southeast—the latter planned on Radburn principles for London's "overspill" population (Miller 2002, 155–60). Much attention was also directed to updating the town center. In 1969–74, Commerce Avenue, east of the original center, was redeveloped as a precinct, including six-story offices, occupied by the NHDC, with a multistory car park and pedestrian links to the town center (Miller 2002, 189–90). The two supermarkets soon became too small to survive: the larger, Sainsbury's, relocated to a peripheral business park in the early 1990s. From 1995, the LGCHF promoted commercial regeneration. The locally renowned Broadway Cinema (1936), an Art Deco structure, was converted into a small multiplex. In the late 1990s, the iconic Spirella Building (1910–22) was successfully refurbished as high-tech offices, retaining an identity as "Castle Corset" with its cast-in-concrete Arts and Crafts lettering proclaiming "High Grade Corsets" (see Plate 5). The Prince of Wales, with retired Spirella ladies in attendance, reopened the building in January 1999 (Miller 2002, 202).

The major regeneration of the 1990s occurred west of Broadway, intended as "Westcheap," beyond the axial Broadway and a mirror image of Eastcheap, which had become a principal shopping street during the 1920s. The 1950s North Hertfordshire College site was redeveloped with Morrison's Supermarket, partly accommodated behind the façades of the former Boys' Club (1914) and Magistrates' Court (1918) fronting Broadway. Compact new College premises were built overlooking Broadway Gardens. The central broadwalks of Broadway and Town Square (renamed Broadway Gardens) were comprehensively re-landscaped in 2002–3 to commemorate the centenary of Letchworth, with a fountain at the focal point of the south end (Miller 2010, 99–100). Further change in 2008–10 was promoted by the LGCHF, notably an £8 million "street scene" redesign of Eastcheap and Leys Avenue, to create a pedestrian-friendly shopping environment, including at the Station Place hub a striking sculptural group by Mel Chantrey, of three bronze verticals symbolizing garden city torches handed on to future generations (Miller 2010, 101). Comprehensive (and controversial) redevelopment proposals for The Wynd (the triangular backland of Leys Avenue and Station Road) and replacement of the 1950s Arena Parade between Broadway and Eastcheap were abandoned due to the 2008 recession. Under John Lewis, appointed as chief executive of the LCGHF in spring 2011, modest community-focused regeneration engaging

stakeholders was adopted in The Wynd in 2012, including a community garden completed in 2014, which reiterated the principle of self-sufficiency.

Recycling of surplus industrial land for housing—a trend that began in the 1980s and has continued up to the time of writing—involved demolition of the massive British Tabulating Machinery factory.[7] While some redevelopments were pastiches of Arts and Crafts designs, they were usually appropriate in scale and context. In 2007, the LGCHF promoted a competition for sustainable housing to commemorate the centenary of the influential Urban Cottages Exhibition (LGCHF 2007). The winning scheme, built by Rowan Homes as Hartington Place, east of Green Lane, was completed in February 2012. It marketed the garden city image as a fusion of past, present, and future, offering a mix of shared equity one- and two-bedroom homes and apartments, financed through the government's HomeBuy scheme, with two- and

Figure 3.6. The fountains in the newly restored Howard Park Gardens, Letchworth, act as foreground to the archetypal Rushby Mead housing, designed in 1911 by Bennett and Bidwell for the Howard Cottage Society. (Photo by Mervyn Miller)

three-bedroom apartments and townhouses for sale. Its restrained modernism presents white-rendered walls, timber panels, and rooftop pods incorporating solar panels, laid out around a central green, with two spur culs-de-sac. To a lesser extent than at Welwyn, escalation of property prices is excluding young families, and the smallest one-bedroom units are unsuitable as long-term family homes. The Howard Cottage Society, founded in 1911 by Ebenezer Howard, manages a portfolio of rental social housing, and North Hertfordshire Homes (a housing association that includes NHDC public housing) is developing new social housing.

Pressure for increased housing land allocation arose as a result of the NPPF obligation for all planning authorities to have an updated Local Plan, within which a five-year rolling allocation of housing land was to be maintained. The NHDC Local Plan dates from 1996 and is long outdated. Work is progressing on its successor covering the period 2011–31, put out as a consultation draft late in 2014. It contained controversial housing land allocations, particularly a 111-acre site north east of the Grange, projected to take 1,000 homes, on land that is in the Metropolitan Green Belt. The land, owned by the LGCHF, custodian of the Howard legacy, was put forward by the Foundation and accepted by NHDC as a preferred option. This raised intense local objection from the Letchworth Garden City Society (LGCS), maintaining that a cardinal garden city principle would be violated. In fact both the Grange and Jackmans Estates, the latter on the southeast, were post-1945 extensions to the original "town area." The latest proposal was perceived as creeping developmentism, alien to the long-held definition by the Garden Cities and Town Planning Association (now TCPA) (which predated the statutory planning approval of the Metropolitan Green Belt by many years): "A Garden City is a town planned for industry and healthy living; of a size that makes possible a full measure of social life but not larger; surrounded by a permanent belt of rural land; the whole of the land being in public ownership or held in trust for the community." A public inquiry held in February 2018 heard evidence by the LGCS (LGCS n.d.). The inspector's recommendation, which may vary the scheme, will be made to the Secretary of State for Housing, Communities and Local Government, and a decision is expected late in 2018. The situation exemplifies the clash between the original garden city concept and national statutory planning policy, localism, and national housing objectives at its most acute.

In May 2012 a £2.7-million regeneration of Howard Park Gardens, the linear green reservation separating the town center from the residential neighborhoods to the east was completed by NHDC, with a £1.84-million grant from Heritage Lottery Funds under the "Parks for People" scheme. This transformed the old paddling pool, with new fountains, providing a fitting setting for the Ebenezer Howard memorial, built in 1930 (NHDC n.d.). Overlooked by the restored and extended Mrs. Howard Memorial Hall, this has proved to be an outstanding and popular amenity, true to garden city credentials (Figure 3.6).

Welwyn Garden City

The traditional character of Welwyn has also faced challenges of regeneration, lately due to more upscale growth pressures. In 1948, it became a first generation New Town, under the postwar program, based upon Patrick Abercrombie's *Greater London Plan 1944*. This increased its population with new social housing neighborhoods to the north, east, and south. Its town center continued along traditional lines until the 1980s (Rook 2001, 89–91, 121–23). The takeover of the Welwyn Stores by the John Lewis Partnership (JLP) left its 1939 Louis de Soissons building facing The Campus externally unaltered. More radical was the WHBC's partnership with the (then) British Rail Property Board to build a massive shopping mall, the Howard Centre, along the railway frontage. It opened in 1990. Its postmodern concrete pediment terminated Howardsgate, a stark change from the domestic scale of the original 1926 station. Welwyn Garden City's town center is compact and tightly constrained, not only by the railway but also by The Campus and Parkway, its most characteristic green vista (see Plate 4). There was trepidation when The Cherry Tree, originally a restaurant and tea garden north of Bridge Road, was redeveloped for a Waitrose supermarket (a JLP subsidiary) with a car park on its former garden, but it has now settled in. To the south, the WHBC encouraged the larger-scale rebuilding of Sainsbury's supermarket, but the possibility of further southward commercial development is blocked by The Free Church.

Opportunist developers looked to the industrial land east of the railway, which contains two iconic listed interwar factories, Shredded Wheat (1925–26) and Roche Products (1938–40). The land between the railway and Broadwater Road had been cleared, and both factories stood empty by spring 2009. WHBC's consultants prepared a brief and master plan for "Broadwater West" (subsequently adopted as a Supplementary Planning Document [SPD]) (WHBC 2008) for a new mixed-use neighborhood, including housing, a community center, and local shopping. Aspirational preservation and re-use of Shredded Wheat's listed grain silos proved to be an intractable conservation problem (Figure 3.7). The objective was regeneration of a derelict area close to the town center by redeveloping redundant industrial and railway land. Although outside the conservation area, the site faces the heart of the original 1920 garden city plan across the railway. Ownership split between two commercial rivals inhibited holistic redevelopment.

In September 2010, a planning application was submitted to the WHBC for mixed-use development on the Shredded Wheat and railway frontage land

Figure 3.7. The view across the railway tracks from the Howard shopping center, Welwyn Garden City, toward the derelict (but historic) Shredded Wheat Factory underlines a major conservation and developmental challenge to the integrity of Ebenezer Howard's second garden city. (Photo by Mervyn Miller)

(WHBC n.d.). Dominant was a 50,000-square-foot Tesco supermarket on the footprint of the single-story Shredded Wheat production building (1937–39), listed but outside the silos and original multistory factory. It was hoped that the base of the silos would be used as a restaurant and heritage center. A second phase on the railway land was to include a leisure center, hotel, YMCA hostel, medical and care facilities, and houses and flats. The massive supermarket infringed the council's brief and was too distant from the original town center, with poor pedestrian access: effectively an alternative town center, provoking objections from most of the established retailers. The Welwyn Garden City Society (WGCS) led a petition campaign through 2011, and contested every aspect of the proposals (WGCS n.d.).

Hertfordshire County Council (HCC), the highway authority, predicted traffic gridlock. In January 2012, the WHBC refused the application. Tesco's spokesperson warned that the site would remain derelict, the time limit to appeal the decision passed, and the buildings remained empty and forlorn.

Subsequent to the above narrative, Spen Hill, Tesco's property development company, and EPR Architects prepared plans for housing on the site. Exhibited for consultation in December 2014, they proposed over 750 residential units on the 20-acre site, with a hotel, restaurants, and community facilities. The listed factory buildings would be retained and converted to apartments. The initial plans showed retention of the silos, although technical problems of their honeycomb construction ultimately precluded this. A poll showed strong support for retention of the factory, but indicated that a majority would accept demolition of the silos. By this time Tesco was in financial difficulties, and in January 2015 announced closure of forty-three stores nationwide. The future of the Shredded Wheat site was once more uncertain.

Renewed concern about the Shredded Wheat site arose following its sale to ZM Land and Capital, specializing in regeneration of brownfield sites. Their proposal for "The Wheat Quarter" was prepared in conjunction with Plutus Estates and the Metropolitan Housing Trust. A scheme for 1500 new homes and mixed cultural and leisure uses (more urban than overtly garden city) was exhibited in the Howard Centre in December 2017 and submitted for planning permission to WHBC in January 2018. There had been meetings with the WGCS and the newly formed WGC Centenary Foundation. However, the WGCS considered that the proposal had strayed too far from garden city principles to be acceptable, notwithstanding promising concepts for community benefit. It presented an inner-city concept challenging the greener, more open characteristics of garden city development (Welwyn Garden City Society n.d.). The application is likely to be decided by WHBC by autumn 2018. Redevelopment, in whatever form eventually approved, will have a profound impact on the character of the center of Howard's second garden city.

The Roche site, further south along Broadwater Road, has been the second contentious urban renewal project in Welwyn in recent years. An initial housing redevelopment was refused, but a revision with increased affordable housing was approved in March 2011. Taylor Wimpey soon commenced development of the "Mirage" neighborhood for 209 dwellings, with one- to two-bedroom flats and three- to four-bedroom townhouses, in the form of an updated superblock, with landscaped quadrangles. Aesthetically, the buildings took their cue from the restrained modernism of the Roche buildings, flat-roofed, with precise modular windows, and a mix of white rendered walls and dark brick cladding. Phased completion over 2012–14, favorable mortgages for first-time buyers, and effective marketing ensured a swift take-up. Regrettably no occupiers have yet (2018) been found for the listed Roche office buildings, marketed for community uses. Although Mirage represented a valuable reservoir of recyclable land, house prices in Welwyn Garden City continued to rise, despite the recession. This cumulatively excluded young families from the verdant traditional neighborhoods west of the town center.

Conclusions

The three best-known iconic English garden city developments are, in their different ways, having to balance conservation with pressure for change, which, if unchecked, would fundamentally damage their very qualities that have been revered since the early twentieth century. Their popularity as a form of residential development is unquestionable, although the working of the property market has incrementally excluded all but the most affluent—most noticeably at Hampstead (ironic, given Henrietta Barnett's emphasis on homes for "all kinds and conditions" of society). As a residential enclave, set in the context of the burgeoning suburban spread of northern London, the suburb did not have to face the challenge of changing national commercial and employment conditions from the late twentieth century onward, which has beset both the garden cities. At Letchworth, and subsequently Welwyn, efforts to develop affordable housing (as a statutory planning requirement) have inevitably brought higher densities and difficulties in rekindling the image of spacious development promoted by the founders. Yet this has also brought a timely reappraisal of the definition of garden city housing. Development of extensive mid-twentieth-century social housing in both garden cities has enabled their survival as mixed communities so far, but, as stated above, longer-term portents are scarcely favorable.

The differing impact of late twentieth-century commercial regeneration in the two garden cities partly resulted from their original master planning. The original planned Letchworth town center was overgenerous in area, amorphous in form, and its development pattern was distorted by the pre-1914 dominance of housing estates on the east. However, the "loose fit" town center plan proved adaptable to development of the Morrison's supermarket adjoining the southwest of the existing town center, using underdeveloped educational land, but only after the more tightly planned 1970s regeneration had proved inadequate to retaining the increasing scale of supermarkets within the town center.

At Welwyn, de Soissons had defined a compact town center, close to the western neighborhoods, the first to be built. Neighborhood centers were added, particularly after the New Town takeover in 1948. This distribution of shopping facilities proved to be vulnerable as national supermarket chains increased in size and dominance from the 1970s. Nevertheless, Welwyn Garden City benefited from the critical mass of the Welwyn stores (now John Lewis), a commercial anchor in maintaining the overall quality of the town center. The challenge of adapting the garden cities' town centers to the increasing pressures of national supermarket chains has created the greatest uncertainty. By ingenious, intensive on-site redevelopment, an enlarged Sainsbury's supermarket was built on the southwestern corner of Welwyn Garden City center, without compromising its garden city character. The trauma of Tesco has currently ebbed with the hope of housing and mixed uses following the sale of their Shredded Wheat site. It would be premature, however, to welcome unreservedly the most recent proposals. The critical comments by the WGCS have been noted above, although they concluded that the latest proposals went much further in meeting the requirements of the WHBC SPD than did the previous plan.

Changing economic conditions have also influenced the viability of regeneration. Letchworth faced an upheaval of its industrial base, as well as commercial recessions during the 1990s and since 2008. Much surplus industrial brownfield land has been redeveloped for housing, but this windfall was largely exhausted by 2014. At Welwyn Garden City, the closure of key industries came later, and was more starkly visible, but housing redevelopment proved an appropriate strategy in principle.

The current situation highlights the pressure for change in communities, which besides (and because of) being garden cities, are also economic hotspots in southeast England, the 2008 recession notwithstanding. How successfully their essential characteristics are retained, and hopefully enhanced, depends on the ability of their planning authorities (and the SoMs) to defend their unique place-specific ambiance, while maintaining a supply of affordable housing. New nationally drafted planning policies overtly encourage enterprise and growth, albeit with a proclamation of sustainability, but they also incorporate heritage elements and reexamine the garden city concept (TCPA 2012).[8]

National developers likewise must recognize that the government is, at the same time, committed to devolve "localism" to communities who invariably have a staunch view of values worth defending. There is also, particularly in Letchworth, a dynamic role for the LGCHF as the freehold owner of much of the valuable commercial and industrial land, to ensure that its role as custodian of the Ebenezer Howard legacy is fulfilled in a manner that balances economic benefit and environmental quality. But this has been challenged through LGCHF's controversial decision to propose the northeast Grange land for housing, and its adoption as a preferred option in the NHDC Draft Local Plan. Conservation legislation and policies have already brought increased recognition of the importance of the principal legacy of the garden city movement and the values it represented. While it would be inadvisable to attempt to use the tenets of the movement as a block to all new development, this should not preclude robust defense of the essential characteristics that have marked the garden city as an enduring and internationally acclaimed contribution to twentieth-century urban development. Conservation has protected the iconic blend of fine housing design and verdant landscape that defines the term "garden city" and its "spirit of place." To date, the three exemplar communities discussed here have succeeded in so doing, albeit often with inherent tension. However, the recent trends summarized above suggest that this may possibly shortly undergo a fundamental and potentially irreversible change.

Table 3.1
Summary of Historical Events and Heritage Benchmarks
of the Garden Cities Letchworth

Year	Event
1903	September: The newly founded Garden City Pioneer Company purchases an estate of nearly 4,000 acres in Hertfordshire. October: First Garden City Ltd. is created to develop the garden city.
1903–4	October 1903–April 1904: Barry Parker and Raymond Unwin prepare a master plan.
1905	Letchworth hosts the Cheap Cottages Exhibition, which features 120 homes and attracts 50,000 visitors.
1908	Letchworth hosts the Urban Cottage and Smallholdings Cottage Exhibitions. The Letchworth Parish Council is formed under the Hitchin Rural District Council.
1910	Spirella Company of Great Britain opens a factory and begins development of its flagship "Castle Corset" building.
1914	Belgian refugees settle in Letchworth.
1919	The Housing and Town Planning Act municipalizes development standards along garden city lines for public housing, which the newly formed Letchworth Urban District Council (LUDC) starts developing.
1928	May 1: Sir Ebenezer Howard dies in Welwyn Garden City.
1946	Rejection of LUDC's request that Letchworth be granted New Town status under the newly passed New Towns Act.
1945–48	Planning and initial construction phase of the Grange estate on Letchworth's north side take place.
1947	February 2: Barry Parker dies in Letchworth.
1955	Letchworth UDC reaches an agreement with the London County Council to build "overspill" housing; the planning of Jackmans Estate (built 1959–73) begins.
1960–61	The Hotel York company wins the takeover battle for First Garden City Ltd.; Letchworth UDC proposes legislation to Parliament in order to place its asset in a public trust.
1962	The Letchworth Garden City Corporation Act passes; the LGC Corporation begins operation in January 1963.
1967	The Leasehold Reform Act passes; it enables householders to purchase freehold of their homes. The LGC Corporation maintains landlord control by applying for a Section 19 Scheme of Management (SoM) (approved by High Court in 1971).
1974	Following a national administrative reform, Letchworth merges into the enlarged North Hertfordshire District Council (NHDC).
1975	The Commerce Way Shopping Centre opens, hosting NHDC offices.
1995	The Letchworth Garden City Heritage Foundation (LGCHF) succeeds the LGC Corporation; it inherits its SoM and starts downtown commercial regeneration.
1999	The Spirella factory building reopens as high-tech offices.
2003	Broadway Gardens and Howard Park are regenerated to celebrate Letchworth's centenary.
2008–15	The survey of all residential properties strengthens the Letchworth Design Guidance initiated in the 1980s.
2012–16	The Letchworth Garden City Society (LGCS) vigorously opposes the Draft District Plan (DDP2011-31) mandated by NHDC.
2018	LGCHF's proposal to extend Letchworth northeast of the Grange estate into greenbelt land meets with public displeasure. The decision is not expected until late 2018. Population (2011 census), 33,249; 5,500 acres [2,225 ha]; 14,213 dwelling units.

Table 3.2
Summary of Historical Events and Heritage Benchmarks
for Hampstead Garden Suburb

Year	Event
1902–3	Alerted by plans to extend underground rapid transit north of old Hampstead, Henrietta Barnett campaigns for preserving an extension to Hampstead Heath. Influenced by Letchworth's promotion, she advocates the creation of an ideal garden suburb "for all classes."
1905	Raymond Unwin prepares a preliminary master plan.
1906	Unwin is appointed as planner, along with Edwin Lutyens as consultant for Central Square.
1907	May 1: Land is purchased from Eton College. The Hampstead Garden Suburb Trust (HGS Trust) is created to administer development of original land (the "Old Suburb"). The Hampstead Heath Extension is conveyed to the London County Council.
1908–13	Lutyens's plan for Central Square and its approaches takes shape. St. Jude's Church, The Free Church, and The Institute are erected (completed 1930).
1911	Unwin outlines the master plan for the "New Suburb." This 412-acre addition is mainly developed during the interwar period.
1926–28	The Ministry of Transport sanctions the construction of a new highway through the New Suburb (designated part of the A1 London-Edinburgh trunk road in 1953).
1936	June 10: Henrietta Barnett dies.
1940	September: An air raid causes extensive damage to residential properties, particularly around Willifield Green, which are fatal to the Club House, one of Mrs Barnett's "social condensers." June 28: Raymond Unwin dies in the United States.
1965	The Barnet London Borough Council becomes the local government planning authority for Hampstead Garden Suburb.
1967	The Leasehold Reform Act is enacted to enable householders to purchase freehold of their homes; the HGS Trust maintains landlord control by applying for a Scheme of Management (SoM) (approved by High Court in 1974).
1968	The Barnet London Borough (Barnet LB) designates a Hampstead Garden Suburb Conservation Area.
1969	Sale of the suburb, split between Suburb Leaseholds and Ashdale. Reorganisation of the HGS Trust.
1971	Approved by the Secretary of State for the Environment, and subsequently strengthened, "Article 4 Direction" ensures detailed control by Barnet LB.
1977	The Residents' Association publishes for the first time design guidance on the conservation of properties.
2007	May 2: Hampstead Garden Suburb celebrates its centennial.
2011	Additions (by Hopkins Architects) to the Henrietta Barnett School (which took over the former Institute site in 2004) open and raise controversy.
2010–13	The HGS Trust, in liaison with Barnet LB, prepares a comprehensive conservation area analysis with community groups, as well as an updated comprehensive design guidance. Population (as of 2011 census), 15,929; 1,169 acres [473 ha]; 4,967 dwelling units.

Table 3.3
Summary of Historical Events and Heritage Benchmarks for Welwyn Garden City

Year	Event
1918	October: Ebenezer Howard walks C. B. Purdom and F. J. Osborn over a site south of Digswell (part of the site for Welwyn Garden City).
1918	Howard buys the city's first 1,688 acres. Creation of Second Garden City Ltd. The site is surveyed.
1920	Formal establishment of Welwyn Garden City Limited; purchase of 689 additional acres.
1921	The master plan by architect Louis de Soissons is adopted. Stores open at the corner of Bridge Road and on the west side of Parkway.
1922	The Daily Mail Model Home Village opens.
1923	Completion of the first fifty public housing units for the Welwyn Rural District Council.
1925	The first phase of the Shredded Wheat factory opens. Health Minister Neville Chamberlain inaugurates the railway station on Howardsgate.
1927	Creation of the Welwyn Garden City Urban District. Ebenezer Howard is knighted.
1928	May 1: Death of Sir Ebenezer Howard in Welwyn Garden City.
1934	Financial reconstruction of Welwyn Garden City Ltd.
1939	The new Welwyn Garden City Stores open at the corner of Bridge Road and east side of Parkway; the city counts 14,000 residents.
1949	Following the 1946 national New Town Act, the Welwyn Garden City New Town Development Corporation (WGCNTDC) replaces Second Garden City Ltd. and takes over its assets.
1949	De Soissons revises his master plan to accommodate 45,000–50,000 residents. Completion of the Templewood School, designed by Hertfordshire County Council (HCC) architect C. H. Aslin,
1953	Erection of the Coronation Fountain at the junction of Howardsgate and Parkway. The town center gradually fills up.
1960	The College of Further Education opens on the Campus.
1962	September: Death of Louis de Soissons.
1966	The assets of WGCNTDC are transferred to the Commission for the New Towns.
1967	Passing of the Leasehold Reform to enable householders to purchase freehold of their homes; WGCNTDC maintains landlord control by applying for a Scheme of Management (approved by High Court in 1974).
1968	HCC designates the Welwyn Garden City Conservation Area, exclusive of original industrial section west of the railway. The Welwyn Hatfield Borough Council (WHBC) subsequently designates the 1930s Woodhall area.
1974	As a result of the reorganization of local governments in England, WHBC is in charge of managing 5,800 subsidized housing units.
1980	The Housing Act's "Right to Buy" provision encourages the sale of public housing units to their tenants.
1983	John Lewis Partnership buys the Welwyn Stores, subsequently redeveloping the Cherry Tree tea garden into a Waitrose supermarket.
1978	Welwyn counts 41,000 residents in about 15,000 homes.

Year	Event
1990	A large shopping mall, Howard Centre, opens at the end of Howardsgate along the railway frontage.
2001	WHBC publishes the Welwyn Garden City Conservation Area Appraisal.
2001	Welwyn counts 43,000 residents in 22,000 homes.
2008	WHBC publishes the Broadwater West Development Brief, which encompasses Shredded Wheat (SW) and railway sites.
2012	Tesco submits a planning application for a large supermarket and mixed development on SW and the railway sites. WHBC refuses permission and Tesco sells the site to ZM Land and Capital.
2018	Fall: WHBC is expected to decide on the planning application for the comprehensive redevelopment of SW (including 1500 housing units)
	Population (2014), 48,380; 2,968 acres [1,201 ha]; c.18,000 dwelling units.

NOTES

1. Standard present-day references are Miller 2002 (on Letchworth Garden City), Miller 2006 (on Hampstead Garden Suburb), and de Soissons 1988 and Rook 2001 (on Welwyn Garden City). Summaries are to be found in Miller 2010. Key historical references are Purdom 1913, 1925 and 1949 (Letchworth Garden City, and Welwyn Garden City—the last taking the latter into the statutory New Town era) and Barnett 1928.

2. This was undertaken by the author as a consultant to the LGCHF in 2008–9, based on research on the original plans during 1974–76, updated by fieldwork. The Letchworth Garden City Building Study has been used as an aid to property and estate management. Further fine-tuning was under way in early 2015, following consultation. Policies for the Heritage Character Area, identifying the buildings covered, were published in LGCHF 2015.

3. Introduced in the 1990s, the grants have achieved greater awareness of the benefits of more authentic repairs in resale values. Following suspension in 2010, they have now been reinstated for the core Heritage Character Area, and the Heritage Awards were reintroduced in September 2015.

4. (Sir) Nikolaus Pevsner, the eminent art and architectural historian, lived in Hampstead Garden Suburb in the 1930s as a refugee from Nazi Germany. He was particularly enthusiastic about the English garden city movement, and he prominently commended the suburb (Pevsner 1951). In 1963 he met officials of the then Ministry of Housing and Local Government to suggest listing buildings in Hampstead Garden Suburb. His oft-quoted plaudit appeared first in a booklet celebrating the suburb's Golden Jubilee.

5. Control of basements is rather complex, as the Trust's management powers deal only with visible external alteration; however, four basements have been refused on the basis of lightwells, vehicle ramps, or skylights. Twenty-six basements were approved during 2007–12. Under planning regulation, basements are defined as development and require planning permission from Barnet Council.

6. Details of the planning application documents for the extensions have been removed from the Barnet Council Planning website; it is customary for some councils to delete applications once determined.

7. Examples include the site of the British Tabulating Machinery Company (one of the pioneers of computer development) in Icknield Way and the Cooperative Creamery site on Letchworth Gate, both in the 1980s. Housing redevelopment of the Phoenix Motors site (later the Government Training Centre) on Pixmore Avenue was completed late in 2011.

8. See DCLG 2012. It is of interest that NPPF contains, in addition to policies requiring good design in new development (section 7, paras. 56–68) and Heritage Protection (section 12, paras. 126–41), mention of "new settlements or extensions to existing villages and towns that follow the principles of Garden Cities." See also DCLG 2014.

REFERENCES

Barnet London Borough Council (BLBC). 2010. *Hampstead Garden Suburb Character Appraisal—Adopted October 2010*. http://www.barnet.gov.uk/info/homepage/107/planning _conservation and building control.

Barnett, Henrietta.1928. *The Story of the Growth of the Hampstead Garden Suburb, 1907–28*. London: HGS Trust. [Facsimile Reprint by Hampstead Garden Suburb Archives Trust, 2006].

Beevers, Robert. 1988. *The Garden City Utopia: A Critical Biography of Ebenezer Howard*. London: Macmillan.

Deakin, Derick, ed. 1989. *Wythenshawe: The Story of a Garden City*. Chichester: Phillimore.

Department for Communities and Local Government (DCLG). 2012. *National Planning Policy Framework*. http://planningguidance.planning.portal.gov.uk.

———. 2014. *Locally Led Garden Cities*. https//www.gov.uk/government publications/locally -led-garden-cities-prospectus.

de Soissons, Maurice. 1988. *Welwyn Garden City: A Town Designed for Healthy Living*. Cambridge: Publications for Companies, Ltd.

English Heritage. 2008. *Conservation Principles, Policies and Guidance*. http://www.english -heritage.org.uk/publications/conservation-principles-sustainable-management-historic- environment.

———. 2010. *Understanding Place: Historic Area Assessments in a Planning and Development Context. Understanding Place: Historic Area Assessment: Principles and Practice*. http:// www.english heritage.org.uk/publications/understanding-place-principles-practice/.

———. 2012. *Good Practice Guide for Local Heritage Listing*.

———. n.d. *The National Heritage List for England*. http://historicengland.org.uk/listing/the list/.

Hampstead Garden Suburb Trust (HGST). 2002. *HGS Photographic Survey 2002–3, Historical Background (n-d), Design Guidance (n-d), Scheme of Management (1974/1983)*. http://hgs .org.uk.

Historic England. 2016. *Conservation Area Designation, Appraisal and Management*. https://his toricengland.org.uk/images-books/publications/conservationare-designation-appraisal -management:Advice-note-1/.

Hopkins Architects. 2010. *The Henrietta Barnett School*. http://www.hopkins.co.uk/projects /2/134.

Letchworth Garden City Heritage Foundation. 2008–9. Letchworth Design Guidance. http:// www.letchworth.com/ heritage-foundation.

Letchworth Garden City Heritage Foundation. 2015. *Design Principles: Heritage Character Area in Letchworth Garden City*. https://www.Letchworth.com/sites/default/files/docu ments/2017-9/let_7392_heritage_character_brochure_june2015_v8_0.pdf.

Letchworth's Exhibition Cottages. n.d. http://www.exhibitioncottages.info/.

Miller, Mervyn. 2002. *Letchworth: The First Garden City*. 2nd ed. Chichester: Phillimore.

———. 2006. *Hampstead Garden Suburb: Arts and Crafts Utopia*. Chichester: Phillimore.

———. 2010. *English Garden Cities, an Introduction*. Swindon: English Heritage.

North Hertfordshire District Council (NHDC). 2001. *Letchworth Conservation Area 18 December 2001*. http://www.north-herts.gov.uk/.

———. n.d. *Howard Park and Gardens*. https://www.north-herts.gov.uk/howard-park-and-gardens.

Osborn, Frederick J., and Arnold Whittick. 1977 (1963). *New Towns and Their Origins, Achievements and Progress*. 3rd ed. London: Leonard Hill.

Pevsner, Nikolaus. 1951. *The Buildings of England: Middlesex*. Harmondsworth, UK: Penguin.

Purdom, C. B. 1913. *The Garden City*. Letchworth: J. M. Dent.

———. 1925. *Garden Cities and Satellite Towns*. London: J. M. Dent.

———. 1949. *Satellite Towns*. London: J. M. Dent.

"RIBA Awards for School." 2012. *Suburb News* 111(Summer). http://www.hgs.org.uk.

Rook, Tony. 2001. *Welwyn Garden City Past*. Chichester: Phillimore.

Town and Country Planning Association (TCPA). 2012. *Creating Garden Cities and Suburbs Today*. http:// www.tcpa.org.uk/data/filesCreating_Garden_Cities_and Suburbs-today.

Ward, Stephen. 1994. *Planning and Urban Change*. London: Paul Chapman Publishing.

Welwyn Garden City Society. n.d. welwynhatfield.co.uk/wgcsocietyhomepage.

Welwyn Hatfield Borough Council (WHBC). 2008. *Broadwater Road West Supplementary Planning Document* [SPD] *Adopted December 2008*. http://www.welhat.gov.uk/article/1027/BroadwaterWestSDP.

———. n.d. http://www.welhat.gov.uk/article/5550/resident.

CHAPTER 4

UPLANDS

A Residential Park in Victoria,

British Columbia, Canada

Larry McCann

Uplands was designed and planned during 1907–8 by the Boston-based landscape architect John Charles Olmsted. Located in Oak Bay, the oldest suburban municipality in the Greater Victoria region, the Uplands neighborhood is distinguished by a picturesque landscape of gently curving streets, varied architecture, and spacious, well-treed lots. It was the first of several large-scale subdivision schemes that John Olmsted crafted for Canadian clients. For Olmsted, the extensive Garry oak meadows of the Uplands Farm site evoked memories of the deer parks that contributed, so pleasingly, to many of the English country estates he studied and photographed while on a sojourn abroad in 1894. Recalling this, he responded to the site's many "natural beauties" by creating an artistic but practical design. Writing to a business associate in 1909, the reserved, usually modest New Englander declared that of his many subdivision projects, Uplands was "unquestionably the best adapted to obtain the greatest amount of landscape beauty in connection with suburban development."[1] In a whirl of promotion, Uplands was touted as "Victoria's Celebrated Residential Park" (Uplands Limited 1921, 1922). Uplands is indeed exemplary; it is a model of its kind. It was the first large-scale, naturalistic, and holistically planned subdivision in Canada to break away entirely from the rectangular-shaped subdivision, the existing city form (McCann 1999, 2006b). The curvilinear street system and protective property restrictions introduced at Uplands spurred immediate imitation, even emulation, in a number of communities across western Canada and along the Pacific Coast of the United States. Uplands fittingly distinguishes John Olmsted's lengthy career; it stands as a masterpiece of subdivision design and planning (McCann 2014a, 2016).

Yet despite a century of private and public efforts aimed at safeguarding Uplands—chiefly through the use of deed restrictions, a unique piece of provincial legislation, zoning regulations, tree-protection guidelines, and simply by persuasion—the potential for unfavorable change remains a constant. Large-scale, single-family redevelopment and remodeling projects are threatening the original vision and established character of Uplands as a residential park. Garry oaks have been cut down, heritage-quality houses replaced, and view corridors blocked. The increase in housing size is due largely to shifts in the architectural preferences of the nouveau wealthy class and to zoning and other regulations that fail to protect all properties in equal ways. This much-admired, much-envied neighborhood deserves stronger and more protection as a unified whole by retaining the distinctive qualities of its residential park character.

Uplands is home to 2,250 of the nearly 17,500 people living in suburban Oak Bay (incorporated in 1906). Oak Bay is the most affluent of the thirteen incorporated municipalities that compose the Capital Region District (CRD; the district's population is about 345,000). Oak Bay occupies a coastal location along the region's southeastern rim, approximately two miles from Victoria's downtown business core and Inner Harbour. This coastal setting is shared by Uplands (Figures 4.1 and 4.2). When the subdivision was laid out, farmland and oak forests kept it apart from built-up areas in Oak Bay and the neighboring municipalities of Victoria and Saanich (McCann 2006a). Today Oak Bay is almost completely built-up and mostly residential in character; it has virtually no industrial land use and few retail nodes or apartment districts. At Uplands, by choice of the original promoters, there are no stores, churches, schools, or other basic community facilities within the neighborhood. This obliges residents to seek goods and services elsewhere. "The Village" is Oak Bay's up-market retail, business, and administrative core, attracting many Uplands residents. Interaction with the wider local community sometimes takes place in more pivotal ways. At critical junctures in Oak Bay's history, elected officials living in Uplands have guided the municipality's policies regarding property assessment, house building, and zoning. Despite its age, Uplands remains the CRD's most exclusive residential enclave (Forward 1973; Sparks 2006). Several waterfront properties recently sold for over $10,000,000; no others are assessed below $1,000,000. The average for Oak Bay's single-family properties in 2015 was $691,000; for the CRD, $550,000.[2]

This chapter focuses on the important design and planning strategies that have shaped and still guard the iconic status of Uplands. Offered first is John Olmsted's philosophy of designing in harmony with the physical environment. For Uplands, he emphasized the use of artistic and practical planning principles to enhance and sustain the native Garry oaks and other "natural beauties" of the Uplands Farm site. Many landscape architects strived to combine beauty and utility in early twentieth-century North America: the Olmsteds were acknowledged masters (Beveridge 1977; Freestone 2011; Hockaday 2009; Levee 2000; McCann 1996). Regulatory devices are considered next. From the onset, a set of private deed restrictions suggested by John Olmsted was the basis for protecting property values and residential park features. Later, in 1936, the administration of deed restrictions

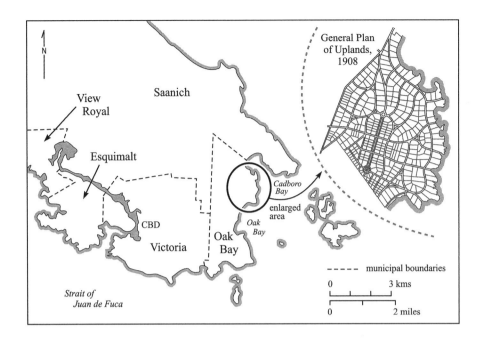

Figure 4.1. The location of Oak Bay Municipality and Uplands subdivision in the Greater Victoria region. (Cartography by Ole Heggen; the map of Uplands is redrafted from the original "General Plan" produced by Olmsted Brothers in 1908)

Figure 4.2. A waterfront view of Uplands from Cattle Point. (Photo by Larry McCann)

was entrusted to the public realm—to the elected municipal council. This was made possible by the provincial government's Oak Bay Special Powers Act (1935). This legislation sanctioned the council to prepare regulations—in the form of the Uplands Regulations Bylaw (1936)—that would protect the subdivision's residential park character *in perpetuity*. The chapter concludes by considering several heritage and conservation-planning strategies available to the municipal council and Uplands residents for protecting both the natural and built environment of Uplands. As with any Olmsted subdivision project, it is the original plan's intent that requires protection, for the whole is greater than the sum of its parts.

A Practical and Artistic Design for Uplands

There is much to admire at Uplands that supports its iconic status. This is especially true of the approach that John Olmsted used to reveal the "genius of the place." Plan elements—lots, street blocks, roads, parklets, and more—were all conceived to support the overall intent of the subdivision's naturalistic design. As the 1908 General Plan for Uplands reveals, roads curve gracefully, shifting directions in pleasing ways, following the lay of the land. Sometimes, while crossing down and through oak-studded meadows, roads bend out of sight. Reappearing, they flow straight towards the sea where, in advance of a parkway located a lot's depth from the shoreline's ragged edge, they arch once more—gently, smoothly, defining the subdivision's all-embracing artistic layout. These roadway tracings reveal picturesque scenes that were enhanced by the designer's thoughtful arrangement of some three hundred amply sized lots, all set within irregularly shaped street blocks (Figure 4.3).

Uplands lots differ in size and shape. This asymmetry was influenced by several key factors, including steep slopes, rock outcrops, and the need to protect Garry oaks. Important too was John Olmsted's belief that a house's placement on a homesite should not obstruct the views of nearby residences. To achieve this goal, he established a spatial hierarchy of views. Views at Uplands were integrated in an orderly sequence that progressed outward, away from the house: *first*, a view of the home-grounds or near foreground; *next*, the middle-distance view of the homesite's surrounding, parklike features; and, *ultimately*, the "far outlook," which for Uplands meant distant views of Haro and Juan de Fuca straits, the Gulf Islands, and, far away on the mainland, Mount Baker and the Coast and Olympic Mountain ranges. This hierarchy is illustrated in the color image selected to represent Uplands (see Plate 6).

Arranging this scheme across a rough landscape was challenging. To aid the design process, surveyors were instructed to plot five-foot contour lines and map the exact location of several thousand Garry oaks. With maps in hand, John Olmsted

Figure 4.3. Midland Road: the curved roads of Uplands are generally quite narrow, incorporating public spaces (e.g., parklets and verges) in their layout. For John Olmsted, landscape architecture was "the Art of improving grounds for use and enjoyment where beauty is an important purpose." (Photo by Larry McCann)

spent almost a full month of days at Uplands contemplating the lay of the land, establishing street blocks, staking roadways, and determining lot boundaries. The resulting picturesque scenes and viewscapes speak to his thorough, careful resolve to preserve the site's many "natural beauties." The overall effect also fully satisfied the psychological benefits associated with residing within a naturalistic, parklike setting (Beveridge and Rocheleau 1995). When laid out, the lot system of Uplands contrasted sharply with the ubiquitous, rectangular subdivisions that had, for so long, dominated the suburban landscape of Canadian cities (Harris 2004; McCann 1999).

Deed Restrictions: A Precursor to Zoning and Neighborhood Preservation

During the pre-zoning era, before town or city planning legislation became established during the 1920s, deed restrictions comprised an essential legal framework for protecting private property in exclusive neighborhoods (Fogelson 2005; Monchow 1928; Sies 1997). For Uplands, John Olmsted devised a comprehensive set of deed restrictions in close discussion with the subdivision's developer, William Hicks Gardner of Winnipeg, who in turn consulted with syndicate partners and legal authorities before seeking approval from the Hudson's Bay Company (HBC, established in 1670). The HBC had optioned, in 1907, to sell Gardner some 465 acres of its 1,100-acre Uplands Farm for $270,000. The HBC originally "acquired" the title to the acreage from aboriginal peoples in 1862. The terms of the "option agreement" stipulated that Gardner must secure the HBC's approval for the restrictions and subdivision plan before the sale could be completed. This was done to protect its adjacent, undeveloped property. The right to do so was relinquished in 1936.

Getting the project under way in "boom" times proved difficult. Lacking development funds, Gardner sold off almost the entire tract in 1911 to a French multinational, the Franco-Canadian Corporation. Astutely, when negotiating the sale, Gardner initiated a far-sighted strategy to preserve the layout of Uplands. The "Agreement of Sale" stipulated that the subdivision plan approved by the HBC and by Oak Bay's municipal officials—that is, John Olmsted's "General Plan for Uplands"—*must* be maintained to guide future development. Minor adjustments in layout were tolerated. By the mid-1920s, in a "twist of fate" linked directly to restrictions imposed by the French government on exporting capital abroad, Franco-Canadian and its subsidiary land company, the Uplands Limited, defaulted on a mortgage held by Gardner. In this way, the Winnipeg entrepreneur regained control of approximately one-third of the subdivision's 465 acres. He thus once again championed and defended John Olmsted's landscape plan, which he did unstintingly until his passing in 1951.

Deed restrictions were central to the early and ongoing defense of Uplands as an exclusive residential neighborhood. Adapted from John Olmsted's original suggestions, these regulated the minimum construction value of a house (initially $5,000), land use (single-family only), the maximum height of a residence (two-and-a-half stories), fence construction (no side-of-property hedges or fences within sixty feet of a road allowance); and front-, back-, and side-lot-line setback distances (various because lots were shaped irregularly). To John Olmsted's way of thinking, setbacks and hedge and fence placement were all-important considerations for creating and maintaining the subdivision's residential park character. Restrictions were established to run initially for twenty-five years, until 1936.[3] Certain of these restrictions, particularly the minimum size of a dwelling, would later become the essential tools of Oak Bay's zoning bylaws.

"Getting the Plan": Adjusting the Layout of Uplands

The comprehensive protection of property at Uplands has always attracted wealthy residents.[4] Early homeowners certainly supported a vision of building in harmony with the natural environment. Their dwellings, very much smaller than today's,

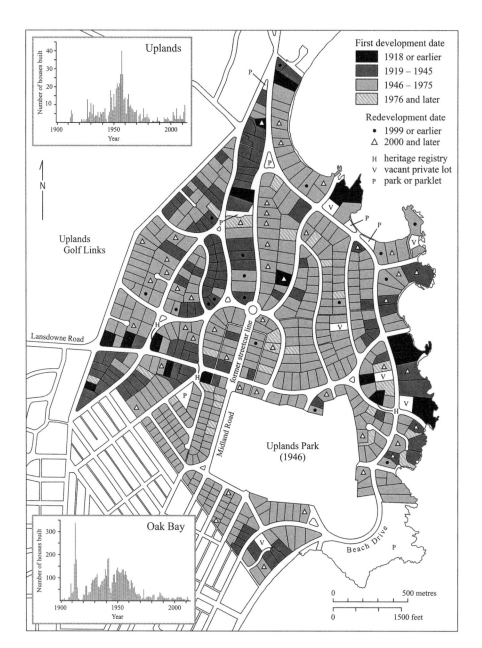

Figure 4.4. The building history of Oak Bay and Uplands to 2012. (Cartography by Ole Heggen, using data compiled by Larry McCann from historical assessment and building permit records in the Oak Bay Municipal Archives)

complied agreeably with existing deed restrictions. Early property owners retained native Garry oaks as a way of reinforcing the subdivision's parklike character. Yet regardless of protective restrictions or praise for the artistic layout, house building at Uplands remained rather sluggish until the post–World War II boom era, when the subdivision was finally built out. Ongoing construction activity is now led by redevelopment and major renovations. Generally, redevelopment (also called in-fill) projects have sought out large properties with splendid views or smaller lots that occupy regulatory zones with rather permissive side-lot setback restrictions (Figure 4.4).

"Getting the plan" is the expression used by the Olmsted firm to describe the process of producing a "General Plan" for projects, such as a land subdivision or park system (Zaitzevsky 1982). In the life course of Uplands, Olmsted Brothers, the land companies, and the municipality, each understood that there would be "twists and turns" in developing the plan before some sort of stasis was eventually achieved. Most layout adjustments at Uplands were usually justified by the ongoing throes of economic uncertainty and the crucial need to sell lots. The technique was densification through re-subdivision. This was done by dividing a few large, undeveloped blocks and adding new streets in the northeastern section of the subdivision. As well, many two- and three-acre homesites were converted to smaller lots. Re-subdivision doubled the total number of lots to just over six hundred. When making these adjustments, the land companies strived to retain a parklike ambience, though sometimes sacrificing neighborhood or "far outlook" views.

The most substantial layout adjustment following World War II was the creation, in 1946, of Uplands Park. Dogged by sluggish lot sales, Gardner (who restructured his land syndicate as Estates Limited in 1934) had lobbied the municipality since the mid-1930s to purchase, for use as public parkland, some fifty acres of difficult-to-develop land located in the subdivision's southeastern section. Strategically chosen, this "buffer" of underused farmland, marsh, and rock outcrops would safeguard the subdivision's "naturalistic" character. By 1946, the two land companies operating in Uplands—Estates Limited and the Uplands Limited—had both fallen behind on their payment of property taxes. To meet their debt obligations, Estates and Uplands, working together, offered Oak Bay an enlarged seventy-six-acre parcel. The asking price was $65,000. In March 1946, the municipality held a referendum, querying Oak Bay taxpayers about purchasing the land for a park. The public's response was overwhelmingly positive (McCann 2016).

Even with these considerable adjustments in layout, by the 1970s the Uplands landscape possessed a rich patina acquired from the maturing of Garry oaks, the making of private gardens, and the building of houses that displayed an eclectic mix of evolving architectural styles. Sequenced historically, the mix of pre-1970s house

types includes Edwardian mansions; Colonial Revivals; English Tudor cottages and bungalows; expansive, low-slung ranchers; and modernist, flat-roofed houses. Some of these houses are widely recognized as architecturally significant and worthy of heritage recognition, but many are rather generic in form, especially the one-story bungalows and ranchers built "on spec" between the mid-1940s and late 1960s.

But the carefully wrought patina of early, prudent development—the "genius of the place"—is becoming somewhat blemished. The emerging situation is a response of property owners and speculative builders reacting to shifting investment strategies and architectural fashions. The razing of several architectural gems, including several of the earliest houses built in Uplands, has dismayed heritage enthusiasts.[5] These and other teardowns have given way to oversized historical revival, neomodern, and postmodern houses of ambiguous form (Figure 4.5). Fortunately, some homeowners have made it incumbent upon themselves to improve older houses in ways that support principles of heritage conservation; and many owners of renovated or redeveloped properties, when making substantial changes in situ, have sought ways to harmonize the grounds of their properties with the wider parklike landscape, even when adjoining the waterfront. Heritage enthusiasts or critics of change often overlook these well-intentioned initiatives. But not all property owners are as conscientious about preserving the character of Uplands. The process of tearing down dwellings and building ever-larger residences continues to remove mature Garry oaks, overwhelm existing houses, and encroach upon long-cherished view corridors at all scales of John Olmsted's system of views, thus marring the essential parklike characteristics. In this way, the relationship between private property rights and the public good is challenged:

assertive property owners are pitted against the scorn of neighbors, the pleas of watchdog heritage buffs, and the sometimes ambivalent stewardship of Oak Bay's elected officials and administrators.

Protection Through the Uplands Regulations Bylaw and Zoning

Most people living in Uplands believe that the single-family makeup and natural beauty of their neighborhood will be protected and sustained well into the future. There is no formal association of Uplands property owners—no board of trustees, as John Olmsted once advised—to speak on behalf of residents. Nonetheless, people are highly organized in unofficial ways to speak out against perceived threats, real or not. Uplands homeowners are well aware that property protection is tied tightly to Oak Bay's regulatory bylaws. The most important are a comprehensive zoning bylaw that governs *all* properties throughout Oak Bay, plus the neighborhood-specific Uplands Regulations Bylaw. Oak Bay was the first municipality in British Columbia to formulate a zoning bylaw. It did so in a rudimentary way in 1924 under authority of the province's Municipal Act. This was followed three years later by a more wide-ranging bylaw, made possible by the provincial government's recently introduced 1927 Town and Country Planning Act. Oak Bay's administrators adapted several of the Uplands restrictions. Until midcentury, a variant of the cost of construction restriction—minimum house size, a strong measure of social class—was the primary tool used to separate various residential zones throughout Oak Bay, not just in Uplands (McCann 2014a, 2016).

From 1936 until the mid-1980s, the most compelling method for safeguarding Uplands was to enforce the full weight of the Uplands Regulations Bylaw. This bylaw stems from a rather unusual, extraordinary piece of provincial legislation. The Oak Bay Special Powers Act authorized the municipality "to make regulations applicable to Uplands."[6] The reasons for Oak Bay taking over management of the Uplands deed restrictions are complex. Following World War I, the financial security of the land companies was in jeopardy. This pressured them in 1926 to relinquish ownership of the subdivision's privately built infrastructure (roads and all utilities, for example), as well as their right to enforce deed restrictions. Sponsors of the Special Powers Act, taking heed that the twenty-five-year timeframe governing the Uplands restrictions was about to expire, stipulated the continued use of restrictions. The act also granted Oak Bay's council the legal right to establish any additional regulations deemed indispensable for protecting the subdivision's *overall* parklike character. In amended versions of the Uplands Regulations Bylaw, one clause has always included words to the effect that "all by-laws of the Corporation of the District of Oak Bay apply to the Uplands except insofar as the same may conflict with this Bylaw, in which case this Bylaw prevails."[7] Clearly, the bylaw still possesses considerable leverage for managing the ongoing protection of John Olmsted's vision of Uplands as a residential park—but only if the council decides to apply the bylaw's full legal mandate.

The first Uplands Regulations Bylaw, comprising twenty-one clauses of "do's" and "don'ts," was put into effect in January 1936.[8] Important clauses placed the minimum cost of constructing a residence at $6,000 (for the house and any appurtenant buildings) and established modest front- and side-lot-line setbacks at thirty-five and ten feet, respectively. No duplex or multiple-family housing was permitted, just single-family dwellings (and only one per property). To maintain a parklike ambience, no hedges or fences over four feet were permitted within thirty-five feet of a road allowance. Other regulatory measures focused on nuisances, the size of re-subdivided lots, and fines. The Uplands Limited, through its parent company, Franco-Canadian Corporation, wanted Oak Bay to sanction racial restrictions, but the municipality refused to do so.[9]

To strengthen the council's ability to deal with newly emerging issues, the Uplands Regulations Bylaw, like zoning, has been amended and consolidated from time to time. In the early 1950s, residents of Uplands became concerned that identical, ranch-styled houses were proposed for a street in a recently realigned area along the subdivision's southern edge. The council responded by introducing a regulation that prohibited the construction of houses of "similar architectural form" within five hundred feet of each other.[10] This rule is still in effect today, but other regulations became ineffectual or unnecessary and were therefore dismissed. These include a dwelling's minimum construction value and its minimum size. Since the 1970s, the number of clauses associated with the Uplands Regulations Bylaw has been whittled down considerably, with most rules transferred to Oak Bay's zoning bylaw because of the evolving, broadening powers granted to zoning under the enabling legislation of the Local Government Act.[11]

During this process of whittling down and transferring, certain regulations have drawn considerable attention. In a 1967 reworking of the Uplands Regulations Bylaw—the most comprehensive version ever put in place—a new rule was introduced to control a dwelling's "ground coverage." The intent was to sustain and preserve the subdivision's natural features and parklike character. Newly built houses in Uplands were becoming bigger, and, because ground-coverage guidelines were now employed by several Greater Victoria municipalities as a method for limiting the size and hence the impact of a building's "footprint," Oak Bay decided to take similar action to manage the irregular size and shape of Uplands lots. Accordingly, a finely differentiated scaling system was devised. It was based on the principle that as lots increased in size,

the permissible ground-coverage percentage of a house and its appurtenant buildings must *decrease*.[12]

This approach worked well for several years, particularly in re-subdivided and realigned street blocks of small homesites. But questions soon arose about the rule's efficacy when applied to early settled sections of Uplands. Historically, residences in these areas never overwhelmed a homesite; here, "designing with the land" apparently satisfied a homeowner's need for space and aesthetic sensibilities (Figure 4.6). But a creeping disregard for this design axiom, coinciding with a Canada-wide building trend favoring very large houses, emerged during the early 1970s. The building of overly large residences—provocatively called "monster" houses by many critics—continued through the late 1970s and early 1980s. Uplands residents spoke out strongly against this building trend, but municipal officials were slow to initiate a solution. One reason for the delay relates to the debate in Oak Bay about house size: what some people considered a monster house, others disputed, claiming otherwise. Terms such as "monster" and even "parklike" are culturally bounded, tied to local knowledge and personal feelings about place.

Setback distances, a long-standing feature of the Uplands Regulations Bylaw, were seized upon as supposedly a better means for controlling the siting of a house

Figure 4.6. Properties in older sections of Uplands were designed and built in close harmony with the physical landscape, as illustrated by 2580 Cotswold Road, by the architect Hubert Savage (1937). (Photo by Larry McCann)

and possibly the house's actual size. Side-lot-line setback distances were deemed more critical than street-front setbacks. Changing tactic, the control of setbacks at Uplands was removed from the Uplands Regulations Bylaw and merged with the municipality's zoning system. This policy shift was initiated through Zoning Bylaw 3531, passed by the council in October 1986.[13] Two types of municipality-wide zones, labeled RS1 and RS2, were assigned to Uplands. Their boundaries matched those of areas previously designated to enforce the Uplands Regulations Bylaw. RS1 zoning covered a small area of very large waterfront lots, as well as several inland streets distinguished by "far outlook" homesites. RS2 zoning covered the rest—and most—of the subdivision. Regardless of zone, a thirty-foot, side-lot-line setback total was applied to a majority of lots. This was ten feet wider than the value assigned to lots under a previous 1970s revision of the Uplands Regulations Bylaw. In the RS2 zone, a number of lots that possessed street frontages of seventy feet or less were permitted a twenty-foot total. Ten years later, in 1996, in a response to calls for improved protection, the thirty-foot, side-lot-line setback total was increased to thirty-five feet. This too proved ineffectual: view corridors were still being blocked and privacy impinged upon. The irregular size and shape of lots designed by John Olmsted had again come into play.[14]

In 2000, after much consultation, Oak Bay tried a slightly different approach. A system of scaled side-lot setbacks was implemented. This was similar in intent to the ground-coverage scheme devised for the 1967 version of the Uplands Regulations Bylaw. For lots with a width of 110 or more feet—*regardless of zone*—the minimum side-lot-line setback total was set at 40 feet. This sum was five feet more than the previous high. To ensure privacy and to maintain existing view corridors, native trees and an overall parklike ambience, one of the side-lot setbacks could not fall below fifteen feet. Any property with a width less than 110 feet was assigned to one of several scaled groups, for example, the 90- to 109-feet category. Side-lot-line setbacks were scaled, that is, reduced, appropriately. For instance, at the bottom of the scale, lots with a frontage of less than seventy feet were assigned a twenty-foot setback total, with two equal ten-feet-wide margins.[15] But this approach too is error-prone. The use of broad categories can work for subdivisions with lots of similar sizes, but the uniqueness of each Uplands homesite creates difficulties. Broadly based areal zoning in Uplands fails to adequately protect *all* properties *equally*.

The Uplands Advisory Design Panel

To remedy this situation, municipal officials wisely sought ways to minimize controversy and uncertainty by improving the methods used to evaluate the specific merits and overall impact of a building project. In particular, a far-reaching policy was set in motion in 1990 when the council established an advisory design panel (ADP). Its purpose was twofold. Comprising architects and other knowledgeable specialists, the ADP was assigned the task of providing the council with "non-binding guidance" on the design, first, of *major* building projects throughout the municipality, and second, of *all* projects in Uplands.[16] The ADP's opinions were expected to supplement, but not replace, those of the council's land use subcommittee, which until 1990 was the sole group charged with evaluating an Uplands building application and bringing forth recommendations to the council.

The need for impartial, objective criteria soon emerged, especially to assist with evaluating the ever-increasing number of new building and renovation applications. For Uplands these sometimes tallied five, six, or even eight or more per month. A process that involved public information sessions and a design charrette was begun in 1998. The goal was to produce a set of comprehensive design criteria for evaluating projects. The resultant Uplands design guidelines focused on three areas of concern: siting the house, designing the house, and landscaping the property. Formally adopted in 2000, the guidelines reiterated the spirit and intent of many of the design and planning principles practiced by John Olmsted almost a century ago.[17] Here was clear recognition that the residential park character of Uplands was valued and should be protected and sustained.

In support of this goal, four years later, in 2004, the Uplands Regulations Bylaw was amended to affirm the ADP's specific functions, to specify its membership (mostly design professionals), and to strengthen certain features of the design guidelines.[18] For example, the ADP was given the added authority—if the project failed to comply with the guidelines—to ask applicants of proposed projects to rework their plans. Oak Bay's planner is currently the ex officio and nonvoting chair of the ADP, and is also the person who reports on a project's evaluation to the land use subcommittee. The strengthened role of the ADP has certainly proven useful in helping the council make more informed decisions. But weaknesses persist. Of most concern, siting decisions in Uplands still rely too heavily on the generalized categories of area-based, setback zoning.

What Role Does Institutional Planning Play?

Institutional planning, as formally constituted within local government, has played only a minor role in shaping and preserving the character of Uplands. Until January 2015, Oak Bay did not employ a professional, university-trained, and accredited planner. Oak Bay's municipal engineer sometimes had partial training as a planner or took an interest in the planning process. For a decade in the postwar era, from 1946 to 1955, an advisory Town Planning Commission offered informed commentary on a wide range of town planning issues. On occasion, the commission was asked to make suggestions about the ongoing planning and build-out of Uplands.[19] The commission's role was superseded by the services of trained planning professionals employed by the Capital Region Planning Board of British Columbia (CRPB), formed in 1955. Local governments in the Greater Victoria region were encouraged to contract the services of the CRPB to complete a town planning study. Informal advice was also offered.

In preparing what is now called an official community plan (OCP)—first in 1967, next in 1981, then in 1997—Oak Bay initially relied on the planning staff of the CRPB. This ceased after the CRPB was disbanded in 1966. Private planning firms have completed post-1967 versions of the OCP.[20] A recently completed fourth OCP was also prepared by private consultants with the aid of mapping technologies and data provided by Oak Bay's engineering and building departments, and it was adopted in 2015. Existing OCPs, even the most recent, have largely ignored Uplands. This omission has no doubt been influenced by the long-standing functions of the Uplands Regulations Bylaw.

Heritage Conservation

At present, government-led heritage practice in Oak Bay—and by extension in Uplands—is associated with two bylaws derived from provincial enabling legislation. British Columbia's Local Government Act (1996) and Heritage Conservation Act (1996) sanction municipalities to adopt policies in support of heritage conservation. Oak Bay's response has been to upgrade older, ad hoc initiatives by instituting two heritage bylaws: the Heritage Register Procedure Bylaw (2004) and the Heritage Commission Establishment Bylaw (2011).

In the mid-1990s, the municipality supported the compilation of an inventory of selected pre–Depression era dwellings found throughout the municipality, including in Uplands (Stark 1995). This was a spur to the Heritage Register Procedure Bylaw. It deals with the registration and follow-up monitoring of publicly identified "heritage" houses.[21] For any house to achieve *official* heritage status—which is different than having public officials or private citizens identify and place a house on the municipality's Heritage Register—its owner must apply directly to the council and request that a bylaw be specifically written to legally confirm and protect the home's heritage designation. Following procedures outlined in the Heritage Conservation Act, the council must hold a public hearing before the bylaw is given a final reading. To nullify heritage status, the council must rescind the bylaw. No property owner in Uplands has requested official heritage designation; only four Uplands houses have been either publicly or privately singled out for inclusion on the Heritage Register.[22] Inclusion does not prohibit a house from being modified in ways that are unsympathetic to its historic character, or from demolition. However, when the owner of a "listed" registry or heritage house applies to have it redeveloped, a month's "stay of demolition" is mandatory. This gives the municipality an opportunity to seek advice and possibly stave off demolition. Few permits have been overturned, whether in Uplands or elsewhere in the municipality.

The more common, well-traveled path to heritage conservation in Uplands is for a homeowner to act independently yet conscientiously in striving to meet heritage standards when restoring a house. Several homeowners have spent millions of dollars upgrading their residences in line with accepted heritage conservation practices (Figure 4.7). By following this *informal* course of action, these self-appointed conservationists cite the desire to "keep their options open" and not be bound by the constraints of a *formal* local government bylaw.

The Heritage Commission Establishment Bylaw supports a broadly based commission that advises the council "on any matter related to the heritage significance of any building, structure or landscape feature within the Municipality of Oak Bay."[23] Spurred to action by heritage advocates, several features of Uplands, but not the subdivision itself, have been accorded heritage status by the municipality. These include the so-called gates (really just stone pillars) that mark three street entrances to Uplands. There are also plaques that commemorate the creation of Uplands Park and mark the historic presence of aboriginal village life and activities within the subdivision. Provincial legislation from the 1970s requires that if aboriginal artifacts are discovered on a development site, the archaeological record must be evaluated before construction proceeds. Oak Bay has only recently begun to officially recognize the role of First Nations people in shaping the local cultural landscape.

Finally, the municipality's Tree Protection Bylaw offers a useful and practical framework for sustaining the parklike landscape of Uplands.[24] The bylaw is rooted, quite naturally, in broader societal concerns about environmental degradation and loss of habitat. Its regulatory goal is to protect native vegetation and "heritage" trees in Oak Bay, especially the venerable Garry oak, so boldly emblazoned on the official crest of the municipality.[25] At one time, Garry oak forests covered nearly 38,000 acres throughout Greater Victoria; today, the total is fewer than 4,000 acres (Acker 2012). The threat of further loss from residential construction and natural aging processes is very real, and the municipality is developing an urban

forest strategy.[26] The ADP refers frequently to Oak Bay's existing Tree Protection Bylaw when it reports to the council about the impact of a building project's "footprint" on the Uplands landscape. The municipality's arborist can be called on to offer expert opinion on the site conditions and health status of Garry oaks threatened by construction activity. Tree protection and zoning regulations can thus work in tandem. In going forward, the Tree Protection Bylaw offers considerable weight for maintaining the natural environment of one of Canada's most prestigious neighborhoods, that is, for preserving the "genius of the place" that prompted William Gardner, more than a century ago, to call the oak-studded Uplands Farm "the most beautiful property in Victoria."[27]

Conclusion: With an Eye on the Future

Throughout its century-old history, the Uplands neighborhood has been lauded for its imaginative layout of curved streets and picturesque homesites, for its desirability, and for attempts to preserve natural habitat. Such praise is well and justly deserved. Uplands was the first subdivision of its kind in Canada; it is John Olmsted's masterpiece of neighborhood planning; and over time it has influenced subdivision design, planning practices, zoning, and preservation techniques both locally and farther afield. Uplands also illustrates that urban planning and heritage conservation is a cumulative and adaptive process (Smith 1979).

The companies that developed Uplands—William Gardner's land syndicate (later Estates Limited) and Franco-Canadian Corporation and its subsidiary, the

Figure 4.7. 3000 Rutland Road, by the architect Charles Hay (1913). The house and garage were recently restored to their original architectural form, in line with accepted heritage conservation practices. (Historical photo reprinted from The Uplands Limited, "There Is No Place Like Home, in *UPLANDS*" [Victoria: Acme Press, 1922]; contemporary photo by Larry McCann)

Uplands Limited—fully supported John Olmsted's dual approach of blending artistry and practicality when designing and planning the Uplands landscape. Similarly, Oak Bay's elected councilors and senior administrators were motivated by the efficacy of the subdivision's protective deed restrictions. These were used for crafting Oak Bay's zoning bylaw and when formulating and amending the Uplands Regulations Bylaw. Initially, the Uplands Regulations Bylaw was the all-important legal instrument for preserving the character of Uplands. In time, certain of the protective measures associated with this unique bylaw were transferred to zoning's realm under authority of the ever-increasing police powers offered by revisions to British Columbia's Local Government Act. Uplands property owners continue to benefit from the ways these planning instruments protect the integrity of the subdivision's parklike features. The Uplands planning and heritage experience is an amalgam of separate policies that—in a cumulative and adaptive way—perform all-important roles for ensuring that this masterwork of residential planning remains true to its original vision.

What of this iconic landscape's future? Will Uplands retain its essential, defining character as a residential park? Most likely, yes. But if there is a broader, overriding concern that emerges from the Uplands experience, it is that in the course of protecting a historic landscape, agents of the private and public spheres must engage fully in an ongoing, productive dialogue to ensure that planning and heritage policies are developed in the best interests of the public good. In serving the public interest, carefully devised legislation, derived from neighborhood and community-wide discussion, is essential.

With an eye on the future, other questions must be asked: In an era of large-scale house building, should a method other than the current, area-based setback system be used to protect the residential park character of Uplands? Is it worth considering a lot-by-lot approach, that is, a system that regulates each lot separately, based on the physical qualities of each lot? Ideally, such an approach would certainly take into account the astuteness of John Olmsted's hierarchy of views. However, evaluating each property separately would be a labor-intensive process and expensive to administer. To avoid these challenges, could the Uplands Regulations Bylaw be used in a more proactive way? Given the bylaw's acknowledged power to safeguard the natural environment by controlling how residences are actually sited on a lot, this bylaw possesses the legal force to encourage further protection, conservation, and preservation of the physical and built environment. The legacy of a century of protective development suggests that Uplands property owners and even the wider Oak Bay community would be receptive to revitalized government strategies directed at retaining the residential park character of this celebrated landscape.

Table 4.1
Summary of Historical Events and Heritage Benchmarks for Uplands

Year	Event
1907	William Hicks Gardner of Winnipeg organizes a syndicate to develop 465 acres of the 1,100-acre Uplands Farm, owned by the Hudson's Bay Company (HBC). The sales agreement requires that the HBC must approve the deed restrictions and plan.
1909	January: Oak Bay's municipal officials approve the "General Plan" by the American landscape architect John Charles Olmsted, complete with a sophisticated set of deed restrictions.
1911	Gardner must sell most of his holdings to the Franco-Canadian Corporation, a French multinational financial and real estate firm, but the agreement ensures that the "General Plan" is preserved.
Mid-1920s	Franco-Canadian defaults on mortgages held by Gardner, who regains half of his original holdings.
1936	Passage of the Provincial Government's Oak Bay Special Powers Act enables that of the Uplands Regulations Bylaw.
1946	The Oak Bay municipality purchases sixty-six acres, on which it creates Uplands Park.
1952	The Oak Bay municipal council passes a regulation prohibiting building houses of "similar architectural form" within five hundred feet of each other.
1967	The Uplands Regulations Bylaw is revised to control a dwelling's "ground coverage" and to preserve the parklike character.
1986	Side-lot setbacks are transferred to the municipality's zoning system.
1990	An advisory design panel (ADP) is created.
1996	Side-lot setbacks are revised to strengthen the protection of view corridors.
2000	A new side-lot setback scaling system is implemented, but problems persist.
2004	Uplands Regulations Bylaw is amended to affirm ADP's role and to reinforce the importance of a revised set of design guidelines. Fearing loss of property rights, Uplands homeowners are reluctant to use Oak Bay's Heritage Register Procedure Bylaw to designate their houses.
2011	Through the Heritage Commission Establishment Bylaw, several street entrances in Uplands and the site of a First Nations villa receive heritage status.
2013	Oak Bay's Tree Protection Bylaw supports the preservation of Garry oaks and other native tree species.
	Population (as of 2014), 2,250; 389 acres [157 ha]; 596 single-family dwellings.

NOTES

A research grant from the Social Sciences and Humanities Research Council of Canada is gratefully acknowledged. Thanks to Ian Buck, Aman Gill, and Esther Parker, who collected housing and social data for a Geographical Information System; and to Professor Peter Baskerville, Bill Cochrane (retired Oak Bay administrator), and Councilor Pam Copley for commenting on an early draft of the chapter. Ideas in this chapter are developed fully in my book, *Imagining Uplands: John Olmsted's Masterpiece of Residential Design* (Victoria: Brighton Press, 2016). The author was a member of the advisory design panel from 1998 to 2007.

1. "John Charles Olmsted to L. Shannon Davis, 12 April 1909," Job File 3276, Folder 3, 1909, "The Uplands Subdivision," Olmsted Associate Records, Series B, Library of Congress, Washington, DC (hereafter, Uplands-OARSB-LC).

2. "Signs of Stability Emerge in Capital Region Market," *Times-Colonist* (Victoria), January 3, 2015.

3. Information on deed restrictions is extracted from "General Report," Job File 3276, Folder 2, 1908, Uplands-OARSB-LC.

4. See Forward 1973. Recently arrived residents include "dot.com" entrepreneurs, onetime professional athletes, and fabulously rich globetrotters, many of whom are part-time residents.

5. "Uplands Home's Colourful Past Fails to Save It," *Oak Bay News*, March 26, 2010.

6. "Oak Bay Special Powers Act, 1935," Legislative Assembly of the Province of British Columbia, S.B.C., Chapter 54, George V (assented to March 23, 1935).

7. The quotation is from Corporation of the District of Oak Bay, "Uplands Regulations Bylaw, 1987," Council Minutes 1987, January 12, 1987, Corporation of the District of Oak Bay Records Service (CDOBRS).

8. See CDOB, By-law No. 775, "Uplands Regulations Bylaw 1936," Council Minutes 1936, January 9, 1936, CDOBRS.

9. "I should like a provision prohibiting Orientals and Negroes from residing within the property. I do not know whether you would think it worthwhile to add a clause to this effect or not." "E. B. Ross [solicitor for the Uplands Limited] to H. G. Lawson, Esq., K.C. [solicitor for Oak Bay Municipality] re: Oak Bay and Uplands," File 8000, "Zoning 1935," CDOBRS.

10. "Crease, Davey and Co. to Municipal Clerk, 3 October 1952: re: Uplands," Municipal Clerk's Files, 1952, CDOBRS.

11. The withdrawal of the minimum value of house construction measure and other restrictive clauses is derived from examining different, historical versions of the Uplands Regulations Bylaw.

12. The scaling system is detailed in CDOB, By-law No. 2626, "Uplands Regulations Bylaw 1967," Council Minutes 1967, September 5, 1967, CDOBRS.

13. CDOB, By-law No. 3531, "Zoning Bylaw 1986," Council Minutes 1986, September 22, 1986, CDOBRS.

14. CDOB, By-law No. 3531, "Zoning Bylaw Consolidated to 1996," Council Minutes, October 28, 1996, CDOBRS.

15. CDOB, By-law No. 4068, "Schedule C: Uplands Setbacks," Council Minutes, March 13, 2000, CDOBRS.

16. CDOB, "Resolution of the Municipal Council of the Corporation of the District of Oak Bay re: Advisory Design Panel," Council Minutes, September 24, 1990, CDOBRS.

17. "Stately Uplands Neighbourhood Soon to Benefit from Guidelines on Future Development," *Oak Bay Star* (Victoria), April 1, 1998; CDOB, *Uplands Design Guidelines*, 2000, CDOBRS.

18. CDOB, By-law No. 4237, "Uplands Regulations Bylaw Amendment Bylaw, 2004," Council Minutes, June 29, 2004, CDOBRS.

19. Oak Bay Town Planning Commission (hereafter, OBTPC), File 620, "Town Planning Commission Minutes, 1946–1955," CDOBRS.

20. Capital Region Planning Board of BC, *A Plan for Oak Bay 1967* (Victoria: EiKOS Group); *Official Community Plan for the Corporation of the District of Oak Bay* (Oak Bay: CDOB, 1981); and Workshop Group, *The Official Community Plan: A Vision for Oak Bay* (Oak Bay: CDOB, 1997).

21. CDOB, By-law No. 4222, "Heritage Register Procedure Bylaw, 2004," Council Minutes, March 22, 2004, CDOBRS; "Heritage on the Line in Oak Bay," *Times-Colonist*, February 27, 2006.

22. The properties currently placed on the Oak Bay Community Heritage Register can be viewed by searching the Heritage Oak Bay website.

23. CDOB, By-law No. 4550, "Heritage Commission Establishment Bylaw, 2011," Council Minutes, November 28, 2011, CDOBRS.

24. CDOB, By-law No. 4326, "Tree Protection Bylaw, 2006," Council Minutes, August 21, 2006, CDOBRS.

25. The forerunner to the current bylaw focused exclusively on the Garry oak. See CDOB, By-law No. 3835, "Garry Oak Tree Protection Bylaw, 1995," Council Minutes, May 5, 1995, CDOBRS.

26. "Oak Bay Moves Toward Forest Protection Plan," *Oak Bay News*, December 18, 2012.

27. "William Hicks Gardner to Messrs. Olmsted Bros., 16 March 1907," Job File 3276, Folder 1, 1907, Uplands-OARSB-LC.

REFERENCES

Acker, Maleea. 2012. *Gardens Aflame: Garry Oak Meadows of BC's South Coast*. Vancouver: New Star Books.

Beveridge, Charles E. 1977. "Frederick Law Olmsted's Theory of Land Design." *Nineteenth Century* 3: 38–43.

Beveridge, Charles, and Paul Rocheleau. 1995. *Frederick Law Olmsted: Designing the American Landscape*. New York: Rizzoli.

Fogelson, Robert M. 2005. *Bourgeois Nightmares: Suburbia, 1970–1930*. New Haven, CT: Yale University Press.

Forward, C. N. 1973. "The Immortality of a Fashionable Residential District: The Uplands." In *Residential and Neighbourhood Studies in Victoria*, edited by C. N. Forward, 1–39. Western Geographical Series, vol. 5. Victoria: Department of Geography, University of Victoria.

Freestone, Robert. 2011. "Reconciling Beauty and Utility in Early City Planning: The Contribution of John Nolen." *Journal of Urban History* 37: 256–77.

Harris, Richard. 2004. *Creeping Conformity: How Canada Became Suburban*. Toronto: University of Toronto Press.

Hockaday, Joan. 2009. *Greenspaces: Olmsted's Pacific Northwest*. Pullman: Washington State University Press.

Levee, Arleyn. 2000. "John Charles Olmsted (1852–1920): Landscape Architect and Planner." In *Pioneers of American Landscape Design*, edited by Charles Birnbaum and Robin Karson, 282–85. New York: McGraw-Hill.

McCann, Larry. 1996. "Planning and Building the Corporate Suburb of Mount Royal, 1910–1925." *Planning Perspectives* 11: 259–301.

———. 1999. "Suburbs of Desire: The Suburban Landscape of Canadian Cities, c. 1900–1950." In *Changing Suburbs: Foundation, Form, Function*, edited by Richard Harris and Peter Larkin, 111–45. London: Routledge/Spon.

———. 2006a. "Oak Bay: The Making of a Suburban Landscape." In *Oak Bay Walks: A Celebration of Oak Bay's Centennial, 1906–2006*, 5–8. Victoria: Black Press.

———. 2006b. "A Regional Perspective on Canadian Suburbanization: Reflections on Richard Harris's *Creeping Conformity*." *Urban History Review / Revue d'histoire urbaine* 35: 32–45.

———. 2014a. "John Olmsted's Uplands: Victoria's Celebrated Residential Park." *BC Studies* 181: 11–39.

McCann, Larry. 2014b. *The Uplands: A Masterpiece of Residential Design*. Victoria: Brighton Press. (This map and architectural field guide is available for viewing and downloading at www.brightonpress.ca.)

———. 2016. *Imagining Uplands: John Olmsted's Masterpiece of Residential Design*. Victoria: Brighton Press.

Monchow, Helen C. 1928. *The Use of Deed Restrictions in Subdivision Development*. Chicago: Institute for Research in Land Economics and Public Utilities.

Sies, Mary Corbin. 1997. "Paradise Retained: An Analysis of Persistence in Planned, Exclusive Suburbs, 1880–1980." *Planning Perspectives* 12: 165–91.

Smith, Peter. 1979. "The Principle of Utility and the Origins of Planning Legislation in Alberta, 1912–1975." In *The Usable Urban Past: Planning and Politics in the Modern Canadian City*, edited by Alan F. J. Artibise and Gilbert A. Stelter, 196–225. Toronto: Macmillan.

Sparks, Jean. 2006. *Oak Bay British Columbia in Photographs, 1906–2006*. Oak Bay: Corporation of the District of Oak Bay.

Stark, Stuart. 1995. *Oak Bay's Heritage Buildings: More Than Just Bricks and Boards*. Victoria: Hallmark Society.

Uplands Limited. 1921. *Victoria's Celebrated Residential Park: Information Concerning Uplands*. Victoria: Buckle & Neill.

———. 1922. *"There Is No Place Like Home" in Uplands*. Victoria: Acme Press.

Zaitzevsky, Cynthia. 1982. *Frederick Law Olmsted and the Boston Park System*. Cambridge, MA: Harvard University Press.

CHAPTER 5

MENTENG

Heritage of a Planned Community

in a Southeast Asian Megacity

Christopher Silver

The first fully planned community in the Dutch colonial city of Batavia was the Menteng neighborhood developed in the early twentieth century. Inspired by the British garden city scheme, the Menteng project attracted leading Dutch architects to create an iconic place that blended Asian and European elements into a modernist hybrid commonly referred to as "Indisch" architecture (Roosemalen 2003). Even though only one-half of the original scheme ultimately was built, the portion constructed adhered closely to the original plan. And in the spirit of garden city proponents, Menteng was to be a socially integrated community serving all ranks of European habitants in an attractive and well-serviced community. In the postcolonial period, Menteng transitioned from a European enclave into a prestige residence for the Indonesian elite. Its location just south of the administrative and commercial heart of the new capital city of Jakarta enabled it to remain a prestige address even as the pressures of rapid urban population growth of the 1950s through the 1970s pushed the urbanized area deep into the surrounding hinterland. Given the physical scale, design integrity, and residential character of Menteng, potential development pressures from Jakarta's nearby major commercial corridor (Jalan Thamrin) only penetrated the outer fringes of the community.

Perhaps the most important source of Menteng's resilience owed to the influence of its prominent residents. Foremost was Indonesia's President Suharto, who lived there from the 1960s until his death in 2008. Menteng served as the primary urban residence of scores of other top governmental, military, and business leaders. In addition, quite a few of its grandest structures were converted into the residences, consulates, and embassies for foreign dignitaries. The offices of Indonesia's National Development Planning Board were housed in a landmark Menteng building, the former Freemasons' lodge sandwiched between a historic Dutch church and the official residence of Indonesia's vice president. And among Menteng's residents in the 1970s was a future world leader, the young Barack "Barry" Obama, whose mother worked for the nearby Ford Foundation (*Jakarta Post* 2010).

The essential character of Menteng as the center of Dutch colonial life in the pre–World War II period survived to form a distinctive residential enclave in the modern megacity of Jakarta. At the same time, changes were apparent. The greatest changes were losses to the original building stock through a combination of neglect and the pressures of an overheated urban land market that encouraged expanding, reconstructing, or demolishing the original structures. As the architectural historian Woerjantari Soedarsono (2005, iii) puts it, "Menteng experience[d] external pressures caused by development in Jakarta, and also internal pressures caused by changes in lifestyle and demands of time." Another change was elimination of some of the original open spaces, including some of the distinctive street landscaping, in order to accommodate new development. But the most significant losses resulted from building renovations either by insensitive upgrading or clearance of the original structures to build new homes (*Jakarta Post* 2009). Because Menteng boasted such a wide range of housing types in its original form, the introduction of new architectural styles proved less visually disruptive than it would have if there had been a single Menteng housing style. Yet concerns persist within Jakarta's small but vocal preservation community that without adequate legal protections through effective conservation, Menteng's survival remains in doubt. Overall, however, the essential core historic fabric of Menteng remains relatively intact.

Menteng represents Jakarta's most iconic community because its architecture embraces the history and contextual physicality of the later stage of the colonial city of Batavia as well as the modern capital city of Jakarta. It was the collective product of Batavia's most talented architects and planners seeking to transform the administrative seat of the Netherlands Indies into a city that its European denizens could understand and take pride in. From the congested residential quarters near Batavia's harbor, affluent Europeans pushed southward in the nineteenth century to the Weltevreden area in search of space to expand in a healthier environment. As the European population in Batavia expanded in size and diversity after 1900, the demand for additional housing increased in the Weltevreden area. Menteng was to meet the demands for new housing of varying scales. A product of early twentieth-century modernism, it diverged sharply from the classical villas surrounding the Koningsplein. It showcased new styles and building techniques to satisfy a broad range of tastes and needs.

This chapter examines the rationale for the original planned enclave, how it developed into a thriving community during the final three decades of Dutch colonial rule in Indonesia, and how it endured assorted development pressures in the national period. Ironically, Menteng developed as a new community at a time when other sections of colonial Batavia—most notably the original old town settlement near the harbor (Kota) and the grand structures of nineteenth-century development around the Koningsplein—were already candidates for protection

Christopher Silver

under pioneering conservation legislation in the 1930s. Further conservation efforts were thwarted by World War II and the Japanese occupation, and the challenges of building a new nation following independence in 1950. Not until the 1970s did the conservation movement re-emerge, initially refocusing on Kota. Attention to Menteng's potential demise followed as new institutional uses began to crowd out its residential functions and nearby commercial expansion.

Precursor to the Modern City

Early in the nineteenth century, Batavia's European community, previously sequestered within the narrow and unhealthy confines of the old city, began a gradual southward migration to higher, drier, more spacious, and healthier places. The migration into the southern suburbs was prompted by the decision in 1809 of Governor-General Herman Willem Daendals to relocate the colonial administrative functions to the more defensible open area commonly known as Weltevreden (Heuken 1982, 151–59). The construction of two large landscaped squares, Waterloo Square (where Daendals began construction of the Governor-General's palace with material taken from the walls of the old city) and the Kings Square (Konigsplein), which was to serve as a military parade ground and community park, provided spatial anchors for the new European settlement. Although Daendals left Batavia long before the palace was completed in 1828 (Heuken 1982, 157), his decision spurred construction of country houses for the wealthy, a new railway station (Gambir Station), a new Protestant church (Willemskerk), the Batavia Society of Arts and Sciences, along with several hotels and social clubs, the most important club being "*de Harmonie*." The streets adjacent to these park areas attracted new dwellings for the European community. Except for the parks and parade ground, the planning and development of this area, known as Weltevreden, was largely the work of individual property owners creating suburban villas. There was a prepared plan. While the now-unwalled old city retained its commercial primacy, the shift of colonial administrative functions to Weltevreden brought infrastructure that supported the development of a modern twentieth-century metropolis. Key civic, commercial, and residential structures built during the nineteenth century around Konigsplein would become the government offices of the new republic after 1950 and the square itself would be renamed Freedom Square where the national monument (*Monas*) conceived under Indonesia's first president, Sukarno, marked the symbolic center of the city (Silver 2008, 41–45).

The European community that was divided between the old city and the Weltevreden suburbs in Batavia expanded rapidly in the early twentieth century. In the

Netherlands Indies as a whole in 1900, the European population was 75,853. By 1920 it had doubled to 169,708 and then to over 240,000 by 1930 (Jessup 1987, 55n27). While dispersed throughout urban areas of Java and to a lesser extent in some of the outlying islands, commensurate growth of the European community took place in Batavia, which accounted for at least 50,000 of the city's 300,000 population by the 1930s. Batavia's population expansion accompanied a fundamental change in the Dutch government's policy toward its Asian colonies, a change that encouraged greater local control and increased attention to quality-of-life issues indicative of intentions to support permanent occupancy. In a 1901 speech from the throne, the Dutch Queen Wilhelmina urged her government to undertake measures to raise the prosperity of the indigenous population of the colonies. Queen Wilhelmina's "Ethical Policy" sanctioned a movement for reform and modernization in the colonies. The key legislative act was the Decentralization Law of 1903, which expanded local authority over governance in Batavia (Silver 2008, 38). Ostensibly motivated by the intention to upgrade urban conditions for all of Batavia's residents, the accompanying increase of public expenditures principally benefited the European community.

With newly granted powers of self-governance, Batavia's European leadership sought to plan a city more in keeping with contemporary European standards. This necessitated a long-overdue program of urban improvements. This included paved roads, upgrading deteriorated native settlements (*kampungs*)[1] through improved sanitation and drainage and access to clean water, a long-overdue program of public health measures, and the development of residential settlements to accommodate the growing European population. The city government's decision to sponsor development of several planned neighborhoods, one of which was Menteng, was a key component of this modernization effort (Nas 1990, 86–112).

The Menteng Plan

The initial plan for Menteng dates from 1910, although formal and more comprehensive planning for a modernized Batavia did not get started until 1918. A site south of the European enclave around Konigsplein, a place known as New Gondangdia, was selected for the new community (Figure 5.1). The New Gondangdia development site was, according to a Batavia developer, G. E. Jobst, "cobbled together by incompetents, where no mortal can find his way [whereas] New Menteng [which grew out of this effort] has become an unusually beautiful residential district" (Akihary 1996, 98). Batavia's city plan of 1918 was prepared by F. J. Kubatz, director of the Municipal Department of Land and Housing in Batavia. The Kubatz

Figure 5.1. Plan of Batavia (1910), prior to the development of Menteng. (National Museum of World Cultures, TROPEN, Amsterdam; coll. no. TM-60001120)

plan altered the original layout of the larger area known as New Gondangdia (which included Menteng) and incorporated a new drainage canal (now Jalan Mohammad Amin) that served as a border between these two areas. The Kubatz plan also modified the form of the original large square in the original Menteng community plan (discussed below). It reduced the neighborhood park, Burgermeester Bisschopplein (now Taman Suropati), that was intended as the central open space for the community. To some, the revised Menteng plan was considered superior to the original Gondangdia scheme in its design and character. As Jobst added, "This was due not only to the good circulation plan but also because it only included substantial houses" (Akihary 1996, 14–15, 19–23, 94, 98).

The city was prepared in other ways to meet the needs of newly platted European residential settlements. In 1918, Batavia formed the Local Water Supply Enterprise of Batavia (Water Leidingen Bedriff van Batavia) to manage a piped water distribution system that brought eighty-nine liters per second of fresh clean water to the city from nine artesian wells in the Ciomas-Ciburial-Bogor area south of Batavia. The local water enterprise extended piped water to some kampungs particularly after the government agreed to fund part of a limited kampung improvement program beginning in 1927. Overall, the European residents received four times the amount of water delivered to native residents (Argo 1999, 43).

The expanded authority of the local administration to guide development of the city provided legitimacy to a proactive planning process during the 1920s. The Kubatz plan was finalized in 1921 and in 1926 a new law gave preference to local authorities over third parties to acquire urban lands if they showed, through a structure plan (*geraamte plan*), that the land was needed for housing. This gave municipalities the capacity to determine where development would occur. It was "the most important legal regulation on which the pre-war town planning activity was based"; the new authority of local government not only expanded the planning function but also led to improved services, especially in the European settlements (Bogarers and Ruijter 1986, 77).

By the mid-1920s there also was an increased Indonesianization of the local bureaucracy, with a small Indonesian elite serving on the municipal councils throughout the Dutch East Indies. In Batavia, this introduced voices of dissent to the European-centric public expenditures and to the neglect of the needs of native kampungs. But these new voices did little to change the local public policy tradition to ignore the needs of indigenous areas (Abeyasekere 1989, 124; Nas 1990, 9). Based on a 1907 law, the municipal administration had no jurisdiction in the native kampungs, even those located within the municipal boundaries. The 1907 act reaffirmed the policy of noninterference in native affairs that had been set forth in the Government Regulation (Regeerings Reglement) of 1854 (Article 75). The 1854 act officially separated European and non-European populations and made the affairs in the kampungs the exclusive responsibility of native officials (Argo 1999, 42). Indigenous communities were subject to traditional law (*adat*) administered by the village head. Also, outside governance authority of the city were the extensive private landed estates (*particuliere landerijen*) that made up the majority of agricultural lands around Batavia. In 1901, there were 304 private estates, 101 owned by Europeans and the rest owned largely by Chinese officials under their separate system of administration. These estates encompassed 800,000 peasant holdings (see deVeer 1904, cited in Marcussen 1990, 74). Because the kampungs and rural plantations were under indigenous control, and the Batavia administration had no authority to create new indigenous settlements, it concentrated on development for its European population.

The planned residential community of Menteng was one of several areas where increased municipal infrastructure investment was targeted. Developed in response to the demand for new, well-designed housing to serve the expanding European middle class, Menteng was the most ambitious residential planning project throughout the East Indies between 1910 and 1939. As Thomas Karsten noted in a 1938 memorandum to the colonial government referring to the development of Menteng and several smaller but equally fashionable residential subdivisions, "land development and the building trade have developed to such an extent that, except for temporary dislocation owing to unforeseen economic fluctuations, a normal and satisfactory provision for the housing needs of the well-to-do seems assured" (Marcussen 1990, 80).

The initial development of Menteng began in 1910, based on a plan by the Dutch architect Peter Adriaan Jacobus Mooijen (Figure 5.2). Mooijen had been practicing in Batavia since 1903 and was a member of a development group established by the Batavia city government, the Commisie van toesicht op het Geheer van het Land Menteng. Under the leadership of Kubatz, the Commisie was responsible for planning and developing the larger area of Gondangdia (Nieuw Gondangdia) of which Menteng was the centerpiece (Heuken and Pamungkas 2001, 88–93).

The land for Menteng was a privately owned estate of 73 hectares situated just south of the existing Betel Garden (Kebun Sirih) neighborhood that accommodated 3,562 peasant inhabitants in the 1890s. Once it was evident that Batavia needed more housing for the Europeans, and to prevent illegal development from encroaching on this area, the city purchased the estate and created a commission to oversee its development. The plan included housing of varying sizes and quality, with more modest houses built around its edges to ensure occupancy by a cross-section of the European community of Batavia (Heuken and Pamungkas 2001, 12–20). Mooijen's original plan bore a striking resemblance to the form of the clas-

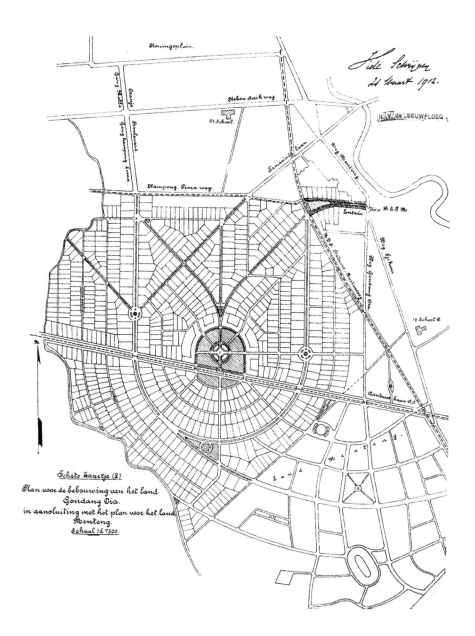

Figure 5.2. Jacobus Mooijen's 1910 plan of Menteng. (Leiden University Library, Archive Moojen, inv. nr. 3)

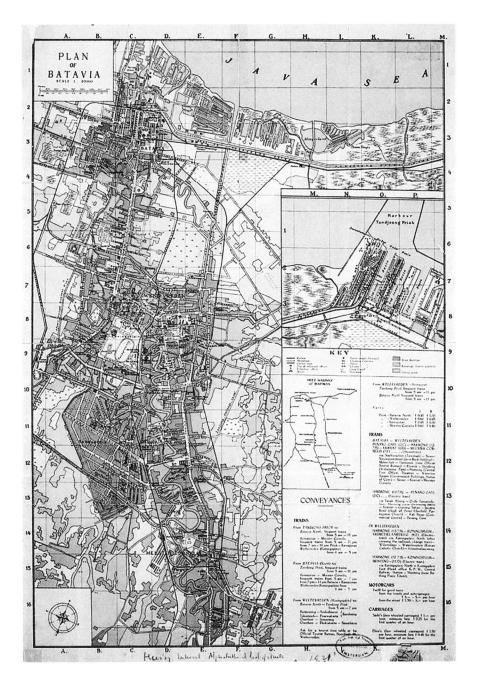

Figure 5.3. Plan of Batavia in 1930, which shows the final layout of Menteng. (National Museum of World Cultures, TROPEN, Amsterdam; coll. no. TM-60001120)

sic garden city model in that it combined wide cross-cutting boulevards with concentric rings of streets and a central public square (Figure 5.3). At the northern entrance to the community, Mooijen designed a modernist civic structure, the Art Center (Gedung Kunstkring), to serve as the cultural center for the European community. In fact, he was first secretary, and then president (1910) of the Bataviasche Kunstkring, an organization created to advance interest in the visual/plastic and decorative arts. The Gedung Kunstkring was made possible through the donation of the land by one of the construction companies that participated in building the neighborhood. Also, it was one of the first concrete structures erected in the Netherlands Indies (see Plate 8). Through rental of the lower floor to commercial uses, the cultural center generated a cash flow for its operations. Nearby, Mooijen erected a three-story building for his architectural firm's office, a building still standing today but later converted to the Cut Mulia mosque (Bellen 1995, 106–7; Jessup 1987, 67).

Although planning for Menteng began in 1910, not until 1912 was Mooijen's revised plan officially unveiled. From the outset, one key difference between the Mooijen plan for Menteng and the garden city model was the absence of any commercial and industrial uses. Rather than a garden city, Mooijen produced a garden suburb but with links to established market areas. For example, the broad boulevard that bisected the community adjacent to the central square (currently named Jalan Imam Bonjul) connected Menteng to an established market nearby in Tanah Abang. Other commercial hubs were in Meester Cornelis and the Cikini, also outside the community area to the east. Menteng's southern boundary was fixed along a flood (*banjir*) canal, which had been proposed in the 1918 Batavia city plan. The flood canal became a priority after the heavy flooding in 1918 and its construction commenced in 1919.

Mooijen's original plan was modified in several other ways by Kubatz's 1918 city plan. In the Kubatz plan, Menteng's street pattern was modified, and a small lake (Lake Lembang) was added to the east of the central park area, originally named Bishops Park (Bischoplein) in honor of G. J. Bishop, who was mayor of the city from 1916 to 1920. The addition of the flood canal eliminated approximately one-third of potentially developable and legally registered sites on Menteng's southern boundary. The Kubatz plan was the final say on the form of Menteng, and it guided the area as it developed during the 1920s and 1930s (Figure 5.4).

Other leading Dutch architects besides Mooijen and Kubatz contributed to the emerging built form of the community through residential and institutional commissions. One of them was the young architect Frans Johan Louwens Ghijsels. Ghijsels had studied at the Technical University in Delft and returned to his place of birth in the Indies to fashion a career in planning and design. Among his peers at Delft were several other architects who later made significant contributions to plan-

Figure 5.4. Jacobus Mooijen's office building at the entrance to Menteng. (National Museum of World Cultures, TROPEN, Amsterdam; coll. no. TM-60042864)

ning and urban development in the Netherland Indies, most notably Henri Maclaine Pont, who designed the buildings for the Bandung Institute of Technology, and Ghijsels's good friend Thomas Karsten, who was the most prominent planner throughout the Netherlands Indies in the 1920s and 1930s. Ghijsels spent his first two years in Batavia assigned to the Municipal Works Department before transferring in 1913 to the architectural division of the provincial government's Department of Public Works (DPW). Ever since the administration of Daendals in the early nineteenth century, the DPW had been responsible for all government-controlled construction. In 1909, the DPW appointed an architect/engineer, Simon Snuyf, to head the architectural division to which Ghijsels was later assigned. Its primary task was to prepare building designs based on standardized forms that determined the form of clusters of houses built in Menteng. Ghijsels left the public works agency in 1916 to establish the consulting firm of General Engineering and Architecture Bureau (Algemeen Ingenieurs en Architectenbureau, or AIA) (Akihary 1996, 10, 14–15).

Figure 5.5. A Freemasons' lodge that was converted to government offices. (National Museum of World Cultures, TROPEN, Amsterdam; coll. no. TM- 60042864)

Through private practice, Ghijsels designed homes for the Municipality of Batavia (1918), the Menteng Property Company (1920–21), the state railway workers' community of Bukit Duri Manggarai (1918), coolie housing for the railway company (1919–20), and a cluster of houses for members of the Indo-Eurasian Association (1923), a group whose members had modest incomes. As Ghijsels wrote about the Indo-Eurasian Association commission, "the living conditions of the lowly civil servant or employee are poor. And if it [his house designs] can be proved to be possible, it could bring about a complete revolution. I shall use all my powers" (quoted in Akihary 1996, 101). These were residential settlements intended to be built in various fringe areas of the city. In addition to house designs, Ghijsels designed the Paulus Church and the adjacent Freemasons' lodge (Logegebouw) in Menteng (Figure 5.5). One of Ghijsels's partners in the AIA, the architect J. F. L. Blankenberg, designed some of the more substantial residences in Menteng between 1926 and 1939 (and after Ghijsels had returned to the Netherlands). This included a home for the owner of Wallenstein, Krausse and Company that later became (and still remains) the residence of the U.S. ambassador to Indonesia. Blankenberg also designed the home of the governor of Jakarta, and several lavish residences for local businessmen along Jalan Imam Bonjul. One of these now houses the National Proclamation Museum (Heuken and Pamungkas 2001, 88–93).

Menteng provided a continuous stream of commissions for the growing cadre of design firms that had set up shop in the city after 1909. The leading architectural firms included M. J. Hulswit, A. A. Fermont and Eduard Cuypers, Biezeveld and Mooijen, Bakker and Meyboom, and Ghijsels's "trendsetting" AIA, all operating in Batavia. In addition, Karsten and Pont had offices in the central Java city of Semarang, and C. P. Schoemaker and Associates was the leading firm in Bandung (Akihary 1996, 12).

The ground plan for Menteng followed a hierarchical system with streets and houses divided into several classes. Parks covered about 30 percent of the area on twenty-three separate sites. During the 1980s, the west edge of Menteng was transformed into a commercial area along Sabang Street (now Jalan Agus Salim), Jaksa Street, Teuku Cik Di Tiro Street, and Menteng Raya Street. There, houses were converted into shops, hotels, offices, and restaurants.

The architectural style of the buildings in Menteng was a hybrid known popularly as "Indies," "Indo-European," or "Indische." This style was characterized by tall pyramid-shaped roofs, front terraces, wide courtyards, and other modern architectural forms influencing the windows, doors, and air ventilation. The residences were distinguished by several classes according to the system governed by the Department of Civil Works (Burgerlijke Openbare Werken). The middle- to high-class residences were classified as class 1 to 3, and they ranged from the largest (1,000 square meters), the midsized from 500 to 800 square meters, and those fewer than 500 square meters. These types were built in the core of Menteng and were targeted for high government officials and the business elite. The architecture of these residential structures was known as "Transitional Period" (*Overgangs periode*), which is the style of architecture between the older "Old Indies House" style (*Oud Indische Huis*), with its typical wide courtyard and wide terraces, and the more modern style called the "European Villa."

The class 1 to 3 areas were situated along several wide boulevards. The layout of a house in the mid-high-class residential area was generally a one- or two-floored freestanding structure (*hoofd gebouw*) with one or two wings/pavilions attached to the main building (Pedoman Perencanaan Menteng). Residences designated as class 4 to 7 served the lower strata of European society. These houses are the most dominant type of residences in Menteng. The architecture of these was a fusion between the Dutch Transitional Period houses and local traditional houses. The areas of class 4 to 7 structures were connected by narrower streets or alleys, classified in Dutch as *laan*, *straat* or *weg*. Another class of residences, class 6 and 7, was targeted for the colonial government staff and was known as *Land Woningen Voor Ambtenaren* (Dutch "country houses for officials"). Generally, this type of house was a single-story structure and sometimes was semidetached (Dutch *koppel*) (Pedoman Perencanaan Menteng) (Figure 5.6).

Figure 5.6. Typical modest house constructed in Menteng. (Photo by Christopher Silver)

There were several distinct variations on the housing styles employed, based on size and amenities. The most modest bungalows were the "Tosari," intended for a small family (only two bedrooms) and one space for a servant, and the "Sumenep," the latter built on a slightly larger lot providing additional space for servant quarters and a backyard garden area. The "Madura," which came in two forms on a larger lot, was a more substantial dwelling, including a large pavilion room to accommodate guests, more and larger bedrooms, and a garage situated at the rear, behind which were the servant quarters. In addition there was villa-style housing, some houses that employed mansard roofs or steep-pitched roofs that made possible second-story spaces, and several in the international style (Heuken and Pamungkas 2001, 45–63). These government-led residential settlements displayed a healthy mix of housing types and residents.

Preserving Menteng

The prestige that Menteng enjoyed in the context of colonial Batavia was transferred to the indigenous urban elite of Jakarta during the postcolonial period. Whereas many emblems of the colonial past were shunned by Indonesians during the first decades of independence, Menteng as a community of prestige persisted. It provided a residential anchor for the central core of the city that remarkably withstood the pressures of commercial encroachment in later years. This should be attributed, in good measure, to the quality of the original plan, which effectively incorporated elements of interconnectedness with adjacent areas while preserving the area's spatial integrity through an ingenious system of streets and boulevards and contiguous structures. Although escalating city-center land values pressured Menteng to convert to more intensive nonresidential uses in later years, the residential core persisted. The community plan of Menteng, and the lifestyle that it was intended to provide, endured as the city around it changed drastically.

Formal efforts to preserve the Menteng community and its distinctive structures rested on a modest legal framework, namely the 1931 Monumenten Ordonantie (No. 238). This ordinance was intended by the Dutch administration to safeguard a handful of historically important structures in the original seventeenth-century settlement. In the decades immediately following independence, there was no political constituency for preservation. Indeed, it was under Sukarno's directives that many vestiges of the colonial past were removed. Jakarta's current preservation movement dates from the post-Sukarno era. Beginning in the early 1970s, there was a government-led effort to undertake a district preservation process. It focused on the area extending from the Fatahillah Square area in Kota, which contains the original city hall (*stadhuis*) northward to the coastal zone around its historic fish market (Pasar Ikan) and its eighteenth-century warehouses (Gill 1995). The district plan was authorized by a decree from the West Jakarta government in March 1972, which created a preservation steering committee (Surat Keputusan Gubernur Kepala Daerrah Chusus Ibukota Jakarta Cd.3/1/2/72, Tanngal, March 3, 1972). With support from the Rockefeller Foundation, two members spent three months touring historic districts, museums, and historic structures in the United States and Europe to identify best practices for Jakarta's historic district (Warmansjah 1973, cited in Cobban 1985, 311). The district plan that followed included rehabilitation of Fatahillah Square as the heart of the district. In addition, the judiciary building became a ceramics museum, a *wayang* puppet museum began in an adjacent building, and a maritime museum was set up in one of the abandoned warehouses near the fish market. But, as James Cobban notes, the broader preservation objectives of creating a tourist-friendly destination had not been realized when he visited the site in the mid-1980s (1985, 312–18).

Renewed effort to preserve the original settlement of Jakarta ignited preservation citywide. In 1975, a governor's decree recognized Menteng as one of Jakarta's treasures to be preserved (Reg. D.IV-6098/d/33/1975), although it was the central government's Ministry of Education and Culture that possessed the real power to protect listed structures and only 18 of the 224 identified historic buildings in Jakarta fell under its jurisdiction. Although Menteng's structures were not subject to the threats posed by new commercial developments adjacent to the community, the serious threat was its booming real estate market and the desire of new property owners to demolish the smaller, old buildings to replace them with new and larger structures.

In the early 1980s, Jakarta preservationists contested the demolition of the landmark Dutch colonial social club De Harmonie (Harmony), located north of Menteng at the northwest quadrant of the Konigsplein area. The private club had been a dominant social institution of the Dutch community in Batavia since the late eighteenth century, initially located in the old city but moved to the Weltevreden area along with the migration of the Dutch residences in the early nineteenth century (see Teeuwen n.d.). The city demolished it in 1985 to make additional space for both road widening and new commercial construction. According to Pauline Roosmalen (2012, 2), even though "the protests were in vain," more significant was "that Indonesians stood up to defend the survival of a colonial building." The failed preservation efforts of the 1970s and 1980s, nonetheless, had built momentum for stronger legal protections. A new law in 1992 updated the 1931 monuments act, with a particular focus on stimulating preservation efforts in Kota (UU No.5/1992 Benda Cagar Budaya). In this case, preservation of the old city was but one part of a grand plan to create a modern waterfront city along the north coast to accommodate the building boom and to expand tourism (Martokusumo 2002, 384–85).

For Menteng, it was the 1999 Bylaw on the Preservation and Utilization of Heritage Buildings that offered local protections to important structures. It divided structures into three classes (A, B, and C). Category A structures were protected from demolition and inappropriate interior and exterior alterations, and category B had to maintain the external form in an unaltered state. Only category C could be removed but ideally should be altered and renovated in accordance with the prevailing designs of neighboring structures (*Jakarta Post* 2011a). But the partial demolition in 2011 of a modest, 350-square-meter historic "Indische" house in Menteng demonstrated the ineffectiveness of the preservation ordinance. This particular house, built in 1932, had been used in films and local television shows as a period structure and was one of the houses protected under the 1992 decree on heritage buildings that allowed new construction on the site but no changes to the original edifice (Figure 5.7). Although the new owner was stopped from completely demolishing it, with its roof largely torn off and the windows removed, nature would finish the job of removing it so that this high-priced real estate (the land sold for U.S.

$1.76 million) could be redeveloped. Ironically, as "Rumah Cantik" (beautiful house) sat in its deteriorated state, prices in surrounding areas of Menteng soared (*Jakarta Post* 2011b).

Figure 5.7. Original Menteng house being removed for new development. (Photo by Christopher Silver)

When the Dutch urbanist Peter Nas revisited Menteng in 2001, he noted the deterioration of another signature structure, Mooijen's Kuntstkring on Jalan Teuku Umar. After the Dutch exodus following Indonesian independence, the culture center was converted into an Indonesian government office building. By 2001, when Nas toured the neighborhood, the Kuntstkring was empty and, in the words of Nas, was in "complete disarray" (Nas and Pratiwo 2003, 277). By 2006, however, the exterior had been thoroughly and tastefully restored under the aegis of the Jakarta Cultural and Museum Agency. It has been restored to its original function as a city-supported culture center known as the Galleri Senin.

It is not just the loss of architecturally valuable structures but a more general challenge to its livability that confronts Menteng today. Traffic congestion during commuting hours generated by motorists seeking an alternative route to the over-subscribed Jalan Thamrin and Jalan Sudirman corridor turns many of the streets of

Menteng into gridlock daily. Many of its finest residential structures, especially along Jalan Imam Bonjol and Jalan Teuku Umar, have been converted to consulates and embassies for Jakarta's substantial diplomatic community, thereby further reducing its residential density. On the positive side, however, some of these institutional conversions have been done with architecturally sensitive rehabilitation of the structures. And despite considerable losses to demolition or sometimes overzealous renovations, reinvestments in housing throughout Menteng have helped to stabilize the area in the face of pressures to convert this valuable city-center land to commercial towers as has dominated the development patterns on the adjacent Thamrin-Sudirman corridor.

Conclusion

When one enters Menteng from virtually any direction, it is still obvious that you are entering a distinctive residential area. It is distinctive because of the unique historic architecture of its buildings, the orderly pattern of its landscaped street system, and the absence of mixed land uses so characteristic of most other sections of Jakarta. Abidin Kusno regards its architecture, the "Indisch architecture," as an example of "syncretic modernism," that is, "neither Indonesian nor Dutch" (2000, 31). In his view, it is neither a confirmation of the value of indigenous design nor strictly modern and international. It represents a symbol of a new colonial society that was forcefully resisting Indonesian nationalism and yet also not entirely comfortable with the colonizing practices over the previous three centuries. The creators of the Indisch motif accepted the technology of the modern but wanted also to respect and express the heritage of the Indies in their work. As the Dutch architect Maclaine Pont put it directly, it is the linking of "west and east together without suppressing either" (Jessup 1987, 211–12; Kusno 2000, 32).

But Kusno stresses that the postcolonial idea (after 1945) was one that still retained links to the colonial past, as reflected in a community such as Menteng. Kusno agrees with Arjun Appadurai (1995; Appadurai's work centers on the postcolonial experience in India) that "decolonization is a dialogue with the colonial past, and not a simple dismantling of colonial habits and modes of life." (Kusno 2000, 212) According to Kusno, this dialogue has helped to create a new colonialism within the postcolonial world. As reflected in preservation efforts, as Marsely von Lengerke Kehoe puts it, "the colonial past remained relevant to modern Indonesian identity" (Kehoe n.d., 19). Menteng performs that function in the constantly changing and rapidly evolving megacity of Jakarta.

Table 5.1
Summary of Historical Events and Heritage Benchmarks of Menteng

Year	Event
1910	Menteng's development begins, based on a plan by the Dutch architect Adriaan Jacobus Mooijen.
1912	Mooijen's revised plan is officially unveiled.
1918	F. J. Kubatz, the director of the Municipal Department of Land and Housing, prepares Batavia's city plan, finalized in 1921. Menteng's street pattern is modified, and a small lake (Lake Lembang) is added to the east of the central park area.
1920–21	Menteng Property Company is created to begin housing construction.
1920s	Johan Ghijsels, architect and planner, designs many houses for the Menteng Property Company through his consulting firm, the General Engineering and Architecture Bureau (Algemeen Ingenieurs en Architectenbureau, or AIA).
1926	A new law gives preference to local authorities over third parties to acquire urban lands if they show, through a structure plan (geraamte plan), that the land is needed for housing. Municipalities are empowered to determine where development will occur.
1926–39	Menteng experiences a period of active residential construction, including large structures adjacent to Taman Suropati.
1931	Monumenten Ordonantie (No. 238, 1931) is enacted to safeguard a handful of historically important structures in the oldest parts of the city.
1950s–1970s	Following Indonesia's independence in 1950, the local gentry replaces the European population in Menteng.
1975	A governor's decree recognizes Menteng as one of Jakarta's treasures to be preserved, in response to increased demolition and modification of houses.
1980s	The western part of Menteng is transformed into a commercial and entertainment area along Sabang Street (now Jalan Agus Salim), Jaksa Street, Teuku Cik Di Tiro Street, and Menteng Raya Street.
1999	The Bylaw on the Preservation and Utilization of Heritage Buildings offers improved local protections to important structures.
2011	The demolition of the iconic "Indische" house (1932), in defiance of preservation bylaws, increases awareness of the challenge of rising real estate values.
	Population (as of 2010), 11,793; 603 acres [244 ha]; 6,918 households (as of 2013; surrogate for Menteng's predominant single-family housing structures).

NOTE

1. A kampung is an indigenous urban settlement on a neighborhood scale, typically composed of makeshift structures, few if any public services, and highly congested living conditions.

REFERENCES

Abeyasekere, Susan. 1989. *Jakarta: A History*. Rev. ed. New York: Oxford University Press.
Akihary, H. 1996. *F. J. L. Ghijsels: Architect in Indonesia, 1910–1929*. Translated by T. Burrett. Utrecht: Seram Press.

Appadurai, Arjun. 1995. "Planning with Modernity: The Decolonization of Cricket." In *Consuming Modernity: Public Culture in a South Asian World*, edited by Carol Appadurai Breckenridge, 23–48. Minneapolis: University of Minnesota Press.

Argo, Teti A. 1999. "Thirsty Downstream: The Provision of Clean Water in Jakarta, Indonesia." Ph.D. diss., University of British Columbia, Vancouver.

Bellen, Marik. 1995. "Cultural Institutions in Batavia, 1900–1942." In *Issues in Urban Development: Case Studies from Indonesia*, edited by Peter J. M. Nas, 98–114. Leiden: Leiden University.

Bogarers, Erica, and Peter Ruijter, eds. 1986. "Ir Thomas Karsten and Indonesian Town Planning, 1915–1940." In *The Indonesian City: Studies in Urban Development and Planning*, edited by Peter J. M. Nas, 71–88. Dordrecht, Netherlands: Foris Publications.

Cobban, James L. 1985. "The Ephemeral Historic District in Jakarta." *Geographical Review* 75(3): 300–318.

Gill, Ronald. 1995. "Jakarta's Urban Heritage: Restoration of the Urban Memory of Kota." In *Issues in Urban Development*, edited by Peter J. M. Nas, 65–97. Leiden: Research School CNWS.

Heuken, Adolph, SJ. 1982. *Historical Sights of Jakarta*. Jakarta: Cipta Loka Caraka, 1982.

Heuken, Adolph, SJ, and G. Pamungkas. 2001. *Menteng: Kota Taman Pertama di Indonesia*. Jakarta: Yayasan Cipta Loka Caraka.

Jakarta Post. 2009. "Menteng Residents Want More Say in Heritage Plan" (August 3).

———. 2010. "Menteng 'Old Friends' of Barack Obama" (November 4).

———. 2011a. "City Blasted for Not Protecting Heritage House" (November 30).

———. 2011b. "Menteng Heritage House Lies in Ruins" (November 29).

Jessup, Helen Ibbitson, 1987. "Netherlands Architecture in Indonesia, 1900–1945." Ph.D. diss., Courtauld Institute of Art.

Kehoe, Marsely von Lengerke. n.d. "The Paradox of Post-Colonial Historic Preservation: Implications of Dutch Heritage Preservation in Modern Jakarta." Unpublished paper.

Kusno, Abidin. 2000. *Behind the Postcolonial: Architecture, Urban Space and Political Culture in Indonesia*. London: Routledge.

Marcussen, Lars. 1990. *Third World History in Social and Spatial Development: The Case of Jakarta*. Aldershot: Avebury.

Martokusumo, Widjaja. 2002. "Urban Heritage Conservation: Experiences in Bandung and Jakarta." In *The Indonesian Town Revisited*, edited by Peter J. M. Nas, 374–89. Singapore: Institute of Southeast Asian Studies.

Nas, Peter J. M. 1990. "The Origin and Development of the Urban Municipality in Indonesia." *Sojourn* 5: 86–112.

Nas, Peter J. M., and Pratiwo. 2003. "The Streets of Jakarta: Fear, Trust and Amnesia in Urban Development." In *Framing Indonesian Realities: Essay in Symbolic Anthropology in Honour of Reimar Schefold*, edited by Peter J. M. Nas, G. A. Persoon, and R. Jaffe, 275–94. Leiden: KITLV Press.

Roosmalen, Pauline K. M. 2003. "Changing Views on Colonial Heritage." In *Identification and Documentation of Modern Heritage: World Heritage Papers*, edited by R. van Oers and S. Haraguchi, 122–28. Paris: UNESCO.

———. 2012. "Confronting Built Heritage: The Appropriation of Colonial Architecture and Planning in Indonesia." Paper presented International Conference, Societies and Cities in Comparative Perspective, Prague (August 29–September 1).

Silver, Christopher. 2008. *Planning the Megacity: Jakarta in the Twentieth Century*. London: Routledge.

Soedarsono, Woerjantari. 2005. "The Streetscape and Building Character Control of Menteng Conservation Area, Jakarta." Ph.D. diss., Institute of Technology Bandung, Indonesia.

Teeuwen, Dirk D. n.d. "The Harmonie Club in Batavia-Jakarta and Much More." http://jakartabatavia-historicalsites.nl. Djakarta Archive Shots, 1940s–1950s, www.sharehouse.wordpress.com/2011/01/15/djakarta-archive-shots-1940s-1950s-jakarta-historical-photos/.

Warmansjah, G. A. 1973. Unpublished report. Department of Museums and History of Jakarta (February 21).

CHAPTER 6

COLONEL LIGHT GARDENS

History, Heritage, and the Enduring Garden Suburb

in Adelaide, South Australia

Christine Garnaut and Robert Freestone

Suburbs are integral to Australia's urban history and the popular aspiration to live and establish a home in the suburbs is long held (Davison 1995). Over the course of the nineteenth century the desired standard of living converged around detached houses on "the quarter acre block." The middle-class showpieces for these ideas were turn-of-the-century model suburbs capturing the rising expectations that came with nationhood (from 1901), civic improvement movements, and improved urban infrastructure. The modern town planning movement, and specifically the garden city idea with its adage of "one family, one house, one garden," delivered a fully developed set of planning and design principles.

While a rich array of planned places has made its impact on the Australian landscape, the heritage of planned communities has been acknowledged only occasionally in official listings by national, state, and local authorities (Freestone 2010). Colonel Light Gardens is one so recognized. Designed in 1917, it was built largely between 1921 and 1927 on the metropolitan fringe of Adelaide, the capital of the state of South Australia. It survives today virtually intact. In 2000 the entire suburb was declared a State Heritage Area, a designation resonating with international efforts to conserve interwar suburban environments (Larkham 1999b; Miller 2010; Whitehand and Carr 1999). This chapter investigates the enduring special qualities of Colonel Light Gardens and the challenges as well as opportunities that have emerged over its nine-decade history in the face of development pressures, changes in governance, and conservation initiatives introduced in the twenty-first century.[1] The major theme is how the original master planning, special administrative provisions, and active civic pride within a property-owning community have combined to forge a "degree of persistence" often witnessed in elite planned suburbs (Sies 1997, 187).

Iconic Status

The mantra of planning "on garden city lines" received widespread support in Australia from the 1910s (Freestone 1989; Stern, Fishman, and Tilove 2013, 646–59). This was promoted through various media, but a critical conduit was a series of lectures delivered in 1914–15 under the aegis of the Australasian Town Planning Tour (ATPT) (Freestone 1998). Sponsored by the London-based Garden Cities and Town Planning Association (GCTPA), the tour was organized by the Association's emissaries, the New Zealand–born journalist turned town planner Charles Reade and the British planner-surveyor William Davidge. Together with related propaganda efforts by state-based town planning associations and individual advocates, the ATPT assisted in activating the garden city idea and eliciting practical experiments.

From the time when the idea was first mooted in the South Australian Parliament that the state should build a model garden suburb, the proposed development that came to be known as Colonel Light Gardens was promoted locally as "a standard to turn to."[2] Indeed, its status as a model planned suburb has persisted if not intensified (Garnaut 1998). Its residents have long acknowledged it as "a special place with its own special environment"[3] and have campaigned assiduously for protection at significant moments in its history. They led the drive for formal statutory designation, pushed for its broader recognition as a place of national heritage significance, and remain vigilant to ongoing threats to its enduring character (Garnaut 2000, 2002, 2007; Henry 1955).

Colonel Light Gardens is iconic among Australian garden suburbs on several grounds: its comprehensive and faithful adaptation of garden city planning principles in the British tradition; its links to the peripatetic town planning missionary, Charles Reade; its endurance and integrity as a complete built environment; its heritage listings; and the impact of residents' contributions on its protection and conservation (Freestone 2010; Garnaut 2002; Home 2013; Miller 2002; Ward 2002).

Adelaide's Model Garden Suburb

In the wake of the ATPT and pressure from the South Australian Town Planning and Housing Association, in June 1915 the state government purchased the three-hundred-acre Grange Farm at Mitcham, south of Adelaide's city center, expressly to build a model suburb according to the best practice principles espoused by Reade (Garnaut 2006; Garnaut and Round 2009). In 1916, the government appointed Reade as its official planning advisor (elevating him in 1918 to the post of

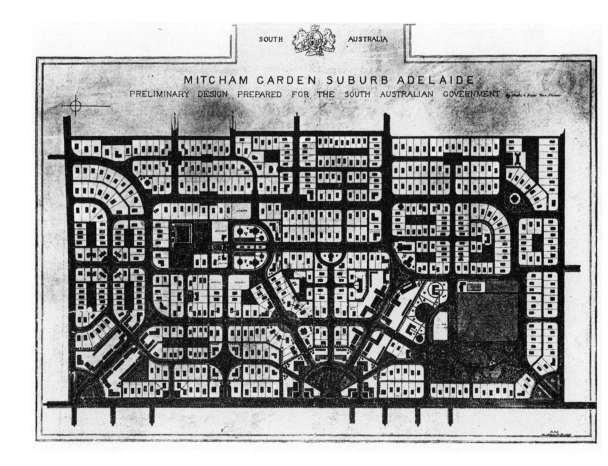

SOUTH AUSTRALIA

MITCHAM GARDEN SUBURB ADELAIDE
PRELIMINARY DESIGN PREPARED FOR THE SOUTH AUSTRALIAN GOVERNMENT

Figure 6.1. Mitcham Garden Suburb ground plan by Charles Reade, drawn by Louis Laybourne Smith. (Reprinted from *Official Volume of Proceedings of the First Town Planning and Housing Conference and Exhibition, 1917*, October 17–24 [Adelaide: Vardon and Sons])

Government Town Planner) and invited him to design the new residential estate. World War I interrupted the suburb's establishment because the Commonwealth government used Grange Farm as an army training camp. In 1917, Reade initiated the processes that led to the preparation of a formal schematic layout as well as a "bird's-eye" perspective for what was named the "Mitcham Garden Suburb." David Crawford, an architect and senior draftsman in the Commonwealth public service, prepared the perspective, which the South Australian government later reproduced in color in a promotional brochure released to coincide with the opening of land sales in the suburb (see Plate 9).[4]

Prominent South Australian architect Louis Laybourne Smith drew the actual ground plan (Figure 6.1), based on details supplied by Reade (Garnaut 1997). It illustrated a vastly different layout from the conventional Australian suburb and represented the "new thinking at the time."[5] Reade was aiming to achieve a visually pleasing, harmonious environment with a strong sense of place. While he drew on the key principles of garden city planning thought, and specifically on Raymond Unwin and Barry Parker's plan for Hampstead Garden Suburb (1907), Reade adapted the principles to embrace Australian preferences, especially for low-density layouts and single-story detached dwellings.

The site was self-contained within distinct boundaries and designed to accommodate residents' everyday needs. A hierarchy of roads fit for purpose supplanted the standardized suburban grid. Areas were also designated for specific purposes. Residential use dominated, but sites were provided for two shopping precincts, administration, churches, a school, a major recreation park with an oval, children's playground and formal gardens, and a smaller recreation reserve for tennis, lawn bowls, and croquet. The school, oval, and one of the shopping precincts formed a center that was expanded after World War II to include several community buildings (Hutchings 2007). Small pocket parks at street corners and internal reserves surrounded by houses were scattered throughout. Buildings were sited as terminal vistas and to break building lines, and ample yard space was allocated to houses. An interconnected network of utility ways (laneways) housed infrastructure—pipes, poles, and wires—for services and communications and created a system of internal pedestrian paths. Street verges were planted with avenues of trees, revealing the planner's intent to create a parklike environment. Although Reade's proposal predated Clarence Perry's neighborhood unit idea, it convincingly anticipated the key principles (Hutchings and Garnaut 2009).

Reade showed the plans for the proposed suburb in a major exhibition associated with the First Australian Town Planning and Housing Conference and Exhibition, which he organized in Adelaide in October 1917 (Tregenza 2007). Promotion intensified when South Australia's Attorney General and Minister for Town Planning delivered a paper about it at a second national conference the following year (Barwell 1918). In November 1919 the South Australian Parliament passed the Garden Suburb Act, which provided specifically for the planning, laying out, and development of a garden suburb at Mitcham. The Act was "unique . . . in its intent to specifically create and guide the development of a single suburb as a model community" (Cheney 1994, 154).

In April 1921 the model garden suburb was named Colonel Light Gardens after South Australia's first surveyor-general, Colonel William Light, whom Reade admired and to whom the plan of Adelaide (1837) is widely attributed. Reade had left South Australia by then to work in the Federated Malay States. Although he played no further part in Colonel Light Gardens' development, he did keep abreast of its progress.[6]

Establishing, Remodeling, and Completing the Garden Suburb: The 1920s and 1930s

The Garden Suburb Act established a unique governance structure: a state-appointed Garden Suburb Commission headed by a single commissioner with responsibility for all aspects of the suburb's administration, financial management, and development.[7] The commission carried out the normal administrative role of a local council, including building approvals, collection of taxes, and improvement and maintenance of the public realm. The inaugural commissioner, Charles Harris, released the first building sites for purchase in August 1921. Initially, land sales and house construction were slow. Meanwhile, the state government was endeavoring to address Adelaide's acute postwar housing shortage and selected Colonel Light Gardens as the site for an innovative affordable housing program. Named the "Thousand Homes Scheme," the program was financed by the State Bank. The government intended to build approximately seven hundred houses in Colonel Light Gardens.[8]

Reade's plan only accommodated six hundred houses so the government purchased additional land abutting the western boundary. Thus the suburb was divided into two parts separated by a major road. Reade's successor as Government Town Planner, Walter Scott Griffiths, was instructed to lay out the new section and remodel the undeveloped southern portion of the original plan so as to achieve the maximum number of residential allotments. Griffiths standardized the residential blocks and eliminated several reserves. However, the underpinning garden city principles were not lost. In designing the western extension, he adopted a largely conventional grid but acknowledged the garden city idea by including several reserves. (Figure 6.4 shows the layout of the original and the new sections of the suburb.) Although the Thousand Homes Scheme hastened Colonel Light Gardens' development, landowners who had already bought in to the suburb perceived that group housing would lower its tone and founded a residents' group to voice their objections. The government pushed on regardless. In approximately three years, nearly seven hundred houses were constructed. Concurrently, individuals continued to build homes on land excluded from the scheme.

Houses erected in Colonel Light Gardens were built predominantly in the bungalow style, the architectural fashion in South Australia in the 1920s (Figure 6.2). In accordance with popular convention, builders rather than architects designed most of the dwellings. The State Bank offered purchasers of the Thousand Homes a choice of fourteen plans. Respecting the garden city maxim of architectural "unity but not uniformity," no two houses in any part of the suburb were the same side-by-side; however, throughout they retained a consistency in single-story detached form, materials, and colors (Garnaut 2006, 2009).

Christine Garnaut and Robert Freestone

Domestic-scale nonresidential buildings, including churches, shops, a police station, two schools, a theater, and two meeting halls, were erected in the 1920s to service the growing population. Development and landscaping of public spaces also occurred in parallel. The principal recreation area, named Mortlock Park, was within easy access of the new government primary school. The smaller reserve set aside for mixed recreation and located in the northern part of the suburb was named after Reade.

Existing trees were preserved and new ones planted in avenues of like species in roadside verges. "Ornamental plots" at street corners were grassed and planted with "hardy shrubs."[9]

By late 1927 most of the available housing blocks in Colonel Light Gardens had been developed. The population had reached about four thousand, and a community identity had evolved in accordance with the original vision.[10] Residents were said to have developed a "conscious pride."[11] This flourished as they embraced common goals of raising families, paying off housing loans, improving houses and gardens, and participating in the suburb's strong sporting and social life (Henry 1955). They formed and joined community groups associated, for example, with the local churches and schools (Miller 1993). Despite the popularity of garden city principles among the professional cognoscenti in Australia at that time, the actual realization of a fully fledged planned community was a major achievement.

But challenges were around the corner. During the Great Depression and its aftermath, numerous residents lost their jobs and experienced serious personal hardship.

Figure 6.3. Looking east across the developing suburb of Colonel Light Gardens about 1930. Piccadilly Circus is the undeveloped semicircular site with radiating roads. (Courtesy Colonel Light Gardens Historical Society; original held at the Mitcham Heritage Research Centre)

Many found it hard to pay mortgages and local rates, as well as to feed and clothe their family adequately. "A few simply abandoned their properties and walked away from their investment" (Garnaut 2000, 85). Commissioner Tom Stephens came to arrangements with individuals about the payment of rates and, remarkably, succeeded in keeping the suburb afloat. He created opportunities for the unemployed to work for the commission and ensured that metropolitan-based social welfare bodies assisted the needy in practical ways (Garnaut and Hutchings 2003).

Residents' financial hardship affected the commission's resources. In the wake of the Depression, a cash-strapped Stephens was forced to implement a provision of the Garden Suburb Act permitting the sale of public land to raise revenue for the suburb's upkeep and maintenance. He indicated in his annual report for 1938–39 that the semicircular area at Piccadilly Circus, which had been reserved during the main phase of the suburb's development for future improvement as a formal entrance, had been subdivided into twenty housing blocks.[12] At about the same time, Stephens sold a portion of the land assigned as the Garden Suburb Commission works depot as well as several allotments proposed for shops. The restrained postwar "austerity style" houses subsequently built in these infill locations contrasted with the bungalow style that was dominant elsewhere. Piccadilly Circus was the last substantial precinct opened up for development in the suburb and the site of the largest of the postwar improvements (Figure 6.3).

The Postwar Suburb: Community and
Physical Development and Change

With Colonel Light Gardens mostly built out by World War II, the postwar years were ones of community consolidation. Physical change was largely incremental infill and minor modifications of land use. The suburb's status as a planned community endured and was enhanced in 1947 when it featured in a promotional film made by the Australian Department of Information to attract British migrants to Australia. Titled *Australia and Your Future: Christmas Under the Sun*, the film depicted everyday life in Colonel Light Gardens as the suburban idyll.[13] In 1948 the famous British planner Sir Patrick Abercrombie made an official visit during a national lecture tour. Abercrombie experienced firsthand the maturing "model garden suburb planned . . . on lines divorced from the more orthodox 'grid-iron' system."[14]

After the war and until about 1975, approximately seventy houses were constructed either on blocks purchased but not built on earlier or reserved initially for other uses but released later for housing (Jamieson 1975). In the early 1990s, the South Australian Housing Trust built ten single-story semidetached units for public housing tenants on the site of the former Garden Suburb Commission works depot.[15] Since the mid-1990s only a handful of new houses have replaced original dwellings demolished primarily because they were structurally unsound.

From the 1950s the suburb's original church buildings were replaced by more substantial structures and existing community groups achieved permanent accommodation. A new basketball stadium constructed on the southern edge of Mortlock Park in 1975 was a venue for district and local basketball as well as a daytime "Kindergym" until its demolition following a major fire in 1998. A two-story building for community purposes was built adjacent to the stadium in the 1980s. A few prominent suburb buildings changed uses: the Garden Theatre was converted to a supermarket in the 1960s and the Congregational Church was adapted in 1996 as a childcare center. Over the years, the types of businesses accommodated in the suburb's two shopping zones have changed. Initially they sold foodstuffs but gradually shifted to services requiring less walk-up business. More recently cafés have revitalized both precincts.[16] Several road changes aimed at improving vehicular traffic safety and managing the increased volume of cars in the suburb altered its finer grain in the 1950s and 1960s. Of note was the closure of the diagonal roads at the two secondary entrances and the conversion of each to a single open space.

Colonel Light Gardens boasted a generous amount of public open space in various forms and at different scales. However, because funding for suburb improvements and maintenance was raised internally from rates, the Garden Suburb Commission was forced to prioritize its efforts in developing and maintaining open space. The commissioners focused on the major reserves in the original scheme, Mortlock Park and Reade Park, and on Hillview Reserve in the western addition. Residents themselves assumed the task of developing internal reserves by variously establishing tennis courts, building children's play equipment, and planting shrubs (Freestone and Nichols 2001). Tennis and netball clubs, the Boy Scouts, and even a nurseryman also used the reserves.[17] From time to time some residents with public reserves adjacent to their properties approached the commission to buy all or part of the land for private use. In 1960 the Garden Suburb Act was amended to make such purchases possible. Subsequently some street garden reserves and portions of several utility ways in the northern part of the suburb were acquired by adjoining landowners. When a local tennis club was disbanded in the mid-1960s, Commissioner Theo Sellars exercised his new powers and sold the site for retirement housing. Although no internal reserves were transferred officially into private hands, from the 1980s Mitcham Council allowed residents abutting two substantial reserves in the northern section of the suburb to include a portion within their properties. As a consequence, the original morphology of, and community access to, those particular reserves was compromised.

Suburb Governance and the Evolution of Heritage Conservation

Colonel Light Gardens was afforded a unique protection mechanism under the regime of the Garden Suburb Commission. As the suburb's custodians, successive commissioners were charged with the responsibility of making all decisions about its development. They made critical administrative contributions and formulated and successfully managed a consensus vision for its improvement and growth.

From the 1930s the South Australian government made four attempts to bring Colonel Light Gardens—one of the smallest local authorities in the state—under the control of Mitcham Council, the larger local government authority that surrounded it (Garnaut 2002). All were unsuccessful, for various reasons. Of critical importance was the persistence of resident resistance. As one unnamed resident stated in the early 1950s, "We don't want to go over to Mitcham because of our civic pride and because we are the Garden Suburb" (quoted in Henry 1955, 182). Residents considered that the commission helped reinforce their suburb's identity, distinctive origins, history, and community spirit and pride in their place.

In the 1970s, however, with commission resources unable to meet adequately the growing demands of the suburb's upkeep, and the state government keen to rationalize local government boundaries, amalgamation with the local council was inevitable.[18] In 1974, prior to the repeal of the Garden Suburb Act in 1975, Sellars, the last commissioner, was replaced by Mitcham Council's town clerk, who assumed the role of administrator.

When the commission was being dismantled, the outgoing commissioner recognized that Colonel Light Gardens would be under threat from developers attracted by its generous housing allotments. In mid-1973 he urged residents to support a proposal for R1 zoning (one house per building block), which would protect the suburb's character and amenity as a "low density single dwelling area."[19]

Faced with the imminent demise of the commission, in February 1974 residents formed the Colonel Light Gardens Residents Association (CLGRA). Thus began a textbook example of the process of active "community-led involvement" in suburban conservation (Larkham 1999a, 264). The founding CLGRA members were either newcomers or second- or third-generation residents who had grown up in the suburb (Garnaut 2002). They pursued the R1 zoning and their efforts were rewarded in March 1975. Having achieved this initial goal, the association pursued another of its founding aims, namely "preserving and promoting many of the [suburb's] desirable, historical, social and cultural features" to ensure that "future development . . . does not destroy . . . [its] character, history and beauty" (Garnaut 1997, 255).

Initially the CLGRA adopted a "watchdog role" over Mitcham Council and decisions that might impact the suburb.[20] Eventually, "concerned that [its] historical integrity . . . was threatened by [inappropriate council-approved] building renovations and redevelopment," the CLGRA applied successfully for Australian government funding for planning consultants Bechervaise and Associates in association with McDougall and Vines, Heritage Consultants to undertake a conservation study.[21] The study was released in 1989 and made two recommendations in recognition of Colonel Light Gardens' cultural significance—that it be nominated in its entirety for inclusion on the Register of the National Estate (RNE) and as a State Heritage Area by the South Australian government. The RNE was a respected, nonstatutory means of recognizing Australian "places to keep of 'aesthetic, historic, scientific or social significance . . .' for present and future generations" (Australian Heritage Commission 1981, 9). Heritage legislation passed in the 1970s by the Australian government and by several state governments, including South Australia in 1978, led to the statutory development of registers of places of significance to the nation and to the state (Mosler 2011). These were then the highest legal levels of heritage recognition and protection available at both the national and state levels. The realization of the consultants' recommendations for Colonel Light Gardens became the CLGRA's goal.

In 1996 the Colonel Light Gardens Historical Society (CLGHS) emerged as another local advocate of heritage listing. Its specific mission was to encourage the suburb's physical development according to "Garden Suburb town planning princi-

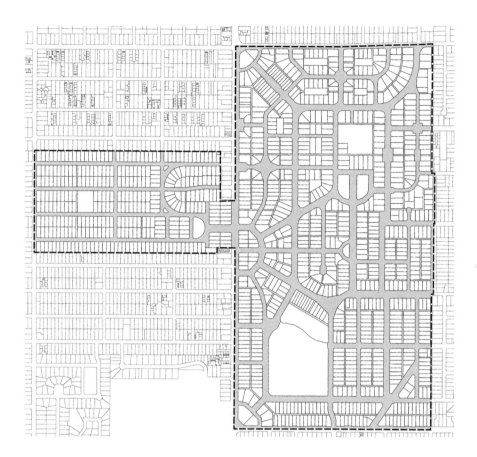

Figure 6.4. Colonel Light Gardens State Heritage Area. (Base map by City of Mitcham; map overlay by Philip Knight)

ples and accepted conservation practices," to promote heritage listing, and to heighten public interest in the suburb's history (Garnaut 1997, 235). The shared goals of both resident-based groups were to be achieved following a prolonged and nationally unprecedented campaign for heritage listing of a planned community. Colonel Light Gardens was entered on the RNE in November 1999. In May 2000 the suburb became a State Heritage Area, in which each building was recognized as an individual State Heritage Place (Figure 6.4).

Heritage Frameworks

Colonel Light Gardens was the first entire suburb in South Australia to achieve State Heritage Area status and it maintains that status today. Although this particular designation is peculiar to South Australia, comparable legislation exists to protect places deemed of state significance in other parts of Australia. Different protections and regulations apply in each state with regard to places of local significance.

A significant component of the community and local council campaign for the heritage listing of Colonel Light Gardens focused on developing a Plan Amendment Report (PAR), which was a requirement of the South Australian legislation before the suburb could be declared a State Heritage Area. In essence, Mitcham Council's plan needed to be altered to include development objectives and policies specific to the suburb. The thrust of the effort in preparing the PAR was to draw on and apply the suburb's planning history in determining a heritage management regime that focused on "managing change, not . . . freezing [the] place . . . in time."[22] The twin emphases were on "continuity as a living place" and ensuring that residents would not view heritage regulations as inhibiting their lifestyle or disadvantaging their financial investment (Garnaut 2007, 277).

Development is now controlled and guided through provisions of the City of Mitcham Development Plan for the State Heritage Area (Colonel Light Gardens) Zone. Every development application must be referred to the state government. Until mid-2012 referral was through a heritage advisor, appointed as the delegate of the state minister responsible for heritage. Following the abolition of the state-government's Heritage Advisory Service in mid-2012, applications are reviewed directly by staff of Heritage South Australia in the Department for Environment and Water.[23]

Colonel Light Gardens' first heritage advisor was appointed in 1992 and remained in the position until 2010. He was involved in preparing the suburb's nominations to the RNE and State Heritage Register and in drafting the PAR. He led the team that prepared the Conservation Management Plan (CMP). In the manner of the Garden Suburb commissioner over an extended period, the heritage advisor provided continuity of advice on development matters affecting both private and publicly driven development. This was yet another arrangement that contributed to the persistence of the garden suburb ideal.

Development objectives, policies, and principles of development control for Colonel Light Gardens within the City of Mitcham Development Plan are informed by the suburb's planning history and by the statement of cultural significance set out in the original Conservation Study (1989). These policy parameters were the subject of broad and prolonged stakeholder consultation during the PAR process (Garnaut 2007). In terms of urban form, a primary principle is that "development should reinforce and complement the desired character and heritage value of the 'Area'" and in this way conserve and underpin the suburb's heritage significance and integrity.[24]

The CMP was also obligatory under heritage legislation in South Australia. A CMP is a practical rather than a statutory (legally binding) document and is used by a local council in conjunction with a development plan. In Colonel Light Gardens its purpose is to provide guidance in relation to the heritage values of the suburb and to the management of public spaces and infrastructure in light of those values. The CMP was officially endorsed by Mitcham Council in 2005 after another protracted consultative process (Garnaut 2007). The CMP identifies the suburb's urban design and landscaping elements, interprets their heritage values, and sets out a framework for detailed management. The council decides its priority projects and allocates funding in its annual budget for its staff to undertake the necessary works. Public instrumentalities like electricity providers carry out and pay for works under their remit.

State government legislation related to the management of community land and introduced after the CMP was adopted has implications for heritage matters in Colonel Light Gardens. For example, the introduction of Community Land Management Plans (CLMPs) into the Local Government Act of 1999 now provides Mitcham Council with a non-heritage-related rationale for reclaiming internal reserves alienated from community use. The council is undertaking a protracted process of consulting with the community about the long-standing and politically difficult matter of recovering two "subsumed" spaces in the northern part of the suburb. While the council has met with opposition from the residents concerned, the CLGRA supports the action.[25] Table 6.1 provides an overall summary of the multiple heritage frameworks canvassed in this section.

Heritage in Practice

Having reviewed the history and governance structures of Colonel Light Gardens, the relationship between heritage and the challenges of physical, social, and administrative change can now be considered. How have residents and local government authorities responded to the challenges of change, including heritage listing? Has listing aided or hindered the suburb's development? And what are the suburb's future prospects?

Resident Buy-in to Suburb Protection and Heritage Listing

The process of heritage listing for Colonel Light Gardens is an example of what Graeme Davison (2000, 125) describes as "democratic heritage". Residents' determination to protect the quality of their built environment has persisted for more than ninety years. From the founding decades, they worked collectively to contribute practically to the development of the suburb and to establish local groups that fostered community engagement, spirit, and pride. Later generations have "treasured" what the pioneers achieved (Cheney 1994, 155). Their actions in leading the charge for heritage listing from the late 1980s were thus in keeping with a long-held local tradition.

Table 6.1
Key Institutions in Governance, Heritage, and
Development Matters in Colonel Light Gardens

Name	Status	Date	Key Foci
Mitcham Council	Local government authority	May 1, 1975–	Is the local government authority. Takes over the roles of the Garden Suburb Commission. Works increasingly with residents' groups for the heritage listing of suburb. Now implements statutory requirements of the City of Mitcham Development Plan for the State Heritage Area (Colonel Light Gardens) Zone and relevant legislation including Community Land Management Plans under the Local Government Act of 1999. Uses the Colonel Light Gardens Conservation Management Plan to guide management and development of public spaces and infrastructure.
Heritage Advisor (representing the Minister for Conservation and Environment)	State government	2000–mid-2012	Advises residents and Mitcham Council regarding development applications.
Heritage South Australia, Department of Environment and Water (formerly Heritage Unit, Department of Environment, Water and Natural Resources)	State government	Mid-2012–	Gives ongoing advice to residents and to Mitcham Council regarding development applications.
Colonel Light Gardens Residents Association	Community group	1974–	Campaigns for heritage listing and for implementing "Garden Suburb Planning Regulations-Planning Proposals." Has taken on a self-styled "watchdog" role over Mitcham Council. Protects the suburb's physical environment and especially its low-density residential amenity.
Colonel Light Gardens Historical Society	Community group	1996–	Campaigned for heritage listing. Encourages the suburb's physical development according to Garden Suburb principles and accepted conservation practices. Heightens public interest in the suburb's history.

Colonel Light Gardens benefited from its particular governance structure, which gave unitary control to the Garden Suburb Commission. The change in governance from commission to regular local authority presented a particular challenge for the suburb's future conservation. Residents had a deep sense of their suburb's history, were confident of its special significance as a planned community, and appreciated the qualities of the built environment that flowed from its planning history. They sought to retain and protect its sense of place. In the years following the shift of governance, residents had disagreements with Mitcham Council. Consequently, through the CLGRA, joined later by the CLGHS, they identified avenues through which to act and secure statutory protection over future development. In time, that process brought residents and the council together as advocates for the same goal and latterly for the suburb's long-term conservation and management.

Heritage Listing and Suburb Development

In the main, current residents of Colonel Light Gardens do not regard heritage as a significant imposition. They understand that the provisions of the Development Plan relating to the suburb's heritage value underpin the sustainability of those values. The wider community (beyond the suburb) is generally aware that heritage legislation applies in Colonel Light Gardens and new residents understand that the regulation of development has a heritage layer.[26]

Although each building in Colonel Light Gardens is a State Heritage Place (SHP), development control policies relate only to what can be seen from the street and do not apply to building interiors as they do for SHPs listed elsewhere in South Australia. This significant departure from normal practice was secured when the PAR was being prepared. It was driven by the residents' and other stakeholders' goal of ensuring the suburb's continuity as a dynamic place attractive to all demographic groups and one where homeowners would not be inhibited by perceived draconian heritage regulations.

The consistency in the number of development applications received by Mitcham Council in the period of 1991–2014 demonstrates that heritage listing has not constrained development in Colonel Light Gardens. Competitive funding to support heritage conservation projects was available through the South Australian government's State Heritage Fund until the fund was abolished from July 1, 2014, and Mitcham Council has offered incentives to encourage development improvements through a Heritage Subsidy Scheme. The council has made available grants for up to several thousand dollars for residents to undertake repairs and to make improvements, like treating rising damp, re-roofing, removing plaster and paint from external brickwork, replacing aluminum windows with timber windows, and installing

appropriate fencing.[27] The scheme is reviewed annually and has been well subscribed. The public realm, and consequently the suburb's amenity, has also benefited from heritage listing (Figure 6.5). In accordance with Mitcham Council's scheme of priority projects for the suburb, a program of staged street-tree and street-garden reserve renewal commenced in 2006 with aged or inappropriate plantings being removed and new species planted in accordance with CMP guidelines. New street-name signs designed as recommended in the CMP were installed in late 2011. Although the plan's policies state that "all footpath and driveway paving within Colonel Light Gardens should be bitumen" (an early paving treatment), as well as recommending "staged removal of concrete unit pavers and any other surfaces other than bitumen," the council has not followed that advice for a combination of aesthetic, economic, and amenity reasons. A community consultation process in 2010 secured significant local support for this pragmatic variation, demonstrating the vital importance of ongoing consultation between the council and residents.

Figure 6.5. Impacts of heritage controls on the public realm: a new street sign, footpath paving, and street garden reserve with new tree species reflect requirements in the 2005 Conservation Management Plan. (Photo by Julia Garnaut 2015)

Looking to the Future

At the time when heritage listing was being mooted in the early 1990s one observer cautioned, "Unless a heritage enactment ensures that there is sensitivity to the real character of the residential mosaic, and its necessity to always respond to refurbishment, and that there is flexibility to meet the changing lifestyle needs of the evolving gentrification, then heritage enactment may become heritage entrapment—a disastrous attempt to freeze in time the dynamic processes of suburb sustenance" (Harper 1991, 69).

These fears have proved unfounded. Indeed, the experience of heritage listing has been so positive that residents and Mitcham Council have even submitted joint nominations for the suburb to the National Heritage List (NHL).[28] Administered by the Australian Heritage Council, the NHL was created under the Environmental Protection and Biodiversity Conservation Act of 1999, and it recognizes places of "outstanding value to the nation." Elevation to the NHL does not impose additional statutory controls, except on actions of the national government; for Colonel Light Gardens it would validate its significance "as a beacon for best practice in the design and layout of early twentieth century suburbs."[29] Furthermore, the CLGRA has expressed the view that the NHL could provide an additional safeguard against development threats in the future. The current metropolitan strategies for Greater Adelaide profess compact city goals and endorse increased density for inner-city suburbs. Parts of the area under Mitcham Council's governance are targeted in the plan. While there is no immediate threat to Colonel Light Gardens, residents are mindful that their suburb is just one within the wider suburban matrix and that even as a State Heritage Area it is not immune to densification pressures. "We want to keep the suburb in the unique way it is. . . . National Heritage listing would protect the suburb for another 90 years"[30] (Figures 6.6a and 6.6b).

At times in Colonel Light Gardens' history, residents have feared that the suburb's character might be eroded through incremental micro-level changes. In recent years, tensions have arisen in relation to the availability of new technologies and materials, an interesting paradox in an era of societal support for sustainable design and development practices. One example is the siting of solar panels installed on dwelling roofs. Consumer interest in running energy-efficient homes and accessing national government rebates on solar energy, coupled with a reduction in the cost of solar panels, have contributed to the panels becoming an attractive investment. The City of Mitcham Development Plan does accommodate new technologies and roof-mounted equipment for Colonel Light Gardens. The variation in siting of dwellings due to the street pattern means that each application for solar panels requires a specific solution. While garage roofs may be used to solve the issue in some instances, they are not always available; inevitably panels become visible from the street, sometimes markedly so. Future challenges include reducing their prominence and—particularly given the loss of the Heritage Advisory Service—ensuring consistency of advice about their location.[31]

Residents' endeavors continue to spring, in part, from the strength of their affection for the suburb and from their affinity with its distinctive qualities as a

Figure 6.6a. East Parkway in 1925, looking south from Windsor Avenue: a street of Thousand Homes Scheme houses. (Courtesy History Trust of South Australia, Adelaide GN7971)

Figure 6.6b. The intact East Parkway streetscape ninety years later with original mature street trees. (Photo by Julia Garnaut 2015)

planned environment. Their community spirit and resilience is expressed not only through initiatives to protect the suburb's heritage values but also in other ways. They have responded enthusiastically to the opening of cafés in the original shopping precincts; both have become thriving informal social venues. Over nearly two decades, the CLGHS has promoted the suburb's history through a comprehensive website, while, more recently, the CLGRA has turned to social media.[32] A CLGRA "I Love Colonel Light Gardens" Facebook page is a popular forum for posting historical information and connecting suburb residents and supporters.[33]

Conclusion

Colonel Light Gardens survives today as a well-preserved and attractive physical environment embodying the distinctive qualities that set it apart in Australia from its 1920s suburban contemporaries. It is an icon of the development of Australian planning on garden city lines, but it remains a living community wherein a variety of facets of everyday life must negotiate its heritage status. In large measure, this is being done successfully due to the enduring culture of the place, which has tended to confine disputes to micro-scale changes.

Colonel Light Gardens has a distinctive planning history, claims a special place in the narrative of the national and international dissemination of the garden city idea, and survives as "the most confident interwar Australian exercise in garden city planning" (Ward 2002, 148). Its original legislative framework and the endeavors of Reade and his supporters, the Garden Suburb commissioners, the suburb's residents' groups, the heritage advisor, historical society, and Mitcham Council have all been pivotal in promoting, sustaining, nurturing, and championing the suburb through its history.

The endurance of Colonel Light Gardens as an intact planned garden suburb demonstrates the strength of the theoretical underpinnings of its original plan captured so evocatively in Crawford's bird's-eye view from 1917 (Plate 9). The plan has formed "a robust frame" for the development of both a resilient community and a physical environment that have responded successfully to, and absorbed changes in, suburban life over nine decades; "the integration of two and three dimensions, of built form and landscape elements, of residential, community and public functions . . . has stood the test of time."[34] Considerably more fortunate than many others, this iconic early twentieth-century planned community still embodies the essence of "planning on garden city lines" and is well positioned to confront future development pressures and other challenges as it looks ahead to its centenary year and beyond.

Table 6.2
Summary of Historical Events and Heritage Benchmarks for Colonel Light Gardens

Year	Event
1915	The state government purchases the three-hundred-acre Grange Farm at Mitcham, south of Adelaide's city center, to build a model suburb along garden city principles.
1916	The state government appoints Charles Reade as its official planning advisor.
1917	While Grange Farm is used as an army training camp, the architectural draftsman David Crawford prepares a bird's-eye perspective, and the architect Louis Laybourne Smith draws a ground plan based on details supplied by Reade.
1919	The South Australian Parliament passes the Garden Suburb Act for the explicit goal of implementing the project. The Garden Suburb Commission (GSC) is placed in charge of development, assuming all roles of a local government authority.
1921	April: Colonel Light Gardens (CLG) is named after South Australia's first surveyor-general. August: land sales start.
1927	Fully fledged community status is achieved with approximately four thousand residents.
1938–39	Land reserved for a formal entrance at Piccadilly Circus is sold for housing.
1940	Garden Suburb Advisory Committee is created, with positions to be filled by residents (operates until 1948).
1947	A film sponsored by the Australian government to attract British migrants to Australia features CLG.
1950s–1960s	Original church buildings are replaced by more substantial structures. A few homes are constructed on vacant lots.
1960	The Garden Suburb Act amendment permits the private purchase of internal reserves.
1974	Faced with GSC's imminent demise, the Colonel Light Gardens Residents Association (CLGRA) is formed.
1975	The Garden Suburb Act is repealed. CLGRA successfully presses for Mitcham Council's adoption of R1 (low-density) zoning.
1989	A federally funded Conservation Study spearheaded by CLGRA recommends the entire suburb's inclusion on the Register of the National Estate (RNE) and designation as State Heritage Area (achieved 1999 and 2000, respectively).
1992	CLG's first state-appointed heritage advisor counsels residents and Mitcham Council regarding development applications.
1992–2000	Residents' groups and Mitcham Council work together increasingly for CLG's heritage listing.
1996	The Colonel Light Gardens Historical Society (CLGHS) is created to promote physical development according to garden suburb principles and accepted conservation practices, to heighten public interest in the suburb's history, and to campaign for heritage listing.
1999	CLG is included on the RNE, administered by the Australian government.
2000	CLG is declared a State Heritage Area in South Australia.
2005	The CLG Conservation Management Plan is approved for public spaces and infrastructure.
2012	The South Australian government abolishes heritage advisors. Staff of Heritage South Australia, Department of Environment and Water review CLG development applications.
	Population (as of 2016), 3349; 1670 acres [676 ha]; 1,220 dwelling units.

NOTES

1. The authors acknowledge the assistance of Mitcham Council staff, including Amy Yardley, Renae Grida, Magnus Heinrich, David Deer, Maggie Ragless (Local History Officer, deceased 2012), Therese Willis (Heritage Advisor, 2010–11, Local History Coordinator 2012–17), Mick Symonds and Graeme Bradley (Colonel Light Gardens Residents Association), Philip Knight (Colonel Light Gardens Historical Society), Simon Weidenhofer (Heritage Advisor, 1992–2010), Mary Corbin Sies, and Isabelle Gournay, and commentary on an early version of this chapter at the Society for American City and Regional Planning History conference, Baltimore, Maryland, in November 2011.

2. Crawford Vaughan, "Second Reading Speech on the Town Planning and Housing Bill," South Australian Parliamentary Debates 1 (1916): 874.

3. Bechervaise and Associates in association with McDougall and Vines, Heritage Consultants, "Colonel Light Gardens Conservation Study" (unpublished, 1989), 23.

4. Crawford was born and raised in Edinburgh, where he undertook his architectural training and worked in private practice. After a period in the Public Works Department in Cape Town, he joined the Commonwealth Department of Home Affairs as a draughtsman in 1909 and became a supervising architect in 1915 (Garnaut 1997; Rowe 1997). For bird's-eye perspective, see [South Australian Government], "Colonel Light Gardens: A Model Garden Suburb." brochure (1921), available from the State Library of South Australia.

5. Stuart Hart, "Address given by Mr. Stuart B. Hart, Director of Planning, South Australia, on the occasion of a ceremony to commemorate the Jubilee of the proclamation of the Garden Suburb Act, 1919" (1970), Stuart Hart Collection S405/74, Architecture Museum, University of South Australia.

6. Although Reade had anticipated returning to Adelaide, his missionary work eventually took him to southern Africa, where he was employed until his death in 1933.

7. Four individuals were appointed as the Garden Suburb commissioner before the role was abolished in 1975. The first, Michael McNamara, accepted another appointment before his duties commenced and was replaced by Charles Harris. Each commissioner was supported by a secretary and a small team of staff employed to build and maintain suburb infrastructure and facilities. In 1940–48 the Garden Suburb commissioner was assisted by the Garden Suburb Advisory Committee, which was not only a conduit between residents and the commission but also a sounding board for the commissioner in terms of identifying community needs and maintenance priorities (Cheney 1994; Garnaut and Hutchings 2003; Henry 1955).

8. The remaining houses were built in the Adelaide suburbs of Rosewater Garden, Flinders Park, and Prospect (Garnaut 2006).

9. Garden Suburb Commission, Annual Report, 1927–28: 1, http://www.clghs.org.au/documents/GSC%20annual%20reports.pdf.

10. C. D. Harris to C. C. Reade, July 27, 1927, Colonel Light Gardens Docket 3282/1927, Mitcham History Research Centre, Adelaide.

11. "Arabian Nights Suburb: Colonel Light Gardens Up to Date," *The Mail*, August 28, 1926.

12. Garden Suburb Commission, Annual Report, 1938–39: 1.

13. The film was released initially in London and shown subsequently in cinemas in Adelaide. See "S.A. Film Being Shown in City," *The Mail*, May 8, 1948, p. 21. The original is held at the National Film and Sound Archives, Canberra, http://www.youtube.com/watch?v=Ceg3Ao_jM5Y.

14. "Sir Patrick Abercrombie," *Advertiser*, November 6, 1948.

15. "Clean-up to Sell Poisoned Land," *Courier Messenger*, May 13, 1992.

16. A café first opened in the Salisbury Crescent precinct in 2010 and was followed by one in The Strand in 2011. "Postcode 5041," *Adelaide Magazine*, September 2011, p. 17.

17. Weidenhofer Architects, *Colonel Light Gardens Conservation Management Plan*, 2005, http://www.mitchamcouncil.sa.gov.au/webdata/resources/files/. Colonel_Light_Gardens_Conservation_Management_Plan.pdf.

18. In the end the amalgamation occurred as a consequence of a 1973 Royal Commission into Local Government Boundaries.

19. Garden Suburb Commission, Annual Report, 1972–73, 1, http://www.clghs.org.au/docu ments/GSC%20annual%20reports.pdf.

20. Colonel Light Gardens Residents Association (CLGRA), newsletter no. 9 (1977): 1.

21. "Plenty of History to Be Found in Colonel Light Gardens," *Mitcham Community News*, March 1990, 15. In 1989 the federally administered "National Estate Grants Programme" offered funding for conservation studies. Such studies are now funded by state and local councils.

22. Brian Samuels, "What Is Heritage Value?" *State Heritage Newsletter* 12 (1998): 3.

23. "South Australian Heritage Advisory Service Axed," http://australia.icomos.org/e-news /australia-icomos-e-mail-news-no-545/#9; City of Mitcham, State Heritage Referral Procedure and Advice, http://www.mitchamcouncil.sa.gov.au/page.aspx?u=1626.

24. City of Mitcham Development Plan, 130. https://www.sa.gov.au/__data/assets/pdf_file /0004/11875/Mitcham_Council_Development_Plan.pdf.

25. Information in this paragraph comes from interviews with key local stakeholders, Magnus Heinrich, David Deer, Philip Knight and Mick Symonds, July 12, 2011.

26. Information in this paragraph comes from interviews with Therese Willis, August 3, 2011; Simon Weidenhofer, October 13, 2011; and Philip Knight, July 12, 2011.

27. Interview with Magnus Heinrich, David Deer, Graeme Bradley, Mick Symonds, and Philip Knight, July 12, 2011.

28. Nominations were made in 2009 and 2011. Neither was successful.

29. Colonel Light Gardens National Heritage List Nomination, Appendix 32 (2011): 8, http://www.clghs.org.au/CLGNHL/CLGNHL2011.pdf.

30. Mick Symonds quoted in "Heritage List Push," *Eastern Courier*, March 30, 2011.

31. Information in this paragraph is from interviews with Philip Knight and Mick Symonds, July 12, 2011; and Therese Willis, August 3, 2011.

32. Colonel Light Gardens Historical Society, http://www.clghs.org.au/.

33. "Move to New Age," *Mitcham and Hills Messenger*, August 8, 2012; "I Love Colonel Light Gardens," http://www.facebook.com/ColonelLightGardensResidentsAssociation.

34. Colonel Light Gardens National Heritage List Nomination, 2011, Appendix 19, 6, http://www.clghs.org.au/CLGNHL/CLGNHL2011.pdf.

REFERENCES

Australian Heritage Commission. 1981. *The Heritage of Australia: The Illustrated Register of the National Estate*. Sydney: Macmillan.

Barwell, Henry. 1918. "South Australia—Soldiers' Settlements." In *Volume of Proceedings of the Second Town Planning and Housing Conference and Exhibition*, 59–75. Brisbane: Government Printer.

Cheney, Susan. 1994. "Colonel Light Gardens. A Unique Suburb in Adelaide: Law Shapes the Urban Environment." *Alternative Law Journal* 19(2): 153–55.

City of Mitcham Development Plan. https://www.sa.gov.au/__data/assets/pdf_file/0004/118 75/Mitcham_Council_Development_Plan.pdf (consolidated February 13, 2014).

Davison, Graeme. 1995. "Australia: The First Suburban Nation?" *Journal of Urban History* 22(1): 40–74.

———. 2000. *The Use and Abuse of Australian History*. St. Leonards: Allen and Unwin.

Freestone, Robert. 1989. *Model Communities: The Garden City Movement in Australia*. Melbourne: Thomas Nelson.

———. 1998. "An Imperial Aspect: The Australasian Town Planning Tour of 1914–15." *Australian Journal of Politics and History* 44(2): 159–76.

———. 2010. *Urban Nation: Australia's Planning Heritage*. Canberra: CSIRO Publishing in association with the Department of Environment, Water, Heritage and the Arts and the Australian Heritage Council.

Freestone, Robert, and David Nichols. 2001. "From Planning History to Community Action: Metropolitan Adelaide's Internal Reserves." *Journal of the Historical Society of South Australia* 29: 21–33.

Garnaut, Christine. 1997. "Model and Maker: Colonel Light Gardens and Charles Reade." Ph.D. diss., University of South Australia.

———. 1998. "'Model Intentions': Colonel Light Gardens—an Object Lesson in Urban Design." *Australian Planner* 35(2): 81–90.

———. 2000. "Tales from the People: At Home in an Australian Garden Suburb." *Oral History Association of Australia Journal* 22: 79–89.

———. 2002. "Not for the Faint-Hearted: Resident Conservation Initiatives in Colonel Light Gardens." In *20th Century Heritage: Proceedings of the Australia ICOMOS National Conference 2001*, edited by David Jones, 450–56. Adelaide: School of Architecture, Landscape Architecture and Urban Design, University of Adelaide, and Australia ICOMOS Secretariat.

———. 2006. *Colonel Light Gardens: Model Garden Suburb*. Reprint ed. Sydney: Crossing Press.

———. 2007. "'A Standard to Turn To': Planning History, Heritage Policy and the Conservation of Colonel Light Gardens." In *Past Matters: Heritage and Planning History. Case Studies from the Pacific Rim*, edited by Caroline Miller and Michael Roche, 270–92. Newcastle: Cambridge Scholars Press.

———. 2009. "'Everyone Was for Bungalows': Suburban Expansion and the Rise of the Bungalow in Post–World War I South Australia." In *The Pacific Connection: Proceedings of the Conference*, edited by Miles Lewis, 150–58. Melbourne: University of Melbourne.

Garnaut, Christine, and Alan Hutchings. 2003. "Building a Planned Community: The Garden Suburb Commission in Colonel Light Gardens." *Planning Perspectives* 18(3): 277–93.

Garnaut, Christine, and Kerrie Round. 2009. "'Pedler of New Ideas': The South Australian Town Planning and Housing Association, 1915–1924." In *Cities, Citizens and Environmental Reform*, edited by Robert Freestone, 120–47. Sydney: Sydney University Press.

Harper, Brian. 1991. "Colonel Light Gardens: Seventy Years of a Garden Suburb: The Plan, the Place and the People." *Australian Planner* 29(2): 62–69.

Henry, F. S. 1955. "Colonel Light Gardens: A Study of the Garden Suburb in Adelaide, South Australia." M.Arch. diss., University of Sydney.

Home, Robert. 2013. *Of Planting and Planning: The Making of British Colonial Cities*. 2nd ed. London: E&FN Spon.

Hutchings, Alan. 2007. "Comprehensive Town Planning Comes to South Australia." In *With Conscious Purpose: A History of Town Planning in South Australia*, edited by Alan Hutchings, 61–84. Adelaide: Planning Institute of Australia (SA Chapter).

Hutchings, Alan, and Christine Garnaut. 2009. "Suburban Design in Metropolitan Adelaide: Principles and Products." *Australian Planner* 46(4): 44–52.

Jamieson, K. M. 1975. *All Saints in the Garden 1925–1975: A Brief History of the Church of England in the Town of Colonel Light Gardens, Adelaide, South Australia.* Adelaide: All Saints Church.

Larkham, Peter. 1999a. "Conservation and Management in UK Suburbs." In *Changing Suburbs: Foundation, Form and Function,* edited by Richard Harris and Peter Larkham, 239–68. London: E&FN Spon.

———. 1999b. "Tensions in Managing the Suburbs: Conservation Versus Change." *Area* 31(4): 359–71.

Miller, Mervyn. 2002. "Garden Cities and Suburbs: At Home and Abroad." *Journal of Planning History* 1(1): 6–28.

———. 2010. *English Garden Cities: An Introduction.* Swindon: English Heritage.

Miller, Robert. 1993. "A History of 'The Colonel Light Gardens Communities.'" Parts 1 and 2. Unpublished.

Mosler, Sharon. 2011. *Heritage Politics in Adelaide.* Adelaide: University of Adelaide Press.

Rowe, David John. 1997. "Building a National Image: The Architecture of John Smith Murdoch, Australia's First Commonwealth Architect." Ph.D. diss., Deakin University.

Sies, Mary Corbin. 1997. "Paradise Retained: An Analysis of Persistence in Planned, Exclusive Suburbs, 1880–1980." *Planning Perspectives* 12(2): 165–91.

Stern, Robert A. M., David Fishman, and Jacob Tilove. 2013. *Paradise Planned: The Garden Suburb and the Modern City.* New York: Monacelli Press.

Tregenza, John. 2007. "Charles Reade: Town Planning Missionary." In *With Conscious Purpose: A History of Town Planning in South Australia*, edited by Alan Hutchings, 45–60. Adelaide: Planning Institute of Australia (SA Chapter).

Ward, Stephen V. 2002. *Planning the Twentieth Century City: The Advanced Capitalist World.* Chichester: John Wiley and Sons.

Whitehand, J. M. R., and C. M. H Carr. 1999. "England's Garden Suburbs: Development and Change." In *Changing Suburbs: Foundation, Form and Function*, edited by Richard Harris and Peter Larkham, 76–90. London: E&FN Spon.

CHAPTER 7

DEN-EN CHŌFU

The First Japanese "Garden City"

André Sorensen and Shun-ichi J. Watanabe

Den-en Chōfu is the most iconic of iconic planned communities in Japan. It was the first planned "garden city" development in Japan, and it was famously successful in combining an innovative plan with a new approach to suburban land development linked to railway construction that later became a dominant mode of suburban development in Japanese metropolitan areas. Den-en Chōfu was initiated by the most famous and celebrated entrepreneur of nineteenth-century Japan, and it has become renowned as a beautiful, distinctive, and prestigious residential enclave inhabited by the wealthy and movie stars. Of the many garden suburbs built during the 1920s and 1930s in Japan, Den-en Chōfu remains the most famous and retains its status as one of the most prestigious residential addresses in the country.

Den-en Chōfu also has a dedicated group of residents who are determined to protect it, and it is the subject of ongoing preservation efforts, but in a number of fundamental ways change is continuing and essential qualities are being lost. In particular, the demolition of old houses is a routine occurrence, re-subdivision and fragmentation of properties continue unabated, and redevelopment of properties is common. Den-en Chōfu is an excellent example of the difficulties facing the preservation of iconic planned communities, especially in the case where planning regulation is weak, and relies primarily on persuasion, peer pressure, and voluntary cooperation in resisting redevelopment pressures.

The case of Den-en Chōfu is of particular interest in comparative perspective, as it is revealing both of profound differences in attitudes toward built history, historical preservation, property rights, and development in Japan compared to some other developed countries, and of the very great differentials in legal and institutional capacity to achieve meaningful preservation of iconic planned communities. While there have always been efforts to "preserve" aspects of Den-en Chōfu, Japan has an utterly different culture of urban environmental management and residential property ownership, in which the idea that preservation of residential areas substantially as they were originally built might be of value is almost unknown. As in much of Asia, urban residential land value is supported by relatively unrestricted development rights, not by a tightly regulated and unchanging environment. So "preservation" has quite a different meaning, practice, and outcomes than in most of the cases examined in this volume.

This chapter first reviews the history and significance of Den-en Chōfu as a premier planned community in Japan, then reviews the legal tools and mechanisms for historical preservation in Japan, and examines the efforts to protect the built form and qualities of Den-en Chōfu. A particular focus is on what aspects of the community are deemed critical for preservation, and who is involved in preservation efforts. The outcomes of preservation efforts are briefly reviewed, and a concluding section then examines the distinctive culture of preservation in Japan, as well as some of the main challenges facing efforts of historic preservation in Tokyo and Japan.

The First and Most Famous Planned Garden Suburb in Japan

It is not an overstatement to suggest that Den-en Chōfu is the most iconic planned community in Japan. Not only is it the first Japanese "garden city," but it was also in some regards the most successful, both financially and in terms of realization of the early conception of its planners. It is important to note that although Den-en Chōfu was built by the Garden City Company (Den-en Toshi Kaisha), and was described as a garden city in promotional materials and elsewhere, it was really a "garden suburb" because it was designed and built as a residential community that depended on central Tokyo for jobs and services. There was never a conception that Den-en Chōfu would be self-contained, with its own industries, services, and full range of occupations and classes (Watanabe 1980). The name itself is also revealing of nuances in the interpretation of the garden city idea in Japan. "Chōfu" is a historic place-name, while "Den-en" suggests countryside, rural, or pastoral landscape, not "garden." So while Den-en Toshi is usually translated as "garden city," it might be more accurately translated as "city set in a countryside landscape."

Although fundamentally different in many ways, therefore, Den-en Chōfu is the Letchworth of Japan, the planned community that established a new model of suburban planned development and that forever altered the pattern of Japanese urbanization by inspiring hundreds of similar planned commuter suburbs outside major cities in the 1920s and 1930s (Katagi et al. 2000). The new suburb was built by the Garden City Company along its purpose-built electric commuter railway, which later grew into Tokyū Railways, in some regards the most successful of the many private commuter-railway companies in the Tokyo region. Den-en Chōfu has continued to be famous as a green, salubrious residential enclave in the sprawl of southwestern Tokyo (Figure 7.1).

The creation of Den-en Chōfu began in 1915 when a group of rural landlords approached the famous entrepreneur Shibusawa Eiichi with the idea of land development in Ebara township, well outside the Tokyo urban area, to the southwest of Shibuya station on the Yamanote loop railway.[1] Shibusawa evidently understood the potential for land development away from the existing urban fringe, where land prices were already increasing rapidly, and agreed to help set up the project.

Shibusawa had established hundreds of new enterprises including banks and manufacturing and shipping companies over the previous forty years, and he had the expertise, access to capital, and stature to carry out such a venture. He had also decided in 1915 at the age of seventy-seven to retire from business and devote his energy to public service, a resolution to which the Den-en Toshi company can be considered the only exception. While the pioneering of a new approach to suburban land development in Japan must certainly be considered a public service, the venture was also highly profitable, so Shibusawa does not appear to have retired his business acumen (Watanabe 1980).

Following three years of organizing, the company promoters released a prospectus that proclaimed urban overcrowding and rural decline as key contemporary problems, and they proposed the building of Den-en Chōfu to restore country life and eliminate urban problems by providing high-quality living environments for the middle class in suburbs with fresh air and with quality infrastructure. The company was formally established in September 1918 with an initial capital of half a million yen, which was increased to 5 million yen by January 1920, contributed by eleven stockholders, of whom six became board members (Watanabe 1980, 132).

The first task was to buy as much land in the target area as possible. By November 1921 the company had succeeded in buying just less than 150 hectares in an irregularly shaped strip about 3.4 kilometers long and from 0.2 to 1.2 kilometers wide. They paid almost 1.8 million yen for the land, which Shun-ichi J. Watanabe (1980, 134) notes amounted to about £480 per acre or about fourteen times the amount paid by Ebenezer Howard for the land for Welwyn Garden City in 1919.

Although the company marketed the whole area as a single development called Den-en Toshi, or Garden City, in fact the land consisted of three main areas, which were developed and sold individually. First was Senzoku, second was Ookayama, and third was the largest area, Tamagawa-dai, that later became known as Den-en Chōfu. The company did not build houses, but subdivided land, built roads, and supplied electricity. The Garden City Company also established a separate company to supply water to the developments. Sewer systems were virtually unknown in Japan at this time, and even in central Tokyo, the first sewers were just being constructed. Crucially to the success of the project, the company also built the railway to provide access to Tokyo, upon which the settlements depended for jobs and services.

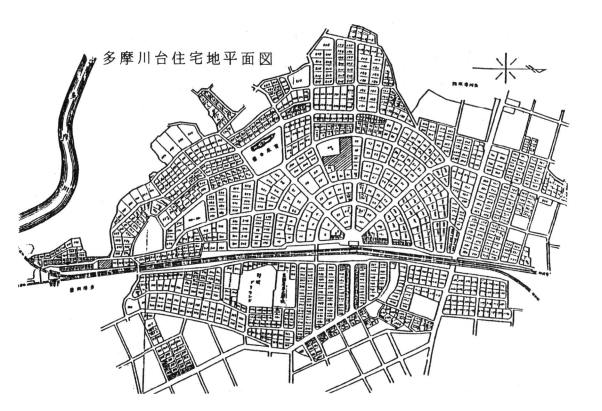

多摩川台住宅地平面図

The company obtained a license to build an electric railway line to link the settlements to Tokyo in 1920, and it had completed the line by the end of 1923, marking the origin of Tokyū Corporation (short for "Tokyo Kyūko," literally "Tokyo Express") that evolved into one of the most dynamic and successful private commuter-railway companies in Japan and indeed the world, perfecting the synergistic combination of rail-way extension, large-scale land development, and department store operation at the railway terminals, which not only provided access to suburban development lands but also ensured a steady base of customers for the railway.

Tokyū was one of the first of the new privately owned electric commuter rail-ways that became the defining element of Japanese metropolitan development. Tokyū was the first to attempt land development on a large scale, linked to railway development. But the company also continued to innovate throughout much of the rest of the twentieth century, using land readjustment (see Sorensen 1999) on an ever larger scale as they moved farther and farther to the southwest from their starting points in the garden city developments. In total, Tokyū developed seven

Figure 7.1. An early site plan of Den-en Chōfu. The irregular site was determined by the land that the Garden City Company was able to buy. One of the iconic features is the radial and circular street pattern, borrowed from St. Francis Wood (Olmsted Brothers, 1913) in San Francisco. (Courtesy Japan General Housing Centre)

Figure 7.2. The current Den-en Chōfu Station is a facsimile of the original iconic station house from the early 1920s. In the 1990s, train lines were buried underground going through Den-en Chōfu and a much larger station was built, including extensive shopping areas and a surface plaza on Tokyū land. The old station buildings were demolished, and this replica was built as a replacement. (Photo by André Sorensen)

train lines to the southwest of Tokyo and to an extensive area of Kanagawa prefecture to the west of Yokohama, an area that continues to thrive based on the Tokyū railway network.

Preservation of the Built Environment in Japan

There are a number of factors that have shaped the development of policies and institutions for historic preservation in Japan. Of the key factors, the first is the high level of urbanization and of material culture in the early modern period, lasting until the collapse of the feudal order and opening to the world beginning in 1868. Second is the highly centralized legal and planning system, which has consistently relied on top-down, national legal systems in the establishment of planning and preservation regulations, supplemented by local voluntary agreements. Third, and not least, is the enduring high level of respect for individual property ownership rights, especially in land, which has powerfully constrained the scope of regulatory infringements on land development initiatives. These factors have combined to create a distinctive approach to historic preservation.

Unlike some of its neighbors in East Asia, serious efforts at historic preservation started relatively early in Japan. Japan was probably the most urbanized country in the world in the eighteenth century, with several very large cities, including Edo (now Tokyo) with a population of approximately one million, and Osaka and Kyoto each with about half a million (Rozman 1973; Sorensen 2002). These great cities each had grand temples, shrines, castles, and other monuments that were the product of a long period of stability, peace, and economic growth, which had also produced a high level of material culture and a sophisticated urban built environment. Cities began to change rapidly with the beginnings of industrialization and the introduction of western building styles and materials at the beginning of the twentieth century, particularly during and after World War I. Recurring large-scale fires, and a deliberate policy of westernization including railway construction, street widening, and the construction of government and commercial buildings in western styles meant that urban change particularly in central areas was relatively rapid. Yet until the passage of the 1919 City Planning Law, the only regulation of urban development and building was the Tokyo City Improvement Ordinance, which applied only to Tokyo and was relatively limited in its impacts even there (see Sorensen 2002).

A primary focus of early preservation efforts was on outstanding buildings such as temples and castles, with priority given almost entirely to structures built prior to the Meiji revolution of 1868. The first law to protect premodern built heritage, including structures from the Edo period (1600–1867) and especially those from even earlier, was the Law for the Preservation of the Old Shrines and Temples, passed in 1897. In 1929 that law was revised and renamed the Law for the Preservation of National Treasures and its scope expanded to include other structures including castles and other government buildings apart from "old shrines and temples" (Seoul Development Institute et al. 2005, 355). Between 1929 and 1950 when the law was again revised into the present Law for the Protection of Cultural Properties, 1,109 buildings were designated, of which virtually all were prominent religious and government structures dating from the Edo period and earlier.

This early and understandable focus on prominent feudal-era structures has had an enduring impact on historic preservation ideas and practice in Japan. Perhaps most important was the clear distinction between the Edo period and after, with the former the target of preservation efforts, and the latter not. It was not until the 1960s that any post-1868 buildings were considered worthy of preservation, and even then almost the sole exception was a vigorous but unsuccessful attempt to save Frank Lloyd Wright's famous Imperial Hotel (completed in 1923) from demolition and redevelopment in 1968.

Also significant was the fact that until the 1960s, virtually all buildings designated were either state-owned or religious structures. These were subject to relatively strictly enforced protections and were provided with significant subsidies for maintenance. Privately owned dwellings and business premises were largely excluded from this model of preservation. This relatively narrow focus of preservation activity began to shift after the widespread destruction of cities during World War II. The Cultural Properties Protection Law of 1950 created a Cultural Properties Protection Commission to administer the law and carry out research and establish priorities for preservation. That focus was revised in the 1960s to include traditional private houses, although still with a focus on those from the Edo period and still targeting individual buildings, not larger townscapes. The major change of the 1960s, however, was a very significant increase in citizen activism in support of preserving the historical built form.

Not coincidentally, this activism was strongest in those cities that had been largely spared destruction by American firebombing during the war, and were still relatively intact, including Kamakura, Nara, and Kyoto, each of which had been an imperial capital city. In Kamakura a planned housing development in the wooded hills behind the famous Tsurugaoka Hachimangū Shrine sparked a vigorous opposition movement, which succeeded in blocking the development by raising funds and buying a portion of the proposed site. At almost the same time active movements emerged in Kyoto to protest the building of the 130-meter-high Kyoto Tower, which was believed to ruin the traditional skyline, and in Nara against a planned prefectural government building, which was seen to pose a similar threat (Hohn 1997; Salastie 1999).

The government responded to these conflicts with the Ancient Capital Protection Law of 1966 that allowed the protection of landscapes around designated protected monuments. This law applied only to the three designated ancient capitals Kamakura, Nara, and Kyoto, however (although it could be applied elsewhere by a special cabinet order), and it focused on the creation of historic landscape special preservation districts (*rekishiteki fūdo tokubetsu hozon chiku*).

This start was extended in the mid-1970s when regulations were created to allow a more effective preservation of larger townscape areas instead of just buildings (Hohn 1997). The creation in 1975 of the important preservation districts (IPDs; *dentōteki kenzōbutsugun hozon chiku*) for groups of historic buildings, as an amendment to Article 143 of the Cultural Properties Protection Act of 1950, for the first time allowed protection of whole areas instead of individual buildings. The designation of such districts is carried out as urban planning decisions (*toshi keikaku kettei*). The first seven designations of larger townscapes were all of prestigious samurai (ruling-class) districts, but designations gradually expanded to include a range of urban types, including merchant towns, temple towns, and craft districts (Hohn 1997). The IPD law was a significant advance on earlier legislation because it allowed the preservation of entire urban areas, not just individual buildings, but only forty IPDs were designated during the first twenty years (Hohn 1997, 224). Hohn argues that the small numbers are mostly because the IPD system provides relatively strict controls over development, but not very generous financial support, so such designation is often opposed by local landowners. Where they were successful it was often because local landowners anticipated significant benefits to local tourism as a result of preservation, mitigating concerns over restricting property rights.

Japan clearly has both a long tradition of historic preservation, and a sophisticated legal infrastructure to achieve it. The focus of those efforts has been on premodern and early modern built forms, however, and not on modern developments. Den-en Chōfu is protected by none of the instruments discussed so far. The area is, however, protected by both a district plan, and a local town making ordinance (*machizukuri jōrei*), and it is to these that we turn next.

District Plans and Machizukuri Ordinances for Historical Preservation

The district planning system was introduced in 1980 as a major addition to the City Planning Law in response to the realization during the 1970s that the new planning law of 1968 (itself a major revision of the 1919 City Planning Law), that had promised much more effective planning and development control, had a number of serious flaws. One was that the zoning and development permit systems did not permit any detailed planning or regulation of the built form of either existing areas or new developments. The new planning law had introduced a much more detailed zoning system (increased from three zones to six), an urban growth boundary system to prevent urban sprawl, a development permit system to regulate proposed land developments, and a significant transfer of planning powers to local governments. Unfortunately, subdivision of land into smaller plots was still as of right, with no minimum plot size, providing great incentives for demolition and the subdivision of older and larger urban plots into smaller ones. The development permit system was also ineffective in allowing the regulation of new developments or redevelopments, because it merely specified a certain minimum standard of road allowances, without providing for any detailed intervention or guidance of the actual design of such public facilities.

The district planning system, modeled on the German Bebauungs Plan system, sought to correct these deficiencies. The new system allowed the designation of a defined area within which a range of new planning restrictions were made possible, including controls over new road layouts, lot sizes, building design, building setbacks, and construction materials. District plans were to be the responsibility of municipal governments, as a way to provide detailed planning of relatively small areas of several hectares or less. District plans have two parts: a statement of policy intent, and a district improvement plan (DIP). The policy statement can include "future images; land use; facility improvement including access roads, small parks and other public open spaces; setbacks and building design; and landscaping" (Japan Ministry of Construction 1996, 42).

The DIP includes specific regulations that will be used to enforce the provisions of the plan. There have been many cases where only the policy statement has been passed, without being followed by a DIP because the policy statement carries no legal power to restrict private building activity, and it is relatively easier for a municipal government to approve such a policy statement, even in cases where the local residents do not agree with it. In practice it is felt that over 90 percent of property owners must agree before a binding DIP is introduced. That has limited the impact of this system on the regulation of urban space both by limiting the area where district plans are in force and by limiting the stringency of regulation in those that do exist.

This approach did, however, have a number of positive impacts. Probably most important is that it provided the first legal mechanism for the detailed regulation of buildings and built form. These powers have been successfully used in a number of locations for historic preservation (see Sorensen 2002, chap. 8). No less important, the requirement to build agreement among those affected was an important factor in the emergence of the very active and broad-based citizen movements, now known as "machizukuri" town-building or community-development movements to improve urban areas and prevent damaging developments (Kobayashi 1999; Sorensen and Funck 2007; Watanabe 2007).

Machizukuri refers broadly to the engagement of citizens in community planning and improvement, but it also refers specifically to a certain style and practice of local government planning in which efforts to improve small areas and neighborhoods in urban areas are supported by local government bylaws or ordinances. Until the significant decentralization reforms of 1999 and 2000, municipal machizukuri ordinances that imposed stronger restrictions on property development rights than specified in national planning law were not legally enforceable in the courts, so they provided a relatively weak influence that was based more on persuasion and peer pressure within a community rather than on legal force. After those reforms, the legal authority of municipalities to pass enforceable municipal ordinances outside of the authorization of national laws was clear, but their application for town planning and historic preservation remained limited. Still, machizukuri ordinances were widely used for historic preservation, in part precisely because with little legal force they were easier to achieve than district plans. When passed in conjunction with a district plan, the machizukuri ordinance could have quite a strong legal force, but it required significant agreement from those affected.

The procedure for passing a district plan–based machizukuri ordinance is relatively simple. A common method is that a local machizukuri residents' council (*jūmin kyōgikai*) is established with a membership of local residents and local leaders for a designated area. The local mayor can then officially recognize both the area and the council. Such recognition gives the council legal status and allows it to receive small amounts of funding support for incidental expenses. The residents' council can submit a machizukuri proposal to the local government. The mayor (and sometimes also the local assembly) examines the proposal and may approve it. Once such a plan is approved, anyone who wants to develop or redevelop a property within the designated area is required to "notify" (*todokede*), "consult" (*kyōgi*), and take "advice" (*kankoku*) from the local government before proceeding with development (Koide 1999). The local government is required to respond to the notification and may or may not respond with advice. In some cases there is also a requirement that the residents' council must also be notified and consulted before a permit for development or redevelopment is issued. The sanctions against those who do not cooperate or do not follow the advice are rather weak. Basically, in most cases the local government can only publish the name of the individual offender to embarrass them.

This system may appear exceptionally weak, but such notification/consultation systems form the core of many machizukuri ordinances and community planning strategies in Japan, and in some cases they have been used very effectively. The key is that because notification is required, the community organization learns of potential problems caused by (re)development at an early stage and can initiate a consultation process. The Japanese take peer pressure very seriously, as maintaining cordial relations with neighbors is a tremendously important cultural value. Unfortunately, most significant development or redevelopment projects are undertaken by development companies, and these are less susceptible to such pressure.

Den-en Chōfu Association

Den-en Chōfu is blessed with a strong residents' association that was established shortly after the creation of the development itself. The Den-en Chōfu Association (Den-en Chōfu Kai) was incorporated as an incorporated nonprofit association (*shakai dantai hōjin*) in 1932, the only neighborhood association so incorporated in all of Japan. The Garden City Company incorporated the Den-en Chōfu Association so that it could grant it legal ownership of a plot of land near the station on which to build a community meeting center. The association still owns that land, just southwest of the train station, which is now occupied by a modern two-story reinforced-concrete community center with meeting rooms and offices.

In the Garden City area, there are nine neighborhood associations (NAs), which are open for everyone living in the area to join. Of the 1,700 households currently living in the area, about 1,100 (over two-thirds) households are currently members. Monthly membership fees are 600 yen (a fairly high fee compared to other NAs in Tokyo). Key services to the membership are a three-time-per-month circulating notice board and quarterly membership meetings.

The main revenues of the association are the membership fees, rental fees for the meeting hall (4,000 yen per two hours), and generous fees from the Ōta Ward government to maintain the public spaces fronting the train station, including the goldfish pond, flower beds, and park benches (100,000 yen per month). Association officers told us that the Tokyū corporation also pays generously for the association's monthly cleanups of the station and its surroundings (15,000,000 yen per year, or about US$150,000 if we convert at 100 yen to the dollar). This seems an extremely generous arrangement, as Tokyū properties tend to be spotless and extremely well maintained, so voluntary efforts by the community are likely just a matter of the street sweeping and litter removal that is done voluntarily by neighborhood associations all over Japan. The main expenses of the association are one office manager, one office staff, and two staff seconded to the Ōta Ward "Silver Centre" day center for the elderly.

When we interviewed the association leadership in June 2011, we were greeted by six members of the association, including the chairperson, two vice chairmen, and the association secretary, all well spoken and distinguished elderly men and women.

Preservation Efforts in Den-en Chōfu

There have been repeated efforts to protect the quality of the neighborhood almost since its creation in the 1920s. The company established restrictive covenants when it sold the lots in the beginning—"gentlemen's agreements" (*shinshi kyōtei*)—but these were not legally enforceable because Japanese law did not provide any way to enforce such restrictions. These covenants included six main provisions. The first specified that buildings should not disturb their neighbors, the second that any fences or garden walls be elegant and refined, the third that buildings should be three floors or fewer, the fourth that buildings should not cover more than half of the plot area, the fifth specified minimum setbacks from the road, and the sixth

specified the minimum construction costs for houses (Oshima 1996; Watanabe 1977). Watanabe (1977) noted that this list contains an odd mix of highly subjective terms, such as "elegant" and "upper class," and more practical building regulations. The constraints of the covenants do appear to have been largely respected in initial building, however, and contributed to the quality of the area.

The Den-en Chōfu Association sees preservation of the garden city as a major part of its mandate and has actively worked to preserve it for many years. From the point of view of the association, the major preservation challenge is preventing the re-subdivision of lots into multiple smaller properties. One of the primary characteristics of Den-en Chōfu is its generously sized lots, which allowed spacious gardens, mature trees, and a general sense of greenery and space that is in great contrast to the rest of To-

Figure 7.3. The last remaining house built in the Taishō era idiom, which combined Art Deco details with western housing patterns in order to create a distinctively Japanese style. Elegant and simple, this house does not benefit from any special preservation measure, and it seems unlikely to survive long. It looks out on a generously sized lawn and a leafy garden, probably the most exceptional feature for a house in Tokyo, reflecting Den-en Chōfu's large original lots. (Photo by André Sorensen)

kyo, which is intensely crowded, with most buildings built to within inches of the property lines, allowing room for potted plants and tightly clipped hedges, but little space for trees.

The two major elements of current preservation policies for Den-en Chōfu are the district plan and the machizukuri ordinance, both passed by Ōta Ward. The plan, first enacted in August 1991, and revised in December 2005, is intended to protect the quality of the area by restricting the possibilities of redevelopment. As the preamble of the plan states: "This district, located on the west side of Den-en Chōfu station at the intersection of the Tokyū Toyoko line and Tokyū Mekama line is Japan's first garden city, built since the late Taisho era with the goal of creating a desirable residential environment set in trees and gardens. This District Plan aims to maintain and conserve a good living environment by imposing restrictions on buildings and green spaces" (Ōta Ward Office 2005).

The district plan divides the area into two districts, namely "Station Front District" of 2 hectares near the station, and "Residential District" of 45.2 hectares for the main residential area. In the Residential District, the plan has eight major and minor provisions:

1. Restrictions on land use, essentially restricting the area to single-family detached homes and prohibiting the building of apartments or commercial uses.
2. Restrictions on the subdivision of land into parcels smaller than 165 square meters.
3. Mandatory setbacks of buildings 2 meters from the road frontage and 1.5 meters on other sides.
4. An absolute height restriction of 9 meters.
5. Reservation of a 1-meter-deep setback on all sides of every plot for greenery, including trees and hedges, prohibiting the construction of garages, buildings, sheds, gates, and such in that space.
6. The shape and color of any part of the buildings and structures that can be seen from the outside should be in harmony with the surroundings.
7. Regulation of garden walls and gates to a height of 1.2 meters, and encouragement of hedges around properties to prevent tall blank walls facing the street.
8. Detailed guidelines for the size, area, and location of hedges, trees, and other greenery in relation to houses to encourage a green environment.

As the members of the Den-en Chōfu Association explained to us, the fundamental problem with the district plan regulations is that the minimum plot size of

165 square meters established in the plan is far too small. Many of the existing plots are well more than twice this size, so the district plan has not prevented the demolition of houses and subdivision of plots. This is a good example of the tendency to implement weak regulations in order to make them acceptable to landowners.

To be able to counter such subdivision, the district plan regulations were supplemented with non–legally enforceable machizukuri ordinance rules to protect the environmental quality. The procedure is a typical notification/consultation type of ordinance, and it works as follows: first, when a landowner notifies the Ōta City planning office of a wish to change something regulated by the ordinance, he or she is told to consult with the Den-en Chōfu Association. That consultation is a legal requirement. The Den-en Chōfu Association can approve or decline to approve the change, but it has no legal power to force people to comply. So it will negotiate and try to convince the applicant to comply with the guidelines in the machizukuri ordinance. Because legal authority is weak, the two parties almost always come to an agreement, even if it is rather less than they hoped for. A very stubborn applicant will normally get everything he or she wants.

Preservation Outcomes

While the efforts of the Den-en Chōfu Association to preserve the essential features of the planned community are undoubtedly sincere, the results are discouraging. Virtually none of the original dwellings remain. There seems to be only one remaining original house in the Taisho Modern residential style (see Figure 7.3). This house has no special preservation orders to protect it. There are more prewar houses in the Japanese style, about a dozen in the district plan area, some of which are very handsome, but others have been renovated and added to in nondescript ways. So preserving the original houses is not such an active preservation issue any more, as there are almost none left. Similarly, the original iconic train station was recently demolished and replaced with a replica (see Figure 7.2).

The biggest problem today is the continued subdivision of parcels into smaller lots. This fragmentation of plots poses a fundamental threat to the character of the neighborhood, as very large houses on small lots leave no room for the spacious gardens that were such an important feature of the original townscape (Figure 7.4). Large houses with large garages also mean that many street trees are cut down to allow access to the garages. Attempts to prevent large concrete walls surrounding gardens have also only been partly successful.

Figure 7.4. Whereas the original dwellings were small houses built on large lots, over recent decades these have steadily been replaced by very large houses on small lots, the impact of which is exacerbated by plot subdivision and fragmentation. (Photo by André Sorensen)

Opposite

Figure 7.5. A major landscape feature that the Den-en Chōfu Association seeks to protect is the green street network with mature trees, a legacy of the generous road allowances and large lots laid out by the Garden City Company. (Photo by André Sorensen)

Figure 7.6. The routine approach to selling real estate in Japan is to demolish whatever structure exists on site, to be better able to sell the land itself. This photograph was taken in 2011, right after a traditional Japanese house belonging to a famous poet had been demolished and subdivided into two parcels. At the time, there were in the district plan area more than a dozen such vacant sites awaiting redevelopment. One can see the footprint of the house on the left, filling virtually the entire lot; this is exactly what the Den-en Chōfu Association seeks to prevent. (Photo by André Sorensen)

Conclusions: Major Challenges Facing Preservation in Japan

Den-en Chōfu has maintained its status as one of the most prestigious addresses in Japan, the "Beverly Hills of Tokyo," with its distinctive radial/concentric street network, handsome avenues of large cherry and gingko trees (Figure 7.5), and the small station-front plaza. The key issue here is "preservation" and what that means in the Japanese context. The basic historic preservation assumption that preserving a part of an urban area more or less intact and unchanged from its initial form is in the public interest is not one that is widely known or accepted in Japan. The idea that a government or planning body should be able to limit the property rights of landowners, or prevent them from demolishing old houses, is not generally accepted.

A central challenge is that the routine approach to selling real estate in Japan is to demolish whatever structure exists on-site, to be better able to sell the land itself, as the buildings themselves are believed to depreciate steadily to zero value in thirty years. An old house therefore almost always reduces the value of the land it occupies. There are, at the time of writing, more than a dozen such vacant sites in the district plan area awaiting redevelopment, as it is routine to demolish all existing structures before a sale of property within the garden city area. Those charged with preserving the settlement see such change as inevitable and unstoppable, even if regrettable. Nothing can be done about it (Figure 7.6).

Preserving the prewar built form might have been achievable in the 1960s or 1970s, but now that moment is long past. Perhaps it is simply unrealistic to expect a strong preservation approach in a situation where land is so valuable, property rights are so strong, and ideas of "historic preservation" still attach primarily to premodern structures and townscapes, not to those of the twentieth century.

The case of Den-en Chōfu raises a number of important questions about the preservation of iconic planned communities, particularly in Asia, or indeed almost anywhere outside Europe. While there is no doubt that those who have taken on the primary responsibility for preservation of Den-en Chōfu are sincere in their desire to preserve this place, the failure to achieve meaningful protection of either the built heritage or even of the parcel configuration is remarkable. It is true that the reasons for that failure are not hard to find, and they include extremely high land prices in Japan and high inheritance taxes that combine to provide powerful incentives to subdivide land, and rather flimsy building methods in the 1920s and 1930s that meant that houses were routinely expected to be demolished and replaced after one generation or about thirty years. Perhaps most important are strong property rights that include the right to demolish dwellings as-of-right, and the right to subdivide existing urban plots into smaller pieces, constrained in Den-en Chōfu only by a minimum parcel size of 165 square meters.

But the fact that this situation is accepted with such resignation seems significant. The conception of preservation prevalent in many other developed countries is that iconic planned communities and historic districts should if possible be preserved essentially as they were first built, including buildings, streetscapes, and other elements that create the character of the place. But there is very little evidence that this idea of preservation is adhered to in Japan. Indeed, such preservation is so far from the realm of possibility in suburban Japan that no one seems to think it worth even articulating as a goal. A strong preservation approach appears to be literally inconceivable.

This is interesting because it is revealing not just of conceptions of preservation, but it also suggests that to a certain extent the goals of preservation advocates are shaped by available tools and rule sets. Knowing that it is legally impossible to impose restrictions on redevelopment or subdivision, and that any district plan that could impose limits would require consent of virtually all property owners, advocates accept with resignation the fact that there is little that they can do to prevent the ongoing loss of much that makes Den-en Chōfu special. This means particularly the large lots and spacious gardens that are so tempting to redevelop. Instead the focus is on enforcing the relatively weak restrictions on garden walls, gates, and shrubbery. Such efforts do not seem likely to result in any significant preservation of this iconic planned community from ongoing transformation into just another suburban residential area.

It does appear, however, that the secret mechanism of the long-term preservation of a high level of living environment in Den-en Chōfu is in fact the relatively weak regulatory framework that for many years encouraged property owners to protect many valued aspects of the local environment, especially the extensive greenery and street trees. It seems clear that the main thing the residents want to save is not the houses but the tree-lined avenues, the prestige of the area, and the high real estate values. It is worth asking whether the efforts at preservation in this area really are about historic preservation at all, or if they are merely an attempt to protect resale values and an element of exclusivity?

Table 7.1
Summary of Historical Events and Heritage Benchmarks for Den-en Chōfu

Year	Event
1915	A group of rural landlords approaches entrepreneur Shibusawa Eiichi with the idea of land development in Ebara township.
1918	The Garden City Company is formally established to subdivide land, build roads, and supply electricity.
1919	The passage of Japan's first City Planning Law in 1919 has very little impact on the development of Den-en Chōfu, as it enables but does not mandate planning schemes.
1920	The initial capital investment of half a million yen is raised to 5 million yen. Six of the eleven stakeholders form a governing board.
1921	Land acquisition proceeds slowly on three settlements; the largest tract is Tamagawa-dai, later renamed Den-en Chōfu.
1923	The electric railway line, funded by the Garden City Company to link its settlements to central Tokyo, begins operation. Kintaro Yabe is the author of the master plan (324 residential parcels averaging 3520 square feet [327 square meters] each for a planned population of 1,600). He also designs the picturesque railroad station. September: The destructive Great Kanto earthquake triggers a major suburban exodus and accelerates plot sales in Den-en Chōfu.
1924	April: About forty-two household (approximately two hundred people) live in Den-en Chōfu.
1928	All parcels are sold, and land prices start rising.
1932	A novelty in Japan, the Den-en Chōfu Association is incorporated as a public interest association. It receives from the Garden City Company land near the station on which to build a community center.
1960s	Japan's preservation legislation begins accounting for private and post-1868 properties.
1975	The Cultural Properties Protection Act of 1950 is amended to allow for the protection of whole areas instead of individual buildings.
1980	The district plan system (*chiku keikaku seido*) is a major addition to the 1968 City Planning Law; it allows the creation of a district plan to help protect Den-en Chōfu from redevelopment.
Late 1980s	The tear-down process accelerates, and lots are subdivided.
1991	A district plan is passed by the Ôta Ward, restricting redevelopment options.
1999–2000	Municipal machizukuri ordinances impose stronger restrictions on property development rights.
2005	The district plan is revised.
2018	Only a small number of the original homes have survived.

NOTE

1. This historical review relies primarily on Watanabe 1980, Ishida 1987, and Katagi et al. 2000.

REFERENCES

Hohn, U. 1997. "Townscape Preservation in Japanese Urban Planning." *Town Planning Review* 68(2): 213–55.

Ishida, Y. 1987. *Nihon Kindai Toshi Keikaku no Hyakunen* [100 Years of Modern Japanese Urban Planning]. Tokyo: Jichitai Kenkyūsha.

Japan Ministry of Construction. (1996). *Urban Land Use Planning System in Japan* (K. Kazunobu, Trans.). Tokyo: Institute for Future Urban Development.

Katagi, A., Y. Fujiya, and Y. Kadono. 2000. *Kindai Nihon no Kōgai Jūtakuchi* [Suburban Housing Areas in Modern Japan]. Tokyo: Kajima Shuppansha.

Kobayashi, S., ed. 1999. *Chihō Bunken Jidai no Machizukuri Jōrei* [Machizukuri ordinances in the era of local rights]. Tokyo: Gakugei Shuppansha.

Koide, K. 1999. "Keikankei Machizukuri Jōrei [Machizukuri ordinances for landscape preservation]." In *Chihō Bunken Jidai no Machizukuri Jorei* [Local community building ordinances in the era of local rights], edited by S. Kobayashi, 73–110. Kyoto: Gakugei Shuppansha.

Oshima, K. T. 1996. "Denenchōfu: Building the Garden City in Japan." *Journal of the Society of Architectural Historians* 55(2): 140–51.

Ōta Ward Office. 2005. "Den-en Chōfu District Plan." O. K. M. Department. Ota: 16.

Rozman, G. 1973. *Urban Networks in Ch'ing China and Tokugawa Japan*. Princeton, NJ: Princeton University Press.

Salastie, R. 1999. *Living Tradition or Panda's Cage? An Analysis of the Urban Conservation in Kyoto*. Helsinki: Helsinki University of Technology.

Seoul Development Institute, Beijing Municipal Institute of City Planning and Design, and University of Tokyo Center for Sustainable Urban Regeneration. 2005. "Historic Conservation Policies in Seoul, Beijing and Tokyo." Seoul: Seoul Development Institute.

Sorensen, A. 1999. "Land Readjustment, Urban Planning and Urban Sprawl in the Tokyo Metropolitan Area." *Urban Studies* 36(13): 2333–60.

———. 2002. *The Making of Urban Japan: Cities and Planning from Edo to the 21st Century*. London: Routledge.

Sorensen, A., and C. Funck, eds. 2007. *Living Cities in Japan: Citizens' Movements, Machizukuri and Local Environments*. London: Routledge.

Watanabe, S.J. (1977). "Nihonteki Den-entoshiron no Kenkyū (1): Den-entoshi Kabushikikaisha (1918-28) no Baai [*Japanese-style Garden City Research (1): The Case of the Garden City Corporation (1918-1928)*]." Nihon Toshi Keikaku Gakkai Gakushū Kenkyū Happyōkai [*City Planning Institute of Japan Transaction of Science Lecture Meeting*] 12: 151–56.

———. 1980. "Garden City, Japanese Style: The Case of Den-en Toshi Company Ltd. 1918–1928." In *Shaping an Urban World*, edited by G. E. Cherry, 129–44. London: Mansell.

———. 2007. "Toshi keikaku vs machizukuri." In *Living Cities in Japan: Citizens' Movements, Machizukuri and Local Environments*, edited by A. Sorensen and C. Funck, 39–55. London: Routledge.

CHAPTER 8

THE JARDIM AMÉRICA AND PACAEMBU GARDEN SUBURBS

Facing the Changes to the Metropolis of São Paulo

Maria Cristina da Silva Leme and

Carlos Roberto Monteiro de Andrade

The first garden cities built in England had a great influence on the reconstruction of cities in Europe after World War I and in the planned expansion of cities in the United States and South America. Some aspects of these garden cities and suburbs—such as mechanisms to control urban growth, a road system layout adapted to topography, and the presence of green areas—were easily assimilated by engineers and architects and inspired projects for new towns and suburbs. It is important to note, however, that none of these aspects were included in the diagrams proposed by Ebenezer Howard in his book *To-morrow: A Peaceful Path to Real Reform*. Conceptual management issues, such as the communal form of ownership and alternatives to give self-support to urban development, proposed in his book in 1898, were not present in these projects and proved to be difficult to grasp and assimilate.

The original garden city concept was split between Howard's original (which took form in the first garden city, Letchworth, in 1904) and the garden suburb of Hampstead in 1907 (see Miller, this volume).

The idea of the city as a whole with multiple functions, which on a regional level sought to bring city and country closer while preventing uncontrolled urban sprawl, changed into the notion of city growth being embraced by the creation of residential areas beyond the existing built-up area, without imposing a limit on urban expansion. The formal aspects of the garden city idea first arrived in Brazil through the work of the English architect Barry Parker, responsible with Raymond Unwin for the project for Letchworth. Parker lived in São Paulo from 1917 to 1919, where he was commissioned by the English real estate company City of São Paulo Improvements and Freehold Land (CSPIFL) to develop a series of garden suburb projects for estates that served as a model for other urban settlements in São Paulo.

This chapter revisits two of Parker's most important projects, Jardim América (Figure 8.1) and Pacaembu,[1] their impact on the city of São Paulo, and the strategies made by the residents, architects, and urban planners to guarantee the preservation of their original characteristics and their permanence.

São Paulo's Transformation at the Beginning of the Twentieth Century

The presence of large foreign companies in Brazil, specifically British companies that were directly and indirectly linked to the construction of cities or the structuring of the territory, played a crucial role in the modernization of Brazil's major cities between the end of the nineteenth century and World War II. The city of São Paulo, which received a significant portion of this foreign capital, underwent extraordinary growth. Among the economic factors that contributed to this process was the fact that the city was a railway hub connecting the country's main regions. The combined interests of big landowners and large foreign companies, like São Paulo Tramway, Light and Power (a British private capital company that monopolized electricity services and public transport by tramway) and the British real estate company CSPIFL, helped to transform São Paulo.

The CSPIFL had London-based bankers as its participants and it was headquartered in England, with offices in Paris and São Paulo. This big business opportunity attracted several respectable local and international figures, such as the chairman of the new company's board of directors, Lord Balfour of Burleigh (also president of the Bank of Scotland and of São Paulo Railway Co., and the future British foreign secretary) and the former president of Brazil, Manuel Campos Salles.

In 1914 CSPIFL contacted the São Paulo Tramway and Light and Power to establish streetcar lines to the areas that they intended to subdivide. The transaction was successful and one year later a contract was signed between the two companies. The new real estate company initially bought twelve million square meters.

The Plan for Pacaembu

Pacaembu was the first development planned by CSPIFL, according to records dating back to 1911. A plan of the city from 1914 (Figure 8.2) showed the Pacaembu development drawn with solid lines—different from Jardim América, which had been drawn with dotted lines and under the name of "Garden City." It is possible that the first plan for Pacaembu and for Jardim América were prepared by the French architect Joseph Antoine Bouvard (1840–1920), who in 1911 was providing

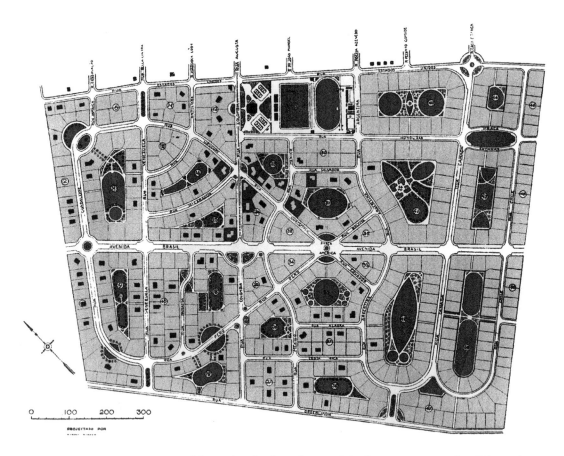

Figure 8.1. Plan showing estates envisioned by the City of São Paulo Improvements and Freehold Company Limited (CSPIFL) in 1912. The existing central city of São Paulo is located outside of this map. (Courtesy Cia CITY Archives)

his services both to the municipal government and to Edouard Fonatine de Laveleye, the founder of CSPIFL.[2] As remarked by Roney Bacelli (1988, 66), "the tracts of land in the southeast of the city have been of special concern for the Company since its foundation." In 1912 Roger Bouvard (the son of the architect Bouvard), Louis Vergé, and Douglas Gurd were sent to Brazil to conduct a new land survey of the properties and study the possibility of developing them.

Regarding Pacaembu, Maria Claudia Pereira de Souza agrees with Bacelli (1988, 67) that "the subdivision project drawn up by CSPIFL was not approved by the municipal government due to failure to meet the required dimensions for street width and minimum street block length" and also because the plan's sinuous layout did not comply with the official straight-line pattern.

In 1916, the Brazilian sanitation engineer Saturnino de Brito mentioned the development in his book *Notes sur le tracé sanitaire des villes*. While praising the avenue at the bottom of the valley, with a channeled stream running down the middle,

Maria Cristina da Silva Leme and Carlos Roberto Monteiro de Andrade

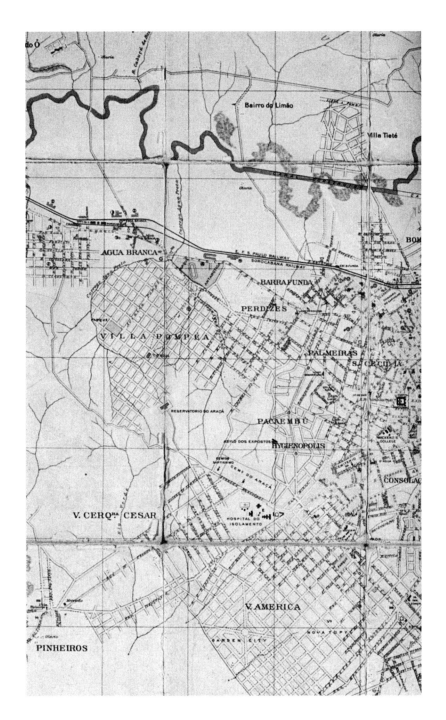

Figure 8.2. A plan of the city of São Paulo in 1914 shows the Pacaembu and Jardim América estates. (Reprinted from *Planta Geral da Cidade de São Paulo da Comissão Geographica e Geologica*, 1914, p. 72)

Brito suggested some changes to the plan, which, according to him, would facilitate rainwater and sewage drainage. However, the development had not been approved by the municipal government, which was one of the reasons why CSPIFL hired Barry Parker. Although several elements of the original plan's layout were incorporated into the final project, Parker does not mention them in any of his notes.

Barry Parker first came to São Paulo on February 2, 1917, and stayed until January 1919. During this period, he worked for CSPIFL, for whom he developed projects that would be used as a model for other urban developments in São Paulo. In one of the articles published about his life in Brazil, Parker recalled that when he first arrived in São Paulo he did not intend to engage in architecture and construction activities. He had come with the sole purpose of acting as CSPIFL's consultant on how to make the best use of their land in Pacaembu. He remarked on São Paulo's quick growth and increase in population, from 47,000 inhabitants in 1886 to half a million in 1919. During this expansion process, Pacaembu Valley, only two miles from the city's central area, like other valleys, was forgotten while the city grew around them.

Parker (1919, 148) believed that the best use for Pacaembu would be to build a public park on the site. However, he realized that turning it into a park would be foolish, given the huge value of the land. On the other hand, he affirmed that in order to best develop Pacaembu there had to be changes to the municipal laws related to streets and buildings. Parker argued that legislation should be modified in order to overcome difficulties in drawing up a satisfactory plan for the valley. The first step was to write a report about Pacaembu, in order to convince the municipal government of the need for these drastic changes. Hence, what appeared to be the most difficult solution to the problem—changing existing legislation—turned out to be Parker's first task in São Paulo. He ended up being much more than just a consultant for CSPIFL, by acting in the capacity of a professional trying to convince the municipal authorities of the need to change the law.

For each project accomplished, he wrote reports and sent them to CSPIFL. The first one was written only one month after he arrived in São Paulo, where he remarked on the company's deep knowledge about the legislation and on the petitions they would have to deliver in order to make the projects in accordance with the best interests of CSPIFL. He also started to make contacts with people who could help him make these changes happen.

In the CSPIFL's archives, four key documents relating to Pacaembu survive. In addition to clarifying the principles adopted by Parker for his projects, they also describe the circumstances surrounding his talks with the municipal government, especially with the director of São Paulo's Municipal Works, the engineer Victor da

Silva Freire. The first three documents were written during the first three months of Parker's stay in São Paulo.

The first one, from March 1, 1917, is a letter from Parker to Douglas Gurd, CSPIFL's managing director in Brazil, and has been filed as "Mr. Barry Parker's Report on Pacaembu."[3] The architect starts the letter by remarking on the inappropriateness of the grid layout for São Paulo. He also affirms that the city layout is a huge mesh sprawling onto hills, valleys, and flat plateaus, with empty valley bottoms and steep hillsides. He points out that the city's development had occurred in areas of easier implementation, which have "blindly" tracked the already delineated development areas, thus evidencing the conflict "between a road's logic and natural pattern and a supposed need for it to conform to arbitrarily drawn lines."[4]

In addition to the grid layout imposed by the colonizers' rigid principles, Parker also criticized the city's unplanned urban development. Based on his observations about the settlement patterns of São Paulo's urban area, Parker defined the principles he later adopted for Pacaembu's plan, as "an antithesis of what has been done until now."[5] He argued that architects as town planners should take into consideration not only architectural but also engineering, sanitary, financial, and other practical aspects and seek to combine them all without sacrificing any one of them. Above all, he claimed that when projecting an estate, an urban planner must emphasize that it had to be pleasant to live in, rather than just a place to impress visitors with symmetrical architectural finishes.[6] He adds that it is not sufficient for it to be cut through by important roads, have a good drainage system (as engineers tend to believe), or be a neighborhood with the biggest possible number of lots. Parker believed that the success of a residential settlement depended on those who lived and enjoyed living there.[7]

In his first report to the company, Parker made it clear that he would not give up on the principles set out in his first writings and on which he had based his projects. The fact that he drew attention to these aspects since starting his job at CSPIFL could be due to a certain degree of suspicion about private companies, which he believed would sacrifice the quality of living in a residential area in order to ensure profits. Except for his plan for the Moorland suburban park in Buxton, built on a property owned by his family, or his projects for the outskirts of Brussels in 1915, all of Parker's residential settlements were based on social, philanthropic, and cooperative principles.

In his report, Parker pointed out two concerns about Pacaembu. The first was in regard to ventilation, as the cool breezes that hit the city from the southeast were blocked by the hills surrounding the area. He also raised the issue of exposure to the sun, as the hills' shadier sides do not face the valley during the hottest hours of the day. His second concern regarded the company, which he feared might adopt a development method based solely on offering a lot of land on which to build.[8]

Parker's suggestion for tackling his first concern was that the valley should be crossed by the smallest possible number of streets, which should retain their tree canopy so that the view from each house would not be a succession of streets but green hillsides and valleys with fresh paths and shade.[9] Additionally, his suggestion would prevent the dismantling of the land areas for the imposition of a grid layout. Regarding the bottom of the valley, Parker proposed that it should be covered with gardens and described the criteria used for this type of project: "once man's work is completed, we must let the land be designed to conform to its natural formations and make it obvious that the work that was done on it was indeed the result of man's manual work."[10]

Regarding Parker's proposed sixteen- and eight-meter-wide street type, he said that countries in which apartment blocks prevail require wider streets. In the case of Brazil, where each family wanted to live in a detached house, eight-meter-wide streets would be sufficient. The layout project criteria would be to follow the land topography, which, according to him, would be the easiest solution for drainage and sewerage. He also suggested that the lots be double-fronted, with the main front facing the valley. While defending double-fronted houses, he also criticized houses with a pleasant front and squalid and unattractive backs.[11] By arguing that such a procedure could only be tolerated through force of habit, he claimed— based on Arts and Crafts principles—that there was no reason why all sides of a house could not be equally pleasant, and that in Pacaembu this would be particularly easy to achieve.

Parker's proposal for houses with raised basements is in line with his ideas for the implementation of residences. Basements could be used as a laundry, kitchen, or dining room, as well as for sewing or even as a billiard room. Above all, Parker wanted to ensure that every house had a nice view of the valley's landscaped and wooded hillsides. He also insisted on the importance of streets lined with trees and on the possibility of creating views for pedestrians. Access to each house must be (at least for most of them) through a green canopy and avenues that open up at intervals and can be seen from roof terraces overlooking the valley.[12]

Parker believed that ensuring a wide view of the Pacaembu Valley's picturesque landscape from houses, streets, stairways, and belvederes—as shown in the architect's sketch (see Plate 11)—would be a way of bringing satisfaction to residents. Furthermore, it would restore the city's old views of open fields and a magnificent mountainous landscape.[13] When comparing the residences in Pacaembu with those in the Avenida Paulista residential avenue (whose spread eastward would mean high expropriation costs), Parker thought the former should not be inferior to the latter. He pointed out Pacaembu's advantages, such as its views, and emphasized Avenida Paulista's connection to the new land lots, projected six years earlier and which would make Pacaembu into a continuation of the avenue (which did not come to fruition).

Parker mentioned the plan for Pacaembu in two other documents in the company's archives. One of them,[14] also from March 1, 1917—and therefore written together with the report mentioned earlier—contains his notes on eight drawings and two sketches, which unfortunately have been lost (although Plate 11 might be one of these sketches). In a more detailed description of his principles for Pacaembu's plan, Parker also mentions a proposal to build colonnaded porticoes on the blocks. In addition to reducing exposure to the sun, these would hold the electric wiring, thus preventing the landscape from being spoiled by exposed electric and telephone wiring. After justifying his choice for a layout with curved streets, Parker remarked that in those days urban planners had to rely on their ability to tackle each problem with an open and unbiased mind, and without showing any predilection for curved or straight streets.[15] In the conclusion to his notes, he affirmed that in Pacaembu curved streets would be more appropriate. He praised them by saying that a curved street always contain some kind of mystery for the pedestrian, while straight, long streets are monotonous.[16]

The other document that Parker wrote about Pacaembu is a letter dated April 10, 1917, addressed to Freire.[17] It is probably no accident that this letter followed a petition written by CSPIFL to the municipal government on the previous day but sent only on the 11th.[18] The text began with the following observation: "The Pacaembu valley is so well known that it is unnecessary to draw attention to the difficulties related to its development."[19] In an attempt to solve this problem, the petition mentioned that the company's board of directors had hired Barry Parker, whose report and drawings on the subject were on their way to the municipal government to be analyzed by its engineers. The document summarized the principles suggested by Parker. The text also said that the streets would be built on one level and then connect to other roads, which is how Pacaembu was, in fact, later built (Figure 8.3). The last paragraph of the petition asked for approval of the eight-meter-wide streets proposed by Parker.

In Parker's letter to Freire, he criticized the legislation that required streets to have a minimum width of sixteen meters and maximum declivity of 8 percent. He argued that it would be impossible to occupy the Pacaembu Valley under the prevailing legislation. After giving a quick analysis of São Paulo's urban plan (the stretch delimited by Paulista, Liberdade, and Consolação avenues), he urged the

Figure 8.3. The estate of Pacaembu during its early implementation stages in the early 1920s. (Courtesy Cia CITY Archives)

municipality to execute a more interesting type of development in Pacaembu, even at the cost of a few concessions.[20]

Although Pacaembu was only effectively opened years later, Parker's proposals were decisive for the project. Several aspects were not carried out; for example, instead of a garden, an avenue was built on the bottom of the valley, with a grass median strip covering the filled-in stream and a football soccer stadium on top of its source. But the overall street layout followed Parker's principles. Figure 8.4 illustrates the neighborhood during its early implementation stages and shows how the project was adapted to the topography of the site, the streets lined with trees, and the bottom of the valley used for the Pacaembu stadium (on land donated by CSPIFL to the municipality).

One week after leaving São Paulo, Parker wrote to CSPIFL's board of directors about his activities for the company: "I found that two of the municipal laws regulating planning and construction prevented the adoption of that type of development

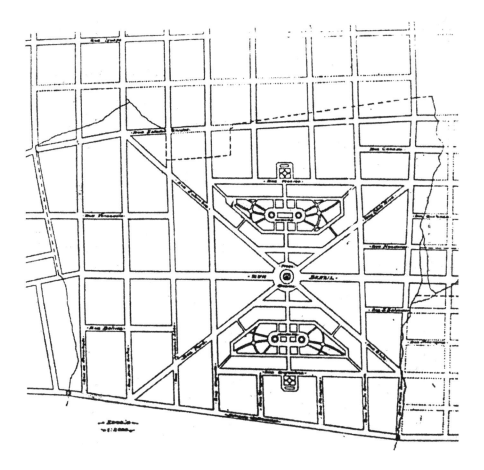

which would best overcome the difficulties and take the most advantage of the opportunities Pacaembu presented and afforded."[21] Parker's writings after his return to England convey a willingness to embrace new ideas and experiences that prevailed among the urban planners in São Paulo in the first two decades of the twentieth century. This realization also appears in the first article he wrote after returning from Brazil. Once again, after praising São Paulo's mayor and Victor da Silva Freire,[22] Parker remarked that his observations about Pacaembu "seemed to convince these gentlemen that the laws relating to the planning and construction of streets must be modified in order that the state might be developed in the way I wished" (Parker 1919, 145, 147). In the same article, he remarked that after handing in the report on Pacaembu and trying to convince the authorities of the need to modify the legislation, he realized that his stay in the city should be extended, so he focused his attention on Jardim América (Parker 1919, 144).

Figure 8.4. The earliest plan of Jardim América, possibly drawn by the French architect Joseph Bouvard in 1911. (Reprinted from H. Segawa, *Prelúdio da Metrópole: Arquitetura e urbanismo em* São Paulo *na passagem do século XIX ao XX* [Cotia, São Paulo: Ateliê Editorial, 2000])

The Plan for Jardim América

The map of São Paulo from 1914 drawn up by the Geographic and Geological Committee shows the first plan for Jardim América. Bouvard is believed to be the author, although there is no confirmation. Hugo Segawa (1988, 71) shows a drawing of this project (Figure 8.5) with Beaux-Arts features, depicting an orthogonal layout crossed by two diagonal lines with gardens in the central area and a central roundabout in the intersection between the two diagonal avenues and the main avenue, which had already been named Avenida Brasil. The estate was only three miles from the city's central area. The failure to approve the first plan of Pacaembu led the company to shift its focus to Jardim América. In 1915, following a recommendation from Bouvard and probably from Freire, Raymond Unwin was put in charge of the development.

The October 1916 issue of the English journal *Garden Cities & Town Planning* contained an unsigned article entitled "South America's First 'Garden City' Development." The text is about CSPIFL's development in São Paulo, which at the time was called Garden City. The article includes pictures of the area with its first houses under construction. An overview of the central square crossed by an electric tramway and the caption "the lawn on the corners was hand planted" indicates that the project was launched before Parker's arrival in São Paulo. The article ends with a plan drawn up by Unwin (Plate 12), with the caption "a well-known English urban planner has been consulted in regards to similar enterprises" ("South America's First 'Garden City' Development," 132). Despite being based on the first project, Unwin's drawing breaks the former's rigidity by introducing curved roads and several gardens and by designing Avenida Brasil as a boulevard with a median strip filled with trees. From a landscape viewpoint, Unwin's plan is very different from the original one. The sinuous roads, which still seemed to be sixteen meters wide, and above all the introduction of internal gardens on the blocks, created a residential suburb very similar to those in England and Germany. As the residential-only suburb would not have a civic center, Unwin created a boulevard that would be the locus of several activities.

CSPIFL's brochure on Jardim América, published in 1923, referred to the development as "the Company's pride and joy" and depicted a brief history of a residential neighborhood described as "one of São Paulo's most picturesque spots." It mentioned Unwin as the author of the "original street layout and the development plan of the garden," adding that "Mr. Barry Parker, another remarkable architect, was called to collaborate in the great enterprise, and had the opportunity to introduce many important improvements to the global plan."[23]

The publication also states that the concept of these notable professionals was fully executed by the company and that Jardim América was a truly original enter-

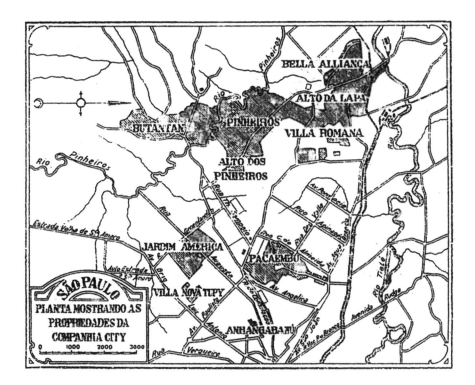

Figure 8.5. Barry Parker's original proposal for Jardim América, 1918. (Courtesy Cia CITY Archives)

prise and the only one of its kind in Brazil.[24] The brochure also drew attention to the fact that "up until then, construction works in São Paulo did not follow a plan, so that urban improvements such as drainage systems, sanitation utilities, paving, electricity, gas, and street lighting were implemented after construction." However, it affirmed that "CSPIFL had changed this old practice by putting on sale tracts of land previously and conveniently prepared both in regards to street layout and to the provision of public improvements, so that the dwellings could be adequately built on those areas." It also emphasized "the public need to carry out these improvements" and that "the first house was built in 1916 and since then over 100 have been built."[25]

With a clearly promotional tone and discourse, the text also pointed out the link between the enterprise and a certain type of housing culture: "The grand boulevards, the extensive lawns with different shapes for public recreation (to be looked after by the owners of the properties facing them) give Jardim América a peculiar aspect like the Anglo-Saxons' homes across the Atlantic Ocean. It is a truly picturesque and charming place and the only garden of its kind in Brazil."[26]

In the same document that he wrote to CSPIFL's board of directors upon his return to England, Parker talks about the knowledge he acquired about São Paulo's residential habits and projects: "A comparison of the plan for Jardim America as I found it on my arrival at Sao Paulo with the plan for Jardim America as I left it will reveal changes which almost amount to an entire remodeling. This came about gradually as the result of experience. We found that the semi-public gardens were what were attracting residents and purchasers, so efforts were directed towards the development of this element of the scheme."[27]

Parker remarked on the residents' habit of having the front of the house exposed to the main street "and turn to the semi public garden the back premises, out building, garages, servant sanitary accommodation, wash houses, garden rubbish heaps, refuse places, dust bins and the like." He would also warn that "the semi public garden will degenerate into nothing more than extensive and rather squalid back premises."[28] His way of solving this problem, as in Pacaembu, was "to make every house a double fronted house, that is to give to each house a road front and a garden front and to place all outbuildings between the houses."[29] But to do so in Jardim América they had to increase the average width of the lots, so many parts of the estate came to be re-platted. The design Parker produced in April or May of 1917, in relation to the former one made by Unwin, amends the layout of the streets, but its basic structure is maintained, further increasing the number of internal gardens on the blocks and setting the division into lots.

Another concern expressed by Parker referred to the possibility of landowners building high walls around their gardens, thus creating long and monotonous streets similar to those found in many English suburbs.[30] Although a fence-free landscape—a common practice in turn-of-the-twentieth-century North American suburbs—was the most desirable alternative, he acknowledged that Brazilians' resistance to this type of neighborhood would make this proposal unfeasible.

The "Clauses for the rights of way for the use of land" that regulated the building works in Jardim América (probably elaborated by Parker) specified the rules for the construction of any type of building. They stipulated the use (residential only); the dimensions of the occupied land for single-story and two-story houses; the building of apartments for domestic staff and other areas; the construction of summer houses and belvederes; the maximum height of 1.5 meters for street barriers—of which 1.2 meters could be hedgerow; and an internal division specification (for a fence, wall, or any other type) built within two meters of the land limit that could not be more than two meters high. The document also regulated the incorporation of land for new developments, with minimum frontage and area of 25 meters and 900 square meters. The residential-only use norms—which were followed closely by CSPIFL—guaranteed the isolation of the houses, while the limits imposed on walls ensured a clear residential landscape, similar to Riverside or Hampstead Garden Suburb.

Figure 8.6. The estate of Jardim América today. (Courtesy Cia CITY Archives)

The zoning of land use was a key factor in the preservation of Jardim América's garden city status. While Parker's plan for Pacaembu was conditioned by the area's hillsides and steep slopes, the curved roads implemented in Jardim América—an area on the floodplains of the Pinheiros River—served a different purpose. In addition to the picturesque views and sinewy streets, both Unwin and Parker wanted to reduce the speed of the vehicles passing through the streets, thus ensuring more tranquility for the residents.

Although Jardim América's urban plan did not embody the communitarian ideals behind the projects of the early British garden cities and suburbs, it still managed to follow other sociability principles and ideas. Instead of the neighborhood unit proposed by Unwin and Parker in their earlier projects (which the North Americans brought back in the 1920s through Thomas Adams, Clarence Perry, and Clarence Stein), the neighborly relationships originally conceived for the Jardim América project mostly took place in the internal gardens (Figure 8.6). Initially conceived as loci for the entertainment of a bourgeois community, the gardens, which were accessed through the houses (but not through the back as, like in Pacaembu, they were all double-fronted) or through direct entrances from the street, remained a reserved and protected area in the centers of a few blocks. However, the streets and squares were scarcely used, except by the nannies of the residents' children.

Their subsequent transformation into closed-in clusters of houses, with smaller lots, indicates that the company's economic interests ended up prevailing. These facts are significant not only because of the distortions to Parker's original plan, but also because of the changes to the settlement's original landscape that had attracted the first buyers.

Between 1918 and 1928, CSPIFL was the owner and keeper of the gardens. The company's original intentions were to hand the gardens over to next-door neighbors or donate them to the municipality. In April 1928 CSPIFL proposed that the residents contribute toward the gardens' maintenance costs, but they were not interested. The company then suggested donating the gardens to the municipality, arguing that it would be better able to obtain a contribution from the residents. Three years later the company reaffirmed the need for the municipality to take on the conservation and protection of the gardens. This was done via a letter to the residents asking for their support in creating a tax to cover these expenses. After a dispute with Mayor Luiz de Anhaia Mello, who refused the proposal, the company decided instead to subdivide the gardens and sell them in small lots, preferably to the neighbors. Thus, the eighteen gardens of Jardim América disappeared.

Ensured Permanence: The Listing of Neighborhoods as a Means of Preservation

During the initial implementation of the Pacaembu and Jardim América settlements, some of the changes suggested by Companhia City were welcomed by the municipality and resulted in changes to urban legislation. This boost to the recommendations of urban planners was defended by Raymond Unwin (1984, 286) as a means of cooperation and a sign of trust between architects, contractors, and the municipality. He also claimed that legislation should be drawn up with the participation of those directly involved, and he mentioned the example of changes suggested and accepted by the local authority during planning of Hampstead Garden Suburb. In São Paulo, in a letter subsequently published in *Garden Cities & Town Planning*, Barry Parker (1919) describes his direct collaboration with the mayor and Freire.

However, acceptance of new ideas gradually faded with the appearance of a new generation of urban planners. A study about the career of the architect and engineer Luiz Ignácio de Anhaia Mello shows progressive maturing and an increase in knowledge about foreign experiences. He introduced urban planning as a subject in an engineering and architecture course at São Paulo's Escola Politécnica. In a course taught beginning in 1927, he referred to the aspects he considered important in the garden city model: the greenbelt dividing the urban and rural areas, and controlling and limiting population growth. The examples used were Letchworth and Welwyn. The program of the course, using Radburn as an example, also refers to the U.S. experience for the introduction of the concept of the neighborhood unit to define the size of parks in local planning.

In his brief tenure as mayor of São Paulo, Anhaia Mello implemented many of the ideas defended in his articles.[31] Through Act 127 of 1931 he enforced zoning for specific urban districts. According to Sarah Feldman (2005, 149), this act introduced two elements that were perceived as the first step toward a new model of control of land use and occupation in the city. The first was the demarcation of a functional zone where only private residential buildings could be built. By following the example of the neighborhood unit, it paved the way for the implementation of commercial centers. The second element was the establishment of a committee presided over by the mayor and entrusted with analyzing the possibility of extending these parameters to the entire city.

Act 127 introduced land-use zoning in São Paulo's urban legislation, which until then was restricted to regulating the relationship between building height and street width in each zone of the city. Anhaia Mello's new approach brought about a significant change to the municipal government's powers. The focus shifted from hygiene and sanitation to controlling the damage caused by various types of land use. This new approach better protected the capital invested and enabled the municipal government to plan its actions accordingly. As described by Feldman, "considering the arguments behind the motives and the area where the first zoning initiative was implemented, we can assume that Act 127 contained a double goal that would become the main target of São Paulo's zoning program as of 1947: to protect the most prestigious areas and the value of their land" (2005, 153).

This regulation was initially restricted to Jardim América. The neighborhood's characteristics, previously guaranteed by the contracts signed between the company and the landowners, were now preserved by the municipal government. This regulation was gradually extended to other settlements in the city through the Building Code. In 1934, the new Code incorporated Act 127 into two articles: Article 40, about the delimitation of the Jardim América zone and the conditions for the creation of a commercial center; and Article 41, about the creation of a committee to elaborate the zoning process. First, this article was applied to the streets, but since 1954 this legislation has been extended to other neighborhoods, especially those projected by the company City of São Paulo Improvements & Freehold Land Company Limited. The legislation was applied also to other neighborhoods developed by local entrepreneurs, in accordance with company city standards, such as Jardim Europa.

These zones became highly valued as residential-only areas and started to attract high-income residents. But their original and distinctive characteristics, such as the residential-only use norms, the isolation of the houses, and the layout of the streets, were threatened by the opposition and pressure of the real estate market to changes in land-use legislation.

At the beginning of the 1980s, a dispute between residents' associations for and against the approval of commercial centers inside these zones became fiercer. In a context of growing political awareness and revival of the democratic process following a twenty-year dictatorship in Brazil, residents' associations in the garden suburbs organized themselves in order to demand the preservation of the characteristics of residential-only neighborhoods. The mechanism used was to request the heritage listing of the neighborhood, an unprecedented initiative for São Paulo. A petition from August 18, 1981, sent by the residents of Jardim Europa, launched an intense debate about the competence of the body entrusted with dealing with the issue, the limits of listing, the relation with zoning, and the neighborhoods' environmental qualities (Prata 2009, 90).

The request for neighborhood listing was re-sent in 1985 by the Sociedade dos Amigos dos Bairros dos Jardins Europa e Paulistano (Association of Friends of Jardins Europa and Paulistano) to Conselho de Defesa do Património Histórico Arqueológico, Artístico e Turístico do Estado de São Paulo (CONDEPHAAT), the state body in charge of cultural heritage preservation. On January 25, 1986, on the grounds of "preserving the area's environmental, landscape, historic and touristic value, as well as its man-made character represented by a dense landscape covered by trees," the Culture Secretary listed the urban layouts of Jardins América, Europa, Paulista, and Paulistano in São Paulo City. These were represented by the streets and squares between the private lots; their vegetation (especially the trees), which is now considered an asset; and the lots' current demarcation lines (these surfaces are also considered to be historic), as the low-population density in these areas is considered to be as important as their urban layout.

In 1985, the residents of Higienópolis and Pacaembu sent a request to CONDEPHAAT. The petition mentions the area's importance as urban heritage and states that "its identity is under threat by imminent aggression from real estate speculators and rampant commercial exploitation."[32] They demanded to include Pacaembu in the same neighborhood listing of jardins. Six years later the process was approved.[33]

Conclusion

During his two years in São Paulo, Barry Parker introduced the garden city model into the architecture and urban planning professional milieu. Commissioned by CSPIFL, he developed a series of garden suburb projects for estates that served as a model for other urban settlements in São Paulo.

Two of his most important projects, Jardim América and Pacaembu, were the first exclusive residential neighborhoods in the city, with large lots, green areas, and the provision of public improvements as drainage systems, sanitation utilities, paving, electricity, gas and street lighting, and streetcar lines. Parker was responsible for sending a series of petitions on behalf of the company to change the municipal regulations regarding the width of the streets and the distance between roads.

The projects introduced new design parameters and standards into São Paulo's urban legislation, with CSPIFL defining the building height and lot coverage parameters, along with other features. The neighborhood's characteristics, previously guaranteed by the contracts signed between the company and the landowners, were later adopted by the zoning legislation of the city of São Paulo. This regulation was gradually extended to other settlements in the city, especially those projected by CSPIFL and those developed by local entrepreneurs, in accordance with the company's standards.

But the settlements' original and distinctive characteristics have been threatened by the growing interest and pressure of the real estate market to changes in land-use legislation. To preserve the settlements, the residents requested that they be given heritage listings. First Jardim América, in 1985, and later Pacaembu, in 1991, have been listed by the state heritage body. This measure has ensured the permanence of the two garden suburbs, by combining in the same argument the neighborhoods' historical architectural and urban heritage qualities and environmental preservation values. Thus, one century after their creation, the original characteristics of the garden suburb layouts are still being valued and preserved.

Today, however, they continue to face pressure from growth and from changes to the metropolis and have been the subject of a fierce debate about the need to preserve their original and distinctive attributes.

Table 8.1
Summary of Historical Events and Heritage Benchmarks
for Pacaembu and Jardim América

Year	Event
1911	The City of Sao Paulo Improvements and Freehold Company Limited (CSPIFL) is created; it is headquartered in England, with offices in Paris and São Paulo.
1911	Records indicate that Pacaembu is the first development planned by CSPIFL.
1914	CSPIFL approaches the São Paulo Tramway, Light and Power company to establish streetcar lines in the areas that it intends to subdivide. A map of São Paulo by the Geographic and Geological Committee shows the Pacaembu development drawn with solid lines—different from Jardim América, drawn with dotted lines and under the name of Garden City.
1915	Following a recommendation from the French architect Joseph Bouvard and probably from Victor da Silva Freire, Raymond Unwin is put in charge of the development of Jardim América.
1917–19	Commissioned by CSPIFL to develop a series of garden suburbs, Barry Parker lives in São Paulo from February 2, 1917, until January, 1919. He reviews and alters the plans for Pacaembu and Jardim América (originally planned with 396 lots) and designs model homes for the latter development. After his return to England, Parker writes a report about his activities for CSPIFL, focusing on Jardim América and Pacaembu.
1919–23	CSPIFL defines rules for the construction of any type of building in Jardim América, stipulating the use (residential only) and the dimensions and forms of occupation of the lots. These rules are extended to CSPIFL's other developments. In 1923 CSPFIL's book *Jardim América* mentions that more than one hundred houses are already built in this community.
1931	March 20: The Municipal Act 127 introduces a new model of control of land use and occupation in the city of São Paulo, with the demarcation of a functional zone where only private residential buildings can be built.
1934	A new Building Code incorporates Act 127 into Article 40 (delimitation of the Jardim América zone and conditions for the creation of a commercial center) and Article 41 (creation of a committee to elaborate the zoning process).
1941	Jardim América is officially completed.
Early 1980s	Disputes for or against the inclusion of commercial centers become fiercer among residents' associations in the garden suburbs. In a context of growing political awareness and revived democratic process following a twenty-year dictatorship in Brazil, these associations organize themselves to demand preservation of the characteristics of residential-only neighborhoods. They request the heritage listing of their neighborhoods, an unprecedented initiative in São Paulo.
1981	August 18: Residents of Jardim Europa, a nearby neighborhood, send a petition challenging the competence of the body regulating landmark listing, zoning, and environmental qualities.
1985–86	The Association of Friends of Jardins Europa and Paulistano re-send a request for neighborhood listing to CONDEPHAAT, the state body in charge of cultural heritage preservation.
1986	January: The Culture Secretary lists urban layouts of Jardins América, Europa, Paulista, and Paulistano in São Paulo.
1991	CONDEPHAAT approves a petition from residents to add Pacaembu to the 1986 listing.
	Pacaembu: Population (as of 2010), 82,788; 352 acres [142,43 ha]; 1,478 dwelling units. Jardim América: Population (as of 2010), 34,384; 266,7 acres [107.92 ha]; 614 dwelling units.

NOTES

1. For a more detailed analysis about the importance of Parker's presence in São Paulo, see also Andrade 1998.

2. This is only a supposition based on Antoine Bouvard's role in CSPIFL.

3. Barry Parker's report on Pacaembu, March 1, 1917, City of São Paulo Improvements Freehold Land Company (CPIFLC) Archives, Box GG 092, Document no. 1, 11 pages.

4. Ibid., 1.

5. Ibid., 3.

6. Ibid., 5.

7. Ibid.

8. Ibid.

9. Ibid., 7.

10. Ibid.

11. Ibid.

12. Ibid., 6.

13. Ibid., 9.

14. Parker's notes on the drawings for Pacaembu, March 1, 1917, CPIFLC Archives, Box GG 092, Document no. 2.

15. Ibid., 7.

16. Ibid.

17. Letter from Mr. Parker to Dr. Freire of the Public Works Department regarding the former's report on Pacaembu, March 10, 1917, CPIFLC Archives, Box GG 092, Document no. 3.

18. Petition sent to the Prefect of São Paulo regarding Pacaembu, April 11, 1917, CPIFLC Archives, Box GG 092, Document no. 4. Despite having been written on the company's behalf, the petition did not contain the signature of any of its directors.

19. Ibid., 1.

20. Letter from Parker to Freire.

21. Manuscript letter from Barry Parker to the directors of City of São Paulo Improvements Freehold Land Company, January 25, 1919, CPIFLC Archives, Box GG 092, Document no. 5, 25 pages.

22. When describing Freire, Parker mentions Freire's education in Paris, the fact that he is a member of the English Institute of Civil Engineers, and his visits to Letchworth and Hampstead. In Freire's library he found many books in English and in other languages about urban planning and correlated subjects.

23. *Jardim America* (1923), City of São Paulo Improvements & Freehold Land Co. Ltd. brochure, 1.

24. Ibid.

25. Ibid.

26. Ibid.

27. Manuscript letter from Parker, 5.

28. Ibid., 6.

29. Ibid., 7.

30. Ibid., 12.

31. There were two brief mandates: the first from December 5, 1930, to July 26, 1931, and the second, which lasted only twenty days, from November 14 to December 3, 1931.

32. Processo CONDEPHAAT 23.972/1985, discussed in Prata 2009, 99.

33. Resolução Secretaria da Cultura 14 May 1991, March 16, 1991, published in Diário Oficial do Estado.

REFERENCES

Andrade, C. R. M. 1998. "Barry Parker um arquiteto inglês na cidade de São Paulo." Ph.D. diss., University of São Paulo.

Bacelli, R. 1988. "Jardim América." In PMSP Secretaria da Cultura, *Série história dos bairros de São Paulo*. Vol. 20.

Barreto, P. 1933. "Uma temerária aventura forense (A questão entre D Amalia Keating e a City of San Paulo Improvements & Freehold Land Co. Ltd.). Alegações finaes do advogado da ultima." In *Revista dos tribunaes*, edited by E. G. São Paulo. 2 vols.

Bouvard, Joseph Antoine. 1911. "O relatório do Sr Bouvard." *Revista de Engenharia* 1: 27– 42.

Brito, F. Saturnino de, and Eduoard Imbeaux. 1916. *Notes sur le tracé sanitaire des villes*. Chaix.

Feldman, S. 2005. *Planejamento e Zoneamento. São Paulo 1947 1972*. São Paulo: EDUSP FAPESP.

Freire, V. S. 1942. "Urbanismo." *Engenharia* 3(November): 76–80.

Howard, Ebenezer. 1898. *To-morrow: A Peaceful Path to Real Reform*. Cambridge: Cambridge University Press.

Mello, L. I. A. 1927. "Problemas de urbanismo mais uma contribuição para o calçamento." *Revista Politécnica* 23: 343–65.

———. 1929. "O recreio activo e organizado das cidades modernas." *Boletim do Instituto de Engenharia* 47.

Parker, B. 1919. "Two Years in Brazil." *Garden Cities & Town Planning* 9(8): 143–51.

Prata, J. 2009. "Patrimonio cultural e cidade: Praticas de preservação em São Paulo." Ph.D. diss., University of São Paulo.

Segawa, H. 1988. "Construção das ordens—um aspecto da arquitetura no Brasil 1808–1930." Master's thesis, University of São Paulo.

"South America's First 'Garden City' Development." 1916. *Garden Cities & Town Planning* 6(7): 130–33.

Unwin, R. 1984. *La pratica del urbanismo: Una introduccion all arte de proyectar ciudades y barrios*. Barcelona: Gustavo Gilli.

CHAPTER 9

GARBATELLA

Heritage, Gentrification, and

Public Policies in Rome, Italy

Sandra Annunziata

Garbatella's iconic status results from the fertile interplay between the aesthetic agenda that informed its construction and the social history of the city of Rome. Known as a "fortress of resistance" against fascism, as a "sociable" and "tolerant" neighborhood, characterized by a sophisticated system of garden spaces, Garbatella is currently completing the transition from public to private tenure—a process that this chapter will argue represents a slow change toward gentrification. This evolution sheds light on the heritage paradox connected with a national policy: the right to buy publicly sponsored rental housing, which in turn relates to the difficulty of ensuring equity and guaranteeing social justice as a city's material and symbolic assets are commodified. This chapter analyzes the historical origins of Garbatella's iconic status, as well as its development, heritage protection, and privatization. Despite protecting the built form, the current preservation framework does not safeguard Garbatella from changes occurring in housing tenure.

Origins and Iconic Status

Garbatella was developed between 1920 and 1933. Its promoters were liberal reformists who favored public ownership as the appropriate form of tenure for working-class housing. It is therefore essential to grasp the ideal of bourgeois reformism that guided Garbatella's origin. By the early twentieth century, the right of the working class to decent housing became a central theme in Italian politics (Vidotto 2001). The consensus government led by Prime Minister Giovanni Giolitti understood that its direct involvement in providing decent housing was crucial to keep an increasingly well-organized working class under control.[1] In 1903 a public autonomous body, called Istituto Case Popolari (ICP), was established for that purpose (Vidotto 2001, 121). ICP's public housing was sophisticated in terms of its massing and decor and the efficient and sanitary planning of living units. Aesthetic quality was aimed at encouraging social responsibility and instilling middle-class family values among low-income tenants.[2]

Garbatella complied with this political agenda. It was viewed as a design experiment as well as a "social laboratory" (Sinatra 2006, 21). It fostered new relationships between the built environment and social structures, as well as between housing experimentation and desirable forms of tenure. With it, a continental adaptation of Ebenezer Howard's garden city ideals (Howard 1965) entered the lexicon of Italian academics and entrepreneurs and, in the mid-1920s, that of bureaucrats of the Ministry of Public Works in charge of allocating funds for ICP housing. Although garden communities have been a minor part of ICP work, the spatial idea of a self-sustained community marked the birth of a major trend in Italian community planning, a trend that evolved into the vernacular style of the Istituto Nazionale delle Assicurazioni (INA) casa experimentation after World War II.[3]

Garbatella was originally called a *borgata giardino*, due to its location at the periphery of Rome's historic core. The term *borgate* refers to planned communities erected in the Roman countryside between 1920 and 1937. These were planned to re-house residents evicted from the city center by urban renewal projects and were very poor in both social and architectural design terms.

Endowed with far more generous garden spaces than its sister communities, Garbatella fitted the bill of an authentic and successful borgata giardino. It provided its working-class residents, immigrants from the countryside (but also displaced city dwellers), with a semi-urban, semirural housing environment.

The creation of Garbatella as a working-class borgata was associated with an ambitious project of industrialization of Rome's southern axis. When the city became Italy's capital in 1887, it already had many of the characteristics of a service and administrative center (Babonaux 1983). However, liberals and progressive business leaders had plans for a major port city. They joined forces with Mayor Ernest Nathan (1907–13) to promote industrial development, by connecting the existing railroad network to the seashore.[4] Several factories and industries had already been erected near Garbatella's site, when, in 1919, the Ente Nazionale per lo Sviluppo Marittimo di Roma (SMIR) was charged with the development of a port-city plan designed by the architects Gustavo Giovannoni and Marcello Piacentini.[5] At the same time, Giovannoni was experimenting with *diradamento edilizio*, a practice involving the judicious "thinning out" of recent buildings in order to restore the glory of Rome's historic core (Giovannoni 1931; Zucconi 1997). This type of selective "purge" entailed residential decentralization; several new neighborhoods, inspired by garden city principles, were planned as companion pieces to the harbor project. Of these, only Garbatella's first phase was implemented.

Development Process

Even though the land occupied by present-day Garbatella was purchased at once, through expropriation of agricultural land, this community never had a full-fledged master plan. Instead, its current plan, bounded to the south by an ancient pilgrimage road, results from incremental additions brought by several phases of development, from 1920 to 1933. Eventually, a total of twenty-nine hectares was subdivided into sixty-nine blocks surrounded by curvilinear streets (Figure 9.1).[6]

Each development phase was characterized by different housing typologies, lot subdivisions, and open-space configurations. Planned by Giovannoni, the initial section (1920–22) entailed five blocks, forty-four buildings (190 residential units), and ample communal space. Streets were curvilinear, to follow the slight slope of the site and avoid uniformity (Giovannoni 1910, quoted in Stabile 2001, 103). Garbatella's original residential type was the two-story, single-family *villino*, in detached or duplex configurations. Ornate façades adopted a vernacular style called *barocchetto romano*,[7] reflecting traditional values by combining urbanity and ruralism and following Ebenezer Howard's

Figure 9.1. Schematic rendition of Garbatella's master plan, emphasizing variety in building footprints. (Drawn by Sandra Annunziata)

Figure 9.2. Garbatella's initial section (1920–22): example of a façade in *barocchetto romano*, a vernacular style, and of the interior courtyards. (Photo by Sandra Annunziata)

desire to marry "town and country." According to Antonella De Michelis, this style "communicated a Roman identity that was not imperial and did not possess the grandeur of the neoclassical Beaux-Arts Style. Rather, it drew heavily upon the still-vital practice of the Roman artisan: a heritage of art and craft" (De Michelis 2009, 510) (Figure 9.2).

Garbatella's earliest residents were factory workers from neighboring industrial districts and artisans: glass makers, printers, and carpenters. Garbatella's inhabitants did not represent the *popolo romano* (the urban poor) but were workers engaged in industrializing Rome. In fact, the ICP's goal was "to ennoble, to improve public housing, and above all to elevate, to educate future citizens" (Costantini 1922, 4) who could aspire to social mobility.

In the borgata giardino of the early 1920s, residents formed a cohesive and self-sufficient community that supplemented its income by cultivating the land allotted with each unit (Rivolta 2010, 63). In Garbatella, each block contained internal spaces for vegetable gardening. Early residents founded a cooperative to trade and sell their products in a collective shop located in Brin Square, the closest point to the railway station that connected the new subdivision to the center of Rome. However, grassroots entrepreneurship did not withstand the advent of the fascist regime in 1922: the cooperative was dismantled and Garbatella as a whole assumed a new character and meaning (Rivolta 2010).

Rome's symbols and monuments from antiquity became the center stage of fascist ideology and propaganda, its industrialization being no longer a priority. Instead, the regime focused on urban renewal projects carried out by clearance schemes. The so-called *sventramenti* entailed the demolition of Rome's medieval fabric and minor architecture. A significant portion of evicted residents were relocated to Garbatella. Meanwhile, Nathan's industrial project was abandoned and the SMIR dismantled.

From 1923 to 1929, the ICP experimented with new forms of housing in its various projects, including Garbatella: the *case rapide* (fast houses), the *case a riscatto* (ransom houses), and the *alberghi suburbani* (suburban hotels), the *villini* all designed by leading figures of Italian architecture (see Plate 13).[8] Garbatella's new development phase of 1923–27 encompassed five hundred case rapide units in single-family villas. This section was dubbed Quartiere dei Baraccati, as it hosted people evicted from the barracks of central Rome. It was championed by the fascist regime, which required that exterior decoration be downplayed. A new era of sobriety had begun for Garbatella, entailing a new kind of self-image and public perception. Again, footprints followed the topography and plans called for curvilinear streets and pedestrian pathways. Collective courtyards functioned as laundry spaces and compensated for the small size of dwellings.

Separate blocks of case a riscatto were erected in 1925–26. These single-family homes, eighty-one residential units grouped within thirty-two buildings, were designed by Plinio Marconi and could be purchased by their lower middle-class residents. The novel principle of ownership of publicly built housing epitomized the transformation of ICP under fascism into what Vittorio Vidotto (2001, 197) has called a "formidable tool for political control and consensus building." This shift from rental to private property would have a lasting impact on Garbatella's formal and informal governance. In the same years the *palazzina*, a four-story apartment building, became a popular residential type in Rome, which landowners and developers adopted for its profitability and its potential to affirm class distinctions (Insolera 1981 [1962], 94–96). In Garbatella, palazzina apartment blocks with Y- and T-shaped footprints and superblocks were built on the outskirts of blocks or along the perimeter of a block. Their front façades defined the public realm while their

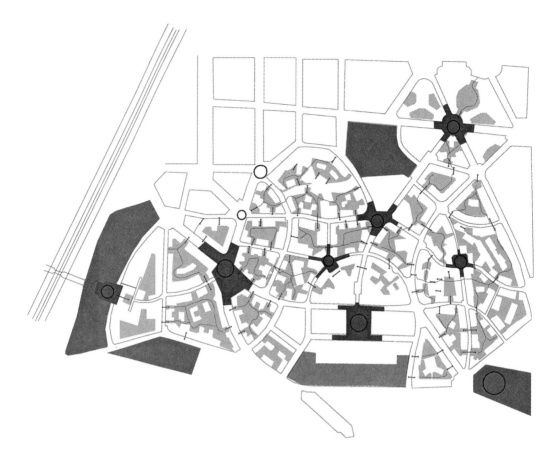

Figure 9.3. Spatial configuration of open space in Garbatella, demonstrating continuity between the internal courtyards, the public parks, and the public squares. This open space configuration results from a complex assemblage between street hierarchy and block composition. (Drawn by Sandra Annunziata)

rear elevations interacted with collective spaces for residents; they acted as nodes at street intersections, providing powerful and inventive corner statements (Rappino 1975, 81).

Greater housing demand in the same years required also the construction of collective facilities and *maggior mole* (literally, bigger buildings). Entrusted to the architect Ignazio Sabatini, the Public Bath and the Palladium Theater exemplified a renewed interest in classical motifs under fascism; they stood in front of a residential block designed by Plinio Marconi. As stated by De Michelis (2009, 9), "two dominant styles of the Garbatella were constructed side by side: the Barocchetto and the new Scuola Romana. . . . Marconi and Sabatini were responding to different layers of the great urban palimpsest of Rome." Experiments in superblock configurations ended with the construction of the alberghi suburbani, which were large and crowded dormitories to house temporarily people evicted from the center of Rome. Like earlier housing types, these hostels contributed to Garbatella's iconicity (Plate 13). At the beginning of the

1930s, with the completion of a kindergarten and several elementary schools, the neighborhood became a self-sufficient urban entity.

With so many typologies and styles, Garbatella was a diverse and complex neighborhood, from both a visual standpoint and a social perspective. As its population increased from 3,500 in 1924 to 15,000 in 1931, it became one of the largest new communities completed under fascism (Sinatra 2006, 51). Its different social groups were named after the type of dwelling from which they had been evicted: *sbaraccati* or *sfollati* (evicted from barracks or shanty houses, respectively). Garbatella hosted wage earners, unemployed workers, or immigrants, but only government employees could afford to purchase case a riscatto (Insolera 1981 [1962], 94). Despite demographic changes, a common visual theme pervaded the entire neighborhood, and its sophisticated system of open spaces acted as a visual and symbolic spine. The distribution and aggregation of buildings in the *isolato* (the perimeter of the block) generated a double spatial hierarchy (Zucconi 2002, 55): one governing public squares and curvilinear streets, the other ordering collective spaces and gardens at the rear of buildings. All spaces—front and back—were interconnected to create a pedestrian-friendly environment and an enduring sense of sociability and community (Figure 9.3).

Heritage Framework and Values

Italy's heritage is protected by a comprehensive national law that incorporates all the pre- and post-unitarian heritage and is monitored by a dedicated Ministry of Cultural and Environmental Heritage.[9] Additionally, the urban fabric of each historic city—ranging from the medieval era to the early twentieth century—is protected at the municipal level by a general master plan that establishes the boundaries of the "historical center"—the so-called zone A—as enforced by the national law.[10] This is a homogeneous area where new buildings, alterations to façades and interiors, and even tree removal are prohibited. The notion of a "historical center" was first coined by Giovanni Astengo for the city of Assisi's general plan. It reflected the desire to safeguard city cores from development as the "premise to ensure modernization" as stated by Carta di Gubbio (the Gubbio charter was signed by local municipalities as a conclusion to the National Congress for the Preservation and Renewal of Historical Centers, held in Gubbio, Italy, September 17–19, 1960). The general plan for the city of Rome was adopted in 1962 (and approved in 1965), and it delimited the "historical center" as the area within the Aurelian wall. Garbatella, at the time, was located in zone B, where buildings (exteriors and interiors) were subjected to a less stringent set of rules. In 1980, Rome's historical cen-

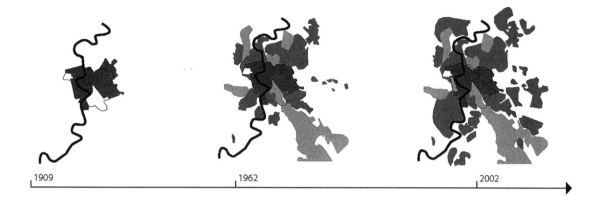

1909   1962   2002

Figure 9.4. Garbatella is located in the southern outskirts of Rome's historical core. This sequence of three diagrammatic land use maps indicates how this district acquired greater centrality over time. (Drawn by Sandra Annunziata from *Nuovo Piano Regolatore Generale di Roma (New General Plan of the City of Rome)* [Planning Department, City of Rome, 2008])

ter precinct became a World Heritage Site. This did not entail stricter protection, but it did heighten international awareness about safeguarding Rome's historic center. In 2008, the Nuovo Piano Regolatore Generale (NPRG) (new general plan) of Rome expanded the protected zone and Garbatella (where few buildings have received national landmark designation) was one of the neighborhoods erected in the late nineteenth and early twentieth centuries, which received the label of "consolidated urban expansion" with a proper set of conservation norms that also entail tax-exemption benefits for restoration (Comune di Roma, 2005) (Figure 9.4).[11]

The extension of Rome's conservation boundaries highlighted the urban qualities of outlying districts such as Garbatella, conferring on them historical and symbolic value. In recent years Garbatella gained even greater attention through media exposure, including a 2010 architecture exhibit prepared by the Sapienza University and the publication of a guidebook (Bonavita et al. 2010).[12] As a result, Garbatella gradually lost its status of an ordinary borgata, becoming a prestigious location. Heritage protection, however, does not guard Garbatella from intangible social change related to the evolution of its housing tenure.

A Desirable Neighborhood and Its Image as a Fortress of Resistance

At present Garbatella is well known for its architecture and for the social experiments it has nurtured. Among Rome's publicly funded residential neighborhoods, it is regarded as a model of good design. Its housing stock and generous open spaces both make Garbatella a vibrant and very desirable place to live. The neighborhood offers a wide range of amenities. The public bath, once transformed into a residential and commercial space, has been claimed recently by the inhabitants as a local library; the theater was renovated in early 2000 by the University of Roma Tre. Nearby, the gardens are all maintained by self-organized management groups. They are all extensively used: some of them are paved and used as playgrounds, others have ornamental planting or are still used for clothes drying.

The metro that runs under Via Ostiense connects the neighborhood with the district built for the Esposizione Internazionale di Roma (EUR) to the south and with the historical center to the north. Today, Garbatella boasts schools, parks, housing for the elderly, and cultural venues. Several community centers, opened to all residents, have been established in formerly squatted buildings. Their diverse activities foster the image of an active community. In addition, local branches of political parties and many associations are actively promoting social and cultural activities.

Garbatella also is home to the Urban Center, a planning agency that documents and publicizes projects and public hearings for the entire eleventh borough. For instance in 2002 it hosted a publicly sponsored plan called the neighborhood contract. This holistic plan for local development (inspired by the French *contrat de ville*) called for participatory budgeting. The restoration of the old market building, the rehabilitation of public parks and two collective gardens, and the revitalization of the pilgrimage street Via delle Sette Chiese were among the public interventions prioritized by the community. Overall, the decision-making process and allocation of funds for initiatives strive to be transparent and to involve residents at every step. However, the plan did not end as expected. When the old market was finally restored, the merchants refused to come back as they had found their temporary relocation along the main commercial corridor more profitable. Consequently the old market now hosts the farmers' markets and the cultural activities sponsored by the council and the local community.

Garbatella has become an icon of community planning not only for its spatial and architectural features, but also for its reputation as a "fortress of resistance" against fascism. A substantial nonacademic literature, in particular the writings of the local historian Gianni Rivolta (Rivolta 2006, 2010; Rivolta and Gori 2003), has cultivated the resistance narrative, which, in turn, has reinforced the image of Garbatella as a cohesive neighborhood. Documents and oral histories preserve and exalt the memory of episodes of intense solidarity, which earned Garbatella its reputation as a unified social block, where partisans, persecuted by the fascist regime and by German occupants during World War II, could find help. Monica Sinatra has reconstructed Garbatella's "foundation myth" and stressed its role as a stage set for political rallies. The local branch of the Italian Communist Party (PCI) was established in its very core and played "a central role in literacy work" and in introducing "the basics for democratic ideals" (2006, 130).

Garbatella for Sale

According to Peter Marcuse, privatization is a "disinvestment of government ownership [in which] property rights lie at the heart of the process" (1996, 119.). Garbatella's privatization process is nowadays particularly delicate, as it is inseparable from its social history and must account for the intrinsic quality of the residential and civic architecture. The "bundle of rights," which, according to Marcuse, can be summarized as those to "use and limit use," "build and limit building," "sell and to tax the proceeds of sale," and provide "transfers after death" (1996, 222, 224), is shared between residents and the public agency in charge of the maintenance of the dwellings and the communal spaces.

During World War II, a housing shortage and impoverishment led many residents to subdivide, share, or sublet their units. After the war, the ICP, which had been renamed Istituto Autonomo Case Popolari (IACP) in 1938, was forced to accept overcrowding, subleasing of units, and transferring of titles to direct relatives. The IACP lost a great deal of its management control, and the eligibility criteria that governed access to public housing started to be altered. As a result, Garbatella has, for several decades, been subjected to a relentless unspoken process of privatization initiated during fascism and later on enacted by the informal practices of its residents.

Privatization is indeed unavoidable because it is the outcome of an ambiguous nationwide economic restructuring process that started during the 1990s with the liberalization of the housing market, the abolition of rent control, and the dismantling of public assets. In 1993, the right-to-buy legislation was introduced by a national law that regulated the alienation of public property, residential and otherwise.[13] Public housing started to be privatized following nationwide constitutional principles, as well as ensuing regional and municipal legislation.[14] Before the right to buy was enforced, entitlement to public housing units was conferred by the IACP in perpetuity to tenants. These tenants were immune from eviction, as long as they did not own residential property in or near Rome and their income was below a certain threshold. Rents were calculated according to unit size and income.[15] This form of tenure did not provide the right to sell units and to profit from ensuing capital gains. As a public agency, the IACP owned the right to profit from Garbatella's entire housing stock while it was its duty to maintain the units and the collective spaces.

What makes Garbatella a contested ground is the fact that, for several decades after World War II, the right to use public housing was transferred after the tenants' death to direct relatives whose income level was increasing, as well as through sublets and *buonouscita* cash payments (an informal practice subjected to few data and therefore hard to document). In addition to such transfers, squatting in empty units became a common, quasi-official occurrence in Garbatella (as in other Roman public housing estates).

In 2001, under Silvio Berlusconi's second mandate, the Minister of Economy and Finance devised expeditious regulations for privatization and fostered the denationalization of public assets as a way to solve the public debt.[16] In 2006 the Lazio region, in charge of Rome's building and planning regulations, approved legislation requiring that the city sell up to 70 percent of its public housing.[17] In 2007, Rome's center-left municipality published a list of properties that were officially for sale.[18] Most of them were situated in what a local newspaper called "prestigious locations," including Garbatella. Garbatella's residents received the right to buy, with the clause that newly purchased units must be owner-occupied for ten years. The Lazio region also approved the so-called *sanatoria* (an act of indemnity) to regularize illegal occupiers of housing owned by the ATER (Aziende Territoriali per l'Edilizia Residenziale), the public entity that replaced the IACP in 2002.[19] Former squatters and subleasers achieved immunity for their acts and were granted the privilege to buy the properties where they lived. In other words, after many years of political leniency regarding informal practices, Garbatella residents were able to legally achieve what Marcuse calls the "power to alter prevailing right, privileges, power of immunities by physical acts and payments" and to increase their "incidents of ownership" (1994, 24; see also Annunziata 2017).

As a result of this long process, Garbatella's population has become more diverse in age and income range. It includes "historical" homeowners living in the case a riscatto (or their direct descendants); legitimate tenants, who regularly pay rent according to their income to the ATER or at market prices to legitimate apartment owners; squatters or households waiting for the regularization of their status; and, finally, tenants illegitimately subletting units at market prices from legitimate ATER tenants. This tenure maelstrom leads to two conflicting interpretations. It can be viewed as the positive outcome of political leniency toward an informal form of welfare, which compensates for the government's inability to provide sufficient moderately priced housing. In other words, Garbatella can be seen as enjoying a type of self-governance that produces a socially mixed environment, typical of urban entities in southern Europe (Allen et al. 2008; Leontidou 1990). The tenure situation can also be viewed as the sign of an uncontrolled form of overconsumption of "housing goods" (Webster 2007). Whichever interpretation is used, Garbatella's public housing is going to be formally privatized because the ATER has stopped managing its properties properly and is facing a serious financial crisis. While some Italian municipalities decided not to sell their residential properties and to devise instead new management policies, the city of Rome required the ATER to sell its housing in order to alleviate a huge financial burden and to garner political consensus among citizens. ATER officials declared that the legalization process would protect citizens' rights while improving their agency's finances by recouping back rents. They also argued that the sale would enable the construction of new public housing in the future.[20]

Opportunities or Threats?

Given its complexity, the process of formal privatization of Garbatella is deliberately slow. Public opinion generally holds that the shift from renting to ownership represents a real opportunity as well as an implicit right for Garbatella's longtime residents. Most of those who benefit from Garbatella's privatization believe this process is legally sound and necessary in order to fulfill their legitimate rights to stay put. They also argue that ATER tenants, in other parts of the city, are already property owners. A small but vocal minority of residents is fighting to implement equitable and transparent criteria for the transfer of public property to private hands. In fact it remains unclear who will actually benefit from the privatization of a collective resource and what the future of the neighborhood will be.

In addition to ignoring and altering Garbatella's social legacy, we can question the fairness of the sale process along three lines of inquiry: the determination of sale prices, the selection of tenants entitled to become homeowners, and the absence of debate about the consequences surrounding this aggregate sale.

The purchase prices were established in 1993 according to estimates by the Catasto, the state agency in charge of the inventory and rent estimation of all the property (real estate and land) throughout Italy, and these prices have been discounted for Garbatella's long-term tenants. Since then, those entitled to become homeowners are all the tenants as well as informal occupants who have satisfied regularization requirements or else their direct relatives had satisfied them before their deaths. While guaranteeing full access to homeownership to those able to pay, even to former illegal occupiers and subleasers who had achieved immunity for their acts, the ATER reserved the right to displace and relocate tenants who could not afford to buy property in Garbatella, generally moving them to a housing estate at a greater distance from central Rome.

Two decades have passed since purchase prices were established. The sale is still in progress and a value gap between the original price and current market prices encourages speculation.[21] Private units are being rented at an increasingly higher price. Purchased units have already been repaired and improved, making them more valuable in the long term. Even though new owners cannot resell Garbatella property for about ten years and the ATER reserves the right to buy it in priority in case of sale, real estate agents have started advertising sales and purchases in the area.

No public debate addressed the following questions. What will be the impact of the aggregate sale of Garbatella's residential units on such a desirable neighborhood? What will happen to the common, open, and adaptable spaces? The sale of this piece of modern heritage of unchallenged value should at least have triggered a debate on viable alternatives and served as a case study for a broader discourse on desirable public neighborhoods under privatization. Instead, the absence of debate played in favor of the "consensus machine" that the right to buy aims to activate and nurture.

Future Scenarios

Garbatella's housing sale is leading to an inevitable, unspoken, and unchallenged process of gentrification. Like elsewhere in Europe (Bridge, Butler, and Lees 2012), the massive sale of public housing was promoted to public opinion through the rhetoric of homeownership and as a means to achieve full citizenship and community empowerment. In reality the ATER sold its housing units to recover from a huge public debt rather than for the public good. Advocates of gentrification argue that its "positive" effects contribute to the regeneration of neighborhoods and will benefit residents of all incomes. It is generally agreed that gentrification has some benefits for a city's built environment. Undeniably, higher-income tenants and homeowners are not going to negatively transform Garbatella's physical integrity. However the re-investment after decades of disinvestment—a practice of gentrification triggered by the process of tenant ownership conversion—comes at a high price for the city: low-income tenants are displaced (forced or not, directly or indirectly); land values and housing costs skyrocket; and, last but not least, the neighborhood loses its social diversity.

So far, no concern has been voiced regarding how to preserve the social mix in Garbatella and the future of its collective gardens when the housing sale will be completed. Garbatella's successful and "nostalgic" urban design and architecture has been taken so much for granted that no one—planners, elected officials, residents—has worried whether the privatization process may have a negative impact on its social fabric. According to Michael Herzfeld (2009, 3), historical conservation theories and practices are at the core of the gentrification of Rome's most historic districts: "cosmopolitan fashion now invests owning and inhabiting a piece of an allegedly universal history of civilization with irresistible appeal; the rhythms of daily sociability surrender to the commercialization of eternity." A generalized process of eviction of moderate-income residents from the center of Rome has been occurring since the 1980s and is currently reaching locations that were considered part of Rome's periphery only a decade ago (Annunziata 2018). Gentrification in Rome is linked to the sale of city-owned property in a so-called prestigious location: an area where sale prices have increased to the point that they have become prohibitive for residents but very convenient for real estate intermediaries (Annunziata 2014). Garbatella was not listed as a prestigious location and the sale prices have remained very low, even though it has an unquestionable architectural and symbolic value well prized by real estate agents. Moreover, the right to buy policy is also at the core of what Herzfeld called the "the corrosion of solidarity" among Romans, which is "happening with the complaisance of the authorities who have surrendered the allure of neoliberal market logic in virtually every aspect of city management and erased all the alternatives to the neoliberal vision of a good life" (Herzfeld 2009, 23–24). In other words, the right-to-buy policy has eroded solidarity among those who have the economic resources to become homeowners and those who do not, resulting in the displacement of the latter.

Besides the complex process of sales and the impending gentrification effect, other changes, all related to Rome's new service economy, are destabilizing Garbatella and threaten its status and image. Media exposure and popular attraction toward a unique urban environment have led local bars and restaurants to start capitalizing on Garbatella being "on the map" as a touristic and leisure site. In recent years, Garbatella has been used as a set for a very popular TV show, leading many viewers to visit the neighborhood. This new image divided residents between those who were enthralled that their local identity was being recognized, those who sought economic advantages from an influx of visitors and tourists, and finally those who considered this change intrusive and a sign of an irreversible change. The president of the borough believes that changes affecting Garbatella will become opportunities only if they are well managed and respect its specificity.[22]

Furthermore, a city-sponsored urban plan (Progetto Urbano Ostiense—Marconi) for the rehabilitation of former industrial sites is radically transforming the south axis of the city and will impact Garbatella. The urban plan was created in 2000 and revised in 2005 and again in 2013. Among the most important interventions it encompasses are the headquarters of the new Roma Tre University, which moved along Via Ostiense and brought a younger population to the district; and the

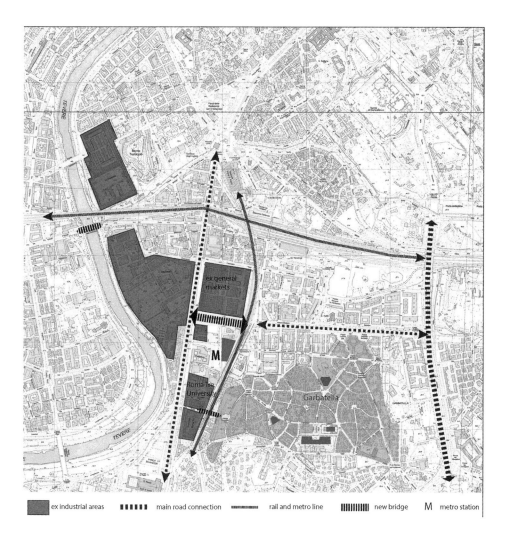

| ex industrial areas | ▮▮▮▮▮ main road connection | ▬▬▬▬▬ rail and metro line | ⦀⦀⦀⦀⦀ new bridge | M metro station |

rehabilitation of the former General Market to include a public library, offices, retail, and entertainment spaces. This latter project was recently interrupted due to a public budget deficit, and the whole urban plan went under revision. In the meantime a new high-tech bridge already connects Garbatella's main commercial street (Circunvallazione Ostiense) to the other side of the railroad tracks (Figure 9.5).

Figure 9.5. This map shows Garbatella today (in the shaded portions), surrounded by former industrial sites currently under redevelopment. (Drawn by Sandra Annunziata)

Conclusion

Today, the iconic garden city of Garbatella, a gem of early twentieth-century urbanism in Rome, described as an example of vibrant urban heritage and as a model

Figure 9.6. Grassroots gardening at Garbatella today. (Photo by Sandra Annunziata)

of good design and collective solidarity, is perceived and treated as a commodity. A slow process affecting rights, immunities, and privileges has ineluctably resulted both in the right to buy housing units and in complete residential privatization, a phenomenon that started before it was legalized, through informal practices. The idea of an open, tolerant, resistant Garbatella, its image as a sociable neighborhood, may become a myth. In actuality it is becoming increasingly exclusive.

At least, the collective open gardens can still remain accessible to all citizens as a collective resource, if a form of self-government based on block organization will prevent the privatization and enclosure of garden spaces and keep them accessible.[23] Such grassroots initiatives are likely to occur when the local activists recall the solidarity and militant spirit that animates Garbatella (Figure 9.6). This approach might offer alternatives to the hegemonic narrative of the "commodified city."

Table 9.1
Summary of Historical Events and Heritage Benchmarks for Garbatella

Year	Event
1903	The state government creates the Istituto Case Popolari (ICP) as an independent public entity in charge of building and managing public housing.
1919	As industries move near Garbatella's site, the Ente Nazionale per lo Sviluppo Marittimo di Roma (SMIR) is founded for the development of an industrial area, designed by the architects Gustavo Giovannoni and Marcello Piacentini.
1920	King Vittorio Emanuele III attends Garbatella's cornerstone ceremony.
1920–22	Giovannoni's first section comprises five blocks, with 190 housing units.
1922	As the fascist regime seizes power, Garbatella counts 3,500 residents.
1923–27	"Fast housing" units are constructed to host people evicted from barracks in central Rome.
1925–26	"Ransom houses" (designed by Plinio Marconi) and apartment blocks target the lower middle class.
1928–29	"Suburban hotels," designed by Ignazio Sabatini, are constructed.
Early 1930s	Kindergarten and elementary schools are erected, ensuring neighborhood identity and autonomy. Garbatella's population reaches 15,000.
1938	ICP is renamed Istituto Autonomo Case Popolari (IACP).
World War II	Episodes of intense solidarity and resistance earn Garbatella its reputation as a unified social block.
1950s	IACP encounters financial difficulties while coping with overcrowding, illegal subleases, and transfers of housing titles.
1965	The general plan for the city of Rome is approved. Garbatella is located in a secondary zone outside the "historic center."
1975	The Ministry of Cultural and Environmental Heritage is created to monitor and implement existing preservation laws.
1993	A national law regulating the alienation of public property introduces right-to-buy legislation. The nationwide sale of public housing ensues. IACP tenants, already granted perpetuity occupation, buy their units at a discounted price.
1999–2000	An urban plan (Progetto Urbano Ostiense—Marconi) calls for the development of the University of Roma Tre headquarters and for the rehabilitation of former industrial structures along Via Ostiense, including the old General Market.
2002	IACP is transformed into ATER (Aziende Territoriali per l'Edilizia Residenziale). The University of Roma Tre renovates the Palladium theater.
2005	The Progetto Urbano Ostiense—Marconi is revised.
2006	Lazio's regional government adopts the most recent *sanatoria* regularization of illegal occupiers of public housing.
2008	Rome's new general plan expands its protected zone to Garbatella, which receives the label of "consolidated urban expansion." This new status entails conservation norms and tax exemption benefits for restoration work.
2010–13	The Progetto Urbano Ostiense—Marconi is newly revised. Budget deficits put the General Market rehabilitation on hold.
	Historic (pre-1970s) Garbatella. Population, approximately 3700; 64 acres [26-ha]; approximately 1900 dwelling units.

NOTES

The present chapter is part of research entitled "Urbanity and Conflict in the Neoliberal City: Rome Neighbourhoods Between Social Practices and Cultural Changes," led by the author at University of Roma Tre, Rome. Part of this work has been developed at Cornell University, Department of City and Regional Planning. The author would like to thank Professor Michael Tomlan for providing the necessary funding to consult the Clarence Stein Papers held at the Cornell University Rare Manuscripts Collection. A special acknowledgment goes to Isabelle Gournay, who provided important suggestions and revisions for this chapter.

1. Giovanni Giolitti was a liberal reformist actively engaged in the extension of democracy and the economic, political, and cultural modernization of the Italian nation-state between 1892 and 1920. In 1903 he passed the law for public housing. See Sabbatucci and Vidotto 2008.

2. In addition to Garbatella, ICP built several new districts in Rome, such as San Saba (1907), the final section of Testaccio (1913–19), and the garden community of Aniene-Montesacro (1923–28), designed respectively by Quadrio Pirani, Ignazio Sabatini, and Gustavo Giovannoni.

3. Community planning in Italy reached its peak with the Fanfani Law in 1949 and the experience of Piano INA Casa. For a detailed work on community planning in Italy during the 1950s, see di Biagi 2010 (2001).

4. The Nathan administration approved the progressive general plan designed by Saint Joust de Teulada. For a detailed planning history of Rome, see Insolera 1981 (1962).

5. Giovannoni and Piacentini were central figures in the field of architecture, planning, and conservation practices in Italy. For a detailed study of the role they played before, during, and after the fascist regime, see Ciucci 1989.

6. Via delle Sette Chiese is an ancient pilgrimage route from S. Paolo Basilica along Via Ostiense, Porta S. Sebastiano, and Via Appia Antica.

7. A fundamental contribution regarding the understanding of the regional style at Garbatella is in Stabile 2001.

8. Among the architects and engineers who contributed to design Garbatella are Gustavo Giovannoni, Innocenzo Sabatini, Plinio Marconi, and Mario Ridolfi.

9. See *Codice dei beni culturali e del paesaggio* art. 10, law July 6, 2002, no. 137. The urban development that occurred before and after the unification of Italy in 1860 is here defined respectively pre- and post-unitarian.

10. The first national planning law in Italy (#1150) was passed in 1942.

11. Property renovation (*ristrutturazione edilizia*) costs can count for up to 36 percent of tax exemption. Since 2012 with the decree of development, the exemption can reach 50 percent.

12. The Modern Observatory in Rome (Osservatorio sul Moderno a Roma) of the Università degli Studi di Roma "La Sapienza" organized an exhibit in 2011 about Garbatella's modern architecture.

13. Law, December 24, 1993, no. 560, Norme in materia di alienazione degli alloggi di edilizia residenziale pubblica. This legislation defines the framework in which the privatization of a public estate should be achieved. It establishes that the regional government will administer the alienation plan for a minimum of 50 percent and a maximum of 75 percent of the total property.

14. Privatization of public residential property occurs in accordance with constitutional norms, in particular art. 47.

15. The income threshold to access public housing in 1999 was 19,000 euros. However, a certain amount of income increase was accepted (until a threshold of 27,000 euros). Theoretically, above this threshold, the household can no longer use public housing.

16. Decreto Legislativo, September 25, 2001, no. 351, Disposizioni urgenti in materia di privatizzazione e valorizzazione del patrimonio immobiliare pubblico e di sviluppo dei fondi comuni di investimento immobiliare.

17. Delibera di approvazione regionale del Piano di vendita triennale degli alloggi di edilizia residenziale pubblica according to *Bollettino ufficiale della Regione Lazio*, no. 36, December 30, 2006, supplemento no. 5, art. 48–54.

18. Delibera consiglio comunale, November 26, 2007, no. 237.

19. In December 2006 the Lazio regional government approved the most recent regularization of illegal occupiers of public housing (estimated to be 5,300 at the time). Other regularizations occurred in 1987–90, 2000, 2003, and 2007, under governments with different political orientations.

20. The revenue from the sale of 2,692 housing units is estimated by Risorse per Roma S.P.A. to be 140 million euros. See http://www.risorse-spa.it.

21. According to the ATER reports, a two-bedroom apartment sold in 2008 for about 40,000 euros in Garbatella. The market value today is 300,000 euros.

22. Interview by the author, with the president of the eleventh bureau of Rome, Marco Catarci, in May 2011.

23. One such case is represented by the garden space called court 51, for which the residents hire a private company to manage the gardens and the utilities (water supplies, electricity, etc.).

REFERENCES

Allen, J., J Barlow, J. Leal, T. Maloutas, and L. Padovani, eds. 2008. *Housing and Welfare in Southern Europe*. Oxford: Blackwell.

Annunziata, S. 2014. "Gentrification in Italy." In *The Changing Italian Cities: Emerging Imbalances and Conflicts*," Urban Studies Working Paper, no. 6, edited by A. G. Calafati, 23–34. Gran Sasso Science Institute, L'Aquila, Italy.

———. 2017. "Exploring the Incidence of Ownership: Evolving Forms of Tenure in Iconic Garden Communities: The Case of Sunnyside, New York and Garbatella, Rome." *Planning Perspectives* 32 (1): 1–22.

———. 2018. "Learning Throughout Comparison: Exploring Gentrifying Neighbourhoods as Political Spaces in Rome and New York City." In *New Developments in Southern European Housing,* edited by E. Bargelli, T. Heitkamp, 167–82. Pisa: Pisa University Press.

Avarello, P., R. D'Errico, A. L. Palazzo, and C. M. Travaglini, eds. 2004. "Il quadrante Ostiense tra otto e novecento." *Roma Moderna e Contemporanea* 12: 1–2.

Babonaux, A. M. S. 1983. *Roma: dalla città alla metropoli*. Venezia: Editori Riuniti.

Bonavita, A., et al. 2010. *Il moderno attraverso Roma: Guida all'architettura moderna della Garbatella, Osservatorio sul Moderna a Roma*. Rome: Palombi Editori.

Bridge, G., T. Butler, and L. Lees, eds. 2012. *Mixed Communities: Gentrification by Stealth?* Bristol: Policy Press.

Ciucci, G. 1989. *Gli architetti e il fascismo: Architettura e città 1922–1944*. Turin: Einaudi.

Comune di Roma. 2005. "Norme Tecniche di Attuazione." In *Nuovo Piano Regolatore Generale di Roma* [New General Plan of Rome]. http://www.urbanistica.comune.roma.it/prg.html.

Costantini, I. 1922. "L'Istituto per le case popolari a Roma. La borgata giardino Garbatella." *Architettura e arti decorative* 3: 121.

De Michelis, A. 2009. "The Garden Suburb of the Garbatella, 1920–1929: Defining Community and Identity Through Planning in Post-War Rome." *Planning Perspectives* 24: 510.

di Biagi, P. 2010 [2001]. *La grande ricostruzione: Il piano Ina-Casa e l'Italia degli anni cinquanta.* Rome: Donzelli.

Giovannoni, G. 1931. *Vecchie città ed edilizia nuova.* Turin: Utet.

Herzfeld, M. 2009. *Evicted from Eternity: The Restructuring of Modern Rome.* Chicago: University of Chicago Press.

Howard, E. 1965. *Garden Cities of To-morrow.* Cambridge, MA: MIT Press.

Insolera, I. 1981 [1962]. *Roma moderna.* Rome: Einaudi.

Leontidou, L. 1990. *Mediterranean Cities in Transition: Social Change and Urban Development.* Cambridge: Cambridge University Press.

Marcuse, P. 1994. "Property Right, Tenure and Ownership: Toward a Clarity in Concept." In *Social Rented Housing in Europe: Policy, Tenure and Design,* edited by Bert Donermark and Ingemar Elander, 21–39. Delft: Delft University Press.

———. 1996. "Privatization and Its Discontents: Property Rights in Land and Housing in Eastern Europe." In *Cities After Socialism: Urban and Regional Change and Conflict in Post-Socialist Societies,* edited by G. Andrusz, M. Harloe, and I. Szelenyi, 119–91. Oxford: Blackwell.

Rappino, S. 1975. "La Garbatella. Logica di formazione del quartiere." In *Lettura progettazione del contesto urbano Ostiense di Roma,* edited by V. Vannelli, 163–207. Rome: Edizioni Kappa.

Rivolta, G. 2006. *I ribelli di testaccio, ostiense e Garbatella.* Rome: Cara Garbatella.

———. 2010. *Garbatella tra storia e leggenda.* Rome: Iacobelli.

Rivolta, G., and E. Gori. 2003. *Garbatella mia.* Rome: La Campanella.

Sabbatucci, G., and V. Vidotto. 2008. *Storia contemporanea, il novecento.* Bari: Edizioni Laterza.

Sinatra, Monica. 2006. *La Garbatella a Roma 1920–1940.* Milan: Franco Angeli.

Stabile, F. R. 2001. *Regionalismo a Roma tipi e linguaggi: Il caso della Garbatella.* Rome: Dedalo.

Vidotto, V. 2001. *Roma contemporanea.* Rome: Laterza.

Webster, C. J. 2007. "Property Rights, Public Space and Urban Design." *Town Planning Review* 78(1): 81–101.

Zucconi, G., ed. 1997. *Dal capitello alla città.* Milan: Jaca Book.

———. 2002. "Un manuale Mancato." In *I classici dell'urbanistica moderna,* edited by P. di Biagi, 55–66. Rome: Donzelli.

CHAPTER 10

SUNNYSIDE GARDENS AND RADBURN

The Common Legacy and

Divergent Experiences of Community Life

John J. Pittari Jr.

As the most tangible physical results of the partnership between leaders of the pioneering Regional Planning Association of America (RPAA) and City Housing Corporation (CHC), the iconic planned communities of Sunnyside Gardens and Radburn share a close heritage. Developed consecutively during the 1920s under the close direction of CHC president Alexander Bing and the architect-planner team of Clarence Stein and Henry Wright,[1] both Sunnyside Gardens and Radburn were conceived as practical experiments to realize the "garden city" ideal in America. They embodied innovative combinations of spatial arrangements and legal instruments as the foundation for their innovative master plans; large-scale production measures, financing mechanisms, and real estate development practices were the basis of their implementation and management. Central to their creation was the firm belief of the individuals involved that the physical design of a development could strongly influence and, in fact, encourage the creation of a social community among the residents. The main purpose of the CHC, as Stein put it, was "to create a setting in which a democratic community might grow" (1957, 34). Thus, while Sunnyside Gardens and Radburn have significantly different layouts, they both utilize a common physical framework of shared open space as their major formative element and intended means of community building. As the initial endeavor, Sunnyside Gardens also provided valuable lessons to be learned and subsequently employed in the planning, construction, and operation of Radburn, giving these "paired" planned communities, both of which represent an ambitious vision of dwelling, an intriguing component of evolutionary development.

Of equal significance, over the course of their nearly ninety-year lifetimes, these two neighborhood communities have substantively sustained their character in the face of change, though in quite differing degrees and manners. While Sunnyside Gardens has witnessed a number of significant clashes of interest among its diversity of residents involving adaptations that have occurred to both the built form and its regulatory mechanisms, Radburn's preservation and aging have been relatively smooth throughout the years—though it has experienced considerable contention during the past decade over important matters of governance. Despite its struggles, Sunnyside Gardens has survived reasonably well as a valued human habitat—a fact made particularly evident by its designation in 2007 as a local historic district by the New York City Landmarks Preservation Commission. Radburn itself has been listed on the National Register of Historic Places since 1975, and it was designated as a National Historic Landmark in 2005—a reflection not only of its well-preserved physical condition, but also of the sizable influence that its conceptual foundation has had on subsequent new town developments throughout the country (and, in fact, around the world). Considered separately or as a pair, these two iconic planned communities have clearly been, and remain today, meaningful places for their inhabitants—as well as valuable real estate properties that command a premium in comparison to their surroundings (Lee and Stabin-Smith 2001).

This chapter explores the historic and contemporary records of Sunnyside Gardens and Radburn, highlighting similarities and differences in their initial conceptions and subsequent experiences, and investigating the particular roles that their spatial arrangements and associated structures of governance have played in not only sustaining their common visions of utilizing shared open space as a means of building community, but also differentiating their methods of doing so as well. The focus herein on the social processes of shared governance as an important key to the past preservation record of these two noteworthy places—and, one might surmise, as an equally important element in their future records—is grounded in several notions. First, the planners' intent that their physical designs would foster social interaction and sound community organization presages a basic correlation between the physical and social realms, an interface that is at least partially embedded in the "private" regulatory framework that requires a close interaction of the residents in order to govern the collective aspects of their environments. Second, both of these iconic places, and especially Radburn, are meaningful elements in the historic continuum of American suburban development and are thereby reflective of significant cultural values regarding homeownership and material well-being. As the preservation scholar David Ames has stated of such historic suburbs, it is hard to grasp their true measure only through their physical plans, for they also "represent the fulfillment of deeply held values about home in American society" (1995, 105), a consideration that gives added weight to the social interactions within these communities, and particularly as they regard preservation-related endeavors. Third, and finally, contemporary ecological studies of sustainable communities indicate that such entities "evolve their patterns of living over time [through] continual interaction" (Capra 2003, 230) among their inherent systems—which, in human communities, includes both physical and social systems. Therefore, an examination of the different ways by which the residents of these two communities have interacted socially in order to govern their respective physical heritages seems an important consideration not only in appreciating their preservation histories, but also in contemplating their associated futures.

Sunnyside Gardens

Despite the desire of the CHC development team to undertake their experimental 1920s design and planning endeavors on a sizable parcel of "greenfield" land that was not yet subdivided, the property purchased for their first effort was located in the borough of Queens in New York City and was already arranged into the standard grid of blocks, streets, and lots (CHC 1930). Unable to substantially alter this fairly ubiquitous urban context, they were forced to fit their desired building arrangements into the preexisting blocks in their attempt to creatively arrange a harmonious whole. Ironically, it is this very framework that contributes much to the physical character and distinction of the neighborhood, as it has allowed the development to simultaneously blend and contrast with its less-sophisticated urban surroundings. An additionally important consideration is that this circumstance also allowed the development team to take advantage of the existing municipal services and employment opportunities, and thus simplified this initial effort in comparison to the later Radburn. While they were limited by the relatively fixed urban pattern of blocks and streets, they were free to experiment with an arrangement of mixed building and housing types because the site was zoned for industrial use rather than residential. Thus, building in modules of singular blocks as their basic planning units, they carefully combined a mixture of simply designed and spatially modest dwelling unit types into handsome, brick, linear structures of human scale arranged around the perimeter of the blocks, with each group composed as a harmonious ensemble of primarily two-story row houses (several blocks also include apartment buildings, which are three or four stories). Notably, construction proceeded without the benefit of an overall master plan, and it was completed incrementally over the course of four years (1924–28), with typically a few entire blocks being built during each phase, so that the neighborhood grew as a progression of discrete wholes.

Conceived primarily to house moderate-income working families in relatively close proximity without crowding, the innovative layout of buildings and grounds can well be considered to be "sub-urban" in character, as it also ensured an abundance of light, fresh air, trees, and lawn for all residents—quite suburban attributes for a clearly urban context. Sunnyside Gardens, moreover, incorporated a novel concept of shared open space that was neither fully public (such as a park owned and run by the government) nor fully private (individual yards maintained solely by their owners), and which deliberately clouded the distinction between those two realms. Perhaps it is not surprising that this same distinguishing concept would prove to be a confusing one over the longer term, particularly to many of the more contemporary residents, and would present a real challenge to the effective governance and preservation of these unique shared spaces.

Going beyond the mere, yet notable, provision of affordable homeownership and possible upward mobility for those of moderate means, the design of Sunnyside Gardens is quite remarkable in several other aspects, including its residential density and diversity, architectural character, and open-space scheme. While representing a significant reduction in the average density of a typical New York City block, for instance, the neighborhood plan employed a density of just over twenty units/acre (1,200 units on about sixty acres of developed land), one that is appreciably higher than the typical suburban model. Even better, this density was achieved by using only 28 percent of the land, leaving the remainder available for use as a communal network of landscaped open spaces, thus giving real substance to the "gardens" moniker.

Placed close to the street edge in a fairly continuous, yet subtly modulated, low-rise wall, the structures were set back just enough to allow a small, semiprivate front garden for each home, with a sidewalk and street trees between it and the curbed roadway. More significantly, this layout provided maximum land behind the homes, each of which had a slightly larger, private rear yard facing the shared central courtyard gardens (Figure 10.1). Probably the most innovative and significant aspect of the master plan, these common grounds (courts) and their connecting pathways formed a simple network of landscaped spaces running throughout the development, and they were created using a pioneering set of easements and restrictive covenants that overlaid the preexisting platted lots, because lending institutions were hesitant to risk changing the underlying lot arrangement. These deed restrictions also included fairly tight controls on building and garden alterations by the residents and were to last for a period of forty years from the time of initial construction, at which time they could be renewed by a vote of the residents. Overall, governance was quite local, as a dozen court/block associations were formed to adopt and administer their own specific rules for each of the central courts and, in turn, to elect a body of representatives (the trustees) to oversee the entire neighborhood. The court associations were typically composed of two residents from that particular block, either owners or renters; two CHC employees; and one person not involved with either entity.

Combined with the neighborhood's aspirations toward a strong sense of community and its basic affordability, the mixture of dwelling types helped to attract

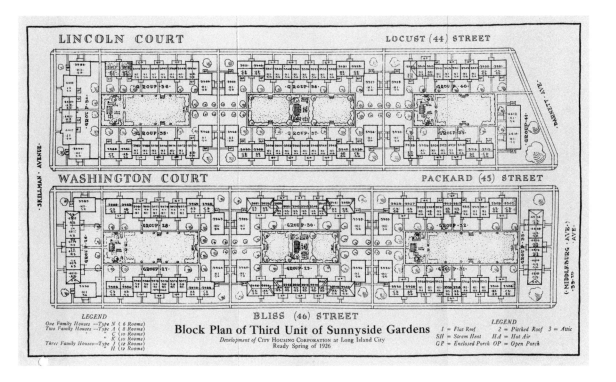

LINCOLN COURT   LOCUST (44) STREET

WASHINGTON COURT   PACKARD (45) STREET

SKILLMAN · AVENUE

·MIDDLEBURG · AVE·

DABNEY AVE.

BLISS (46) STREET

GROUP 36 · *GROUP 38* · *GROUP 40*

GROUP 35 · *GROUP 37* · *GROUP 39*

GROUP 26 · *GROUP 30* · *GROUP 32*

GROUP 27 · *GROUP 29* · *GROUP 31*

LEGEND

One Family Houses —Type N (6 Rooms)
Two Family Houses —Type A (8 Rooms)
"   "   C (10 Rooms)
"   K (10 Rooms)
Three Family Houses—Type J (12 Rooms)
"   H (12 Rooms)

Block Plan of Third Unit of Sunnyside Gardens
Development of City Housing Corporation at Long Island City
Ready Spring of 1926

LEGEND

1 = Flat Roof   2 = Pitched Roof   3 = Attic
SH = Steam Heat   HA = Hot Air
GP = Enclosed Porch   OP = Open Porch

what was a fairly diverse group of early inhabitants.[2] Aside from the attached single-family homes, Sunnyside Gardens notably contains two- and three-family houses, plus separate, yet integrated, apartment buildings (including some of the first cooperative units in the country); and all units were targeted for residents of moderate means, either as owners or tenants. This provision, in turn, helped allow for a resident population with various incomes, occupations, backgrounds, and household sizes—they were largely working families (two-thirds earned less than the median income) comprising laborers and professionals, intellectuals and artists, and a healthy dose of both children and political activists. Nearly half of the initial inhabitants were immigrants from Manhattan's Lower East Side, including some members of the Labor and Communist parties who brought along their political bent. Interestingly, while the neighborhood has seen periods of homogenization over the years, it is again quite diverse demographically, and it includes a sizable population of new international immigrants from a broad range of ethnicities.[3]

In addition to housing and the shared courts, the planners ensured the provision of additional community facilities such as a school site, parking garages, and retail spaces and meeting rooms in the ground floor of some of the apartment

Figure 10.1. Block layout for Sunnyside Gardens (1924) showing housing units arranged around the perimeter and interior court spaces. (Clarence Stein Papers, #3600, Division of Rare and Manuscript Collections, Cornell University Library)

buildings. This reflected their wish to create the framework for
a truly democratic community, one with plenty of social interaction and shared responsibility, a desire obviously enhanced
by the inclusion of community spaces, both built and open.
Based on their subsequent decision that outdoor space other
than the courts was needed for active recreation, a three-acre
neighborhood park was built in 1926 for the sole use of Sunnyside Gardeners—it included several areas for active sports and
a children's playground, which then allowed the central courts
to remain as more intimate spaces for passive recreation (see
Figure 10.2). This private park was maintained with low membership fees charged by the newly formed Sunnyside Gardens Civic Association,
which served to manage the park and to facilitate and host numerous social endeavors for the benefit of the entire neighborhood.

Radburn

Even as the middle phases of Sunnyside Gardens were still being completed, the
planning team (in 1926) was already developing designs for their next experiment
in housing and community building, a more complete conception that they char-

acterized as the Radburn Idea, to be undertaken as a planned new town in suburban New Jersey.[4] Based more directly and fully on Ebenezer Howard's garden city prescriptions, Radburn was initially intended to be a stand-alone new community, one in an eventual regional network of planned garden city developments. Unable to realize the essential elements of an industrial/employment base and a surrounding greenbelt, however, the developers moved forward with shaping as complete a community as possible, and one that would still incorporate a remarkably novel scheme, the basic features for which Radburn would become internationally known. What that would also mean, however, was that Radburn would quickly come to function as a more conventional suburban bedroom community within the metropolitan region, albeit one with a distinctive physical arrangement and program of community facilities and activities. The planners' aspirations were enhanced by the fact that there were no physical or regulatory constraints as there had been with Sunnyside Gardens—the Radburn site was neither subdivided nor zoned. Thus, the Radburn Idea could be fully conceptualized into the master plan for the intended town of Radburn, carrying forward some basic concepts from Sunnyside Gardens, but also introducing a new and radical revision to the conventional relationships among the roadways, blocks, houses, pathways, and parks.

The fundamental planning unit in this case was the superblock, which comprised parkland at the core (as a direct extension of a core Sunnyside Gardens principle), an array of short culs-de-sac with adjoining homes clustered around the edge, and narrow park "fingers" with pedestrian pathways situated between each pair of culs-de-sac. When these superblocks were then grouped together, they provided a continuous ribbon of parkland that served as the backbone of the development—in effect, the notion of a surrounding greenbelt turned inside out. The so-called reverse-front homes had entries onto both the cul-de-sac, for automobile and service access, and the park "finger," for connection via the pathway to the central parkland; their internal plans were organized accordingly, with kitchen and service areas adjoining the cul-de-sac, and living and sleeping areas fronting the pathway to the park, along with a private backyard (Figure 10.3). Safety from the automobile was a primary planning concern, particularly for children using the park pathways, so vehicular and pedestrian circulation routes were separated within the superblock by designing overpasses for connecting through-roadways (Figure 10.4). In total, these elements were combined into a revolutionary but very pleasant composition wherein no house was more than four hundred feet from either park or major roadway (Figure 10.5); the parklands comprised more than 15 percent, and the roadways only 21 percent, of the total site area; and a residential density of just under five units per acre was achieved (680 units on about 150 acres—a much lower density than Sunnyside Gardens, but slightly higher than comparable suburban developments).

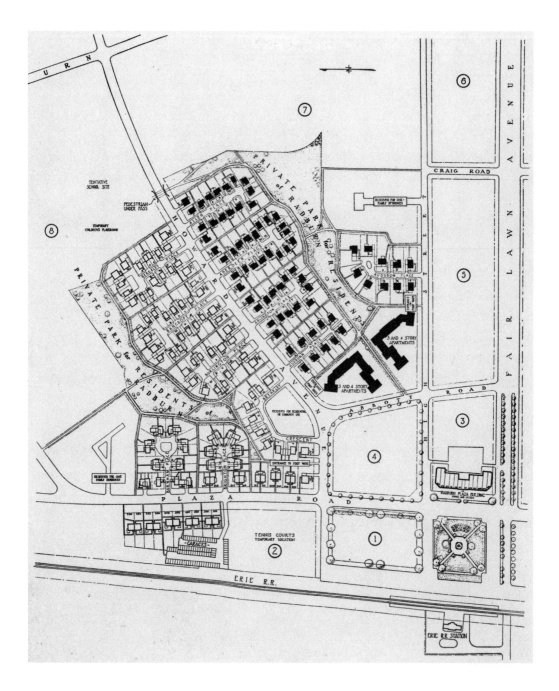

Figure 10.3. The Radburn plan as originally conceived in 1928—only the buildings in black were actually constructed. (Clarence Stein Papers, #3600, Division of Rare and Manuscript Collections, Cornell University Library)

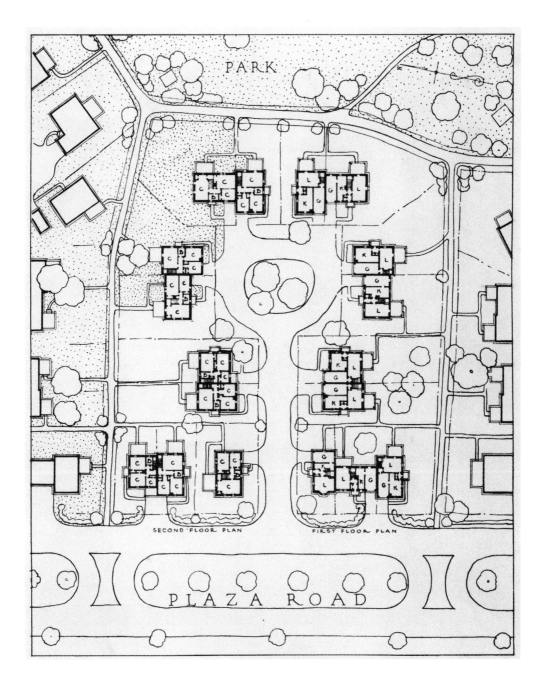

Figure 10.4. A layout of a single Radburn cul-de-sac, showing "reverse front" houses with automobile access from the street (in the rear) and pedestrian access to a large interior park via pathway in the park "finger" (in the front). (Clarence Stein Papers, #3600, Division of Rare and Manuscript Collections, Cornell University Library)

Figure 10.5. A current view of an interior park and inner pathways at Radburn. (Photo by John Pittari Jr.)

The architecture was generally more conservative than that of Sunnyside Gardens, a deliberate decision by the designers, who felt that they were introducing enough unusual ideas in regard to the plan and community organization that the residents needed a style (typically Colonial) that was more familiar and reassuring. While apartment houses were located on the periphery, the dwelling units were mostly detached single-family homes, which were again subtly mixed in both type and style—but in contrast to Sunnyside Gardens, they were designed for middle- to upper-middle-class families. The development team's increased focus—in conjunction with the growing national trend toward mass suburbanization for the middle classes—on planning for families, especially children (who composed 28 percent of the early residents), and the resultant costs involved with providing high-quality (yet still modest) housing plus an ambitious program of community facilities for this resident population, made it largely unaffordable for those of moderate means. The mounting disparity with Sunnyside Gardens was made even more evident in the early population of Radburn, which was quite homogeneous in terms of background, income, education, and occupation. Most of the men were upper-middle-class executives and professionals working in white-collar business or corporate jobs and commuting into New York City on a daily basis; more than three-fourths of both men and women were college-educated, at a time when the vast majority of Americans were not. Some of this was a reflection of the aforementioned national trends, but it was also an expression of the planners' increased consideration, based on their early observations of Sunnyside Gardeners, that shared values and experiences seemed to be important attributes for the type of cohesive community life they intended. In order to ensure this condition, in fact, realtors hired by the CHC encouraged those of like mind to buy, and discouraged those who were not (including blacks and Jews), a policy that was apparently met with indifference by the developers and residents alike (Schaffer 1982).

Further based on their experience with Sunnyside Gardens, the developers also proposed an approach to community management and organization that was more singular, centralized, and controlled. In fact, they purposefully wanted to avoid what they saw as a highly personal policing of each other by Sunnyside Gardeners, a monitoring that was stricter than they had intended and that produced its share of tension among neighbors. The use of deed restrictions for individual homeowners continued as at the prior development, though in addition to addressing matters of architectural and garden regulation, they were expanded significantly to include the provision of necessary public services that were as yet unavailable from the local borough of Fair Lawn. The fees required for these additional services were tied to the specific home value and collected by the Radburn Association, a nonprofit governing body incorporated not only to administer these monies (which would later expand in scope to become the Radburn Fund) and arrange the public services, but also to maintain the common property, enforce the deed restrictions, set general policy, and provide recreational programs (Radburn Association 1929).

A separate Radburn Citizens Association, with membership open to all residents, was also created to serve as a forum to discuss matters of public interest, to communicate citizen opinion to the Radburn Association, and to foster the development of community life. From the start, the CHC purposefully composed the governing Radburn Association largely of nonresidents, either civic-minded volunteers or CHC employees, because they felt the residents would not yet be able to manage their community—but would hopefully grow into that position. Only the trustees themselves were allowed to nominate prospective new members for election by the larger community, giving the Radburn Association an additional measure of control over this important, and supposedly democratic, political process. Given the relatively traditional values and concerns of the early residents—protection of property values, maintenance of homes, continuance of family and community activities—this arrangement was also apparently none too problematic.

The Nature of Community Life

Given the evolutionary, yet conceptually related, physical designs that resulted in the development of these two communities, what is particularly interesting are the remarkably different social histories their residents have since experienced. Almost from the start, Sunnyside Gardeners have consistently, and quite intimately, faced a set of challenges involving the interfaces between individual and collective needs, between private and "shared" (public) property, and between living within the planned framework and adapting it to suit changing conditions (Place in History 2001) (Figures 10.6 and 10.7). On the other hand, residents of Radburn, while certainly facing important challenges of their own, have had what could be considered a more conventional experience with suburban community life. The first significant challenge both communities would face was the severe economic hardship brought on by the Great Depression, wherein many inhabitants, who were carrying a mortgage for the first time, were now struggling severely to make payments. This would quickly become a circumstance that led not only to the abbreviation of Radburn's development, but also to the early demise of the CHC itself due to financial ruin— and a clear indication of the different social natures of the two resident populations.

In Sunnyside Gardens, many of the early residents already shared a vigorous sense of political activism, a trait that clearly came into play during this troubled time. They banded closely together and quickly formed the Consolidated Home Owners Mortgage Committee, to which over half of the homeowners belonged. They participated collectively in zealous rent and mortgage payment strikes against the developer, filed suits against the CHC in federal court, publicly heckled CHC directors (such as Eleanor Roosevelt); and engaged in acts of disorderly conduct such as blockading their doors against law enforcement officials serving foreclosure notices on them. Despite these rather vigorous engagements, over half of the residents lost their homes over the next decade (Lasker 1936). While facing similar financial hardships, the residents of Radburn conducted themselves in a more conservative manner and merely petitioned the CHC to postpone mortgage payments. There were no violent confrontations or legal actions, and in fact, decades later, residents still commend the CHC for their efforts and fondly recall the episode as a time of sacrifice, cooperation, and community spirit. Perhaps the primary issue that lingered from this episode for Radburn residents concerned their future governance structure, especially in terms of representation on overseeing the Radburn Association, particularly after the CHC was defunct. In line with their prior collective action, however, they allowed for the gradual transformation of their political framework such that by 1948, all Radburn Association members were residents of Radburn, and the Citizens Association president became a de facto member

Figure 10.6. Interior court in Sunnyside Gardens (2010) broken up by "fenced-off" individual lots. These disruptions occurred after the 1960s lapse of easement agreements and deed restrictions. (Photo by Isabelle Gournay)

Figure 10.7. Interior of a "preserved" block in Sunnyside Gardens (2015), showing (from right to left) a small private garden/deck in the rear yard, a walkway, and a court. (Photo by John J. Pittari Jr.)

(today there is also a full-time paid manager position). For the most part, other than a battle around this same time with local non-Radburn residents over the need for a new high school, the revision of their governance structure would be the biggest issue the early residents of Radburn would face as they settled into advancing their own domestic pursuits during the coming decades.

Both neighborhoods, fortunately, had recovered well from the Depression years by the time of the postwar economic boom of the late 1940s. Sunnyside Gardens, however, now took on a distinctly middle-class character, earning a nickname as "the maternity ward of Greenwich Village" due to the prevalence of young couples from Manhattan moving in to start families (along with many from other locations) (Rappaport with Saltzman 1991). A healthy and neighborly social life took hold again there, though the level of collective political action subsided in line with the prosperity of the time. Some of the public and common spaces saw minor disrepair as a partial result, and individual owners began to impinge on their deed restrictions, constructing small building additions or paving over front gardens for private driveways. Recognizing that the framework of open-space easements, along with all the other restrictive covenants and related civic organizations, would soon expire without a vote to continue them, many court associations also undertook discussions to renew these shared agreements, which meant so much to the fundamental identity of the neighborhood.

Unable to accomplish this important task, however, the community witnessed the widespread expiration of these rules in the mid-1960s (only one court association voted for full renewal), an occurrence that meant that the city's municipal building code now became the primary regulatory mechanism for individual owners. Apparently quite comfortable with this new situation, many residents made long-desired, and now legal, alterations to their properties, including substantial façade renovations, the addition of porches and decks, curb cuts and driveways, and, perhaps most ominously, fencing off portions of the common courts for private use (see Figure 10.7). Not surprisingly, the community became badly split between those who favored allowing such changes and those interested in preserving more closely the intended identity and character of the neighborhood. With residents still unable to resolve this serious dispute during the coming years, the City Planning Commission declared the neighborhood a Special Planned Community Preservation District in 1974, a zoning designation that recognized its distinctive planned qualities and mandated the approval of special permits for any further physical alterations. Previous changes were allowed to remain, however, and the new designation gave no provision for refurbishing the damaged central courts, which would soon amount to just over half of their original number, nor for restoring the integrity of most of the court associations.

Slowly, the community began to re-organize itself with the formation of a neighborhood land conservancy, the Sunnyside Foundation for Community Planning and Preservation, in 1981. Structured around the old court associations and composed of both older and newer residents, the foundation utilized a "backyard strategy of enlightened self-interest" (Robbins 1985, 18) and sought to rekindle the cooperative community spirit by offering financial incentives to owners who returned their yards to the common courts, by sponsoring larger community events, and by undertaking preservation endeavors and revitalization activities. These efforts achieved a measure of success on the ground, including the reactivation of many court associations and a neighborhood listing on the National Register of Historic Places, and they helped somewhat to restore the community spirit. The Historic Place designation, while another mark of distinction, brought with it no binding legal implications for individual residents (Havelick and Kwartler 1982). On the other hand, the special zoning requirements did carry the rule of law, and a number of residents who continued to view them as too restrictive promoted a rezoning proposal that would allow as-of-right construction for minor physical alterations to their properties. This move, in turn, inspired preservation-minded counterproposals from the foundation, again putting the City Planning Commission in the position of having to consider these competing visions (Ferris 2003).

With no resolution coming forward, however, the Landmarks Preservation Commission (LPC) eventually became the forum for these battles (Efthimiades 2004), and its 2007 decision to designate Sunnyside Gardens as a local historic district was a clear indication that, despite prior incursions to the fabric of the buildings and courts, much of the basic physical framework remained extant (Betts and Caratzas 2007). This decision, which also carried the rule of law under New York City codes, made the LPC the primary administrator of the neighborhood's built environment (NYC LPC 2007), a position reinforced by a 2009 amendment to the special zoning district provisions that eliminated duplicate reviews and ensured a complementary relationship between zoning provisions and landmark regulations. Since the local historic district designation, nine applications have come before the LPC. Most of these requested relatively minor building alterations and often related to the rear façade or an area within the rear yard. Only one application was denied, and that one was unusual in seeking the approval (or forgiveness) of already-installed security doors and windows on the front façade. While this new public regulatory framework may best ensure the neighborhood's physical preservation, the question of whether or not it will perhaps diminish the close, and sometimes conflicted, interaction of neighbors that has sustained, in part, the community's social vitality for over eighty years is yet to be seen—but so far, so good.

Either way, despite their frequent note of discord, the temporal ebbs and flows of the attempts undertaken by Sunnyside Gardeners to accommodate change while retaining their neighborhood identity is a legacy of Stein and Wright's original consideration of this pioneering development as a social experiment in building better homes and communities. They firmly believed that "guaranteed open space and pleasing buildings, offered to a socially and economically diverse collection of urban dwellers, would diminish differences in income, education, and culture, and in turn lead to improved community morale and the possibility for collective action" (Turner 2001, 7). Although they could not foresee the measure of conflict that has sometimes resulted, the planners also generally felt that any such challenges to the cooperative spirit of the community would eventually serve to strengthen the cohesive fiber of the residents. As Wright proudly said of the "neighborly considerations" needed to enforce the pathway easements, shared open space, and deed restrictions during the early years in Sunnyside Gardens, they "helped to weld [it] into a thoroughly conscious and workable community unparalleled in any similar experiment in this country" (Wright 1933, 92).

Based on the experience with Sunnyside Gardens and its resident population, however, it is clear that the planning team deliberately sought—or, at the least, allowed for—a more homogenized and centralized community life at Radburn. One conclusion is that they felt there was a clear threshold to such character-building conflict and that they hoped to minimize any such controversies in their second effort while still ensuring a strong community identity and spirit. Radburn's past has given merit to these aspirations, as throughout the years, physical changes have mostly involved both a not-surprising increased vehicular presence in the culs-de-sac and minor home alterations, and residents have generally experienced a more peaceful community life (McClelland and Reed 2004). There hasn't been much controversy of note in regard to enforcement of the deed restrictions, and the residents largely supported both of its historic designations (onto the National Register of Historic Places in 1975 and as a National Historic Landmark in 2005), as desirable and noteworthy marks of distinction—though, again, these designations carry no binding legal implications for individual residents.

An issue that has flared periodically, however, has been that of community governance, particularly regarding representation on the Radburn Association—and the past decade has witnessed the eruption of these lasting concerns, the result of which has been a very serious, contentious, and litigious battle over this important issue. While the residents' viewpoints differ on the specific catalyst, the record suggests a strong link between rising concerns by members of the Citizens Association over the composition and financial decision making of the governing Radburn Association

Top

Plate 1. Current view of New Lanark village and mills on the River Clyde. (Photo by John Minnery)

Bottom

Plate 2. Bird's-eye view of New Lanark, from a series commissioned by Robert Owen in 1818. While using period conventions for spatial rendering, this watercolor by the art teacher John Winning, who worked for the New Lanark Textile Mills, is an accurate rendition, which current visitors can identify with. (Courtesy New Lanark Trust; www.newlanark.org)

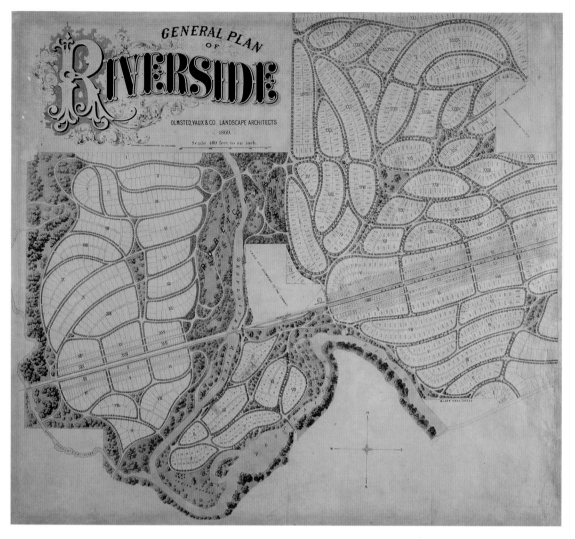

Plate 3. General Plan of Riverside, by Olmsted, Vaux & Company Landscape Architects, 1869. (Courtesy of the United States Department of the Interior, National Park Service, Frederick Law Olmsted National Historic Site)

Opposite

Plate 4. The Parkway in Welwyn Garden City is the key central vista of Louis de Soissons's iconic layout of 1921; it flourishes in springtime in this view looking south toward the Jubilee Fountain of 1970. (Photo by Mervyn Miller)

Plate 5. The Spirella Corset Factory, built 1912–22 by the architect Cecil Hignett. In 1996–99, this landmark of Letchworth underwent an award-winning £10-million regeneration by its owners, Letchworth Garden City Heritage Foundation. (Photo by Mervyn Miller)

"There is no place like home" in UPLANDS

Plate 6. Cover of a promotional pamphlet depicting the "far outlook" view of Mount Baker in Washington State, seen through the picture window of a house on Beach Drive in Uplands. (Reprinted from The Uplands Limited, "There Is No Place Like Home in *UPLANDS*" [Victoria: Acme Press, 1922])

Plate 8. Designed by Jacobus Mooijen, the Dutch architect in charge of Menteng's plan, Kuntskring (1914) served as the cultural center for Batavia's European community. Renovated in the early 2000s, it currently houses an upscale restaurant. (Photo by Christopher Silver)

Plate 7. Detail of the *La Redenzione dell'Agro* (The redemption of the Pontine area), painted in tempera on Eternit panels by Duilio Cambellotti in 1934 on three adjacent walls of the Council room of the Palazzo del Governo in Littoria (now Latina). Around the city center, one can see the network of roads and canals with the individual farmhouses (*poderi*). On the bottom edge are soldiers, farmers, and cattle, symbolizing the fascist renewal of the region. (Photo by Jean-François Lejeune)

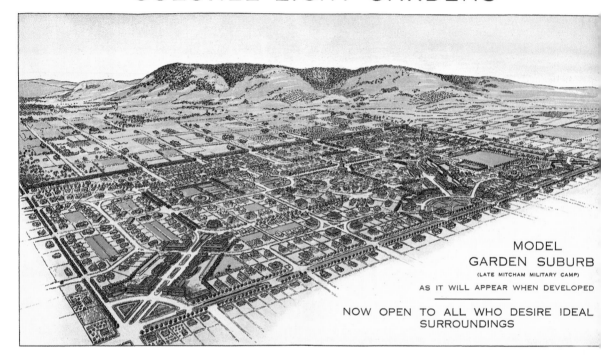

SOUTH AUSTRALIAN GOVERNMENT

COLONEL LIGHT GARDENS

MODEL
GARDEN SUBURB
(LATE MITCHAM MILITARY CAMP)

AS IT WILL APPEAR WHEN DEVELOPED

NOW OPEN TO ALL WHO DESIRE IDEAL
SURROUNDINGS

Plate 9. "Colonel Light Gardens Model Garden Suburb as it will appear when developed." Color image produced by the South Australian government and based on the Mitcham Garden Suburb bird's-eye perspective, drawn in 1917 by D. W. Crawford. (Courtesy Colonel Light Gardens Historical Society; original held at the Mitcham Heritage Research Centre)

Plate 10. In Den-en Chōfu, a few remaining original houses were built in the 1920s in the Japanese style, such as this one, which is almost impossible to photograph because it is surrounded by carefully manicured trees. (Photo by André Sorensen)

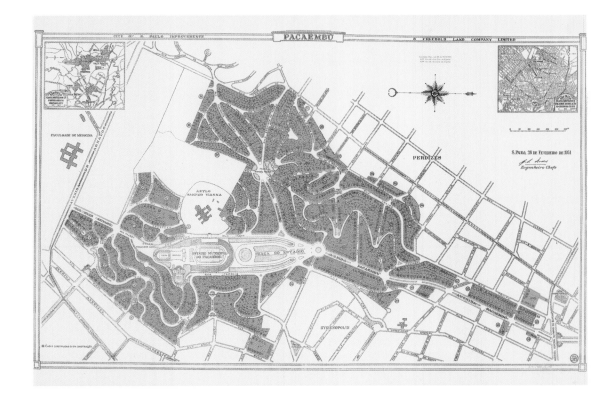

Plate 13. The 1920s witnessed remarkable housing experiments at Garbatella, ending with the *alberghi suburbani* (suburban hotels), designed by Ignazio Sabatini. This "red hotel" was a dormitory designed to temporarily house people evicted from the city center. After World War II it became a socially stable apartment block. (Photo by Sandra Annunziata)

Opposite

Plate 11. This 1951 plan reflects São Paulo's Pacaembu district as built. (Courtesy Cia CITY Archives)

Plate 12. Current aerial view of Pacaembu. The soccer stadium was erected on land that planner Barry Parker intended for a garden. (Courtesy Cia CITY Archives)

Plate 14. The separation of vehicular and pedestrian circulation in Radburn (planned in 1928) is accomplished via roadway overpass and this picturesque walkway underpass. (Photo by John J. Pittari Jr.)

Plate 15. Partial axonometric view of the Cité Frugès, published in *L'Architecture Vivante* in 1927. Le Corbusier combined garden city planning with an urban residential typology and with his distinctive approach to architectural polychromy. (Courtesy Fondation Le Corbusier)

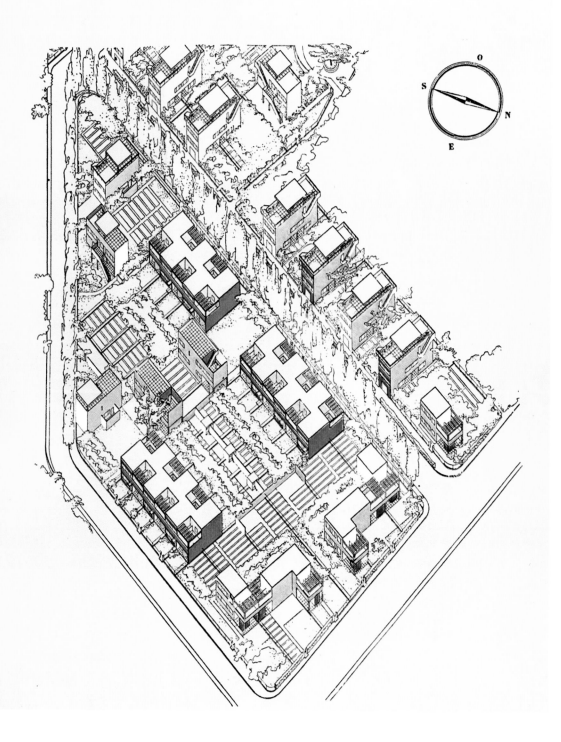

Plate 16. Current view of Frankfurt's Römerstadt housing estate (1927). The front yards to the left are obscured by parked cars, and shrubs and trees of unorchestrated variety mar the once-cohesive street design. (Photo by Susan R. Henderson)

Opposite

Plate 17. This type of "elephant house" (the curved roof rounds like an elephant's back) accommodates two to three families in Soweto's Mofolo/Jabavu and in Orlando West township areas. (Photo by Angel David Nieves)

Plate 18. Wythenshawe in 2016: cottage housing evokes garden city roots, while the plane presages the new hub role of the Enterprise Zone. (Photo courtesy Ian Canham/ Alamy Stock Photo)

Plate 19. Children enjoy themselves as parents look on at a festival held in Roosevelt Center. Historic Greenbelt's shopping and entertainment hub opened in 1937, and its plaza was refurbished in 2000. (Courtesy Eric Zhang, photographer, 2015)

Opposite

Plate 20. Partizánske's orginal Baťa housing (c. 1940) and Catholic church (1942–47) designed by Vladimir Karfík. In the background, the socialist-era housing of the Šipok district was built across the Nitra River from the historic company town. (Courtesy Monuments Board of the Slovak Republic)

Plate 21. Tapiola, shown here in 1969, attracted worldwide attention because of the integration of well-designed buildings with the natural environment. (Photo by Arnold R. Alanen)

Plate 22. This picturesque roofscape view of Seaside (planned in 1980) communicates its coherence, variety, and uniqueness. The town's Architectural Code limits the roof shapes, materials, and some vernacular details. Allegiance to these restraints, slow growth, avoidance of repetitive speculative builders' houses, and a Town Architect together yield a rare qualitative distinction. Residential height limits do not apply to towers, limited in plan to 215 square feet. (Photo © Steven Brooke Studios)

and that body's ruling nearly ten years ago to tentatively approve the sale of an adjacent and sizable parcel of Radburn-owned land for a proposed residential development. The parcel in question (Daly Field) was largely vacant and not fully utilized, but the lack of public notice for the Radburn Association's decision and the lack of confidence in the merit of the decision piqued the ire of some in the Citizens Association. A rancorous battle ensued regarding not only the composition and budgetary practices of the Radburn Association, but also the association's lack of conformance with New Jersey's state regulations concerning the governance of planned communities—a clash that has included lawsuits, subsequent legal appeals to the courts, and citizen appeals directly to state legislators. Although headway has been made in regard to improved budget-making procedures, a 2010 decision by the state Supreme Court upheld the Radburn Association's position in regard to governance and effectively supported the status quo. In addition, the Fair Lawn Planning Board gave final approval in November 2012 to the proposed housing development on the Daly Field parcel—with the seemingly minor condition that it maintain landscaping consistent with the Radburn neighborhood, but without any similar architectural guidelines, as had been suggested by some members of the Citizens Association in order to better integrate it and to help preserve the community character.

Ultimately, this battle comes down to a simple desire for a more fully democratic form of governance within the community. As was stipulated in the original by-laws of the Radburn Association, membership therein is confined to trustees and former trustees, and only that group can nominate candidates to the board or change election rules—and, currently, that group includes a small circle of only about fifty of the more than 1,400 adult residents. Their bias in this regard was made particularly evident in 2005 when the residents voted in two write-in candidates by a wide margin over the "official" nominees, but who were, in turn, refused seats on the board by the Radburn Association membership—with no recourse for the electorate. Despite the apparent finality of the ruling by the state Supreme Court on the matter, it seems clear that relations between the Citizens Association and the Radburn Association are severely strained, to say the least, and what that means for the community's future social interactions as regards governance—including its ability to undertake continued and effective preservation measures—remains unclear. Interestingly, there has not yet been an indication of serious and sustained interest in pursuing designation for Radburn as a local historic district, a status that would remove any potential future threats to heritage protection as might be caused by further conflict over governance—but that would, of course, also bring binding legal implications for individual residents in terms of making changes to their properties.

Conclusion

The maturing of any planned residential community presents the challenges of retaining a vision and preserving a place intended to provide an enhanced quality of life, while avoiding it becoming just like any other neighborhood with merely a bunch of people living in close proximity. An added challenge for iconic communities like Sunnyside Gardens and Radburn, which attempt a larger societal mission, has been the difficulty of maintaining their particular arrangements (some of which are quite uncommon) for an extended time through a "private" regulatory framework enforced by associations made up of a potentially changing array of property owners. As has been eloquently affirmed, the "handing down [of] social ideals from generation to generation is hard enough within families, let alone communities. They need to be reborn outside the formality of deeds and restrictive covenants" (Robbins 1985, 16). For Sunnyside Gardens, at least, the LPC's designation of that neighborhood as a local historic district—and its ensuing role as the new administrator of the built environment—may have effectively done that, though with the concurrent loss of Wright's "neighborly considerations" that played such a meaningful role in bonding that community together socially, at least regarding local governance of preservation issues.

To various degrees, both communities have struggled with this "handing down" process, though in different magnitudes and manifestations. Perhaps it is none too surprising that the intricate nature of Sunnyside Gardens' physical plan, which required that residents agree to "share" a portion of their already-subdivided private property with their neighbors, would meet with sizable challenges; whereas in Radburn, the shared space was already built into the plan and was never perceived as anything but "public" land. In turn, it could perhaps also be expected that residents, no matter how pleasant the physical arrangements of their community, would chafe significantly when their ability to participate equitably in the governance of that same community is stunted, as has been the case at Radburn.

Interestingly, both of the debated issues—private property and democracy—are as iconic, in the United States, as are the two community designs themselves. In the end, and without any clear preservation threats on the horizon, both places, bestowed with distinctive physical plans and social identities, have weathered their particular degrees and types of change and largely sustained their legacies as meaningful human habitats. Perhaps it is merely a reflection of the special qualities found in these places that their inhabitants would tussle with such voracity over issues that might threaten those qualities—a fitting tribute to the power of place.

Table 10.1
Summary of Historical Events and Heritage Benchmarks for Sunnyside Gardens

Year	Event
1924	The City Housing Corporation was created. It is a limited dividend company, headed by Alexander Bing. Clarence Stein and Henry Wright draw the master plan.
1924–28	Original owners sign forty-year restrictive covenants prohibiting physical alterations to buildings and courts.
1926	Sunnyside Gardens Park (also designed by Stein) opens for use by residents only.
1931	Stein's Phipps Garden Apartments opens on the outskirts of neighborhood.
1934	The City Housing Corporation goes bankrupt.
Mid-1960s	Original restrictive covenants are set to expire; numerous residents vote not to renew them and pave over front gardens for private driveways or construct small building additions.
1974	The New York City Planning Commission approves rezoning for the neighborhood as a Special Planned Community Preservation District, mandating special permit approval for further physical alterations.
1981	Sunnyside Foundation for Community Planning and Preservation is created as a community land conservancy advocating for neighborhood restoration.
1984	Sunnyside Gardens is listed on the National Register of Historic Places.
2003	The Sunnyside Gardens Preservation Alliance is founded; it is dedicated to safeguarding the National Register Historic District.
2007	The New York City Landmarks Preservation Commission designates the neighborhood as a local historic district.
2009	The New York City Council approves zoning text amendment to ensure a complementary relationship between zoning provisions (Special Planned Community Preservation District) and landmark regulations.
	Population (as of 2014), 3,450; 56 acres [22,66 ha]; 1,200 dwelling units.

Table 10.2
Summary of Historical Events and Heritage Benchmarks for Radburn

Year	Event
1928	January: Architects of the City Housing Corporation, under the leadership of Clarence Stein and Henry Wright, draw the preliminary superblock diagram illustrating Radburn design elements and adapt the diagram to fit the existing site.
1929	March: The Radburn Association is incorporated as a governmental community organization managed by a self-perpetuating board of trustees, which includes nonresidents; ongoing membership is restricted to new and former trustees. May: The first residents move in; they sign deed restrictions prohibiting physical alterations and mandating a yearly assessment (with automatic renewal January 1, 1960, unless rescinded by majority vote of the Radburn Association). July: The Radburn Citizens Association is created to support community life; membership is open to all residents but this association has no enforcement power.
1930	The new Plaza Building opens, housing shops and a community center.

(continued)

Table 10.2 *(continued)*
Summary of Historical Events and Heritage Benchmarks for Radburn

Year	Event
Early 1930s	Construction continues at a much diminished rate, due to the Great Depression.
1934	The City Housing Corporation goes bankrupt; only a small portion of Radburn's plan gets built.
1938	At the recommendation of the Radburn Citizens Association, the Radburn Association is reorganized to give residents better representation, control, and responsibility.
1960	Original deed restrictions are automatically renewed, with similar renewal arrangement every twenty years going forward.
1975	Radburn is listed on the National Register of Historic Places.
2004	The Radburn Association gives its tentative approval to sell the Daly Field parcel for new housing development, upsetting members of the Radburn Citizens Association; a decade-long battle ensues over Radburn Association's powers.
2005	Radburn is designated a National Historic Landmark.
2010	The New Jersey Supreme Court upholds governmental authority of the Radburn Association.
2012	The Fair Lawn Planning Board gives conditional approval to a new housing development (Landmark at Radburn) on the Daly Field parcel.
2014	The Radburn Association ratifies the sale of the Daly Field parcel to Landmark at Radburn LLC. As of early 2018, the 165 residential units planned for the twelve-acre site have not been built.
	Population, 3,100; 150 acres [56,7 ha]; 675 dwelling units.

NOTES

1. Bing, Stein, and Wright were all founders of the RPAA and served as its leading members, along with Lewis Mumford and Benton MacKaye. Bing, a real estate developer and philanthropist, served as the first president of the RPAA and CHC, and he was the primary source of funding for the CHC. Stein and Wright were both trained as architects and had collaborated on a number of the most recognized housing designs of the early twentieth century.

2. See Wright 1933 and Stein 1957. Wright noted that "the sales emphasis was addressed to moderately skilled manual or trade workers, many of foreign birth," and both men characterized the early resident population as comprising largely a broad range of nonprofessional workers of moderate means.

3. Susan Turner Meiklejohn, personal interview regarding her demographic study of Sunnyside Gardens, January 2005.

4. See Stein 1957 for further discussion of the Radburn Idea.

REFERENCES

Ames, David L. 1995. "Interpreting Post–World War II Suburban Landscapes as Historic Resources." In *Preserving the Recent Past*, edited by Deborah Slaton and Rebecca A. Schiffer, 105–9. Washington, DC: Historic Preservation Education Foundation.

Betts, Mary Beth, and Michael Caratzas, eds. 2007. *Sunnyside Gardens Historic District: Designation Report*. New York: New York City Landmarks Preservation Commission.

Capra, Fritjof. 2003. *The Hidden Connections: Integrating the Biological, Cognitive, and Social Dimensions of Life into a Science of Sustainability*. New York: Doubleday.

City Housing Corporation. 1930. *Sunnyside Gardens: A Home Community*. New York: City Housing Corporation.

Efthimiades, Michael. 2004. "Sunnyside Gardens Considers Landmarking." *Preservation Issues*. Queens, NY: Greater Astoria Historical Society. www.astorialic.org/preservation.

Ferris, Marc. 2003. "Trouble in Paradise: Some in Sunnyside Gardens Want Landmark Distinction." *New York Newsday* (November 4). http://www.newsday.com.

Havelick, Franklin, and Michael Kwartler. 1982. "Sunnyside Gardens: Whose Land Is It Anyway?" *New York Affairs* 7(2): 65–80.

Lasker, Loula D. 1936. "Sunnyside Up and Down." *Survey Graphic* 25(July): 419–23, 439–41.

Lee, Chang-Moo, and Barbara Stabin-Smith. 2001. "The Continuing Value of a Planned Community: Radburn in the Evolution of Suburban Development." *Journal of Urban Design* 6: 151–84.

McClelland, Linda F., and Paula S. Reed. 2004. "Radburn." National Historic Landmark Nomination. Washington, DC: U.S. Department of the Interior, National Park Service.

New York City Landmarks Preservation Commission. 2007. *Sunnyside Gardens Historic District Designation Report* (June 26).

Place in History. 2001. *Sunnyside Gardens Neighborhood History Project*. Brooklyn, NY: Place in History. www.placeinhistory.org/projects/sunnyside_gardens/.

Radburn Association (Radburn, NJ). 1929. *Declaration of Restrictions No. 1 Affecting Radburn, Property of City Housing Corporation* (March 15). https://www.radburn.org/images/residents-area/declaration_of_restrictions_no.pdf.

Rappaport, Nina, with Steven Saltzman. 1991. "Sunnyside Gardens." *Metropolis* (June): 15–19.

Robbins, Tom. 1985. "The Democratic Vision of Sunnyside Gardens." *City Limits* (March): 16–19.

Schaffer, Daniel. 1982. *Garden Cities for America: The Radburn Experience*. Philadelphia: Temple University Press.

Stein, Clarence S. 1957. *Toward New Towns for America*. Cambridge, MA: MIT Press.

Turner, Molly. 2001. "A Thoroughly Conscious and Workable Community." *Sunnyside Gardens Neighborhood History Project*. Brooklyn, NY: Place in History. www.placeinhistory.org/projects/sunnyside_gardens/.

Wright, Henry. 1933. "Housing—Why, When, and How? Part Two." *Architecture* 68(2): 79–110.

CHAPTER 11

CITÉ FRUGÈS

Le Corbusier's Paradoxical Appropriation

in Pessac, France

Gilles Ragot

From 1924 to 1926 Le Corbusier and his cousin Pierre Jeanneret designed and erected the Cité Frugès, an experimental subdivision of fifty-three homes in Pessac, a town adjoining the city of Bordeaux.[1] Among architectural historians, the Cité Frugès is regarded as an ambitious aesthetic, technical, methodological, and social undertaking. However, as soon as they moved in, residents began undertaking major alterations, which underscored the cultural gap between France's artistic avant-garde and its ordinary citizens. Transformations were of such magnitude that, in 1969, the sociologist Philippe Boudon conducted an enlightening study of the residents' takeover. Boudon's book altered perceptions about the subdivision. Critics stopped assessing the Cité Frugès for its design qualities but as evidence of the presumed demise of the modern movement, to such an extent that Charles Jencks did not hesitate to designate Pessac and Saint Louis's Pruitt-Igoe high-rise housing complex as modern architecture's two most illustrious failures (Jencks 1977, 50).

The gradual reassessment of the Cité Frugès began in the early 1970s, culminating in a recent and successful petition for World Heritage Site status. This petition, however, did not entail a consensus on issues of significance and protection status. On the contrary, it exacerbated conflicts among the 110 residents, split between two organizations championing different heritage philosophies. Pessac's elected officials have surrendered their negative feelings toward the Cité Frugès; seeing in Le Corbusier's subdivision a promotional asset, the current municipality has spearheaded an ambitious strategic plan that represents a major benchmark in its polarized critical fortune.

We shall first summarize the tenets of this experimental work, from a formal, spatial, and technical, as well as sociological, standpoint. Second, we shall account for its construction and highlight this project's specificity, before alluding to its reception by architectural critics and original residents. We shall then examine how the cité, after having been somehow overlooked and maligned, was rediscovered through the very unique lens of a sociological study. Finally we shall demonstrate how, starting three decades ago, heritage awareness has enabled a slow process of rehabilitation, but has also triggered contradictory and sometimes adversarial reactions among residents.

An Experiment

There has always been a back-and-forth synergy between Le Corbusier's designs and writings. Writings articulated a coherent doctrine, spearheading new designs, which in return enriched new publications. The Cité Frugès represents an early example of such interactions. Its history began on November 3, 1923, when Henry Frugès wrote to Le Corbusier, "I am an industrialist from Bordeaux, about to build a small worker's housing project near a factory which I just purchased in the moorlands of Arcachon. . . . Your book, *Vers une architecture*, conveys ideas of logic and progress dear to my heart far better, ideas that I have, so far, been unable to express them myself."[2]

In *Vers une architecture*, published in 1923, Le Corbusier irrevocably condemned academicism. He called for a modernity challenging the status quo, based on a new architectural language derived from principles of Purist painting, which he and the painter Amédée Ozenfant had articulated in a 1919 pamphlet called *Après le Cubisme*. Le Corbusier advocated "invariant" qualities: pure geometric forms endowed, in his mind, with emotional values of a "primal" and universal nature.

Vers une architecture conveyed a three-fold agenda, summarized by Le Corbusier in catchphrases that have become clues to understanding his work and the modern movement in general. His formal agenda was encapsulated in his definition of architecture as "the masterly, correct and magnificent play of masses brought together in light" (Le Corbusier 1977, 16). Design could dispense with styles and relate to elementary forms instead. In Pessac, Le Corbusier advocated a radical break from both the "high" and "vernacular" idioms of his time.

As far as process was concerned, Le Corbusier's agenda was summarized in his dictum "A house is a machine for living" (Le Corbusier 1977, 73). He declared that architects had failed to address issues raised by the house in the same straightforward manner as engineers had addressed those related to machinery. In Pessac, Le Corbusier wanted to reinvent not only forms but also interior layouts, spatial configurations, construction methods, and the way inhabitants would use their homes.

Le Corbusier's utopian social agenda was raised in his famous quandary "Architecture or revolution?" (1977, 243).[3] His reply was that "revolution is preventable." How would this be possible? Le Corbusier's answer was through high-quality architecture and urbanism. Design against social turmoil: such is the utopia at the core of the modern movement. To support his discourse, Le Corbusier illustrated *Vers une architecture* with his own theoretical proposals for standardized homes.

This book—architecturally innovative but conventional from a political stand-point—was bound to appeal to the Bordeaux-based industrialist Henry Frugès (1879–1974). A dynamic businessman as well as an artist, Frugès shared Le Corbusier's belief that working-class housing was an aesthetic as much as a social issue. Since 1920, Le Corbusier had unsuccessfully tried to see his name connected with major French companies—Michelin, Peugeot, Citroën, Saint-Gobain—in order to prove the relevance of, and implement, his research on standardized housing. Frugès was not so prominent but offered him the first opportunity to implement his ideas at the scale of a subdivision.

Frugès's initial commission was not his cité in Pessac, but a more modest project in Lège, a small village near Arcachon, southwest of Bordeaux. There, Le Corbusier and Jeanneret erected a small company town with seven single-family homes, a community center, and a wall to play pelota, a very popular sports activity in southwestern France. In Lège, and subsequently in Pessac, Le Corbusier initiated a fruitful dialogue with his client, contradicting popular views of the architect entrenched in his own convictions (Benton 2004). Frugès and his designers also took into account visitors' reactions toward an experimental home erected in Bordeaux, in the courtyard of a factory owned by the industrialist. This small dwelling had a post-and-beam reinforced concrete structure. The American technology of sprayed cement was used to erect the walls.[4] Upon Le Corbusier's request, Frugès acquired a cement gun manufactured in the United States by Ingersoll Rand. The architect was wooed by what appeared to be a straightforward construction process as well as by the cement gun's iconic American modernity. However, Le Corbusier's enthrallment was supplemented neither by an in-depth examination of the process nor by an evaluation of its appropriateness for this particular operation. More instinctive than rational, such a mind-set would have grave repercussions at Pessac.

From his trial run in Lège, Le Corbusier drew lessons for Pessac, particularly with regard to the standardization and prefabrication of the beams, using two modules of five and two-and-a-half meters. At the time, Le Corbusier advocated a takeover of construction by industrial means. His research focused on defining standardized elements and a dwelling module, the various combinations of which would generate diversity. To supervise the Lège site, in anticipation of that at Pessac and, possibly, for subsequent commissions, Frugès formed an in-house building department, whose incompetence, along with the ill-adapted use of the cement-gun technique, would hamper the technical success of these projects. In the early 1920s, while a housing shortage was rampant in France, Le Corbusier kept producing theoretical studies of low-cost standardized houses, a program overlooked by most French architects.[5] The Cité Frugès was the last in a long series of projects and propelled him from theory to practice.

When Frugès approached Le Corbusier, the latter had only completed high-class single-family homes. From 1905 to 1916, six of these were erected in Switzerland; with the exception of the Villa Schwob (1916), their styles fluctuated between regionalism and neoclassicism. In 1923, the house-studio Le Corbusier designed for Ozenfant in Paris was under construction and the Maison Benus was nearing completion in the Paris suburbs. The purist aesthetic of this last house was unique in France and very unusual in Europe, where only Adolf Loos had already demonstrated such radicalism. During the erection of the Cité Frugès, Le Corbusier and Pierre Jeanneret designed five other houses, including the La Roche and Jeanneret houses in Paris (1923–25) and Le Corbusier's parents' house in Corseaux, Switzerland (1923–25).

Originally intended for 135 families, the Cité Frugès was a one-of-a-kind commission and certainly one of the first major workers' housing communities in the history of the modern movement. J. J. P. Oud's 343 row houses in Oud-Mathesesse (1922–24) were semitemporary dwellings and remained indebted to traditional aesthetic notions. His Hoek van Holland group also in Rotterdam, the first to demonstrate Oud's definitive move toward the avant-garde, comprised forty-one units; its construction began in May 1927, one year after the official dedication of the Cité Frugès. In Germany, where many apartment buildings were commissioned to modernists, communities comparable to that at Pessac were not built until 1928, as was the case with Walter Gropius's famous Siedlung Törten in Dessau (1926–28). Only one, albeit less progressive, example was completed slightly prior to Pessac: Victor Bourgeois's 275-unit Cité Moderne (1922–25) in the Berchem-Sainte-Agathe section of Brussels, consisting of fifteen types of single-family houses.

None of these residential projects were as challenging and perilous as the Cité Frugès, where technological experimentation, formal radicalism, spatial and interior planning innovation, and novel use of color combined to serve a powerful social agenda. As opposed to the above-mentioned Belgian, Dutch, or German rental projects, which were sponsored by public or nonprofit backers, the Cité Frugès was privately funded and all its houses were to be purchased by private individuals. These two conditions would facilitate change in houses with no strict covenants checking the actions of successive owners.

An Ambitious Project Plagued by Quality-Control Issues

In May 1924, Frugès purchased a large meadow on the outskirts of Pessac. The original site plan of July 24, 1924 called for 135 houses divided into four neighborhoods. A small central square was surrounded by shops and included a wall to play pelota. Countless difficulties prevented the first neighborhood, which connected the access road to the central square, from being implemented. Fifty-three houses were eventually built. The original placement of the access road and central square remains visible today, but the fact that stores were never built worsened the poor sales of housing units.

The color axonometric drawing published in the journal *L'Architecture Vivante* in 1927 (Plate 15) shows two of the three built neighborhoods: one with the staggered (*maisons en quinconces*) and Z-shaped homes; the other with the "skyscrapers." Houses line tree-planted streets. Each of them takes advantage of private front and back yards, used as pleasure or vegetable gardens, some of them with rabbit hutches. Despite the design's modular principle, the site conveys an overall impression of variety, as opposed to uniformity. Starting with his studies for Hellereau in France (date unknown) and for the Crétets in La Chaux-de-Fonds (1914), Le Corbusier had produced many designs for garden cities and grouped workers' housing, altogether nearly ten projects, which had all remained on paper until those for Lège and Pessac. Pessac's *quartiers modernes* borrowed from garden city concepts its greenfield character, but Pessac departed from this model by adopting a regular street network and shunning the picturesque. Houses are townhomes, some of them—the "skyscrapers"—pertaining to the type of the multifamily apartment to a greater extent than to that of the country house. Le Corbusier favored continuous rows, as opposed to freestanding units. He devised a variety of connections between houses and roadways and some dwellings turn their back to the street. Most importantly, Le Corbusier conceived his architectural design as an urban composition. The masses of his houses, designed according to regular modular proportions, echo each other to form a harmonious whole. Rhythmical variety was achieved by manipulating massing, but also by hollowing out ground floors, to create extended front, back, and side vistas. Colors enhanced the distinctive massing of each dwelling. It was through his refined manipulation of voids and color that Le Corbusier was able to connect his architectural language to a broader urban vision. Reacting against contemporary trends to adopt "generic" garden city plans and house designs for low- and middle-income subdivisions, Le Corbusier devised an urban neighborhood in which he fused modern architecture and low-density planning.

For economic reasons, Frugès and his architects favored a row-house configuration. However Le Corbusier envisioned this workers' housing community as a work of art and progressively departed from the basic, cost-efficient precedent of Lège. He added new bays, arched roofs, terraces, and pergolas, enhancing variety as well as urban and spatial sophistication but multiplying construction costs three to four times. The result was five principal house types: "arcade," "skyscraper," staggered, Z-shaped, and freestanding (Figures 11.1, 11.2, and 11.3).

Figure 11.1. "Arcade"-type house. The modular composition is legible on the elevation: full module; half-module; and a quarter-module used below the depressed vault that connects two residential units. (Photo by Gilles Ragot)

Figure 11.2. "Skyscraper"-type house comprising two back-to-back dwelling units. Only the street-side unit, which is owned by the municipality and is open to visitors, was repainted according to the original color scheme. (Photo by Gilles Ragot)

Figure 11.3. *Quinconce* (staggered) houses. The reason for the plan reversal from one unit to the other is twofold: from a functional standpoint, it prevents wall-to-wall juxtaposition of high-occupancy rooms; from a visual standpoint, it breaks the monotony of row housing. (Photo by Gilles Ragot)

Le Corbusier's artistic pursuits led him to paint houses, using color schemes he had experimented with in his easel paintings. The connection with the experiments of the Dutch De Stijl movement was obvious, although Le Corbusier used a different chromatic palette and granted a different function to color. As opposed to De Stijl, Le Corbusier did not use color to disintegrate actual spatial proportions or dematerialize walls, but to alternatively enhance or dissolve surfaces forming a three-dimensional composition. Color was meant to highlight the interplay between voids and masses, to arbitrarily break the bulk of attached housing units, and to bring variety to the modular composition: "Allow me to repeat this: nothing is more demoralizing than uniformity, a sign of stupidity. Nothing is more powerful and moving than unity" (Le Corbusier 1931).

Frugès gave himself credit for the color scheme. However, at the time, Le Corbusier was already experimenting with polychromy in both his Parisian villas and the small house for his parents. He viewed color and light as materials in and of themselves. In Pessac, a subdivision where, according to Le Corbusier, houses were "exceedingly squeezed," polychromy became a planning tool, intended to "open perspectives, to shatter the embrace of walls too close to each other" (Le Corbusier 1931). According to Le Corbusier, colors were meant to "rejoice" residents. Joy, however, was short-lived. Houses were hurriedly painted in time for the dedication ceremony. Poorly prepared, the paint peeled quickly and had to be scraped before being reapplied, resulting in another unforeseen expenditure.

The originality of Pessac's houses related to the implementation of the "free plan" concept, where the internal arrangement of rooms, freed from structural considerations, varied from one floor to another. Le Corbusier and Jeanneret eliminated corridors and juxtaposed rooms to achieve smooth connections; this feeling of fluidity was enhanced by rounded corners, even piano-shaped curved partitions. Detached from their traditional position against walls, freestanding fireplaces became autonomous plastic elements enlivening rooms and creating spatial subdivisions. The walk-through interiors, which Le Corbusier called an "architectural promenade," were devised to allow residents to experience space through multiple viewpoints. The internal staircase is freed from "its hall" and becomes an added element in the spatial composition. In the "skyscraper" houses, the stair leads directly to the living rooms, which one did not encounter frontally upon climbing the last step, but by making a 180-degree turn. A visitor apprehended this reception space in its largest dimension, from a diagonal, while standing at the tip of one of the corners of this room. On one side, a horizontal ribbon window enhanced the impression of spatial openness. Finally, most of the houses enjoyed a covered deck under the stilts, on the ground floor, as well as an accessible roof terrace, both of these spaces lending themselves to multiple uses. All these design features were not grandiose but demon-

strated Le Corbusier's care for residents' customs. At the time such concern was unusual or nonexistent among designers of low-cost housing, including European colleagues such as Oud or Gropius, whose designs were informed to a much larger extent by strict notions of rationality.

From a technical standpoint, Le Corbusier and Jeanneret were audacious trailblazers, their research being far ahead of those of their contemporaries. However the inexperience of local contractors, worsened by the incompetence of Frugès's construction-site supervisor, led construction to an impasse (Figure 11.4). The cement-gun technique proved expensive, difficult to implement, and did not allow for the erection of walls of consistent width. The placement of metal window frames, fabricated in two standardized sizes, stumbled against this lack of dimensional consistency.

Figure 11.4. The construction site of the Cité Frugès (c. 1925). Notwithstanding Le Corbusier's statements advocating industrialized methods, procedures remained in large part craft-oriented. (Courtesy Fondation Le Corbusier)

In 1925, to finalize construction, Le Corbusier decided to hire an experienced Parisian contractor. The latter almost entirely abandoned the cement gun in favor of more traditional methods, thereby confirming that the Cité Frugès was a partial technical failure. Hiring a Parisian contractor headquartered six hundred kilometers from Bordeaux represented another major additional expenditure, worsening the client's financial hardships.

Completed in 1926, the Cité Frugès remained vacant until 1929. Its design puzzled many observers. More importantly, the architect and his client had not complied with regulations and neglected proper studies for street infrastructure and drainage. It took Frugès nearly three years to obtain running water. Deprived of water, the expensive houses proved unsellable. This situation was unblocked, thanks to the financial conditions offered by a new social housing policy, the Loi Loucheur, enacted in 1928.

A Scapegoat of the Modern Movement

Homes sales started at the end of 1929. Vacant for nearly four years, houses had deteriorated. Despite enticing prices that were below-cost estimates, sales were slow. Returning to Pessac in June 1931, after having heard alarming rumors about how new owners treated their houses, Le Corbusier deemed the situation "truly horrific." Houses had been repainted according to each resident's taste. Many open spaces below the *pilotis* and arcades had been filled to gain additional living space. Exterior decoration had been added on façades. Le Corbusier denounced such "regrettable carelessness"; for him, residents should not have been allowed to indulge their "fatal incompetence."[6] Homebuyers were enticed by the low sales prices resulting from the Loi Loucheur to a far larger extent than by the architectural assets of the cité, which the local press and public opinion denigrated by comparing its design with that of cities in Morocco.

However, the residents themselves did not refer to their houses in such derogatory terms. Even though they were not familiar with Le Corbusier's theories, some of them were aware of living in a special place that singled them out from the broader community of Pessac. As early as 1931, many of them joined an association spearheaded by J. Gabriel, a lawyer from Bordeaux, to defend the interests of the Cité Frugès.[7] Gabriel and Le Corbusier were intent on "rehabilitating" its physical integrity and the public image. Their correspondence bears witness to recognition of positive improvements on the part of residents. This recognition was demonstrated by these residents' decision to pay homage to the creators of the cité, by naming streets after Le Corbusier, Frugès, and Vrinat in 1931.[8]

Nonetheless, Pessac was from the start presented as a failure. Paradoxically, by victimizing the Cité Frugès, Le Corbusier himself contributed to creating the image of a scapegoat of the modern movement. He constantly stressed attacks directed against it, and he kept silent about his share of responsibility and that of Frugès in the conceptual flaws and the regulatory breaches that were the major reasons behind physical damage and poor sales and that had delayed the provision of running water, road infrastructure, and public lighting. By the same token, Le Corbusier was not willing to stress the "cluelessness" of residents who, in his own mind, had been left to their own devices "without directions, nor advice."[9] This situation gave birth to the idea, which other modernists would often endorse, that modern architecture demanded educating laymen unaware of its assets, including in terms of well-being and comfort. Le Corbusier deplored that covenants for the Cité Frugès included no provisions to safeguard the integrity of his work.[10] This absence of aesthetic regulations in a group of homes purchased by persons of modest means explains in great part its adverse transformation in comparison with contemporary Dutch or German housing projects, where public or nonprofit sponsors exercised strict control over the maintenance of rental units.

From Rejection to Oblivion

In 1926, the Cité Frugès was written about in several major architectural journals, including *Wasmuths Monatshefte*, *Das Neue Frankfurt*, and *Werk* in Germany; *Arkitekten* in Denmark; and *La Construction Moderne*, *L'Intransigeant*, and *L'Architecture Vivante* in France. The German critic Siegfried Giedion praised the project at length in his 1928 book *Building in France, Building in Iron, Building in Ferroconcrete*. Commentaries were positive, far from the negative consensus that Le Corbusier complained about. The sole early dissenter was Henry Russell Hitchcock, who stated that the Pessac experiment hampered the development of modern housing in France: Le Corbusier's adaptation to modest dwellings of spatial devices originally intended for luxury villas was ill-advised (Hitchcock 1929). In fact, the free and open planning, which Hitchcock regarded as an unrealistic transposition, could also be regarded as a mark of benevolence on the part of Le Corbusier. It would later surface, as evidenced in Boudon's 1969 study, as an asset, enabling appropriation and individualization by residents.

Le Corbusier himself illustrated the Cité Frugès in the first volume of his *Oeuvre complète* (*Oeuvre complète 1937*, 78–86). However, he seemed to have turned a page and be in mourning. This project was a "severe, harmful lesson" that demonstrated that "novel initiatives clash with public opinion," which in return "declares war against ideas." Le Corbusier strongly resented this stillborn project. To the editor of *Stein Holz Cement* in Frankfurt, he wrote, "You always cared about Pessac, this stillborn village near Bordeaux."[11] He also wrote to Gabriel that Pessac was "like a bereavement" among the work of the avant-gardes.[12]

In Pessac, houses were radically altered in prosaic and ordinary ways according to the taste and needs of their owners. In 1942, an aerial bombardment destroyed three houses and shattered all the windows in the subdivision, considerably speeding up the process of replacing ribbon windows with traditional openings as well as the filling in of some openings.

A Sociological Case Study

The cité's slow return to its original condition began in 1964, when the owner of the house at 3 Rue des Arcades started significant restoration on the façades and interiors of his unit. With Le Corbusier's death in August 1965, the historical significance of the architect and the Cité Frugès reached a new level. The French Minister of Culture, André Malraux, sponsored national funerals. Demonstrations of admiration and gratitude streamed from the entire world, altering Le Corbusier's public image. Four days after his death, J.-C. Dalbos, *député-maire* of Pessac, accompanied by the editor of the region's major daily newspaper, paid a visit to the Cité Frugès. A few months later, on the fortieth anniversary of its opening, Dalbos sent a petition to Malraux, requesting landmark designation for the Cité Frugès. His request would be examined for more than three years but was eventually denied.

The first official protection measure, related to 3 Rue des Arcades, would not happen for another fourteen years. This time lapse witnessed the publication of two major works. In 1969, Philippe Boudon, an architect and sociologist, published *Pessac de Le Corbusier: Etude socio-architecturale*. In 1972, Brian Brace Taylor organized an exhibition on Pessac at Harvard University; the catalogue, using material from Taylor's remarkable doctoral research, was also released in French, in a small publication with a limited circulation (Taylor 1972). By contrast, Boudon's book reached a larger readership. It was translated into German in 1971 and published the following year as *Lived-in Architecture: Le Corbusier's Pessac Revisited*. A French reprint came out in 1985.

Coinciding with the advent of postmodernism, Pessac's rediscovery was sociological in nature. Beginning with the "failure" argument, a premise strengthened by his compelling illustrations, Boudon ended his inquiry with a more qualified conclusion. He reinterpreted the physical changes, which had so far been identified as many proofs of failure, as positive assets demonstrating how adaptable Le Corbusier's design really was. Boudon contended that by accommodating change,

Figure 11.5. Plate comparing an original view of the "staggered" units with their appropriations by residents. (Reprinted from P. Boudon, *Pessac de Le Corbusier* [Paris: Dunod, 1969], 132)

Pessac's housing demonstrated its respect for individuality. Therefore, Boudon's book invalidated the ludicrous connection Jencks would subsequently establish between Pessac and Pruitt-Igoe. The Cité Frugès was never subjected to vandalism, but was transformed according to the wishes of its residents, who willingly acknowledged some of its assets. Additionally, it was never plagued with crime issues and, from Boudon's standpoint as a sociologist, its adaptability favored a positive appropriation of modern architecture on the part of residents. According to Boudon, residents sensed they belonged to a specific visual and social community: in 1969, despite their transformation, all of their homes had a formal kinship.

Despite its nuanced conclusions, Boudon's study had the adverse effect of reinforcing the failure hypothesis. Its spectacular photographs of transformed houses (Figure 11.5) may have been in great part responsible for this misunderstanding. In fact Boudon's book had the enduring effect of postponing heritage measures, as it led the Cité Frugès to be viewed from a sociological, as opposed to an urban or architectural standpoint. The lack of publicity around Taylor's study, which reinstated the avant-garde character of its architecture, ruled out launching a discussion on the design assets of the Cité Frugès, which Boudon's photographs obliterated. Most of the articles published in the 1970s and 1980s on the Cité Frugès were indebted to Boudon's research and under no circumstance advocated a heritage reassessment.

Placing the Cité on the Heritage Map

The decisive turning point toward placing the Cité Frugès on the heritage map occurred in the 1980s. In 1980, the house at 3 Rue des Arcades was designated as a historic landmark (*monument historique*). In France, landmark designation is granted by the Ministry of Culture upon examination of a preliminary historical and heritage study established by one of its regional agencies. Designation is generally granted with the approval of the property's owner, who benefits from state subsidies for restoration and renovation work. Repairs are not compulsory but they must follow criteria of authenticity and integrity and be monitored by a government-appointed *Architecte en Chef des Monuments Historiques*. In 1982, another Pessac homeowner sought advice from a regional public agency involved with residential rehabilitation. This request gave rise to a survey of the entire subdivision, entrusted to a team composed of several architects and one historian-sociologist (Ferrand, Feugas, and Le Roy 1985). The survey had a triple agenda: to establish a technical assessment; to transform one house into a visitors' center, through a trial restoration; and to harmonize initiatives emanating from diverse stakeholders. The goal was to involve residents in order to "salvage the Quartiers Modernes Frugès without displacing residents" (Ferrand, Feugas, and Le Roy 1985, 5). Released in 1985, the report confirmed that residents felt they belonged to a community and a neighborhood. It also highlighted their concerns that public authorities would challenge their prerogatives as homeowners. Residents were willing to act as a group, but income discrepancy between them created a fracture that has never been mended, despite repeated efforts on the part of elected officials. Many residents had moved to the cité for its affordability and accessibility to Bordeaux, rather than for its architecture. Their preference went to maintaining and improving existing conditions, including additions, instead of returning to the original design.

The 1985 report resulted in the establishment, in 1994, of a *zone de protection du patrimoine architectural et paysager* (ZPPAUP); it was published in book form in 1998 (Ferrand, Feugas, Le Roy, and Veyret 1998). The principle of a ZPPAUP pro-

Figure 11.6. "Skyscraper" house on rue Le Corbusier. Because they do not entail compulsory repair policies, ZZPAUP regulations yield ad hoc restoration work, which precludes visual unity and triggers slow-paced improvement. (Photo by Gilles Ragot)

tection area was instituted in 1983 and is generally, as was the case in Pessac, initiated by a municipality. The survey work is conducted by a multidisciplinary team, including architects, historians and sociologists, whose final report must meet the approval of a regional commission monitored by the Ministry of Culture and including not only representatives of this ministry, but also architects, historians, and elected officials. The ZPPAUP regulatory system entails protection and design advice aimed at safeguarding urban and architectural ensembles of distinction. ZPPAUP regulations affecting the Cité Frugès do not compel homeowners to undertake restoration work, but they define a precise and mandatory framework for any type of intervention on an existing building. Highly specific guidelines target a gradual return to original conditions (Figure 11.6). Restoring open public spaces is a priority, followed by the restitution of exteriors in terms of massing, façade decoration, and polychromy.

Figure 11.7. The rue Le Corbusier, lined to the left by "skyscraper" houses and to the right by "staggered" units. Priority is given to restoring the streetscape as a safeguard for the original garden city atmosphere. (Photo by Gilles Ragot)

Since 1995, the ZPPAUP framework has enabled a long-range, wide-encompassing, and incremental rehabilitation, as opposed to a quick and coercive restitution. In the course of two decades, the Cité Frugès has changed; the most striking alterations, which Boudon had illustrated in his book, have for the most part been expunged, through individual initiatives that, to a large extent, comply with the regulatory framework. Restoration work was also given a push when, in 1983, the municipality of Pessac purchased one of the two units in a "skyscraper" model for restoration as a visitor center, which now welcomes more than three thousand visitors every year.[13] In 1995, a public housing agency purchased four houses, restored them, and currently offers them as rental units.[14] Positive changes are evident, but the final results remain mixed and precarious, as elected officials are hesitant to fully enforce the ZPPAUP regulations, which some residents do not wholeheartedly endorse. In a ZZPAUP sector, no subsidies are available, but repair and restoration work is not compulsory. In the event that work is performed, it must comply with ZPPAUP regulations. The Architecte des Bâtiments de France, in charge of the district and under the tutelage of the Ministry of Culture, as well as each city's planning office monitors, exercises regulatory and quality control. In Pessac, ZPPAUP regulations aim toward the incremental reestablishment of original conditions (Figure 11.7), in terms of massing, colors, fenestration, fences, and so on. Homeowners benefit from subsidies only if their houses have been landmarked as monuments historiques.

This gradual restoration process is championed by the Association des Amis de Le Corbusier et des Quartiers Modernes Frugès, which was formed in 1990 to protect the neighborhood and guide residents willing to restore their homes through the administrative steps required. This nonprofit group, which includes several architects, also monitors compliance with ZPPAUP regulations, counteracting the deficiencies of local enforcement agencies. However, the way some residents try to monitor others, who are less cognizant of, or interested in, preserving the cité and restituting its original condition, is not devoid of tensions. Divisions worsened with the idea of placing Le Corbusier's subdivision on UNESCO's list of World Heritage Sites, launched in 2002.

The Cité Frugès: A World Heritage Site

The proposal to list as World Heritage Sites nineteen works by Le Corbusier exemplifying his seminal contribution to the modern movement was submitted to the vote of the World Heritage Council and denied twice, in 2009 and 2011; finally a revised list of seventeen sites was approved in 2016 (Ragot 2012). The presence of the Cité Frugès among the listed sites represents a complete reversal in terms of the nearly one-hundred-year-old attitude toward this project. Pessac's houses may be modest in terms of size, cost, and social standing. However, they exemplify a revolutionary quest on the part of architects: to go beyond prestigious commissions and work for the common man. This new objective shattered our attitude toward architectural history and heritage. The World Heritage Council establishes its heritage criteria on singling out iconic works, deemed as "masterpieces," and therefore did not account for this major evolution in the history of architectural practice. The cité's candidacy marked a determinant rise in its heritage status. Any World Heritage Site petition process requires the drafting of a strategic plan. The city of Pessac is requested to implement the first comprehensive, long-term plan of action ever devised for the Cité Frugès and therefore to serve as its cultural, social, and financial steward.

The management plan mandated by UNESCO entails organizing new cultural and tourism activities, closer monitoring of repairs and construction work undertaken by homeowners, and improving visitors' accommodations with the opening of a visitor center. It calls for raising the protection status of all houses in the cité. Nine additional homes have been landmarked in 2009 and thirteen are being considered for designation in 2012. Protection procedures raised expectations and sometimes disappointment among those homeowners whose houses were not selected for designation. At the same time residents are also afraid to see their subdivision become too much like a museum and be depleted of its everyday life. In 2009, a second residents' association called Vivre aux Quartiers Modernes Frugès was founded. It is less favorable to a quasi-archeological restitution than the Association des Amis de Le Corbusier et des Quartiers Modernes Frugès. Paradoxically, the enhanced heritage status, referred to as *patrimonialisation*, which was spearheaded to a larger extent by academics, Parisian cultural bureaucrats, and Pessac's elected officials than by residents themselves, led to reinforce preexisting divisions among the 110 residents of the cité.

In March 2018, the municipality made public that it was working on a "management plan" for the Cité Frugès, a survey of buildings and landscapes, studies for signage, and online documentation for school groups, in collaboration with the Regional Office of Cultural Affairs (DRAC Nouvelle-Aquitaine). The municipality is also preparing an application to the Cultural Routes program sponsored by the Council of Europe, in order to implement "La route Le Corbusier" (Ville de Pessac 2018).

Conclusion

A key benchmark in Le Corbusier's career, the Cité Frugès marked the end of his experiments to create urban compositions with small single-family homes. However, the cité fell into oblivion, including on Le Corbusier' part, as his research interest shifted during the same time period from mass-produced houses to multi-family dwellings.[15] From 1922 to 1925, he had devised the *Immeuble-villas*, based on the principle that "each apartment unit is in reality a small house with a garden, located at any height above the pavement" (Petit 1970). Amenities shared by residents complemented the program of this vertical village, which anticipated the *Unités d'habitation* erected after World War II. At the Exposition des Arts Décoratifs, which was held in Paris in 1925, Le Corbusier was able to exhibit a full-scale dwelling unit for an *immeuble-villa*. Consequently, the Cité Frugès represented the culmination but also the end of a design phase, marked by a sentiment of failure and by Le Corbusier's shift toward apartment living. As far as heritage is concerned, the historian Bruno Fayolle-Lussac, at a 2003 conference, expressed his concerns that media coverage and emphasis on preservation would lead to the influx of residents which, "from a cultural standpoint, would conform to its designer's wishes to the expense, at least partially, of the cité's original social agenda" (Fayolle-Lussac 2005). The social status of residents has changed since 1930, their income has risen, but the cité has not been gentrified. The social mix that today's planners call for is a reality and makes heritage stakes all the more complex.

Table 11.1
Summary of Historical Events and Heritage Benchmarks for Cité Frugès

Year	Event
1923	Bordeaux industrialist Henry Frugès approaches Le Corbusier to build seven homes and a community center in Lège near Arcachon.
1924	May: Frugès purchases land in Pessac near Bordeaux. July: Le Corbusier's master plan calls for 135 houses in four neighborhoods and a few stores.
1926	Official dedication of the Cité Frugès, reduced to fifty-three units.
1929	Vacant homes find buyers, thanks to the 1928 Loi Loucheur, a national homeownership incentive.
1931	The Bordeaux lawyer J. Gabriel spearheads an association aimed at protecting Le Corbusier's design: although it is joined by many homeowners, it does not prevent future alterations and additions.
1942	Three homes are destroyed by aerial bombing and are not rebuilt.
1964	The owner of #3 Rue des Arcades initiates its restoration.
1969	Philippe Boudon's sociological reevaluation of residents' alterations attracts professional and media attention.
1971	The Ministry of Culture denies the historic district designation requested by Pessac's mayor.
1980	#3 Rue des Arcades is awarded historic landmark designation.
1983	The municipality of Pessac purchases a unit as a visitor center.
1985	A government-sponsored survey advocates restoration and revitalization.
1990	The Association des Amis de Le Corbusier et des Quartiers Modernes Frugès is created. It assumes leadership in the rehabilitation process.
1994	The Cité Frugès becomes a *zone de protection du patrimoine architectural et paysager* to ensure an incremental reestablishment of original conditions.
1995	A housing agency purchases and restores four homes.
2009 and 2011	UNESCO denies the cité's listing as a World Heritage Site.
2016	UNESCO lists the cité as a World Heritage Site among seventeen international works by Le Corbusier.
	Population (as of 2018), approximately 150; 5,4 acres [2,18 ha]; fifty single-family dwellings.

NOTES

This chapter was translated by Isabelle Gournay.

1. From 1922 to 1940, Le Corbusier was associated with his first cousin, the architect Pierre Jeanneret.

2. Henry Frugès's letter to Le Corbusier, November 3, 1923, Fondation Le Corbusier, FLC H1-17-1.

3. This question and its reply were the last sentence in *Vers une architecture*.

4. The sprayed-concrete technology was invented in 1907 by Carl Akeley. It was patented in 1909 to erect artificial rocks in a Pennsylvania zoo. It was used essentially for engineering works, such as canals, mines, or stabilization of embankments or cliffs. It was brought to France after World War I to consolidate or rebuild ruins.

5. These projects were workers' housing in Saintes (1917), Maison Monol (1919), a subdivision at Le Vouldy (1919), "cités ouvrières" at Saint-Gobain and at Grand Couronne (both dated 1920), Maison Citrohan (1920 and 1922), Maison d'artiste (1922), Maison en série (1922), Maison Loi Ribot (1923), Lotissement Peugeot (1923–24), and Maison en série pour artisans (1924). From this impressive series of projects, only one house, designed in a regionalist style but already designed after a five-meter-square grid, was erected in 1917 in Saint-Nicolas d'Aliermont near Dieppe, Normandy.

6. Le Corbusier's letter to M. Vrinat, an engineer hired by Frugès in Pessac, no date, but written a few days after Pentecost, 1931, FLC H1-20-019.

7. The organization, still in existence, was an initiative of the first residents of the Cité Frugès, but it encompassed members from the broader quartier du Monteil. It plays no significant role in current heritage debates.

8. René Vrinat was an engineer employed by Frugès at Pessac.

9. Le Corbusier's letter to Vrinat, undated.

10. Le Corbusier's letter to Vrinat, undated: "The covenants was supposed to include a clause demanding respect toward neighbors and the entire project. I read some covenants: nothing of the sort is specified."

11. Le Corbusier's letter to the editor of *Stein Holz Cement*, February 11, 1931, FLC H1-20.

12. Le Corbusier's letter to J. Gabriel, March 10, 1931, FLC H1-20.

13. The address for this visitor center is 4 Rue Le Corbusier.

14. This nonprofit independent agency is called OPAC Aquitanis. At the same time, the Cité de Lège was landmarked in its entirety in 1990, as it was purchased by another agency involved with subsidized housing (Habitat-Girondin). It was restored in 1994–97 before being rented.

15. The Cité Frugès was not published in the special issue of the journal *L'Architecture d'Aujourd'hui* (no. 10, 1933) that was devoted to Le Corbusier and Pierre Jeanneret.

REFERENCES

Benton, Tim. 2004. "Pessac and Lège Revisited: Standards, Dimensions and Failures." *Massilia* 3: 64–99.

Boudon, Philippe. 1969. *Pessac de Le Corbusier: Etude socio-architecturale.* Paris: Dunod. (Translated as *Lived-in Architecture: Le Corbusier's Pessac Revisited* [Cambridge, MA: MIT Press, 1972].)

Fayolle-Lussac, Bruno. 2005. "De la stigmatisation à la monumentalisation du Mouvement Moderne: L'Oeuvre de Le Corbusier en Gironde." In *The Reception of Architecture of the Modern Movement: Image, Usage, Heritage, Actes de la Septième Conférence Internationale de DOCOMOMO*, 201–6. Saint-Etienne: Publications de l'Université de Saint-Etienne.

Ferrand, Marylène, Jean-Pierre Feugas, and Bernard Le Roy. 1985. "Pessac. Le Corbusier. Sauvegarde et réhabilitation des quartiers modernes Frugès." CEREL/ARIM Aquitaine, with the assistance of Marie-Cécile Riffault and Jean-Luc Veyret. Typewritten document.

Ferrand, Marylène, Jean-Pierre Feugas, Bernard Le Roy, and Jean-Luc Veyret. 1998. *Le Corbusier: Les quartiers modernes Frugès*. Paris: Fondation Le Corbusier.

Hitchcock, Henry-Russell. 1929. *Modern Architecture: Romanticism and Reintegration*. New York: Payson and Clarke.

Jencks, Charles. 1977. *The Language of Post Modern Architecture*. New York: Rizzoli.

Le Corbusier. 1931. *Polychromie architecturale*. FLC B1-19-95/123. First published in Arthur Rüegg, *Le Corbusier. Polychromie architecturale. Les claviers de couleurs de Le Corbusier de 1931 et 1959*. Basel: Birkhäuser Verlag.

———. 1977 (1923). *Vers une architecture*. Paris: Crès et Cie. Translated by Jean-Louis Cohen and John Goodman as *Toward an Architecture*. Los Angeles: Getty Research Institute, 2007.

Oeuvre complète de 1910–1929. 1937. Le Corbusier; Pierre Jeanneret; Willy Boesiger; Oscar Stonorov. Zurich: H. Girsberger.

Petit, Jean. 1970. *Le Corbusier lui-même*. Geneva: Editions Rouseau.

Ragot, Gilles. 2012. "The Nomination of the Architectural Work of Le Corbusier for Designation as a World Heritage Site: Chronicle of a Double Refusal." In *Shifting Paradigms in Modern Heritage*, edited by Marie-Stella Casciato and Emilie D'Orgeix. Liège: Editions Pierre Mardaga.

Taylor, Brian Brace. 1972. *Le Corbusier at Pessac: The Search for Systems and Standards in the Design of Low Cost Housing*. Cambridge, MA: Harvard University / Fondation Le Corbusier.

Ville de Pessac. 2018. *Compte-rendu sommaire du Conseil Municipal du 26 mars 2018*. http://www.pessac.fr/sites/default/files/upload/documents/pdf/mairie/conseils-municipaux-2018/compte-rendu-sommaire-du-conseil-municipal-du-26-mars-2018.pdf.

CHAPTER 12

THE RÖMERSTADT SETTLEMENT

The "New Life" in Frankfurt am Main, Germany

Susan R. Henderson

The settlement program of Frankfurt am Main (1927–31), named by its chief planner Ernst May the "New Frankfurt" (Neue Frankfurt), was one of the most significant European housing initiatives of the 1920s, parallel to the great modern housing campaigns in Berlin and Vienna. The Frankfurt program found its most ideal expression in the settlement called Römerstadt (Roman City). It remains a highly desirable residential enclave and in recent years has been the subject of conservation initiatives and professional discussion. This chapter gives an overview of the settlement, its origins, subsequent history, and current state; what original features are intact or remain legible; and, further, which of these features are relevant, either to the preservation process or to contemporary life.

Römerstadt: Origins

Römerstadt was one of the New Frankfurt model settlements encircling a new greenbelt in the Nidda Valley in the northwest of the city. Römerstadt, Praunheim, Westhausen, and Höhenblick were four among the seventeen settlements, large and small, built during the program between 1927 and 1930. Conceived along with the park as a garden satellite, they were the best embodiment of the social ideals and modernizing impetus of the New Frankfurt initiative as conceived by Ernst May and the visionary mayor Ludwig Landmann. As an entity, this Nidda Valley satellite represented a reform of the industrial city that integrated "Nature" with "settlement" while dissolving dense urban fabric.[1]

Ernst May was a staunch advocate for an urban design strategy based on the garden city suburb as exemplified by the work of his mentor, Raymond Unwin. Hampstead Garden Suburb had been a revelation to May when he began working for Unwin in 1911. It was not just the site design that had impressed him. In Hampstead's housing, he discovered the architectural counterpart to the garden landscape—a crafted neo-vernacular where comfort and convenience were preeminent considerations. And in its social program, which mixed the classes, and provided community buildings and outdoor spaces, he found a blueprint for his interpretation of a reform lifestyle to parallel the new suburb:

> In current urban design theory, we are inclined to categorize Unwin as romantic. But far more important than his formal modeling of master plans and buildings was that, in his large settlements, he succeeded in creating an authentic domestic climate, that is, he succeeded in bedding the housing—single family houses or apartment blocks—in a humane, attractive atmosphere, and he succeeded in incorporating the larger community's social institutions within a single settlement. All this, which today passes as accepted ingredients of the modern neighborhood, Unwin, with his far-sighted intelligence, had already recognized and realized in that time. (Ernst May, quoted in Buekschmitt 1963, 19)

The reforming paternalist was a type May recognized and admired, and Unwin presented a particularly apt hero as the professional activist in pursuit of a social vision. Ten years later, when the Weimar Republic declared its mission to build a new, modern, and democratic Germany, May certainly must have aspired to be a German Unwin.

For May and his Frankfurt team of designers, life in the new suburb would center on a healthy, largely outdoor life, in which the inhabitants occupied leisure time exploring their cultural and spiritual horizons. Dubbed the "New Life" (Neue Leben), it was a lifestyle based on the liberal concept of self-development, or *Bildung*.[2] The New Life expanded Bildung beyond the individual undertaking once reserved for the privileged bourgeois into a prescription for the masses, and expanded its aspirations to include much of the material comforts also associated with a middle-class life. The New Life was a chief promise of the Weimar Republic, a "third-way" solution to the political and economic turmoil of the early 1920s, and a redress to the hardships the population had suffered during World War I. It offered physical, spiritual, and intellectual fulfillment, and material well-being—in housing and social amenities—all this in lieu of the revolutionary promises of socialism. As it evolved as social policy, the New Life needed to assume a more specific content and form. This was the self-appointed task of the New Frankfurt.

Thus, the New Life became for a brief time the ideal of postwar life. And in so becoming it was joined to another utopian ideal: the garden city. In itself a destination for a multitude of life and land reform initiatives, the German garden city movement captured the popular imagination and its organization, a wide membership (Bergmann 1970). Founded in 1902, the German Garden City Society was "at once more utopian, and more realistic than its English original," a "breeding ground for socialist, cooperative and reformist ideals, but also for nationalist, capitalist and idealized vernacular values" (Lejeune 1996, 53; Bollerey and Hartmann 1980).[3] It was a determined lobby for private allotments and parkland, and it held fast to the ideal of the single-family homestead as the ideal dwelling for the German family.

To the garden city, May harnessed the contemporary creed of rationalization. The economic and sociological driver of German modernization in the postwar years, rationalization had inspired a virtual cult among housing designers, who envisioned that efficiency and the "one best way" would work the same economic miracle in everyday life that the industrialist Walter Rathenau had in the production of wartime materiel. In the Frankfurt settlements, rationalization resulted in a series of strictly configured house and garden types, flat roofs, and simplified construction methods. Its corollary, domestic economy, shaped a rationalized household that included the Frankfurt Kitchen, simple lightweight furnishings, and the banishment of ornament in favor of color. The push toward modernization drove May's insistence on unusual amenities such as electricity, hot running water, modern bathtubs, sinks and showers, cable radio, and electric laundry facilities.

In July 1925, May wasted little time on ceremony in his inaugural presentation to the Frankfurt city council as the new director of Frankfurt's housing and settlement office. The practice of city planning, he said, must be reconsidered. He called to task the previous generation of planners who had focused on the image of the city, on plazas, broad streets, and monumental buildings; and the engineers and physicians whose reforms had ignored the humanistic values pleaded by garden city advocates (Boehm 1926–27; Schürmeyer 1928). He called for the abolition of both rental barracks and the land speculation that had led to an overcrowded and insalubrious city. He challenged the domination of traffic concerns. What the modern city most needed was a setting for the New Life, based in the residential fabric of garden settlements. By harnessing the power of modern technology, Frankfurt could instead realize a new, contemporary urban beauty based in the everyday ("Sitzungsbericht" 1925). New streetcar lines would facilitate the workers' daily commute; electric laundries and modern kitchens would lighten women's housekeeping burdens; allotments provided a respite from urban life and a means of self-provisioning; parks enabled contemplation and sport; and community buildings and libraries would foster a vital social and intellectual life (Henderson 1996).

Römerstadt in 1927

Even among the Nidda Valley settlements, Römerstadt was exemplary. It was completed within one building campaign and before the economic downturn that led to the minimal dwelling and the simplified site plan installed in later projects.

Figure 12.1. Aerial view of the Römerstadt settlement in 1927. The Nidda River is in the foreground; the Nidda Valley Park is to the upper left. (*Städtebau* [1929])

Thus, the density was low, its design cohesive, and its white-collar and professional population were less contentious and demanding than their blue-collar counterparts in settlements nearby. The housing of single-family row houses with attached allotment gardens—then considered the ideal social incubator for the nuclear family—made up more than half of its 1,220 units. Even those living in apartments had garden allotments in the valley colony below, and there was a generous allowance for streets and pedestrian pathways. The 1927 plan included extensive community facilities as well: two schools and a day-care center, shops, a cooperative store, a community center, a church, a guesthouse, a communal laundry, a theater, cable-radio, and a youth clubhouse. Many of these facilities went unrealized—the theater, the second school, and the church, for example—but the housing and gardens went forward and enough of the amenities that Römerstadt was still the most complete and generously equipped among the Frankfurt settlements.

Figure 12.2. Römerstadt looking east. A bastion overlooking the park is visible in the distance. Its long body closes the street view. One can also discern the color highlighting massing and building orientation, and the distinction—in the lawn and porch designs—of house fronts between north and south. (*Das Neue Frankfurt* [1928])

The site plan was a remarkable essay on the Unwinian design principles. Responding to the shape and slope of the site, May and his colleague Herbert Boehm divided the settlement into two parts—a large circular quadrant and a slightly tapering, triangular spit—binding them with the sinuous main street called Hadrianstrasse. The curving lanes of the circular quadrant created a certain insularity and intimacy; the long blocks had down-the-street views curtailed by a jog in the street.

In both, periodic breaks in the house rows accommodated paths that led out to the bastions overlooking its southern bounding wall, a battered concrete rampart. Above it, terraces projected out toward the valley, and staircases led down to a promenade and the allotment colony below. The rampart was one of Römerstadt's most vital features. Practically, it protected the settlement from the floodplain, and, with a wall of apartment blocks along the northern boundary, it completed the settlement's strong borders and distinct outline. Mnemonically, the wall evoked the ancient Roman town that once inhabited the site, and marked, not the edge between town and a hostile countryside, but the boundary between a reformed domesticity and the wanderer's imaginative reach. Developing the theme were its bastions, along with the stepped-block profiles, attic stories, and towers of nearby buildings. Even the street names were evocative: An der Ringmauer (Along the Encircling Wall), Mithrasstrasse, and Hadrianstrasse. It was here, on a bastion terrace, that residents and the housing society, the Aktienbaugesellschaft für kleine Wohnungen (ABG; Housing Society for Small Dwellings) erected a bust in May's honor after his departure for the Soviet Union in 1930.[4] It was executed in the "simple style of a Roman herm" ("Die Römerstadt" 1932) but quickly disappeared with the rise of fascism.

This masterful design extended to the massing and arrangement of the entire settlement. Along its length, views from Hadrianstrasse opened to the left and right into streets lined with tidy row houses. The north-facing houses that sat close to the lane had low concrete walls that shielded the landings, with narrow planting troughs at their base. South-facing houses had trellised porches, front lawns, and flowering trees. Special elements articulated unique aspects of the plan: there were framed beds on the terraces, and a concrete trellis at Am Forum, likely a contribution by the Swiss architect Mart Stam (Henderson 2013). An assortment of building elements, including concrete plates and steel roll bars, lent both variety and consistency to the entryways.

While the landscape treatment was exquisite, it was in the dialogue between novel form and nature that Römerstadt's modernism departed from Hampstead Garden Suburb. On the main street of Hadrianstrasse the great curving profile of an apartment block and cooperative store designed by Carl Rudloff emerged to the north. A hinge was effected by the primary school—an L-shaped and sharply rectilinear block, punctuated with a clock tower—that aptly embodied New Education goals. It was designed by Frankfurt's chief city architect, Martin Elsaesser.

Next came the long curving wall and stepping profile of the southern apartment block, which traced the remaining curve of Hadrianstrasse, 190 meters to the south. It was designed by the Viennese architect Franz Schuster. Early plans showed that Hadrianstrasse was to continue as a pedestrian way through the Nidda Valley and link Römerstadt with the settlement of Ginnheim.

Römerstadt captured the popular imagination like no other, and it earned the New Frankfurt international acclaim. Professionals and the public flocked to see it. In 1928, three staff architects were occupied fulfilling requests for tours. The next year, the Garden City Society, under its director Hans Kampffmeyer, sponsored a course for professionals: for four days visiting architects were schooled in the particulars of the *Neue Bauen* and the satellite suburb, with Römerstadt as a primary model ("Frankfurt Kurse" 1929). At the opening of the 1929 Stuttgart Werkbund exhibition, May encouraged visitors to complete their tour of experimental housing with a visit to the settlement; delegates to the Frankfurt Congrès Internation-

Figure 12.3. An apartment block on Hadrianstrasse, Carl Rudloff, architect (1927). (*Das Neue Frankfurt* [1927])

aux d'Architecture Moderne toured in 1930. Locally, the housing was in great demand, despite relatively high rents. Its eventual residents were mostly professional people and upper-level white-collar workers. In 1929, Mart Stam was living at 145 Im Burgfeld, one of the bastion apartment blocks looking out over the Nidda Valley. In the same year, a new hire, the architect Walter Schwagenscheidt, moved with his family into 101 Mithrasstrasse: he wrote, "We were agreed that it is the most beautiful [settlement] that Frankfurt has produced. In what other settlement houses could you find a living room of 25 square meters with broad windows and terraces on the garden and to the south? Built-in electric kitchen, central heating, warm water, and all the rest?!"[5]

Römerstadt met with serious challenges only a few years after its construction. With the onset of the Great Depression, many settlers were unable to pay their utility bills, and the accusations that May had imposed luxuries beyond the means of the average household seemed substantiated. Under the Nazis, New Frankfurt settlements were labeled structurally faulty, ugly, and un-German. Subsequent coats of painted stucco emerged in an oppressive gray. Neither did the settlements escape the brutality of the fascist regime. House-to-house searches for "political enemies" began as early as 1933. Römerstadt was luckier in the war, escaping the bombing, unlike some other settlements, although as a precaution cuts were made in the cellar party walls to provide an emergency escape route through neighboring houses.

Römerstadt: Then and Now

Römerstadt's iconic status lies in its achievement as a modern garden city scheme, and it reflects the grand reform ideals of "New Era" Frankfurt. Preservation will look to those aspects necessary to this "reading" of its landscape. At the same time, the settlement currently faces distinct issues of viability as a community and as housing stock. In 2016, some of Römerstadt's amenities are more precious than ever, while others are anachronisms, whose preservation must be held in balance with present needs. The following sections outline these essential features and report on their current state.

Parks and Gardens

Beginning at the scale of the household, the fundamental component of Römerstadt's landscape was the allotment. Every household in the Frankfurt settlements built in the first two years, and in many others across the country, was provided an allotment intended for the cultivation of fruits and vegetables. These were rationalized gardens analogous to the Frankfurt Kitchen; indeed, the Frankfurt allotment was consciously based on the same concepts. The back-to-the-land landscape architect Leberecht Migge provided a standardized series of garden plans to partner New Frankfurt house types, plans in which no space was "wasted," and the order and arrangement of the beds facilitated a fully efficient project in the growing of food (Barnstone 2008; Gröning and Wolschke-Bulmahn 1995; von Reuss 1981).[6] In the allotment colony below the wall, each plot was additionally provided with a standardized garden cabin, designed by Grete Lihotzky (Margarete Schütte-Lihotzky).

In every plot, the ABG planted perennial berry vines and fruit trees, bordering hedges, and defined plant beds such that all the tenant had to do, as was quipped, was use them. The ABG further strictly controlled the uses and appearance of the gardens and cabins. Allotments had been popular among the working class during the post-war crisis, but they often had a motley appearance; in the settlements they assumed a guise of middle-class propriety and industrial efficiency alongside their homelier purpose.

The love of gardening runs deep in Germany, and as late as the 1980s, many of Römerstadt's plots still produced a rich array of fruits and vegetables. With the high

Figure 12.4. Römerstadt allotments and sheds in 1927. (*Das Neue Frankfurt* [1928])

level of gardening skill among the resident population, and a continued investment in the maintenance of hedges and pathways by the ABG, the gardens and landscape have remained remarkable features of the settlement. But as the decades have worn on, postwar consumer culture has had its influence. The homely tradition of the allotment garden began to wane such that, today, an aerial inspection turns up virtually no sign of the original scheme. These long, narrow strips, so conducive to vegetable gardening, are hard to configure as nonutilitarian pleasure gardens, and yet every household has its lawn set about with decorative planting and children's play sets, many attempting a more gardenesque aspect with a wavering path or curved shrubbery beds. The allotments below the wall, once strictly regulated and provided with identical, rationalized garden cabins to avoid the "chaos" of unregulated allotments, have also been altered and some even abandoned to weeds, while the cabins have expanded in size, number, color, material, and form to an extent that would have appalled their makers.

Figure 12.5. Römerstadt allotments and sheds in 2012. (Photo by Susan R. Henderson)

The original purpose of the allotment was to ensure that tenants could provide themselves with food in times of crisis; it was also believed that the food crop would defray some of the burden of rent and utility payments. Culturally, the kitchen garden provided a "reform" outlet for working-class leisure, bringing the settlers back in touch with nature in a productive way. Neither of these ideas has particular resonance today, although in the evolving green economy, that seems poised to change, if only in a limited resurgence of home gardening. Still, it is doubtful whether green initiatives will revive the self-sufficiency strictures embodied in the garden plots of Römerstadt. Meanwhile, the long narrow garden patches behind each row house, and even the garden colony, itself, are outmoded. What the settlement really needs is off-street parking, and it may be sensible to remove cars from the settlement's narrow streets to new alleys and parking behind the houses. This would eliminate some garden areas, but the new plots would have a usable proportion.

Römerstadt's streets are indeed overwhelmed by cars (see Plate 16). Once intimate and neighborly, the streetscapes are now occluded by high banks of curb-parked metal. A less dramatic, but still significant, blurring of the streetscape has been the planting of shrubs and trees, effected by the relaxed garden regulations. Originally, each south-facing row house was fronted by a small lawn planted with

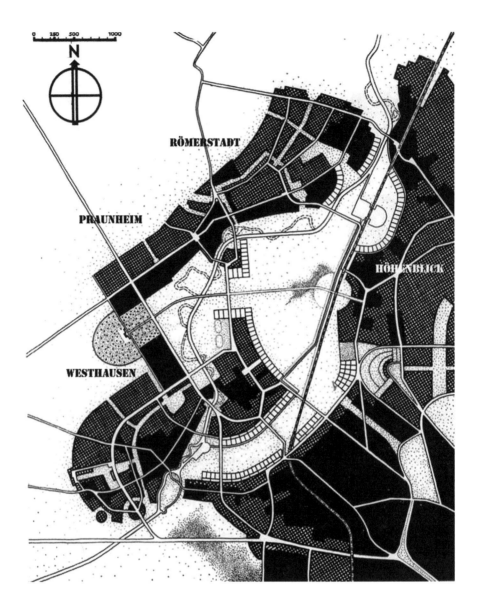

Figure 12.6. Nidda Valley Park plan (1927). (*Das Neue Frankfurt* [1927])

a single fruit tree. Today, a look down a lane in mid-summer presents a rich but jumbled array of green.

The original Nidda Valley greenbelt scheme designed by May and Boehm in 1926 presented a complete and beautifully choreographed narrative of the role of the park in the New Life. To the north, the crescent of settlements ringed the horizon. Sports facilities and allotment colonies occupied the perimeter and the banks of the Nidda River running through the valley center. From the city-side cliff, looking across to the white walls of the settlements in the distance, paths descended into the park, leading through open meadows, past a holding pond to allay floodwaters (and forming part of a new swimming facility), and continuing up into the settlements, one leading to the great S-curve of Hadrianstrasse. To the south was a vast new cemetery, while a string of small islands in the river were transformed into a chain of outdoor classrooms for scientific experiments and school outings. Although the grand scheme was never realized in all the rich variety of elements that the plan suggested, enough was achieved to make it truly the leisure realm of the New Life, a celebration of the modern ideal of the body and its self-realization through exercise, sport, and the outdoor life. Fitness culture has spawned a renaissance for the park in recent decades. Its paths, bike lanes, meadows, and playing fields now serve an even more robust and certainly better-outfitted population. The park's design, however, has suffered numerous erosions of its grand terrain. May and Boehm's plan had anticipated the pressures of urban growth, and they attempted to protect the Nidda Valley through zoning. Predictably, the park has nevertheless met with persistent challenges. In the 1930s, the fascists built housing in the valley. More serious incursions came after the war. Among these were a rail line, two highways, and a U-Bahn line, with serious consequences for Römerstadt.

Traffic and Its Impact

In 1925, Römerstadt was serviced by one end-of-the-line streetcar stop on the Nidda canal. From there, passengers transferred to a bus bound east for the settlement. It was a laborious journey for daily commuters, and the scheduled connections between streetcar and bus were undependable. The bus route ran along the northern boundary of the settlement, with periodic stops at cross streets. May and Boehm designed the settlement with this in mind. Römerstadt would be approached primarily on foot, from its northern boundary. Departing from the bus, one would have passed the tall wall of apartment blocks comprising the northern boundary, then turned into a residential street where the scale became more intimate. Or one might disembark at the intersection with the main street of Hadrianstrasse as the S-curve descended toward the park past its three dramatic buildings. The original scheme also called for a second school and a church at the top of the street.

In 1968, the city built a U-Bahn line stretching to the north to Nordweststadt, a settlement of some seven thousand units built in 1962.[7] The new line bisected Römerstadt at the point where the school meets the southern apartment block on Hadrianstrasse. The line's crippling impact on the coherence of the settlement was dealt a final blow by the addition of a raised, four-lane highway in 1980, dubbed, ironically, the Rosa-Luxembourg Stadt Autobahn. The highway and U-Bahn are now both encased within high walls on their passage through the settlement; at street level, another wall runs along Hadrianstrasse on the eastern side, blocking

Figure 12.7. Current view of the highway wall and U-Bahn cables from the school, with the southern apartment block designed by the Viennese architect Franz Schuster in the background. (Photo by Susan R. Henderson)

off secondary streets. The U-Bahn station has also created a new and primary entry point into the settlement: one set in the middle of the settlement amid a disorienting landscape of concrete ramps, walls, and stairs. From there, one passes into one side of the settlement or the other beneath the highway viaduct.

The walled U-Bahn and highway create the major blight on the integrity of today's Römerstadt, and they destroy a key moment in the poetical narrative of its landscape, not to mention its logistics. Revisiting the often-published photograph of the juncture of the school and the southern apartment block, one sees how the school sits astride the border between the parkland and the settlement. It is an image that exemplifies the New Life as comprising two sustaining forces: nature and community. Today, the school no longer faces the valley, the playground no longer wheels out into the open air, and the school windows, intended to bring in an abundance of light and air, look out on a massive concrete wall. An expansion of the school by Gunther Behnisch in 1995 extended the original school into the park with a long spit of a building. Elsaesser's school was now enclosed.

Raymond Unwin observed the significance of boundaries in the definition of identity: "Many ancient towns derive exceptional beauty from their enclosure by ramparts or walls. To this enclosure is due . . . the absence of that irregular fringe of half-developed suburb and half-spoiled country which forms such a hideous and depressing girdle around modern growing towns. . . . Even the wall itself may find some modern counterpart" (Unwin 1971 [1909], 154). Unfortunately for Römerstadt, the walls of the highway and U-Bahn have now had the opposite effect, destroying both the functioning entity of the settlement and its narrative.

Architecture and Color

Of all the features giving Römerstadt its character, its buildings have fared best. ABG and city regulations, now in combination with its conservation status, have rendered this fundamental aspect of Römerstadt inviolable to a great degree. There have been minor changes to house fronts, but nothing has seriously marred or challenged their basic appearance, and the three unique buildings of Hadrianstrasse remain intact.[8]

The joy in this architecture, however, has been significantly diminished with the loss of the original color scheme. The color plan of Römerstadt was one of its most distinctive features. Ernst May and the graphic designer Hans Leistikow had begun collaborating on the settlement color plans in Silesia in 1924. Their concept was to employ a coordinated color scheme for settlement buildings in order to articulate the boundaries, massing, and rhythm of the buildings and blocks and to enhance spatial readings. Much of this agenda might previously have been achieved by ornament. Color was also plotted and coordinated among buildings to confirm hierarchical order, define forms and boundaries, and enhance light conditions. The three major compositional principles were these: the settlement should float above a green setting, so the south-facing walls would be white; large blocks or towers would define boundaries—they were articulated in red or yellow; shady and sunny sides of the interior streets were painted accordingly, with north- or west-facing street walls deeply colored, generally in a brick red, and south- or east-facing walls in white. In addition, brightly colored details created rhythm and defined individual houses with the blue or red of railings, downspouts, doors, and window frames. In this way, the Römerstadt site plan was made legible through color. Elsewhere, the red wall of the southern apartment block, with its contrasting, blue window bands, made for a deep swath of color that met the blue and white horizontal stroke of the school; beyond were red bastions that stepped forward and drew attention out over the valley. Further along Hadrianstrasse, the northern apartment block was perhaps an ochre color—the settlers called it the "banana" or "cigar"— and was a deep color, either red or blue on the garden façade, with contrasting balcony and window framing (see Figures 12.1, 12.2, and 12.3).

The appreciation for the color plan has not been revived along with an appreciation for the settlement. The house rows were for some time a depressing and undistinguished gray; the ABG recently repainted the "cigar" in a uniform, bright white, walls and details alike, and ongoing repainting promises more of the same. The bastion blocks retained a brick-red color until recently, but current work indicates that even this modest recognition of the color plan will soon be overtaken.

Neighborhood Characteristics

Römerstadt's initial success as a community was sustained over the decades by tenants who clung to their houses and apartments over long spans of time. In 1945, the U.S. Army appropriated the settlement, as it did a number of others, to house its personnel; it was returned to the ABG in two stages, the second as late as 1956. Even with this long interim, many of the original residents returned (Lauer 1990, 110ff.). Current residents tend to stay settled as well: many have tenancies running from five to more than fifteen years. In 2008, about 60 percent of the population were adults of working age; 21 percent were over sixty-five. One remarkable feature of Römerstadt has always been its low density. In 1930, it had the lowest density among the city settlements, numbering 4,000 residents in 1,200 units. In 2008, the population had dropped nearly by half, reflecting the general tendency toward smaller households. Indeed, only about a quarter of the residences were households with more than two people (Wörner and Schröpfer 2009).

Known from the outset for its educated and middle-class population, Römerstadt's claim to be an "Akademikersiedlung" ("College Graduates' Settlement"), when compared to, for example, the neighboring settlements of Praunheim or Westhausen, was the result of its more lavish and roomier houses and more expansive and articulated grounds, which drew accordingly higher rents. In the 1960s, an overview of the population numbered 17 percent as college graduates, and 60 percent of parents planned for their children to attend college. Among its 1,259 working residents in the postwar years, 988 were white-collar workers.

Governance of the settlement remains close to what it was in 1927. The ABG still manages the property. There is a residents' advocacy group, though much of its functions are volunteer initiatives, such as small beautification projects. Significant policy changes are made by the ABG in consultation with the advocacy group.

Iconic Status

In 1972, Römerstadt was declared a federally protected property; it is recognized for its cultural significance and is protected against "significant changes and falsifications," as the preservation law states. Accordingly, any significant alterations require permission from the city. What is interpreted as "iconic" are the exterior envelope of the houses and apartment blocks and the regulation of exterior features like windows and entrances and balconies. The creation of the Ernst May Gesellschaft in 2005 further established its iconic status. The society had the goal of gaining local recognition for the achievements of Ernst May and the New Frankfurt settlement program. The society focused on restoring the Römerstadt row house into a museum, which it also occupies. The interior colors along with the materials have been refurbished, typical furnishings acquired, and its Frankfurt Kitchen and allotment garden restored.[9] The society's polemical stance is the celebration of Römerstadt, with Ernst May as the hero figure of Frankfurt's *Neue Bauen*. It hosts a yearly party on May's birthday and gives regular tours of the settlement and other buildings and settlements built under New Frankfurt auspices. Meanwhile, Frankfurt's Deutsche Architektur Museum (DAM) and the Institut für Stadtgeschichte (Institute for City History) have hosted a series of exhibitions on subjects related to the New Frankfurt, including two major exhibitions at DAM. One exhibition in 2009 looked at the work of Martin Elsaesser (Elsaesser et al. 2009), and, a second, in 2012, focused on the career and work of Ernst May himself (Quiring et al. 2011). Altogether, these projects have given the New Frankfurt initiative a prominence it has not had since its original construction.

In the final assessment, Römerstadt stands as the clearest statement of New Frankfurt modernity; it was *the* essential proving ground for the New Life. Its complex site plan, modern amenities, technological conveniences, and ample row houses still reflect this vision. Thus, the value achieved in preserving this property is in maintaining something of its New Life aspirations, as expressed in its landscape, gardens, and walks, and in the area's cohesive site and massing plans. Over time, the settlement has lost a good deal of this special character—through the erasure of its color scheme, the invasion of automobiles, and wear and tear effected by the U-Bahn and the highway. Some amelioration is possible. A solution to the parking problem would be a great gain in recouping the visual quiet of its streets. And a reinstitution of some version of the color plan would bring back the dynamic relationship between the various blocks of the settlements and its expression of the simple joy of color. This, indeed, is one of the most unappreciated, but most easily recouped, aspects of its original form. On the other hand, the damage wrought by transit lines seems irredeemable under present circumstances. There have been proposals of late to lower the highway to grade, but this will be of little help in mending the settlement's rent fabric.

The name "Römerstadt" was chosen in recognition of the Roman *castrum* that once occupied the settlement site and surrounding area. The street Im Forum was the site of the forum, and "Mithrasstrasse" referred to the theater and two small Mithraic temples once sited there. In the nineteenth century, local amateur archaeologists were so excited about these discoveries they talked about Frankfurt as the new Pompeii. The construction of Römerstadt unearthed more artifacts, but pressures exerted by May's office meant the loss of archaeological material to the excavators. In the 1950s, further remnants to the north of the castrum were bulldozed to build Nordweststadt. The losses continued with the construction of the highway, when a pottery kiln was unearthed on the embankment, and a bath building on its path. Today's Römerstadt is a scarred palimpsest of Roman remains, the 1920s New Life settlement, and late twentieth-century highway and exurban development. With a little more wisdom, the many modernizing builders who shaped this site might have divined a cautionary tale in the fate of the Roman castrum under their stewardship.

Table 12.1
Summary of Historical Events and Heritage Benchmarks for Römerstadt

Year	Event
1911	Ernst May works for Raymond Unwin on Hampstead Garden Suburb.
1925	Mayor Ludwig Landmann hires May as the director of Frankfurt's housing and settlement office.
1927	May's plan for the Nidda Valley settlement satellite, which includes Römerstadt, is under construction. His design team includes Herbert Boehm (site plan), Carl Hermann Rudloff (house types and cooperative store building), Martin Elsaesser (school), Grete Lihotzky (kitchen), Hans Leistikow (polychromy), and Leberecht Migge (landscape).
1928	Römerstadt is completed. The Aktienbaugesellschaft für kleine Wohnungen (ABG; Housing Society for Small Dwellings) owns and manages the residential units.
1928	Through *Das Neue Frankfurt* and numerous other publicity venues, New Frankfurt and Römerstadt gain international recognition.
1930	Assembled in Frankfurt, delegates to the Congrès Internationaux d'Architecture Moderne visit Römerstadt. May leaves Frankfurt for the Soviet Union.
1945	The U.S. Army houses its personnel in Römerstadt, which has escaped bombings.
1956	Römerstadt housing is fully returned to the ABG.
1968	The U-Bahn transit line reaches Römerstadt, eroding the integrity of the settlement plan.
1972	Römerstadt is declared a federally protected landmark.
1980	Paralleling the U-Bahn line, the raised, four-lane Rosa Luxembourg highway, encased in high walls, bisects the settlement.
1995	The new school addition (Gunther Behnisch architect) alters the original impression of openness and visual clarity of the original school building.
2005	Created to gain local recognition for the New Frankfurt program, the Ernst May Gesellschaft organizes tours and focuses on restoring a Römerstadt row house and its gardens into a museum.
	Population (as of 2018), 2500; 74 acres [2,83 ha]; 1,200 dwelling units.

NOTES

1. For a more detailed discussion of Römerstadt and the New Frankfurt, see Henderson 2013.

2. Among many "new" tropes—the New Life, the New Woman, the New Building—the New Life was in common currency in the 1920s. It was appropriated with such insistence in the case of the New Frankfurt that it assumed a particular association with it.

3. The founders of the Deutsche Gartenstadt Gesellschaft (DGG; German Garden City Society), Heinrich and Julius Hart, campaigned for the dissolution of industrial cities into a landscape of economically autonomous settlements. These would return workers to a "truly German" way of life and thereby end the political turmoil and chaos of the cities.

4 Today, the ABG comprises a larger consortium of formerly independent housing societies and is called ABG Frankfurt Holdings.

5. Walter Schwagenscheidt to Hermann Schauffler, January 1, 1929, quoted in Preusler 1985, 79.

6. Not all the allotment gardens were designed by Migge. Some of those directly adjacent to the row houses were the work of landscape architects from the municipal offices; these were less stringently rationalized, even having patches of lawn. May and Migge began their collaboration in the early 1920s when May was the head of the rural housing authority in Silesia.

7. Ironically, Nordweststadt was the work of May's former team member, Walter Schwagenscheidt. It is a large Zeilenbau settlement typical of the period.

8. The interiors are quite changed, of course, and have been further modernized, with remodeled kitchens and baths, and featuring new wallpapers, floor coverings, and light fixtures.

9. The society was awarded a silver medal by the Deutsches Nationalkomitee für Denkmalschutz (German National Committee for Preservation).

REFERENCES

Barnstone, Deborah Ascher. 2008. "The Prehistory of Environmentalism: Schlesischer Bund für Heimatschutz." In *The Architecture Annual: Delft University of Technology*, edited by Henco Bekkering, 64–69. Rotterdam: 010 Publishers.

Bergmann, Jean Klaus. 1970. "Agrarromantik und Großstadtfeindschaft." In *Marburger Abhandlungen zur Politischen Wissenschaft*, vol. 20, 135–63. Meisenheim am Glan: Verlag Anton Hain.

Boehm, Herbert. 1926–27. "Baulanderschliessung in Frankfurt, Früher und Heute." *Das Neue Frankfurt*: 107–8.

Bollerey, Franziska, and Kristina Hartmann. 1980. "A Patriarchal Utopia: The Garden City and Housing Reform in Germany at the Turn of the Century." In *The Rise of Modern Urban Planning*, edited by Anthony Sutcliffe, 135–64. New York: St. Martin's Press.

Buekschmitt, Justus. 1963. *Ernst May*. Stuttgart: Alexander Koch.

De Michelis, Marco. 1985. "Naissance de la Siedlung." *Les Cahiers de la recherche architecturale* 15/16/17: 138–53.

Elsaesser, Thomas, Christina Gräwe, Thomas Schilling, and Peter Cachola Schmal, eds. 2009. *Martin Elsaesser und das Neue Frankfurt / Martin Elsaesser and the New Frankfurt*. Tübingen: Wasmuth.

"Frankfurt Kurse für neues Bauen." 1929. *Baumeister* 27, supp. (August): 153.

Gröning, Gert, and Joachim Wolshke-Bulmahn. 1995. *Von Ackermann bis Ziegelhütte: Ein Jahrhundert Kleingartenkultur*. Vol. 36 of Studien zur Frankfurter Geschichte. Frankfurt am Main: Verlag Waldemar Kramer.

Henderson, Susan R. 1996. "A Revolution in Woman's Sphere: Grete Lihotzky and the Frankfurt Kitchen." In *Architecture and Feminism*, edited by Debra Coleman, Elizabeth Danze, and Carol Henderson, 221–48. Princeton, NJ: Princeton Architectural Press, 1996.

———. 2013. *Building Culture: Ernst May and the New Frankfurt, 1926–1932*. New York: Peter Lang.

Lauer, Heike. 1990. *Leben in Neuer Sachlichkeit*. Frankfurt: Notizen.

Lejeune, Jean-François. 1996. "From Hellerau to the Bauhaus: Memory and Modernity of the German Garden City." In *The New City*, edited by Jean-François Lejeune, 53–68. Princeton, NJ: Princeton Architectural Press.

May, Ernst. 1913. "Unwin as a Planner for Social Welfare." *Town and Country Planning* 21 (November): 427–28.

Noever, Peter, ed. 1996. *Margarete Schütte-Lihotzky. Soziale Architekture: Zeitzeugin eines Jahrhunderts*. Vienna: Böhlau Verlag.

Preusler, Burghard. 1985. *Walter Schwagenscheidt, 1886–1968. Architektenideale im Wandel sozialer Figurationen*. Stuttgart: Deutsche Verlags-Anstalt.

Quiring, Claudia, Wolfgang Voigt, Peter Cachola Schmal, and Eckhard Herrel, eds. 2011. *Ernst May 1886–1970*. Munich: Prestel.

"Die Römerstadt ehrt ihren Schöpfer." 1932. *Frankfurter Nachrichten* (April 1).

Schürmeyer, Walter. 1928. "Siedlungspolitik, und Stadterweiterung in Frankfurt a.m." *Deutsche Bauzeitung,* supp. "Stadt und Siedlung" (January): 1–2.

"Sitzungsbericht." 1925. *Frankfurter General Zeitung* (July 24).

Unwin, Raymond. 1971 (1909). *Town Planning in Practice*. New York: Benjamin Blom.

von Reuss, Jürgen. 1981. "Leberecht Migge—Spartakus in Grün." In *Leberecht Migge, 1881–1935. Gartenkultur des 20. Jahrhundert*, 10–32. Worpswede: Worpsweder Verlag.

Wörner, Anke, and Waltraud Schröpfer. 2009. "Frankfurter Siedlungen 2008." *Frankfurter Statistische Berichte 2/3 2009*. www.frankfurt.de/sixcms/media.php/678/2009.

CHAPTER 13

SOWETO

Planning for Apartheid and Preserving the Garden City

Townships of Johannesburg, South Africa

Angel David Nieves

Townships have developed an *iconic profile* in South African
society, representing the very heart of where the struggle for
freedom was waged, where many of today's leaders, including
famous politicians, artists, business icons, sportsmen and women
were born and grew up.
—Shisaka Development Management Services 2009
  (emphasis added)

1976 Uprising

On the morning of June 16, 1976, black African students were gunned down by
members of the South African police and security forces as they marched to protest the adoption of Afrikaans as the primary language of instruction within
schools across Johannesburg's "South Western Townships," better known as
Soweto (Figure 13.1).[1] The subsequent release of Sam Nzima's iconic photograph
(Figure 13.2) depicting the death of Hector Pieterson—an early casualty of the
protests—coupled with the deaths that day of many other schoolchildren, would
catalyze the Student Uprisings and spark the global anti-apartheid movement
(Bonner and Segal 1998, 83; Cillie 1980; Gerhart 1994; Hlongwane 2006). The
physical backdrop to these events, a so-called model native township, was made up
of a series of systematically planned would-be South African garden cities, with
the primary purpose of reinforcing the powers and capacities of the state system of
apartheid (Robinson 1990). Physical spaces such as these, which were built under
the apartheid system, have provided the social, political, and economic context for
black urban life since the founding of Johannesburg in 1886 to the present. Few
studies have considered the historical significance of these townships as extant
physical artifacts of a difficult past; however, they now face the complex heritage
issues and concurrent pressures of the international tourist market. This chapter

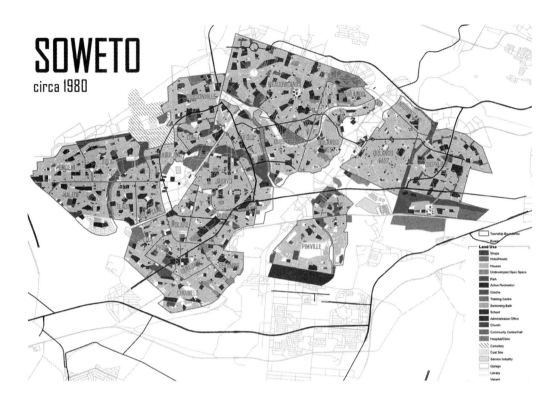

SOWETO
circa 1980

Figure 13.1. A Soweto (South Western Townships) map. (Photo by Angel David Nieves)

attempts to look beyond some of the perceived "ebb and flow in planning iconicity," as observed by Isabelle Gournay in her chapter within this volume, and to instead consider how Soweto can carry "non-visually driven meanings" for a variety of stakeholders since its founding. This initial foray is part of a multiyear study and collaboration for the Soweto Historical GIS Project (SHGIS; http://dhinitiative.org/projects/shgis). Dona Stewart (2003, 219) has argued in her work on Egypt's metropolis, Cairo, that "rarely, if ever, are Cairo's multiple heritages conceptualised as an integrated fabric of overlapping historic landscapes." Similarly, in Johannesburg's Soweto, the meaning and significance of these planned communities defer to the competing interests of urban redevelopment, large-scale heritage planning, and globalization.

To the casual western observer, Soweto, with its endless iterations of the garden city's concentric and radial plan, remains manifestly familiar yet always resolutely the other. Our understanding of it now seems bookended by the images of Pieterson's slaying and Nelson Mandela's memorial service at FNB Stadium just outside Soweto's eastern Orlando District (FNB, of course, stands in for First National Bank, as opportunistic a corporate naming opportunity as the first world's Citi-Field in New York or AT&T Park in San Francisco) with the hellish images of the filmmaker Neill Blomkamp's *District 9*'s squatter slums sandwiched in-between.

Soweto is a vision typically framed at bottom by a swath of divided highway, a dusty bedroom community of rusted metal roofs stretching endlessly on a flat plain. Soweto is always there—the iconicity of the images emerging from the anti-apartheid struggles of decades ago ensures this—but there is seemingly no way inside Soweto, bounded as it is by mining refuse, ring roads, railways, and highways. Once inside, its labyrinthine, concentric blocks, so unlike the avenues of Manhattan that stretch to the horizon, foil any effort of the eye to take it all in or even to navigate it intuitively.

Figure 13.2. The Hector Pieterson Memorial in Soweto, Johannesburg, opened in 2002. (Photo by Angel David Nieves)

It is difficult to determine exactly where to begin a discussion of Soweto's iconicity, because so little has been done on this particular topic (Figure 13.3). Soweto fits the definition of "iconic," as suggested by Gournay in this volume: a community must offer "highly recognizable visual representations, encapsulating its physical and social tenets." In Soweto's case, it depends on who you ask and on which particular moment of the life cycle of this community is under investigation. Soweto itself has been the subject of countless studies, but few have looked critically at the kinds of design intentions, realized and imagined, that allowed for the eventual Student Uprisings of 1976 (Jurgens and Donaldson 2012, 155). This is now just one of many ways that geographic methodologies are applied to the study of the anti-apartheid movement. My research examines the micro-geography of resistance and the layer-

Figure 13.3. Orlando extension, Soweto (1950). (Courtesy Museum Africa Collection, Johannesburg)

ing of meaning and action between the apartheid state and township residents across its built form. Some of my early hypotheses regarding the influence of the garden city movement suggest that the densities resulting from these planned interventions might have likely encouraged empowerment among its residents. Soweto, more than 18 miles southwest of Johannesburg's central business district (CBD), at more than 77 square miles and today with more than 1.2 million residents—at about 15,500 persons per square mile, it is almost twice as dense as Los Angeles and approaching the density of San Francisco—is the most metropolitan township in the nation. The indigenous black population, specifically in Johannesburg, which had been widely dispersed and even landless before arriving in this newly emerging megacity, could organize politically and culturally here in ways that permitted them to enact forms of resistance to the Nationalist Party. City officials, health reformers, and Nationalist Party leaders envisioned townships (what I refer to here as "black labor-machines") as icons for progressive, modern planning principles for the betterment of "natives," yet that, over time, inadvertently provided the network of densely organized communities that upended a system of domination and oppression.

Early Townships

Segregation was nothing new, of course, in South Africa—racial segregation was already in practice as far back as the white settlers' permanent landing at what is now Cape Town in 1652. Entrenched structural segregation came about after the 1850s and is often attributed to the growth in racialism among the dominant classes of the British Empire and the age of imperialism (Christopher 1983, 146; Department of Native Affairs n.d., 193). The earliest formal townships were in Kimberley, where migrant laborers came to work in the mines following the discovery of gold in 1867. The infamous hostel system was introduced. Each hostel typically housed sixteen workers per sleeping room for eleven months of the year, with a one-month break to visit families back in the rural homelands. The indigenous black population was lured or forcibly moved from rural areas using tactics common to colonialism, including dispossession of farmland, the expropriation of livestock, periodic war, and many other forms of manipulation to address the needs of rapid industrialization and the expansion of cities.

The demands for a cheap labor force and the outbreak of the Boer War, at the turn of the twentieth century, resulted in the uprooting of large rural populations, including blacks and poor whites (white Afrikaners). After gold was discovered, a "poor white problem" emerged during the first three decades of the twentieth century. Sanitation crises, massive housing shortages, and the spread of public health epidemics led to an array of racial and moral panics about the proximity of black workers who lived in the same urban neighborhoods as whites. Water-borne sanitation was first introduced in Johannesburg in 1908, but the disposal of human waste for the entire city occurred near black neighborhoods. English settlers and officials regarded non-Europeans as unhygienic, giving rise to the "sanitary syndrome" whereby the local authorities sought to remove nonwhites and establish separate African residential areas at some distance from the European town. As A. J. Christopher (1983, 188) has noted, "The result was the construction of the [nonwhite] location, regularly laid out and physically isolated from the town it served." Urban segregation of the African population was enforced under the Natives (Urban Areas) Act of 1923, which established the settler doctrine that "the town is a European area in which there is no place for the redundant Native" (188). By February 1933 the Provincial Administrator for Johannesburg, J. S. Smit, compared the planning of the Witwatersrand to the recent "regional movements" taking place in the Greater Ruhr region (of Germany), London, and New York, referring directly to the work of garden city planners from Europe (Home 1990; Mabin 1993, 313; Myers 2003). Other legislative acts and government policy mandates that required black South Africans (or black Africans), colored (or mixed-race) individ-

MuseuMAfricA Johannesburg. PH2002-420

Figure 13.4. Matchbox houses, Meadowlands, Soweto (ca. 1954). (Courtesy Museum Africa Collection, Johannesburg)

uals, and Indians to live separately included the Land Act of 1913, the Natives Urban Areas Consolidation Act of 1945, the Immorality Amendment Act of 1950, and the Group Areas Act of 1950 (Lewis 1966, 38). By 1950, well over forty acts and amendments were passed to secure the Nationalist Party's formal control over the urban landscape and its growing urban population (Figure 13.4). However, these acts also ensured that over the course of several generations the majority of the black population would develop long-standing ties to—and a rich cultural heritage within—their respective townships as the struggle against apartheid was waged.

Apartheid Garden Cities

South African industrialization had brought with it crime, disease, degradation, and prostitution, all of which were seen as incompatible with the emerging civic order. Local municipal authorities sought new ways to address the problem of residential segregation and town planning developments. Ebenezer Howard's *Garden Cities of To-morrow*, released in 1902, would provide a template for solving the crisis of the industrial city through the design of ideal towns built as separate satellites away from the parent city and surrounded by agricultural greenbelts on land held in common by the community. Howard's proposal was determined to be a viable solution to the urban crisis across South Africa by employing town planning with layouts at relatively low density (although Soweto today is slightly denser than greater London), ample gardens, allotments for open space, voluntary cooperation between landowners and local authorities, and self-management by residents. Garden city ideals were promoted all over the world through the International Garden City Association. In South Africa local authorities turned to Britain in search of solutions to their urban problems—to use the romanticized ideals of the English village to "uplift" social others (Coetzer 2009, 1).[2] The idea of improving the conditions of "native" housing and asserting control soon required the systematic application of the town planning principles first proposed by Howard and later reinterpreted by Raymond Unwin and Barry Parker. By 1922 the Joint Native Townships and Housing Estates Committee of Cape Town prepared a contract for an African township that "had been designed [using] the best examples of modern town planning" (Demissie 1992, 233). In Johannesburg the Western Native Township, along with the housing scheme near Langa in Cape Town, was among the first to incorporate low-density housing development using town planning principles in the design of "garden cities." Both schemes incorporated a buffer zone to separate the African townships from white residential and commercial areas. By 1925, the slumyard population of Johannesburg was estimated to be nine thousand, and by 1927 the figure reached forty thousand. Garden city design models (Figure 13.5) were intended to veil the strong impulses of government-sponsored social control and racial segregation (or the government-sponsored architectural project of social control and racial segregation). Many of the design intentions of the garden city movement in South Africa were undermined by the lack of available public funding or even private support from mining interests. An important question remains still unanswered: should the ideals of the garden city movement, a largely underdeveloped or unrealized model housing scheme in Soweto, be preserved for future generations? Or should efforts to adapt what was actually built by apartheid planners, architects, and social scientists, by local residents, be preserved instead? (See Figure 13.6.)

Indeed, Soweto, today comprising twenty-nine townships, demonstrates attributes of a planned community or, more specifically, a series of segregated planned communities. The 1927 amendment of the Native Urban Areas Act enabled the government to relocate people without first providing them with alternative accommodation and without paying attention to the growing need for more hous-

Figure 13.5. Garden city model in a propaganda photograph, Orlando, Soweto. (Courtesy Museum Africa Collection, Johannesburg)

Figure 13.6. "Main Street," Western Native Township, Soweto (ca. 1921). (Courtesy Museum Africa Collection, Johannesburg)

ing. The city government provided emergency camps with basic water and sanitary services. However, in the early years planning at what would become Soweto was rudimentary: it was little more than an improvised civil engineering exercise of lot and block plans, along with shocking sanitary conditions. There were no provisions for utilities, nor was there model housing—options included municipality-built V-shaped huts but no adequate alternative housing (Bonner and Segal 1998,

Figure 13.7. A typical native cottage, the Type J1 brick house. (Photo by Angel David Nieves)

13, 15). The Orlando housing plan for African workers consisted of two or three rooms with no kitchens or bathroom (Figure 13.7) (Connell 1947; Demissie 1992, 235; Johannesburg Citizens' Housing Committee 1953; Union of South Africa 1937, 21, 23). However, publications in South Africa at the time were replete with images of the ideal living conditions being provided for native workers (Bonner and Segal 1998, 17).

Residents in what would become Soweto were tenants and not landowners and were responsible for the development and maintenance of their own housing. For myriad reasons, they were unable to engage with planners, architects, or other design professionals; instead they resorted to subsistence strategies to erect better shelter, however temporary.

Urban Regeneration

"Subaltern urbanism," the study of postcolonial and postimperial cities of the developing world, has now emerged as a means to further theorize the Global South's megacities and the subaltern spaces and classes (spaces and classes conventionally perceived as inferior because of race, class, gender, sexual orientation, ethnicity, or religion) that constitute a majority of their populations. The informal settlements of the twenty-first century that today command much of our scholarly attention in the fields of urban and regional planning are in many ways very similar to the settlements and cities such as Johannesburg at the turn of the twentieth century. The creation and expansion of all-black townships as a series of iconic, planned, urban would-be greenbelt communities have received only sporadic attention in the post-apartheid era, in lieu of a more common neoliberal view of the antihomogeneous, symbolic, and material meaning of the global megacity. For some, Johannesburg exemplifies the characteristics of an African "megacity," due to its "post-colonial, Pan-African dynamics, which emphasise diversity, hybridity and transformational processes of cultural exchange" (Farber 2008). The apartheid system that demanded orderliness and a stringent urban management style focused on functionality has resulted in a certain level of neglect concerning the future of township growth and change, particularly in terms of preservation planning and policy (Donaldson 2001, 226). According to some studies, townships currently house more than 40 percent of South Africa's urban population, and 20 percent live in informal settlements and low-income housing estates. (See Plate 17.) In Johannesburg, 43 percent of residents live in Soweto, and 73 percent live in townships, informal areas, and low-cost housing estates (Neighborhood Development Programme 2009, 7). A quarter of South Africa's population (11.6 million), now upward of 47.8 million people, lives in the country's seventy-six largest townships. Because of historic social compression in racially segregated areas, older townships are seen as socially, culturally, and economically more diverse, often containing middle- and lower-income areas and scattered middle-income households. Soweto provides an example of this sort of diversity of socioeconomic profiles.

Images and other documentation of early Soweto remain largely out of circulation, as Soweto's bibliography and heritage continue to remain unexplored—all part of an untold countrywide narrative of township development. For example, the visitor center for greater Soweto, a likely showcase for tourists seeking to acquaint themselves with Soweto's narrative, is not in Orlando (or Orlando West)—the most heavily trafficked tourist district of the townships and the former home of two Nobel laureates, Nelson Mandela and Desmond Tutu—but is instead located in Kliptown at the Walter Sisulu Square. The narrative provided at the visitor center says little about the broader history of Soweto, except for a brief mention on its website that "Kliptown is the oldest residential district of Soweto, and was first laid out in 1891 on land which formed part of Klipspruit farm."[3] While the Kliptown Open Air Museum uses multimedia to tell the story of the drafting of the Freedom Charter in 1955, it fails to convey Soweto's complex spatial history to the public. Annual events commemorating the Student Uprisings of 1976 do not focus on the ways in which the everyday built environments of the townships contributed to local forms of resistance.

Planning documentation for Soweto remains particularly obscure. There is, as yet, no definitive history for Soweto, much less about its planning history. The two most recent publications, *Soweto: A History* (1998) by Phil Bonner and Lauren Segal, and *Orlando West, Soweto: An Illustrated History* by Noor Nieftagodien and Sally Gaule (2013) do not necessarily focus solely on this greater-than-120-year period of planning history (Jurgen and Donaldson 2012, 154). The great majority of maps and plans that accompany this chapter—all relics from the decades of apartheid and segregation—were uncatalogued (both digitally and otherwise) and were secured by chance at a provincial government office in Pretoria in 2010. *The Soweto '76 Archive* prototype, developed between 2006 and 2008 at the Maryland Institute for Technology in the Humanities and SHGIS, are the only archival venues for these planning maps and images.

Soweto is a "garden city" in a metropolitan area replete with suburban typologies. The original Soweto garden city plan has proved resilient. Originally overwhelmingly residential, Soweto's plan made allowances for schools, commerce, and sporting areas and, over the decades, Soweto has accommodated such later large-scale interventions as Orlando Stadium (originally built in 1959, it seats 24,000 and was rebuilt for soccer's 2010 FIFA World Cup for R280 million or US$30.8 million) and today's Maponya Mall. Soweto is no longer strictly a bedroom community—mass employment centers within the townships were generally outlawed under the apartheid state—as the local economy today hosts both formal and informal activities. Heritage and other tourist offerings include black-owned bus tours, local restaurants, and local arts and crafts found both in stands and at retail storefronts (Jurgen and Donaldson 2012, 204).

Over the past ten years, Soweto has undergone major renewal and redevelopment. Today, Soweto is witnessing upgrades to its local social and economic infrastructure (Sibiya 2012, 7), with additional investments coming from the private sector and from state entities such as the City of Johannesburg (COJ). Urban renewal and redevelopment have, in turn, led to increased property prices in the Soweto residential market. There is also an influx of higher-income earners, or what recent research identifies as an emerging black middle class (Shapiro 2009; Sigonyela 2006). Soweto has also experienced an influx of wealthier residents and an out-migration of original residents (Sigonyela 2006; "South Africa" 2007, 1), as suburbs across Johannesburg begin to reflect the demographic changes brought on by the emerging black middle class.[4] In the past, the out-migration of residents had been linked to the search for a better life and a greater number of amenities found only in the suburbs. However, as townships now have amenities similar to the suburbs, wealthier residents are moving back to Soweto (Visser 2002).

While Soweto was intended as little more than containment housing or, more generously, as a bedroom community, amenities and multiuse set-asides have developed over the decades. Amenities at Soweto have included parks, playfields, commercial districts, and even commercial strips developed in tandem with the FIFA 2010 World Cup. The Gauteng commuter train (or Gautrain) to the international airport was developed along with other light-rail and commuter-rail projects. Highways to and around Soweto were also expanded. But for most, public transportation on buses or taxis remains the method of choice. However, distances into the city are considerable (Soweto is more than thirty kilometers outside the CBD) and a one-way trip into the city during rush hour may take as long as an hour. With white flight from Johannesburg into the suburbs, Soweto's service workers are now similarly dispersed outside the CBD. Bus networks from Soweto to Johannesburg's suburbs have grown to accommodate this urban sprawl. Eighty-seven formal taxi ranks and a further fifty informal taxi ranks were identified in Soweto in February 1990. Because of the structure of the route system, passengers living in the western part of Soweto usually must use two taxis to get into town. On a typical weekday, some four thousand taxis with passengers arrive and about two thousand taxis loaded with passengers leave one of the largest taxi ranks at Baragwanath Hospital daily. Many passengers arrive by taxis from various parts of Soweto and transfer to buses leaving for destinations in Johannesburg (Khosa 1993, 191). Under apartheid, the national government paid huge subsidies for bus and train fares to help facilitate the spatial reorganization of urban areas.

Proximity to brownfields such as former gold mines and their mountains of refuse might veto development back in the United States, but, apparently, this has not been the case in Soweto. Maponya Mall, an R$70 million, 700,000-square-foot megamall in Kliptown, has stores such as Nike, McDonald's, Timberland, and the Gap. The mall's website proclaims "Maponya Mall is in the heart of true South African Culture and after enjoying first class shopping we urge you to visit the various historical sites around Soweto. The foundation of a democratic South Africa was mined and refined around this bustling Township which now, in its true right, is a City."

While the state upgraded infrastructure, local organizations continued to pressure for basic improvements in sidewalks, paved roads, street fixtures, and lighting. Challenges remain formidable in Soweto. Parts of Soweto remain among the poorest in Johannesburg. Unemployment there is believed to be above the national average of 25 percent. New informal settlements for immigrants from Zimbabwe and other African countries continue to draw from scarce resources. Violent crime and the demands of illegal immigration into Soweto remain hugely problematic.

For undocumented arrivals from surrounding towns and farmlands, and those from countries nearby South Africa, particularly from Zimbabwe, the dream of a better life often fails to materialize. The COJ introduced a number of urban renewal initiatives, including an upgrade of Vilakazi Street (where Mandela and Tutu lived), the rebuilding of the FNB Stadium for the 2010 FIFA World Cup, the development of the Kliptown Walter Sisulu Square of Dedication (Freedom Square), the Bara Taxi and Bus Facility, the Soweto Empowerment Zone, and the R1-billion Orlando Ekhaya project.[5] The adoption of neoliberal planning policies over the past two decades has led to local and regional governments across the Global South clamoring to become part of the world economy and to be designated as global cities—and Johannesburg is no exception. Although the COJ spearheaded these redevelopment efforts, other partners, including the national government, Gauteng Province, and the private sector, have all poured additional resources toward the redevelopment of Soweto. What this means for the major tourist attraction of Soweto Township, still at a considerable distance from the CBD, remains unclear.

In 2012 the Department of Arts and Culture forecast the one hundredth anniversary of the African National Congress as a way to promote "a forward thrust in our efforts to identify, collect, protect and promote our heritage to deepen social cohesion and nation building and to serve as both catalyst and driver of sustained development."[6] Urban regeneration, or "third wave gentrification," as seen in Soweto, has meant the creation of even greater contrasts between the "haves and have nots" and between the old and new residents. Traditionally, some economists have argued that the "institutional agents" (the COJ, Gauteng Province, etc.) and the influx of capital (foreign and domestic) are the key role players in the gentrification process. However, in the case of Soweto's urban regeneration, the spending and investment of foreign tourists seem to act only as occasional or short-term agents of gentrification, seeing as these monies do not necessarily become reinvested in new modern housing schemes or even act as long-term catalysts for heritage development. Many of the urban regeneration schemes, such as Kliptown or the Red Location Museum (in Port Elizabeth, Eastern Cape), have made little difference in the efforts to preserve extant historic fabric or in necessarily changing the way heritage organizations might redefine the parameters of significance, especially for black South Africans.

The historian Sue Krige's recent work (2010) on industrial heritage provides a new way of conceptualizing the neglected history of these planned communities for workers as worthy of further study vis-à-vis their cultural value and significance. In a city such as Johannesburg, industrial heritage should be recognized as having cultural value and significance. According to the National Heritage Resources Act (NHRA) of 1999, the measures of cultural significance are aesthetic, architectural, historical, scientific, social, spiritual, linguistic, or technological. The act also promotes a more holistic approach to heritage management, where the physical site and its tangible, material remains are meant to be coupled with the preservation of intangible heritage, which can relate to the history and culture of African and other marginalized communities living in townships (Marschall 2008, 360).

The conservation of industrial heritage is certainly not about buildings only. Oral histories (which often reclaim invisible/neglected voices) provide an incredibly important dimension to such work. According to the NHRA of 1999, the *association* of a person or particular community or communities with a place is a measure of cultural significance. The act recognizes that heritage significance resides in the whole (the precinct), its landscape, as well as in the parts (the buildings). The idea of a heritage precinct or area adds to how we understand and work with cultural heritage. The NHRA specifically states that a local authority can "assess the intrinsic, comparative and contextual significance of a heritage resource." Finding ways to ensure that the urban heritage resource is both worthy of preservation and also a means of generating income for local township residents through local tourism efforts is still much debated. As Krige has argued, "[In some cases] working with industrial heritage allows us to foreground the many categories that the SAHR [South African Heritage Resources] Act provides of what constitutes 'cultural' significance, and how it can be assessed. The history of industrialization and urbanisation, viewed through the lens of its physical remains, shows how people (not only Black people) had to adapt one of the many aspects of their identities, their culture, to urban living" (2010, 108).

The urban geographer Ronnie Donaldson (2001, 226) has noted that, since 1994, "A kaleidoscope of post-apartheid urban outcomes, including spaces of integration, redevelopment spaces, restitution and redistribution spaces, control spaces, and spaces of decadence, has been observed during [the] transition [to democracy]." Despite the new political order of concern for the "well-being of the majority of the population," much of that concern has "been marked by disappointment, and in many cases disillusionment." Instead, many city policies put into place in the years immediately following the first democratic elections (and, perhaps, some would argue, over the last seventeen years) across South Africa's cities have focused on issues of densification, corridor development, and mixed land uses. Donaldson (2001, 229) raises an important question: "how are these practices implemented, or how will they be implemented in a sustainable manner that would take into consideration the conservation of historically significant areas?" The answer is particularly important as we attempt to understand the significance of township design and planning. Desegregating society, creating new infrastructure, and building houses in underdeveloped areas were of critical importance to the early success of the African National Congress, but the conservation of certain historical urban spaces received little attention until the new millennium. Internationally, historic districts and the sense of place inherent to these living and working communities had been well established as marketable tourist attractions by the early 1990s. By then, urban tourist attractions also included museums and heritage sites. However, in South Africa, whites still controlled access to the heritage tourism industry, leaving marginalized communities outside the emerging heritage conservation realm. The overall disrespect for black heritage during the apartheid regime in which "Afrikaner mythology along with its icons and monuments was 'romanticized' within an entirely Eurocentric approach" meant that few efforts were made to focus on black historical living spaces that might be incorporated into a citywide heritage program (Donaldson 2001, 229). Reaching some kind of consensus for the historical artifacts that survived apartheid becomes critically important. If that history "is too charged and too recent, when architectural value is seen to be irrelevant in the face of desperate need," new strategies will be needed (Donaldson 2001, 230).

Gentrification is a fact in Soweto as surely as it is a fact in Harlem in New York City, or in northwest Washington, DC, or in Oakland, California, or in myriad cities across the globe (Visser 2002, 205). Huge swaths of Kliptown have been bulldozed for the creation of Freedom Square. Elsewhere in Klipspruit, whole blocks of "matchbox houses" were demolished for the construction of Maponya Mall. Most certainly, the material culture of the original black garden city that embodies the narrative of the Uprisings of the 1970s and other resistance to the apartheid state is in jeopardy. Unlike other gentrifying neighborhoods, however, Soweto represents an overwhelmingly black ethnicity with widespread house and car ownership. Today, the former impoverished apartheid set-aside is now a neighborhood of choice for the emerging black middle class of Johannesburg. African National Congress liberation heroes are even building high-end family compounds there, and the Sowetan matchbox-house archetype has been reimagined in one real estate listing as a "Great Deal! Neat starter home for first time buyers with 2 neat bedrooms, spacious lounge and Kitchen fully walled with sliding gates. Close to schools, Shops and Public transport."[7] To state it provocatively, the regeneration of the iconic containment housing quarter of Soweto—to the casual eye, it appears that every other existing matchbox house has been reimagined from the old matchbox archetype—is proceeding in South Africa much as the Levittowns of the United States have transformed since their post–World War II creation.

While the ubiquitous policing and surveillance of the apartheid state have been officially dismantled, privatized security is today widespread and is a fact of life in middle-class or affluent neighborhoods in South Africa. The township police stations that were once staffed by whites—typically, the only white faces in apartheid-era townships were police or soldiers—are now staffed by blacks. Township entry and exit points, that is, checkpoints, are gone. In the new South Africa, freedom of movement for all citizens is guaranteed, and the pass offices that restricted passage in the apartheid state have been repurposed, abandoned, or razed. In one unique instance of repurposing, the former Albert Street Pass Office in Johannesburg's CBD now houses a women's shelter.

There is still no complete accounting for the dead and missing in the Uprisings. Even the youth Tsietsi Mashinini, who carried Pieterson in Nzima's iconic photograph, remains missing. (It is believed that Tsietsi soon fled from South Africa after being harassed by security forces there. He has not been heard from since his mother last received a letter from him from Nigeria in 1978.) Preservation in Soweto must find a way to make the liberation struggle of a generation ago relevant to the students of today. Preservation must also make clear that the history of the Uprisings and other resistance is interconnected with contemporary events in South Africa and must help ensure that, never again, will the kind of oppression that existed for more than four hundred years return there. The black/white ethnic divide in South Africa is still omnipresent. Yet, today, the formerly marginalized have a real presence in culture, business, and government.

How does one preserve the narrative of the "traumascape" when the material narrative of the new South Africa is so oftentimes indifferent to it? Blomkamp's movie *District 9* vividly revisits an imagined South African traumascape. Shot on location amid now emptied matchbox houses of Chiawelo in Soweto (whose residents were slated to be relocated to new public housing), just south of the mastaba-like tailings of Johannesburg's earliest gold mines, *District 9* depicts a barren, impoverished built landscape no longer inhabited by the human other but by "others" literally from outer space.

Are there ways to harness pro-poor tourism or the dark tourism movement? Soweto's residents are eager to preserve the memory of their successful resistance. Hence the question "Should the culture of apartheid planning be conserved or should it be adapted and developed in some way that more closely benefits those living there?" The question may be academic as Soweto is in every way "in play" from a development standpoint. Rather, one might ask what material narratives are left to preserve, and is there a way to mediate the objectives of either of the above? Today, most sites in Soweto that memorialize resistance to apartheid are connected to an individual person or hero of the movement, as it were. And yet the actual site of Pieterson's shooting on Moema Street in Orlando remains unmarked—instead the heritage tourist is referred to the sites on Vilakazi Street. Another case in point is Mandela's house. The Soweto Heritage Trust, which runs the Mandela house site, is now under the auspices of the city. However, when the house site was administered by the Mandela family, contemporary photographs documenting shifting collections, artifacts of questionable provenance, and so on demonstrated how problematic on-site preservation actually was.

Today, Soweto's iconicity, like so much other development in Asia and the Global South, is a moving target. Case in point: as I made final revisions to this chapter the former website text of Maponya Mall, with its proud, not quite familiar syntax, was replaced by this bit of corporatese: "with many South African retail 'firsts' [Maponya Mall] . . . has secured strong commitment from local business, as well as top national retailers who have several flagship stores here. Since inception, the Mall's design and concept guaranteed retail and office space not only to well-known retailers, but also to local Soweto businesses. In this way, Maponya Mall aims to capture the flow of an estimated R4.3 billion per annum in potential revenue currently being spent outside of Soweto, and boost the local economy."[8]

Who could anticipate mass infrastructure such as FNB Stadium, by Johannesburg's Boogertman + Partners and U.S. architects HOK Sport, which was the global stage for Nelson Mandela's memorial service? Its designers likened the building's form to the calabash, the iconic, ubiquitous African cooking pot. This stadium, something that seems to my eye a sly African reworking of the frantically constructed Beijing National Stadium (or "Bird's Nest," created by the architects Herzog and de Meuron), is of a globally monolithic scale, open to the elements, its rusty red panels invoking the earth of Soweto, an infrastructure proudly gap-toothed and seemingly improvised.

Soweto already reflects its residents. Here, Sowetans fought against the hegemonic control of the apartheid state and transformed dense, controlled landscapes into viable space where black institutions and political organizations could grow. It was the anti-apartheid activist Walter Sisulu who believed that the country's modern history is impossible to separate from its most famous township. In 1998 he wrote, "The history of South Africa cannot be understood outside the history of Soweto. . . . The development of the township, and the trials and tribulations of its people are a microcosm of the history of this country. Industrialisation, apartheid policies and the struggle of South African people all find their expression in that place called Soweto" (Roberts and Thloloe 2005, 4). Sowetans are proud of both their contributions to the liberation struggle and their unique role in shaping that history across the African continent. For many, South Africa's story is very much the story of Soweto and its integral role in the liberation struggle as a physical site that raised an awareness of apartheid on a global stage. A "garden city" bereft of gardens—in reality, a dormitory for black Africans—was transformed into an iconic homeland of resistance.

Table 13.1
Summary of Historical Events and Heritage Benchmarks for Soweto

Year	Event
1886	April: Gold is discovered on the Langlaagte Farm. October: Present-day central Johannesburg is declared a township; its first building plots are subdivided on a grid-iron pattern.
1899–1902	South African War (Boer War or Anglo-Boer War) fought between Britain and the colonies of the South African Republic and the Orange Free State.
1905	The Klipspruit farm on the margins of Johannesburg is declared a native settlement.
1909	Most of Johannesburg's northern suburbs have already been proclaimed.
1913	The Land Act requires black South Africans (or black Africans), colored (or mixed-race) individuals, and Indians to live separately.
1923	The Natives (Urban Areas) Act reinforces segregation in South African cities. In Johannesburg, the Western Native Township is among the first to incorporate low-density housing development and "garden city" planning principles.
1927	An amendment of the Native Urban Areas Act enables the government to relocate people without first providing them with alternative accommodation and without paying attention to the growing need for more housing. The Johannesburg City Council decides to create a Department of Native Affairs.
1939	World War II paves the way for an influx of black people to Johannesburg.
1944	James Mpanza leads members of the Sofasonke Party to protest housing conditions in Orlando.
1945	The Natives Urban Areas Consolidation Act (No 25 of 1945) tightens influx controls and is one of the many follow-up laws to the 1923 Natives (Urban Areas) Act.
1948	The Nationalist Party comes to power with D. F. Malan as prime minister.
1950	The Immorality Amendment Act prohibits adultery, attempted adultery, or related immoral acts (extramarital sex) between white and black people. The Group Areas Act enforces the segregation of the different races to specific areas. It also restricts the ownership and the occupation of land to a specific statutory group. Blacks cannot own or occupy land in white areas. While the law is supposed to apply in converse, it is essentially land under black ownership that is appropriated by the government for use by whites only.
1955	Forced removals begin; African families resettle from western areas to Soweto.
1959	The Orlando Stadium is erected, with a capacity for 24,000 spectators.
1963	First use of the name "Soweto" for "southwestern townships."
1976	June 16: A student uprising opposes the adoption of Afrikaans.
1990	February: The government begins to dismantle the Nationalist Party's apartheid policies.
1990s	Heritage tourism initiatives are on the rise.
1994	As the African National Congress wins the election, apartheid comes to an end.
1997	The Soweto Heritage Trust begins with Nelson Mandela as its founder.
1999	The National Heritage Resources Act is enacted.
2002	The Hector Pieterson Memorial and Museum is opened.
2004	The Soweto Heritage Precinct is created.
2007	September: Maponya Mall officially opens.
2010	Orlando Stadium is rebuilt for the 2010 FIFA World Cup.
	Population (as of 2011), 1,271,628; 49,427 acres [20,000 ha]; 355,331 households.

NOTES

1. In South Africa, the term "township" usually refers to an urban living area that, from the late nineteenth century until the end of apartheid in 1994, was reserved for nonwhites on the periphery of cities.

2. A. J. Thompson, a protégé of Raymond Unwin, worked on Pinelands in Cape Town.

3. Walter Sisulu Square eKliptown, http://www.waltersisulusquare.co.za.

4. Chris Needham, "Runaway Prices Get Stuck," *Sunday Times*, December 3, 2006, http://www.cyberprop.com/cyber1_08122006_2.shp.

5. Lucille Davie, "Development Zones—Soweto," http://www.joburg.org.za/index.php?option=com_content&view=article&id=5613&catid=30&Itemid=58#ixzz12mx1lcfb.

6. Heritage Projects, Arts and Culture Department, Republic of South Africa, http://www.dac.gov.za/projects/heritage2012-projects.html.

7. This property was for sale for R250,000 (US$27,500) on www.property24.com.

8. "About Maponya Mall, http://www.maponyamall.co.za/.

REFERENCES

Bonner, Phil, and Lauren Segal. 1998. *Soweto: A History*. Cape Town: Maskew Miller Longman.

Christopher, A. J. 1983. "From Flint to Soweto: Reflections on the Colonial Origins of the Apartheid City." *Area* 15(2): 146.

Cillie, P. M. 1980. *Report of the Commission of Inquiry into the Riots at Soweto and Elsewhere from 16th June to the 28th February 1977*. Cape Town: Government Printer.

Coetzer, Nicholas. 2009. "Langa Township in the 1920s—an (Extra)ordinary Garden Suburb." *South African Journal of Art History* 24(1): 1–19.

Connell, P. H. 1947. "Native Housing and Its Architectural Aspects." *South African Architectural Record* 32(6): 166–72.

Demissie, Fassil. 1992. "The Politics of a Place to Live: Determinants of African Housing in South Africa, 1923–1976." Ph.D. diss., University of California, Los Angeles.

Department of Native Affairs. n.d. *Survey of the Bantu Tribes of South Africa*.

Donaldson, Ronnie. 2001. "Challenges for Urban Conservation in the Historical Pretoria Suburb of Clydesdale." *Urban Forum* 12(2).

Farber, Leora, et al. 2008. "Johannesburg and the Megacity Phenomena." *FADA Research Newsletter* 10. University of Johannesburg. http://www.uj.ac.za/EN/Faculties/fada/research/Documents/research%20jul%2008.pdf.

Gerhart, Gail M. 1994. "The 1976 Soweto Uprising." Institute for Advanced Research, University of the Witwatersrand.

Hlongwane, Khangela Ali. 2006. *Soweto '76: Reflections on the Liberation Struggle—Commemorating the 30th Anniversary of June 16, 1976*. Johannesburg: Mutloatse Arts Heritage Trust.

Home, R. K. 1990. "Town Planning and Garden Cities in the British Colonial Empire 1910–1940." *Planning Perspectives* 5: 23–37.

Johannesburg Citizens' Housing Committee. 1953. *A Place to Live: Some Aspects of . . . Native Housing in Johannesburg*. Johannesburg.

Jurgens, Ulrich, and Ronnie Donaldson. 2012. "A Review of Literature on Transformation Processes in South African Townships." *Urban Forum* 23(2): 155.

Khosa, Meshack M. 1993. "The Black Taxi Industry." In *The Apartheid City and Beyond: Urbanization and Social Change in South Africa*, edited by David M. Smith. New York: Routledge.

Krige, Sue. 2010. "'The Power of Power': Power Stations as Industrial Heritage and Their Place in History and Heritage Education." *Yesterday & Today* 5.

Lewis, P. R. B. 1966. *A City Within a City: The Creation of Soweto.* Johannesburg: Johannesburg City Council.

Mabin, Alan. 1993. "Conflict, Continuity and Change: Locating 'Properly Planned Native Townships' in the Forties and Fifties." In *Proceedings of the Symposium on South African Planning History.* Pietermaritzburg.

Marschall, Sabine. 2008. "An Inspiring Narrative with a Shadow: Tangible and Intangible Heritage at the Phoenix Settlement of Mahatma Gandhi." *Southern African Humanities* 20(2): 353–74.

Myers, Garth Andrew. 2003. "Designing Power: Forms and Purposes of Colonial Model Neighborhoods in British Africa." *Habitat International* 27: 193–204.

Neighborhood Development Programme. 2009. *Introducing the Township Renewal Challenge,* National Treasury Department, Republic of South Africa, 7. http://ndp.treasury.gov.za /TTRI/Township Renewal Sourcebook/Township Renewal Sourcebook/Module 1—Intro ducing the Township Renewal Challenge.pdf.

Nieftagodien, Noor, and Sally Gaule. 2013. *Orlando West, Soweto: An Illustrated History.* Johannesburg: Witwatersrand University Press.

Roberts, Adam, and Joe Thloloe. 2005. *Soweto Inside Out.* Penguin Global.

Robinson, Jennifer. 1990. "'A Perfect System of Control'? State Power and 'Native Locations' in South Africa." *Environment and Planning D: Society and Space* 8(2): 135–62.

Shapiro, Lauren. 2009. "The New Urban Geography: The Changing Face of Suburbia." Future-facts. http://www.futurefact.co.za/index.php?option=com_phocadownload&view=cate gory&id=1:2008-conference-downloads&download=10:the-changing-face-of-subur bia&Itemid=132.

Shisaka Development Management Services. 2009. *Township Transformation Timeline.* Johannesburg: Shisaka Development Management Services.

Sibiya, Philile Nkosikhona. 2012. "Gentrification in the Former Black Townships: The Case of Soweto in South Africa." M.A. thesis, University of the Witwatersrand.

Sigonyela, Mboniso. 2006. "Soweto Swept Up in SA Property Boom" (February 20). http:// www.iol.co.za/news/south-africa/soweto-swept-up-in-sa-property-boom-1.267035# .UToo-XygljQ.

"South Africa: The Rise of the Buppies." 2007. *Economist* 1 (November 3). http://www.econo mist.com/node/10064458.

Stewart, Dona. 2003. "Heritage Planning in Cairo." *International Development Planning Review* 25(2): 219.

Union of South Africa. 1937. *Report of the Department of Native Affairs for the Years 1935–36.* Pretoria: Government printer.

Visser, Gustav. 2002. "Gentrification and South African Cities." *Cities* 19: 419–23.

CHAPTER 14

WYTHENSHAWE

Manchester's Municipal Garden City

James Hopkins and Michael Hebbert

One of the sorrier chapters in recent British housing history has been the steep decline of garden suburbs built by councils in the early twentieth century in a spirit of social and environmental idealism. Anne Power of the London School of Economics was one of the first British researchers to reveal the extent of neighborhood decline in these low-density council estates. A surprising number of the "estates on the edge" in her book of that title (Power 1997) were suburban—thus on the edge in a physical as well as a metaphorical sense. Martin Crookston's study of the characteristic problems of these cottage estates shows how heritage awareness may help them to meet the challenges of change. His study, with a title *Garden Suburbs of Tomorrow?* that deliberately echoes Ebenezer Howard's work, shows how the historical legacy of these estates might be harnessed to the urgent task of urban renewal (Crookston 2014). Here we follow the challenges of heritage, preservation, and change in just such a setting, perhaps the most iconic of Britain's cottage estates, Wythenshawe.

Conception of a Garden City

Wythenshawe is Manchester's very own garden city, created by the municipality in response to the housing problem as it existed in the early twentieth century: there was no longer the human degradation witnessed by Friedrich Engels in 1844, but rather a confinement of working-class families to an unalleviated mineral landscape of stone-flagged streets and cramped brick and slate terraces, heated by coal fires and punctuated by the giant smokestacks of coal-burning factory boilers, depositing carbon at a rate of three hundred tons per square mile: people lived in the "classic slum" of Robert Roberts (1971), the "dirty old town" of Ewan McColl (Engels 1993; Thompson 1970). By the measure of occupants per room, the Manchester conurbation had lower overcrowding rates than Glasgow or the East End of London, but nothing could match the sheer scale of its repetitive terraced housing (Harrison 1981; Williams 1996).

Already before World War I, social housing providers had experimented around Manchester at Burnage Garden Village (1910), Blackley Estate (1911), and Chorltonville (1911) with accommodation in a radically different cottage-and-garden style. The 1919 Addison Act normalized this dwelling type and established a national subsidy framework for large-scale municipal construction on greenfield sites. Manchester Corporation became a major social housing provider and within twenty years was outstripping private provision two to one (Kay 1993).

The core municipality of the Manchester conurbation was more tightly bounded than its counterparts in Leeds, Liverpool, or Birmingham. Fully urbanized neighbors blocked any possibility of growth to the west, north, east, and southeast. Obliged to look outside its limits for building land, Manchester was amenable to the garden city doctrine that improved housing should be built in freestanding settlements rather than suburban extensions. Rural Cheshire, to the southwest, had been favored since the early nineteenth century as premier commuter country for successful Manchester businessmen. Upwind of the conurbation, Cheshire's smokeless atmosphere and unimpeded solar radiation meant a drier climate and temperatures two to three degrees above the city average. Wythenshawe had already been selected as the site for Manchester's tuberculosis hospital in 1902. In 1920 Patrick Abercrombie was commissioned by the Manchester Corporation to report on the feasibility of developing a garden city beyond the municipal limits on the rural Tatton Estate south of the River Mersey. He recommended the purchase of 4,500 acres and expressed his hope that it would become "a model community for the whole country" (Abercrombie 1920, 9). Despite local objection and strenuous opposition from Cheshire County Council, Manchester Corporation acquired most of the land in 1926 and incorporated it under an Extension Act of 1930 (Simon 1926).

The driving forces behind this project were the engineering industrialist and local politician Ernest Simon and his wife, Shena, who was a sister of the Fabian cofounder of the London School of Economics, Beatrice Webb. Simon was one of the last generation of British business leaders to make local government their political arena. As a member of Manchester Corporation from 1911 and as its Lord Mayor from 1921, he was both a powerful spokesman for the Mancunian interest and an articulate spokesman for local democracy as a whole. He applied a keen problem-solving approach to Manchester's coal-smoke pollution, substandard housing, and dismal public health record. As a pragmatic Liberal, he believed city corporations should become large-scale providers of affordable working-class housing, following the latest principles of hygienic design and using municipal procurement and direct labor to achieve economies of scale (Hughes and Hunt 1992; Olechnowicz 2000; Redford 1940; Stocks 1963). The Simons were enthusiastic believers in town planning and demonstrated their personal commitment to the garden city project by purchasing 250 acres of the Wythenshawe estate from the Tatton family in 1926 and presenting it, without conditions, to the city. Shena Simon served on the Wythenshawe Estate Special Planning Committee from its inception in 1926, and she was its chair from 1931 to 1933 (Miller 1992).

Wythenshawe was an intentionally and boldly iconic project, commissioned from the leading practitioner in the field, Barry Parker. His joint practice with Sir Raymond Unwin designed New Earswick, Letchworth Garden City, and Hampstead Garden Suburb. While Unwin became a civil servant after World War I, shifting his attention to regional planning and housing-policy work (Miller 2004), Parker continued at the drawing board, designing the Jardim América garden suburb in São Paulo, Brazil (1917–19) and numerous British municipal housing schemes, Wythenshawe being the largest and boldest. He served as its consultant planner between 1927 and 1941 and was given significant freedom in its design. His plan required an area of 5,500 acres—necessitating additional purchases by the Corporation—of which over a thousand would constitute a greenbelt, permanent agriculture, and open parkland. The plan spanned the three ancient parishes of Baguley, Northenden, and North Etchells and would accommodate 107,000 residents in 25,000 homes, employed in two industrial zones (Rodgers 1986).

Two unique features of the project were its municipal genesis and its scale, "perhaps the most ambitious programme of civic restructuring that any British city has ever undertaken" (Rodgers 1986, 44). Other cities were building suburban estates, some very large, but here the intention was different: the model community would be self-contained, with its own employment base and services. In contrast to the single tenure of the London County Council's vast out-county estates, Manchester wanted to emulate the social mix of Letchworth and Welwyn. A fifth of the housing was intended for owner-occupation. It was the first time that the garden city formula had been applied by a local government. The project would be able to draw on Manchester Corporation's borrowing powers and the increment on the land would return to the community, as Ebenezer Howard intended. In addition, the Corporation could, in principle, lay down the infrastructure of local services and amenities in logical sequence (MacDonald 2002).

The design showed Parker's familiarity with the latest American planning principles (Stern et al. 2013). Parker followed Frederick Law Olmsted's use of parkways as distributor roads to residential areas, linking them to local parks. The Princess Parkway was an arterial link to Manchester while the Western Parkway circled the edge of the town, defining its outer boundary. Instead of the incessant intersections and stop-lines of the Mancunian street grid, Wythenshawe had clover-leaf intersections (England's first) or roundabouts, and its roads curved in subtle response to landscape and topography. There would be no shabby ribbon development—housing was to be set back at least 150 feet from the main thoroughfares behind wide verges graced by mature trees (Heywood 1933; Manchester Guardian 1929).

Walter Creese shows how carefully Parker applied Clarence Perry's neighborhood unit principle (Creese 1966). His plan was based on ten primary school and shopping clusters, each serving a half-mile radial catchment. Housing was shaped around small greens or in varied polygonal patterns with inner culs-de-sac to achieve a Radburn-style level of pedestrian protection. Arts and Crafts ideals were evident in the fine detailing and specification of the dwellings, while the indoor toilets, bathrooms with hot and cold running water, and modern kitchens expressed a progressive ideal of gender relations, offering the woman "a clean, well-planned home, which will be her palace—so well and wisely planned that her labour will be lightened and her strength and intelligence reserved for wider interests" (*Woman's Outlook* 1934). True to its name, the garden city gave every family space at the front and a back garden at least thirty feet long. Housing densities of between four and twelve houses per acre marked an extraordinary contrast with the characteristic forty to fifty homes per acre of inner Manchester (Macfadayen 1933). Shena Simon took great interest in the practical and aesthetic details of the project, with the aim that working-class families should live in homes that were "as healthy as . . . the mansion of a millionaire" (Olechnowicz 2000).

So Parker's plan built on Wythenshawe's salubrious reputation. The industrial area was designated a smoke-free zone, one of the first in the country. The tuberculosis sanatorium would become the nucleus of an extended hospital quarter. The cottages and handsome farmhouses of the former bucolic landscape were preserved, along with many of its mature trees. The buildings and parks of the area's three ancient manor houses—Peel Hall, Baguley Hall, and Wythenshawe Hall—were retained as urban amenities, skilfully framed by parkways and avenues to emphasize continuity with the rural past (Deakin 1989; Dougill 1935; Kay 1993; Manchester and Salford Better Housing Council 1935).

Development: The Prewar Phase

House building began in 1932 and progressed quickly. By 1934 the preexisting population of approximately 5,500 had increased to 25,000, greater than Letchworth and Welwyn garden cities combined. By the outbreak of World War II, Wythenshawe contained a third of the city's entire stock of social housing. The first new churches had been built, providing a striking architectural focus. Progress was slower on the industrial sites intended as the primary source of local employment, not least because the smoke-control policy limited them to light industry. At the outbreak of World War II, Wythenshawe had attracted only seventeen plants. So the majority of residents commuted out to work; two-thirds went to the Trafford Park Estate alongside the Manchester Ship Canal. That was an awkward journey, but so was access to central Manchester's labor market, because the Corporation trams did not reach past Withington, some four miles north, and buses did not circulate the vast estate. The two existing railway stations—Northenden and Baguley—were on the east-west line between Stockport and Altrincham but offered no direct connection to Manchester (Hughes and Hunt 1992; Interview 4).

Wythenshawe homes were set at the highest band of municipal rents, restricting them to skilled workers in regular employment. The Corporation applied strict eligibility criteria and a postoccupancy inspection system to weed out tenants with "slum habits." The aspirational blue-collar families who populated the garden city seem to have judged that—on balance—home comforts and a fine landscape setting made up for the various disadvantages of life on the periphery. A 1935 survey found 90 percent of residents to be happy: some positively reveled in their quasi-rural lifestyle by "playing on the parkway, making dens in the bushes and hiding amongst all the lovely blossom trees" (Interview 4). The housing design had created possibilities of privacy unimaginable in dense terraced streets. In their cottage-style homes with gated and hedged gardens (Figure 14.1), Wythenshawe's pioneers discovered a family-centered lifestyle hitherto enjoyed only by the bourgeoisie. When men returned home from work, the front door was shut for a night beside the fire (Hughes and Hunt 1992; Interview 4; Interview 5; Manchester and Salford Better Housing Council 1935).

The rigors of the early years encouraged solidarity and collective action. The early pioneer settlers found themselves living without basic roads and sewers. Trips to shops, pubs, cinemas, and medical services involved long walks to Northenden or Gatley over fields or unmade roads (Figure 14.2). The early comers mobilized to protest about the lack of facilities and transport, especially when, in 1934, Manchester Corporation sought to increase rents that were already the highest in the conurbation. In a spirit of resilience, the new Wythenshavians realized Parker's vision of a self-reliant community: neighborhood associations, sports clubs, and church groups flourished as residents entertained, educated, fed, and cared for themselves. An old farm became the home of the Residents' Association and offered guidance and tools for vegetable growing, while men's clubs, women's guilds, and lads' clubs used whatever land and equipment they could.

As a founder of the Association for Education in Citizenship and a leading light in the National Council of Social Service, Sir Ernest Simon had a keen interest in grassroots organization, which he saw as a school of citizenship and a bul-

Figure 14.1. Pioneers in
Wythenshawe (1938). (Courtesy
Manchester Libraries, Information
and Archives, Manchester City
Council)

Figure 14.2. Hall Lane Baguley
(1945). (Courtesy Manchester
Libraries, Information and Archives,
Manchester City Council)

wark against fascism. Initially he nurtured grassroots activities in Wythenshawe, but he became concerned that the garden city had developed into a one-class estate, lacking in social leadership. Andrzej Olechnowicz has provided a wry account of the ambivalence of Ernest and Shena Simon as champions of participatory democracy vis-à-vis its expression in their own Wythenshawe. Residents' demands for a greater say in decision making—"home rule" for Wythenshawe—were sternly declined (Olechnowicz 2000).

Development: The Postwar Phase

Wythenshawe was half-built at the outbreak of World War II. Signing off from the project in 1941, Parker declared it to be the premier example of an actually existing garden city. War production boosted local investment in light industry and manufacturing, filling much of Sharston's 110-acre industrial estate. The magnificent municipal transport depot, completed in 1939, with space for 100 double-decker buses beneath its 165-foot-span barrel-vaults, became a bomber factory. Other construction paused during hostilities, but the mid-forties mood was optimistic. The *City of Manchester Plan* of 1945 included a survey finding that 93 percent of Wythenshavians considered themselves happy, and it took the garden city as the benchmark against which all future neighborhood reconstruction should be measured (Nicholas 1945). Despite pressure for emergency building at high densities, the postwar plan kept faith with Parker's vision, improving the rail link, increasing the industrial land allocation, and relocating the future civic center, envisaged as a Beaux-Arts set-piece of public architecture amid an expanse of lawns and formal shrubbery. The Corporation's vision was reaffirmed in *Wythenshawe: Plan and Reality* (1953), which compared the garden city to the new wave of state-funded New Towns and increased its target population from 80,000 to 100,000 (Deakin 1989; Hughes and Hunt 1992).

In reality, austerity thwarted the intentions of the postwar plans, and the requirements of the 1946 Housing Act brought significant shifts. The year 1946 saw 1,900 building starts, a high production rate that was to continue over the next two decades. Various forms of prefabricated steel-framed and concrete houses were introduced, with open-plan fronts instead of private gated gardens; Parker's density limits were relaxed as cottage provision gave way to denser typologies: first, walk-up flats and maisonettes and then tower blocks. The inflow of new residents became more intense as Manchester's large-scale slum clearance developed momentum. Unlike the closely vetted pioneers and immediate postwar incomers, slum clearance tenants were allocated to housing en masse. The translation was not easy: the pioneers were keen to differentiate themselves from the incoming welfare tenants, who in their turn

Figure 14.3. Postwar flats on cul-de-sac (1955). (Courtesy Manchester Libraries, Information and Archives, Manchester City Council)

complained that the early settlers were "nowt but a load of snobs" (Hartwell 2002, 91; Hughes and Hunt 1992, 90) (Figure 14.3).

In 1964, Wythenshawe's population hit its maximum of 100,000 and house building began to slow. Thirty years after the start of construction, attention turned at last to the creation of a civic center. Parker's original design, relocated and modified in 1945, took eventual shape as a 1960s megastructure. Designed by the city architect and constructed between 1969 and 1971, it was described in Sir Nikolaus Pevsner's *Buildings of England* series as "nothing special" (Hartwell et al. 2004, 91, 492). The center was named "the Forum" and it incorporated a retail complex and multistory car park with a library and arts center, the first of its kind in the Manchester area. For a while the new center offered a remarkable cultural program, attracting international performers and a wide catchment audience. But the size and social profile of Wythenshawe was a challenge: it was still being run as a housing estate by top-down management. The rector of Benchill spoke of it as "the opposite of community" (Deakin 1989, 158). The Residents' Association continued to call for home rule, arguing that they had a larger population than most self-administering towns yet less say than other Manchester neighborhoods. The establishment of a consultative committee on matters such as planning applications did not allay the grievance.

Then the community was hit by a cruel physical intrusion. England's spinal M6 motorway had opened in 1965, and its M56 spur to Manchester passed close by the city's fast-growing international airport. The once elegant Princess Parkway was transformed into a heavily trafficked arterial freeway. Its construction in 1969–71 ripped up fifty thousand trees and shrubs, obliterated the carefully designed connections between the neighborhoods and the Olmstedian parkway landscape, and severed the east from the west (Figure 14.4). Worse, this process was repeated when a second motorway, the orbital M60, was built along the Mersey Valley between Wythenshawe and Manchester, cutting off minor roads and leaving the Northenden neighborhood as a giant traffic island accessible for pedestrians only by subway. And despite all the visual, sonic, and atmospheric intrusion of transport infrastructure,

Figure 14.4. Princess Parkway before (top, 1960) and during (bottom, 1970) conversion to a motorway. (Courtesy Manchester Libraries, Information and Archives, Manchester City Council)

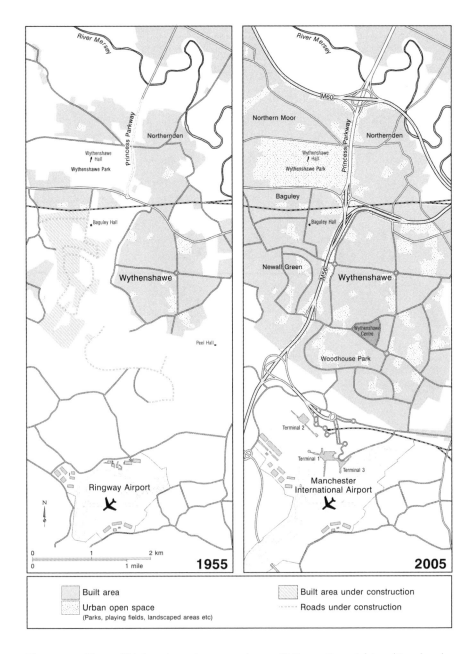

Figure 14.5. Maps of Wythenshawe in 1955 and 2005. (© Crown Copyright and Landmark Information Group Limited [2018]. All rights reserved. [1954, 1955 and 1996]. University of Manchester Cartographic Unit based on Ordnance Survey National Grid 1:10560, 1st Imperial Edition 1948–1977 [TIFF geospatial data], County/Tile: sj88nw, Published: 1954 and County/Tile: sj89sw, Published: 1955, and Ordnance Survey N.G. 1:10000/10560 Latest Edition [TIFF geospatial data], County/Tile: sj88nwm7, Published: 1996, and County/Tile: sj89swm7, Published: 1996 Landmark Information Group, Using: EDINA Historic Digimap Service, http://digimap.edina.ac.uk/, downloaded September 2011).

local transportation remained poor—the only railway station closed in 1965, and bus travel into Manchester was still a fifty-minute journey (Deakin 1989, 145–46).

The physical quartering of Wythenshawe by highway infrastructure reinforced a process of differentiation already evident in the housing sector (Figure 14.5). Some of the ten neighborhoods were becoming notorious. Derick Deakin describes worsening problems of petty crime, rubbish dumping and vandalism, housing voids, and internecine tensions (Deakin 1989, 145–46). The city faced requests for barriers and gates to stop criminal access between Wythenshawe and neighboring Gatley. The introduction in 1980 of tenants' right-to-buy accelerated the polarization between owner-occupiers and social renters (Interview 3). Rent arrears and evictions led to vacancies and boarded properties in one area, while extensions and new porches were added in another (Interview 4; Interview 5).

Despite its location in the desirable commuter belt and surrounded by the prosperous suburbs of Sale, Didsbury, Gatley, and Altrincham, Wythenshawe's population fell by a third between the 1971 and 2001 censuses (Manchester City Council 1985, 2008; Office for National Statistics, 1971, 2001). Significantly, it was no longer described as a garden city. It had become a "problem estate"—iconic for all the wrong reasons.

The Endless Housing Estate

Sir Peter Hall's widely read *Cities of Tomorrow* combined an account of Wythenshawe's development with observations of present-day graffiti and vandalism: "Manchester has not dealt kindly with its masterpiece. . . . The place looks down-at-heel in that distinctively English way, as if the city has given up on it" (Hall 2002, 115). Another great contemporary geographer, Doreen Massey, grew up in the garden city and wrote perceptively of how "that open spaciousness of the fresh air can be closed down in a myriad of daily ways"—the cracked curbstone, the vandalized bowling green, the security grill on the kitchen window (Massey 2001, 464). The sense of poverty was more marked in the context of a buoyant local labor market of more than 52,000 jobs—20,000 at Manchester Airport, 5,000 at Wythenshawe Hospital, and others with Microsoft, Shell, Virgin Media, and the soapmaker PZ Cussons. Wythenshawe residents came to have one of the lowest economic activity rates in the city-region, with half of those of working age receiving an incapacity benefit. Four of the neighborhoods were ranked in the top 1 percent most deprived nationally, with high rates of gun, knife, and drug crime (Manchester City Council 2009). A former resident reflected, "I'd never want to go back. There are such a lot of problems because there are problem families every-

Figure 14.6. The future prime minister David Cameron on a visit to Wythenshawe and the "nation's most notorious hoodie," February 2007. (Courtesy Press Association)

where, because drug abuse is so rife. I just tend to think that they sort of gather in places like Wythenshawe" (Interview 2).

Most cities have estates with such a profile, but Wythenshawe's notoriety became iconic, just like the everyday environment of Mancunian working-class terraces in the long-running Granada TV Studios soap opera *Coronation Street*. In the blackly comic television series *Shameless*, first aired in 2004, a motley cast of chavs, slags, scallies, hoodies, and layabouts pursued their chaotic lives on the "Chatsworth Estate." Filmed on outdoor location in Wythenshawe, *Shameless*'s irreverent characters reinforced every stereotype of the Wythenshavian: their families were dysfunctional and their alcohol and drug abuse was funded by welfare and crime. The estate's media profile was inadvertently reinforced by the Conservative leader David Cameron, who visited in February 2007 and was caught on camera with a hooded teenager making a gun sign behind his head (Figure 14.6). Boasting of his criminal exploits on television news, seventeen-year-old Ryan Florence immediately became "the nation's most notorious hoodie" (*Manchester Evening News* 2007). The "Cameron 'gun' teenager" photograph was a front-page story in the national press and was picked up internationally. The *New York Times* used it to illustrate why Britain had come at the bottom of a UNICEF league table of industrialized nations: this "endless housing estate" epitomized the failed social order of feckless youngsters betrayed by "absent fathers, the mothers on welfare, the drugs, the arrests, the incarcerations, the wearying inevitability of it all." As one teenager summarized, "When you live in Wythenshawe, you don't expect any better" (Lyall 2007).

The affair even took a royal dimension. In 2009 the Duchess of York made an ill-judged television documentary on youth unemployment and disaffection. Entitled *Duchess on the Estate*, it involved a visit to open a community center at Northern Moor. She interviewed locals and was shocked: "I knew it was bad but I didn't realize they are proud of their disgraceful behavior.... Young people go out with their mobile telephones and their knives now.... Literally, you can't get some young people to do joined up writing, let alone joined up sentences." The encounter did nothing for her reputation or for Wythenshawe's either (BBC News 2009; Greer 2009; Wylie 2009a, 2009b). Of course, that reputation was an unfair representation of the everyday reality of life for many Wythenshawe residents and businesses (Interview 1; Interview 3). But iconicity is not about fairness.

Myth-Busting and Recovery

Wythenshawe belongs to Manchester, and Manchester has led the way among older industrial cities in positive urban regeneration and civic boosterism. A long-established system of partnerships with the private sector has earned it a reputation as a city that can "make it happen" (Hebbert 2010).

As statistical indicators tracked the decline of Wythenshawe, regeneration policy kicked in (Manchester City Council 2004). The decade from 1998 onward saw more than £800 million of special funding invested in the area's hospitals and health programs, recreation facilities, schools and education, police, and transport. The Forum was gated to prevent nocturnal vandalism, and the civic center was branded and relaunched as Wythenshawe Town Centre. A symbolic new greenway for cyclists and walkers provides, for the first time, a direct link between the Forum and Manchester Airport, and a new line on Manchester's tram (streetcar) network between the city and airport via Wythenshawe opened in November 2014, forging the link that Parker had always envisaged. A new Enterprise Zone was created in March 2011 in and around the airport, offering discounted business rates, simplified planning rules, and super-fast broadband (Drivers Jonas Deloitte 2011; McKeegan and Linton 2011; see Plate 18). The volume of international cargo is being expanded, with space allocations to "broaden the airport's appeal to first and second tier logistics operations and compete more effectively in the Value Added Logistics (VAL) sector" (Drivers Jonas Deloitte 2011, 2). The horseshoe-shaped perimeter, which Parker laid out as a greenbelt melding the garden city into a rural landscape, has been reconfigured as an employment zone for high-end technology, research and development, training, and headquarter functions. Wythenshawe's strategic regeneration plan seeks to connect it and allow it to benefit from the prosperity and economic dynamism of the communities that surround it in South Manchester (Manchester City Council 2004). The beginning of the twenty-first century saw a reversal to Wythenshawe's population decline: mid-2013 estimates showed Wythenshawe's population at 74,600, up from 66,062 in the 2001 census (Office for National Statistics 2001, 2011, 2013).

Meanwhile, a branding and marketing campaign has been launched to address Wythenshawe's reputational problems. *Real Lives—Wythenshawe* is sponsored by a partnership of Manchester City Council, Parkway Green and Willow Park Housing Trusts, St. Modwen, Marketing Manchester, and the Forum Trust. In an attempt to dispel misconceptions and "build a community feel where residents feel safe and engaged," the advertisements feature the interests and activities of local residents, emphasizing the tradition of self-organization and community association left to Wythenshawe by its early pioneers (Ward 2008). They play on Wythenshawe's location at the affluent end of town, sprinkling the stardust of the "south Manchester effect." And crucially, the campaign invokes the garden city element of Wythenshawe's heritage: its lower population density compared with Manchester's average (24.9 people per hectare compared with Manchester's 39.1), its higher-than-English-average tree coverage (15.3 percent), a park of 270 acres, a community farm, and three hundred allotments and homes with gardens.

The marketing vision appeals directly to the planning origins of Wythenshawe, offering its rebirth as "Manchester's 'Garden City'—a distinctive part of the City of Manchester characterised by a unique environment and a new dynamic of growth and development the idea brings together the positive aspects of housing and green space (Garden) with the sense of growth and change in the economy" (Manchester City Council 2008). Wythenshawe's heritage-led revival could best be described as a work in progress. So far, the lead has come from branding and public relations teams capitalizing on the suburb's most obvious selling point: its greenspace and tree cover. The ancient freestanding trees and mature woodlands that were artfully protected within Parker's original plan are indeed a remarkable endowment, and good work is now being done to protect them by the nonprofit Red Rose Forest in partnership with the City Council and residents' groups. Preservation of architectural heritage is more problematic. The garden city encompassed an extraordinary range of structures, including the mid-fourteenth-century timber-framed hall at Baguley, the fifteenth-century parish church of St. Wilfred Northenden, the great manor house built at Wythenshawe by Robert Tatton around 1540 that was his descendants' home for six centuries, a handsome red-brick farmhouse at Newall Green Baguley carrying the date 1594 upon its lintel, the eighteenth-century Moor Farm with its seventeenth-century outbuildings, and the classically detailed Sharston Mount farmhouse dating from 1800. Though all these monuments have statutory protection—they are "listed buildings" in British parlance—several have suffered neglect or vandalism, the difficulties of location being aggravated by inadequate stewardship on the part of Manchester City Council. Their best hope lies in grassroots mobilization such as from the Friends of Wythenshawe Hall, who have worked tirelessly to keep the hall open to the public even after an arson attack in 2016.

Of the architectural legacy of the twentieth-century garden city, only a handful of iconic buildings are listed: the Assembly Hall of Jehovah's Witnesses, originally designed as an Art Deco cinema in 1933 by Charles Hartley; the 1938 Church of St. Luke the Physician; N. F. Cachemaille-Day's breathtaking church of St. Michael and All Angels, of 1937; the 1939 bus garage in Sharston, with its innovative shell-concrete barrel vaults; and a virtuoso design of 1964, G. G. Pace's William Temple Memorial Church. Reporting on a tour of these sights for the *Guardian* newspaper, Owen Hatherley (2012) commented that they had not seen Wythenshawe itself—Parker's vast exercise in residential design. Despite its significance in planning history, most of the garden city has no preservation policy. Northenden is the only part to be designated as a Conservation Area, a status reinforced by the establishment of a Northenden Neighbourhood Forum with planning powers. Elsewhere the chief preservative of the scale and architectural character of the cottage estate has been its residents' relative poverty. One thing is sure, however: as the area's fortunes improve, it will face new challenges of change, and a more assertive policy for heritage preservation will be needed.

Conclusion

Wythenshawe earns a special place in town planning history as the largest garden city built by municipal enterprise. That genesis was its undoing. It took shape as a semidetached suburb of (mostly) council housing subject to the shifts in allocation rules and design standards. Its peripheral situation gave it neither the standing of a satellite town nor proper connectedness to the city's employment and amenities. Treated as a city ward, and without a civic center to give a focus for the first thirty-nine years, it never developed an identity to match its size. It seemed a place on the

Figure 14.7. Wythenshawe *Real Lives* campaign. The man in this photo said, "I've lived in Wythenshawe since 1950. That's 58 years in all. Since I retired I've been on my allotment practically every day. I'm happy there. I grow everything there. Potatoes, fruit, corn, sprouts, all sort." (Photo Gavin Perry, *Real Lives* campaign, 2008)

edge, protruded into the Cheshire countryside. Resident interviews defined Wythenshawe in terms of peripherality: "I would say Manchester was the . . . you know, the centre, and we're a suburb of Manchester"—one felt it was best described as Manchester's "overspill" (Interview 2; Interview 5).

It is in this context that Parker's garden city is being revalorized. Lost in middle age to a vast and fractured housing estate, its regeneration returns to the tangible assets of the Arts and Crafts design, with its retained woodland, gardens, allotments, and out-of-town ambience. As Massey writes, it is "green and spacious still: the clarity of the air, the freshness of the (constant) breeze still strike me each time I arrive" (2001, 465). Passengers landing from international flights at Manchester Airport are greeted by the heartwarming *Real Lives* images of Wythenshawe folk growing geraniums, displaying prize vegetables, tending allotments (Figure 14.7), buying fresh fish, walking the whippets, adjusting the pony's cheek-straps and a horse looking over a stable door at Wythenshawe Hall:

> It's the kind of place where you can put down roots. Family homes with gardens and easy access to both city centre and countryside, plus a huge investment in new schools and community facilities, make Wythenshawe a good place to live. . . . Wythenshawe is Manchester's original Garden City— built on the principles of being "close to town and country," and this re-

mains true today: only seven miles from Manchester's City Centre but surrounded by South Manchester's most affluent suburbs and directly linked to the Cheshire countryside . . . Wythenshawe is one of Manchester's greenest places—with mature tree lined roads, parks, allotments and gardens, it's a place where you can breathe. . . . Wythenshawe is proud of its community values, whether it's saying hello over the garden fence or over 100 community groups and clubs. (Manchester City Council 2009)

Today's publicity campaign for a distressed suburb appeals back to its original garden city vision. There's life in the old icon yet.

Table 14.1
Summary of Historical Events and Heritage Benchmarks for Wythenshawe

Year	Event
1920	The Manchester Corporation commissions Patrick Abercrombie to conduct a feasibility study for a satellite garden city beyond municipal limits on the 2,468-acre Tatton Estate.
1926	The Manchester Corporation purchases land; Mayor Ernest Simon and his wife Shena donate 250 additional acres to the city.
1927	August: Barry Parker is appointed consultant planner.
1930	Manchester's Extension Act incorporates Wythenshawe within the city boundaries.
1932	The first housing units are constructed.
1934	The preexisting population of approximately 5,500 increases to 25,000. Residents mobilize against rent increases.
1935	A survey indicates a high degree of satisfaction among residents.
1941	Parker's role as consultant planner ends.
1945	The *City of Manchester Plan* calls for improved rail links, increased industrial land allocation, and a new location for the civic center.
1946	An intense cycle of building activity begins.
1964	Wythenshawe reaches a maximum population of 100,000. Provision of new housing units slows, while residents begin to increasingly resent top-down management.
1965	The train station serving Wythenshawe closes.
1969	A civic center, the massive Wythenshawe Forum, is created; it incorporates cultural and retail activities.
1971	A heavily trafficked arterial freeway opens on the site of Princess Parkway.
1980	Tenants' right-to-buy legislation enhances the polarization between owner-occupiers and social renters.
1998	£800 million of public funds are reinvested.
2001	The population falls by a third, from 97,105 in 1971 to 67,836 in 2001. The civic center is rebranded as "Wythenshawe Town Centre."
2011	March: The government announces the Manchester Airport Enterprise Zone.
2014	November: A new tram line between Manchester and the airport via Wythenshawe is opened.
	Population (as of 2011), 74,200; 6,880 acres [2784 ha]; 33,144 dwelling units.

REFERENCES

Abercrombie, P. 1920. *Report on the Wythenshawe Estate.* March 10, 1920, included in the Housing Committee minutes, March 29, 1920.

BBC News. 2009. "Anger over ITV Duchess Programme." http://news.bbc.co.uk/1/hi/england/manchester/8207003.stm.

Creese, W. L. 1966. *The Search for Environment: The Garden City, Before and After.* New Haven, CT: Yale University Press.

Crookston, M. 2014. *Garden Suburbs of Tomorrow? A New Future for the Cottage Estates.* London: Routledge.

Deakin, D. 1989. *Wythenshawe: The Story of a Garden City.* Chichester: Phillimore & Co.

Dougill, W. 1935. "Wythenshawe: A Modern Satellite Town." *Town Planning Review* 16(3): 209–15.

Drivers Jonas Deloitte. 2011. *Manchester Airport City: Development and Infrastructure Framework.* Manchester.

Engels, F. 1993. *The Condition of the Working Class in England.* Oxford: Oxford University Press.

Greer, S. 2009. "Estate Fury at Duchess TV Show." *Manchester Evening News* (August 18).

Hall, P. 2002. *Cities of Tomorrow: An Intellectual History of Urban Planning and Design in the Twentieth Century.* Oxford: Blackwell.

Harrison, M. 1981. "Housing and Town Planning in Manchester Before 1914." In *British Town Planning: The Formative Years,* edited by A. Sutcliffe, 106–53. Leicester: Leicester University Press.

Hartwell, C. 2002. *Pevsner Architectural Guides: Manchester.* New Haven, CT: Yale University Press.

Hartwell, C., M. Hyde, and N. Pevsner. 2004. *Lancashire: Manchester and the South-East.* New Haven, CT: Yale University Press.

Hatherley, O. 2012. "On the White Bus to Wythenshawe—Council Housing by Design." *Guardian* (May 22).

Hebbert, M. 2010. "Manchester: Making It Happen." In *Urban Design and the British Urban Renaissance,* edited by J. Punter, 51–67. London: Routledge.

Heywood, L. 1933. "Municipal Housing at Wythenshawe." *Town and Country Planning* 1.

Hughes, A., and K. Hunt. 1992. "A Culture Transformed? Women's Lives in Wythenshawe in the 1930s." In *Workers' Worlds: Cultures and Communities in Manchester and Salford, 1880–1939,* edited by A. Davies and S. Fielding, 74–101. Manchester: Manchester University Press.

Kay, A. 1993. "Wythenshawe Circa 1932–1955: The Making of a Community." Ph.D. thesis, University of Manchester.

Lyall, S. 2007. "How the Young Poor Measure Poverty in Britain: Drink, Drugs and Their Time in Jail." *New York Times* (March 24).

MacDonald, E. 2002. "Structuring a Landscape, Structuring a Sense of Place: The Enduring Complexity of Olmsted and Vaux's Brooklyn Parkways." *Journal of Urban Design* 7(2): 117–43.

Macfadayen, D. 1933. *Sir Ebenezer Howard and the Town Planning Movement.* Manchester: Manchester University Press.

Manchester and Salford Better Housing Council. 1935. *Wythenshawe: The Report of an Investigation.* Manchester.

Manchester City Council. 1953. *Wythenshawe: Plan and Reality.* Manchester.

———. 1985. *Population Survey.* Manchester: Manchester City Council Planning Department.

———. 2004. *Wythenshawe Strategic Regeneration Framework.* Manchester.

———. 2008. *Economy, Employment and Skills Overview and Scrutiny Committee: Report for Resolution*. Manchester.

———. 2009. *Real Lives Wythenshawe—Mythbusting*. Manchester.

Manchester Evening News. 2007. "Cameron 'Gun' Teenager Behind Bars" (March 6).

Manchester Guardian. 1929. "A Model Suburb: Manchester's Plans for Wythenshawe" (September 3).

Massey, D. 2001. "Living in Wythenshawe." In *The Unknown City: Contesting Architecture and Social Space*, edited by I. Borden et al., 459–75. Cambridge, MA: MIT Press.

McKeegan, A., and D. Linton. 2011. "Manchester Airport Enterprise Zone Will Generate 'Mini-City' with 10,500 Jobs." *Manchester Evening News* (March 25).

Miller, M. 1992. *Raymond Unwin: Garden Cities and Town Planning*. Leicester: Leicester University Press.

———. 2004. "Parker, (Richard) Barry." In *Oxford Dictionary National of Biography*, edited by H. C. G. Matthew and B. Harrison. Oxford: Oxford University Press.

Nicholas, R. 1945. *City of Manchester Plan*. Norwich: Jarrold and Son.

Office for National Statistics, London. 1971. *Census. Aggregate Data (England and Wales)*.

———. 2001. *Census. Aggregate Data (England and Wales)*.

———. 2011. *Census: Aggregate Data (England and Wales)*.

———. 2013. *Ward Level Mid-Year Population Estimate*.

Olechnowicz, A. 2000. "Civic Leadership and Education for Democracy: The Simons and the Wythenshawe Estate." *Contemporary British History* 14: 3–26.

Power, A. 1997. *Estates on the Edge: The Social Consequences of Mass Housing in Northern Europe*. Basingstoke: Macmillan.

Redford, A. 1940. *The History of Local Government in Manchester*. London: Longmans.

Roberts, R. 1971. *The Classic Slum: Salford Life in the First Quarter of the Century*. London: Penguin.

Rodgers, H. B. 1986. "Manchester: Metropolitan Planning by Collaboration and Consent, or Civic Hope Frustrated." In *Regional Cities in the United Kingdom, 1890–1980*, edited by G. Gordon, 41–57. London: Harper and Row.

Simon, E. D. 1926. *A City Council from Within*. London: Longmans.

Stern, R. A. M., D. Fishman, and J. Tilove. 2013. *Paradise Planned: The Garden Suburb and the Modern City*. New York: Monacelli Press.

Stocks, M. 1963. *Ernest Simon of Manchester*. Manchester: Manchester University Press.

Thompson, E. P. 1970. *The Making of the English Working Class*. London: Penguin.

Ward, D. 2008. "Biting the Bullet: How Locals in Wythenshawe Are Trying to Change Public Perceptions of the Estate." *Guardian* (November 5).

Williams, G. 1996. "City Profile: Manchester." *Cities* 13: 203–12.

Woman's Outlook. July 1934.

Wylie, I. 2009a. "The Duchess on the Estate." *Manchester Evening News* (August 11).

———. 2009b. "Duchess Talks About Life on the Estate." *Manchester Evening News* (August 14).

INTERVIEWS

Interview 1. 2011. Interview with former female resident of Wythenshawe by James Hopkins (July 31).

Interview 2. 2011. Interview with former female resident of Wythenshawe by James Hopkins (July 31).

Interview 3. 2011. Interview with former female resident of Wythenshawe by James Hopkins (June 15).

Interview 4. 2011. Interview with female resident of Wythenshawe by James Hopkins (November 16).

Interview 5. 2011. Interview with former female resident of Wythenshawe by James Hopkins (November 16).

CHAPTER 15

SABAUDIA

Foundation, Growth, and Critical Memory

in the Last Italian City

Jean-François Lejeune

How much did we laugh, us intellectuals, about the architecture
of the Regime, about such cities as Sabaudia! And yet, nowadays,
analyzing them, we cannot but experience an unexpected feeling.
The architecture of Sabaudia has nothing unreal, nothing ridiculous:
the passing of time has given its architecture of Fascist origin a
modern character between the metaphysical and the realistic. . . .
A city that we saw as preposterous and Fascist suddenly appears
to us as haunting and delightful.

The date of May 26, 1927, marked a momentous turning point in fascist urban
policy. In his notorious Ascension Day's speech, Benito Mussolini argued that
metropolitan industrialization and concentration induced, among other ills, the
"sterility of the population."[1] A year after, in his article "Sfollare le città," the Duce
outlined the regime's radical goals to limit metropolitan growth by re-equilibrating
city and countryside and "ruralizing" the country (Mussolini 1928). A major program of public works was initiated to restructure older neighborhoods through
demolition and reconstruction, as well as to modernize towns and cities with a
new infrastructure of post offices, train stations, and other representative buildings, such as the *case del fascio*.[2] The reclamation of the Pontine marshes and the
subsequent founding of agricultural new towns and villages, along with new industrial towns in Sardinia and the aeronautical city of Guidonia near Tivoli, followed
this line of ideological and technical planning. "With both types of towns," Diane
Ghirardo (1989, 24) wrote, "Fascism seemed to be promising a new and bright future with up-to-date, hygienic living conditions and improved agricultural and
industrial productivity." About one hundred and seventy new communities were
created in Italy (including Sardinia and Sicily) between 1928 and 1942.

This chapter focuses on the most iconic case, Sabaudia, one of the five towns
founded in the 1930s within the Pontine region in the province of Lazio (Figure

Figure 15.1. View along the civic axis of Sabaudia in the mid-1930s. In the foreground are the city hall and its tower; midway to the right is the tower of the casa del fascio; in the background are the church and its campanile. (Courtesy Archivio Fotografico Touring Club Italiano)

15.1).[3] It highlights the process of settlement and growth of the original agricultural center, now also an important tourist center on the Tyrrhenian Sea. It analyzes Sabaudia's unique iconic image—a combination of the modernity of its architecture and the "metaphysical" image of its urban spaces—as well as the use of propaganda-driven photography, painting, and films to promote it nationally and internationally during the fascist era. Finally, it examines the role played by a post-1960s generation of scholars who initiated the ideologically complex process of critical rehabilitation. Nowadays, Sabaudia has been recognized as historical heritage of the twentieth century. However, the restoration of its often-degraded buildings and public spaces remains an intellectual and technical challenge.

New Cities and Landscape in the Pontine Region

Plans for the reclamation of the Pontine marshes, the malaria-infested region to the south of Rome between the Via Appia and the Mediterranean Sea, go back to antiquity. Rulers like Julius Caesar, Augustus, and Renaissance Popes like Leo X (with the likely help of Leonardo da Vinci) and Sixtus V developed more or less

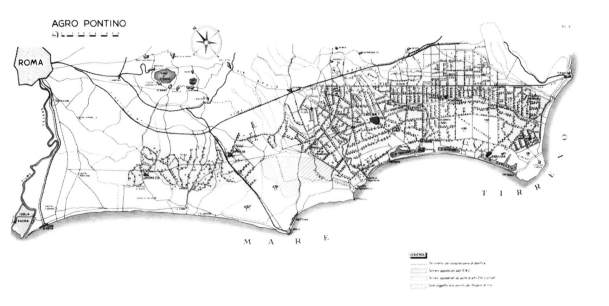

AGRO PONTINO

ROMA

T I R R E N O

M A R E

LEGGENDA

ambitious but aborted projects to sanitize the area. Eventually, it was accomplished by the fascist regime, which from 1927 embarked on the *bonifica integrale*, a multipronged public works program to engage a "total war" against malaria, drain the marshes, and colonize the reclaimed areas (Linoli 2005; Snowden 2006) (Figure 15.2). The first years focused on vast works of hydraulic engineering. After 1931, the Opera Nazionale dei Combattenti (ONC) was put in charge both of managing the newly created parcels of land and of installing more than four thousand

Figure 15.2. General plan of the colonization of the Agro Pontino. Littoria is slightly at the center of the region (in black); Sabaudia is visible to its right along the coast (in black). Clearly visible is the gridded network of roads and canals that service and drain the region (the roads are known as *migliari* as they are generally one kilometer apart). (*Architettura* [June 1934])

homesteads. The farms were distributed to thousands of colonists who were encouraged (at times through coercion) to move, like the Peruzzi family in the novel *Canale Mussolini* (Pennacchi 2010), from the impoverished provinces of Veneto, Friuli, and Emilia-Romagna.[4]

The hierarchical organization of the region was structured at three levels by the ONC. First, there were the *poderi*, or farms, each with an isolated farmhouse (*casa colonica*). Second, there were the districts, each centered on a *borgo* or hamlet consisting of a small church, a small casa del fascio, and a school. These hamlets were not inhabited but were surrounded by the poderi. Third were the new towns, also called *città di fondazione* (cities of foundation). The five towns, built from 1932 to 1939—Littoria, Sabaudia, Pontinia, Aprilia, and Pomezia—were primarily conceived as service centers.[5] They contained houses and apartments, but those were reserved for shop owners, employees, and civil servants. The Roman artist Dullio Cambellotti saw and depicted this rural urbanism—or urban ruralism—as the purest expression of fascist modernity (Carli and Bragaglia 1994). The central section of *La Redenzione dell'Agro*—the large narrative triptych painted in 1934 at the Prefecture in Littoria—shows the central nucleus of the city-region in construction: in the background, the network of roads, farms, and hamlets is clearly visible and inscribed within the rigor of the geometric division of the territory in *migliari* (parallel roads at intervals of one kilometer) and canals; in the foreground, groups of soldiers/farmers and animals struggle to create a fascist new nature, new city, and new society (Caprotti and Kaïka 2008).[6] (See Plate 7.)

Reflecting on the Pontine foundations, Luigi Piccinato, one of the urbanist-architects of Sabaudia, wrote in 1934 that "neither Littoria nor Sabaudia were cities in the usual urbanistic significance of the term" (Malasurdi 1993, 355). They were not walled or closed in opposition with the countryside, but "authentic agricultural centers, with an indissoluble link to their territory and to the soil that produces" (Malasurdi 1993, 357). In other words, the traditional concept of a city was, in Piccinato's words, to be replaced by a new "city-region, city-province, city-nation" (Malasurdi 1993, 357). As Mussolini declared one month before the inauguration of Sabaudia: "The rallying cry is the following: within a couple of decades all the residents of the Italian countryside will have a large and healthy house. . . . Only in this way can we fight against the nefarious urbanization; only in this way will we be able to bring back to the fields and villages all those dreamers and disappointed ones who have left their established families in order to follow the urban mirages of the salary in cash and easy recreation" (Martinelli and Nuti 1981, 154).

To be sure, this negative vision of urbanization and urban life preceded the advent of Italian fascism and had deep roots in the industrialization of cities in the second half of the nineteenth century. During the interwar period, Oswald Spengler's *The Decline of the West* (1918) was a major source of inspiration for anti-urban policies and for Mussolini, among other actors. The debate was international in nature and influenced major experiments such as the socialist *Siedlungen* of Ernst May in Frankfurt and of Bruno Taut and Martin Wagner in Berlin, the de-urbanist projects in the Soviet Union, and the rural aspirations of the New Deal in the United States (Ghirardo 1989; Martinelli and Nuti 1981). The program of new foundations within the Pontine region partook in these international trends. At the same time, their unique program and form were the result of a complex negotiation between two tendencies of fascist politics: on the one hand, a ruralism that aimed at ascribing "a new dignity to every form of work, particularly agricultural," and on the other hand, the attraction of a vernacular and urban monumentalism that strove to express the lineage of fascism with the antique and medieval past (Ciamarra 2006, 39).

Iconicity: The Plan and Towers of Sabaudia

In April 1932, the ONC's president, Valentino Orsolino Cancelli, commissioned the Roman architect Oriolo Frezzotti to design the master plan and main buildings of the first Pontine city, Littoria. Frezzotti prepared the plan in less than sixty days.[7] Six months later the town was inaugurated with its main public buildings and spaces in place. Seen from the air, Frezzotti's radio-concentric design brought to mind Palmanova and the Ideal City of the Renaissance, re-actualized in light of Ebenezer Howard's and Raymond Unwin's theories (Figure 15.3). Littoria became an international sensation. In the fifth issue of *Quadrante*, Pietro Maria Bardi reported the excitement that the presentation of the new town at the international congress CIAM IV had generated: "Our report on Littoria is ready, the maps and photographs have been attached to the boards. Van Eesteren has asked the architect Bottoni to make the presentation. After London, Berlin, Paris, now Littoria. We are truly at the

Figure 15.3. Aerial view of the first Pontine city, Littoria (now Latina), in 1934. The radial structure of Frezzotti's master plan is clearly visible and focuses on the central square with the city hall and its tower. In the foreground to the right are the civic and religious square with the church, the veterans' house, and the day-care center; on the right is the administrative square with the Palazzo del Governo. (Courtesy Archivio Fotografico Touring Club Italiano)

SABAUDIA
DOTT: ARCH : G. CANCELLOTTI - E. MONTUORI - L. PICCINATO - A. SCALPELLI

■ EDIFICI PUBBLICI
■ COSTRUZIONE INTENSIVA
▨ COSTRUZIONE SEMINTENSIVA
▨ GIARDINI
1 COMUNE
2 CHIESA - BATTISTERO - CANONICA - CASA DELLE SUORE - ASILO
3 CASA DEL FASCIO - DOPOLAVORO - SINDACATI
4 CINEMA TEATRO
5 ALBERGO
6 CASERMA RR.CC
7 POSTE E TELEGRAFO
8 CASERMA M.V.S.N
9 ASSOCIAZIONE COMBATTENTISTICHE
10 SCUOLE E O.N.B
11 DIREZIONE AZIENDALI O.N.C
12 OSPEDALE
13 OPERA MATERNITÀ E INFANZIA
14 CAFFE RISTORANTE
15 CIRCOLO IMPIEGATI
16 MACELLO
17 CIMITERO
18 SERBATOIO IDRICO
19 CAMPO SPORTIVO
20 MERCATO COPERTO
21 CLUB SPORTIVO
22 PRATO DELLE FESTE

1: 2000

Figure 15.4. Plan of Sabaudia, the outcome of a 1933 competition. The black lines represent the mixed-use buildings defining the primary public spaces; clearly visible are the freestanding houses on the west side of the town. The housing shown to the east of the entry axis was never built. (*Architettura* [June 1934])

center of a very curious attention" (Carli 2002, 31).[8] Littoria was planned for five thousand residents, yet it presented a highly urban image, one that contradicted the regime's goal of "de-urbanization." However, Mussolini quickly understood the political and propagandistic value that could be derived both nationally and internationally. On the day of its inauguration, the Duce announced the foundation of a second new town, Sabaudia.

Sabaudia was the result of a one-month design competition held in early 1933 and won by a team of young architect-urbanists who had graduated from the new School of Architecture of Rome and were members of the Gruppo degli Urbanisti Romani (GUR): Luigi Piccinato, Gino Cancellotti, Alfredo Scalpelli, and Eugenio Montuoti (Ciucci 1989).[9] The town plan, its tridimensional construction, and the Rationalist architecture of Sabaudia gave it an immediate iconic image (Figure 15.4).

The plan was structured on three principles: first, a modern reinterpretation of the Roman colonial diagram with two axial streets—*decumanus* and *cardo*—intersecting at the Piazza della Revoluzione; second, the balanced asymmetry of building masses and the careful termination of the visual lines characteristic of the medieval city; and, third, the loose arrangement, on both sides of the main axis, of two paradigms of modern housing—the organic garden neighborhood and the rational grid of the modern housing movement of the 1920s (Bocchi and Guidoni 1988; Burdett et al. 1981, Muratore, Carfagna, and Tieghi 1999; Piccinato 1934). Key to the planning of Sabaudia was Camillo Sitte's book *Der Städtebau*, first published in 1899 and popularized in Italy since the 1910s by Gustavo Giovannoni and the Associazione Artistica fra i Cultori di Architettura. As Richard Etlin (1991, 101) wrote, "the theories of Sitte enabled architects and cultural groups to find in the city—and its renewed artistic spirit—the 'powerful magnet capable of collecting the scattered fragments and arranging them in order.'"

The first axis, decumanus, enters the town from Littoria and the reclaimed countryside at the end of a four-kilometer-long perspective that terminates at the city hall's tower; the other and shorter axis, cardo, connects the military headquarters to the church. Sabaudia's "medieval" image was exalted in the complex of two central squares: the civic one at the intersection of axes with the tower of the town hall, the hotel, the shops, and the cinema; and, isolated but visually connected, the religious one, complete with the church and its detached campanile and baptistery. The whole organism was oriented according to modernist requirements of light and air, and it was surrounded by a system of parks equivalent to a greenbelt.

Whereas Littoria's urban spaces were fundamentally introverted, Sabaudia's response to the regime's concept of "de-urbanization" was clever and made physical with direct visual links between city, the man-made countryside, and the mythical landscape to the south. This is demonstrated by the long entrance axis; the "transparent" patio of the city hall opening on the waterway and the dunes; the subtle articulation of the central square with the public garden—a sort of Piazza San Marco, where the Canal Grande would be replaced by a green and distant view of Monte Circeo; and, last but not least, the tall and slender towers of the city hall and the church's campanile aiming at establishing a connection with the flat landscape. For Alessandra Muntoni (2006, 27), this physical concept was conceived "to make the void speak, to render quasi physically this re-conquered territorial space, new protagonist of a reversed relation country-city."

Arguably, the iconicity of the town was significantly different than most planned pre-1940s communities, whose public image was mostly related to a modern concept of housing and dwelling, as in the case of Garbatella, Greenbelt, the Red Vienna, or the New Frankfurt. Sabaudia's ensemble was resolutely modern and one of the first examples of Rationalist architecture in the country. Its architecture was "in its correct sobriety and beauty, well adapted to the simple and rural character of the place" (Piacentini 1934). However, it is the public architecture of the city hall, the church, the towers, and the "metaphysical" image of the urban spaces that were first built, advertised, and ultimately recorded in the "collective memory" of residents, visitors, and readers. As Piccinato explained, "The building of these institutions should be proportioned to the needs of the entire agricultural center and not only to those of the communal town center itself: this explains the apparent disproportion between the size of the public buildings and the number of houses that together with the public buildings comprise the true and characteristic urban aggregate. . . . Sabaudia is seen comprehensively in its territory, or rather as a strongly decentralized building pattern that has its center in a large central district" (Malasurdi 1993, 358).

Sabaudia was founded on August 5, 1933, and inaugurated after 253 days of labor, on April 15. In 1936, it counted about 4,800 residents, but only a couple hundred nonagricultural workers lived in the town itself. The ONC built fewer than one hundred housing units of type A, the most urban one with two floors of housing above a commercial ground floor and a maximum height of twelve meters. This type took the form of simple and thin housing bars that lined the two axes and the central square and whose modern horizontal lines recalled "the horizon line and the tranquility of the countryside" (Piacentini 1934). Moreover, the manner in which Piccinato and his colleagues used those bars typical of the modern movement to create well-defined public spaces was unique and distinguished their works from most of their European counterparts. They shaped modern public spaces in a typologically new way, that is, not as carved spaces out of a dense fabric but as skillful assemblages and articulations of thin and interconnected linear buildings. On the northern side of the town, the master plan prescribed the least dense type (type C), a single- or double-family villa with setbacks on all four sides and a maximum height of nine meters. Not surprisingly, Piccinato (Malasurdi 1993, 363) portrayed it as "the richest type, distributed on the edges in direction of the most important vistas, and penetrating within the center, in particular around the church." It was the type that corresponded best to the anti-urban objectives of the regime, and most blocks were built in the 1930s.

To be sure, if the war had not interrupted the implementation of the master plan, the overall image of Sabaudia might have become more complex. To the east of the center, the architects planned a neighborhood whose main typology was the *casa a schiera* (type B, two and a half floors in height, at a maximum height of twelve meters), a row house with a small setback of four meters, to be used along narrow residential streets. Starting from the central axis in the middle of the town, a green led to the school complex and continued diagonally toward Migliara 54 and the countryside. On both sides of the diagonal, the plan showed parallel bars of attached row houses with rear gardens, connected by footpaths and small articulation squares. The repetitive nature of this arrangement showed obvious influences from the 1920s Siedlungen by the German architects Bruno Taut, Ernst May, and Martin Wagner.[10]

The propagandistic and programmatic values of Littoria and Sabaudia did not escape international attention. The experimental communities were widely published and discussed, especially in countries where issues of de-urbanization were at the core of the agenda, such as the United States during the New Deal or post–civil war Spain. Le Corbusier himself took notice. In 1934 he traveled to Italy and lectured in Rome with the avowed goal of meeting with Mussolini and soliciting the commission for the third town, Pontinia. His criticism of Littoria was expectedly negative. On one of his sketches, he wrote: "a poor little town in the garden city manner, a garbage dump for the schools of architecture" (Ciucci 1980, 68). But, contrary to the Italian Rationalists who had high praise for the city, he was equally critical of Sabaudia. Le Corbusier recognized that, in spite of the architects' efforts, it was not "the village of modern times, but a dream, a sweet and somewhat romantic poem, a 'shepherds' dream" (Ciucci 1980). Unsurprisingly, Le Corbusier's interest in and priority for the modern housing unit and its assemblage into *unités d'habitation* did not match the fascist regime's primary interest in a modern monumentality that gave no emphasis on issues of housing. His sketches for Pontinia showing two large housing bars and a series of modern farm facilities were directly inspired by his project of 1934 for agrarian reorganization in the French Department of Sarthe, later to be redeveloped as the "Radiant Farm" (*Ferme radieuse*). From the high floors of the apartments, farmers would have been able to admire the reclaimed lands (Le Corbusier 1953). In doing so, he intended to reverse the iconic image of the town from public monumentality to the private monumentality of the housing block.

Iconicity: Futurist and Metaphysical Space

In the late 1920s, the metropolitan, technology-driven tenets of the first Futurism, epitomized by Antonio Sant'Elia's *La Città Nuova* (the New City) and the first Futurist manifestos of Filippo Marinetti and friends, increasingly contradicted the rural tendencies and aspirations of the fascist state (Oliva 2009). In contrast with *Stracittà*, which championed progress, technology, and the urban environment, *Strapaese* was a movement that extolled nature and rural values and glorified a heroic and mythical past (Martinelli and Nuti 1981). In the 1930s, in search of a renewed vision to counter the developing Rationalist movement, the Futurists, still with Marinetti at their head, redirected the movement closer to the Strapaese side of the regime and embraced the de-urbanization agenda.[11] The Futurists praised the "Fascist speed" of town construction in stylistic hyperboles: "November 10, 1931-X; beginning of the reclaiming works; June 30, 1932-XI, first stone of Littoria; December 18, 1932-XI: Benito Mussolini inaugurates Littoria. . . . Heroic rhythm, because, to win, every day is one of fight against malaria, funeral goddess of the Pontine Marshes, and against its invisible armies of fever-giving mosquitoes and putrid miasma" (Vittori and Carli 2000, 128).

In this evolving context, the new towns reconciled the apparently contradictory presence of modernism and ruralism, of city and country, and of experimenting between modernity and reference to tradition. Not surprisingly, the iconic urban form of Sabaudia, as well as its integration within the new fascist landscape, attracted the unique gaze of Aero-Futurist painters and photographers (Lejeune 2008). Following the Manifesto of Aero-painting of 1929 (Oliva 2009), the airplane and the aerial gaze became the symbolic means and tool of Futurism. Faced with the sickness, ugliness, and poverty of the traditional cities, altitude allowed seeking for relief, by abstracting the multitude and the masses in movement on the earth. Works like *Bonifica integrale* (1933) by Peruzzi, Tato's *Sorvolando Sabaudia* (1934), Prampolini's *Cuore aperto di contadino bonificatore* (1935), or Di Bosso's *Spiralando su Sabaudia* (1936) situate the Aero-Futurist movement at a point of reconciliation between the two antagonistic factions of Italian culture during fascism (Strapaese and Stracittà). As Emily Braun wrote, "It was not *Strapaese's* intention to reject modernity in its entirety, but rather to absorb it through the filter of tradition, and in this way to counter the complete eradication of the past" (1995, 95).

Most observers, historians, and critics have emphasized the even more explicit connection with the other great movement in Italian modern art, that is, the metaphysical painting of Giorgio de Chirico and Carlo Carrà and, after World War I, other artists like Mario Sironi. The città di fondazione formed, in the architect Luigi Prisco's words, a *metafisica costruita*, or constructed metaphysics (Besana et al. 2002). Prisco, like many historians and critics before him, equated the "metaphysical" character of the urban spaces of the Pontine cities with the series of paintings produced, mostly by de Chirico, between 1914 and 1925, under the general title of *Piazze d'Italia*. De Chirico himself was very aware of architecture and landscape, as he wrote in *Valori Plastici*: "In the construction of the city, in the architectural form of the houses, the squares, the gardens, the public promenades, the ports, the train stations, etc., can be found the fundamental elements of a great metaphysical aesthetic" (Carli 2002, 36).

De Chirico's abstracted architectural language was at once traditional and modern. As such, and with various degrees of intensity, it was strongly reflected in the architectures of Littoria, Sabaudia, Aprilia, and others like Pomezia. Likewise, the opening of the traditionally enclosed urban spaces toward the rural environment displayed in the construction of the Pontine cities what Muntoni (2006, 27) has called "involuntary metaphysics." It was undoubtedly another critical element of de Chirico's painting and vision: "The landscape, framed in the arcade of a portico, as in the square or the rectangular of a window, acquires a major metaphysical value, as it solidifies and becomes isolated from the space that surrounds it. So, architecture completes nature" (Carli 2002, 36).

The period photographs, mostly produced by and for the Touring Club Italiano (TCI), and some of the architect's drawings, consciously exploited these standard elements of metaphysical painting (Figure 15.5). From their very start the Pon-

Figure 15.5. Aerial view of Sabaudia in 1934. The town center is complete with the three towers visible on the civic axis; the park is not yet planted. The only housing visible is the apartments lining the central street; the lots for single- or double-family houses are already laid out. In the upper right is the temporary housing for construction workers. (Courtesy Archivio Fotografico Touring Club Italiano)

tine cities were scenically, urbanistically, and politically conceived as urban objects of propaganda and as such were extensively photographed. In contrast with Tato's *Sorvolando Sabaudia* and other aerial works that suggested or effectively showed the masses that were supposed to fill the large spaces imagined by the architects as points of gathering for the regime, most TCI photos were precisely constructed to emphasize the illusion of one or more vanishing points; they were more often than not either empty of human beings, or featured an enigmatic figure standing in isolation, a statue as in one of de Chirico's metaphysical squares, or even, as an iconic element of modernity, the silent presence of an automobile.

Cinema was perhaps the most efficient medium of representation during the fascist period. Sabaudia's cinema faced the main piazza and functioned as a center of both community and propaganda. Federico Caprotti has carefully researched the hundreds of 1930s documentary newsreels that have survived. He has argued that the success of transforming the Pontine swamps owed as much to the careful staging of every step of the project through cinematographic representation as to the extensive investment of labor power, capital, and technology. Better than any other medium, cinema could illustrate how integrated the new fascist cities were with the "ideal Fascist landscape," which had replaced territories of poverty, disease, and sterility (Caprotti and Kaïka 2008).

Postwar Expansion and Change

The 1943 Battle of Anzio left the region in a state of devastated chaos. Farms were in ruins, the canal system had been sabotaged by the German army, and malaria returned for a short time. The reconstruction of the infrastructures was fast, and in a couple of years the Agro Pontino system was functioning again. Except for Latina (as Littoria was renamed after 1945), which had been promoted to a provincial capital, Sabaudia and the three other new towns grew slowly. Sabaudia's superb location on the coast of the Tyrrhenian Sea, its visual connection with the Monte Circeo protected as a national park, and its proximity to a mythological past added a major touristic importance to its agricultural role. In fact, the fascist planners had already imagined Sabaudia as an exclusive seaside destination for the elitist tourism of the regime's apparatus. Yet little happened during the 1930s, and Sabaudia provided an unexpected but important support to the military as a temporary garrison for troops to embark toward Africa and Spain.

In the manner of all Italian cities, whether large, small, or middle-sized, the post-1945 expansion of Sabaudia and the other Pontine cities broke away from the concept of the continuous city, which had dominated the history of western urbanism since the medieval times. The theoretical foundations of this radical change went back to the *Zeilenbau* diagrams of Walter Gropius and to the works of Le Corbusier, but it is the Legge Urbanistica (Urbanistic Law) of 1942 that gave it legal and administrative power. The law specifically stated that its objectives were to favor deurbanization and "reverse the tendency toward urbanism." Even though it was passed during the fascist period, it was not challenged after the war. In practice, the law ended the urbanism of the 1930s, and more generally centuries of continuous urban growth and invention, characterized by the care taken in establishing a close relationship between architecture and urban spaces, and proceeded towards a more abstract, analytical, and disciplinary culture of city planning which increasingly broke its ties with architecture (Bocchi and Guidoni 1988). Hence, the first decades of Sabaudia's expansion slowly filled up the spaces left unbuilt in the master plan; however, the urban code, the block alignments, and the original building types were set aside. All the development that followed eventually found its roots in a new ideological conception of urbanism. In this case the modernist antistreet ideology—and to some extent the 1960s–70s anticapitalist ideology—replaced the fascist one.

In the late 1960s, Luigi Piccinato, now a major figure of postwar urbanism, was called on again to conceive a new master plan. In a 1971 report, he rightly criticized the fact that a chaotic and unsightly juxtaposition of villas and new apartments, often in the typology of the *palazzina*, had sprung up within the core with no respect for the uncompleted housing section of the city, originally planned to be built with the case a schiera.[12] Likewise, outside of the original city limits, green areas were invaded by more unplanned development. Expectedly, Piccinato's plan, even though loaded with good intentions in terms of ecological protection, lacked any physical sense of place. The plan did not envision the form of the urban expansion, favoring to rely instead on a rather vague definition of the new housing areas without any awareness of urban image and iconicity. To his credit Piccinato was keen on protecting the surrounding landscape, both around the towns, the lake, and the coastline. Unfortunately, his plan went against the intentions of the municipal authorities and most developers. As a result, its impact was quite limited (Malasurdi 1993, 371–74).

Since the 1950s and in the absence of any serious growth control, the original center of Sabaudia was increasingly besieged by the abysmal quality of its surrounding periphery. The situation was dramatically worse in Latina.[13] However, in both cases, the foundational cores continued to be lived in as the original colonist families became increasingly rooted into the region and acquired more freedom and economic independence. In fact, as Sabaudia and Latina transitioned from purely agricultural centers into more diverse economic entities, their commercial and residential importance grew in a more traditional way. To some extent, Sabaudia's and Latina's foundational nuclei became de facto "historic centers." Their public image remained practically unchanged. There was no *damnatio memoriae*—in the sense that no buildings were deliberately destroyed or defaced—but all Pontine cities have suffered from neglect, indifference, and ignorance.[14]

Sabaudia's population has been in constant and linear augmentation since the war. In the 1970s, half of the population worked in the touristic sector; out of the nine thousand residents, half lived in the hamlets surrounding the town and the littoral villas. Nowadays, Sabaudia houses more than twenty thousand permanent residents, of whom 10 percent are foreigners, including a small but sizable Indian community of about one thousand. During the tourist season, the population more than doubles with the usual and problematic impact on the infrastructures of water, public spaces, parking, and traffic. In light of their ideology of de-urbanization, the fascist planners did not connect Sabaudia to the railway system (similarly, Latina's train station is located four kilometers outside of the center). The consequences of these ideological decisions continue to weigh negatively on a vision of sustainable transportation and development.

Fascist or Not Fascist; Modern or Not Modern

Periodicals and critics of the 1930s admired Sabaudia for its unornamented and modern architecture, for the clarity of its conceptual plan, and for the newness of its urban spaces. Two of the most important periodicals of the 1930s—Pietro Bardi's *Quadrante* and Giuseppe Pagano's *Casabella*—especially gave this praise. Yet, interestingly, the fascist hierarchy attacked the town in a famous debate of 1934 and accused it of ugliness and un-Italian aesthetics (Rifkind 2012). During the 1950s and 1960s, the architectural community came under the influence of Bruno Zevi, an architectural historian and longtime newspaper critic for *L'Espresso*, who was a biased critic of the relation of fascist architecture with tradition and modernity. Because of its modern Rationalist architecture, Sabaudia was seen by Zevi as an exception. It was, shamefully, described as the "non-fascist" town, while Latina was all "heavy monumentalism" and the other towns—Pontinia, Aprilia, and Pomezia—were seen as mere "vernacular and populism" (Zevi 1997, 428). In that sense, Zevi and his friends agreed to ignore or to minimize the fascist affiliation of those architects who had been at the modernist avant-garde.

Intellectuals, writers, and artists as diverse as Alberto Moravia, Mario Schifano, and Pier Paolo Pasolini were more direct and more honest. Many of them chose the Pontine area, and in first place Sabaudia and its littoral, as vacation places. In the early 1970s, Pasolini made very public and critical remarks against postwar modern urbanism and architecture. In contrast, he referred positively to Sabaudia and commented, "Sabaudia, even though the Regime influenced its design with deliberate Rationalist, estheticizing and academic aspects, has its real roots in that very Italian reality that Fascism was unable to influence. In truth, it is not Fascism which created Sabaudia, but the reality of provincial Italy, rustic and paleo-industrial."[15]

Zevi's one-sided interpretation of architectural history started to fade with the rise of a new generation of Italian and foreign historians who initiated the rehabilitation of fascist architecture as a whole. In the 1970s and 1980s, Giorgio Ciucci, Luca Nuti, and Alessandra Muntoni brought to light a large archival material about the pontine cities but remained mostly critical of their layout as not being modern enough. Giorgio Muratore and others (1999), Luigi Prisco and Giuseppe Strappa (1996), and, in the English language, Richard Burdett (1981) and Diane Ghirardo (1989) brought a more positive and balanced assessment. In Ghirardo's case, the comparison between the New Deal and fascist Italy brought attention to the parallelism of de-urbanization theories between the United States and Italy. In 1988 the urban historian Enrico Guidoni dedicated a milestone volume of the collection *Atlante storico delle città italiane* to Sabaudia, followed two years later by a volume on Littoria.[16]

In 2002, the Regione Lazio financed a large exhibition and an extensive catalogue under the title *Metafisica Costruita* (Constructed metaphysics). The project was curated by Luigi Prisco and with the critical participation of both the Touring Club Italiano (the largest photographic repository of architecture during the fascist period) and the Istituto Luce, which, created in 1924, became the major instrument of cinematic propaganda under Mussolini. This visually spectacular exhibition adroitly exploited the public recognition of de Chirico and other metaphysical artists in order to de-link architecture and fascist symbolism in favor of a larger artistic-cultural context. Yet, more than the architecture of Sabaudia and the other towns on display, the exhibition emphasized the quality and contemporary value of their urban concepts.

Fascist or not fascist. Modern or not modern. These contested identities were established during the fascist era, accentuated after the war, and, to some extent, have remained unresolved. After more than five decades of research and scholarship, a very large part of the contemporary Italian critic continues to be driven by nostalgia. On the one hand, the rather conservative ideology anchored in the fascist origins of the towns is at work in the Pontine region; the creation of the publishing house Novecento, dedicated to promoting the archives of the region and based in Latina, is a case in point. On the other hand, many writings by well-known architects and authors remain tainted by the nostalgia for a modernist urbanism that did not take place. The recent laments of critics such as Massimo Ciamarra and Franco Purini who admire the bravura of Sabaudia and its architects but found them "lacking in courage," "not modern enough," or a "modern travesty of a traditional structure," strangely parallel with Le Corbusier's criticism in the 1930s. Paradoxically, they also bring to mind the

advocacy of the absolutely modern *città corporatista fascista* (corporatist city), advocated by the avant-garde of fascist architects like Bottoni and the *Quadrante* group in
the 1930s (Ciamarra 2006, 41; Purini 2006, 42–43).

The postwar history of urbanism has been systematically directed toward a linear
and progressive positivism that tends to equate the notion of progress with any formal organization that puts into question or rejects the hegemony of the street as a
basic organizing principle of urban space. And, precisely, Sabaudia and the other città
di fondazione are at odds with that ideological agenda. They are made of streets,
squares, parks, public buildings, and private structures. They are in fact the last genuine Italian cities, modern and traditional, successful and problematic at once.[17]

While academic criticism of Sabaudia and the neighboring towns has swayed
for decades, their recognition by both the intellectual and general public, Italian
and foreign, has been increasing steadily. Film directors like Marco Ferreri and
Federico Fellini have made it so that their urban landscapes have entered the collective memory of many. For the thousands of architecture and urban design students and professionals—Italians and foreigners alike—Latina and Sabaudia have
become necessary stops on the modern version of the Grand Tour.

New Steps Toward the Physical Restoration of Sabaudia

Against all odds, the debate about those identities—fascist and modern—had no
direct effect on the protection and preservation during the twentieth century. In
practice, the Italian architectural heritage is one of the best protected in the world,
and this also includes Sabaudia and the other pontine towns. The Legge Bottai of
1939 established the concept of *tutela e protezione dei beni culturali* in Italy and the
law, even though it was originally limited to "works of art," has remained the primary
legislation in favor of the protection and restoration of artistic and architectural heritage. It was consolidated in article 9 of the Constitution of 1949 and was concretized
in the creation of the Ministerio dei Beni Culturali (Ministry of Cultural and Environmental Heritage) in the 1970s.[18] By default, the buildings of Sabaudia were auto-
matically included, even though the legislation offered few incentives toward active
protection and preservation. After 1945, Sabaudia's historic fabric suffered no major
demolition with the exception of the market and its Rationalist hypostyle-like grid of
columns. Yet, as mentioned earlier, the overall environment deteriorated because of a
lack of investment despite the town's increasing touristic appeal.[19]

The definitive step toward the official recognition and physical preservation of
Sabaudia was the Regional Law no. 27, approved by the Regione Lazio in 2001 and
overseeing the "interventions for the knowledge, the recuperation and the valori-

Figure 15.6. View of the outdoor staircase of the original post office by the architect Angiolo Mazzoni. Completed in 1934, the now-restored masterpiece of Pontine futurism currently houses a center for documentation of the architecture and urbanism in the region. (Photo by Jean-François Lejeune)

zation of the cities of foundation." In his comments, Prisco, the architect in charge of the program's implementation, argued that the importance of the law relies "in the desire to recuperate the comprehensive character of the artistic and architectonic Italian culture during the 1930s as well as encourage a critical reading of its achievements, including on the level of its economic, social and anthropological aspects" (Prisco 2006, 5–6). In its comprehensiveness and the diversity of financing it offers, the law has encouraged a new interest for the study, preservation, and potential renovation of the landscape. The Pontine cities, hamlets, and farms are increasingly analyzed, not in isolation, but rather as a part of a much larger and complex *Kulturlandschaft* (cultural landscape) that comprises the network of canals and roads, the hydraulic infrastructures such as the locks, and the natural and man-made landscape itself.[20]

Since the early 2000s, maintenance and respect for the civic heritage have marginally improved, and some actions have been taken toward rehabilitating the most iconic structures. With joint municipal and regional financing, the Palazzo delle Poste e Telegrafi in Sabaudia has been fully restored (Figure 15.6). Built in 1933–34, the post office was the work of Angiolo Mazzoni, one of the best and most neglected architects of twentieth-century Italian architecture (Mazzoni 2000). The spectacular blue mosaics that cover the façades of the building, the horizontal windows, and the beautiful outdoor staircase, inspired by the vernacular examples of Capri and Amalfi, were brought back to their original beauty in 2011. Under the name Centro di Documentazione Angiolo Mazzoni, the building now houses the historic archives of the city. It completes the museum system already in place in and around the city, with the ruins of the Roman Villa di Domiziano, the historical museum of the region known as Museo Civico del Mare e della Costa, and the Museo Emilio Greco, dedicated to the twentieth-century sculptor and graphic artist (Carli et al. 2010).[21]

The battle for and the protection of iconicity took a dramatic turn in 2010 when a proposal for the redesign of the central square surfaced in the press with the apparent support of the municipality. The project proposed to repave most of the piazza's surface with slabs of stone and "activate" the square with umbrellas and other urban furniture: "The architects' pretention is to make 'contemporary'—i.e., in fact 'consumerist'—an urban space whose profound poetry resides in fact in its lauded impermeability to the totalitarianism of the image."[22] The uproar that this aseptic project created among citizens and cultural groups, such as the Fondazione CESAR, Italia Nostra, and others, was quite unexpected. The press even called it *la piazza della rivolta* (the square of the revolt). As Italia Nostra commented in a press release, "The Piazza of Sabaudia, located on the ambiguous ridge of the Italian Rationalism between humanness and hyper-reality, just like the city that was laid out between the city and the sea, and its story set between civic dream and political barbarism, is now a trench. If it were taken over we would have lost another part of Italy."[23]

Following this wave of criticism, the restoration of the plaza was completed in the spring of 2013 in the respect of the original design and materials (Figure 15.7). The rationalist Hotel Sabaudia al Lago, occupying the eastern side of the piazza and closed for more than twenty years, has been partially restored but remains empty. Last but not least, in February 2012, thirty-seven years after a judgment that mandated their removal, the abusive outdoor staircase and second-floor addition that defaced the loggia wing at the entrance of the square were demolished to great applause.[24] The elegant loggia designed by Piccinato and his colleagues has now been revived with its superb perspective of columns. The spirit of Giotto and Piero della Francesca (see his *Flagellation of Christ* of 1455–60) that inspired the Italian Rationalist movement may be nascent again in Sabaudia, the "last Italian city."[25]

Figure 15.7. Photograph of Sabaudia's main square. To the left is the town hall with its tower. To the right is the loggia attached to the cinema/theater, which was restored in 2013 with the removal of the outdoor staircase and covered terrace. (Courtesy Archivio Fotografico Touring Club Italiano)

Table 15.1
Summary of Historical Events and Heritage Benchmarks for Sabaudia

Year	Event
1923	December: National legislation passes that defines the concept of *bonifica integrale* (integral reclamation) for road construction, irrigation, and the fight against malaria.
1927	May 26: Mussolini's Ascension Day's speech launches a vast public works program to drain the Pontine marshes, eradicate malaria, and cultivate and colonize the reclaimed areas.
1931	The Opera Nazionale dei Combattenti (ONC) is put in charge of the colonization of the Pontine region, with new town foundations and settlements of more than four thousand small farms by colonists from impoverished provinces.
1932	April: The architect Oriol Frezzotti receives the commission for the master plan and main buildings of Littoria. December: Littoria is inaugurated in the presence of Mussolini.
1933	The Gruppo degli Urbanisti Romani (GUR)—Gino Cancellotti, Eugenio Montuori, Luigi Piccinato, Alfredo Scalpelli—wins the competition organized by the ONC. August 5: Sabaudia is officially founded and construction starts according to the plans of the GUR's four architects.
1934	April 15: Sabaudia is inaugurated. The civic and religious centers are built, but most of the planned housing is not completed. Littoria becomes the provincial capital.
1935	The third new town, Pontinia, is completed.
1936	Sabaudia counts 4,890 residents, but only a couple of hundred reside in the town.
1937	The fourth new town, Aprilia, is inaugurated.
1939	The fifth and last Pontine new town, Pomezia, is inaugurated.
1942	First General Urbanistic Law favors de-urbanization and modernist antistreet ideology.
1943	The Battle of Anzio devastates the region. Aprilia is heavily damaged.
1945	Littoria is renamed Latina.
1945–50	Full restoration of the Pontine region and partial reconstruction of Aprilia take place.
1971	Sabaudia counts 10,359 inhabitants. A new master plan (*piano regolatore*), submitted by Luigi Piccinato, is critical of uncontrolled new construction. The historic section is heavily degraded, but the demolition of the original covered market is the only major landmark loss. One half of the residents live in peripheral hamlets and seaside villas. Expanding tourism is the major employer.
1970s	Critical rehabilitation of Sabaudia and of the architecture and urbanism of the Pontine towns takes place.
1974	The RAI (Radio Televisione Italiana) broadcasts a film by Pier Paolo Pasolini on Sabaudia.
1975	The Ministry of Cultural and Environmental Heritage (Ministerio dei Beni Culturali) is created to monitor and implement existing preservation laws.
2001	Regional Law no. 27 is passed to support "interventions for the knowledge, the recuperation and the valorisation of the cities of foundation."
2002	A large exhibition titled *Metafisica costruita* (Constructed Metaphysics) and financed by the Lazio region takes place in Rome.

Year	Event
2010	A proposal to "modernize" the central square meets with strong opposition and is abandoned.
2011	Angiolo Mazzoni's original post office is restored and reopens to house city archives and historic exhibits. Sabaudia continues to grow chaotically.
2012	The upper restaurant that defaced the loggia closing the square is demolished. The restoration of Hotel Sabaudia al Lago on the square starts slowly; sold by the municipality, it remains closed as of 2018.
2017	A referendum to change the name of Latina back to Littoria is postponed.
	Population (as of 2017), 20,500 (10 percent are foreigners, most of Indian origin); 35,840 acres [14504 ha].

NOTES

The epigraph for this chapter is translated from a pronouncement by Pier Paolo Pasolini in the 15-minute film *Pasolini e la forma della città*, directed by Paolo Brunetto and completed in 1973. The film can be seen at https://www.youtube.com/watch?v=btJ-E0Jxwr4.

1. For the Ascension Day's speech, see http://cronologia.leonardo.it/storia/a1927v.htm.

2. The case del fascio (houses of the Fascist Parti) were built throughout Italy, from villages to cities, as local seats of the National Fascist Parti. The most discussed is the Casa del Fascio in Como, built by Giuseppe Terragni from 1932 to 1936: see Etlin 1991 and Rifkind 2012.

3. See, among others, Etlin 1991, Ghirardo 1989, Caprotti 2007, Rifkind 2012, and Ciucci 1989.

4. The ONC was established at the end of World War I to help veterans. The law of April 9, 1931, created the Commissariat for Migrations and Interior Colonization (Commissariato per le Migrazioni e la Colonizzazione Interna), an organization involved with the policies of internal migrations and transfers. See Novello 2003, Treves 1976, Ghirardo 1989, and Pennacchi 2010.

5. I use the original name when writing about Littoria during the fascist period, and I use the new name of Latina for events after 1945.

6. See Massimilano Vittori, "La conquista della terra, ciclo eroico misconosciuto," http://www.borghidilatina.it/main/la-storia.htm?id=11.

7. On Littoria, see Carli and Vittori 2002, Cefaly and Muratore 2001, and Bocchi and Guidoni 1990. When Littoria was given the status of a provincial capital in 1933, Frezzotti signed the first expansion plan of the city.

8. The quote is from Bardi 1933. Littoria's early critical fame was eventually short-lived as its plan and its architecture were increasingly seen as too traditional in comparison with Sabaudia. Yet, for many fascist leaders, Littoria better reflected the aesthetic goals of the regime.

9. On the GUR and its professional profile, see Ciucci 1989.

10. The competitions for Aprilia and Pomezia, held in 1936, further revealed the extent of the typological and morphological inventions of Italian new town planning, but once again, the housing areas were left unbuilt. It is only in the case of the aeronautical city of Guidonia near Rome that housing became essential in defining the public image of the town: see Lejeune 2008.

11. The major protagonist of the controversy was Curzio Malaparte, who corresponded with the Strapaese journal *Il Selvaggio* and created the Stracittà journal, *900*, with Massimo Bontempelli.

12. The palazzina is a unique typology that developed in Italy from the late 1930s. It is a transformation of the isolated villa type into an apartment building with four façades separated by

small alleys or gardens. The much-maligned speculative type is finally undergoing critical reha-bilitation.

13. The new *piano regolatore* of Latina (Piccinato 1993) was a frontal attack on the radial model, considered as formalistic and outdated. Instead of better controlling the growth from the center, the plan imagined a linear organism, made up of autonomous zones lacking any morphological or typological definition. Moreover, the plan rejected all continuity with the codes and principles of 1932–33, leading to some disastrous interventions. As of 2011, Littoria had 115,895 inhabitants. It remains a major center for agricultural production; it has an impor-tant pharmaceutical and chemical industry, and it offers a strong service sector, both public and private.

14. In Sabaudia, the defaced fascist dedication carved on the tower of the city hall was even-tually restored in 1984.

15. This quote is from Pier Paolo Pasolini from the film *Pasolini e la forma della città*.

16. Following the publication of the volume on Sabaudia, the choice of Latina was definitely a more challenging project. It is to the authors' credit that they departed from the ideological position of many peers. See http://www.casadellarchitettura.eu/index.php?do=atlante.

17. From the mid-2000s, the Rome-based Fondazione C.E.S.A.R., the weekly blog main-tained by the late historian Giorgio Muratore, and La Sapienza University professor Giuseppe Strappa have regularly developed strategies to reevaluate the urbanism of the Pontine cities for the current practice of urban design.

18. In 2002, the law known as Codice Urbani rationalized the process of conservation and protection, while expanding the reach of the concept of *beni culturali* to the landscape, environ-mental areas, archives, and so on. See Barbati and Cammelli 2004 and Tamiozzo 2004.

19. Those buildings were designed by Gino Cancelotti, Eugenio Montuori, Luigi Piccinato, and Alfredo Scalpelli in 1933.

20. For a recent project relative to the discipline of landscape urbanism, see Berger and Brown 2012.

21. Another post office, also designed by Mazzoni, stands at the center of Latina in close proximity to the Piazza del Comune. Completed in 1932 with its arched outdoors staircase and its tall vertical windows protected by segment-circle antimalaria screens, it was enlarged by Maz-zoni two years later. In the 1960s, the arched outdoors staircase was removed, thus reducing the structure to a shadow of its original design. The example of Sabaudia has now generated a series of calls in favor of a similar demolition/restoration study of Latina's post office.

22. Gruppo Salingaros, http://biourbanismnotes.blogspot.com/2010/10/salviamo-la-piaz za-di-sabaudia.html.

23. Ibid.

24. See http://www.youtube.com/watch?v=CtFCUFvA3dA. See also the recent ordinance at http://www.comune.sabaudia.latina.it/index.php/component/content/article/461-ordinan za-n24-tutela-patrimonio-storico.

25. On the influence of early Renaissance painting and representation on Italian Rational-ism, see for instance Etlin 1991, and particularly chap. 8, "Rationalist Architecture: A Contex-tual Avant-Garde."

REFERENCES

Barbati, Carla, and Marco Cammelli. 2004. *Il codice dei beni culturali e del paesaggio: Commento al decreto legislativo 22 gennaio 2004, n. 42*. Bologna: Il Mulino.

Bardi, Pier Maria. 1933. "Cronaca di viaggio." *Quadrante* 5 (September).

Berger, Alan, and Case Brown. 2012. "A New Systemic Nature for Mussolini's Landscape Urbanism." In *Dirt*, edited by Megan Born, Helen Furján, and Lily Jencks, 252–61. Philadelphia: PennDesign; Cambridge, MA: MIT Press.

Besana, Renata, et al. 2002. *Metafisica costruita. Le città di fondazione degli anni Trenta dall'Italia all'Oltremare: Dagli archivi storici del Touring Club Italiano e dell'Istituto italiano per l'Africa e l'Oriente e dai fondi locali.* Milan: Regione Lazio, and Touring Club Italiano.

Bocchi, Francesca, and Enrico Guidoni. 1988. *Atlante storico delle città italiane/Lazio 3: Sabaudia.* Rome: Multigrafica.

———. 1990. *Atlante storico delle città italiane/Lazio 5: Latina.* Rome: Multigrafica.

Braun, Emily. 1995. "Speaking Volumes: Giorgio Morandi's Still Lifes and the Cultural Politics of Strapaese." *Modernism/Modernity* 2(3): 89–109.

Burdett, Richard, et al. 1981. *Sabaudia 1933: Città nuova fascista.* London: Architectural Association.

Caprotti, Federico. 2007. *Mussolini's Cities: Internal Colonialism in Italy, 1930–1939.* Youngstown, NY: Cambria Press.

Caprotti, Federico, and Maria Kaïka. 2008. "Producing the Ideal Fascist Landscape: Nature, Materiality and the Cinematic Representation of Land Reclamation in the Pontine Marshes." *Social and Cultural Geography* 9(6): 613–34.

Carli, Carlo Fabrizio. 2002. "La koiné metafisica: Novecentismo, Razionalismo, Futurismo nelle città nuove pontine." In *Metafisica costruita. Le città di fondazione degli anni Trenta dall'Italia all'Oltremare: Dagli archivi storici del Touring Club Italiano e dell'Istituto italiano per l'Africa e l'Oriente e dai fondi locali.* Milan: Regione Lazio, and Touring Club Italiano.

Carli, Carlo Fabrizio, and Egisto Bragaglia. 1994. *Duilio Cambellotti e la conquista della terra.* Latina: Edizioni Agro.

Carli, Carlo Fabrizio, and Massimiliano Vittori. 2002. *Oriolo Frezzotti: 1888–1965: Un architetto in territorio pontino.* Latina: Novecento.

Carli, Carlo Fabrizio, et al. 2010. *Palazzo delle Poste e Telegrafi di Sabaudia. Contributi per un restauro.* Rome: Palombi.

Cefaly, Pietro, and Giorgio Muratore. 2001. *Littoria 1932–1942: Gli architetti e la città.* Latina: Casa dell'architettura.

Ciamarra, Massimo Pica. 2006. "Occasioni mancate." In *ArchitetturaCittà: rivista di architettura e cultura urbana*, no. 14 (Città Pontine), edited by Giovanni Marucci. Università degli Studi di Camerino. http://web.unicam.it/culturaurbana/cittapontine2006.pdf.

Ciucci, Giorgio. 1980. "A Roma con Bottai." *Rassegna* (July).

———. 1989. *Gli architetti e il fascismo: Architettura e città 1922–1944.* Turin: Einaudi.

Etlin, Richard. 1991. *Modern Architecture in Italy 1890–1940.* Cambridge, MA: MIT Press.

Ghirardo, Diane. 1989. *Building New Communities: New Deal America and Fascist Italy.* Princeton, NJ: Princeton University Press.

Le Corbusier. 1953. "La fattoria radieuse. Il villaggio radieux." In *Oeuvre complète, 1934–38.* Zurich: Les Editions d'Architecture.

Lejeune, Jean-François. 2008. "Speed and Rural Poetics: From Littoria to Guidonia, Aero-Futurist City." *Angiolo Mazzoni e l'architettura futurista.* Bollettino Fondazione CESAR 5/6 (September–December): 59–74.

Linoli, Anatolio. 2005. "Twenty-six Centuries of Reclamation and Agricultural Improvement on the Pontine Marshes." In *Integrated Land and Water Resources Management in History: Proceedings of the Special Session on History, May 16th, 2005*, edited by Christoph Ohlig, 27–56. Schriften der Deutschen Wasserhistorischen Gesellschaft. Norderstedt: Books on Demand.

Malasurdi, Federico. 1993. *Luigi Piccinato e l'urbanisticá moderna*. Rome: Officina Edizioni.

Martinelli, Roberta, and Lucia Nuti. 1981. *Le città di Strapaese: La politica di "fondazione" nel ventennio*. Milan: FrancoAngeli.

Mazzoni, Angiolo. 2000. *Angiolo Mazzoni: Architetto futurista in Agro Pontino*. Latina: Novecento.

Muntoni, Alessandra. 2006. "Urbanistica e architettura nelle città dell'Agro Pontino." In *Architettura città rivista di architettura e cultura urbana*, no. 14 (Città pontine), edited by Giovanni Marucci. Università degli Studi di Camerino. http://web.unicam.it/culturaurbana /cittapontine2006.pdf.

Muratore, Giorgio, Daniela Carfagna, and Mario Tieghi. 1999. *Sabaudia, 1934: Il sogno di una città nuova e l'architettura Razionalista*. Sabaudia: Comune di Sabaudia.

Mussolini, Benito. 1928. "Cifre e deduzioni. Sfollare le città." *Il Popolo d'Italia* (December 22).

———. 1934. "Sintesi del regime." In *Scritti e discorsi* 9 (March 18). Milan: Hoepli.

Novello, Elisabetta. 2003. *La bonifica in Italia: Legislazione, credito e lotta alla malaria dall'unità al fascismo*. Milan: FrancoAngeli.

Oliva, Achille Bonito. 2009. *Futurismo manifesto 100 x 100: 100 anni per 100 manifesti*. Milan: Electa.

Pennacchi, Antonio. 2010. *Canale Mussolini*. Milan: Mondadori.

Piacentini, Marcello. 1934. "Sabaudia." *Architettura* 6 (June): 321–23.

Piccinato, Luigi. 1934. "Il significato urbanistico di Sabaudia." *Urbanisticà* 1 (January).

———. 1993 (1971). "Relazione al Piano regolatore di Sabaudia." In *Luigi Piccinato e l'urbanisticá moderna*, edited by Federico Malasurdi. Rome: Officina Edizioni.

Prisco, Luigi. 2006. "La legge regionale per le città di fondazione." *Architettura Città: Rivista di architettura e cultura urbana*, no. 14 (Città pontine), edited by Giovanni Marucci. Università degli Studi di Camerino. http://web.unicam.it/culturaurbana/cittapontine2006.pdf.

Prisco, Luigi, and Giuseppe Strappa. 1996. *Architettura moderna a Roma e nel Lazio, 1920–1945*. Rome: Edilstampa.

Purini, Franco. 2006. "Questioni pontine." In *Architettura Città: rivista di architettura e cultura urbana*, no. 14 (Città pontine), edited by Giovanni Marucci. Università degli Studi di Camerino. http://web.unicam.it/culturaurbana/cittapontine2006.pdf.

Rifkind, David. 2012. *The Battle for Modernism: Quadrante and the Politicization of Architectural Discourse in Fascist Italy*. Milan: Marsilio.

Snowden, Frank. 2006. *The Conquest of Malaria: Italy, 1900–1962*. New Haven, CT: Yale University Press.

Tamiozzo, Raffaele. 2004. *La legislazione dei beni culturali e paesaggistici: Guida ragionata per studenti, specializzandi e operatori, amministrativi e tecnici, delle pubbliche istituzioni di tutela*. Milan: Giuffrè.

Treves, Anna. 1976. *Migrazioni interne nell'Italia fascista: Politica e realtà demografica*. Turin: Einaudi.

Vittori, Massimiliano, and Carlo Fabrizio Carli. 2000. *Futurismo e Agro Pontino*. Latina: Novecento.

Zevi, Bruno. 1997. *Storia e controstoria dell'architettura in Italia*. Rome: Newton Comton.

CHAPTER 16

GREENBELT

Sustaining the New Deal Legacy

Mary Corbin Sies and Isabelle Gournay

Greenbelt, Maryland, the most fully realized of the three Green Towns that the federal government erected to jump-start Depression-stricken building industries, is an anomaly in the history of U.S. profit-driven real estate. Its designers—the planner Hale Walker, the architects Douglas Ellington and Reginald Wadsworth, and the gardener Angus MacGregor—fashioned a comprehensively planned suburban town for low-income white residents that projected a bold physical and social agenda, not unlike that of Römerstadt[1] (Dreysse 1988; Williamson 1997, 54). The Resettlement Administration (RA)—renamed the Farm Security Administration (FSA) in 1937—located Greenbelt twenty kilometers northeast of the White House. From 1935 to 1937, the RA constructed 574 brick or concrete-block houses and 306 garden apartment units on 217 acres, a public school, and a shopping complex (Figure 16.1). There were 641 acres of parkland and active recreation space featuring an artificial lake and a swimming pool (Gournay, this volume, Figure 20.2). In 1941, the FSA added one thousand smaller wood-frame "defense homes" for workers associated with the World War II buildup.

Seventy-five years later, Greenbelt remains an anomaly, especially when compared to the more ubiquitous forms of suburban development in the United States. Its distinctive heritage stems from its intentionally intertwined tangible and intangible cultural heritage. The International Council of Monuments and Sites (ICOMOS) defines tangible forms as buildings, landscapes, or artifacts and intangible heritage as customs and oral traditions, languages, festivities—the ways that people create meaning and express their cultures.[2] With respect to Greenbelt, we can think of these two categories in turn as the built environment and the social fabric and lifeways of the community. Greenbelt's brain trust intertwined both dimensions when they designed the new town.[3] After reviewing Greenbelt's genesis, distinctive features, and post-sale growth, this chapter analyzes how well its stewards—citizen volunteers and activists, the Greenbelt Homes, Incorporated (GHI) housing cooperative, dedicated elected officials, and city employees—have succeeded in conserving the new town's heritage, as well as what challenges Greenbelt faces today.

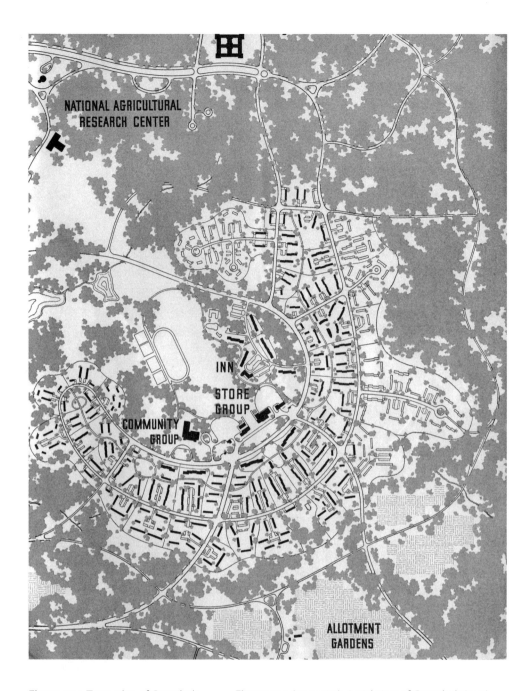

Figure 16.1. Town plan of Greenbelt (1935). The planned inn was not built. From Resettlement Administration, *Greenbelt Towns: A Demonstration in Suburban Planning* (Washington, DC: Resettlement Administration, 1936). (Courtesy Greenbelt Museum)

Figure 16.2 (opposite). Aerial view of Greenbelt (1941). From left to right: the access road (Southway), with defense homes under completion, the original super-blocks, Roosevelt Center, Greenbelt Center School, and, at top right, Greenbelt Lake. ("Greenbelt, Maryland, Aerial View, probably early fall," Library of Congress, Farm Security Administration, LC-USF344-007788-ZB)

Federal Greenbelt: A Benchmark of Community Planning and Cooperative Living

Greenbelt embodied and updated the physical and social ideals of the garden city movement (Arnold 1971; Namorato 1992; Parsons 1990; Stein 1957; Sternsher 1964). Its designers created a walkable and scenic suburban town, albeit designed for the automobile age. Five superblocks formed the heart of its iconic plan, which adapted the Radburn idea of dwellings—row houses in this case—clustered around cul-de-sac lanes (Mayer 1936) (Figure 16.2). Most rows were short and arranged in open courts along parallel crescent roadways. A network of walkways ensured that pedestrians circulated separately from automobiles; five underpasses gave them safe access to the town center and schools.[4] Clusters of garages were interspersed throughout the superblocks for the two-thirds of original residents who owned cars. There were varied floor plans, from single-story, one-bedroom end units to 1,500-square-foot downhill models with a live-in basement (Mach 1997, 34). All-electric kitchens anchored the service sides and culs-de-sac, while living rooms and

master bedrooms looked out on the common reserves, many with playgrounds.[5] Visually distinctive International Style apartment buildings lined the lower perimeter road.[6] Following Clarence Perry's concept for Neighborhood Unit planning, the town center offered an elementary school doubling as a community center, a shopping plaza, known today as Roosevelt Center, and a recreational complex (Perry 1929). The school gymnasium, its library, the movie theater, drugstore soda fountain, outdoor swimming pool, tennis courts, and baseball fields helped to compensate for the modest size of dwellings. The wooded greenbelt and lake welcomed adventurous youths, like those filmed in the documentary named *The City* (Steiner and Van Dyke 1939).

Cooperatives and democratic progressivism strongly shaped Greenbelt's history as well. In 1937, the FSA contracted Edward Filene's Consumer Distribution Corporation to provide commercial services in the form of jointly owned and democratically operated consumer cooperatives.[7] These included a grocery store, gas station, drugstore, movie theater, barbershop, beauty parlor, credit union, newspaper, and nursery school. In 1937, the Maryland General Assembly authorized Greenbelt to pioneer the first council-manager form of government in the state, based on the town charter devised by the FSA. Under this progressive system that splits governing responsibilities between elected officials and technocrats, the city council, elected every two years in nonpartisan contests, appoints a city manager, who can hire and fire members of his staff.

The radical agenda behind Greenbelt's physical and social environment made it distinctive among American suburbs in several ways. Although the planners and architects integrated landscape, architecture, and planning to form a single design entity, the landscaping of the superblocks and greenbelt eclipses the plain architecture. Residents have incorporated the walkability, parks, allotment gardens, and green surroundings into their lifestyles. Greenbelt was created for lower middle-class residents and has remained affordable. Greenbelters are joiners, quick to join cooperatives, contribute volunteer labor, interact with their council and staff members, and organize social and political infrastructure when needed. Democratic traditions are strengthened by the free cooperative newspaper, the *Greenbelt News Review* (*GNR*). The militantly nonpartisan weekly, which volunteers have published without interruption since 1937, covers council and GHI meetings; planning, development, and community issues; as well as opportunities and threats generated by the city's location in a burgeoning metropolitan corridor. As one long-term resident put it, *GNR* is "our major source of information in the city . . . a huge factor in the city's integrity" (Havekost 2012).

Because the federal government provided so many public services and amenities to the pioneer residents, current Greenbelters expect and seem willing to pay for a high level of services, from recreational programs, parks, and playgrounds, to community policing, holiday celebrations, pedestrian pathways, and landscaping. These expectations have been passed down through the generations, and the entire package of features, amenities, and distinctive Greenbelt lifestyle composes an informal credo of "Greenbelt principles" that guide residents when controversial issues arise and constitute a distinctive lived reality.

Post-1952 Development: Old Greenbelt, Western and Eastern Districts

By 1942, Greenbelt totaled 1,895 dwelling units, and it represented the country's most comprehensive combination of modern community design and social engineering.[8] From its inception, however, the community was controversial.[9] County residents were outraged that their tax dollars were subsidizing its lavish recreational amenities. The real estate industry and many local, state, and national elected officials opposed any direct federal input in housing.[10] All of these parties lobbied the government to divest the new towns. In 1952, the Public Housing Authority, which then managed Greenbelt, sold the town. The original and defense row houses as well as 708 acres of undeveloped land went to the Greenbelt Veteran Housing Corporation (GVHC), a citizens' housing cooperative. The apartment buildings, commercial properties, and 850 additional acres were sold to private entities. The City of Greenbelt gained ownership of the lake, pool, playfields, allotment gardens, and water and sewage facilities.[11] In 1957 GHVC changed its name to GHI, which continues as the town's principal co-op today.

Once the federal government sold Greenbelt, both the municipal government and residents fought to ingrain expectations that the Greenbelt principles would prevail in subsequent development. Financially strapped, the housing co-op sold to private homebuilders a significant portion of the greenbelt it acquired in 1952. Between 1955 and 1990, what is now called Old Greenbelt (see Figure 16.3) was built out, mixing subdivisions of single-family houses, garden apartments, townhouses, and one controversial high-rise overlooking the lake. New developments shifted residential density from the original superblocks to the lake and its park. Many residents moved from the original housing to larger homes, demanding that private developers provide the amenities they expected: wooded backlots, parks, and pedestrian walkways connecting to the lake and Roosevelt Center (Gournay and Sies 2010, 207–9).

Modern churches were erected along the original double-crescent roadway. In the 1960s, a new municipal building and public library were sited perpendicular to

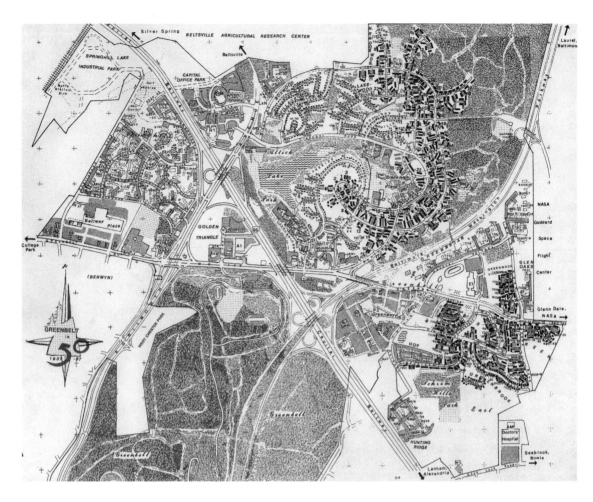

Figure 16.3. "A Map of Greenbelt, Maryland, 20770," prepared by the drafting committee of Citizens for Greenbelt, Inc. (1987). This fiftieth anniversary map shows the post-1952 development of central Greenbelt as well as the Springhill Lake garden apartment complex in Greenbelt West (upper left) and the beginnings of townhome and condominium development in Greenbelt East (center right). Greenbelt National Park is to the south (lower left). (Collection Isabelle Gournay)

the school, forming a mall to host civic events. An aquatic center and exercise facility adjacent to the pool opened in 1992. A few intrusions have occurred near Roosevelt Center: a professional building, rear parking lots, and mundane red-brick apartments. Today, Old Greenbelt boasts a successful farmers' market, several recent co-ops, including the New Deal Café (a live music venue), affordable housing, and an impressive portfolio of amenities and public services for a middle-class community.[12] To ensure survival, the movie theater was purchased by the city in 2002, restored in 2015, and its operations entrusted to a local nonprofit organization. The latest leisure amenity is a skateboard park between the community and youth centers.

The opening of the Baltimore-Washington Parkway and the Capital Beltway, in 1954 and 1964, respectively, placed Greenbelt at the hub of a major interstate highway system (Figure 16.3). In 1959, the National Air and Space Administration's (NASA) Goddard Space Flight Center opened just beyond the town's eastern boundary, attracting many employees looking for homes ("Goddard Space Flight Center" 2013). Four new sections developed beyond Old Greenbelt.

First was Greenbelt West, which comprised the Beltway Plaza shopping mall (1962–85) and Springhill Lake Apartments (1962–70) (Williamson 1997, 230). Thanks to consistent pressure from the city, this rental complex, totaling 2,900 units in 250 apartment blocks and 120 row houses, was almost a "second Greenbelt"; it included an elementary school, shopping center, indoor-outdoor recreation facilities, and pedestrian pathways winding through the landscaped acreage (Gournay and Sies 2010, 212).[13]

A second section from the 1960s was Greenbelt Park, an 1,100-acre recreational area and campground administered by the National Park Service; its physical alienation from Old Greenbelt across an eight-lane roadway represents a missed opportunity ("Greenbelt Park, MD" 2013).

The 1970s saw the creation of Greenbelt East, adjacent to NASA. A key project was Greenbriar (1974–80), a luxury garden apartment complex of roughly 1,200 condominium units, which became a well-planned community after the city pressured the developer (Gournay and Sies 2010, 213). Other condominium complexes followed in Greenbelt East, most with more amenities than would typically be included by private developers. There were also conventional subdivisions of detached single-family houses, a few apartment complexes, a professional condominium complex, a shopping center anchored by a major grocery store, and the Maryland Trade Center, a forty-five-acre high-rise office park.

The final section of Greenbelt to develop was the Golden Triangle, a fifty-seven-acre tract of commercial real estate wedged between three major roadways. Begun in 1977, this area is home to hotels, a car dealership, corporate office complexes, and a large chain restaurant (Wilson 1997, 217). Commercial tax dollars help to underwrite and make affordable the amenities and facilities that Greenbelters have come to rely on.

Stewards for Old Greenbelt

Despite steady growth, the physical and social environment of the iconic New Deal community provides an anchor of continuity and cultural heritage. Old Greenbelt would look and feel different, however, had developers and county planners gotten their way, and had several generations of stewards not counteracted threats to its physical plan, original housing, and social fabric. The key stewards—the City of Greenbelt, its Department of Planning and Community Development, GHI, citizen activists, citizen volunteers, and the *GNR*—mobilize and work simultaneously, if not always together. We present four case studies of stewardship: the "battle for Greenbelt";[14] the protection of Old Greenbelt's iconic housing and landscape; the establishment and operation of the Greenbelt Museum; and the campaign to preserve the Center School by converting it to a community center. Each endeavor brought its own challenges and lessons, allowing some stewards to grow in stature and effectiveness.

Fighting to Preserve the Greenbelt Principles

The "battle for Greenbelt" is the most dramatic example of stewards defending the physical environment of the planned community. In 1957, a plan prepared by the local planning authority, the Maryland-National Capital Park and Planning Commission (M-NCPPC), called for redevelopment of the defense housing area, additional commercial buildings in Roosevelt Center, and a new arterial road routed through the heart of Old Greenbelt. M-NCPPC's 1964 sector plan projected much higher densities, 124 acres of high-rise dwelling units, 297 acres of garden apartments, and a population of 52,000, compared to the 11,000 residing there. If implemented, these plans would have compromised the integrity of the historic core.

The key steward in this battle was the city itself. In the early 1960s, neither the city council nor the city manager was overseeing planning closely; each focused on governance issues still being worked out after the 1952 sale. The updated plan that Hale Walker completed in 1954 served as a guiding document for town planning (Giese 2012). Although Greenbelt was an independent municipality, it did not then and does not now control its own zoning or planning. Zoning was regulated at the county level and worked in a convoluted way. M-NCPPC could draw up and advise on plans but its Prince George's County Planning Board did not have authority to approve them. Decision making was vested in the county council.[15] Stewards for Old Greenbelt were forced to appeal for relief to county officials promoting a conflicting credo of economic development and demographic growth.

In 1962, Greenbelt hired a manager with a unique service ethic: Jim Giese, who served for twenty-nine years, and built a staff that worked diligently on behalf of the community (Craze 2012; St. John and Young 2011, 112). Giese marshaled the city's official opposition to the 1963 master plan, hiring consultants, launching legal challenges to overturn zoning decisions, and successfully requesting that the county planning board meetings be opened to the public (Giese 2012). The *GNR* joined him, attending meetings and reporting carefully on planning matters throughout the controversy. Led by city officials, citizen activists protested the 1964 plan at every possible occasion. They turned out by the hundreds at hearings, confronted developers at rezoning request meetings, and formed Citizens for a Planned Greenbelt to lobby for growth that extended rather than destroyed the New Deal planning vision (Skolnik and Zubkoff 1997, 192–95).[16]

Under pressure, the county officials denied developers' rezoning requests and the "battle for Greenbelt" was won, inspiring much greater respect for planning and city officials' ability to uphold the Greenbelt principles (Giese 2012). Had there been no iconic plan, no history of civic engagement, little agreement about the Greenbelt principles, and less dedicated stewards, Old Greenbelt would have been dramatically altered by 1970.

Once the battle was over, the city reacquired incrementally a number of parcels that GVHC had sold to private developers and that M-NCPPC had proposed for high-density development. These actions restored a portion of the original greenbelt (Skolnik and Zubkoff 1997, 195). The city established its own Department of Planning and Community Development (DPCD) and hired its first full-time planner, Celia Craze, in 1986. DPCD oversees all physical development in the city; it reviews development proposals, manages capital projects, prepares population and housing projections, undertakes code enforcement of housing units, and coordinates planning and development activities with other public bodies inside and outside the city (DPCD 2013). Craze, like Giese, a technocrat who exercised considerable power in shaping Greenbelt's development and shepherding its planning heritage, still headed the department in 2017. She considers parts of the iconic plan "fundamental," while recognizing that new development should not just replicate Old Greenbelt but evolve to meet residents' current needs and desires (Craze 2012). As DPCD has battled with developers to get what Greenbelters wanted, both the office and Craze herself have grown in stature in Prince George's County.

DPCD worked with the county planners to amend the county's master plan of 1989 in order to protect residential development and the commercial core in Roosevelt Center. The mechanism of protection is declaration of most of Old Greenbelt as an RPC (Residential Planned Community) zone.[17] Working at macro and micro levels, this powerful zoning tool "locks in" the density and footprint of Old Greenbelt, ensuring maintenance of the 1937 iconic plan (Craze 2012).[18] It prevents GHI from constructing new buildings or cellphone towers in the superblocks, for example, and the current landowners of commercial property in Roosevelt Center cannot infill or change the footprint of the 1937 buildings (Craze 2012).

At different times, the city and GHI have sought and failed to obtain local approval for a National Register Historic District designation for the New Deal–era town. Neither National Register status nor Greenbelt's designation as a National Planning Landmark in 1987, however, offers the protection and enforcement afforded by RPC zoning.[19] Although the Historic District designation attests that a neighborhood has special significance, it cannot prevent landowners from altering or demolishing their property, unless they use federal funds to do it. Despite this weak level of protection, many city officials and citizens oppose the National Register Historic District designation because they believe it will prevent them from doing what they want with their property.[20] Most Greenbelters we interviewed seemed unaware of the protection and enforcement powers of RPC zoning; indeed, most do not know that it prevents substantial change to the town's historic footprint. Prior to the city's opposition, GHI was inclined to seek Historic District designation because it would enable them to apply for low-interest loans and grants to assist with maintenance and rehabilitation of housing. To date, however, groups promoting Historic District designation have been unable to obtain the necessary approval of the majority of citizens.

The Housing Cooperative's Stewardship

As the owner of the most iconic part of Greenbelt's landscape, GHI, one of the largest co-ops that manages historically significant housing in the nation, is the key steward of the original housing and superblocks. In the United States, housing co-ops are rare; they undermine established American values that lionize individual property ownership. GHI dedicates itself to providing quality homes for its members and "celebrating and respecting the historical legacy and ideals of the original Greenbelt plan" (GHI 2018b). It is collectively owned and democratically operated for its members on a nonprofit basis. Its stewardship involves managing and protecting its physical assets—1,600 dwellings and private yards, as well as open acreage—*and* attending to its social/cultural ethos by screening prospective members for their willingness to care for their share of the cooperative and to participate actively in its life.

Governed by an elected nine-member board, GHI provides and updates its rules and regulations through a substantial *Member Handbook* (GHI 2016). Units must be owner-occupied and may only be resold at a profit after two years. New applicants attend orientation meetings to learn about the rules and operation of the co-op as well as what residents value about Greenbelt's iconic legacy. Monthly fees pay for salaried staff assistance, including a maintenance department, which handles "repair requests and implements many scheduled capital improvement programs," and technical services, which "regulates modifications to GHI homes and yards and performs pre-sale inspections" (GHI 2018a). The inspections, begun in 1968, were implemented to correct an earlier period of neglect of the co-op's physical fabric; members must address GHI's demands before putting their units on the market (Lewis 2012). Like the city, GHI maintains a formal structure of volunteer standing and ad hoc committees supported by staff liaisons. The Architectural Review Committee evaluates requests to add to or remodel a unit, or to erect a garden shed or fence. The Woodlands Committee develops management schemes for land in common ownership, including the pocket parks. The Finance Committee maintains the co-op's assets. GHI has been "quite conservative" and successful in preserving its members' equity, and it commits considerable effort to keep its homes among the most affordable in the region (Lewis 2012). Through its Greenbelt Development Corporation, GHI is strategizing how to gain additional income in order to afford its next round of improvements without exceeding its members' ability to pay for them. It already owns and rents two 1930s garden apartment buildings and has tried to acquire others from private owners to generate a steady stream of rental income to mitigate its members' expenses (Lewis 2012).

For the most part, GHI has managed well a unique planned landscape of buildings, common areas, collective woodlands, playgrounds, and front and back yards. In 1983, the co-op instituted a Community Beautification Program. This annual, strictly enforced inspection of external façades and private gardens requires members to bring their property into conformity with the *Member Handbook*. A voluntary program to restore the commons of the superblocks and return courts to the low, natural hedging that the federal government required from pre-1952 tenants has begun. GHI and the city split the cost of maintaining internal playgrounds and both entities take an active interest in managing their respective woodlands (City of Greenbelt 2013).

Managing its architectural assets presents a greater challenge for GHI; the aging housing stock has acquired an array of problems, and modern residents desire more space and individual expression than most units provide. GHI's record of preserving design integrity is mixed. While its 1980s utility upgrade removed the original multipaned metal-casement windows—key character-givers—GHI recently invested in new slate roofs for the brick gabled units, despite the expense. Additions and alterations to the small units raise a quandary, as GHI weighs heritage concerns against the yearning of members, especially families with children, to follow today's lifestyle standards. Added ornamentation, such as "Colonial" shutters, siding, bay windows, and porch enclosures, have passed architectural review (Figure 16.4). For every member who has hired an architect to design a harmonious addition blending with its surroundings, many more have created bland bump-

Figure 16.4. Greenbelt Museum, 10B Crescent Road, one of the original concrete block houses; it is part of a pair of units. 10B (left) has been restored to its original 1937 appearance; 10A (right), which the city is transforming into a visitor center, has been "Colonialized." (Courtesy Eric Zhang, photographer, 2015)

outs or bulky wings that mar the rhythm of residential rows, contradicting their logical expression and unassuming character (Figure 16.5). Looking ahead, GHI must contemplate whether to devise stricter guidelines and oversight.

GHI remains a key steward of Old Greenbelt's social heritage as well. It fosters citizen volunteers and activists, and it informs members about the Greenbelt principles. Its annual general assembly is well attended, hosts lively debates, and encourages the dedication of volunteers, staff, and the general membership in the democratic process of resolving problems and facing challenges, a vital Greenbelt tradition. For years, the recently reinstated Marketing Committee has overseen recruitment and socialization; it holds open houses, new member socials, maintains a website, and travels to area festivals to spread the word that Greenbelt remains a thriving and affordable place to live (see http://www.ghi.coop/content/marketing-committee for a promotional video). As one of its former members explained, the idea was that "we're not really selling our houses, we're selling a [Greenbelt] way of life" (Havekost 2012).

Campaigns for the Greenbelt Museum and the Community Center

From the beginning Greenbelt's brain trust planned to foster a community of civically engaged citizens. Two case studies delineate the stewardship whereby Greenbelt's intangible heritage—its social fabric, socialization about the Greenbelt principles, engaged citizenry, and cooperative democratic traditions—supports the adaptive reuse and interpretation of its tangible architectural assets.

Establishing the Greenbelt Museum was a grassroots effort that commenced in the 1970s. The idea took hold during the lead-up to the fiftieth anniversary celebration of 1987. Citizen volunteers associated with the anniversary committee began promoting the idea of a house museum in earnest. Giese, keen to have a fiftieth anniversary project that would outlast the celebration, supported the effort. The volunteers handled every aspect of the founding: phoning neighbors to build support, consulting museum professionals, sending out letters to residents living in two-family units to inquire whether they might sell their unit to the city, doing research in special collections to obtain pictures and plans of the original concrete-block units, and shepherding the idea through GHI (Havekost 2012;

Figure 16.5. This inharmonious alteration obscures the original concrete block flat-roofed house; such extensive transformation is unusual, though. (Courtesy Eric Zhang, photographer, 2012)

Lange 2012). The owners of 10B Crescent agreed to sell their unit and the two-bedroom house was restored to its original 1937 appearance using volunteer labor (Figure 16.4). Although there was some opposition from GHI members who felt it misused city funds to take an affordable housing unit out of circulation, the museum opened on October 10, 1987, as part of the homecoming weekend for the anniversary celebration (Giese 2012; Havekost 2012).[21] Thereafter the museum opened regularly on Sunday afternoons, staffed by a volunteer coordinator with a script interpreting the everyday life of a typical Greenbelt family between 1937 and 1952 (Lange 2012; St. John and Young 2011, 110–11). The Friends of the Greenbelt Museum (FOGM) incorporated in 1985 as a nonprofit organization to manage the museum, build its collections, and raise funds (Knepper 2001, 194–95). Today the museum is staffed by a full-time museum director who works for the city and by a part-time education and volunteer coordinator and a part-time office assistant, both compensated by FOGM. Volunteers serve as docents, give special tours, and support other efforts, such as maintaining the gift shop and fundraising (*Greenbelt Museum* 2013).

As the product of volunteerism, the museum takes a leading role in educating people about Greenbelt's unusual legacy of community history and citizen engagement. In addition to the historic house and guided walking tours, the museum provides rotating exhibits that interpret Greenbelt's history in its community center gallery, and it also sponsors bimonthly educational lectures. For publications and historical documents, it reprinted a New Deal brochure (Gournay, this volume, Figure 20.1), placed historical markers along the landscape, issued a walking-tour map, and recently published its first book (*Greenbelt Museum* 2013; St. John and Young 2011). These activities instruct citizens and visitors about Greenbelt's iconic planning vision, inform them about the Greenbelt principles, and market the community to tourists and would-be residents. The museum has substantially raised the profile of Greenbelt throughout greater Washington, DC (Lange 2012).

While volunteers contribute the ongoing work that enables both the city and GHI to stay on course, activists organize, sometimes quite militantly, in response to perceived threats or controversial issues confronting the town. As more than one Greenbelter explained to us, "citizen activists are the heart of any successful community" (White 2012). One of the most contested issues to arouse activists, after the "battle for Greenbelt," was whether to renovate the original elementary school or build a new structure to replace the long vacant North End School (1942) and turn the character-defining Center School (1937) into a community center (Ryberg et al. 2005; Williamson 1997, 294) (Figure 16.6). This controversy showcased Greenbelt's brand of democracy in action.

Figure 16.6. Greenbelt Community Center (the original Center School, completed in 1937). (Photo by Mary Corbin Sies)

A good sampling of the debate took place in the pages of the *GNR* in the form of letters to the editor and reporting by the newspaper's nonpartisan journalists. Greenbelters were divided between those who insisted that the Center School was always intended to be "the" school "from day one" and those who argued that the building had been intended and used as a school *and* community center during the iconic era (Giese 1997, 294–95). Those focused more on educational issues thought the Center School could be renovated more cost-effectively to meet students' needs while others felt only a new and technologically up-to-date facility could serve that purpose. Activists warned that converting the Center School to a community center would "place a $4 to $6 million dollar burden plus astronomical maintenance costs on city taxpayers" (Giese 1997, 295). Each side accused the other of misrepresentation, "dealing in pure fantasy," and turning their backs on the Greenbelt principles, and both sides blasted the *GNR* for maintaining its characteristic neutrality (Beauchamp 2012; Giese 1997, 295).

Throughout the controversy, the newspaper steadfastly provided citizens with coverage of the range of perspectives on the schools, occupying the center of Greenbelt's public sphere.

In the end, a special election was called in June 1989 and Greenbelters approved the conversion of the Center School to a community center by four percentage points. When the election results were in, both sides accepted the decision and moved on. In 1992, the North End School was demolished and construction on the new school began. The city appointed an advisory task force of citizen volunteers to work with architects to review the conversion of the Center School to a community center. The project serves as an object lesson in adaptive reuse, preserving the integrity of the classrooms, dramatic stairwells, and hallways. Florance Eichbaum Esocoff King Architects used a light touch in adjusting the building to its new functions, maintaining the school's historic character both outside and inside. It opened its doors in the fall of 1995 and remains heavily used for recreation, meetings (including those of the city's advisory boards), the arts, senior services, childcare, summer camps, performances, assemblies, and civic celebrations. With the lake park, the community center stages the activities that bring Greenbelt citizens into contact and cements the city's social fabric.

Achievements and New Challenges

Today Greenbelt can take pride in the fact that most of its iconic planning, architecture, and ethos of community spirit and civic engagement remain intact. While its stewards—the city, its planning office, GHI, citizen volunteers, citizen activists, and the *GNR*—may not always see eye to eye on every issue, they have constructed the protections necessary to safeguard Greenbelt's landscape and legacy *and* an organizational infrastructure for arousing the citizenry should any further defense be needed. Residents who arrived in the 1960s and 1970s admit that they came by accident but express satisfaction with what a wonderful and affordable place Greenbelt was to raise children and how easily they were welcomed into community life regardless of their personal circumstances and income (Beauchamp 2012; Havekost 2012; Lewis 2012). Today many residents starting families seek out Greenbelt because of its sociability, lower costs, liberalism, pedestrian friendliness, green ethos, excellent public services, and abundant programs and recreational opportunities for children (Giese 2012). Of those who reside in Greenbelt for a finite period, a critical number infuse their skills, professional expertise, and temporal and emotional resources into the community.

Greenbelt still faces several small and large challenges as it moves toward its one hundredth anniversary, however. Most pressing is securing the social and commercial viability of Roosevelt Center (Plate 19). This challenge has two dimensions: designing a successful community gathering space and boosting the patronage of the center's businesses. In 1999, the city hired the landscape architect Sharon Bradley to restore clarity and focus to the center's plaza.[22] She blended historic and modern elements with innovative and sustainable construction and planting techniques (Bradley 2012). Using original blueprints, Bradley reconstructed the 1937 benches, brought in tables with patio umbrellas, and replaced trees that obscured commercial signage. The *Mother and Child* sculpture by Lenore Thomas—which long-term residents consider a sacred symbol—was beautifully restored. The city and the New Deal Café sponsor several festivals in the plaza, with performers using a stage that frames the statue. Bradley advocates a second phase of enhancement that would terrace the hillside behind the plaza to create a natural amphitheater and more generous performance space (Bradley 2012; Forgey 2000; Zhang 2012a).

The city must also address Roosevelt Center's commercial challenges. A marketing study concluded that Roosevelt Center has not succeeded in attracting sufficient residents from the three sections of Greenbelt to patronize its enterprises, despite its historic movie theater, café/live music venue, arts center hosting a community theater company, farmers' market (Figure 16.7), and restaurants (Davis 2012; Urban Information Associates 2003, 10–11). It remains a best-kept secret from neighboring communities as well. The "Greener Greenbelt Charrette" (2007), a presentation created through a partnership between GHI and the Potomac Valley Chapter of the American Institute of Architects, worked up several citizen-generated ideas for ensuring the town center's success: opening a visitor center, filling vacant commercial spaces, adding residential and live/work units near Roosevelt Center, bringing more cooperatives into the center, and improving signage on major highways indicating the center's location (GGI 2007). As of this writing, a nonprofit has revitalized the movie theater, and a new makers' space is providing STEM (science, technology, engineering, mathematics) and other educational opportunities for all ages. To create more robust patronage, however, Greenbelt needs to develop a denser residential district within walking distance of Roosevelt Center.

Improving pedestrian access through Roosevelt Center constitutes another priority. The challenge is to connect Greenbelt's commercial and civic centers while maintaining the iconic planning principle of separating automobile and pedestrian circulation. The pedestrian pathway system fails at the town center bus stop, which has pedestrians disembarking from public transportation into vehicu-

Figure 16.7. The farmers' market was established as a nonprofit in 2008. It is located in the Roosevelt Center parking lot and is open every Sunday between May and November. (Photo by Mary Corbin Sies)

lar rather than pedestrian pathways (City of Greenbelt 2012).[23] The council has approved a Pedestrian and Bicyclist Master Plan, prepared by the Advisory Planning Board, that would improve connectivity between the three sections of Greenbelt (City of Greenbelt 2014). Better circulation for pedestrians, bicyclists, and drivers would bring more residents—including those moving into Greenbelt Station, a new upscale townhome/apartment district on the city's western boundary—to Roosevelt Center for shopping and leisure.

An emerging challenge for transportation circulation, economic viability, and housing affordability concerns whether the General Services Administration will in the near future reactivate its plan to relocate the Federal Bureau of Investigation (FBI) to Prince George's County or northern Virginia. If Greenbelt is selected, the FBI headquarters will anchor transit-oriented development on what is now surface parking for the Greenbelt station of the Metro mass transit system. Prior to President Trump's decision to cancel the new headquarters, the city council, planners, and citizen advisors had reviewed preliminary designs for an accompanying multiuse complex with new parking and bus amenities to be built adjacent to the Metro tracks (Malouff 2014; Renard Development/Gensler 2016). With the new transportation master plan in place, if the FBI relocates or if Greenbelt attracts another major enterprise to the site, the employees could boost Roosevelt Center's economic viability and reinforce its role as a performance and restaurant hub.

Another urgent challenge is the aging of the iconic era's housing and infrastructure. An emblematic example is GHI's effort to find solutions to prohibitive energy costs, which hamper its members' physical and financial well-being. Its 1980s utility upgrade replaced radiators with electric baseboard heating. Subsequent deregulation of electricity distribution has made the heating system unaffordable and baseboards—like many types of windows and doors—are at the end of their life cycle. To prepare for the upgrade begun in 2015, GHI initiated a pilot program, accompanied by an educational campaign, to audition different structural and mechanical solutions on a sample of brick, concrete, and frame houses without compromising their "unique and historic character" (GHI 2012). The technical and aesthetic challenge was how to weatherize those concrete-block homes and still retain design integrity. The overall affordability of Greenbelt's housing remains a critical issue as well, as pre-2008 Great Recession property values began to put purchasing GHI units out of reach for lower middle-class residents and as previously affordable garden apartment complexes undertake renovations and raise their monthly rentals.

Other challenges abound. How can Old Greenbelt become an inclusive community by race, class, sexuality, and age as its demographic profile continues to diversify? Can Greenbelt's tradition of volunteerism and activism persist as the residents who waged the "battle for Greenbelt" and the museum and community center campaigns continue to age? There are encouraging signs that new generations are contributing to the social fabric, as younger volunteers have recently joined the *GNR*, organized the farmers' market, and formed the nonprofit operating the restored movie theater (Giese 2012). The Greenbelt stewards' ability to socialize residents about both the community's democratic traditions and what makes Greenbelt special is the vital element in preserving the city's intangible heritage. In an age of multimedia forms of communication, Greenbelt's stewards are becoming more resourceful about getting their message out about what they consider their Greenbelt principles, what the city does for its residents, and what its residents do for the city. So far, Greenbelters have acted to protect the city's iconic landscape and architecture and to uphold their unique pedestrian-friendly, affordable, green way of life. If there is a singular lesson from Greenbelt's story for other iconic planned communities, it is that robust, inclusive, and continuous citizen engagement is a crucial component of the preservation formula.

Table 16.1
Summary of Historical Events and Heritage Benchmarks for Greenbelt

Year	Event
1935	The Resettlement Administration (RA), an agency of the federal government, launches the Greenbelt Town Program. Greenbelt's superblock plan calls for 574 townhouses and 306 garden apartment units; a commercial center, including a movie theatre; a primary school/community center; and a public pool.
1937	October: The first tenants of the Farm Security Administration (FSA; RA's successor) move in. Cooperative enterprises include a grocery store and citizen-run newspaper. Greenbelt receives Maryland's first council-manager form of government.
1938	Experimental construction of ten detached manufactured houses (Parkbelt Homes) takes place.
1938–42	FSA photographers document Greenbelt's growth and community life.
1941	FSA appends rows of one thousand "defense homes" to the original plan in response to the World War II build-up and the need to house defense workers close to Washington, D.C.
1952	The federal government sells Greenbelt: original and defense townhouses go to a citizens' housing cooperative that is renamed Greenbelt Homes, Incorporated (GHI) in 1957.
1954	The nearby Baltimore-Washington Parkway opens. The first private subdivisions of single-family homes on parcels of the original greenbelt are erected.
1957	The Maryland-National Capital Park and Planning Commission (M-NCPPC) unveils a drastic redevelopment and roadwork plan for Old Greenbelt.
1960–70	Greenbelt integrates African American residents into the town.
1964	The nearby Capital Beltway opens. A massive garden apartment complex and regional shopping mall in Greenbelt West are constructed.
1964–70	"The battle for Greenbelt": citizen involvement defeats county planners and private developers advocating drastic densification plans.
1974	The Greenbelt East district begins with a 1,200 condominium apartment group.
1987	Historic Greenbelt is designated a National Planning Landmark. The Greenbelt Museum opens to celebrate the town's fiftieth anniversary.
1990	Special Residential Planned Community (RPC) zoning is implemented to protect the original footprint of Historic Greenbelt.
1992	The aquatic center adds an indoor pool and exercise facility to the original outdoor pool.
1995	A citizen referendum approves the reopening of the original primary school as a community center. A new elementary school is built on the north end.
1999	The Roosevelt Center plaza is revitalized; the *Mother and Child* statue is restored.
2002	The city purchases the original movie theater in response to a citizen campaign.
2009	The city council expands from five to seven to increase diversity; Greenbelt citizens elect their first African American councilmember.
2010	A citizen-run farmers' market opens.
2014–15	An American Heritage Areas Authority Grant helps fund the restoration of the Greenbelt movie theater; the city awards its operation to a nonprofit organization spearheaded by local citizens. City of Greenbelt: Population (2010 U.S. Census), 23,068; 4057 acres [1642 ha]; 9,747 dwelling units. Historic District: Population, approximately 2500; 741 acres [3.2 ha]; 1885 dwelling units.

NOTES

1. Walker (1891–1981) trained under John Nolen, whose office planned many celebrated communities. Ellington (1886–1960), educated at the University of Pennsylvania and the Ecole des Beaux Arts, is best known for his work in Asheville, North Carolina. Wadsworth (1885–1981), born in Montreal, received a certificate in architecture from the University of Pennsylvania. In Philadelphia he worked for Bissel & Sinkler. MacGregor (d. 1949) was a British-trained landscape specialist with previous commissions for J. Pierpont Morgan and English aristocrats. See "Biography: Douglas D. Ellington, Architect," D. H. Ramsey Library and Asheville Art Museum and Pack Library, Asheville, NC, http://www.library.thinkquest.org/J0112120/; "A Word for Douglas Ellington," *Greenbelt Cooperator* (December 8, 1937), p. 6; "Wadsworth, Reginald Jeffrey (1885–1981)," *Philadelphia Architects and Buildings*, http:///www.design.upenn.edu/archives/collection_list.htm; "Hale J. Walker," *Washington Post* (August 17, 1967), p. B10; "MacGregor Rites Today," *Washington Post* (December 22, 1949), p. B2.

2. ICOMOS, Fourteenth General Assembly and Scientific Symposium, "The Interdependence of the Tangible and Intangible Cultural Heritage," http://openarchive.icomos.org/468/1/2_-_Allocution_Bouchenaki.pdf.

3. Greenbelt's political champions and design consultants belonged to the pantheon of prewar American reformers: the economist Rexford Tugwell and First Lady Eleanor Roosevelt; the consultants Clarence Stein and Henry Wright, creators of Radburn; Tracy Augur of the Regional Planning Association of America; and the housing reformer Catherine Bauer.

4. The fifth underpass, under Edmonston Road, leading to the original high school is documented in Zhang 2012b.

5. As in Radburn, house plans were reversed so that kitchen and utility spaces looked out on the "service-side," and living and bedroom spaces looked out on the "garden-side" of the property.

6. Originally pristine white, some buildings have been painted inharmonious colors by current owners; original windows have been replaced and some balconies have been glazed. For a fuller discussion of housing types, plans, and styles in Greenbelt, see Gournay and Sies 2010.

7. See "Edward A. Filene," *Encyclopedia Britannica Online Academic Edition*, http://www.britannica.com.proxy-um.researchport.umd.edu/EBchecked/topic/206821/Edward-A-Filene.

8. This figure includes the New Deal townhomes and garden apartments, the five single-family detached homes of 1937, the ten Parkbelt homes of 1938, and the defense housing units. Greenbelt's iconicity is discussed in Gournay's chapter in this volume.

9. Examples of negative coverage include "Strange Housing Subsidies," *Washington Post* (August 6, 1936), p. X8; "Greenbelt Open," *Washington Post* (April 21, 1937), p. 12; "Byrd Attacks," *New York Times* (July 5, 1937), p. 4; and "Costly Greenbelt," *Washington Post* (July 8, 1937), p. 8.

10. The federal government exercised several kinds of indirect support of housing during the New Deal era. See Freund 2010 and Jackson 1985.

11. GHVC formed in 1949 when the government made official its intention to divest the Greenbelt towns. See "Greenbelt May Be Offered," *Washington Post* (August 2, 1945), p. 1.

12. By 2010, Greenbelt had 23,068 residents: 47.8 percent black, 25.9 percent white, 14.3 percent Hispanic/Latino, 9.7 percent Asian, 3.3 percent two or more races, and 0.3 percent American Indian/Alaska Native. There were 9,450 households in Greenbelt, a homeownership rate of 49.1 percent, and an average of 2.43 persons per household. The median household income was $61,854; 10 percent of residents lived below the poverty line. See "Greenbelt City Quickfacts" from the U.S. Census Bureau, quickfacts.census.gov/qfd/states/24/2434775.html.

13. "Huge Rental Project," (Washington) *Evening Star* (October 7, 1961), pp. B-1, B-12; "This

Community Will Offer a Village Atmosphere," *House & Home* 21 (April 1962): 154–55; "New Opportunities in Rental Housing 1," *House & Home* 25 (May 1964): 90–91.

14. The best secondary account of the "battle for Greenbelt" is chapter 5 in Knepper 2001.

15. In the United States, there is considerable variation in how planning and zoning authority is vested. These powers may be given to the municipality, the county, or a regional or metropolitan planning authority. The arrangement differs from state to state, and different states may have robust or weak regulations. In Prince George's County, MD, the power to approve or disapprove zoning and development proposals is vested in the district council, which is identical to the county council, a board of elected officials representing each district in the county. Plans and development proposals are drawn up, however, by the M-NCPPC and then submitted to the Prince George's County Planning Board—a division of M-NCPPC—which advises the county. The five members of the planning board are appointed by the county executive and confirmed by the county council for four-year terms. Controversial matters are reviewed by the district council; municipalities may also appeal plans and zoning decisions forwarded by the planning board to the district council. Conversation with Terri Hruby, assistant director of planning, City of Greenbelt, April 22, 2013. See also the county planning board's website, http://www.pgplanning.org/Planning_Board/About_The_Planning_Board.htm.

16. During the 1960s, Greenbelt developed a reputation for having aggressive citizen activists who fought any developers' proposals they deemed against their town's best interests. See White 2012. See also "Master Plan for Greenbelt Assailed," (Washington) *Evening Star* (July 22, 1964); "City Girds to Fight," *Greenbelt News Review* (July 16, 1964), p. 1; "Greenbelt Area Zoning," (Washington) *Evening Star* (March 13, 1965); "Master Plan Is Protested," *Washington Post* (May 8, 1965), p. B2; " 'Save Greenbelt' Campaign," *Greenbelt News Review* (April 1, 1965), p. 1.

17. The RPC zone covers Old Greenbelt, including the parcels between GHI and the Baltimore-Washington Parkway, but excludes the subdivisions erected after 1960. At this writing, the county is developing a new zoning code. Greenbelters are watching its development closely, but expect the new zoning to impose a similar level of protection in Old Greenbelt.

18. *Adopted Sectional Map Amendment: Langley Park, College Park, Greenbelt to the Approved Master Plan of October 1989* (Upper Marlboro, MD: M-NCPPC and Prince George's County Planning Department, May 1990).

19. See American Planning Association, http://www.planning.org/awards/landmarks.htm.

20. Many Americans believe, incorrectly, that the National Register or National Landmark designation will impede a property owner's rights to determines what happens to his or her property.

21. During the second weekend in October, many "pioneer families" visit Greenbelt to commemorate the original move-in date for the town.

22. The Bradley site design firm specializes in community redevelopment. See http://www.asla.org/guide/LAGuide.aspx?id=39575.

23. Judith Davis (2012), the former mayor of the City of Greenbelt, told us that the charrette, particularly ideas for creating more residential density in or near Roosevelt Center, scared people.

REFERENCES

Arnold, Joseph. 1971. *The New Deal in the Suburbs: A History of the Greenbelt Town Program, 1935–1954*. Columbus: Ohio State University Press.

Beauchamp, Virginia. 2012. Interview by Mary Corbin Sies and Isabelle Gournay (September 14). Tape recording and fieldnotes in authors' possession.

Bradley, Sharon. 2012. *75th Anniversary Symposium: Sustaining Greenbelt's Legacy*. Symposium

DVD: "Session 1: A Living Community: Greenbelt's Enduring Legacies: Roosevelt Center Mall Renovation." Available from the Greenbelt Museum collection, Greenbelt, MD.

City of Greenbelt. 2012. *75th Anniversary Symposium: Sustaining Greenbelt's Legacy.* Symposium DVD: "Session 4: Greenbelters on the Move." Available from the Greenbelt Museum collection, Greenbelt, MD.

———. 2013. "Forest Preserve Management and Maintenance Guidelines." http://www.greenbeltmd.gov/documentcenter/view/208.

———. 2014. "Pedestrian and Bicyclist Master Plan." http://www.greenbeltmd.gov/DocumentCenter/View/1733.

Craze, Celia. 2012. Interview by Mary Corbin Sies (June 13). Tape recording and fieldnotes in author's possession.

Davis, Judith. 2012. Interview by Mary Corbin Sies and Isabelle Gournay (August 21). Tape recording and fieldnotes in authors' possession.

Department of Planning and Community Development (DPCD). 2013. City of Greenbelt website. http://www.greenbeltmd.gov/planning_code/.

Dreysse, D. W. 1988. *Ernst May Housing Estates. Architectural Guide to Eight New Frankfort Estates.* Frankfurt: Fricke.

Forgey, Benjamin. 2000. "In Greenbelt's Town Center, a Fine New Deal." *Washington Post* (July 8), p. C5.

Freund, David. 2010. *Colored Property: State Policy and White Racial Politics in Suburban America.* Chicago: University of Chicago Press.

Giese, James. 1997. "Greenbelt: The Sixth Decade, 1987–1997." In *Greenbelt: History of a New Town, 1937–1987*, edited by Mary Lou Williamson, 290–315. Greenbelt, MD: City of Greenbelt.

———. 2012. Interview by Isabelle Gournay and Mary Corbin Sies (May 30). Tape recording and fieldnotes in authors' possession.

"Goddard Space Flight Center." 2013. NASA History Program Office. http://history.nasa.gov/centerhistories/goddard.htm.

Gournay, Isabelle, and Mary Corbin Sies. 2010. "Greenbelt, Maryland: Beyond the Iconic Legacy." In *Housing Washington: Two Centuries of Residential Development and Planning in the National Capital Area*, edited by Richard Longstreth, 203–28. Chicago: Center for New American Places.

Greenbelt Homes, Incorporated (GHI). 2012. "The Upgrade." Greenbelt Homes, Incorporated website. http://ghi.coop/content/upgrade.

———. 2016. *Member Handbook.* Greenbelt Homes, Incorporated website. http://ghi.coop/content/member-handbook-greenbook.

———. 2018a. "GHI Departments." Greenbelt Homes, Incorporated website. http://ghi.coop/content/ghi-departments.

———. 2018b. "Historic Preservation Task Force." Greenbelt Homes, Incorporated website. https://www.ghi.coop/content/historic-preservation-task-force.

Greenbelt Museum: A National Historic Landmark Planned Community Built in 1937. 2013. www.greenbeltmuseum.org.

"Greenbelt Park, MD." 2013. National Park Service. http://www.nps.gov/gree/index.htm.

Greener Greenbelt Initiative (GGI). 2007. "Greener Greenbelt Charrette" (September 30). PowerPoint presentation in authors' possession.

Havekost, Barbara. 2012. Interview by Isabelle Gournay and Mary Corbin Sies (September 28). Tape recording and fieldnotes in authors' possession.

Jackson, Kenneth. 1985. *Crabgrass Frontier: The Suburbanization of the United States.* New York: Oxford University Press.

Knepper, Cathy. 2001. *Greenbelt, Maryland: A Living Legacy of the New Deal.* Baltimore: Johns Hopkins University Press.

Lange, Sandra. 2012. Interview by Isabelle Gournay and Mary Corbin Sies (September 26). Tape recording and fieldnotes in authors' possession.

Lewis, Sylvia. 2012. Interview by Isabelle Gournay and Mary Corbin Sies (September 7). Tape recording and fieldnotes in authors' possession.

Mach, Leta. 1997. "Constructing the Town of Greenbelt." In *Greenbelt: History of a New Town, 1937–1987,* edited by Mary Lou Williamson, 28–36. Greenbelt, MD: City of Greenbelt.

Malouff, Dan. 2014. "If the FBI Moves to Greenbelt, Here's What It Will Look Like." *Greater Greater Washington* (July 31). http://greatergreaterwashington.org/post/23801/if-the-fbi-moves-to-greenbelt-heres-what-it-will-look-like/.

Mayer, Albert. 1936. "Green-belt Towns for the Machine Age." *New York Times* (February 2), p. SM 8.

Namorato, Michael Vincent, ed. 1992. *The Diary of Rexford G. Tugwell: The New Deal, 1933–1935.* New York: Greenwood Press.

Parsons, Kermit C. 1990. "Clarence Stein and the Greenbelt Towns: Settling for Less." *Journal of the American Planning Association* 56(Spring): 161–83.

Perry, Clarence. 1929. "The Neighborhood Unit." Vol. 7 of *Regional Survey of New York and Its Environs, Neighborhood and Community Planning.* New York: New York Regional Plan.

Renard Development/Gensler. 2016. Conceptual Renderings: "WMATA|Greenbelt Station." https://www.wmata.com/about/public-hearings/upload/2b-Renderings.pdf.

Ryberg, Stephanie, Mary Corbin Sies, and Isabelle Gournay. 2005. Greenbelt Center School and Community Center (1937). National Register level documentation prepared for the Maryland Historical Trust, Modern Movement in Maryland Survey, Phase Two. https://mht.maryland.gov/secure/medusa/PDF/PrinceGeorges/PG;67-4-1.pdf.

St. John, Jill Parsons, and Megan Searing Young. 2011. *Greenbelt.* Charleston, SC: Arcadia Publishing.

Skolnik, Elaine, and Harry Zubkoff. 1997. "Growing Pains." In *Greenbelt: History of a New Town, 1937–1987,* edited by Mary Lou Williamson, 214–27. Greenbelt, MD: City of Greenbelt.

Stein, Clarence. 1957. *Toward New Towns for America.* Cambridge, MA: MIT Press.

Steiner, Ralph, and Willard Van Dyke. 1939. *The City.* Documentary short, 43 min. American Documentary Films, Inc. (for the American Institute of Planners).

Sternsher, Bernard. 1964. *Rexford Tugwell and the New Deal.* New Brunswick, NJ: Rutgers University Press.

Urban Information Associates. 2003. *Roosevelt Center: Market Study* (January). Baltimore: Urban Information Associates.

White, Tom. 2012. Interview by Isabelle Gournay and Mary Corbin Sies (August 27). Tape recording and fieldnotes in authors' possession.

Williamson, Mary Lou, ed. 1997. *Greenbelt: History of a New Town, 1937–1987.* Greenbelt, MD: City of Greenbelt.

Wilson, Richard A. 1997. "Greenbelt in the 1970s and 1980s." In *Greenbelt: History of a New Town, 1937–1987,* edited by Mary Lou Williamson, 214–27. Greenbelt, MD: City of Greenbelt.

Zhang, Eric. 2012a. "Greenbelt 75th Anniversary Symposium, Session I." *Greenbelt in 2012* blog (May 4). http://greenbelt2012.wordpress.com/2012/05/04/greenbelt-75th-anniversary-symposium-session-1/.

———. 2012b. "Greenbelt's Pedestrian Underpasses." *Greenbelt in 2012* blog (December 17). http://greenbelt2012.wordpress.com/2012/12/17/greenbelts-original-pedestrian-underpasses/.

CHAPTER 17

BAŤOVANY-PARTIZÁNSKE

A Functionalist Company Town in Slovakia

Alena Kubova-Gauché and Isabelle Gournay

Originally called Baťovany, the Slovak city of Partizánske is among the best preserved of Tomáš Baťa's company towns. It showcases a fascinating interplay between functionalist design and the capitalistic ethos of what was then the world's largest shoe manufacturer. Baťa, who founded this industrial empire in 1894, was killed in an airplane accident in 1932, but his successor and half-brother, Jan Baťa, pursued his expansionist and paternalistic policies. In 1938, when Baťovany was being planned, Baťa's production was growing at an annual rate of more than 20 percent. It employed 65,064 workers worldwide, including 41,814 in Czechoslovakia, where its headquarters was located, in the city of Zlín (Pokluda 2004, 13). In addition to maintaining regular stores, the company erected stylish retail emporia (complete with pedicure services) in several European cities. Czechoslovakia was leading the world in the field of shoe manufacturing and Baťa's products were available in eighty-two countries.

Baťa's company towns formed a network of "serial" subsidiary cities, conceived in and administered from Zlín, whose mayor was Tomáš Baťa himself, from 1923 to his death. Each town specialized in a production sector, from rubber to stockings. Each boasted similarly designed brick and concrete factories and cubical workers' housing. In what is presently the Czech Republic, Baťa erected the towns of Otrokovice—Baťov (1930–34), Trebíc (1933), Zruč nad Sázavou (1938), and Sezimovo Ústí (1939); in Slovakia, in addition to Baťovany, Batizovce (presently Svit, 1934). Production sites were established in several European countries—including Borovo (1931–35) in Yugoslavia (presently Croatia); Chelmek (1932) in Poland; Ottmuth (1932) in Silesia (presently Krapkowice, Poland); Möhlin (1933) in Switzerland; East Tilbury (1933–34) in Great Britain; Hellocourt (1933–35) in France—and as far afield as India (Batanagar, 1934–35), the United States (Belcamp, Maryland, 1936–39), and Canada (Batawa, 1938–39). Today, only Zlín cultivates the Baťa mystique, as an incentive for tourism. The demolition of the Belcamp site around 2000, to make room for upscale waterfront residences, passed unnoticed, and attempts to create federal heritage issues in several of Baťa's European towns and to petition for a collective World Heritage designation have proven unsuccessful.

Originally planned for five thousand residents, Partizánske is presently a city of twenty-five thousand. Its history reflects dramatic changes in the region's political makeup. The original master plan for Baťovany, which was built near an existing village, Šimonovany, dates back to August 1938. The Slovak state, which was a protectorate of Nazi Germany, was created in March 1939, after Czechoslovakia was dismantled. Czechoslovakia was reconstituted in 1945, at a time when Baťovany already counted 2,800 residents and its factories employed 3,555 workers.[1] Baťa's factories were nationalized as early as May 1945, but local shoe production continued and kept expanding. In 1949, as socialism had taken over and the country was firmly rooted in the Eastern Bloc, Baťovany was renamed Partizánske, to honor the Slovak National Uprising, which originated in this city on August 29, 1944. From the 1950s to the 1970s, political, economic, and ideological changes did not prevent Partizánske from thriving as a manufacturing center nestled in beautiful scenery.[2] In 1989, the Velvet Revolution propelled Czechoslovakia toward democracy; four years later, the country was split into two republics and Partizánske became part of Slovakia.

Baťovany-Partizánske has therefore experienced three consecutive economic frameworks with differing ideological underpinnings and stewards. From 1938, when the first factory was built, to 1948, when the new city had already achieved significant growth, Baťa successfully implemented a functionalist and capitalistic ethos driven by cost-effectiveness and industrial productivity. From 1948 to 1989, the socialist regime imposed a nationally planned agenda that furthered Partizánske's economic and demographic growth. Since the 1990s, the city has struggled to adapt its industrial apparatus to the new globalized economy.

Changes in the social makeup of the city have followed its political and economic fortunes. Baťovany's original iconicity related to a socially homogeneous "community of labor" dominated by a single employer. As Eastern Bloc socialism promoted the idea of a society without class divisions, Partizánske's image was that of a prosperous town, where a cohesive group of skilled workers and their families enjoyed a high quality of life. Since the Velvet Revolution, ideals of social cohesion have given way to expressions of individualism and conspicuous consumption, and more recently to distress due to deindustrialization and unemployment. This loss of identity is also felt in terms of heritage awareness and initiatives, which, so far, have emanated from isolated individuals and have had little impact.

Unfavorable social and economic circumstances are not the only reasons why heritage awareness is limited. More than specific architectural landmarks, what makes Partizánske so significant and iconic in the historiography of Baťa's company towns, as well as Czech functionalism and modernist planning in general, is its linear plan (Kubova 2016). Jiří Voženílek, an avant-garde Czech architect on Baťa's payroll between 1937 and 1949, authored its 1938 plan and revised it in 1946. The program of a modern industrial town like Baťovany was conducive to implementing such functionalist thinking. Today, Partizánske's urban core remains governed by a very legible functional diagram, where open spaces and buildings connected with specific activities—work, housing, leisure, worship—are clearly delineated while enjoying strong visual connections. This chapter discusses the city's historical, formal, and ideological ties with Baťa's planning and design ethos, before analyzing Voženílek's singular contribution, its implementation and enduring legacy. The conclusion explores how to preserve the original spirit of the plan while achieving economic revitalization.

Modernism as Insignia: The Baťa Connection

By the late 1920s, Zlín, where Baťa was headquartered, counted 12,300 Baťa employees among its sixteen thousand inhabitants. Buildings were regulated by a modular grid measuring 6.15 x 6.15 square meters. This functional and aesthetic template dictated the composition of façades for every building type erected by Baťa in Zlín, as well as in subsidiary company towns, including Baťovany: these were factories, the famous "Schools of Work" for vocational training and their companion student dormitories, community centers, social and health care institutes, sports and recreational facilities, even workers' housing. This standardization flowed into the public domain, marking a radical departure in the field of civic design, from traditional European urbanism toward the creation of a purely "industrial city." The idea of a city shaped over centuries by highly individualized buildings housing prestigious institutions had lost its currency. Baťa was inventing a new paradigm for company towns, which complied with modernist visions for planning and architecture. Baťa opened in Zlín an in-house planning, architecture, and engineering department, which also trained the men who supervised construction and controlled expenditures in its subsidiary company towns. If changes were made to the standard Zlín type in one of these towns, as was the case for some of Baťovany's early houses, they were implemented anonymously.

Tomáš Baťa's ideal industrial settlement was a "garden city full of sun, water, refreshing greenery, a clean city, city of the highest salaries, prospering small businesses, flourishing trade and crafts, a city with the best schools" (Baťa 2002, 111). His vision was interpreted by an architect he employed for many years, František Lydie Gahura, in a 1925 project for Zlín named "A Factory Among Gardens" (Kubova 2005c). A key member of Baťa's design team was the Czech architect Vladimír Karfík who had worked in the United States, including for Frank Lloyd

Wright, as well as on Pessac in Le Corbusier's office. Karfík designed Baťa's most iconic building, its sixteen-story headquarters office tower in Zlín. In Partizánske, he was responsible for the monumental Catholic Church, and he designed row houses along the main esplanade.

In Zlín, the close physical and visual connection between Baťa's starkly modernist factories and workers' houses became truly iconic, translated into countless photographs published throughout Europe. The city's experimentation with a new urban image, where buildings formed a standardized kit of parts, enthralled the avant-garde. Baťa's planning ideas and architecture were heralded by some of Europe's most influential architects and critics, including Auguste Perret and Le Corbusier. In 1935, the latter proposed a linear city plan for Zlín that was never implemented. The French journal *L'Architecture d'aujourd'hui* marveled at this "experimental cell for a new organization of labor, economics and social life" (Vago 1935, 48). Indeed, the corporate branding of Baťa, which advertised its goods and services in forty languages, relied heavily on this image of cutting-edge modernity.

The site selection for Baťa's company towns was based on exacting surveys of demographic data and basic human needs, as well as on production and transportation strategies that were primarily determined by industrial development policies. Avoidance of social conflicts was a key consideration, leading to the creation of new towns *ex nihilo* in agricultural regions distant from traditional industrial centers with powerful trade unions. At Baťovany, the topography, preexisting railroad infrastructure, and availability of cheap labor drawn from the surrounding countryside all proved very favorable.[3] New opportunities were provided for the local population: "Education, work, social benefits, independence and liberation from the Christian patriarchal tradition of [the] Slovak countryside—these were the values that lured hundreds of young people to Baťa's schools and factories" (Moravčíková 2004, 519).

Beyond the company town image, the planning significance and iconic power of Baťa's cities relate in great part to the deliberate logistical, visual, and social inclusion of factories into the cityscape. By 1935, this inclusion was implemented according to a functionalist schema, which Voženílek would later describe as a linkage between "decentralized factories" and "individual residential areas" (Voženílek 1947). Voženílek's challenge was to devise ideal plans for new industrial cities, which would meet Baťa's numerous requirements. He was entrusted with several master plans, including those for Baťovany, Svit, Martfü in Hungary, and Best in the Netherlands. His inspiration came from Le Corbusier's unrealized plan for Zlín. In the 1940s, when commissioned to design an extension for Zlín, he would once again adopt a linear diagram.

Voženílek's Linear City Theories

Prior to Baťovany, most of Baťa's towns had been devised within a finite plan dictated by a circular layout. In Partizánske, Voženílek introduced a new formal and functional vision, as he coalesced two major trends of European modernist planning, which both deeply resonated among members of the Czech avant-garde: the Functional City and the Linear City. Partizánske's iconic status lies in this unique and rich synthesis. For Voženílek, ideas put forward by proponents of the Functional City, which crystallized during the fourth meeting of the Congrès Internationaux d'Architecture Moderne (CIAM) in 1933, were appropriate to devise a modern industrial city like Baťovany (CIAM 1979). He concurred that the demands of everyday life, work, and recreation had to be accommodated as inexpensively as possible and that a strategy of industrial development, based on precise economic and demographic data, ought to inform the plan of a company town. Using this approach entailed forsaking traditional methods of urban design. Voženílek also appreciated how Linear City schemes offered a new type of urban form, conceived in terms of regional planning and relying on careful examination of transportation needs and industrial growth strategies. Nonetheless, he went beyond the basic idea of a Linear City stretching long distances, which had been expounded by the Soviet planner Miliutin and subsequently by Le Corbusier. Baťovany was planned as a series of open-ended "functional rows" (Figures 17.1 and 17.2) that, instead of being relentlessly parallel and uniform, formed a rhythmical figure-ground pattern, where both industry and open public space were given pride of place and where separate functional realms were kept within walking distance of each other.

The aesthetic and symbolic potency (and iconicity) of Baťovany's plan reflected Voženílek's training, talent, professional connections, and mixture of idealism and pragmatism. He had been a member of the Left Front, a highly structured Czech avant-garde movement founded in 1929 (Kubova 1992). Despite a long and productive career under socialism, his is not a household name, even in his own country.[4] Voženílek was detail-oriented, as evidenced in his exacting studies of the shape and height of windows to provide optimal illumination. Yet he showed limited interest in promoting his work in Baťovany. In 1948, when he presented in the French journal *Techniques et architecture* his novel concept of a "typical floor" for a factory building, which he had implemented for this town, he did not mention its precise location (Voženílek 1948).

Voženílek's 1947 article, entitled "Contribution to the Development of the Linear City," published while he was working on an extension plan for Zlín, helps us understand his theories. There he likened linear schemes to "the functional merging of a structure into a higher organism." He continued: "By its clear division

Alena Kubova-Gauché and Isabelle Gournay

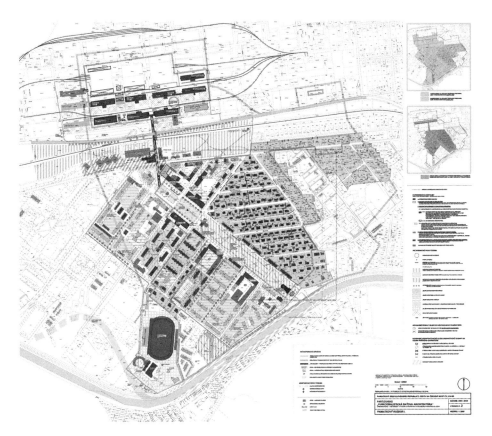

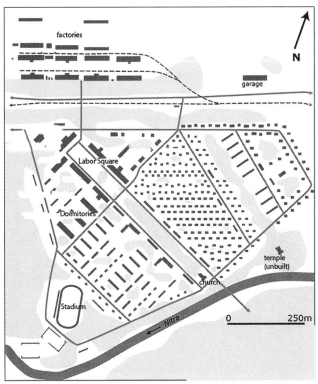

Figure 17.1. Diagrammatic plan of Partizánske (1946–47), redrawn from Jiří Voženílek's original, demonstrating his belief that "the best position for public institutions [along Labor Square] is at the boundary between a greenbelt and residential areas, and along the axis leading to the production unit." (Courtesy Monuments Board of the Slovak Republic)

Figure 17.2. Diagrammatic plan of Partizánske (1946–47), redrawn from Jiří Voženílek's original plan and used in 2011 as an overlay for suggested protection zones. (Courtesy Monuments Board of the Slovak Republic)

as well as general use which can fulfill many quantitative and qualitative requirements, the linear city is the basis of socialist architecture for the future, which will
offer the richest variety of spatial solutions, thanks to a rational exploration of
functional relations" (Voženílek 1947, 236).

For Voženílek, built form was a result of external requirements to realize savings
in infrastructure and to ensure productivity, as well as to accommodate a variety of
lifestyles. Functional but flexible planning would be achieved by combining a production strategy with the provision of numerous amenities. The ideal plan was an
open system, where conjoining workplace and housing into a single social and visual
unit opened new possibilities for organizing the physical fabric of a city. Voženílek
believed that his diagram could be used to both create a town of five thousand or a
city of twenty-five thousand and could accommodate harmonious growth. He
agreed with Karfík's idea that a building is not properly planned unless it complies
with "today's needs of production, not counting the possibility that tomorrow both
the production system and the product might change" (Karfík 2001, 41).

Voženílek realized that a Linear City scheme was conducive to uniformity and
that standardized architecture was monotonous. He always put a premium on the
concept of community and sought to inject urbanity into his diagrammatic plan.
Contrary to advocates of the Functional City, he preferred pedestrian distances
between various activities, as opposed to those dictated by motorized traffic. For
him, the Linear City concept could limit commuting to work, either on foot or by
public transportation, to about twenty minutes. Voženílek also embedded architectural diversity in his plan. Foregoing Thomas Baťa's credo of "collective work,
individual housing," he envisioned housing of different sizes and heights in his
1946 plan. Stating that "the principle of a linear city is not linked to any particular
residential typology," Voženílek believed that the appropriate placement of apartment buildings would enhance the significance of the urban center: "The most
logical arrangement for a residential row is from large-scale to individual housing
and according to the decreasing density of built-up area. . . . The ratio of built-up
areas for each kind of residence depends on the age and kind of workforce employed in production plants" (Voženílek 1947, 241).

Voženílek's critique of urban sprawl became more vocal, along with his desire
to see industrial cities develop within a regional framework. In the political context of 1947, his conception of a city that would be both functional and socialist
was not an easy proposition:

> The condition of contemporary cities as well as the results of current urban
> studies show that to date the state of settlements is a serious barrier to indus-
> trial and social advancement, and neither in the future will it be adequate to

support the organization of industry or living conditions in a socialist society. However, there have been introduced completely contradictory concepts for further development. Namely, satellite garden districts on the outskirts of large cities, the radical rebuilding of city centres, new and larger concentrations of inhabitants, and high density of inhabitants, de-urbanization and complete spread of settlements. (1947, 229)

Voženílek wanted to find a common principle behind all projects for industrial cities: "It is highly probable that a common urban principle will exist for a socialist society established on a common base of industrial civilization, and that its variations will logically correspond to the various qualitative and quantitative compositions of its individual settlement units" (1947, 229).

Designing Baťovany-Partizánske

The planning of Baťovany-Partizánske (Figures 17.1 and 17.2) is informed by three major and complementary concepts:

- an ideal plan, opened to the surrounding landscape and addressing issues of regional planning;
- an emphasis on community planning, with many shared amenities;
- typological and, consequently, social diversity in the architecture, with housing intended both for single people and large families (the erection of multifamily apartment buildings departing from Baťa's garden city vision).

Baťovany was surrounded by hills and bounded by the meandering Nitra River to the east. Voženílek's highly legible master plans were a skillful combination, as opposed to a mere diagrammatic juxtaposition, of functional requirements. To the north, above the railroad tracks, a monumental factory district consisted of parallel rows of identical brick structures. The earliest residential districts with flat (Figure 17.5) or pitched (Plate 20) roofs stretched to the east. On paper, as well as in aerial photographs, single-family or duplex houses, originally rented by Baťa to its workers, read as many evenly spaced dots. Their small gardens were not intended to produce vegetables, as Baťa's well-paid employees were encouraged to spare their energy for producing shoes and to rest outside of the factory. This dense residential landscape complied with Voženílek's ideals of pedestrian friendliness.

Below the factories and the original housing, Voženílek devised a wide-open space. Originally called Labor Square, it was renamed People's Square after World War II. It consists of a plaza (Figures 17.3 and 17.4), known today as the Slovak

Figure 17.3. SNP (formerly Labor) Square, with a remodeled "community house" in the foreground and school buildings in the background. (Courtesy Monuments Board of the Slovak Republic)

National Resistance, or SNP, Square, continued by a parklike strip, where Voženílek translated into a linear space Baťa's demand for ample green spaces within its new towns. By the Nitra River, Labor Square ended with Karfík's monumental Catholic Church, erected between 1942 and 1947.[5] It was connected to the factories by a diagonal "promenade" crossing the railroad tracks.

Voženílek's goal was to devise an urban structure with a clear hierarchy, which would indicate how the industrial city ought to function. He turned to the history of European cities to devise a clearly defined system of public spaces, therefore adding a new dimension to the concept of the Linear City. Following a tradition dating back to the Middle Ages, that of market squares as spaces for the exchange of goods and for personal encounters, the civic section of Labor Square was lined with monumental but low-lying buildings of varied but unified design, which housed administrative, commercial, and recreational amenities. One building type along this esplanade, which had no equivalent in Zlín, was a hotel designed, according to Jean-Louis Cohen (2004) and Stefan Šlachta (2006), by Karfík and which still serves as Partizánske's social hub.[6] Stark and dignified flat-roofed structures housing vocational schools, also found in

Zlín and other Baťa company towns, were located closest to the factories. To the north, Labor Square's landscaped section was lined by Karfík's four-unit row houses, which mediated between the scale of this large open space and that of single-family homes behind; to the south, state-of-the art primary and secondary schools, as well as a gymnasium, were erected according to Voženílek's 1946 plan.

This plan offered a well-defined pedestrian network formed by the original Labor Square, by the secondary transverse axes toward the factories and the sports complex (with a swimming pool completed in 1948 and a soccer stadium), and by subsidiary streets. To the south, streets were lined by rows of four-story garden apartments with projecting balconies, based on a type conceived for Zlín by Karfík. Altogether, Voženílek devised a hierarchy of

Figure 17.4. SNP (formerly Labor) Square today, with the former Baťa factory complex in the background: to the left, the city hall, erected in the 1950s; in the middle, the railroad station dating back to the 1960s; to the right, the former "communal house" (designed by Vladimir Karfík and F. Kučera, 1939–40), currently housing a hotel and stores. (Courtesy Monuments Board of the Slovak Republic)

public spaces (again, not unlike those of historic towns) and implemented his idea that "the best position for public institutions is at the boundary between a green-belt and residential areas, and along the axis leading to the production unit" (Voženílek 1947, 236). Believing that the traditional relation between the center and the periphery could be lost in a purely linear organization, he reintroduced the concept of centrality into his plan. To this day, life-sustaining activities—administrative offices, social and cultural amenities, retail and services—are concentrated in Partizánske's center.

The Socialist City

In late 1945, the Czech arm of the Baťa company was nationalized. Renamed Svit, it catered essentially to the Eastern Bloc market while following the same production strategy as before and during World War II (the quality of its shoes tended to decline, however). Partizánske remained a single-product manufacturing center. In a very short period, the second half of the 1940s, planning modern industrial cities came to define Czechoslovakia's political strategy and national identity. Changes affecting this country raised a crucial issue: could the idea of the Functional City for a single capitalistic employer persist and evolve under a centralized socialist regime, and at what price? Voženílek believed that his linear diagram matched ideals for a "Socialist City" and, indeed, his 1946 plan for Partizánske served as a template for a new generation of Czech industrial cities.

Voženílek was able to ease Partizánske's transition from company town to Socialist City while refusing to revert to traditional urban design and architecture, as prescribed by socialist realism (Kubova 2009). For his revised 1946 master plan, he took stock of information on the most recent foreign experiences related to industrial cities, both in terms of postwar rebuilding and ex nihilo construction.[7] In July 1953, the government approved new prospects for the development of industrial towns, including Partizánske. The first Five-Year Plan anticipated doubling industrial production and the construction of more than 350 industrial plants and 177,000 apartment units. By then, the notion of the Socialist City had acquired its full meaning in connection with this overall economic plan.

Because of the flexibility of its original urban scheme, Partizánske was able to accommodate substantial growth without experiencing the sprawl so prevalent in socialist-era Czechoslovakia. Amenities continued to be built according to the 1946 plan. From the late 1940s to the late 1980s, residential growth (essentially multifamily apartment buildings) occurred south of SNP Square, in compliance

Alena Kubova-Gauché and Isabelle Gournay

with Voženílek's plan. The geometrical rationale of this plan was potent enough to dictate logical extensions, and new construction kept clear visual connections with People's Square. Partizánske's system of parallel visual and functional rows was compromised in a single but major way: in the 1970s, the central promenade was split into two parts, with the erection of the kind of high-rise apartment building constructed in so many Czechoslovakian cities at the time. The rationale behind erecting this tower was to house many residents in a small footprint and in a central location. However, its placement had the effect, whether intentional or not, of obfuscating the then "politically incorrect" link between the Catholic church building and the factory complex. By 1963, high-rise apartment buildings started being erected on the other side of the Nitra River (Plate 20), outside the original core. Expansion also continued of the former villages that were annexed to the city, some of which regained their autonomy after 1989. The new district had its own schools and stores and no visual connection with the original plan, but its residents continued to patronize SNP Square for administrative, specialty shopping, and leisure activities.[8]

Current Challenges and Recent Initiatives

Today SNP Square, where the fountain was restored and the hotel was renovated, remains an attractive downtown, with cafés and restaurants. The municipality has renovated the twenty-five-acre sports complex inherited from Baťa. Karfík's spectacular church received a historic landmark designation in 1995, and it remains to this day Partizánske's only building to benefit from this national protection status. However, the post-1989 return to a liberal economy under Slovakian rule has negatively affected Partizánske's original industrial and residential districts.

Baťa's historic factories were all privatized, the municipality being barred from purchasing any of them. Their current ownership and stewardship are fragmented and unstable. A few buildings have been renovated (in particular, by the French manufacturer of protection equipment Bacou-Dalloz); others are used for storage management, but many sit empty. Exteriors are unchanged, but reuse options that have been envisioned so far offer short-term and ad hoc, as opposed to comprehensive, solutions. Adapting Baťa's 120-acre industrial district to new production processes entails major functional difficulties. Adaptive reuse respectful of its modernist character is a difficult financial, aesthetic, and sociocultural proposition. Difficulties are also compounded by the completion of a 140-acre industrial site benefiting from government incentives outside Partizánske's municipal boundaries, with no

Figure 17.5. Recent addition to an original flat-roofed Baťa house. (Courtesy Monuments Board of the Slovak Republic)

connection with the downtown. Today there are only three thousand workers in the old factories and the unemployment rate hovers around 20 percent.[9] The original industrial district has been directly and adversely affected by global changes in manufacturing. Its partially disaffected factory buildings act as scapegoats for the commonly held belief among Partizánske's residents that their current economic woes relate to the failure of post-1989 privatization policies.

Baťa's environmental control over its workers' housing was not unlike that of the U.S. federal government in Greenbelt (see Chapter 16 in this volume): fences had to remain natural hedges, and pets and garden sheds were prohibited. In both communities, a network of pedestrian pathways (leading to wells in Baťovany) nurtured everyday socialization and remain in use. Changes in Partizánske's original residential districts started as early as the 1950s, with the erection of permanent fences. They intensified in the 1990s, when private citizens could purchase Baťa's single-family houses at low prices. Alterations and additions are often quite radical; for instance, residents of attached twin houses have repainted the original red-brick or light-colored stucco walls with mismatched and garish colors (Figure 17.5).

Although no house has been torn down and rebuilt, less than a handful preserve their original aspect. Looking for increased comfort, in particular, improved

Alena Kubova-Gauché and Isabelle Gournay

thermal insulation, and willing to enhance their social status, homeowners did not hesitate to compromise the simplicity and integrity of Baťa's worker housing. They were, and still are, offered no guidance when considering altering or enlarging their dwellings and siting new detached garages. These changes have not compromised the original street alignments, however, and Voženílek himself thought of housing as having a limited life cycle (Kubova 2005a, 12). Changes also relate to a loss of collective memory, with the passing away of the generation of Baťa's renters and of their children. Alterations to garden apartments built at the beginning of the socialist era have been less conspicuous, consisting mostly of the screening of projecting balconies, and the municipality has enforced provisions preventing the erection of additional stories.

The "Culture 2000" program, sponsored by the European Community, generated reports and publications on the part of Slovakian academics who focused on Partizánske's early workers' housing without considering post-1948 resources (Šlapeta 1992; Moravčíková 2004; Topolčanská 2005). But the interest manifested by the Slovak branch of Docomomo (International Working Party for Documentation and Conservation of Buildings, Sites and Neighbourhoods of the Modern Movement) was short-lived, as it was only narrowly connected to the European program.

The broader issue of raising awareness about Partizánske's planning significance had yet to be addressed. In 2004, Alena Kubova, with the active support of city officials, organized the exhibition and eponymous symposium "Partizánske: Reinventing the Functional City," which took place in France, in Saint-Etienne, and in the smaller industrial city of Firminy, where Le Corbusier had built an apartment block and a church (Kubova 2004, 2005a, 2005b).[10] At this 2004 conference, Ján Podmanický, Partizánske's mayor at the time, whose key concern was economic revitalization for his city, demonstrated his interest in Voženílek's planning contribution; the city's current mayor and the head of its architecture office had also attended.

In 2007, Kubova organized an international symposium in Paris, with Partizánske's officials in attendance. Called "How to Reinvent the Industrial City," this conference convened architects, planners, and academics from six European countries who addressed issues related to both the past and future of Rationalist industrial planning, beginning with Baťa's experiments in the 1930s. The direct outcome of the 2004 and 2007 events was a draft for a citywide plan for the protection and preservation of Partizánske (Figure 17.2), elaborated by the Monuments Board of the Slovak Republic, in connection with its subsidiary for the Trenčín region, where Partizánske is located. This plan aimed at creating a shared identity and heritage awareness by heralding both the city's efficient planning armature and its modernist architectural landmarks. Unfortunately, this initiative

Figure 17.6. The cover of a conference pamphlet (2005), using a 1941 photograph of Baťa factories. (Courtesy Alena Kubova)

stalled with the arrival of a new municipal team in 2009, which still ponders whether enforcing protection measures would deter new investors and employers.

The posters and pamphlets for these 2004 and 2007 events exploited the iconic potential of not only Voženílek's plan for Partizánske, but also that of historic photographs. Commissioned by the factory leadership in 1941, a highly contrasted black and white photograph shows women with baby carriages walking along the diagonal promenade connecting Labor Square to the factories (Figure 17.6).[11] The promenade's abstract linearity is accented as it seems to float above an empty and flat terrain, awaiting the "greenbelt" envisioned by Voženílek. The young mothers strike a pose in front of the compound where the fathers of their children work. This photograph symbolizes the existence of a community of labor and hints at

Alena Kubova-Gauché and Isabelle Gournay

Partizánske's novel urban diagram and organization of social relations. It emphasizes large-scale production ideals, of babies as well as shoes. In the current context of deindustrialization, this iconic photograph encapsulating a major tenet of the Baťa ethos seems surreal and obsolete. Partizánske's current logo and branding image, devised in 1963, is an elegant high-heeled woman's shoe. This memento of the city's industrial past and original raison d'être has been translated into a monumental floral ornament (Figure 17.7), planted by the municipality at the symbolic "hinge" of Voženílek's plan: the public park located at the diagonal crossing of the aforementioned "workers' wives and baby carriages" promenade and SNP Square, opposite City Hall.

Figure 17.7. A floral shoe ornament planted on SNP Square as a reminder of Partizánske's origin story. (Courtesy Monuments Board of the Slovak Republic)

In the last decade, awareness of Partizánske's architectural and planning significance has risen among design professionals, such as members of the Association of Slovakian Architects (which until recently was headed by the Karfík scholar Stefan Slachta), European architecture students participating in a workshop co-organized by Kubova in 2006, and architecture professors at the Slovak University of Technology who supervise master's thesis proposals to adaptively reuse the old factories. Beyond academic architectural circles, Partizánske does not have dedicated heritage champions. Besides a Baťa "School of Work" Alumni Association, which administers an archive of school writings and photographs, there is no Baťa-centered heritage movement at the European scale. Only Zlín has been able to benefit economically and culturally through its association with the shoe company. In the early 1990s, attempts to resurrect the Baťa mystique in Partizánske, such as an initiative to rename the city Baťovany, were short-lived and ineffectual, as new generations of residents without personal connections to the shoe company would not identify with the city's origin story. No new narrative or collective identity has emerged, however.

As elsewhere in Slovakia, there is no grassroots heritage involvement in Partizánske, no historical society or concerned resident groups that would sponsor regular events or special celebrations of its social, urban, and architectural legacy. It is therefore crucial for Partizánske's municipal stewardship to step in: elected officials, as well as the town architect who collaborates with the regional heritage office, and the technical planning service, which is in charge of the decennial updating of the city's master plan mandated by the Slovak government. City officials and staff must also find ways to rally public opinion beyond design and heritage specialists, to make citizens aware of the social and aesthetic values of Partizánske's modernity. Outreach has so far been sporadic. A concerted effort is needed; it should consist of conferences taking place in the town itself, as well as a range of publications, markers, and maps.

Using its own funds, the municipality has begun rehabilitating some of the 1950s apartment buildings it owns near the sports complex. The restoration of Baťa's boarding houses into apartment units represents a more significant expenditure, and a request for European Community funding by the former municipality proved too complex from a logistical and bureaucratic standpoint to be finalized. The focus of the current mayor is to provide a better economic future for Partizánske. Preserving and enhancing his town's historic *genius loci* seems to him a lesser priority. However, it would be worth pondering the role of tourism in the city's economic regeneration, especially if touristic activities lead to the adaptive reuse of Baťa's factories and the provision of steady local employment. Partizánske is only a two-hour drive from Slovakia's vibrant capital city, Bratislava. It can establish a

Alena Kubova-Gauché and Isabelle Gournay

heritage network with other cities in the region, such as the historic town of Trnava. Nearby attractions include a spectacular nineteenth-century neomedieval castle at Bojnice, which Baťa owned in the interwar period: thermal sources and a spa, fishing lakes, and winter sports amenities. However, Partizánske is too large and too new a city, and its original housing has been too much altered to become a "museumized" company town like New Lanark in Scotland (see Chapter 1 of this volume) or a workers' housing settlement like Margarethenhöhe in Germany.

Because the social, planning, and architectural significance of Baťovany-Partizánske relates less to specific buildings than to its overall diagrammatic plan, its stewards must think outside the conventional heritage box. Devising creative ways to protect and enhance its planning diagram seems to be the only way that the city can regain iconicity. The delineation of one or several specific protection zones would not reflect Voženílek's holistic view of a Linear City, and it would not necessarily help preserve his goal to devise functional and green zones without finite physical and visual boundaries. In order to implement effective heritage and economic uplift policies, Partizánske ought to celebrate its distinctive brand of urbanity, by raising awareness of its unique "origins story" as a Baťa company town, as well as a Linear City and Socialist City. It ought to respect the spatial integrity of the 1946 master plan, to preserve vistas and open spaces, and to maintain the height gradation between buildings, all intended by Voženílek. To avoid the densification of the downtown, which would compromise the clarity of Voženílek's diagram, alternate districts should be identified, where new amenities could be built. New methods and tools, such as mapping of existing conditions and efficient visualization of demographic and econometric data, should also be considered.

Unfortunately, the current economic downturn precludes, at least for the foreseeable future, the removal of the high-rise apartment building hiding the church from SNP Square and the factory complex. Today, the political and economic situation is not conducive to promoting and celebrating Partizánske's modernity and iconicity. Its role as a planning exemplar raises very little interest on the part of its residents and other stakeholders. Priority goes to solving economic woes and to the "extensive reconstruction" of the moated castle in Šimonovany, for which the town received funding from the European Union.[12] The interest manifested by the Slovak branch of Docomomo was short-lived, narrowly connected to the European "Culture 2000" project.

Partizánske's municipality is faced with two major socioeconomic and environmental challenges: regaining prosperity by finding a new raison d'être for its factories while also acknowledging the Linear City concept inherited from the 1930s. Rising to this challenge would allow this Slovak city to rebuild its image and identity by drawing on its unique planning legacy.

Table 17.1
Summary of Historical Events and Heritage Benchmarks for Baťovany-Partizánske

Year	Event
1938	Jiří Voženílek plans Baťovany for five thousand residents. Construction begins on the factory compound.
1939–45	Development and factory production proceed under pro-Nazi Slovakian rule.
1946	After Baťa's nationalization by the Czech Socialist regime, Voženílek revises his master plan.
1949	Baťovany is renamed Partizánske.
1953	The first national Five-Year Plan monitors Partizánske's growth.
1970s	A residential tower encroaches on the main square.
1980s	The residential district of Šipok rises to the south of the original plan.
1989	The Velvet Revolution entails the privatization of the original factories and housing. Economic decline ensues, and Baťa-built houses exhibit major additions and alterations.
1993	Partizánske becomes part of Slovakia.
2004	Docomomo documents pre-1949 structures with funding from the European Commission's "Culture 2000" program. An exhibition and a symposium in Saint-Etienne, France, exemplify renewed scholarly interest for Baťa's rationalist planning and architecture.
2007	"How to Reinvent the Industrial City," a symposium held in Paris, focuses on Partizánske's future.
2008–11	The Monuments Board of the Slovak Republic prepares a preliminary preservation report.
2010	The new municipality takes no action on preservation recommendations.
	City of Partizánske: Population (as of 2013), 23,709; 5530 acres [2240 ha]. Envisioned preservation precinct: Population, 4,000; approximately 60 acres [24.3 ha]; 900 historically significant dwelling units.

NOTES

Thanks to Ms. Katarina Kosova, Director-General of the Monuments Board of the Slovak Republic.

1. Proclaimed on October 28, 1918, the Czechoslovak Republic was, until its dismantling by the Nazis in 1938–39, one of the most industrialized countries in Europe. It was reinstated on May 9, 1945.

2. In the late 1950s, Partizánske had 8,000 residents while the factories employed 7,700 persons.

3. The first passenger railroad station was erected in 1950.

4. Voženílek studied architecture at the Czech Technical University in Prague. He headed the design team in charge of Zlín's 1946–47 Regulation Plan, which remains implemented to this day. His best-known building remains the Collective House (1947–51) in Zlín. In the 1950s, Voženílek held several official positions and was Architect-in-Chief for the city of Prague from 1961 to 1970. He also taught planning at the Prague Architecture School. For additional information, see Voženílek 1957; Svoboda 2010; Kubova 1992, 233.

5. Presently Partizánske's population is nearly 74 percent Catholic. A Protestant temple planned on a smaller parallel promenade to the north was never built.

6. For an expanded version of Cohen's essay, see Cohen 1980.

7. Among advocates of functionalism, the division of Europe between western and Soviet blocs did not stop exchanges of information and a yearning for international cooperation, in order to implement reconstruction efforts. For instance, one of the Czech architectural journals published all details of Le Corbusier's Unité d'Habitation in Marseille at the time when Voženílek implemented the same type of collective housing in Zlín.

8. A significant number of residents averse to this rather high-density residential growth moved to nearby villages where they renovated old farmhouses.

9. Speech by Ján Podmanický, mayor of Partizánske, "How to Reinvent the Industrial City" symposium, Paris, 2007.

10. A ten-minute video extolling the city's planning assets was also commissioned for the occasion from one of Slovakia's most promising film directors, Juraj Krasnohorsky.

11. Along the same route, Moravčíková 2004, 525, illustrates a parade of uniformed students of the Baťa-administered School of Work, which had opened in September 1939.

12. See http://www.partizanske.sk/?id_menu=0&module_action__95386__id_ci=64750 #m_95386.

REFERENCES

Baťa, Tomáš. 2002. *Úvahy a Projevy*. Zlín: Univerzita Tomáše Bati ve Zlíně.

Cohen, Jean-Louis. 1980. "Nostro cliente é il nostro padrone, Le Corbusier e Baťa." *Rassegna* n.3, 347–60.

———. 2004. "Les projets de Le Corbusier pour Baťa, entreprise mondiale." In *Biennale internationale du design 2004 Saint-Etienne*, 119. Exhibition catalog. Azimuts, n.s.

Congrès Internationaux d'Architecture Moderne. 1979. *Dokumente 1928–1939*. Basel, Stuttgart: Martin Steinmann, Birkhäuser.

Karfík, Vladimír. 2001. "Organizace moderniho prumyslu." In *Vladimir Karfik 1901–2001. Zbornik prispevkov z vedeckej konferencie*. Bratislava: Faculty of Architecture.

Kubova, Alena. 1992. *L'avant-garde architecturale en Tchécoslovaquie, 1918–1939*. Liège: Mardaga.

———. 2004. "Partizánske: Réinventer la ville fonctionnelle." *Biennale internationale du design 2004 Saint-Etienne*. Exhibition catalogue. Azimuts, n.s.

———. 2005a. *Partizánske: Réinventer la ville fonctionnelle, Znovuobjavenie funkcneho mesta*. Exhibition catalogue. Bratislava/Paris.

———. 2005b. "Partizánske à Saint Etienne." *L'Architecture d'aujourd'hui* 357: 14–15.

———. 2005c. "Une ville nouvelle comme une 'Usine dans la verdure.'" *Les Annales de la Recherche Urbaine* 98, special issue, "Les visages de la ville." http://www.annalesdelarechercheurbaine.fr/IMG/pdf/18kubova98.pdf.

———. 2009. "Modernity of the 'Functional City', the Beliefs and Doubts of Architects at the Turn of the 1950 in Czechoslovakia." In *The Values and Perspectives of the Preservation of 1950s and 1960s Architecture and Urbanism*, 52–58. Conference proceedings. Bratislava: Monumentorum Tutela, the Monuments Board of the Slovak Republic. (Includes English-language abstracts.)

———. 2016. *Ville industrielle vs paysage habitable, Tchécoslovaquie 1918-1956*. Paris: Éditions de la Villette.

Moravčíková, Henrieta. 2004. "Social and Architectural Phenomenon of Baťaism in Slovakia." *Slovak Sociological Review* 36:519–43. http://www.sav.sk/journals/uploads/02061144Moravcikova.pdf.

Pokluda, Z. 2004. *Ze Zlina do sveta, Pribeh Tomáše Bati*. Zlín: Tomáš Baťa Foundation CR-\ MZA Brno, Statni okresni archiv Zlín (Departmental archives, Zlín).

Šlachta, Š. 2006. "Baťa and Karfik-Zlin and Batovany (Partizanske)." *Future of Towns with Monofunctional Industry Examples of Baťa Towns.* Conference abstract.

Šlapeta, V. 1992. *Baťa: Architecture and Urbanism 1910–1950.* Zlín: PETIT.

Svoboda, Jiří. 2010. "Jiří Voženílek in Zlin." Doctoral diss., Brno University of Technology.

Topolcčanská, Mária. 2005. "Consistency of Serial City: Baťovany (Slovakia) Designed by Architects of Baťa Co." *Revista de crítica arquitectònica.* upcommons.upc.edu/revistes/.../1/182 _191_maria_topolcanska.pdf.

Vago, Joseph. 1935. "Zlin, phénomène social." *L'Architecture d'aujourd'hui* 11: 48–49.

Voženílek, Jiří. 1947. "Prispevek k vývoji pásového mesta" [Contribution to the development of the Linear City]. *Architektura ČSR* 6: 229–41.

———. 1948. "Le nouveau bâtiment standard industriel à Zlin." *Techniques et architecture* 3–4: 64–66.

Voženílek, Jiří. 1957. "Zásady socialistické výstavby sidlišt." *Stavba mest a vesnic, urbanisticka príručka.* Výskumný ustav výstavby a architektury, skupina územního planovani, s.23, Brno.

CHAPTER 18

TAPIOLA

From Garden City to National Landscape Icon

in Finland

Arnold R. Alanen

In 1957, a brief article, "Tapiola Garden City, Finland," appeared in the British journal *Town and Country Planning*. Written by Heikki von Hertzen, the director of a Finnish nonprofit organization known as Asuntosäätiö, or the Housing Foundation, the article reflected the social concerns and garden city ideas that the lawyer-turned–housing and community activist had been voicing for more than a decade. When von Hertzen became director of the Housing Foundation in 1953, he began overseeing the new garden city suburb of Tapiola, located ten kilometers (six miles) west of Helsinki. Also spelled out in the article was von Hertzen's overarching and ambitious goal for Tapiola: "to establish a small town in unspoiled country, pointing a new way to plan and build modern communities" (von Hertzen 1957, 108). Deployed throughout the publication was the colorful and hyperbolic language that von Hertzen often used when depicting postwar urban conditions in Finland and elsewhere: Tapiola, he claimed, would serve as an antidote to everything that made cities "unfit for human life"—namely, "terrorizing traffic, persistent nervous tension, exhaust gases, soot and dust" (1957, 108–9). Von Hertzen did not shy away from even more provocative language; several years later he asserted that poor planning, throughout the world, was leading to "the rape of our cities" (1976, 98).

Tapiola's reputation grew quickly over subsequent years, often more so outside of Finland than within the country. Visiting planners recognized elements of both the English garden city and American neighborhood concept in the layout and organization of the town; architects were impressed by Tapiola's buildings, several of which exemplified the finest features of Finnish modernism; landscape architects and environmental planners marveled at the attention given to nature and natural features in the town's development (Plate 21); and journalists searched for superlatives when describing the community—including a writer for Philadelphia's *Evening Bulletin*, who called Tapiola "the beautiful sister" in the New Town family, "the Vanessa Redgrave, the Jane Fonda of the lot" (Toland 1967).[1]

Also of note were the impressions of numerous American New Town developers, several of whom undoubtedly saw something of themselves in von Hertzen—brashness, tenaciousness, strongly held opinions, and a forceful personality. They also expressed their appreciation for the Housing Foundation's market-driven orientation, especially its reliance on private rather than public (i.e., socialistic) funding sources. "Von Hertzen's free market concepts and design individuality particularly impressed us," wrote a planner involved with the New Town of Irvine, California, who visited Tapiola in 1965.[2]

Tapiola continued to garner favorable international attention for several years thereafter, even as several Finnish architects, planners, and social scientists launched a vigorous critique of the community during the late 1960s. These naysayers, who identified themselves as Finland's "angry young men" (this was the 1960s after all), claimed that the planning of Tapiola was based on "feeling, not reason," and that its socioeconomic characteristics—"a village for better people"—were out of step with the Finns' egalitarian concepts of social democracy (Hiisiö 1970; Nyman 1968, 52–53).

Passions cooled by the 1980s as Tapiola became a commercial and cultural center for Espoo (the larger municipality to which it belonged) and was integrated into the Helsinki metropolitan region (Lapintie 2005). Likewise, as interest in New Towns subsided throughout much of the western world, the pilgrimages of visiting planners and architects to Tapiola declined. Tapiola became passé. But then, when Tapiola's historic planning, design, and environmental features were threatened by neglect and development pressures during the early 1990s, a wave of appreciation for the community, some of it undoubtedly fueled by nostalgia, emerged within Finland. In 1993 Tapiola was designated as one of Finland's twenty-seven "National Landscapes"—places that have "great symbolic value and widely recognized significance in cultural and historical terms" (Finnish Ministry of the Environment 2015). The only "modern" landscape in the group, Tapiola was defined as the most representative example of "Finland's high quality community planning, which, even in its early stages, received extensive international acclaim" (Future of Tapiola Workgroup 2003, 18). Tapiola had indeed come full circle: from an internationally renowned garden city during the 1950s to an often-criticized community one decade later, it then emerged, after a quarter century, as a major symbol of Finnish identity.

The ensuing discussion provides an overview of a garden city—often called a "forest town" (*metsäkaupunki*) in Finland—that is now more than six decades old (Pakkala 1994, 223). It begins with a brief summary of Finland's postwar economic and housing situation and von Hertzen's garden city visions for Finland. An overview of Tapiola's initial twenty-five years of history follows, including highlights of the striking dichotomy between the plaudits of international observers and the criticisms of several Finnish intellectuals. The conclusion features the period since 1993, the year Tapiola was designated a National Landscape. It is apparent that Tapiola faces a conundrum that many iconic communities encounter today: how to accommodate significant change and development while simultaneously conserving historic planning, architectural, and landscape attributes.

The Family Federation of Finland, Heikki von Hertzen, and the Emergence of Tapiola

Finland was immersed in two wars with the Soviet Union from 1939 to 1944. Although the Finns emerged from these conflicts with their independence preserved, the country had to deal with extensive war-related devastation and the deaths of more than seventy-five thousand soldiers. The Finns were also forced to cede 10 percent of their land area and make huge monetary reparations to the Soviet Union; furthermore, more than four hundred thousand Finns who fled the ceded area required housing and employment.

In 1941, while Finland engaged in war, twenty social interest groups and organizations came together to form Väestöliitto (the Finnish Population and Family Welfare League; renamed the Family Federation of Finland in 1993). During the 1940s and 1950s most social policy legislation in Finland was written by Väestöliitto, which forwarded its proposals to Parliament for consideration. In 1951 Väestöliitto came together with six other public service groups to form the Housing Foundation (Asuntosäätiö), the organization that sponsored and financed Tapiola's development (Väestöliitto 1960, 4, 11).

Tapiola, however, would never have emerged as a world-renowned garden city without the vision, energy, and political astuteness of Heikki von Hertzen. Von Hertzen received his law degree in 1940 and soon started working as a banker in Helsinki and the industrial city of Tampere. As a loan officer, von Hertzen quickly gained firsthand knowledge of the housing problems encountered by Finnish working-class families, and he also wrote articles for journals and newspapers that included commentary about population policy and civic responsibility; these journalistic endeavors were noted by Väestöliitto officials, who hired him as the organization's executive director in 1943. This position gave von Hertzen opportunities to travel and observe housing issues throughout Finland and the other Nordic nations, and he familiarized himself with well-known British and American achievements in community planning and landscape architecture (Ruokonen 2003, 90; Tuomi 2003a, 43–44, 47; von Hertzen and Spreiregen 1971, 73). Furthermore, a

1945 exhibition, *Amerikka rakentaa* (America builds), which appeared in Helsinki, was widely applauded by Alvar Aalto and other Finnish architects: "American living culture," Aalto wrote, "made up of small, elegant, lightly built wooden buildings, [is] blended with a plan that recalls a free-form country environment" (Aalto, cited in Nikula 1994, 219).

In 1946, von Hertzen summarized his observations and proposals in *Koti vaikko kasarmi lapsillemme* (A home or barracks for our children?), a brief polemic that was somewhat similar to Ebenezer Howard's *Garden Cities of To-morrow*. Von Hertzen, however, quite naturally focused on Finland and its urban housing problems, all of which, he later wrote, led to "social pathology with such symptoms as malaise, indifference, crime, and vandalism." These problems, von Hertzen argued, could be resolved only by adopting "a real community building effort" that would result in "an environment conducive to healthful social interchange and personal enrichment for persons of all ages and all interests" (von Hertzen and Spreiregen 1971, 73).

Since von Hertzen had little, if any, familiarity with architectural and planning theory, he sought advice from a friend and mentor, Otto Meurman, a well-known architect, professor, and "Finland's grand old man of town planning" (Pantzer 2011). Just as Meurman had done when preparing his own 1947 Finnish-language town planning textbook, *Asemakaavaoppi* (Theory of town planning), von Hertzen featured several examples of Swedish housing and suburban development, including Friluftstaden in Malmö and Guldheden in Gothenburg (Meurman 1947; von Hertzen 1946). Von Hertzen was also inspired by Meurman's portrayal of the planning and landscape architecture displayed at two well-known planned communities of the 1920s and 1930s: Radburn, New Jersey, and Greenbelt, Maryland (von Hertzen and Spreiregen 1971). He later remarked that *The Culture of Cities*, by Lewis Mumford (1938), had provided a framework for his ideas. However, the most influential source was the documentary film *The City* (1939), with a script adapted by Mumford and produced for the 1939 New York World's Fair. In 1982 von Hertzen recalled how *The City* influenced his thinking: "I have used the film's theme quite often, underlining the fact that we are biological beings and that the most important environment for the majority of us in our lives is the town or city.... At the moment it is not the right environment. With pollution it is not biologically correct, it is not a sociologically pleasing place either, and we can be quite certain from a mental or spiritual point of view that this environment doesn't give the right impulses for a happy kind of life" (von Hertzen, cited in Alanen 1983, 43–44).

Mumford's pronouncements about the "mythic admiration of nature and . . . criticism of technology" found a receptive audience in Finland and all the Nordic countries (Nikula 1994, 220). Indeed, Mika Pantzer's review of the Housing Foundation's archives reveals that Tapiola's planners and builders drew substantially from American "reformist thinking," primarily as voiced by Mumford (Pantzer 2011). Although Mumford himself made few comments about Tapiola, he did, in a 1984 interview, compare the community favorably to the postwar New Towns of England. Tapiola displayed a "town of architectural variety, liveliness, and human warmth," Mumford stated, and he demonstrated that "living in a new town did not have to be like living in a grimly gray housing estate; Heikki von Hertzen, Tapiola's creator, had made that stunningly clear" (Mumford, cited in Miller 1989, 471).

Tapiola: Buildings and Landscapes

In 1950–51, when von Hertzen located an undeveloped 267-hectare (660-acre) estate of fields and forests just west of Helsinki, he "prevailed" on Väestöliitto's board of directors to purchase the land. The board agreed and also supported von Hertzen's proposal for a new garden city that would become Tapiola; this decision, wrote a board member decades later, represented a "courageous example" of a "calculated risk" (Hulkko 2006, 10).

Von Hertzen and the Housing Foundation, from the very outset, sought to create "a microcosm of Finnish society" at Tapiola. This would be accomplished by providing a range of housing sizes and types—detached residences, row houses, and multistory apartment blocks—and assisting lower-income applicants in securing low-interest government loans (Tuomi 2003a, 10–11). As a nonprofit entity, the Housing Foundation built Tapiola by following a "simple strategy": constructing new residences whenever funds were available, and then generating more income through the sale of houses (Lahti 2008, 154). The foundation's publicity department also prepared numerous brochures and publications that described Tapiola's house types and floor plans; these items not only assisted prospective home buyers in making choices, but also provided the general public with new information about contemporary design and housing standards in Finland (Tuomi 2003a, 18, 20). The Housing Foundation's ambitious publicity campaign, however, was not only self-serving. In fact, the organization had reason to tout its early efforts, something that has been acknowledged by both admirers and critics. One commentator noted, in 1980, that Tapiola's buildings were "truly new," especially the "technical innovations" that pointed "to a brilliant future for housing production." Furthermore, the Finnish architects who designed the buildings "were free to experiment with arrangements and materials that had never been used elsewhere" (Suhonen 1980, 76). Tapiola succeeded because "different architects worked consciously to achieve a common good" (Nikula 1994, 222).

Figure 18.1. The initial 1950s plan for Tapiola included three neighborhoods (east, west, and north), grouped around a town center; a small neighborhood to the south was added later. (Collection Arnold R. Alanen)

In 1954 the architect Aarne Ervi won the design competition for Tapiola's town center, the signature district that would serve the community's residential neighborhoods. Ervi's proposal was unusual for the time because it anticipated the growth of automobile ownership in Finland: roads encircled Tapiola's center, which made it a pedestrian-friendly zone; and accommodations were provided for the opening of Finland's first American-style shopping mall in 1968. A thirteen-story office building that exemplified Ervi's ability to express modernist design features in a "delicate" manner soon became the key landmark of Tapiola's suburban landscape. Adjacent to the office tower was a large orthogonal pool, formed out of an abandoned gravel pit, which provided the setting for three other major structures: a hotel, church, and swimming hall (Lahti 2008, 154–56).

The former owner of the landholding had, already in 1945, commissioned Otto Meurman to prepare a master plan for the entire area—"a large-scale application of the Anglo-Saxon garden city ideal set in a Finnish forest and field landscape" with small buildings, "all located within low and spacious residential areas fitted into nature" (Tuomi 2003a, 10, 14). This plan served as a guide for the four architects who started designing Tapiola's first neighborhood unit in 1953. While each architect developed site plans and housing proposals for different sections of the neighborhood, all were "designed to the smallest detail to fit into the landscape." Unlike the 1945 plan, however, these architects included several modernist tower blocks, thereby increasing the overall population density (Tuomi 2003a, 12, 14). Nevertheless, when build-out was reached during the late 1960s, Tapiola's density averaged a relatively low twenty-three people per acre, or fifty-seven per hectare. At that time the community included 4,600 dwelling units: 130 single-family homes, 500 in terrace or row houses, and 3,970 in blocks of flats (Hiisiö 1970, 39; Nikula 2003, 123) (Figure 18.1).

The second neighborhood, dating to the mid- to late 1950s, followed the pattern of its earlier counterpart; it was a free-form plan displaying buildings that coexisted with the terrain in an "animated way." The winning entry in the 1958 design competition for the third neighbor-

Figure 18.2. Tapionraitti (Tapio's Road) seen here in 1969, a distinctive avenue used by pedestrians and bicyclists, extends through the heart of Tapiola over a distance of 1.5 kilometers. It links the eastern and western neighborhoods to the town center. (Photo by Arnold R. Alanen)

hood, however, offered a quite different solution: an orthogonal grid plan that rejected the organic outline of previous efforts. This proposal was one of the first indications of the general philosophical change that would become more widespread when suburban communities were planned in Finland during the 1960s. The dense orthogonal grid of the northern neighborhood, at least to some planners and proponents, represented a Finnish manifestation of democratic egalitarianism (Desjardins 2003, 118; Tuomi 2003b, 24) (Figure 18.2).

Parks and forested areas separated the neighborhoods, and both local and through traffic were segregated within each unit. In von Hertzen's view, Tapiola's innovative architectural and physical planning features, characterized by "the mixed placement of high-rise and low-rise housing in both a methodical fashion and following the topography," were responsible for making the community an international sensation (von Hertzen and Itkonen 1981, 62). Tapiola also "opened the doors to landscape architecture in Finland," inspired, at least in part, by von Hertzen's earlier interest in the garden cities of Sweden, Britain, and the United States. (Prior to this time, Finnish landscape architects primarily focused on small parks and gardens.) Two of Tapiola's early landscape architects—Nils Orénto and Jussi Jännes—gave form to von Hertzen's recommendations, notably an uninterrupted system of greenways between the buildings, utilizing the agricultural and forest land that had characterized the former estate. The distinctive angular form of one major park, Silkkiniitty ("silk meadow"), for example, followed the outline of a former farm field, but the "open park-like areas around which the buildings were gathered" also paid homage to Radburn and Greenbelt (Ruokonen 2003, 90, 98). The park continues to accommodate residents who engage in numerous pursuits, ranging from walking and cross-country skiing to active games of soccer and *pesäpallo* (a Finnish version of American baseball); the design of Silkkiniitty also provides walkers with a variety of visual experiences as they perambulate through the twelve-hectare (thirty-acre) site (Figure 18.3).

Tapiola Through Visitors' Eyes

By the early 1960s, as Tapiola approached its targeted population of sixteen thousand residents, untold numbers of visitors and onlookers arrived from throughout the world. As the British economist-planner D. E. C. Eversley wrote in 1961, all planners should see Tapiola—"probably one of the most advanced town-building projects in Europe today" (Eversley 1961, 164). Because his article was simply titled "Tapiola," Eversley apparently believed the community needed no further explanation or description, at least within the ranks of British planners. Two years earlier,

the Yugoslavian writer Ivanka Beševi, after viewing a
museum exhibition of Finnish architecture in Belgrade,
termed Tapiola "a genuine fairy-tale idyll" that reflected
the Finns' alleged affinity for nature. Noting that Ervi and
other architects had sensitively incorporated Tapiola's
streets and houses into a forest, she continued: "Squirrels
jump from branch to branch, foxes hide in the courtyards
and it may well be that from time to time even goblins
find their way there. This settlement, naturally acquired
the name of the Sibelius symphony and the name of the
Finnish god of the forest, Tapiola" (Beševi, cited in Čeferin 2003, 134) (Figure 18.4).

Figure 18.3. Aerial view of Tapiola in
the early 1960s, looking west toward
the town center. Many residences
were located within existing
woodlands, whereas former farm fields
provided space for parks, gardens, and
recreational activities. Overlooking the
water-filled basin is a thirteen-story
office building, still the tallest structure
in Tapiola. (Collection Arnold R. Alanen)

Americans, however, were most captivated by Tapiola. Von Hertzen recognized
this phenomenon and expressed deep gratitude to the "man who 'invented' Tapiola . . . [and] put Tapiola on the world map": Frederick Gutheim, an urban planner,
historian, and writer who served as president of the Washington Center for Metropolitan Studies from 1960 to 1965 (von Hertzen, cited in Alanen 1983, 47). Gutheim

Tapiolan puutarhakaupunki
Tapiola Garden City

Figure 18.4. The "good life" promoted in Tapiola during the 1950s included allotment gardens for residents. In the background are several row houses, designed by the architect Aulis Blomsted and completed in 1955. (Courtesy Postcard Collection, Espoo City Museum)

became familiar with Tapiola while compiling information for a biography of Aalto during the 1950s, and Gutheim met von Hertzen in 1960, the year the book was published (Gutheim 1960). Later, in 1963, Gutheim would identify Tapiola as "one of the most important of the world's New Towns" when writing to Robert Simon, who began developing Reston, Virginia, during the early 1960s.[3]

In October 1963 Gutheim organized an exhibition at the Architectural League of New York that displayed models, photographs, and plans of Tapiola. Soon thereafter, Ada Louise Huxtable, America's best-known architectural critic, identified Tapiola as "probably the finest of the New Towns that have been a postwar phenomenon abroad, most notably in England and Scandinavia." Despite Tapiola's relatively small size, the *New York Times* reviewer contended that "its housing and planning principles are expandable. And Tapiola proved that it could be done with success and sensitivity. To American viewers of the exhibition, it is an example and a rebuke" (Huxtable 1963). When the exhibit moved to the National Housing Center, Wolf von Eckardt of the *Washington Post* termed Tapiola "an example of how sound planning and good architecture can provide a beautiful setting wherein an eventual 15,000 people can not only live and play but also work, and stay put" (von Eckardt 1963).

Similar comments were made four years later when Tapiola received the first R. S. Reynolds Memorial Award for Community Architecture (shared with Stockholm and the Scottish New Town Cumbernauld) from the American Institute of Architects. "Tapiola without a doubt is one of the most pleasant living environments ever built with private funds," stated the jurors, but noted that "its greatest success" might very well be "the quality and strength of its social and economic plan and program" (Ketchum et al. 1967, 36–58).

The positive evaluations made by Gutheim and others led more observers to Tapiola during the mid-1960s and thereafter. Two "European New Towns Traveling Seminars"—both organized in 1965 for American planners, academics, and community developers, as well as "brisk and hard-nosed" New Town promoters, building supply contractors, and journalists—subsequently influenced the design of several planned communities in the United States (Gutheim 1966, 100). Ann Louise Strong of the University of Pennsylvania, who headed one group, later summarized her sentiments (and undoubtedly those of her colleagues) in a 1971 book that reviewed New Town planning in five countries: "Of all new towns and new communities," she wrote, "Tapiola is thought by many to be the most beautiful and humane [and] may be the most successful new community yet built" (Strong 1971, 98). Among the participants were representatives of such American New Towns as Valencia, Mission Viejo, and Irvine, California; Columbia, Maryland; and Reston. Raymond Watson, Irvine's chief planner, still had vivid impressions of Tapiola more than thirty years after going on the tour: "Tapiola was one of the most architecturally impressive towns we visited. Its mix of densities and housing types and integration with the natural landscape was extremely attractive and mitigated against any feeling of being a project similar to the Soviet new towns and housing projects" (see Plate 21). The Finnish garden city's design features also captivated Robert Simon of Reston. When viewing Tapiola's thirteen-story office tower in 1965, Simon decided "we need one of those for Reston." Soon, a sixteen-story building arose in Lake Anne Village, Reston's first neighborhood. According to Simon, Lake Anne's Heron Tower House (designed for condominiums, not offices) "was a way to tell the world that Reston would be something more than just an ordinary subdivision."[4]

From the mid-1960s and into the early 1970s the tireless von Hertzen preached the gospel of Tapiola whenever he spoke at American housing conferences and universities. He also visited other New Towns. In September 1966, Simon informed an American colleague about the Finn's forthcoming visit: "The Eastern Seaboard of the United States is certainly getting excited over the arrival of Heikki von Hertzen." The Finnish visitor then toured Reston and several other recent New Towns during a seven-week-long journey. After viewing Reston's Lake Anne Village in 1966, von Hertzen termed the development a "success" and informed Simon that it was the "best" New Town he had seen in the United States. The Finnish garden city advocate described several parallels between Tapiola and Reston, including the intermixing of low- and high-rise housing, and the combination of commercial and community facilities in each town center. "But most important" in both communities, wrote von Hertzen, were resident "opportunities for the fruitful use of leisure time and cultural needs."[5] In 1969 von Hertzen briefly served as a consultant to two Minnesota planned communities: the "new town in-town" of Cedar-Riverside in Minneapolis, and suburban Jonathan (Alanen 1983, 48).

Critics and Defenders

While some Finnish architects and planners questioned the garden city character of Tapiola as early as the 1950s, the critique reached a crescendo during the latter years of the subsequent decade. The criticisms, some substantive, others trivial, were expressed in conferences, newspapers, journals, and books, although a 1967 seminar, "Mitä opimme Tapiolasta?" (What can we learn from Tapiola?), organized by the Finnish Association of Architects, drew considerable attention. Typically, the architects claimed that Tapiola revealed "nothing of what traditionally is regarded as townscape"; lacked "architectural order"; and was not a "rational" solution for an "urbanized culture" (Nyman 1968, 52–53). Social scientists and journalists often viewed Tapiola as being "too natural, quiet, clean, and uncluttered to be urban or a real town instead of a 'make-believe' community"; to them it was an "upper-class . . . or 'one-class community'" for "better people" that might be appreciated by a unique population—those who were "dynamic, extroverted, educated upper-class people"—but could be highly unsatisfactory "for real workers," that is, the majority of citizens "who are not that rough and tough or sophisticated" (Hiisiö 1970; Heideman 1975, 28–29). Even the landscape design of Tapiola's parks received criticism for the visual "disharmony" caused by a "heretical" use of foreign plants; much more preferable, these critics inferred, was the "restful overall picture" offered by native forest landscapes of spruce, pine, and birch (Ruokonen 1994, 232). Because of the community's position "as a kind of ideal," wrote one commentator, Tapiola continued "to haunt Finnish planning" (Suhonen 1980, 76).

Von Hertzen obviously took offense at the assault, arguing that Tapiola's opponents used "the means that any Mafia has ever employed" to discredit both him and the community (von Hertzen, cited in Alanen 1983, 47). While von Hertzen and the Housing Foundation certainly had many advocates in Finland, one of the strongest supporters was an American community health planner, M. Lawrence Heideman. In a lengthy 1975 article that appeared in *Urban Ecology*, Heideman set out to dispel the "unrealistic criticisms" leveled against Tapiola, most of which he believed had been promoted by "personal and official opponents [who] . . . have systematically spread falsehoods about it, and uninformed, defensively oriented people have believed and spread them." After Heideman listed numerous arguments that, at least to him, successfully refuted each criticism, he summarized the community's "unique success story": Tapiola's natural features, he wrote, were "spellbinding," and it "truly" served as "a town of and for all classes of people" (Heideman 1975, 27).

Tapiola as a District Center

Much of the passion cooled by the late 1970s and early 1980s, which also coincided with the time that the municipality of Espoo assumed many of the Housing Foundation's public service functions. A sleepy, rural commune of some 15,000 inhabitants that exerted little control over Tapiola when the garden city was spawned during the early 1950s, Espoo's population reached 137,400 by 1980, grew to 213,300 in 2000, and then to 279,000 in 2017. Today Espoo is Finland's second largest city, although in reality it is "a composition of suburbs scattered around a seashore, and which, despite continuous planning, never seems to settle into a unity" (Nikula 2003, 119). Logically, Tapiola might have been designated as Espoo's major center during the 1970s, but government officials chose to concentrate most municipal functions in the original village. The greater Tapiola area, nonetheless, became larger and more visible than the governmental center once the nearby campus of Helsinki's University of Technology (Aalto University since 2010) grew into a major technological and educational center. As Espoo expanded during the 1970s and 1980s its growth was directed toward five district centers, including Tapiola. While the community's business center continued to serve local residents and people living throughout southeastern Espoo, district designation resulted in the emergence of Tapiola as a center for cultural and specialized retail activities that served the entire municipality (Future of Tapiola Workgroup 2003, 9) (Figure 18.5).

When Tapiola's residential development was completed during the 1970s, the population peaked at about sixteen thousand. The town center footprint, however, expanded considerably. The planning directive that was adopted to guide this effort—"a compact city is a contact city"—resulted in a center that had higher building densities than in the past. When the project was completed in 1987, Tapiola's center offered 54,000 square meters (581,250 square feet) of retail and office space—an increase of 19,500 square meters (248,650 square feet) in eight years. This expansion,

Figure 18.5. The 1954 plan for Tapiola's town center, prepared by Aarne Ervi, called for the transformation of an abandoned gravel pit into a water-filled basin. At the northeastern end of the basin is a swimming hall; also bordering the basin to the south (right), but outside the image, are a church and hotel. In 1989, a cultural center was built proximate to the northwestern (lower left) corner of the basin. (Photo by Arnold R. Alanen)

however, had a negative impact on many of Tapiola's neighborhood-level services. At least ten small grocery stores had closed by 2003, and almost all other commercial properties that formerly housed services were converted into office space (Future of Tapiola Workgroup 2003, 9, 16; Niemi 2003; Nikula 2003, 135–38).

When writing in 2003, Ritva Nikula, one of Finland's leading architectural historians, and herself a resident of Tapiola from 1972 to 1998, decried "the pretensions of the expanding shopping mall." While Tapiola's residents were formerly able to purchase "everything they needed from the now-dead shops" and specialized outlets in the original center (Tapiontori Square), "the disappearance of local services . . . meant that convenience and common responsibility . . . disappeared from the everyday lives of families with children" (Nikula 2003, 135). Other changes, as noted by Mika Pantzer in 2011, have occurred more recently: "rain shelters and benches in front of shops that were meant to act as meeting places . . . are turning into empty stage sets, whose original function will soon be recalled by no one"; the information center that served as the nerve center for international visitors who descended upon Tapiola during its period of "grandeur" has been replaced by a pizza emporium; and the panoramic view once provided from the restaurant located atop the original tower block, a place that "the fathers of Tapiola envisioned as the hub of the area's civic activity, has moved out of the building and now serves as office space." Much of what remains of Tapiola's "bygone life" is only a collection of "mere facades," including "public clocks that have stopped working, waterfalls without water, [and] vacant shelters where the young used to (and were planned to) gather" (Pantzer 2011). Furthermore, the decline in household size between 1965 and 2013 (3.2 to 2.2 persons) and an increase in the square meters of dwelling space per inhabitant (17.6 to 36.0) have resulted in a total population decrease: Tapiola's population as of 2016 stands at ten thousand.

Protecting a National Landscape

As mentioned earlier, Tapiola was named one of Finland's twenty-seven National Landscapes in 1993. Specifically mentioned in Tapiola's designation were its excellent architectural and landscape design features, the sensitive relationship between buildings and landscape, and the positive influence of the community in shaping subsequent suburban development throughout Finland (Finnish Ministry of the Environment 2015). While National Landscape status was not accompanied by any new preservation regulations, Espoo's city planning office recognized the town's importance during the early 2000s when it organized a workgroup to consider "the values that have made and still make Tapiola a model of community planning"; the group also developed guidelines that would simultaneously lead to sensitive "preservation and further development" (Future of Tapiola Workgroup 2003, 10, 15).

The workgroup described three factors that distinguished Tapiola: the high standard of its physical surroundings, which also enhanced the quality of the social environment; the community's value "as a source of inspiration and example"; and its status as "an important historical document and a symbol of post-war optimism" (Figure 18.6). Also noted were five major threats faced by Tapiola: a decline in population numbers and services; the competition posed by nearby commercial centers; an increase in traffic volumes; a deteriorating environment; and plans to expand the historic commercial center (Future of Tapiola Workgroup 2003, 10).

Figure 18.6. The center of Tapiola, looking west. Just behind the trees is the basin; to the left is the Tapiola Office Building (Aarne Ervi, 1961); and to the right is the Espoo Cultural Center (Arto Sipinen, 1989). Immediately behind the two buildings is a section of Tapiola's shopping center (late 1960s) and at the rear are four "Hip Flask" (*Taskumatti*) apartments, named for the shape of the buildings (Viljo Revell, 1960). (Courtesy Tapio Heikkilä)

Overriding all preservation and development issues was a concern about the potential erosion of Tapiola's "structural" identity as a garden city. Specifically, the recommendations called for the protection of Tapiola's "well-planned residential living [spaces], enjoyable green areas and exercise venues, [and] . . . diverse commercial services, jobs, and high-level culture." Restoration of the "garden city image," it was argued, could be accomplished through "the unity of buildings and outdoor areas" whereas future development activities would require even greater awareness of Tapiola's already-established role as the district center for Espoo's cultural services and specialized retail activities (Future of Tapiola Workgroup 2003, 17, 34) (Figure 18.6).

Official action on some proposals was evident by 2006 when Espoo's planning department produced a document, *Recommendations and Guidelines for Repair and Maintenance of Tapiola's Older Areas*; shortly thereafter, landscape maintenance proposals for public spaces were developed after residents and media outlets severely criticized existing inadequacies (City of Espoo 2006, 2007). These activities, however, were dwarfed when, in 2006, plans were announced to extend a metro line from Helsinki to the center of Tapiola and other nearby communities; the line, which opened in 2017, includes a stunning metro station in Tapiola. The decision spawned a host of proposals that almost immediately demanded simultaneous consideration by both preservation and development agencies. Public involvement has been facilitated throughout Tapiola and Espoo by a planning process that begins with a "participation and assessment plan," which spells out goals and targets for the ensuing year (City of Espoo 2018). Numerous meetings were organized for residents of Tapiola and Espoo, as well as various groups and associations; some gatherings that drew overflow audiences reportedly occurred in a "good atmosphere" and generated "lively dialogue" (*Espoo Magazine* 2012, 8–9). Residents were also encouraged to post their comments and concerns on the internet—a logical and common practice for Finns, whose propensity is to utilize electronic media in all facets of their lives.

Most of the discussions concerning the management and protection of Tapiola's cultural resources and built environment are conducted and overseen by the Espoo City Museum, a research institution that includes staff members who prepare inventories and local databases and who participate in the municipal planning and building permitting process. However, because of Tapiola's national significance and importance, these plans and projects often require further review by other agencies. Representatives from the Finnish National Board of Antiquities, for example, participate in meetings concerning proposals and actions that might affect Tapiola's heritage resources, and they negotiate the division of related tasks and responsibilities on a case-by-case basis with the Espoo City Museum.[6]

Much attention has been given to recent plans that call for the addition of at least one million square meters of building space to the three million square meters now found in Greater Tapiola—an area with 46,000 people that, besides the historic garden city, includes several communities with numerous facilities for science, technology, art, and business. Only a very small amount of new construction will

Figure 18.7. A computer-generated perspective of Tapiola as envisioned when restoration and new development projects are completed during the 2020s; the view is from the northeast and looking west and southwest. The historic town center (right) essentially remains intact, whereas the new commercial center (left) replaces most of the former buildings that date to the 1970s and 1980s. The angular planting beds in the forefront, part of Leimuniitty (Flame Meadow Park, 1959), are being restored, as is the roundabout that was removed during the 1970s. (Courtesy Arkkitehtitoimisto SARC, OY, Helsinki)

occur above ground in the historic center; much more development will take place underground, where space has been created for the metro station, a bus terminal, and a parking garage. Almost all new retail and office space, however, will occur on the footprint of those buildings that emerged just south of the historic center during the 1970s and 1980s. The architectural and structural qualities of these buildings, considered inferior to those in the original commercial district, will be converted into "a lively and comfortable city centre in the midst of greenness" that includes "a high-quality transportation terminal, efficient parking and maintenance services, and cozy pedestrian areas and meeting places" (Mäkinen 2017). The new buildings will be responsive to the architectural character of the historic environment, and in a concession to local and national preservation concerns, none will exceed the height of the original tower, designed by Ervi in 1953[7] (Figure 18.7).

Once all development is completed by the early 2020s, the population of the historic center, which now accommodates several hundred people, is expected to have two thousand. (Tapiola's overall population is expected to reach fifteen thousand residents by 2050.) The expanded center will include a covered "gallery"—a shopping boulevard that links all Tapiola's major retail outlets. When opened, also in the 2020s, it will be the largest pedestrian-oriented urban center in Finland. Because the plan calls for the elimination of most motorized traffic from the center, energy use and ecological conditions will return to their 1950s levels (Mäkinen 2017).

Conclusion

Countless words have been written about Tapiola since it began emerging west of Helsinki during the early 1950s. Certainly no other postwar community in Finland has received more attention from scholars and writers. Most of these publications have focused on the community's garden city features, its architectural accomplishments, its social and economic characteristics, and its founder, Heikki von Hertzen. Recently, however, Tapiola has also become part of the discourse that considers the origins of the "good life" in postwar Finland. Among the most meaningful aspects of this assessment are those that question the "paradox" of Tapiola: how could the "anti-urbanism and anti-consumerism" represented in its early planning philosophy eventually evolve into a community that serves as the definitive example of Finland's "modern, urbanized consumer society"? There is a particular irony in this observation, given that Tapiola "is now recognized as a model for a consumption and work-centered community" in Finland (Pantzer 2010, 122; 2011).

Much of the "good life" discussion looks back to the 1950s and 1960s, a time when Tapiola's planners, particularly von Hertzen, sought to define "the boundaries of good and bad, necessary and unnecessary consumption." Indeed, von Eckardt, who devoted most of a chapter to Tapiola in his 1967 book *A Place to Live*, wrote that "Tapiola in Finland is the happiest place to live I have seen built in recent years" (1967, 347). Tapiola's critics, on the other hand, claimed that its residents "lived in an illusionary awareness of happiness" that reflected a "rather paternalistic garden-city system" (Pantzer 2010, 122). While explanations for the paradox are still being formulated, it is clear that Tapiola, like many other iconic planned communities throughout the world, is a complex, multilayered place that often reveals contradictory themes and messages.

Table 18.1
Summary of Historical Events and Heritage Benchmarks for Tapiola

Year	Event
1943	Heikki von Hertzen is appointed as executive director of Väestöliitto (Finnish Population and Family Welfare League); he observes housing in Nordic countries and familiarizes himself with British and American achievements in community planning and landscape architecture.
1945	The owner of the future Tapiola landholding commissions Otto Meurman to prepare a master plan for the entire area.
1946	Von Hertzen's polemic, *Koti vaikko kasarmi lapsillemme* (A home or barracks for our children), focuses on Finland's urban problems, and offers solutions that guide the development of Tapiola.
1950–51	Von Hertzen locates an undeveloped 660-acre (267-hectare) estate of fields and forests just west of Helsinki, prevailing on Väestöliitto's board of directors to purchase the land.
1951	Väestöliitto comes together with six other public service groups to form the nonprofit Asuntosäätiö, also known as the Housing Foundation, which sponsors and finances Tapiola's development.
1953	Von Hertzen becomes director of the Housing Foundation. The four architects who plan Tapiola's first neighborhood unit, "designed to the smallest detail to fit into the landscape," are inspired by Meurman's 1945 plan.
1954	The architect Aarne Ervi wins the design competition for the town center. His thirteen-story modernist office tower emerges as Tapiola's key landmark.
Mid- to late 1950s	The free-form plan for the second neighborhood follows the pattern of its earlier counterpart.
1958	The winning entry in the design competition for the third neighborhood rejects the organic outline of previous efforts, forecasting a philosophical change in Finnish suburban planning.
Early 1960s	Tapiola begins attracting visitors from all over the world, including Reston's developer, Robert Simon.
1968	Finland's first American-style shopping mall opens in Tapiola.
Late 1960s	Tapiola continues to garner favorable international attention, even as several Finnish architects, planners, and social scientists launch a vigorous critique of the community. When build-out is reached during the late 1960s, Tapiola's population approaches six thousand; its density averages twenty-three people per acre (fifty-seven per hectare), with 4,600 dwelling units (130 single-family homes, 500 in terrace or row houses, and 3,970 in apartment blocks).
1970s	Tapiola's residential development is completed, and its population peaks at twenty thousand.
1980s	As Tapiola becomes a commercial and cultural center for Espoo (the larger municipality to which it belongs), it is integrated into the Helsinki metropolitan region.
1987	Tapiola's center offers 581,250 square feet (54,000 square meters) of retail and office space—an increase of 248,650 square feet (19,500 square meters) in eight years.
1993	A wave of appreciation for the community, sometimes fueled by nostalgia, emerges in Finland when Tapiola is designated as one of the nation's twenty-seven "National Landscapes."
2003	Almost all remaining commercial properties that formerly housed services have been converted into office space. A Future of Tapiola Workgroup is formed; it develops guidelines for sensitive preservation and future development.
2006	Plans are announced to extend a metro line between Helsinki and Tapiola.
Early 2020s	The expanded historic center is expected to host two thousand residents. It will include a shopping boulevard linking all major retail outlets. As most motorized traffic will be prohibited, energy use and ecological conditions will return to their 1950s levels. The overall population will stabilize between eleven thousand and twelve thousand.
	Population (as of 2016), 10,000; 865 acres [350 ha]; 6,200 dwelling units.

NOTES

I am indebted to the following Finns, who provided information for this chapter: Tapio Heik-kilä, Antti Mäkinen, Mika Pantzer, Ria Ruokonen, Laura Tuominen, and Mari Vaattovaara. My wife, Lynn Bjorkman, also shared many useful observations during our visits to Tapiola.

1. As a young undergraduate student during the 1960s, I was also intrigued by Tapiola, so much so that I wrote a thesis (Alanen 1963) and my first published article about the community (Alanen 1967). I also met with Heikki von Hertzen in 1963 and had more substantive discussions with him in 1969 and 1982; parts of our 1982 meeting, conducted as an interview, were published one year later (Alanen 1983).

2 Letter from Raymond Watson to author, October 16, 1999.

3 Letter from Frederick Gutheim to Robert E. Simon, October 7, 1963, Frederick Gutheim Papers, George Mason University (hereinafter cited as Gutheim Papers).

4. Watson, letter to author; author's interview with Robert E. Simon, October 19, 1998.

5. Letter from Robert E. Simon to William Conklin, April 11, 1966; letters from Hubbard H. Cobb to Robert E. Simon, August 18, 1966, and October 6, 1966; and letter from Heikki von Hertzen to Robert E. Simon, October 6, 1966, all in Gutheim Papers.

6. Email message from Laura Tuominen to author, February 13, 2013.

7. Author's interview with Antti Mäkinen, October 9, 2012.

REFERENCES

Alanen, Arnold R. 1963. "Finland's Garden Cities." B.A. thesis, Student Project for Amity Among Nations Library (SPAN), University of Minnesota.

———. 1967. "Tapiola: Finland's Contribution." *Northwest Architect* 31: 30–35.

———. 1983. "An Interview with Heikki von Hertzen: The Man Behind the Garden City of Tapiola, Finland." *Landscape Journal* 2: 40–51.

Čeferin, Petra. 2003. *Constructing a Legend: The International Exhibitions of Finnish Architecture, 1957–1967.* Helsinki: Suomalaisen Kirjallisuuden Seura.

The City. 1939. Documentary film. Directed by Ralph Steiner and Willard Van Dyke, with music by Aaron Copeland; adapted by Lewis Mumford from a story by Pare Lorentz. New York: New York World's Fair.

City of Espoo. 2006. "Tapiola—Vanhojen asuntoalueiden korjauksen ja hoidon suuntaviivat." http://www.espoo.fi.

———. 2007. *Tapiola Projects Review.* https://www.scribd.com/document/253594807/Tapiola -Projects-Review-2007-ENG-Screen11.

———. 2018. "Town Planning Process." https://www.espoo.fi/en-US/Housing_and_environ ment/City_planning/Town_planning/Town_Planning_Process.

Desjardins, Susan Wiksten. 2003. "The City Centre and the Suburb: City Planning During the 1950s and 1960s in Stockholm and Helsinki." M.A. thesis, Åbo Akademi University, Turku, Finland.

Espoo Magazine. 2012. "Tapiola." https://www.yumpu.com/en/document/view/8170382/read -about-tapiola-espoon-matkailu.

Eversley, D. E. C. 1961. "Tapiola." *Town and Country Planning* 29: 161–64.

Finnish Ministry of the Environment. 2015. "Legislation on Building and Landscape Protection." http://www.ym.fi/en-US/Land_use_and_building/Legislation_and_instructions/Leg islation_on_building_and_landscape_protection.

Future of Tapiola Workgroup. 2003. *Tapiola Tomorrow: Report by the Future of Tapiola Workgroup.* Espoo, Finland: Kaupunkisuunitelukeskus.

Gutheim, Frederick. 1960. *Alvar Aalto.* New York: George Braziller.

Gutheim, Frederick. 1966. "Europe Offers New Town Builders Experience." *Public Management* 48: 99–107.

Heideman, Lawrence, Jr. 1975. "Tapiola: A Model, Myth, or Happenstance? A Personal Investigation." *Urban Ecology* 1: 5–47.

Hiisiö, Ossi. 1970. *Tapiola—parempien ihmisten kylä*. Helsinki: Tammi.

Hulkko, Jouku. 2006. "100-Year Anniversary of the Birth of J. J. Sukselainen, Founder of Vaestoliitto." *Finnish Yearbook of Population Research* 42: 5–12.

Huxtable, Ada Louise. 1963. "Architecture: Virtues of Planned City." *New York Times* (October 24).

Ketchum, Morris, Jr., et al. 1967. "From Three Emerged One: Stockholm, Tapiola, Cumbernauld." *Journal of the American Institute of Architects* 48: 36–58.

Lahti, Juhana. 2008. "The Helsinki Suburbs of Tapiola and Vantaanpuisto: Post-War Planning and the Architect Aarne Ervi." *Planning Perspectives* 23: 149–69.

Lapintie, Kimmo. 2005. "New Towns, Suburbs, and Urban Sprawl—Struggling for Integrity in the Helsinki Metropolitan Region." In *International Conference on New Towns*, edited by Iraj Etessa et al., 315–23. Tehran, Iran: Ministry of Housing and Urban Development.

Lukkarinen, Päivi. 2007. "Tapiolan puutarhakaupunki." Museum of Finnish Architecture. http://www.mfa.fi/tapiola.

Mäkinen, Antti. 2017. "Tapiola—Hub of Culture, Arts, and Sports." https://www.espoo.fi/en-US/Jobs_and_enterprise/A_dynamic_city/Locate_in_Espoo/Urban_Development/Metro_Zone/Tapiola.

Meurman, Otto I. 1947. *Asemakavaoppi*. Helsinki: Otava.

Miller, Donald D. 1989. *Lewis Mumford: A Life*. Pittsburgh: University of Pittsburgh Press.

Mumford, Lewis. 1938. *The Culture of Cities*. New York: Harcourt, Brace and Company.

Museovirasto. 2018. "The Finnish Heritage Agency." https://www.museovirasto.fi/en/.

Niemi, Lauri. 2003. "From Suburb to District Centre: Tapiola's Transformation from a Garden City into a District Centre of Espoo." In *Roots and Seeds: Tapiola 50th Anniversary Celebration Conference*. Espoo, Finland: Tapiola Development Project.

Nikula, Ritva. 1994. "Housing Policy and the Urban Environment—Programme and Reality." In *Heroism and the Everyday: Building Finland in the 1950s*, edited by Riitta Nikula and Kristiina Paatero, 217–22. Helsinki: Museum of Finnish Architecture.

———. 2003. "Housing Policy, Architecture and the Everyday." In *Tapiola: Life and Architecture*, edited by Timo Tuomi, 116–43. Espoo, Finland: Housing Foundation and City of Espoo.

Nyman, Kai. 1968. "Espoo, Tapiola, Helsinki Rural Commune." In *Seminar on Finnish Architecture*, 49–57. Helsinki: Finnish Association of Architecture.

Pakkala, Pekka. 1994. "Neighbourhood Planning." In *Heroism and the Everyday: Building Finland in the 1950s*, edited by Riitta Nikula and Kristiina Paatero, 222–27. Helsinki: Museum of Finnish Architecture.

Pantzer, Mika. 2010. "Tapiola as a Breeding Ground for Modern Consumption and Consumers." In *Modernism: Essays on Finnish Modernism*, edited by Marianne Aav, 125–33. Helsinki: Designmuseo, 2010.

———. 2011. "What Are We to Do with Our New Affluence? The Making of Modern-Day People in Postwar Finland—A Short Introduction to a Project Studying [the] Making [of] a Model City." In *Material World: Topics for Discussion Archives* (June 27). http://www.materialworldblog.com/2011/06/what-are-we-to-do-with-our-new-affluence.

Ruokonen, Ria. 1994. "Landscape Design in Tapiola." In *Heroism and the Everyday: Building Finland in the 1950s*, edited by Riitta Nikula and Kristiina Paatero, 228–32. Helsinki: Museum of Finnish Architecture.

———. 2003. "The Handworked Landscape—the Green Areas of Tapiola." In *Tapiola: Life and Architecture*, edited by Timo Tuomi, 90–111. Espoo, Finland: Housing Foundation and City of Espoo.

Strong, Ann Louise. 1971. *Planned Communities: Sweden, Finland, Israel, the Netherlands, France*. Baltimore: Johns Hopkins University Press.

Suhonen, Pekka. 1980. "The '40s and '50s in Finnish Architecture and Cultural Life." In *Problems of Co-ordination in Urban Planning and Architectural Design: Seminar on Architecture and Urban Planning in Finland 1980*, 67–78. Helsinki: Society of Finnish Architects.

Toland, Henry G. 1967. "A Visit to Tapiola: 2-Month Loans Began This Beauty." *Evening Bulletin* (Philadelphia) (November 24), J edition.

Tuomi, Timo. 2003a. "Heikki von Hertzen and Tapiola." In *Tapiola: Life and Architecture*, edited by Timo Tuomi, 40–51. Espoo, Finland: Housing Foundation and City of Espoo.

———. 2003b. "Tapiola—Garden City." In *Tapiola: Life and Architecture*, edited by Timo Tuomi, 6–29. Espoo, Finland: Housing Foundation and City of Espoo.

Väestöliitto. 1960. *Väestöliitto: The Finnish Population and Family Welfare League*. Vammala, Finland: Vammalan Kirjapaino Oy.

von Eckardt, Wolf. 1963. "Finland Leads Way in Urban Planning." *Washington Post* (December 1).

———. 1967. *A Place to Live: The Crisis of the Cities*. New York: Delacorte Press.

von Hertzen, Heikki. 1946. *Koti vaiko kasarmi lapsillemme*. Helsinki: Werner Söderström Osakeyhtiö.

———. 1956. "Tapiolan puutarhakaupungin suunnittelusta" [The planning of Tapiola Garden City]. *Arkkitehtilehti*: 1–2.

———. 1957. "Tapiola Garden City, Finland." *Town and Country Planning* 25: 108–14.

———. 1976. "The Rape of Our Cities." *Building Research and Practice*: 98.

von Hertzen, Heikki, and Paul D. Spreiregen. 1971. *Building a New Town: Finland's New Garden City*. Cambridge, MA: MIT Press.

von Hertzen, Heikki, and Ulovi Itkonen. 1981. *Raportti kaupungin rakentamisesta: Tapiolan arkea ja juhlaa. Asuntosääatiö 1951–1981*. Tapiola: Asuntosääatiö.

CHAPTER 19

SEASIDE

Iconic Community of the New Urbanism

Steven W. Hurtt

The plan for Seaside, a somewhat remote beach-resort community in Florida, burst onto the scene in 1984 by winning a *Progressive Architecture* Design Award.[1] Almost immediately, Seaside's Plan (Figure 19.1), Code (Figure 19.2), and emerging architecture earned both the admiration and enmity of architects and critics, stirring both hope and skepticism in U.S. professional, academic, and media circles, thus quickly achieving iconic status.

Seaside's Plan offered a compact, single-family residential density akin to older towns and city neighborhoods, a density largely abandoned in a post–World War II preference for sprawl. The geometric formality of Seaside's Plan was reminiscent both of the Beaux-Arts–influenced City Beautiful and of garden city movements such as Letchworth, Welwyn, and numerous plans by John Nolan. Seaside's developer, Robert Davis, possessed a knack for hiring untried architects whose work earned recognition across vernacular, avant-garde, and traditional styles, a seeming contradiction that helped keep Seaside in the press.[2] Some saw the Code as an inspired strategy for promoting community and aesthetic coherence as a framework for the individualistic while others saw it as oppressive of artistic license.[3] Its unabashed embrace of traditional town planning principles and architectural imagery stuck in the craw of modernist devotees while drawing the enthusiasm of those disenchanted with modernism. It engendered controversy.

Seaside remains iconic today, on its own merits and as a symbol of the leadership that its designers, Andrés Duany and Elizabeth Plater-Zyberk (DPZ), have provided to the elaboration and promotion of the ideas it represents. For the past thirty-plus years, Seaside, similar developments, and the principles of New Urbanism have represented both critique and better alternatives to the deleterious effects of sprawl.[4]

Seaside is located in Florida's panhandle, which lies along the north coast of the Gulf of Mexico and stretches westward toward New Orleans, Louisiana. Birmingham, Alabama, is several hundred miles to the north, and Atlanta, Georgia, is about 350 miles to the northeast. Closer cities include Pensacola and Tallahassee. The coast's *genius loci* is captured by place-names along it, many ending in the word

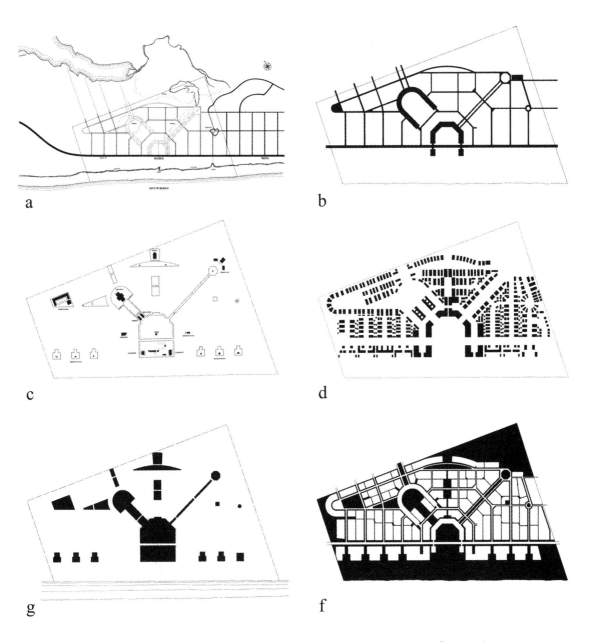

a

b

c

d

g

f

Figure 19.1. Andrés Duany's and Elizabeth Plater-Zyberk's planning concepts for Seaside, 1980: (a) Intended street linkages to Route 30A, to Sea Grove to the east (right), connection to the inland lake to the north (top) beyond the property boundary; all have been achieved. (b) Block and street structure. (c) Location of intended public or clubhouse buildings related to the formal pattern of public space. (d) Location of lots for houses. (g) Open space, that is, public space independent of streets and beach. (f) Private development areas (white) to public areas (black). (Courtesy DPZ Partners LLC)

URBAN CODE

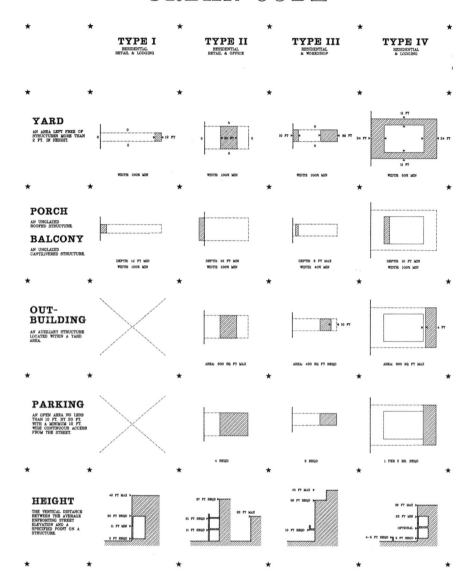

Figure 19.2. Three sheets of paper describe the Seaside Code: Urban Code, Architectural Code, and Landscape Code. Shown here is one half of the Urban Code, which is linked to the Regulating Plan. Specific building types are connected to specific lot types, which in turn are related to specific streets. Visually prominent lots are not regulated by type, but by design review. The combination of the Codes, Regulating Plan, slow growth, and architectural guidance results in both visual coherence and variety. (Courtesy DPZ Partners LLC)

"Beach." A coastal state highway, 30A, connects these places. Stretches of undeveloped land between them are interrupted by roadside attractions, cottage communities, and high-rise condominiums that presage privatization of the beach. Route 30A gives access to the Davises' eighty-acre parcel but cuts through it, separating most of the developable land from its primary attraction, a stunning beach of fine white sand.

In its earliest years in this unsettled place, Seaside existed more as idea than reality: a few modest summer cottages, a scruffy landscape, a highly idealistic Code, an improbably ambitious Plan, and a committed landowner and developer (Figure 19.3). But, if Seaside's 1980s reality was unconvincing, its Plan and Code were inspirational because they indicated solutions to the myriad problems of sprawl, including social and economic segregation, separation of land uses, environmental degradation, auto dependency, and loss of community: problems long identified but not rectified. Moreover, Seaside represented solutions that seemed equally applicable to those of struggling cities where investment and social capital had decamped to expanding commute sheds.

Figure 19.3. This tiny building, with "United States Post Office Seaside FL" emblazoned in its architrave, was designed by Seaside developer Robert Davis himself. It signaled a pretension to civic grandeur and community that may have seemed preposterous when it sat in lonely isolation facing Route 30A, backed by a swath of grass marking a future town green. Today Seaside's public realm of formally linked spaces and distinctively white "civic" buildings is substantially complete. (Photo by Isabelle Gournay, 1985).

Seaside recalled viable towns and city neighborhoods. What stood in the way of making such places again? Two things: zoning regulations that segregated land uses and a modernist stricture against traditional urban and architectural forms. Seaside demonstrated that these regulations and mind-sets could be challenged, perhaps changed, and implied there was a waiting market for developments offering a mix of uses, a mix of residential types, and the prospect of neighborly community.

Seaside's founders, architects, and those of like mind began a process of rediscovering what made older villages and towns work. The storied "red Pontiac convertible" tour of small southern towns by Robert and Daryl Davis, along with Andrés Duany and Elizabeth Plater-Zyberk, provided a romantic model for the necessary effort, one that included exacting measured analysis and typological categorization along with photographic documentation. Sharing such discoveries among an expanding group of allies enriched the range of planning techniques and solutions.[5] A growing number of projects that would come to illustrate the principles of the New Urbanism demonstrated that sprawl, far from being driven by market demand, resulted from a nationwide codification of the suburban vision gone awry: the result was segregated land uses, an ever-expanding highway network, and a cascade of detailed engineering standards, all dictated by rules that could be subjected to change (Duany et al. 2000).

In thirty years, Seaside has achieved economic success, gained notoriety, created influence, and served as a cultural magnet for the region. A host of similarly principled projects in the United States, Canada, and abroad, varied as they are, seem not to have diminished Seaside's iconic status. After a brief history, this chapter describes the intellectual milieu from which Seaside emerged; the nature of "community" at Seaside; its governance and institutional structure; how and why it remains a model of New Urbanism; its discernible impacts; and whether, how, and to what extent historic preservation should be invoked.

Shaping Seaside's Vision

While Robert Davis and his wife Daryl created Seaside, Robert credits his grandfather with the initial concept for developing "80 acres of arid land and scrub" to provide a summer camp for the employees of his Birmingham, Alabama, department store. He remembers how "JS would show us the place that, in his vision, would one day be a great human settlement" (Davis 2013b, 33).

The Davises' early imaginings included "a conservative business plan and a progressive, perhaps radical, social plan . . . compact cars and clotheslines . . . tiny bedrooms but expansive porches . . . outdoor kitchens and outdoor showers . . . small

Airstream trailers . . . bed and breakfast inns. . . . Porch sitting . . . friends and family spending extended evenings sharing time with each other and passing on tales and traditions to children and grandchildren." Seaside was to be a place capable of "enticing people into the public realm by making strolling more pleasant and convenient than driving" (Davis 2013b, 34–39).

The recently published *Visions of Seaside*, edited by Dhiru Thadani (2013), reveals that even after the Davises discovered DPZ, turning their word picture into the Plan for Seaside did not come readily. Numerous more conventional schemes were investigated.[6] Eventually Seaside's fundamental forms emerged: a sweeping arc indicative of today's Town Center, a variety of residential plot sizes, and axially related spaces. But connections beyond the site boundaries were rare and streets tended to form radial concentric patterns around the central arc. These early plans were unrelated to the surroundings, the usual sprawl pattern of autonomous developments.

Duany attributes a lecture given by the Luxemburg-born architect Léon Krier visiting Miami for major changes to Seaside's plan.[7] The shape of the Town Center became a partial octagon and embraced rather than avoided 30A. The radial concentric geometry was eliminated, replaced by two grids: one aligned with 30A and the beach, the other with the diagonal sides of the central partial octagon. Axes explored earlier became three radials emanating from three adjacent sides of the partial octagon. Street connections to the community of Sea Grove to the east and to the undeveloped property to the north became clearly indicated.[8] No longer was Seaside imagined as an autonomous, insular place. Additionally, residential lots were proposed along and against the north and west property boundaries to the rear of the eighty-acre plot, where a wide shallow arc of open space emphasized the central axis as did a public space at its terminus.

With this revised plan, the Davises' verbal picture became tangible. Encouraged by DPZ, Robert Davis solicited a critique of the revised plan from Krier. The architect responded primarily by reinforcing the DPZ plan. Among Krier's suggestions were greater emphasis on the formal geometry of the public realm; more explicit indication of honorific buildings related to that realm; and introduction of a pedestrian pathway system that lay parallel to the street system but was located between and behind the residential lots. The several suggestions by Krier that most significantly influenced and were incorporated into the DPZ plan that won the 1984 *Progressive Architecture* "Citation" were, first, the pedestrian pathway system; second, Krier's suggestion of a space along the axis between the Town Center and its northern terminus; and third, that terminus marked by a public building, not simply a public space. That space and public building have now been realized as Ruskin Place and the Chapel (Figure 19.4).

Figure 19.4. The central axis of Seaside runs north from the Town Center through Ruskin Place and visually terminates at the bell tower of the Seaside Chapel. Ruskin Place is surrounded by live-work row houses; the option of commercial space on the ground level increases the sense of urbanity adjacent to the Town Center. (Photo © Steven Brooke Studios)

An Epochal Project

In 1984, Seaside synthesized a handful of heady theories and emerging practices that had been developing in architecture and urban design over the past two decades, encapsulating them in a single, small, easy-to-comprehend, picturesque community. The community is described on four sheets of paper: a Regulating Plan and a simple set of graphically described Codes, one each devoted to Urban Design, Architecture, and Landscape. Figure 19.2 illustrates approximately half of the Urban Code.

By the 1980s, the critique of modernist planning and architecture had matured. Former devotees of the Congrès Internationaux d'Architecture Moderne (CIAM) had withdrawn from advocacy of many of its principles (Mumford 2009). The richness of past architectural vocabularies was being tentatively explored anew.[9] A revalidation of architectural typologies tightly linked with urban morphologies had emerged,[10] particularly in Europe but also in the United States.[11] Related to these was an emerging pattern in urban history that placed emphasis on municipal, somewhat anonymous author-ity, in contradistinction to emphasis on the hero-architect or patron.[12] And urban and architectural context was once again seen as a contributing foundation for the new rather than as a contrasting foil to modern architecture's abstract, skeletal, platonic forms.[13] Genius loci was asserted as equal to, or more important than, ex-pressions of the zeitgeist (Norberg-Schulz 1979). In different ways, projects by Robert Venturi, Charles Moore, Michael Graves, Aldo Rossi, Ricardo Bofill, Mau-rice Culot, Rob and Léon Krier, Michael Dennis, Koetter-Kim, Cooper-Robertson, and Peterson-Littenberg illustrated the shift in sensibility that Seaside likewise demonstrated.

The Sense of Community

Is Seaside a "real" community? Skeptics say "no," implying that Davis's descriptor "resort-community" is an oxymoron. This criticism presumes that "real commu-nity" depends on residential and institutional propinquity and membership.[14] But "community" means many things. Belonging is paramount. People belong to many "communities," some place-based but many interest-based (Brower 1996, 2011). Seaside welcomes both visitors and homeowners, fulfilling the Davises' "resort-community" objective. But the criticism raises reasonable questions: What is the social character of Seaside? What are its social institutions and what role do they play? Does the physical form of Seaside promote community?

While the Davises intended Seaside as a resort community and it is one, and while their ambition and plan for Seaside outstripped the childhood memories that inspired them, changing times and the Davises' responses to these changes have also contributed to the sense of community one finds at Seaside today.

Resort communities are no longer only active in short summers and shuttered up in long winters. Winterization and air-conditioning make them habitable and active year-round. An active "resort community" can support quality-of-life oppor-tunities that most neighborhoods cannot. The planned commercial Town Center and Lyceum, devoted mainly to educational programs as envisioned in the initial Plan, speak to the Davises' ambition for a year-round, complex "community." Sea-side's Town Center was intended to grow into a commercial center, including many restaurants and boutiques, drawing from a much larger population than Seaside's 355 residential units. That goal has materialized, partially aided by Jaquelin Robert-son, whose firm, Cooper Robertson, designed Watercolor, the large community growing to the north and west around Seaside. Robertson reasoned that Seaside's Town Center would logically serve Watercolor as well (Figure 19.5).[15] Similarly, the

Figure 19.5. Cooper Robertson designed the development of Watercolor to the west and north of Seaside. Jaquelin Robertson saw Seaside as the "town center" for the entire area and argued against its duplication in Watercolor. As with many post-Seaside examples of New Urbanism, some suburban-sprawl regulations still dictate Watercolor's final form. (Courtesy DPZ Partners LLC)

Lyceum area meeting rooms and auditorium provide regional "community spaces." They are supported by the Seaside Institute's scheduling and staging of events, and a charter school is now included.

The first cottages were modest and evocative of a slow-paced, warm-weather, summer-activity sort of place. Davis's idea of "cottage" had considerable latitude in imagined size, cost, grandeur, and income capability, as is attested by the planned variation in house-lot sizes and allowable lot coverage. Seaside has drawn a wealthier clientele than the Davises initially anticipated. This has amplified financial success and reduced socioeconomic diversity, but increased the availability of housing supporting short-term or "resort" visitors, independent of length of stay. All these people—visitors, homeowners, and renters—support activity, and many of them also contribute to the making of community.[16]

I have visited Seaside a half-dozen times over the course of its development and have always felt a strong sense of community there. Granted, my visits have usually included professional colleagues, but, still, warmth and welcome were encountered everywhere. Likewise, two psychologists, the authors of a 1996 article in the *American Journal of Community Psychology*, reported similar experiences at Seaside, leading them to further research on and within the community. Exceptional to most community psychology literature, their article pointedly makes the assertion that "the place makes the people. The environmental context induces the shared emotional connection and feeling of belonging" that the deliberate planning and architecture of Seaside both symbolizes and promotes community in multiple ways. Their interviews found a consistently strong "sense of community among those who reside, work, and visit within the town." They describe Seaside as a successful design effort that "strove to strike a balance between the individual and collective and to mediate between the individual and community." What initially seemed a contradiction to the idea of community, that only twenty residential owners reported Seaside as their primary residence, was offset by "an additional 70 families . . . in residence for the greater portion of the year . . . almost three times that figure . . . in residence for 3 to 4 months each year . . . and the majority of . . . rental residents . . . repeat visitors" (Plas and Lewis 1996, 111, 117).[17]

These patterns are partially explained by U.S. tax laws that have favored investment in second homes. While roughly half the properties at Seaside are available for rent,[18] the other half are being utilized by their homeowners or extended families and friends, thereby contributing to a high "homeowner presence." There is also the prospect of future community. Many second- home investors/owners, currently renting their properties for various periods of time, are planning that their Seaside property will be their future retirement home, their primary or permanent residence. Thus many different residential owners are more "present" and engaged in matters of community than the percentage of rental property would suggest. A further testament to that "presence" is the existence of two swimming and recreation (tennis) areas, both membership clubs.

Perhaps more than any other single factor, the design, the spatial layout, closely knit houses, their generous porches and shallow front yards, the easy walkability of the entire place, the narrow, pedestrian scaled streets with delimited vistas, the wide range of inviting places to walk to—beach, shops, cafés, restaurants, or cultural venues—all conspire to afford neighborliness that in turn begets community. The houses are all real houses and owned by people, not corporations. Stores and restaurants are locally owned businesses. Seaside looks like, feels like, and acts like a town, not a single-owner resort. It is a town in all the socio-mythic ways except governance (Langdon 1988; Low 1998; Manzo and Perkins 2006; Sexton 1995).

Private Governance

Community is one thing, governance another. Sometimes they are synchronous but sometimes not. Lest there be any question about it, Robert and Daryl Davis own the two companies that have created and manage Seaside: Robert Davis, the Seaside Community Development Corporation (SCDC); Daryl Davis, the Seaside Associated Stores (SAS).[19] Doris Goldstein (2013) has described who has what authority at Seaside. Goldstein calls herself a "founding resident" and has been legal counsel to the SCDC since 1986. She writes, "The Town of Seaside is an optical illusion. There is no town government, only a system of private covenants and restrictions, each a jurisdiction, nestling up to the next. . . . No structure ties it together. Instead, each exists as a parallel universe, adjacent but not connected" (587). There are nine separate homeowner associations, most based on a street of facing properties, each created as development proceeded. Each association has limited authority over the property along its street; this authority mostly relates to Urban Code development types. Neither these residential associations nor the Town Council has any authority over areas of nonresidential use. The nonresidential areas include the Lyceum, Ruskin Place, the Chapel, the membership-based swim and tennis clubs and all the commercial areas, including the Town Center and the long strip of property between 30A and the beach, all presided over by the SCDC or the SAS, which is to say, Robert and Daryl Davis.

On their own initiative, the nine residential associations created the Seaside Town Council made up of the presidents of each association. The town council's limited authority comes from the consensus the presidents can build and extend over each of their residential areas, utilizing the covenants and deed restrictions granted to them. Goldstein informs us that all rights of development were accorded to SCDC when Walton County approved the development plan. Likewise, the right of architectural review is held in perpetuity by the SCDC in eight of the nine residential associations. Moreover, the SCDC has the right to change the governing codes. Goldstein writes, "Despite the expense, SCDC has kept architectural review for more than 30 years, mostly because Robert cares deeply about architecture and wants it to be right" (588). Davis has maintained a Town Architect ever since the inception of Seaside. Eight Town Architects served for a year or two between 1983 and 1992. Subsequently three have served much longer terms. According to Thadani, the Town Architect "serves as a member of the Seaside Architectural Review Committee that reviews submitted projects for code compliance. . . . As Seaside has evolved the position of the Town Architect has changed from one of championing adherence to the master plan vision and designing and drafting cottages, to the more expansive role of helping to shape the character of Seaside by serving as an architect-of-record, educator, public space overseer, and to working with architects to continue to shape the public realm" (Thadani 2013, 137).

An attentive walk through Seaside makes clear that nothing in the visual realm has escaped scrutiny. The emphasis is on the pedestrian environment: brick paver street surfaces limited to the drive aisle; intentional absence of curbing; street signage and fire hydrants at a reduced size; the required, regulated, nonrepetitive picket fences; short streets that often culminate in a visual terminus, most memorably in the "Gateway Beach pavilions" (Figure 19.6). The scrutiny of the Town Architect and the Davises is present everywhere.

Figure 19.6. Emblematic of the public realm and of community, the gateway beach pavilions symbolize Seaside. Functionally, they protect the dunes by designating where to climb over them and they disguise the showers needed for washing away sand and salt. Architecturally, they celebrate the threshold moment of gaining a panoramic vista of sea and sky, offer benches for restful contemplation, and provide an identity to each street that leads from and to the beach: (a) Obelisk, (b) Savannah St., (c) Tupelo St., and (d) East Ruskin St. (Photos © Steven Brooke Studios)

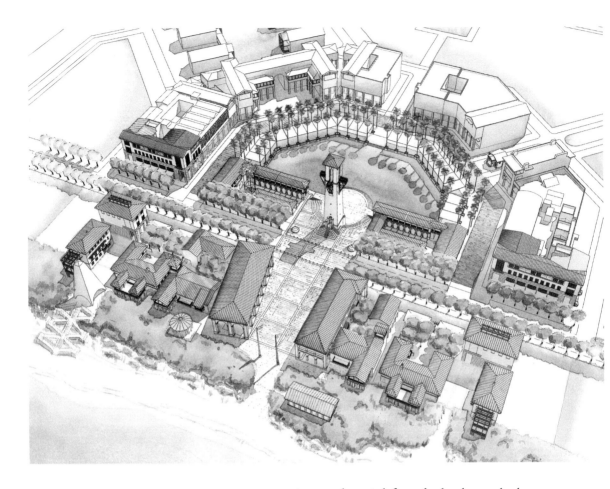

Figure 19.7. This rendering shows a next phase of the Town Center development. Vaguely modeled on the Piazzetta San Marco in Venice, it adds commercial space while providing a stronger link between the Town Center and the beach. Seaside's continuing development demonstrates how prevalent preservation strategies may conflict with what Robert Davis calls "successional urbanism." (Courtesy Opticos Design Inc., opticosdesign.com)

A recent lawsuit left no doubt about who has what authority at Seaside. A group of residents objected to the auditorium long slated for the terminus of the Lyceum and went to court against the SCDC. They did not prevail. But their action revealed homeowner anxiety about the future. The upshot was a design charrette to vet and address those anxieties (Goldstein 2013). The results were agreements to bring the Code up to date, make it more uniform across all residential areas, establish a professional architectural review board to oversee all applications and schematic designs that advanced the vision of the Town Center (Figure 19.7). The Léon Krier–designed tower, long a figment of Seaside's imagined future, appears at the focal point of the Town Center. Across from the Town Center, on the Gulf Coast side of 30A, is a plaza vaguely modeled on the Piazzetta San Marco in Venice. And where the colonnaded half octagon defining the Town Center abuts 30A, identical buildings book-end and announce it.

Reflecting on Seaside's regulatory strategies, Goldstein recommends against the multiple and separate residential ownership associations in favor of one to assist singularity of community, but also warns that homeowner associations can be antithetical to New Urbanism, opposing its guiding principles of inclusivity and open access by arguing and voting against them. Some of Seaside's homeowners wanted to privatize the beach and also pushed to prevent a through street connection to Watercolor, long part of Seaside's Plan. The beach remains open to the public but that street connection is now open only to pedestrians and bicyclists. Goldstein also advises that as "a practical necessity" legal authority for commercial areas should be clearly separate from residential authority because responsiveness to market opportunities and demand is not something likely well managed by homeowner associations.

So, Seaside looks like a town, but legally it is not one. The Town Council has no municipal authority. Seaside remains a real estate development corporation, authority residing with the SCDC and SAS under the Davises' enlightened leadership. The Davises have sought institutional governance forms to achieve desired ends, instigating clubs, commercial enterprises, corporations, management entities, and institutes. The Seaside Institute is among Davis's earliest institutional inventions. Davis has told me that he knew the Chautauqua model and saw it as a way to expand the limited benefits of sun, sea, and sand (Low 1998). The Seaside Institute was intended to provide various forms of intellectual stimulation and entertainment, making Seaside a locus of year-round events and supporting its commerce as well.

The institute has regularly reconceived its mission: planning, incubating, and running programs. To date, two incubated programs have become permanent and independent: Escape to Create, which brings artists to a residency program, and the Seaside Repertory Theater. Hosted events have included a number related to Congress for the New Urbanism (CNU) events, recalling elders, attracting scholars and honorees, and educating novitiates by bringing them to what someone recently called the "cradle" of New Urbanism. According to its website, the institute's mission increasingly focuses on promoting the ideas and forms that increase the probability of "places" becoming "communities." Understanding Seaside's iconic importance, the institute has also assumed the self-conscious role of documenting its history in cooperation with the University of Notre Dame's School of Architecture (seasideinstitute.org).

Is Seaside Still a Good Model?

With the thousands of New Urbanist communities built, what things about Seaside remain peculiarly instructive, allowing it to continue serving as a preeminent model? Seaside broke the rules of conventional subdivision development regulations nearly ubiquitous across the United States, but luckily those rules were not in force in Walton County, Florida, when Davis sought plan approval. Why not? Walton County had not yet experienced the economic or political pressure to adopt such regulations. Seaside's Plan and Codes were approved without running the usual gauntlet of suburban regulations, negotiating and compromising on numerous requirements. Free of such compromises, Seaside is a very pure version of built New Urbanism and so continues to inspire and instruct. More broadly, Seaside symbolizes six major impacts related to New Urbanism.

Inspiring New Developments

In appearing to break the rules of conventional suburban subdivision development, Seaside seemed to demonstrate that it was possible to build again in the manner of historical villages, towns, and city neighborhoods. Its Plan and Code had shown how. A handful of similar projects followed, proving there was pent-up demand for like-minded communities not satisfied by the offerings of sprawl. The willingness of buyers to pay a premium for housing that was part of a mixed-use, walkable "place" demonstrated that sprawl resulted from man-made regulations, not irrefutable market forces. The success of each new Seaside-like development strengthened resistance to the regulatory status quo and emboldened both developers and citizens who became an expanding clientele for a new form of practice.

New Rules and Practices

Seaside challenged convention and inspired both DPZ and like-minded firms to devise new frameworks, new rules to allow mixed-use, town-like places. Standard architectural and planning practices operate within conventional legal and regulatory frameworks, or "the rules." Through practice, client-architect teams discovered a key part of the framework: that an early, well-planned, intense, and inclusive working meeting lasting approximately one week, that brought together community stakeholders, authority, and technical people in a public venue, provided the best assurance of design success. This process served to educate people about the status quo and reasons for and alternatives to it; solicit ideas about alternatives and illustrate them; facilitate discussion to reduce polarization; galvanize support for designs that addressed issues and goals; accelerate approval for developers; and simplify approvals and public review by authorities. Andrés Duany appropriated the word "charrette" from architectural education to describe this process.[20] New commissions for DPZ and similarly inclined professionals came from two related groups: town guardians and developers. Both groups shared an interest in protecting the best "places" found in their locales, analyzing and emulating them as a guide for development, and resolving seemingly intractable conflicts caused by proposed developments that legally met existing codes but ran counter to the character they wished to protect or extend. Even when agreements were reached, existing regulations sometimes stood in the way. In one instance, development of an alternate code provided a model ordinance for what has come to be known as Traditional Neighborhood Development (TND).[21]

Codification of Traditional Neighborhood Development

Neighborhood or community design has long been seen as a fundamental societal unit in planning. Seaside's size, character, form, and intention corresponded nicely with those interests. Between 1990 and 1992 a DPZ-led town planning process in Bedford, New Hampshire, codified this approach by creating an addendum to the town zoning ordinance describing in legal terms the characteristics of the intended development, based on "traditional neighborhood design." This ordinance, subsequently referred to as TND, was promoted as a model for other jurisdictions that needed to devise similar ordinances providing the legal framework that could be used to affirm a *contextual* approach to reinforcing the character of existing older neighborhoods and/or basing the design of new neighborhoods on forms and principles derived from desired models.[22]

Shortly after the publication of Seaside, similar projects began to appear. Some, such as Kentlands in the Maryland commuter shed of Washington, DC, were new developments while others related to existing communities. Among the latter was Mashpee Commons in Mashpee, Massachusetts, a DPZ design that turned a proposed small suburban shopping center adjacent to its main street into an expansion of the town's historic core, incorporating residential in its mix of low-rise, multi-story uses. Mashpee Commons was one among a number of early projects that demonstrated the viability of the Seaside idea—that new/old, mixed-use, walkable communities could be built across a spectrum of development densities and preexisting patterns, whether town or suburb, strip shopping area, or older town center, to better local communities like Mashpee, eroded or threatened by sprawl-type development.[23]

Communities of Increasing Importance and Scale

Another of Seaside's impacts is the increasing scale of projects it has inspired. Two stand out: Poundbury in England and Celebration in Florida. Both began construction circa 1994. Poundbury demonstrates Prince Charles's advocacy for the environment, particularly his defense and promotion of the social and environmental sustainability of the village-rural patterns in England. He hired Léon Krier, whose critical theory had contributed significantly to the plan of Seaside, as Poundbury's lead designer, a position he retains today. Poundbury demonstrates the international reach of the Seaside idea and promises to serve as a test case and model in England and Europe, just as Seaside served the United States.

If zoning was the first major impediment to New Urbanism, conservative banking practices was the second. Without capital investment, New Urbanism communities of significant size could not be built. Thus Celebration, because of its sheer size and notoriety, marked a turn-about in the willingness of the banking community to invest in New Urbanism developments. Celebration's founder was Michael Eisner who, as its president, had the financial resources of the Disney Corporation behind him. Near Walt Disney World Resort, Celebration covers 4,900 acres and has 4,566 residential units; by 2010, it had achieved a population of nearly 7,500 including just over 3,000 households, one-third with children. Celebration proved that the market for communities inspired by Seaside was there; big finance could safely invest.

Congress for the New Urbanism

In addition to new communities, Seaside inspired a key new organization. The CNU, the principal organ for promoting the ideas represented by Seaside, was formed nine years after the publication of Seaside's plan. Seaside's success led to new commissions for DPZ. They and others kept encountering the myriad regulations that thwarted the building of similar places. Common frustration became common cause, a cause that led to the creation of the CNU. What were the critical steps leading to the CNU's formation?

Seaside initially met with critical opposition from the architectural avant-garde and a cold shoulder both in planning circles and in most schools of architecture. But the popular press (as opposed to professional reviews) gave Andrés Duany a public platform. He engaged the avant-gardists, with Peter Eisenman at their helm. Duany then moved on from debating the avant-garde contrarians, arguing that the cause of urbanism would be better served by focusing critical discussion among those committed to its advancement. A few architecture schools hosted conferences focused on solutions to the problems of sprawl, thus helping to build an academic as well as professional constituency.[24] Circa 1990, a serendipitous meeting of consorting protagonists provided the opportunity for them to hammer out what they called the Ahwanee Principles,[25] which became the foundation for CNU's Charter. Of equal consequence was the publication of *The New Urbanism: Toward an Architecture of Community* (Katz 1993), explaining the principles, illustrating a number of projects based on them, and including essays by the movement's leaders. Subsequently, the CNU has been the principal organ for the continued development of New Urbanism ideas, strategies, and techniques of implementation, outreach, and education.[26]

Form-Based Codes

The *idea* of form-based codes, like Seaside's, may prove to be Seaside's greatest impact and enduring legacy. Form-based codes rely on four principles: the *form* of the environment is as important as any other factor; *form* must be intended, not just consequential; the *form* of many historic places demonstrates desired ends; and such ends can be achieved through the use of *form-based codes* intended to produce new environments that emulate these older ones (Hamer 2000; Parolek, Parolek, and Crawford 2008).

The Seaside Code revived the idea of form-based codes, as opposed to use-based zoning regulations that had prevailed since 1926 in the United States. While well intended in their time in segregating egregious uses from less egregious ones, use-based zoning has come to be seen as one of the factors generating sprawl, largely due to the combination of segregation of uses, large-scale enterprise, and insistence on highway transport, all contributors to the deterioration of towns and cities.[27]

Emily Talen (2013, 194–95), writing in *Visions of Seaside*, describes the impact of the Seaside Code:

> Its graphic presentation stood in sharp contrast to previous generations of codes that were not only excessively long and bureaucratic, but failed to provide any clues as to how rules would translate into physical form. The Seaside Code argued, in effect, that it was legitimate to enact rules for the purpose of creating predetermined places, patterns, and forms. . . . The idea caught on . . . a "typological" or "form-based" approach to coding was seen by many as the best option for achieving real results—i.e., a renewed, more sophisticated approach to city-making in the U.S. This was essential because Americans lacked, in many places, vernacular building traditions, cultural agreement, and technological limits . . . the antidote to conventional zoning, subdivision regulations, and myriad "flexible" techniques . . . which had been introduced in compensation for the inflexibilities and limitations of use-based codes.

Form-based codes have come to be well regarded in the United States. As regulatory documents, they are easy to follow. Simple illustrations eliminate much uncertainty for both developers and communities. If followed, by-right approval is easy to obtain. To existing villages, towns, and cities, form-based codes offer regulations potentially more suitable to their historic development and character than use-based codes. That such codes had been around for thousands of years was rediscovered; understanding that they had been largely supplanted by use-based codes led to restoring form-based codes to effective utilization.

Increasingly, the professional U.S. planning community, which had eschewed the importance of form for decades, has embraced the idea that form matters, increasingly understanding that form-based codes can help create aesthetic and socioeconomic environments that are purposefully envisioned, can promote mixed uses including a mix of residential opportunities, can maintain and strengthen the form-use character of "special districts,"[28] and that similitude of form can host a diversity of uses and peoples by giving them a common visual identity that transcends their individual purposes. (See Plate 22.)

A New Urbanist Landmark for the Twenty-First Century?

How will Seaside endure? Should it be preserved? What problems does it face? Having changed the paradigms of planning and urban design throughout the United States, Seaside as fact and symbol is iconic. Therefore, a case could be made that it is a candidate for historic preservation, including Historic District designation. But this raises both practical and philosophical questions. The practical questions include the following: Is its historic preservation either logical or urgent? If urgent, when, how, and who might act? What challenges are there, what approaches can be imagined? The philosophical questions are those raised in many chapters in this volume: they argue for more flexible ideas about preservation, critically addressing the questions of what to preserve, why, and for whom? The philosophical conflict is whether to preserve the artifact either "as is" or restored to a "selected period in history" to represent it, as opposed to an emphasis on preservation of the culture itself, which inevitably means embracing its evolution, its changes, as well; and that means accepting changes to its material culture as well, a seeming contradiction to the idea of "preservation." In imagining Seaside as an environment where some of these practical and philosophical preservation challenges may be faced, it can be imagined as a test case including alternate scenarios. As such, Seaside's future may prove as instructive as has its past.

As a practical matter, Seaside is not yet "finished," so the preservation issue might seem premature, but certainly it is coming, partially because change is coming. The Town Center and beach-front areas can accept more and bigger buildings, as evidenced by the recent charrette and as illustrated in Figure 19.7. Likewise, the Lyceum buildings could become far more substantial. These imagined futures seem more desirable than the present condition, so stopping development for preservation purposes in these areas makes little sense. And who would promote it? The residential area presents a knottier problem. It is almost entirely built out; only one lot remains to be sold, and only a handful remain to be built on. But there is the specter of tear-downs: none so far, but Seaside's success could soon threaten the cottages and small houses that are among its earliest buildings and that contribute much to Seaside's character and diversity, the physical evidence of its "culture." According to the Code, many residential lots are "underbuilt."

How might we feel and think about this? I am uncomfortable with such a prospect. I like seeing the tangible record of the slow-growth development of this place, the affordability that was its beginning, its mixed variety of scales. I'd be inclined to side with those loyal to the relationship between the original idea and its original artifacts. On the other hand, Duany says he is unconcerned, that bigger houses, while "blockier" and less picturesque, would be more "urban," which he finds prima facie good. Robert Davis knows that bigger houses would take a toll on the broader socioeconomic spectrum he and Daryl intended. But, he reassures himself, imagining that over time bigger houses would become boarding houses or bed and breakfast inns bringing socioeconomic diversity once again. I can rationalize that bigger and blockier would still conform to the Code, so some aspects of the existing character would be lost but others retained—I would see the culture in evolution. Views such as those expressed by Duany and Davis, placing emphasis on balancing cultural evolution with cultural/artifact preservation, have been uncommon in preservation discussions but are creeping in (Hamer 2000; Lamprakos 2014; Semes 2009).

What of timing? For now it seems reasonable to trust that Seaside as-it-is-still-becoming outweighs its Seaside-as-it-is iconic state; the same slow-growth approach that has served the Davises and Seaside so well will continue for a time and the specter of tear-downs will not overtake that continued development. If and when it does, that will be the time to act. Then what? Isn't the whole of Seaside significant, not just a bit here and there? If so, that means designating Seaside a Historic District: every building considered "contributing," some more important than others. Because the public and commercial sectors are the least complete, and need more flexibility than residential areas, the residential areas alone might be designated a Historic District. One scenario is that some citizen group or the Seaside Town

Council applies for Historic District status for the entire residential area. Another is that one or another of the nine residential associations does so. In either case, application for Historic District designation could come from a citizens group as among the surest legal forms of resistance to change of the entire residential area or selected streets (residential associations). A third alternative is the spotty designation of specific houses for different "historic" reasons. For the immediate future, it seems reasonable to trust in Robert Davis's guidance. He is age-aware, knows a transition will come, imagines ideal scenarios himself, and pursues them. Davis has already established a professional design review group made up of nonresidents. This can be thought of as guiding change to the culture in the same way the culture of the place came into being—through the guidance of Daryl and Robert Davis.

For the entire region from Pensacola to Appalachicola, Davis envisions preservation of the fragile coastal ecology along with its development. He cites the Burnham Plan for Chicago commissioned by the Commercial Club and the importance of the *Wacker Manual* in informing and rallying political support for much that the 1909 Plan of Chicago envisioned. He hopes Walton County finds a similar future. Nonprofit organizations have begun work in diverse areas: Davis hopes their work will yield a unified effort. He cautions that "highest-and-best-use" measured monetarily is rarely "best" for a community (Davis 2013b, 603–7).

Davis thinks about how Seaside might best support a healthy, aging-in-place life, supported by intellectual, social, and physical activities. He has begun to pursue the integration of good health care systems not presently in place. He imagines that a number of Seaside's civic buildings now made of wood may be succeeded by structures of brick and stone, a long tradition in American urbanism that nevertheless contradicts most current preservationist practice and thinking (Davis 2013b, 603–7) and again raises the very questions addressed throughout this book.

Davis calls his view "successional urbanism," accepting an evolving relationship between culture, place, and history, thus expressing an approach toward which the preservation community is struggling but has not yet arrived, trying to answer the difficult question, how do we preserve the physical representations of our culture, place, and history, hold onto the material culture of the past, while the culture itself evolves—an evolution that inevitably changes the material culture? (Davis 2013b, 603; Lamprakos 2014). Seaside may add to its iconic status by playing yet another role, contributing to the debate and eventual resolution of this very question as the preservation community and our society confronts it. Davis himself, in establishing the professional design review group and the Seaside Institute, has possibly created the kind of vehicles for urban design and planning conversations that might generate ideas for how to ensure Seaside's continued inspiration as a model, while both its community and its built environment continue to evolve.

Table 19.1
Summary of Historical Events and Heritage Benchmarks for Seaside

Year	Event
1979	Robert S. Davis inherits eighty acres of land purchased by his grandfather in 1946.
1980	Andrés Duany and Elizabeth Plater-Zyberk devise the master plan after they took with Davis and his wife Daryl a "red Pontiac convertible" tour of small southern towns.
1981	Ground breaking for Seaside occurs.
1982	The Seaside Institute is founded.
1983	Teófilo Victoria becomes the first Town Architect.
1984	The Seaside Plan wins a *Progressive Architecture* Design Award Citation.
1986	The Prince of Wales establishes the Prince's Foundation for Building Community, an educational charity with goals similar to those represented by Seaside.
1988	Philip Langdon's *Atlantic Monthly* study raises public awareness of Seaside.
1991	David Mohney and Keller Easterling publish the first scholarly book on Seaside.
1993	The Congress for the New Urbanism (CNU) is established to share knowledge and educate others about ideas represented by Seaside.
1994	Peter Katz publishes *The New Urbanism: Toward an Architecture of Community*. It features Seaside and similarly principled developments.
1996	Construction starts on the neighborhood charter school.
1998	*The Truman Show* is filmed within the town's boundaries.
2001	Seaside's Interfaith Chapel opens. The Repertory Theater is organized.
2008	*Views of Seaside* is published with sumptuous illustrations and a multitude of short essays by many well-known architects, urban designers, and critics.
2013	*Visions of Seaside*, an encyclopedic publication edited by Dhiru Thadani, records Seaside's development and celebrates the community's iconic status.
	Population (estimate), 400 (winter)–1600 (summer); 80 acres [32 ha]; 355 dwelling units.

NOTES

1. *Progressive Architecture*, P/A Awards (January 1984): 138–39. According to Gosling and Gosling 2003, 176, "the jury praised the high intensity of land use and the proportions of squares, avenues, streets, and alleys." Technically speaking, this "planning" project received a "Citation." Architectural projects received "Awards."

2. Brooke (1995) counts twenty national and/or regional awards or equivalent accolades between 1983 and 2003 and articles in *Smithsonian* and *Newsweek*. In 1990 *Time* magazine declared Seaside "Best of the Decade" in design. *Metropolitan* marked its twentieth anniversary (Marshall 2001). Also see Bressi 2002.

3. A 1984 architecture studio directed by Peter Hetzel (1994) and Dhiru Thadani (2008) at the Catholic University of America "tested" the Seaside Code. The studio design model illustrated Seaside in its early years.

4. Katz, Scully, and Bressi (1993) first made an elaborately illustrated and well-reasoned book arguing the merits of New Urbanism.

5. Professional, academic, and collegial alliances became the Congress for the New Urbanism.

6. False starts and early schemes, rarely documented in architectural/planning literature, are for Seaside exceptionally illustrated in Mohney and Easterling 1991, 86–107, and Thadani 2013, 160–227.

7. Krier's lecture was part of a series spearheaded by Peter Eisenman. According to Duany (in Thadani [2013, 69–71]), "this tour brought Massimo Scolari, Rob Krier, Léon Krier, and Rem Koolhaas to Miami. . . . The ideas were terribly exciting. . . . In the Post-Modernist era, architecture's history was being rediscovered. . . . Krier really connected. He was crystal clear about ideas and ethics . . . none of us had understood urbanism until we saw Leo's now famous diagrams."

8. Thadani 2013, 172–73.

9. Brolin (1976) and Norberg-Schulz (1979) challenged the presumption of universality in modern architecture and planning in conflict with place and genius loci. Venturi (1977) incited a re-exploration of architectural imagery (iconography) and associated meanings.

10. For typological versus program-driven design, see Colquhoun 1981, Rowe 1982, Thadani 2010. The P/A Awards circa 1984 reveal a broad interest among architects in the relationship between city form and architectural typologies that gave rise to the Seaside Code.

11. Typological and morphological relationships between architecture and historic existing city forms emerged in the writings and work of Leonardo Benevolo, Giancarlo di Carlo, Mark Girouard, Léon Krier, Rob Krier, A. E. J. Morris, Paolo Portoghesi, and Aldo Rossi, among others, and urban design emerged as a professional practice and academic discipline with a developing literature (Barnett 1974, 1986; Bothwell 2004; Broadbent 1990; Gosling and Gosling 2003; Hurtt 1982; Krier 2009; Mumford 2009; Ockman 2012; Thadani 2010; Trancik 1986).

12. At a seminar, I recall Spiro Kostof countering the great-man theory of urban form by arguing the importance of municipal authority and civil servants in creating beautiful and functional cities in Europe.

13. Contextualism emerged from Colin Rowe's teaching at the Cornell University School of Architecture. See Schumacher 1971, Rowe and Koetter 1978, Cohen 1974, and Hurtt 1982.

14. For a demonstration of strong "community" action in a DPZ-designed New Urbanism development, see the history of Kentlands, Gaithersburg, MD (www.kentlandsusa.com: "About"; "History of Kentlands").

15. Jaquelin Robertson headed the innovative urban design offices that become part of New York City's Department of Planning during Mayor Lindsay's administration and thus was partially responsible for the Battery Park City team and design that also won a P/A jury "Citation" the same year as Seaside (1984): it shared with Seaside the characteristic references to traditional urban forms, specifically extending New York street, block, and parcel types, and use of an urban code.

16. Diane Dorney, executive director of the Seaside Institute, remarked, "I think there is a very high sense of community among the visitors. Many have been coming here for decades and have developed a fondness for the town that may far exceed the fondness they have for their year-round community. . . . Sense of community is something you can find in a vacation spot, and that shouldn't be dismissed." Robert Davis followed with, "Diane talked about the way that summer places like Seaside create bonds within families across generations and often are places young people meet each other, from which meetings new families are sometimes formed. Seaside owners and rental guests who came with their children continue to return, with their kids and grandkids now" (email exchanges with the author).

17. Plas and Lewis, psychologists, were impressed by their personal experiences of community at Seaside. They researched and put forward their Seaside-based argument to the develop-

ing field of community psychology, pushing its boundary regarding the influence of the physical environment on the development of "sense of community."

18. The primary rental property management group at Seaside handles 176 properties; Diane Dorney reports that "some owners now use VRBO (Vacation Rentals By Owner) as well," so exact information on rentals is not possible.

19. Personal conversation with Robert Davis.

20. Regarding the origin of the charrette as an efficient process in professional practice, I recall Duany citing a similar student experience while attending the École des Beaux Arts in Paris.

21. The TND type of development plan originated in the United States as a model legal form in 1990 through 1992 in the Town of Bedford, New Hampshire. Recognizing that, for the design to be implemented, zoning laws needed to adapt, Rick Chelman, the Honorable Norman Stahl (U.S. Federal Court of Appeals), Andrés Duany, and Scott Brooks wrote and sought passage of the first "TND Ordinance." It was then promoted as a model ordinance that could be modified and adopted elsewhere, thus putting into zoning's legal terminology the mixed-use principles of traditional town planning.

22. For other critical precedents for the TND, see the AD Profile Issue, *The Anglo American Suburb* (Stern and Massengale 1981), *Paradise Planned* (Stern, Fishman, and Tilove 2013), and *The Urban Design Handbook* (Gindroz, Levine, and Urban Design Associates 2003).

23. I observed part of the charrette in Mashpee.

24. Schools and sympathetic deans then included University of Miami (Elizabeth Plater-Zyberk); University of Virginia (Jaquelin Robertson); University of California, Berkeley (Harrison Fraker); University of Michigan (Douglas Kelbaugh); and University of Maryland (Steven Hurtt).

25. "In 1991, the Local Government Commission, a private nonprofit group in Sacramento, California, invited architects Peter Calthorpe, Michael Corbett, Andrés Duany, Elizabeth Moule, Elizabeth Plater-Zyberk, Stefanos Polyzoides, and Daniel Solomon to develop a set of community principles for land use planning. Named the *Ahwahnee Principles* (after Yosemite National Park's Ahwahnee Hotel), the commission presented the principles to about one hundred government officials . . . at its first Yosemite Conference for Local Elected Officials" ("New Urbanism" at en.wikipedia.org).

26. My involvement with CNU since its foundation has made me aware of its self-critical attitude, search for new challenges and solutions, and publication policies.

27. In 1926, the U.S. Supreme Court decision *Village of Euclid v. Ambler Realty Co.* (272 U.S. 365) validated use-based comprehensive planning and zoning ordinances in the interest of "public health, safety, morals or general welfare."

28. New York City was the forerunner of "special zoning district" designations by using floor area ratio incentives to maintain, enhance, and induce complementary uses along with use-related form requirements. See Elliott and Marcus 1973 and Barnett 1974, 1986.

REFERENCES

Barnett, Jonathan. 1974. *Urban Design as Public Policy*. New York: McGraw-Hill.

———. 1986. *The Elusive City: Five Centuries of Design, Ambition and Miscalculation*. New York: Harper and Row.

Bothwell, Stefanie, et al., eds. 2004. *Windsor Forum on Design Education*. Washington, DC: New Urban Press.

Bressi, Todd W., ed. 2002. *The Seaside Debate: A Critique of the New Urbanism*. New York: Rizzoli.

Broadbent, Geoffrey. 1990. *Emerging Concepts in Urban Space Design*. London: Van Nostrand Reinhold.

Brolin, Brent C. 1976. *The Failure of Modern Architecture*. New York: Van Nostrand Reinhold.

Brooke, Steven. 1995. *Seaside*. Gretna, LA: Pelican Publishing.

Brower, Sidney. 1996. *Good Neighborhoods: A Study of In-Town and Suburban Residential Environment*. Westport, CT: Praeger.

———. 2011. *Neighbors and Neighborhoods: Elements of Successful Community Design*. Chicago: APA Planners Press.

Cohen, Stuart. 1974. "Physical Context, Cultural: Including It All." *Oppositions 2, Journal of Institute for Architecture and Urban Studies*: 1–40.

Colquhoun, Alan. 1981. "Typology and Design Method." In *Essays in Architectural Criticism, Modern Architecture and Historical Change*. Cambridge, MA: MIT Press.

Davis, Robert Smolian. 2013a. "Prologue." In *Visions of Seaside: Foundation/Evolution/Imagination: Built & Unbuilt Architecture*, edited by Dhiru Thadani, 31–47. New York: Rizzoli.

———. 2013b. "The Last Word." In *Visions of Seaside: Foundation/Evolution/Imagination: Built & Unbuilt Architecture*, edited by Dhiru Thadani, 603–7. New York: Rizzoli.

———. 2014. Interview with Steven W. Hurtt (January 14). Seaside, FL.

Duany, Andrés, et al., ed. 2008. Views *of Seaside: Commentaries and Observations on a City of Ideas*. New York: Rizzoli / Seaside Institute.

Duany, Andrés, Elizabeth Plater-Zyberk, and Jeff Speck. 2000. *Suburban Nation: The Rise of Sprawl and the Decline of the American Dream*. New York: North Point Press.

Elliot, Donald H., and Norman Marcus. 1973. "From Euclid to Ramapo: New Directions in Land Development Controls." *Hofstra Law Review* 1(1): 56–91.

Gindroz, Ray, Karen Levine, and Urban Design Associates. 2003. *The Urban Design Handbook: Techniques and Working Methods*. New York: W. W. Norton.

Goldstein, Doris. 2013. "The 2012 Charrette." In *Visions of Seaside*, edited by Dhiru A. Thadani, 587–99. New York: Rizzoli.

Gosling, David, and Maria-Cristina Gosling. 2003. *The Evolution of American Urban Design: A Chronological Anthology*. London: John Wiley and Sons.

Hamer, David. 2000. "Learning from the Past: Historic Districts and the New Urbanism in the United States." *Planning Perspectives* 15(3): 107–22.

Hetzel, Peter J. "Imagining Seaside." In *Visions of Seaside,* edited by Dhiru A. Thadani, 101-3. New York. Rizzoli.

Hurtt, Steven. 1982. "Conjectures on Urban Form, The Cornell Urban Design Studio 1963–1982." *Cornell Journal of Architecture* 2: 54–141.

Katz, Peter, Vincent Scully Jr., and Todd W. Bressi. 1993. *The New Urbanism: Toward an Architecture of Community*. New York: McGraw-Hill.

Krier, Léon, Dhiru A. Thadani, and Peter J. Hetzel. 2009. *The Architecture of Community*. Washington, DC: Island Press.

Lamprakos, Michele. 2014. "The Idea of the Historic City." *Change over Time, an International Journal of Conservation and the Built Environment* 4(1): 8–38.

Langdon, Philip. 1988. "A Good Place to Live." *Atlantic Monthly* 261(3): 39–60.

Low, Thomas E. 1998. "The Chautauquans and Progressives in Florida." *Journal of Decorative and Propaganda Arts* 23: 306–21.

Manzo, Lynne C., and Douglas D. Perkins. 2006. "Finding Common Ground: The Importance of Place Attachment to Community Participation and Planning." *Journal of Planning Literature* 20(4): 335–50.

Marshall, Alex. 2001. "Seaside Turns Twenty." *Metropolis Magazine* (June): 68–72.

Mohney, David, and Keller Easterling, eds. 1991. *Seaside: Making a Town in America*. New York: Princeton Architectural Press.

Mumford, Eric Paul. 2009. *Defining Urban Design, CIAM Architects and the Formation of a Discipline, 1937–69*. New Haven, CT: Yale University Press.

Norberg-Schulz, Christian. 1979. *Genius Loci: Towards a Phenomenology of Architecture*. New York: Rizzoli.

Ockman, Joan, ed. 2012. *Architecture School: Three Centuries of Educating Architects in North America*. Cambridge, MA: MIT Press.

Parolek, Daniel G., Karen Parolek, and Paul Crawford. 2008. *Form Based Codes: A Guide for Planners, Urban Designers, Municipalities, and Developers*. Hoboken, NJ: John Wiley and Sons.

Plas, Jeanne M., and Susan E. Lewis. 1996. "Environmental Factors and Sense of Community in a Planned Town." *American Journal of Community Psychology* 24(1): 109–43.

Rowe, Colin. 1982. "Program vs. Paradigm, Otherwise Casual Notes on the Pragmatic, the Typical, and the Possible." *Cornell Journal of Architecture* 2: 8–20.

Rowe, Colin, and Fred Koetter. 1978. *Collage City*. Cambridge, MA: MIT Press.

Schumacher, Thomas. 1971. "Contextualism: Urban Ideals and Deformations." *Casabella* 359–60. Milano. Editrice Casabella S.p.A: 78–86.

Semes, Steven W. 2009. *The Future of the Past: A Conservation Ethic for Architecture, Urbanism, and Historic Preservation*. New York: W. W. Norton.

Sexton, Richard. 1995. *Parallel Utopias: The Quest for Community: The Sea Ranch, California, Seaside, Florida*. San Francisco: Chronicle Books.

Stern, Robert A. M., David Fishman, and Jacob Tilove. 2013. *Paradise Planned: The Garden Suburb and the Modern City*. New York: Monacelli Press.

Stern, Robert A. M., and John Massengale. 1981. *The Anglo American Suburb*. London: Architectural Design.

Talen, Emily. 2013. "The Seaside Code." In *Visions of Seaside*, edited by Dhiru A. Thadani, 193–213. New York: Rizzoli.

Thadani, Dhiru A. 2010. *The Language of Towns and Cities: A Visual Dictionary*. New York: Rizzoli.

———. 2013. *Visions of Seaside: Foundation/Evolution/Imagination: Built & Unbuilt Architecture*. New York: Rizzoli.

Trancik, Roger. 1986. *Finding Lost Space: Theories of Urban Design*. New York: Van Nostrand Reinhold.

Venturi, Robert. 1977. *Complexity and Contradiction in Architecture*. New York: Museum of Modern Art.

CHAPTER 20

ICONICITY IN PLANNED COMMUNITIES

The Power of Visual Representations

Isabelle Gournay

Selecting a title for this book, Robert Freestone, Mary Sies, and I had in mind a specific modality by which a planned community could be deemed "iconic": that of being endowed with highly recognizable visual representations, encapsulating its physical and social tenets. These representations were not working documents—such as surveyor's plans or blueprints—buried in archival file cabinets, but images for public consumption, redrawn plans or photographs that pop up in all sorts of publications and may have sufficient artistic merit to be on public display. We believed that "iconicity," understood as visual specificity and recognition, was one among several valid parameters to select case studies, and we sensed that it also played a role in the heritage issues that they are facing.

At different times in their history, potent images—those conducive to "iconic" status—have been devised to "sell" planned communities to varied constituencies: those who have the political or financial leverage to implement it (elected officials, investors, home buyers); residents and public opinion; planning and design professionals, who can ensure its becoming and remaining a "classic" case study in their discipline; current stewards; and consumers of cultural tourism.

In the previous chapters, the photogenic assets (and sometimes liabilities) of our case studies have been captured in a wide array of illustrations. Visual representations matter. Unless we are residents or neighbors, looking at them on a printed page or on a computer screen constitutes our first and perhaps only acquaintance with a planned community. After having seen this community with our own eyes (sometimes not long enough to truly capture its physical, social, and regulatory strengths and weaknesses), we still have to be reminded of it by visual representations that we or others have recorded.

It is true that "icon" has become a buzzword and "iconic" a substitute for "famous." According to the *Oxford English Dictionary*, the original meaning of "icon" is "an art form associated with the Orthodox Church": hieratic (highly stylized) paintings on wood, which have become objects of collective or individual devotion. An updated definition is that of "a person or thing regarded as a representative symbol, especially of a culture or movement . . . considered worthy of admiration or respect."[1] Using this second definition, the term "icon" can be applied to a planned community, which can therefore be deemed "iconic" from various physical, social, or symbolic perspectives. Our oldest case study, New Lanark, is a "representative symbol" of benevolent paternalism and of the company town movement at its beginnings. Our most recent case study, Seaside, which was immortalized in the 1998 movie *The Truman Show*, is undeniably the first and major "representative symbol" of New Urbanism. The qualifier "iconic" is not universal, however. For instance, reflecting slightly different meanings, the French use *emblématique* and the Spanish, *simbólico*.

Seaside is also the first planned community that the media deemed "iconic," an adjective often used for spectacular buildings and megacities but yet to be adopted for districts or towns at an intermediate scale, between a distinct structure and a populous urban entity. A presentation drawing or a photograph for a given planned community can become a "representative symbol" of its visual and social characteristics, therefore becoming "iconic" itself. Bird's-eye views of New Lanark (Plate 2), which Robert Owen commissioned from a local art teacher, John Winning, are such enduring icons. They continue to capture New Lanark's *genius loci* (spirit of the place) and are extensively used for scholarly and publicity purposes.

One can also argue that the original meaning of "icon" as hieratic representation and object of devotion applies to some planning images, such as the ultra-famous photograph of Walter Gropius's exceedingly long and stark apartment block, which became "the" visual representation of Berlin's Siemenstadt district among design professionals.[2]

This chapter delineates the contours and appraises the significance of visual iconicity for planned communities, by referring to our book's case studies and additional examples. It explores the visual effectiveness, as well as the practical and symbolic agency, of representations of real places (as opposed to conceptual diagrams and drawings), which have been reproduced and commented upon over many years. It does not address alternate, non–visually driven, meanings with which authors of previous chapters may have endowed the term "iconic." Its exploratory nature and mandated brevity explain why this text studies large- or medium-scale exterior views, created to illustrate planning concepts and the enactment of community ideals, and why it sets aside images that focus on a landmark building or artwork without encompassing its planned surroundings, as well as interior scenes, film clips, and computer-generated images.[3]

After surveying the ups and downs of planning iconicity from the garden city movement to New Urbanism, I shall analyze concurrently two types of images that enable a planned community to become iconic from a visual standpoint: those of the master plan itself, and those with residents benefiting from the planned environment. Readers will find these images reproduced in color plates or in previous chapters. A discussion revolving around issues of agency will follow, suggesting lines of inquiry and offering hypotheses, more than firm conclusions, on the positive and sometimes negative impact that well-known images exercise on the sustainability of the planned community they represent.

To characterize iconographical analysis and iconological interpretation, one can borrow the definition offered by the *Oxford Companion to Western Art* (Timmerman 2001, 353), by substituting "planned communities" for "works of art": "While iconography is a descriptive and classificatory discipline, iconology is an interpretative method, which aims to contextualize planned communities culturally and explore their possible meanings." Iconology has been integrated into the theoretical spectrum of the multidisciplinary field of visual studies, which puts a premium on "visuality," as opposed to "textuality."[4] However, a purely academic foray into images produced by design or media professionals, to be found in printed sources, seemed too abstract.[5] Fortunately I happen to live in Greenbelt, where residents can experience on a daily basis visual representations that have evolved from propaganda tools to grassroots agents. Focusing on Greenbelt's imagery, the following section provides a reality check as to why visual representations matter in the history and life of a planned community.

Images of Greenbelt

Even before ground was broken in 1936, Greenbelt was already intentionally iconic. To promote its Greenbelt Towns program, which faced national and local opposition from elected officials and public opinion, the Resettlement Administration (RA) and its successor, the Farm Security Administration (FSA), deployed a phenomenal visual arsenal, with illustrated brochures, exhibition panels, and posters. At first the RA promoted imagery from existing planned communities, which could advance its agenda. For instance, its 1936 brochure *Greenbelt Towns: A Demonstration in Suburban Planning* was replete with alluring housing and planning photographs from Europe; it included an already-famous aerial view of Römerstadt's School and Schuster apartment block (Figure 20.1) with this caption: "Every family has its own garden in the huge housing projects near Frankfurt, Germany" (Resettlement Administration 1936).

This brochure, which the Greenbelt Museum has reprinted and sells in its gift shop, featured a highly legible master plan for Greenbelt. Dictated by the topography, this plan's crescent shape (Figure 16.1) became iconic even before it was visible and has remained the backbone of current printed and outdoor maps provided to

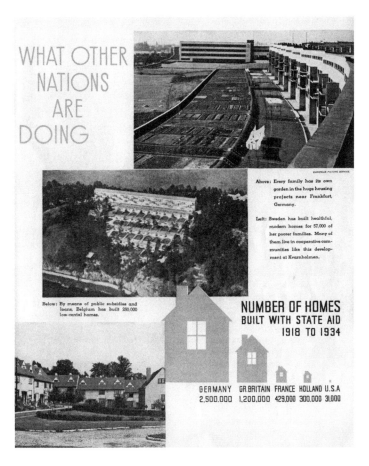

Figure 20.1. Page from *Greenbelt Towns: A Demonstration in Suburban Planning*, a brochure published by the Resettlement Administration (Washington, DC, 1936). Römerstadt's iconic view (top right) exemplifies Weimar Germany's leadership in affordable housing erected with public funds. (Courtesy Greenbelt Museum)

visitors. Greenbelt's version of the superblock concept gained enduring visual recognition in a 1941 aerial photograph of its central commercial and residential section (Figure 16.2), commissioned by the federal government from a company specializing in such photographs (Duany et al. 2003; Hamlin 1952; Sert 1942; Stein 1951). The same oblique panoramic viewpoint unfolded, in slow motion, in the movie *The City*, which was initially screened at the 1939 New York World's Fair.

Because it was the New Deal's earliest green town and so close to Washington, DC, Greenbelt regularly hosted "documentary" photographers on the staff of the RA and FSA. They visited several times a year, from 1935 to 1942, when a second set of defense homes had been erected and when Greenbelt had become a real community for its residents. Many of these official photographs have been reproduced in books and periodicals, while becoming a template for Greenbelt's self-image. They may have started as politically motivated depictions of highly socialized residents, all white and handsome like movie stars.[6] However, through the camera lenses of Marion Post Wolcott and Marjorie Collins, Greenbelt's self-proclaimed pioneers are not shallow silhouettes but energetic individuals: children drag a

Figure 20.2. Greenbelt's swimming pool in June 1939. Marion Post Wolcott's photograph of active and joyous recreation, a stone's throw from residential units, was commissioned by the Farm Security Administration to deflect fiscal and ideological opposition against direct public sponsorship of model housing and community planning. (Library of Congress LC-USF346-051999-D-A; courtesy Greenbelt Museum)

small wagon by the shopping center, dash out of pedestrian underpasses to go from school to home, use playground equipment next to their houses. Embedded in Greenbelt's physical and social fabric, RA and FSA photographs have shaped its origin story and are reenacted by current residents in their daily lives. Some are presently hung in the community center; others are on historic markers and have pride of place in Greenbelt's latest celebratory publication in the popular Arcadia series "Images of America" (Parsons St. John and Searing Young 2011).

The FSA photograph selected among more than eight hundred others on the Library of Congress website was taken in 1939, most likely from the diving board of the swimming pool (Figure 20.2). It layers this outdoor pool full of bathers, a buffer zone of greenery, and housing units. In 1947, this image of active leisure in an orderly, pristine, and healthy setting appeared in France's major design journal, *L'Architecture d'aujourd'hui*. It was subsequently used by Clarence Stein—with the caption "In the summer the swimming pool is the real social center of Greenbelt"—in *Towards New Towns for America* (1951), in Paolo Sica's *Storia dell'urbanistica* (1978), and in the "Images of America" book. This photograph carries greater significance when its viewer is made aware of the uphill battle entailed in erecting what was the first public swimming pool in the county. This key amenity, which continues to afford country-club living to Greenbelt's moderate-income residents, would have been scrapped by Congress without Eleanor Roosevelt's direct appeal to her influential husband, the president of the United States.

To these period images, various genres of planning- or community-based images were added over the years, including photographs published in the weekly citizen-run *Greenbelt News Review* and midcentury cartoons by resident Izzy Parker. Through a recent revitalization and tree-trimming process, the shopping center's esplanade (Plate 19) fulfills again its role as a stage set for iconic community photographs. The celebration of the town's seventy-fifth anniversary was seen by many residents as an opportunity to expand and renew Greenbelt's visual iconicity. In particular, Eric Zhang created a fantastic blog about life in Old and New Greenbelt throughout 2012, replete with site-specific photographs.

The Greenbelt chapter in this volume studies how stewards devised and nurtured strong physically and socially driven "principles," which helped people maintain their low-density, amenity-rich, and nature-friendly environment beyond its New Deal nucleus. There is strong evidence that these principles were shaped by visual representation as much as by written words. The Greenbelt case study also indicates that iconic images can shape a resident's understanding and experiences of a place. As the city's population has increased, becoming more ethnically and racially diverse and including many transient tenants, its origin story and socialization agenda, as translated in historic images, are not familiar for every resident. But grassroots efforts, such as the photographs by Zhang, who was born in China (and was named Greenbelt's Outstanding Citizen for 2013, an honor generally reserved for much older residents), demonstrate the beneficial agency of a living legacy of visual representations, which avoids the pitfalls of nostalgia.

Highlights of Planning Iconicity

Contrary to Greenbelt's swimming-pool photograph, it is often difficult to document the critical fortune of an image, from its production, reproduction, distribution, and eventual recognition as a specialized or popular icon. It is evident, however, that visual iconicity in the field of planning became a full-fledged and international phenomenon with the advent of the garden city movement.[7]

This movement's golden age (1905–35) coincided with the rise of the planning profession, with its own graphic conventions, related literature, and transatlantic networking of conferences, exhibitions, and site visits—all factors increasing the implementation and diffusion of a specialized iconography for a global multilingual audience. Prepared in the office of Louis de Soissons, Welwyn's map was conceived as an "illumination" (with its scripted border reminiscent of medieval manuscripts), or an icon in the original sacred and artistic meaning of the term, as much as a master plan (Figure 3.3). Featured on the covers of two scholarly books (Buder 1990; Whittick 1987), it still reigns supreme among planning illustrations for its graphic harmony and sophistication.

First published in 1909 by Raymond Unwin in *Town Planning in Practice*, the layout for the artisans' quarters in Hampstead Garden Suburb (Figure 3.2) is beautifully composed and highly readable, even in small-scale reproductions, and it has become the foundational icon to present superblock and cluster planning concepts. "Pochéed" in black ink, the building blocks convey a sense of community, while the graphic pattern of yard lines expresses privacy. The conflation of several geometric grids alludes to the quality and diversity of vistas and the dots of tree trunks to a green canopy along streets.

The advent of the garden city movement also coincided with an influx of photographic illustrations in the publishing world at large. Many period photographs of Letchworth, Hampstead Garden Suburb, and Welwyn have achieved iconic status, because they succeeded in expressing the melding of city and country, landscape and architecture. They harked back to English pictorial and cultural traditions of landscape design and painting, as well as to Arts and Crafts imagery, but they were also photogenic in a crisp and modern way. Just like its theoretical underpinnings, garden city imagery was adaptable and versatile, making such communities as Colonel Light Gardens, Garbatella, Jardim América, and Den-en Chôfu visually distinctive.

Indebted to the garden city movement, Frankfurt's planning and housing program, of which Römerstadt is the crown jewel, was particularly photogenic. Many New Frankfurt photographs that achieved iconic status did not originate with Ernst May's highly effective propaganda machine. Michael Stöneberg (2011) notes that, in 1927, two professional photographers took it upon themselves to shoot almost identical axial views of the zig-zag courtyard in the Bruchfeldstrasse *Siedlung*. Both placed a group of small children "by the paddling pool towards the community center." Each photograph was extensively reproduced, and other similar views (Figure 20.3) ensued, contributing to the creation of one internationally known icon. The zig-zag courtyard was the background for photographs of adults lounging on terrace roofs, which addressed the larger debate between advocates and detractors of the modernist flat roof. Stöneberg concludes that the "visual rhetoric" of New Frankfurt photographs "was never specially commissioned or authorised,"

and "had a larger reach than the written arguments of its propagandists, since the photos were often used uncritically by publicists who were independent or somewhat skeptical about the Modernist movement."[8]

In the ever-increasing body of planning manuals and textbooks published after 1945, the number, size, and quality of period documents generally declined; the production and exploitation of alluring images for new planned communities mattered less to their planners and stewards. Indeed, as stated by Michael Neuman (1998, 61), "images and plans, historically important carriers of planning knowledge and tools for urban change[,] [had] gotten the short stick." Notwithstanding the townscape movement in England, when ocular "pleasure" and "serial vision" were put to the fore by Gordon Cullen and his associates, visually driven planning was generally distrusted, on the premise that alluring renderings on paper were produced with little thought about their implementation and did not necessarily equate with spatial quality in completed projects.

A reevaluation of iconicity among planning practitioners and writers occurred in the 1980s, coinciding with the rejuvenation of urban design as a planning disci-

Figure 20.3. Anonymous photograph of children playing by the wading pool of the Bruchfeldstrasse group, in Frankfurt's Niederrad Estate, soon after its completion in 1927. Several commercial photographers created almost identical views, placing still or active children in front of this iconic zig-zag project. Notice the hanging laundry, which also humanizes the abstraction of the architecture. (Photo courtesy Susan R. Henderson)

pline. Seaside's Plan (Figure 19.1) was at the core of this phenomenon: it was drawn to convey a wealth of practical and theoretical information and could be printed at a small scale while remaining meaningful. Like their garden city predecessors, Unwin and de Soissons, Andrés Duany, Elizabeth Plater-Zyberk, and their Seaside advisor, Léon Krier, had an architecture background and a knack for didactic imagery. Seaside found its "iconographer" in the professional photographer and resident Steven Brooke. Rendered in a soothing maritime palette of blues and whites, his photographs set iconic benchmarks for this resort. In particular Brooke's views of rooftops (Plate 22), with turrets and belvederes enabling views of the Gulf of Mexico, hark back to picturesque images of nineteenth-century towns and attest to the refusal of Seaside's planners to let automobiles control the community.

The advent of New Urbanism and neotraditional design also helped reevaluate visual iconicity in print, both from a quantitative and qualitative standpoint, and marked the return to lavishly illustrated treatises. Spearheaded by the designers of Seaside, *The New Civic Art* juxtaposes 1,400 images of old and new planned communities. Its didactic plates and extensive captions revive iconic plans, such as that for the World War I community of Hilton Village in Virginia, whose "small houses have retained high value over the decades" (Duany et al. 2003, 90). *The New Civic Art* is also replete with little-known plans that did not achieve iconic status at an international level but have local significance. Subtitled as a "visual dictionary," Dhiru Thadani's *The Language of Towns and Cities* (2010) is also significant; it has entries on "cone of vision," "visual comprehension," and "deflected vista," which reflect the rehabilitation of visuality in planning practice. *Paradise Planned* (Stern, Fishman, and Tilove 2013) has raised the iconographic bar even higher, while demonstrating that leafy streetscapes are notoriously difficult to individualize in photographs.

Rendering the Plan Iconic and Visualizing Its Livability

The essence of a "planned" community is to be created with an intentional and legible layout, which can be visually rendered in artistic two-dimensional master plans as well as bird's-eye views and aerial photographs. This plan's specific devices—such as Letchworth's curving streets, Welwyn's housing "closes," Greenbelt's pedestrian underpasses, or Seaside's beach pavilions (Figure 19.6)—may be quite photogenic, acting as both visual attributes and pictorial motifs in memorable images.

Greenbelt's FSA photographers convincingly portray both individuals going about their daily lives and groups enacting a collective ritual. Images they created translate how routine and ritual are accommodated by Greenbelt's planning infrastructure and by the layout of its buildings and open spaces. This is no small accomplishment, as personifying the human component of the community concept in a still image is challenging. Happy, healthy, carefree, and protected childhood (Figures 20.2 and 20.3) is a key visual theme that planned communities have frequently sought to convey convincingly in their visual representations. But this is not always the case: photographs of Wythenshawe's lonesome tricycle rider (Figure 14.1) and Soweto's barefooted girls in their Sunday best (Figure 13.5) are not entirely persuasive.

Many planned communities have been endowed with an iconographic apparatus combining memorable visual representations of their plan and of their residents within this plan. An early example is that of Riverside, whose original developers printed 2,500 copies of the General Plan prepared in Frederick Law Olmsted's office (Plate 3). Although it was not entirely implemented, this large, colored rendering, which Riverside's "Images of America" picture book describes as "at once a work of art and a masterplan of urban planning," has achieved iconic status (Sacchi and Guardi 2012). The rendering technique adopted by Olmsted draws from his earlier plans for public parks and private estates, but the embellished lettering and great diagonal of the railroad tracks are original and distinctive. The graphic display gives pride of place to lines bounding the lots, which Riverside's land-rich but capital-poor investors gave to Olmsted, and to others who implemented his plan, in lieu of an honorarium. In addition to being the most ubiquitous illustration of Riverside in the planning and landscape literature, the General Plan is reproduced on refrigerator magnets sold by the local historical society and serves as an overlay for the city's bicycle route map. In 1871, Riverside's investors issued a separate prospectus (which did not include a plan). Recently reprinted, this pamphlet is Riverside's second foundational document: its text has never stopped being quoted and its engravings reproduced. The view depicting the twisting and turning central road (Figure 2.3) is quite accurate (the house to the right still exists). It depicts the social and recreational ritual of the promenade by foot, horseback, or carriage, which Olmsted admired in Europe and wanted Riverside residents to enact.

By the late 1920s, photographs became a popular iconic genre to depict new greenfield communities, often superseding drawn master plans. Endowed with the aura of modernity and mechanical accuracy, they attested to the implementation of new planning concepts that would lead to new lifestyles. Two of our case studies, Partizánske and Tapiola, offer interesting pairings of iconic aerial views and photographs taken at ground level, incorporating residents enacting routines expected of them by planners. Aerial visualizations of Baťa's ideal "community of labor" strikingly collapses and condenses the dimensional and symbolic relationship between factory, church, and workers' housing. These visualizations are complemented by the photograph where factory buildings and baby strollers collide (Figure 17.6). These images are haunting and powerful but also unsettling in their stark-

Figure 20.4. Through the lens of the photographer Gretchen van Tassel, from whom Clarence Stein commissioned updated views of Radburn in 1948, life in a cul-de-sac is treated as a "genre scene." (From Clarence Stein, *Towards New Towns for America* [Liverpool: Liverpool University Press, 1951], plate 16; courtesy Division of Rare and Manuscript Collections, Cornell University)

ness and emphasis on the sweeping diagonals envisioned by planner Jiří Voženílek. The far more comforting harmony between man and nature achieved in Tapiola is rendered in its aerial photographs encompassing the lake, tower, large park, and low-density housing, and in photographs of residents working on their vegetable gardens (Figure 18.4).

Radburn offers an interesting visual dynamic between images of plans and residents. While drawings of its plans (for the original project and the completed neighborhood) were instant icons (Figure 10.1), which reached European audiences just as the community was being built (Benoit-Lévy 1928), its early photographic views lacked specificity and charm. In 1948, bothered by the fact that he "really had no pictures that represented the present beauties" of the community he had designed with Henry Wright, Clarence Stein commissioned "a very intelligent young woman photographer," Gretchen Van Tassel, to produce photographs that he used extensively in *Toward New Towns in America*, which appeared in the British *Town Planning Review* in the late 1940s before its publication as a book in 1951 (Stein 1998, 507). Accompanied by substantial and informative captions (most likely authored by

Stein himself), Van Tassel's photographs are idealized but not unrealistic, leading us to believe that residents took pleasure in being asked to pose for them. They are referred to in the main text and unfold thematically, like a film documentary. The happy childhood theme takes pride of place: two young girls sit and chat in an inner park; healthy boys and adorable toddlers ride their bikes or tricycles on pathways; a gang of teenagers in their bathing suits, towels on their shoulders, dash out of the beautifully crafted, stone-arched underpass. Two men walk energetically along a "hedge-lined path"; family groups are depicted at work and at play in their "private garden, close to, but independent of, the community life in the inner parks" (Stein 1951, 59). A pool scene, replete with lean, bikini-clad women, alludes to the same summer ritual depicted in Greenbelt. One of Van Tassel's plates for Stein's book consists of two views from the "service lane" in Burnham Place, Radburn's most spacious cul-de-sac. The foreshortened bicycle in the foreground, the man kneeling in front of his car, the white dot of the little girl under the tree, the balance between pavement and greenery: the top photograph (Figure 20.4) is almost as well composed as a street view of Delft by Vermeer and makes the idea of dead-ending streets very palatable.

The Long-Term Agency of Iconic Images

Many questions remain to be addressed concerning images presented in this chapter, as well as those illustrated in the previous chapters of this volume. For instance, why, among dozens or sometimes hundreds of meaningful visual representations for a particular planned community, did only a few become truly iconic? Is this due to their superior artistry or photogenic character, to their subject matter, or to the effectiveness of their distribution channels? Or can this be pure serendipity? Allow me to focus on two questions that are central to this book and can be adequately addressed. Why do strong visual representations with iconic potential matter for a planned community? And what are their assets and liabilities for its long-term viability?

The direct agency of visual representations pertaining to the built environment is a topic debated by historians of art, architecture, and material culture. Images have strong and long-lasting meanings and impacts, with or without an accompanying text. There are, however, instances of planned communities for which iconic images have mattered little, if not at all. These images may have been produced in too small numbers or too far apart in time. Or, despite their visual allure, they have lost their experiential or symbolic relevance due to rapid physical or social change, generally triggered by the free-market economy. This is true for prime real estate locations such as Menteng and Den-en Chôfu, but also for communities designed for low-income residents. For instance, revitalization efforts for the World War I housing community of Yorkship Village (currently Fairview) near Philadelphia, have been cut short by the latest economic downturn, despite this community's strong visual iconicity and its endorsement in New Urbanist literature (Duany et al. 2003). There are also a few counterexamples of planned communities that lack strong early visual representations, at least alluring ones, and are nonetheless good places to live at present. Coming to mind is the Frankfurt housing colony of Westhausen, which was erected just after that of Römerstadt, in relentless *zielenbau* and *existenz-minimum* fashion. Early iconic views of Westhausen depict a mechanical, apparently dehumanized environment, which current photographs available online show as softened by vegetation and eminently livable.

Overall, however, iconic images matter, for some not-so-good and many more compelling reasons. There are a few obvious liabilities. When views of the pioneering construction phase prevail in a community's iconic spectrum, districts erected at a later date do not receive due credit for their physical and social assets, as for Welwyn's post–World War II neighborhoods. Liabilities may relate to the very essence of the photographic medium, for instance, to its propensity to distort distances. Black and white period photographs do not account for rich color schemes in both buildings and landscapes. The adage that "a photograph is worth a thousand words" had a negative outcome in Pessac, where, as stated by Gilles Ragot in this volume, Philippe Boudon's influential book of 1969 (Figure 11.5) "had the adverse effect of reinforcing the failure hypothesis. Its spectacular photographs of transformed houses may have been in great part responsible for this misunderstanding."

Adverse agency may occur when visual representations, idealized to excess, raise the bar for heritage standards too high. This point is illustrated in Sunnyside Gardens. Before World War II, published photographs depicted the open common areas as pleasant but rather mundane spaces. Taken in the late 1940s, Van Tassel's photograph of a woman lounging in perfect isolation on one of the internal reserves (Figure 10.2) became "the" iconic image of Sunnyside Gardens. In Kevin Lynch's *Site Planning* (1962), it was contrasted with neighboring streetscapes, and it was recently used by Caroline Constant (2012) to compare Sunnyside Gardens with Römerstadt. The mature vegetation hiding the bland brick façades, the perfectly balanced shadows on the impeccable lawn, the undisturbed sun worshipper—all these visual characteristics converge in a view far too idealized to serve as a realistic guideline for the current stewardship of Sunnyside Gardens' common areas (Figure 10.3), discussed in this book by John Pittari. In *The New Civic Art,* Andrés Duany uses this same 1940s photograph with the following caveat: "Unfortunately, these wonderful common places have been privatized by subdivision into yards. It is curious that this type of communal pattern, while perfectly feasible in Europe and elsewhere, seems to be unpopular in the United States. Perhaps it is because it gives to the private backyards which Americans value, as they have no problems with squares in front of their dwellings. As an urbanist, it is futile to bemoan such transformations" (Duany et al. 2003, 175).

Images can forecast the blossoming or demise of a planned community. For instance, two high-rise projects were erected in France in the 1930s, each receiving international accolades. Early photographs of the Centre Urbain in Villeurbanne show how it was served by public transportation, street-level shopping, and public health services. Recent plans to extend its central artery pay tribute to the longevity of this scheme.

The widely reproduced photograph of the so-called garden city of Drancy-la-Muette (Figure 20.5) in the far suburbs of Paris, with skyscrapers amid corn fields, hints at the physical isolation, which led to its use as a German internment camp during World War II and its nearly complete demolition in the 1970s.

Among planning and architectural professionals, visual representations can exercise a straightforward and significant agency. To reuse Neuman's expression, iconic rendered plans and images act as direct "carriers of planning knowledge" in the early career of key practitioners. In 1914, Le Corbusier transposed the celebrated photograph of the entrance of Margarethenhöhe in Essen in a bird's-eye view for an unrealized garden city in his native town of La Chaux-de-Fonds, the Cité-jardin aux Crétets. To devise Seaside's plan, Duany and Plater-Zyberk referred to John Nolen's compositional strategies and graphic standards. To represent his design for Poundbury (1993), Krier returned to New Lanark's tradition of colorful bird's-eye view making. The distinctive visuality of certain plans and views allows them to play a direct and beneficial role in the borrowing of planning and architectural ideas from one planned community to another. While Ernst May's plan for Römerstadt borrows from that of his former employer Raymond Unwin at Hampstead Garden Suburb, Römerstadt's Hadrianstrasse rounded buildings (Figure 12.3) are echoed at the Cité de la Butte Rouge in Chatenay-Malabry near Paris, views of which influenced designers of French new towns and residential districts in the 1970s. In addition to Bruno Taut's apartment buildings in Berlin, it is hard to believe that staff architects of the Resettlement Administration had not come across the image of Walter Gropius's Siemensstadt block and J. J. P. Oud's rounded corner stores at Kiefhoek and Hook of Holland near Rotterdam (1924–27) when they designed Greenbelt's garden apartments and shopping center (Plate 19).[9]

Among those who write about planning and design, iconic master plans can become agents of debate, even controversy. While sparing older artistic maps and plans, such as those of Riverside (Plate 3) and Welwyn (Figure 3.3), the planning

Figure 20.5. The garden city of Drancy-la-Muette near Paris, photographed just after its completion (c. 1937). The "tower in the cornfields" imagery was not a good omen for the community, which became a German internment camp during World War II and has since lost its iconic battery of high-rise buildings. (Jose Luis Sert, *Can Our Cities Survive? An ABC of Urban Problems, Their Analysis, Their Solutions; Based on the Proposals Formulated by the C.I.A.M., International Congresses for Modern Architecture* [Cambridge, MA: Harvard University Press, 1942], 59; courtesy Architecture Library, University of Maryland)

literature has often reduced intricate plans to a few lines or patches of color. Authors seek to avoid copyright issues and decrease reproduction costs, or to comply with the latest graphic conventions. Some want to challenge or even desecrate the iconicity of the plan they discuss.

For instance, in their influential book *Communitas,* Paul and Percival Goodman traced a cartoonish sketch (Figure 20.6) of Greenbelt's iconic crescent layout to illustrate the "disconnection of domestic and productive life" (Goodman and Goodman 1947, 4). In doing so, they pinpointed veritable commuting hurdles faced by residents of Greenbelt and many other planned communities in the United States. In countless diagrammatic renditions—some of them turned upside down, some totally devoid of descriptive captions—Radburn's neighborhood plan (Figure 10.5) became an "idea" or a "principle" (as opposed to the representation of a real place), used by both advocates and detractors of the superblock and cul-de-sac concepts.

Iconic images are no panacea against gentrification (in fact, they may encourage this phenomenon in places like Garbatella) or deindustrialization (how would a young woman living in todays' Partizánske identify with wives of Baťa workers in the baby stroller photograph?). Nevertheless, iconic images are natural "branding" agents for planned communities that rely on cultural tourism for economic sustainability: New Lanark, of course, where the Winning images are so ubiquitous, and other historic company towns like Guise or Margarethenhöhe. Using authentic period documents with heightened visual allure to attract outside visitors is perfectly legitimate, as long as their historical interpretation is accurate.

But the transformation of a few planned communities into cultural venues or resorts, their de facto "museumization," raises a larger issue for all planning landmarks: should visual iconicity be primarily a promotional tool for outsiders—visitors or scholars—or a grassroots agent targeting residents? And are both agendas compatible? There are no easy answers to this quandary. For all its vitality, Greenbelt's iconic apparatus tends to remain, like the town itself, a "best kept secret" enjoyed by those who live in and next to its New Deal nucleus. Greenbelt could promote itself more aggressively to attract business for its historic shopping center, eateries, and movie theater. A publicist would most likely recommend Art Deco–

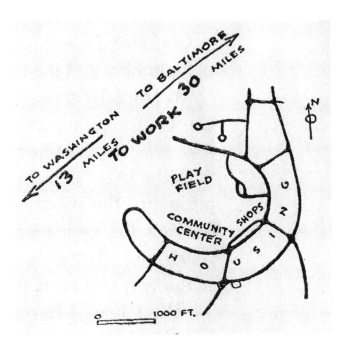

Figure 20.6. In their influential manifesto, *Communitas*, the sociologist Paul Goodman and the architect Percival Goodman added commuting distances to a minimalist rendition of Greenbelt's plan, using this planned residential community as a counterexample. (Paul Goodman and Percival Goodman, *Communitas: Means of Livelihood and Ways of Life* [Chicago: University of Chicago Press, 1947]; courtesy Architecture Library, University of Maryland)

inspired imagery, as in Miami Beach. Banking on the popular nostalgia for this glamorous but hybrid style would, in my opinion, obfuscate Greenbelt's origin story, which combines garden city and International Style aesthetics and ideals.

Powerful period images can help stewards of a planned community rally against external attempts to compromise its defining physical and social characteristics (such as low-density housing, a parklike environment, and walkability), while limited visual documentation becomes a major heritage hindrance. One can argue that any type of accurate and legible period document could be used to devise guidelines for landmark designations and for the restoration of open spaces and key buildings. I suggest, however, that the most iconic and symbolic among these documents play a distinct role. With their skillful composition and high contrasts, professional and aerial photographs highlight the genius loci and essential elements of a plan, including regulatory frameworks and vistas.

Even if they were not entirely implemented, beautiful and meaningful "foundational plans" reflect the unadulterated intention of their designer. Le Corbusier's colored axonometric drawing (Plate 15) was the key document to reestablish the Cité Frugès's original polychromy and implement a coherent landscaping vision. Its intricate line rendering encapsulates the formal and theoretical complexity of this small group of homes, a feat that no black and white period photograph has achieved. Iconic images not only act as tools for protection and restoration, but also allow a community to extend and update its environmental, artistic, or social legacy. For instance, the 1871 series of engravings (Figure 2.1) depicting very accurately Riverside's first buildings (church, houses, business block, and water tower) inspired an enduring legacy of high-quality civic and residential design, in complete agreement with Olmsted's landscape philosophy. Documents like those mentioned in this chapter can help planned communities rise to the difficult challenge that lies at the very core of this book: preserving the essence of their planning concepts without becoming "frozen" in time.

In addition to exhibition material and posters, images reproduced at a large scale can be embedded in the physical fabric. Common in medieval Italy, the tradition of city views that municipalities commissioned to decorate town halls was reinstated in Littoria's stunning murals for the Palazzo del Governo (Plate 7). In Lyons, the Musée Urbain Tony Garnier mainly consists of magnified drawings of this architect's epochal Cité Industrielle project painted on the blind side walls of his Cité des Etats-Unis apartment complex. One wall represents an early scheme for the neighborhood itself (www.museeurbaintonygarnier.com). Every community has a space that a self-celebratory mural could enliven.

At present, computer screens have become the most ubiquitous portal for old and new views of planned communities. Historical postcards, once key channels of popular iconicity, resurface in online commercial outlets. Google Earth provides aerial photographs that, when juxtaposed with their iconic counterparts, clearly address issues of physical change and vegetation growth. Updated images of iconic spaces and buildings are found on photo-sharing sites, such as Flickr, and in sites and blogs maintained by municipalities, homeowner associations, historical societies, and residents. Surfing the web, I was finally able to comprehend the planning, architectural, and chromatic variety and vitality of Siemenstadt, a far cry from Gropius's stark façade. And one can discover places that have not reached an international level of visual recognition but that have significant iconic potential. Resources available on the internet can be volatile, and texts accompanying images may be misleading or erroneous. Only a few of all recently produced electronic images will reach enduring iconic status. The benefits of this grassroots imagery overcome liabilities, however. The experiential and conceptual approach in this chapter leads us to believe that an embarrassment of visual riches is far less detrimental for the livelihood and heritage of any planned community than a depleted iconography.

NOTES

I would like to thank Mary Corbin Sies for her invaluable encouragement and advice.

1. *Oxford English Dictionary*, http://www.oed.com/view/Entry/90879.

2. Publications illustrating this view of Siemenstadt range from the cover of Carol Aronovici, *America Can't Have Housing* (1934), to Thomas Sharp's *Town Planning* (1940) and Peter Gay's *Modernism: The Lure of Heresy from Baudelaire to Beckett and Beyond* (2008).

3. William Le Baron Jenney's water tower in Riverside (Figure 2.7), Edwin Luytens's twin churches in Hampstead Garden Suburb, Le Corbusier's "skyscraper" unit in Pessac (Figure 11.2), and Angiolo Mazzoni's post office in Sabaudia (Figure 15.5) can all be deemed "iconic." Most of our case studies feature at least one "landmark" structure: a school (Römerstadt; Greenbelt), a theater (Garbatella; Greenbelt), a railroad station (Den-en Chôfu; Radburn), a place of worship (Menteng), or an office tower (Tapiola). Images of urban furniture (benches, lampposts, street signs) can also evoke and nurture the spirit of a planned community. Interiors having reached iconic status include the hall in New Lanark's Institute and the "Frankfurt Kitchen" in Römerstadt.

4. This approach is found among cultural geographers; see Cosgrove and Daniels (1988).

5. I pored over primary and secondary sources, in printed or electronic form. I perused monographic studies, as well as general works of planning literature: "treatises," "textbooks," "sourcebooks," "handbooks," "encyclopedias," and "general histories." A wide array of images—many of them unpublished or having not been circulated for many years; some pertaining to planned communities that have not reached an international level of visual recognition—can be retrieved on websites prepared by planning professionals, archival and museum repositories (such as the Reston Archives), academic visual resources collections, and commercial vendors. Academic search engines, like ProQuest and JSTOR, lead to illustrated articles in professional and scholarly journals, as well as newspapers. "Enthusiast websites" can be useful research tools, such as that placing online books, maps, and aerial views related to Welwyn. http://cashewnut .me.uk/Home/home.php.

6. Images of Greenbelt residents have not achieved the cult status of Dorothea Lange's and Walker Evans's photographs of migrant workers. Although Greenbelt's photographers may have been slightly less talented, the depiction of misery may carry greater artistic weight than that of happiness.

7. Upon first examination, images of Bournville (begun 1895) and Port Sunlight (begun 1888) forward planning agendas to a lesser extent than those of Letchworth, Hampstead Garden Suburb, and Welwyn. In their published form of 1898 and 1902, Ebenezer Howard's garden city diagrams are a perfect match for the "graphic symbol" definition of icons in computing: "Sign whose form suggests its meaning"; see Miller 2005.

8. In the *Architectural Review* (July 1959): 21–35, Roehampton, the tower-block community sponsored by the London County Council, was hailed by Nikolaus Pevsner for its visual connections with the English Picturesque tradition and for its departure from "drawing board" planning. See Pevsner 2010.

9. The Kiefhoek and Hook of Holland shops were illustrated within Henry Russell Hitchcock's *Modern Architecture; Romanticism and Reintegration* (1929); Kenneth J. Connant's *Modern Architecture* (1930); Henry Russell Hitchcock and Philip Johnson's *The International Style: Architecture Since 1922* (1932); *Architectural Record* (June 1931): 506–7; Catherine Bauer's *Modern Housing* (1934); and Sheldon Cheney's *The New World Architecture* (1935). There is no evidence that Greenbelt's designers visited Europe in the 1930s.

REFERENCES

Benoit-Lévy, Georges. 1928. "Le Bréviaire du lotisseur." *La Technique des Travaux* 4 (April).

Buder, Stanley. 1990. *Visionaries and Planners: The Garden City Movement and the Modern Community*. New York: Oxford University Press.

Constant, Caroline. 2012. *Modern Architectural Landscape*. Minneapolis: University of Minnesota Press.

Cosgrove, Dennis, and Stephen Daniels. 1988. *The Iconography of Landscape: Essays on the Symbolic Representation, Design, and Use of Past Environments*. Cambridge and New York: Cambridge University Press.

Duany, Andrés, Elizabeth Plater-Zyberk, and Robert Alminana. 2003. *The New Civic Art: Elements of Town Planning*. New York: Rizzoli.

Goodman, Paul, and Percival Goodman. 1947. *Communitas: Means of Livelihood and Ways of Life*. Chicago: University of Chicago Press.

Hamlin. Talbot. 1952. *Forms and Functions of 20th Century Architecture*. Vol. 3. New York: Columbia University Press.

Lynch, Kevin. 1962. *Site Planning*. Cambridge, MA: MIT Press.

Miller, Mervyn. 2005. "Celebrating an Icon of Planning History: Raymond Unwin's Seminal Diagram, *The Garden City Principle Applied to Suburbs*." Unpublished paper, Society for American City and Regional Planning History, Miami.

Neuman, Michael. 1998. "Planning, Governing, and the Image of the City." *Journal of Planning Education and Research* 18 (Fall): 61–71.

Parsons St. John, J., and M. Searing Young. 2011. *Greenbelt*. Charleston, SC: Arcadia Publishing.

Pevsner, Nikolaus. 2010. *Visual Planning and the Picturesque*. Edited by Mathew Aitchison. Los Angeles: Getty Research Institute.

Resettlement Administration. 1936. *Greenbelt Towns: A Demonstration in Suburban Planning*. Washington, DC: Resettlement Administration.

Sacchi, L., and C. Guardi. 2012. *Riverside*. Charleston, SC: Arcadia Publishing.

Sert, Jose Luis. 1942. *Can Our Cities Survive? An ABC of Urban Problems, Their Analysis, Their Solutions; Based on the Proposals Formulated by the C.I.A.M., International Congresses for Modern Architecture*. Cambridge, MA: Harvard University Press.

Sica, Paulo. 1978. *Storia dell'urbanistica*. Il Novecento. Rome: Laterza.

Stein, Clarence. 1951. *Towards New Towns for America*. Liverpool: Liverpool University Press.

———. 1998. *The Writings of Clarence S. Stein: Architect of the Planned Community*. Edited by Kermit Carlyle Parsons. Baltimore: Johns Hopkins University Press.

Stern, R. A. M., D. Fishman, and J. Tilove. 2013. *Paradise Planned: The Garden Suburb and the Modern City*. New York: Monacelli Press.

Stöneberg, Michael. 2011. "The Photographers of the New Frankfurt." In *Ernst May 1886–1970*, edited by C. Quiring et al., 79–90. Munich: Prestel.

Thadani, Dhiru A. 2010. *The Language of Towns and Cities: A Visual Dictionary*. New York: Rizzoli.

Timmermann, Achim. 2001. "Iconology." In *The Oxford Companion to Western Art*, edited by Hugh Brigstocke, 353–54. New York: Oxford University Press.

Whittick, Arnold. 1987. *Practical Idealist. A Biography of Sir Frederic Osborn*. London: Town and Country Planning Association.

Zhang, Eric. 2012. "Greenbelt in 2012." http://greenbelt2012.wordpress.com/.

CHAPTER 21

AFTERWORD

Lessons of the Iconic Planned Community

R. Bruce Stephenson

Webster's Dictionary defines an icon as a "religious image" and an "image of uncritical devotion."[1] The iconic planned community is rooted in the evangelical creed of the early twentieth-century reformer, who believed that rationally ordering the physical environment would improve urban life. The first generation to confront Darwin, university-trained experts dismissed the industrial order's contention that competition ensured the survival of the fit. The city's sordid conditions and the factory's desensitizing labor system threatened the human potential, and planning was a tool to guide human evolution to a higher plane. The early planners viewed the urban environment as an organism of interdependent parts, and to procure a "fit" society they designed human-scaled communities integrating town and country. Letchworth, the first garden city, was their prototype. Referenced in several of the book's twenty-one chapters, it became the icon of an international crusade to build heavenly cities on secular dimensions. "The civilization characteristic of Christendom has not yet disappeared, yet another civilization has begun to take its place," George Santayana noted shortly before the start of World War I (Santayana 1913, 1).

Garden city advocates were staunch physical determinists but they also cultivated a humanistic seed—the ideal of the organic community that lay at the heart of western civilization. Beginning with Robert Owen's industrial village in Scotland and concluding with Robert Davis's neotraditional tourist haven in Florida, this book documents the effort to translate optimal design into a sustaining common life. Early residents instilled meaning in their environs, while future generations worked to safeguard their inheritance. They experienced success and failure, as the effort to translate the reasoned genius of the past into a template for the future sparked reaction, resolution, and unintended consequences. The lessons are profound. In the twenty-first century, sustainability and resilience are the watchwords but, as the preceding chapters demonstrate, the desire to balance individual rights and the public welfare remains the key to the "good life" that Aristotle envisioned for a civilized people. In the whirlwind of an ever-morphing global economy fueled by instant communication and privatization, the iconic community is a harbinger of the future. The question is will these special places stand as beacons of enlightenment or will they fade away, relics of an age we can no longer fathom or appreciate?

The Fitness of the New Jerusalem

The struggle to adjust to a world of declining resources and unending demands is timeless, but it is only in the last century that a field of expertise arose to direct the Faustian imperative for development. The transition to the modern age was chaotic, profitable, and violent. By the late nineteenth century the industrial world was urbanizing at an unprecedented rate, and the city was the point of challenge; it was a disordered environment where profit-seeking produced unmatched squalor and affluence, conflict beset labor and capital, and municipal governments struggled to provide basic services and essential infrastructure. City planning was the response. Like other professions, it drew on precedent, established a lexicon, and instituted a rational system of procedures to solve problems. It was also imbued with utopian ambitions. Not unlike the ministry, practitioners experienced a calling to the profession. They had to be prophets with the capacity to envision the future and the skill to guide urban expansion on rational and sustaining lines. Drawn from the first class of university students educated on Darwinian precepts, the novice planners valued expertise but were not bereft of spiritual aspiration. If the Kingdom of God no longer informed the basis of a better city, they labored to create a heavenly city on an earthly foundation, a city made more "fit" for human evolution.

The Origin of Species (1859) restructured concepts of social cohesion as well as biological principles. By the 1870s, the idea of fitness had moved to the center of intellectual thought. The universal "laws of nature" of the Social Darwinists at Anglo-American universities dictated that unfettered competition determined the "fitness" of those seeking to master the free market's "jungle." German scholars, led by Johannes Conrad, countered the laissez-faire directives of "English economics" with a contextual analysis derived from Darwinian evolution. Competition was not the sole measure of a species; the environment also determined a species' fitness for evolution. If modern industrial society was to reach its potential, government and university expertise, the German economists concluded, must direct urban expansion to procure a fit environment (Lindenfeld 1993; Rodgers 1998).

The German university incubated the theory of environmentalism, which drew its logic from biological principles. The concept of the "niche," the unique role an organism plays in procuring the health of an ecosystem, set the framework for drawing comprehensive plans to integrate urban components and advance human evolution. The physical environment and social improvement were interdependent and, as science proved, species survival was a product of both living conditions and genetic coding. Environmentalism advanced the idea that the city was a collection of organic parts that could be systematically planned to secure profits, health, and better lives. By the early twentieth century, university-trained experts on both sides of the Atlantic were proselytes of city planning and civic salvation was the goal. They were determined to clean, order, and sanctify a discordant environment that lay at the center of human progress (Buder 1990; Ellefsen 2010).

Like any movement bent on creating a better world, city planning needed a sacred text that illustrated the path to redemption. In 1898, the publication of Ebenezer Howard's *To-morrow: A Peaceful Path to Real Reform* presented a compelling framework for turning utopian ideals into bricks and mortar. Howard's genius was to meld other men's ideas into a blueprint—the garden city—that extended the traditions of civic art, park planning, suburban design, and conservation. The second edition of *To-morrow* was re-titled *Garden Cities of To-morrow* to reflect the garden city's central role in advancing "real reform." Integrating its essential components—greenbelts, industrial districts, town centers, and picturesque neighborhoods—defined the expert's practice, but it was the provision of worker housing and a communitarian approach to land development that stirred reformers (Bullock and Read 1985; Hall 1988). Howard challenged the status quo, but he was also tactful, placing the garden city on a continuum with a sacred vision. The opening lines of the first chapter of *Garden Cities* quoted William Blake's illuminated 1808 poem, "Milton": "I will not cease from mental strife, Nor shall my sword sleep in my hand, Till we have built Jerusalem In England's green and pleasant land" (Howard 1902, 20).

The quest to build a New Jerusalem—a city of optimal design that fostered health, altruism, and civic loyalty—enlivened the rhetoric of the early planners (Dennis 2008; Hunt 2004). In 1895 John Nolen, in his first public address, said that if experts directed municipal policy, "civic faith" could be grounded on a rational foundation and the city could become as healthy as it was just, and "every man would be both laborer and capitalist." "We might then be tempted to believe," he proclaimed, "in the words of St. John that we saw the Holy City, the New Jerusalem; coming down from God out of Heaven."[2] In 1902 Sylvester Baxter, the Boston journalist who popularized *Garden Cities* in the United States and helped Nolen write *New Towns for Old* (1926), announced that Americans stood at "the dawn of a great civic awakening" (Baxter 1902, 255). Like the religious awakenings of the early eighteenth and nineteenth centuries, the evangelical fervor of the early twentieth century was enlivened by a vision of redemption but it was better living conditions—not eternal salvation—that awaited.

Over the next two decades, the rhetoric of the New Jerusalem would fade but only after city planning was ensconced in the machinery of municipal government. The reforms initiated in the late nineteenth century: building codes; the control of building densities; the planned extension of cities; and the construction of sewerage, water, and transportation systems had coupled with the provision of worker housing by the 1930s in most major cities. The neoteric tool of early city planners, the comprehensive plan, guided these improvements. At the same time, standards were established for designing new towns and suburbs. The garden city keyed this endeavor. It provided a blueprint and the rationale to step beyond the tenets of Victorianism and set the framework for a fit, urban civilization.

The garden city was undoubtedly a response to the "dark satanic" city of Victorian England, but Howard was also a student of Darwin and social evolution. His vision of a future metropolis of interconnected garden cities replicated the function of a community of living organisms. By contrast, Victorians considered the city to be an artificial environment that produced "un-natural men." The response, perhaps best personified in the work of Frederick Law Olmsted Sr., was to create artistically arranged expanses of idyllic landscapes to "re-create" a benighted humanity (Wilson 1990). The prototype suburb of Riverside melded nature and urban form to house "suburban yeoman, who would stand," Olmsted wrote, against "the nihilistic tendencies" of urban life (Beveridge and Rocheleau 1995, 99–100). Howard built on Olmsted's model, but he also presented a more far-reaching vision of the future city. "The object," he wrote, "is to raise the standard of health and comfort of all true workers of any grade." With limited dividend companies, prescribed plans, and municipally owned land, it would be possible to direct growth and to synergize "the natural and economic combination of town and country" (Howard 1902, 22). But for Howard's reforms to reach fruition, it would require, as Olmsted put forth in 1868, "the best application of the arts of civilization" (Olmsted 1992, 275).

By the early 1900s, civic art had made significant inroads since Baron Haussmann oversaw the planning of Paris a half-century before. Camillo Sitte's pathbreaking text, *City Planning According to Artistic Principles* (1889) championed the concept of "organic design." A critic of Haussmann's Beaux-Arts formalism, Sitte traced the source of urban vitality to the historic city's choreographed sequence of streets and public spaces. It was incumbent on the planner, Sitte argued, to modify the urban grid to create the intimacy and picturesque beauty missing in the expansive spaces of Paris, Barcelona, and Vienna (Hanisch 2010). At Sitte's death in 1903, Beaux-Arts plans remained dominant, as witnessed by the McMillan Plan for Washington, DC, but the art of town planning stood at the forefront of the reform agenda. In September 1903, the First Pioneer Garden City Company, which Howard headed, hired Raymond Unwin and Barry Parker to plan Letchworth.

While committed to Howard's concept, Camillo Sitte and William Morris inspired Unwin and Parker (Fishman 1982). The medieval English village informed the vernacular architecture they fashioned to invoke a sense of order and stability. Careful site planning structured the community along natural contours, while the analysis of soil and topography identified lands most conducive for development, preservation, and agriculture. Streets and neighborhoods were aligned to ensure efficient movement and provide access to nature, business, and civic institutions. Unwin, a student of the Renaissance and Baroque city, valued the Beaux-Arts approach, and he had axial avenues terminate at the town center to heighten its viability (Scully 1991). Letchworth's precise dimensions and spacing sought to secure the ancient promise of the beloved community, the point of civic equanimity where residents invest in both their place and each other. Letchworth and sister communities, including Hampstead Garden Suburb and Jardim América, presented a New Jerusalem for a secular age, and their appeal helped legitimize the fledgling city planning profession. In 1913, Howard was elected the first president of the International Garden City Association, a position he held until his death in 1928. Unwin succeeded Howard and, in 1931 John Nolen, the American garden city aficionado, followed Unwin to the organization's presidency.[3] By then, garden cities had been built on six continents, town planning had risen to an art form, and city planning was an established profession and an academic discipline.

The very fact that Letchworth was built according to a plan brought it renown, but it was not the exemplar Howard had envisioned. The economics of real estate development negated the ideals of cooperative landownership and the desired range of working-class housing. At the same time, Letchworth was a practiced work of art that verified the investment in professional planning. "The loving attention that the architects gave to the residential environment," Stephen Ward (1992, 5, 8) writes, "added a new micro-dimension to the garden city idea that marked the beginnings of its conceptual and practical fragmentation as a holistic strategy." Letchworth became the iconic planned community of its time, a Mecca for the first generation of professional city planners.

In 1906 John Nolen, a recent graduate of Harvard University's Landscape Architecture Department, traveled to Europe to document the basis of good town planning. Letchworth was an early destination. Although far from complete, the American was intrigued by the picturesque setting that Unwin and Parker had produced by configuring groups of attached housing and aligning streets, civic buildings, and greens on subtle sight lines. More important, the integration of urban components created an efficiency of movement and a communal aesthetic seldom found in private real estate ventures. Nolen labeled Letchworth the "perfect city" and, upon returning to the United States, he shifted his practice from designing parks to pursuing commissions in town and city planning (Nolen 1909; Stephenson 2015). If the first garden city failed to meet Howard's lofty goals, it enjoined Nolen and scores of other reformers to take up the challenge of urban planning.

In 1909, Nolen joined the Garden Cities and Town Planning Association of England and, in June 1911, he returned to Letchworth as a member of the Boston Chamber of Commerce European Tour. The first order of business for the sixty businessmen, municipal officials, and urban experts (who spent a month studying European urban reform) was a tour of Letchworth and Hampstead Garden Suburb led by Howard and Unwin. In the following weeks, the Americans joined their counterparts in France, Italy, Switzerland, and Germany studying policies and projects (e.g. municipal utilities, industrial housing for workers, zoning studies) designed to create a city that was "fit and fair," Nolen asserted (Stephenson 2015; Hancock 1986). Reciprocal tours were launched and a fertile cultural exchange ensued as municipal leaders on both sides of the Atlantic advanced the practice of modern city planning.

Within a week of returning to the United States, Nolen sent a survey to the planners he had met. It was one step in what became a torrent of interest in a novice discipline (Saunier 1999). By World War I, an international network was in place and a cadre of planning experts was contributing to "a world mart of useful and intensely interesting experiments," writes the historian Daniel Rodgers (1998, 4). An intense optimism pervaded the effort, as city planning promised to usher in a golden era of peace and prosperity. Rather than test their fitness on the battlefield, nations were destined, planners believed, to prove their superiority by building cities of unmatched fitness. "The whole world could become engaged in internal improvements and urban rivalry to such an extent that, during the time required for carrying out the civic plans, international peace would rule and even become a permanent guest upon our planet," wrote the German planner Werner Hegemann (Collins 2005, 31).

The mechanized brutality of World War I terminated the hopes for a new millennium, but, even as civilization fell into disrepair, plans were drawn to improve the human condition. Factory production was a key to victory and employers were cognizant that a well-housed worker was a better worker. To aid the war effort, the British and American governments established agencies to plan and build communities for workers laboring in industries vital to the military machine (Lang 1999). Government investment in "industrial housing" gave planners some hope that human evolution could still progress. They perceived the Great War to be a natural disaster and, just as in the animal world, the human species would survive and adapt to new conditions. It was imperative, then, that waging war should aid in obtaining a future fit for a people who had lost their evolutionary bearing.[4]

In the United States, the federal planning agency adopted the garden city as its model. Nolen, who earned the most government commissions, laid out a path to deliver victory in war and peace in *New Ideals in the Planning of Villages, Towns and Cities* (1919). Upon returning home, servicemen would find "a new and better type of workman's home," he wrote. Using the "British formula," a "new order of life" was destined to arise, with "the construction of new villages and towns after the declaration of peace" (Nolen 1919, 134–37).

If the Great War stilled the prewar era's benign humanism, it also advanced innovation and raised expectations for peace in a world where the ranks of class and privilege had been rent. In 1918, the Prussian Parliament passed a law that made adequate housing a right that was summarily written into the Weimar Constitution (Ellefsen 2010). In Britain, "the elders have been pretty thoroughly discredited," Unwin wrote Nolen in 1920. After helping lead the wartime housing initiative, Unwin had been named his nation's deputy director of housing. He was drawing plans to "break down the difference between classes" and "bring a greater equality and understanding between the brain worker and the hand worker."[5] Unwin was charged with coordinating dwelling design, site planning, surveying, and costing work for worker housing, the centerpiece of Britain's domestic agenda. That summer twenty thousand housing units were under construction with tenders for an additional one hundred thousand. By decade's end, six hundred thousand dwellings were constructed for the working class, much of it on suburban lands, once the province of the upper and middle classes (M. Miller 1992).

Unwin's shift from socialist reformer to government bureaucrat embodied planning's acculturation. The garden city had been compromised, interpreted, and assessed and, in the end, its ideals were translated into principles of practice. In the decade before the Great Depression, an unmatched body of work took shape as construction commenced at places like Den-en Chôfu, Cité Frugès, Sunnyside Gardens, Radburn, Garbatella, Römerstadt, Zlín, Menteng, Johannesburg's Western Native Township, Colonel Light Gardens, and Wythenshawe. New legal and financial tools were employed and, in the case of Radburn, special care was made to accommodate the automobile. Better building materials, advances in architecture and engineering, and innovations in communication and energy production extended the profession's bounds, but there was a point of origin. The plans drawn, even the Cité Frugès, Le Corbusier's experiment in modernist architecture, drew inspiration from the garden city (M. Miller 2002).

Expectations ran high after the Armistice was signed. "There was a tremendous enthusiasm to build a new and better world," Clarence Stein recounted (quoted in Hancock 1964, 627). Stein's colleagues in the Regional Planning Association of America (RPAA), Lewis Mumford and Henry Wright, took up residence in Sunnyside Gardens to test the viability of their experiment. By then Unwin, who moved from Letchworth to Hampstead Garden Suburb in 1906, had long been in study, cultivating and documenting his expertise. Unwin was an effective propagandist and writer who humanized a technical discipline and transformed it into an art. Town planning constituted "finding a beautiful form of expression for the life of the community," he wrote in *Town Planning in Practice* (Unwin 1994 [1909], xiv).

Still in print, *Town Planning in Practice* (1909) is a seminal work that extended the Victorian conscience to encompass a comprehensive environmentalism. Unwin created a sophisticated design regimen, where, Walter Creese writes, "The width of the streets, species of trees, grass verges, gardens, walls, schools, and shops had to be definitely responsive to the dwellings that surrounded them" (Creese 1994, xxiv). Like Sitte, Unwin took his cue from historical precedent, but it was folly, he warned, to merely replicate the past. *Town Planning in Practice* presents an iconic imagery illustrating how time-worn configurations could be transformed into new forms of beauty and efficiency. Inspired by the French Post-Impressionists, Unwin used a variety of shapes, solids, and diagonal planes to communicate the spacing of buildings and their relationship to the public realm. Unwin fashioned an art form that, not unlike the Post-Impressionists, raised the perspective of human achievement. Planning, by World War I, was an attempt to give the modern city a vernacular identity that venerated the landscape and linked neighborhood, town, and region on a common bond (Creese 1994). *Town Planning in Practice* also set the structure for what was to follow. Just as Paul Cézanne's brightly hued landscapes unveiled the parameters for modern art, modernist architects reduced Unwin's design template to its essence and created plans depicting streamlined hygienic cities. In the process, the garden city's picturesque architecture was shed, written off as a romantic nostalgia with no place in a world of precise mechanical function.

During the 1920s, the planning profession worked through a tumult of ideas and schemes as practitioners embraced the new and old. Colonel Light Gardens, built immediately after World War I, was a faithful adaptation of garden city planning principles. Garbatella, established as a "social laboratory" to test garden city principles, had its mission redefined after Italy's 1924 fascist takeover. Römerstadt, which started construction in 1927, gave a modernist twist to the garden city template. The global economic depression accelerated the shift to modernist principles, especially in Europe, where efficient, cost-effective housing schemes appealed to municipal governments desperate to provide work and shelter. In the United States, despite its affinity for the new, a Jeffersonian attachment to the land slowed the transference of Le Corbusier's and Walter Gropius's concepts. An enlivening dialectic ensued in the Resettlement Administration, which oversaw the Roosevelt administration's town planning initiative, and Greenbelt was the synthesis (Alanen and Eden 1987; Arnold 1971; Knepper 2001; Z. Miller 1981).

The new town on the outskirts of Washington, DC, set Weimar modernist architecture within a free-flowing system of green, which harkened to the Olmsted plans for Riverside and the Uplands. Without a formal civic center, Greenbelt lacked the crisp geometry of Hampstead Garden Suburb but this did not deter the effort to create and sustain social community. Residences were aligned on mews and linear greens to foster casual acquaintances with the hope that more long-lasting relationships would take root and foment an organic democracy. The iconic film *The City* (1939) documented Greenbelt's aspirations. Aaron Copland's music and Lewis Mumford's narration celebrated the placement and use of functional buildings and of lives lived close to industry and nature. Most of all, *The City* featured Greenbelt's children: iconic images of them being educated in an open, free-form style, biking safely and effortlessly across the community, and enjoying an idyllic afternoon swimming in a facsimile of Walden Pond. Mixing the life affirmations of Walter Gropius and Henry David Thoreau, Greenbelt provided convenience and comfort for adults, while striking a new course for nurturing children in a democracy (Christensen 1986; Knepper 2001).

Sabaudia, the Italian fascist New Town built in the same period as Greenbelt, also mingled tradition and modernism but the goal, of course, was not to advance democracy. A modernist monumentality centered a town tied to the countryside in the effort to show how fascism was reviving the power and aesthetic of ancient Rome. The fascist dream, like Rexford Tugwell's Resettlement Administration, was short-lived.

Baťovany, the Slovak community founded by the shoe manufacturer Thomas Baťa, was renamed Partizánske to honor a 1944 rebellion against fascism. Inspired by a capitalist and defined by Soviet Bloc communism, this modernist community of factory districts and axially aligned neighborhoods was expected to create a society bereft of class divisions and democracy. Ironically, the industrial city inspired by the efficiency of Henry Ford fell victim to capitalism. Since the Velvet Revolution, the Baťa factories produce only a fraction of the shoes they once did, which has left the residents of Partizánske struggling to maintain their town's identity and to profit in a world of free markets and hyperconsumerism.

Tapiola, a mix of precise modernist architecture, forest, and Arcadian landscape, was designed to mitigate the consumer impulse to indulge in materialistic delight. Quite the opposite happened, as residents invested in a community that secured status and a lifestyle that delivered consumerism in an unmatched setting. Tapiola brought the issue that Ebenezer Howard and Raymond Unwin confronted full circle: it was expertly designed but was it a town for "real workers"?

The Iconic Community in the Consumer Age: Bastardization or Enlightenment?

The conflict between consumer desires and social good bedevils communities across the globe in a world that has grown, according to Thomas Friedman, "hot, flat, and crowded" (2008). The demand for a middle-class lifestyle will not abate, and China, slated to have the world's largest economy, is ground zero for those trying to harmonize urban development. Henry Paulson, an expert on crisis (he oversaw the Wall Street bailout as the secretary of the treasury under George W. Bush), claims that China must initiate a new regimen of planning or risk economic and environmental catastrophe. China's "potential is choking on traffic and pollution," Paulson notes; its cities are layered in superblocks where arterial roadways generate traffic jams and contaminate the environs. The solution: building "livable cities" with "smaller blocks and mixed-use neighborhoods and accessible public transportation." Only then, Paulson believes, can China "balance economic development with energy efficiency, improve air quality and reduce congestion" (Paulson 2012).

When a Republican Wall Street stalwart advocates building "livable cities," a harmonic convergence is in motion. From the United States to China, building transit-based, human-scale, mixed-use communities keys the desire to construct the "resilient city," the moniker for twenty-first-century utopian aspirations (Newman, Beatley, and Boyer 2009). With superblocks and autocentric development in disrepute and traditional town planning resurgent, this book helps clarify a history that is inspiring a profession in transition.

Andrés Duany, in the preface to the reissued *Town Planning in Practice* (1994), traced the "central tragedy" of American city planning to Radburn and the superblock. It was there that Unwin's "sophisticated and complex system" fell victim to Stein's "simple minded-slogan, demanding the moving cars be separated from moving pedestrians." Radburn, Duany contends, "choked on the three-car garage" (1994, v). A practiced polemist, Duany has a keen historical eye as witnessed by his encyclopedic text, *New Civic Art* (2003). But he is not a historian and the march of events is more nuanced than he would have us believe. Radburn was a thoughtful response to the times, a model that the RPAA put forth to capture urban expansion in communities that were safe, affordable, and integrated with nature. Radburn's plan was ingenious; the problem occurred when "many elements of the Stein-Wright garden suburb model were easily bastardized for mass consumption by the production-oriented American real estate development industry," writes William Fulton (2002, 163). Bastardization of ideals was endemic to planning after World War II, especially in the United States where the profession suffered a loss of principles, direction, and eventually identity (Alofsin 2002; Campanella 2011). Its legitimacy besmirched by urban renewal and modernist failures, the profession is redefining itself, due in no small part to Duany—who made and celebrated history at Seaside.

Seaside, the most studied New Town project of the last quarter century, is a pedestrian-oriented community with short blocks, a mixed-use town center, interconnected neighborhoods, and a multifaceted park system. It has inspired dismissal, debate, New Urbanism, and, most important to this book, a reexamination of history. Early in his career, Duany chastised the planning profession for ceding its birth rite of physical design to become processors of development. In a prescient 1989 article, "Repent Ye Sinners, Repent," Ruth Knack (1989, 6) noticed that while Duany had his detractors, he also brought "new attention and focus to such figures as Elbert Peets, Raymond Unwin, and John Nolen." In the quarter century since, the practice of town planning and civic design has been re-invigorated, even in once-recalcitrant academic departments.

Randall Arendt (2012) recently made a plea to refocus planning education on place making and the physical planning of the natural and built environment. Arendt laments that students seldom evaluate historic planned communities, and they do not "analyze how the scale and arrangement of a community's component parts (such as neighborhoods, streets and boulevards, parks and open spaces) contribute to its functioning as a livable, walkable, bikeable, sustainable place." Arendt's article had 111 co-signatories, including Thomas Campanella, who argues planners risk irrelevance unless they embrace the profession's founding mission: creating "physical settings . . . to bring about a more prosperous, efficient, and equitable society. . . . We are entering the uncharted waters of urbanization on a scale the world has never seen. And we are not in the wheelhouse, let alone steering the ship. We might not even be on board" (2011, 149).

This book documents the identity—the iconicity—that increasing numbers of planners seek to recover. Emulation defines both flattery and iconicity. Olmsted's plan for Riverside anticipated Howard's concept of the garden city, and it became a point of study among design professionals. At Harvard University in the early 1900s, the Chicago suburb was employed to teach landscape architecture students the intricacies of laying out residential subdivisions. Graduates of the seminal program, such as John Nolen, integrated this knowledge with garden city principles to develop a template for the new town planning profession (Stephenson 2015). Letchworth, as noted, was reinterpreted across the industrial world, as the construction of communities such as Den-en Chôfu, "the Letchworth of Japan," inspired a new pattern of urban development. Menteng, a suburb of Jakarta, inspired imitation but also had a transcendent iconicity. Its modernist architecture not only integrated vernacular and international forms in a garden suburb but also merged east and west in a sustaining unity. Such pragmatic art is essential, especially in a megacity like Jakarta that is defining the urban future.

Menteng's special sense of place is both revered and threatened. Like in other elite communities (e.g., Hampstead Garden Suburb, the Uplands, and Jardim América), mansions have replaced smaller dwellings and private development has encroached on the public realm. The forces of change and development are relentless, and innovative policies have been implemented to safeguard the iconic community. Historic preservation has moved from preserving endangered buildings to protecting neighborhoods, which has led to establishing Conservation Areas in Great Britain, National Landscapes in Finland, Heritage protection in Italy, District Plan Systems in Japan, Conservation Management Plans in Australia, Cultural Heritage Sites in Brazil, the *Denkmalschutz* in Germany, *zones de protection du patrimoine architectural et paysager* in France, Heritage Conservation sites in Canada, and National Register Historic Districts in the United States. Yet, even with government protection, self-interest has imposed its will as "super houses" replace historic residences, private ventures impinge on public spaces, and autocentric schemes eviscerate environments scaled to foster face-to-face encounters and social capital. Den-en Chôfu offers the most unsettling testament, as André Sorenson and Shun-ichi J. Watanabe question within this volume "whether the efforts at preservation in this area really are about historic preservation at all, or if they are merely an attempt to protect resale values and an element of exclusivity."

Designed to procure the "good life," the iconic community has attracted residents desiring the "goods life." Gentrification is endemic, even in less elite sites with democratic pedigrees such as Garbatella (the "fortress of resistance" against fascism) and Soweto ("an iconic homeland of resistance"). Disinvestment, of course, is the most debilitating problem. In Wythenshawe, ill-conceived urban renewal and highway "improvement" projects damaged the communal fabric and dissipated the solidarity of its pioneering blue-collar residents. A functioning garden suburb devolved into a "problem estate" with a complex set of economic and social problems. Wythenshawe's rebirth is predicated on establishing new connections, from greenways to a tram system linking it to Manchester. Its iconicity, however, remains moored in its historic spaces. Wythenshawe's community gardens market its viability to potential investors, in the same manner that Sabaudia's public squares, Riverside's commons, Letchworth's interior greens, Tapiola's Silkkiniitty, Radburn's pedestrian underpass, Greenbelt's shopping-center esplanade, Römerstadt's allotment gardens, Sunnyside's courtyard gardens, Garbatella's intricate system of gardens, and Seaside's Ruskin Square create value and instill a sacredness of place.

The prescience of this book was to document how residents translated their sacredness of place into a set of principles to navigate the future. Restrictive deeds and regulations were not enough. If a people are to imbibe in its inherited social ideals, these ideals had to be celebrated and acted on. Civic activism is contingent on connections to people and their environs, and the iconic community was designed to procure face-to-face interaction. Laneways, greenways, parkways, and pedestrian paths were expected to foster social interconnections and, ideally, a reverence for place would take hold. The physical environment alone cannot inspire civic activism, but it can foment an aggressive stewardship of history, a "power of place" that galvanizes citizens to action.

Colonel Light Gardens and Greenbelt are especially instructive. In Australia, a state-appointed commission initially oversaw the garden suburb's development. By midcentury the community had taken form and, in the 1970s, a democratic governing system was in place. By then an active civic pride had forged, "the 'degree of persistence' often witnessed in elite planned suburbs," Robert Freestone and Christine Garnaut write in Chapter 6. Over the last quarter-century, Colonel Light Gardens is a textbook example of civic engagement. Its history is honored, as its plan continues to guide development on the "middle way" that Howard envisioned. Greenbelt, a community also designed for a range of incomes, never had the protections afforded its Australian counterpart. When the regional planning authority proposed running an arterial thoroughfare through Greenbelt's historic core, a battle ensued. Working in concert with city officials, hundreds of citizens turned out to successfully contest rezonings and autocentric roadway projects in the mid-1960s. This instituted a practice of "aggressive stewardship" that has helped Greenbelt evolve in a manner that met the needs of residents while protecting its unique cultural fabric. The establishment of the Greenbelt Museum testifies to the celebration of place that is endemic to a beloved community, the endpoint of the early planners' visions (Blake 1991).

Soweto, with its array of problems and its potential, might best portend the urban future. City officials and local residents established a training program to develop the expertise to transform the township into a system of "sustainable neighborhoods." The planning enterprise's best hope is to ground sustainability—which has become a ubiquitous buzzword—in reality (Owen 2009). Sustainability must take iconic form and the preceding pages offer a cue. The iconic community is a story of quality design and contested space. Residents disputing issues that impinge on their quality of life is "a fitting tribute," John Pittari contends in Chapter 10, "to the power of place."

The early planners designed communities to activate the human instinct of "adaptive fitness." They believed improved living conditions would translate into better social relations and a heightened sense of human dignity. World peace was the ultimate goal. Despite their wildly utopian aspirations, the planner's concept of environmentalism had merit. Genes are passed through individuals, but human evolution is predicated on the formation of complex groups. Thus, the brain is wired in two basic ways: individuals focus on either their immediate self-interest, or they think in a more reflective and rational manner on how to improve their communal existence. These impulses are in perpetual conflict and theologians, not surprisingly, argue that religion is intrinsic to survival because it translates our propensity for altruism into ritual (Sacks 2012). In the midst of the Industrial Revolution, urban reformers replaced mystic sacrament with plans to embed humanity's altruistic impulse into the daily walk of life. They envisioned a civic sacredness arising in communities that were both fit and fair. Their greatest accomplishment—establishing a system of collaborative international planning—is a legacy this book has brought to life.

Over a century has passed since experts drew prototype plans to secure the health, material security, and emotional well-being of people adapting to a new urban world. The iconic planned community remains a work in progress; it is both a treasure to preserve and a vital mix of humanity that must evolve. Whatever the future brings, this book offers an important guide for creating and maintaining places designed to sustain life and nurture our elemental instinct for communal life.

NOTES

1. *Webster's New Collegiate Dictionary* (Springfield, MA: G & C Merriam Company, 1973), 567.

2. *Philadelphia Evening Telegraph* (May 5, 1895).

3. In 1924, the International Garden City Association was renamed, becoming the International Federation of Town and Country Planning and Garden Cities. In 1931, the organization changed its name to the International Federation of Housing and Town Planning. See Buder 1990, 148.

4. Garden City Movement Hearing, *Senate Resolution 305 Sixty-Fourth Congress*, February 9, 1917 (Washington, DC: Government Printing Office).

5. Raymond Unwin to John Nolen, January 12, 1920; Unwin to Nolen, August 30, 1920, Box 8, Nolen Papers (NP), Special Collections, Cornell University, Ithaca, NY.

REFERENCES

Alanen, Arnold R., and Joseph A. Eden. 1987. *Main Street Ready-Made: The New Deal Community of Greendale, Wisconsin*. Madison: State Historical Society of Wisconsin.

Alofsin, Anthony. 2002. *The Struggle for Modernism: Architecture, Landscape Architecture and City Planning at Harvard*. New York: W. W. Norton.

Arendt, Randall. 2012. "Planning Education: A Better Balance." *Planetizen* (October 31). http://www.planetizen.com/node/59072.

Arnold, Joseph L. 1971. *The New Deal in the Suburbs: A History of the Greenbelt Town Program, 1935–1954*. Columbus: Ohio State University Press.

Baxter, Sylvester. 1902. "A Great Civic Awakening in America." *Century Magazine* (June): 255–64.

Beveridge, Charles, and Paul Rocheleau. 1995. *Frederick Law Olmsted: Designing the American Landscape*. New York: Rizzoli.

Blake, Casey. 1991. *The Beloved Community*. Chapel Hill: University of North Carolina Press.

Buder, Stanley. 1990. *Visionaries and Planners: The Garden City Movement and the Modern Community*. New York: Oxford University Press.

Bullock, Nicholas, and James Read. 1985. *The Movement for Housing Reform in Germany and France, 1840–1914*. New York: Cambridge University Press.

Campanella, Thomas. 2011. "The Death and Life of American Planning." In *Reconsidering Jane Jacobs*, edited by Max Page and Timothy Mennel, 141–60. Chicago: American Planning Association.

Christensen, Carol A. 1986. *The American Garden City and the New Towns Movement*. Ann Arbor: University of Michigan Research Press.

Collins, Christiane Crasemann. 2005. *Werner Hegemann and the Search for Universal Urbanism*. New York: W. W. Norton.

Creese, Walter L. 1994. "Introduction: An Extended Planning Progression." In Raymond Unwin, *Town Planning in Practice*, vii–xxvi. New York: Princeton Architectural Press.

Dennis, Richard. 2008. *Cities in Modernity: Representations and Productions of Metropolitan Space, 1840–1930*. New York: Cambridge University Press.

Duany, Andrés. 1994. "Preface." In Raymond Unwin, *Town Planning in Practice*, v. New York: Princeton Architectural Press.

Duany, Andrés, Elizabeth Plater-Zyberk, and Robert Alminana. 2003. *New Civic Art: Elements of Town Planning*. New York: Rizzoli.

Ellefsen, Karl O. 2010. "Exploring the German Model: Managing Urban Growth at the Turn of the 1900s." In *Manifestoes and Transformations in the Early Modern City*, edited by Christian H. Cordua, 105–24. Burlington, VT: Ashgate.

Fishman, Robert. 1982. *Urban Utopias in the 20th Century: Ebenezer Howard, Frank Lloyd Wright, Le Corbusier*. Cambridge, MA: MIT Press, 1982.

Friedman, Thomas. 2008. *Hot, Flat, and Crowded: Why We Need a Green Revolution—and How It Can Transform America*. New York: Farrar, Straus, and Giroux.

Fulton, William. 2002. "The Garden Suburb and the New Urbanism." In *From Garden City to Green City: The Legacy of Ebenezer Howard*, edited by Kermit C. Parsons and David Schuyler, 159–70. Baltimore: Johns Hopkins University Press.

Hall, Peter. 1988. *Cities of Tomorrow: An Intellectual History of Urban Planning and Design in the Twentieth Century*. Oxford: Blackwell.

Hancock, John. 1964. "John Nolen and the American City Planning Movement." PhD diss., University of Pennsylvania.

———. 1986. "What Is *Fair Must Be Fit*: Drawings and Plans by John Nolen, American City Planner." *Lotus International* 50: 20–39.

Hanisch, Ruth. 2010. "City Planning According to Artistic Principles, Vienna 1889." In *Manifestoes and Transformations in the Early Modern City*, edited by Christian H. Cordua, 125–36. Burlington, VT: Ashgate.

Howard, Ebenezer. 1902. *Garden Cities of To-morrow*. London: Swan Sonnenschein.

Hunt, Tristam. 2004. *Building Jerusalem: The Rise and Fall of the Victorian City*. London: Weidenfield and Nicolson.

Knack, Ruth. 1989. "Repent, Ye Sinners, Repent." *Planning* 44(8): 4–9.

Knepper, Cathy D. 2001. *Greenbelt, Maryland: A Living Legacy of the New Deal.* Baltimore: Johns Hopkins University Press.

Lang, Michael. 1999. *Designing Utopia: John Ruskin's Urban Vision for Britain and America.* New York: Black Rose Books.

Lindenfeld, David F. 1993. "The Myth of the Older Historical School of Economics." *Central European History* 26(4): 405–16.

Miller, Mervyn. 1992. *Raymond Unwin: Garden Cities and Town Planning.* Leicester: Leicester University Press.

———. 2002. "Garden City and Suburbs: At Home and Abroad." *Journal of Planning History* 1(1): 6–28.

Miller, Zane L. 1981. *Suburb: Neighborhood and Community in Forest Park, Ohio, 1935–1976.* Knoxville: University of Tennessee Press.

Newman, Peter, Timothy Beatley, and Heather Boyer. 2009. *Resilient Cities: Responding to Peak Oil and Climate Change.* Washington, DC: Island Press.

Nolen, John. 1909. *Montclair: The Preservation of Its Natural Beauty and Its Improvement as a Residence Town.* Montclair, NJ: Montclair Municipal Art Commission.

———. 1919. *New Ideals in the Planning of Villages, Towns, and Cities.* Boston: American City Bureau.

Olmsted, Frederick Law, Sr. 1992. "Preliminary Report upon the Proposed Suburb Village at Riverside." In *The Papers of Frederick Law Olmsted*, edited by David Schuyler and Jane Censer, vol. 6, 272–78. Baltimore: Johns Hopkins University Press.

Owen, David. 2009. *Green Metropolis.* New York: Riverhead Books.

Paulson, Henry. 2012. "How Cities Can Save China." *New York Times* (December 4).

Rodgers, Daniel T. 1998. *Atlantic Crossings: Social Politics in a Progressive Age.* Cambridge, MA: Belknap Press of Harvard University Press.

Sacks, Jonathan. 2012. "The Moral Animal." *New York Times* (December 23).

Santayana, George. 1913. "The Intellectual Temper of the Age." In *Winds of Doctrine.* New York: Charles Scribner.

Saunier, Pierre-Yves. 1999. "Atlantic Crosser. John Nolen and the Urban Internationale." *Planning History* 21(Spring): 23–31.

Scully, Vincent. 1991. *Architecture: The Natural and the Manmade.* New York: St. Martin's Press.

Stephenson, Bruce. 2015. *John Nolen Landscape Architect and City Planner.* Amherst, MA: University of Massachusetts Press.

Unwin, Raymond. 1994 (1909). "Introduction to the Second Edition." In Raymond Unwin, *Town Planning in Practice*, xi–xviii. New York: Princeton Architectural Press.

Ward, Stephen V. 1992. "The Garden City Introduced." In *The Garden City: Past, Present, and Future*, edited by Stephen V. Ward, 1–27. London: E & FN Spon.

Wilson, William H. 1990. *The City Beautiful Movement.* Baltimore: Johns Hopkins University Press.

CONTRIBUTORS

Arnold R. Alanen is Professor Emeritus of Landscape Architecture at the University of Wisconsin–Madison. The winner of several academic awards, he has written extensively on cultural landscapes and planned New Towns.

Carlos Roberto Monteiro de Andrade is Professor in the Institute of Architecture and Urbanism at the University of São Paulo, Brazil. His scholarship focuses on the theory and history of urbanism, nomadism, and the Situationist International.

Sandra Annunziata is Adjunct Professor at the Department of Architecture, University of Roma Tre, Rome. Her main research field is about urbanity and conflict in the neoliberal city with a focus on antigentrification policies and practices in Rome.

Robert Freestone is Professor of Planning in the Faculty of Built Environment at the University of New South Wales, Sydney. His research has focused on Australian planning history within an international context.

Christine Garnaut is Associate Research Professor in Planning and Architectural History and Director of the Architecture Museum at the University of South Australia in Adelaide, South Australia. Her research focuses on twentieth-century Australian planned environments.

Isabelle Gournay is Associate Professor of Architecture Emerita at the University of Maryland. Her publications continue to explore connections between urbanism, architecture, and housing in France and the United States.

Michael Hebbert is Professor Emeritus at the University of Manchester and the Bartlett School of Planning at University College London. His research interests span urban design, regeneration, governance, and development.

Susan R. Henderson is Professor of Architectural History at the School of Architecture, Syracuse University, New York. Her publications range from early twentieth-century esotericism to social architecture in Weimar Germany and Islamic architecture.

James Hopkins is University Historian at the University of Manchester, where he is responsible for researching and conserving the university's past. His research focuses on the history of knowledge institutions and their built environments.

Steven W. Hurtt is Professor and a former Dean in the School of Architecture, Planning, and Preservation at the University of Maryland. He has practiced architecture and held professional registrations in Washington, Indiana, Michigan, and Maryland.

Alena Kubova-Gauché formerly taught in the École Nationale Supérieure d'Architecture de Lyon, France. Her research explores avant-garde architecture, preservation, and industrial heritage.

Jean-François Lejeune is Professor of Architecture, Urban Design, and History at the University of Miami School of Architecture. His publications focus on architecture and urban design in Florida and Latin America, as well as New Town planning in Italy and Franco's Spain.

Maria Cristina da Silva Leme is Professor in the School of Architecture and Urbanism at the University of São Paulo, Brazil. Her research focuses on Brazilian and Latin American urbanism and planning history.

Larry McCann is Professor Emeritus of Geography at the University of Victoria in Canada. His research interests focus on the historical geography of the Canadian urban landscape.

Mervyn Miller is a practicing architect and town planner based in Hertfordshire, England, and he is a Fellow of the Royal Institute of British Architects. He has forty-five years of experience in practice and research in conservation of the historic built environment and the garden city movement.

John Minnery is Honorary Associate Professor in the School of Earth and Environmental Sciences at the University of Queensland, Brisbane, Australia. His research and publications are mainly in the areas of planning history and urban policy.

Angel David Nieves is Associate Professor in the History Department at San Diego State University. His research and community activism engage with issues of race, memory, preservation, gender, and nationalism in cities across the Global South.

John J. Pittari Jr. is Associate Professor in the School of Architecture, Planning and Landscape Architecture at Auburn University, Alabama. His research bridges city planning, landscape architecture, and architecture through a focus on community design, both past and present.

Gilles Ragot is Professor in Contemporary Art History and Chair of the Department of Art History and Archaeology at the Université Bordeaux-Montaigne.

He has published extensively on French architectural history and is a leading authority on the work of Le Corbusier.

David Schuyler is Arthur and Katherine Shadek Professor of the Humanities at Franklin & Marshall College, where he teaches American studies. His research has focused on urban planning and landscape history, Andrew Jackson Downing, and Frederick Law Olmsted.

Mary Corbin Sies is Associate Professor of American Studies at the University of Maryland. Her scholarship focuses on urban and planning history, historic preservation, and suburbia.

Christopher Silver is Professor of Urban and Regional Planning, and the former Dean, of the College of Design, Construction and Planning at the University of Florida, Gainesville. His research encompasses historical and contemporary issues in Indonesia and the United States.

André Sorensen is Professor of Urban Geography at the University of Toronto (Scarborough Campus), Canada. His research areas include metropolitan planning and governance, East Asia, and comparative historical analysis of the roles of institutions in shaping planning outcomes and cultures.

R. Bruce Stephenson is Professor of Environmental Studies at Rollins College in Winter Park, Florida. He has written extensively on New Urbanism, environmental history, John Nolen, and Lewis Mumford.

Shun-ichi J. Watanabe is Adjunct Professor of Urban Planning in the Department of Architecture, Tokyo University of Science. He has published and lectured widely on topics of comparative planning among the United States, Britain, and Japan.

INDEX

Page numbers followed by an *f* refer to figures; page numbers followed by a *t* refer to tables.

ACKNOWLEDGMENTS

This book has been a long time in the making and a labor of love for many people. We would like, first, to thank our contributors for their dedication to scholarship on the heritage of iconic planned communities and for their diligence and patience in responding to our many publication requests and deadlines.

This project has been supported by many institutions, whose generous grants and donations have made it possible to include the images and color plates that illustrate the character-defining features of iconic places and how they have fared over time. We are grateful to the Clarence S. Stein Institute for Urban and Landscape Studies at Cornell University and to Professor Eugenie L. Birch and the Penn Institute for Urban Research at the University of Pennsylvania for their generous grants. Special thanks go to Professor David Gordon (Queens University, Canada), who gave a strong endorsement of the project for our Stein Institute proposal.

Our home institutions also provided strong support for our book. We owe thanks to Dean Bonnie Thornton Dill and former Associate Dean Sheri L. Parks and the College of Arts and Humanities at the University of Maryland for a DRIF grant. Also at the University of Maryland, Professor Emerita Nancy Struna (former chair) and Budget Coordinator Julia John helped to shepherd through a grant from the Department of American Studies. Academic Coordinator Tammi Archer assisted with the preparation of grant applications and supplied astute trouble shooting and problem solving. The School of Architecture, Planning, and Preservation at the University of Maryland provided grants from the Architecture and the Preservation programs and from the Steven W. Hurtt Fund. We are grateful to Director Brian Kelly and Interim Dean Don Linebaugh and to Assistant Dean Ingrid Farrell for this support. We also received funding from the Faculty of Built Environment at the University of New South Wales in Australia, and from the Dean of Faculty at Hamilton College in Clinton, New York. Thanks go to Robert Freestone and Angel David Nieves, respectively, for facilitating those book subventions.

At the University of Pennsylvania Press, we benefited from the sage advice, expert knowledge, and patience of our editor, Robert Lockhart. Elizabeth S. Hallgren and, especially, Erica Ginsburg contributed perspicacious guidance through the production process.

We trace the origin of this volume to a meeting of the International Planning History Society (IPHS). In a session, "Iconic Planned Communities and the Challenges of Change," moderated by David Gordon, Isabelle Gournay and Mary Sies, John Pittari, Antonella de Michelis, and Mervyn Miller presented papers and Bruce Stephenson provided the comment. Robert Freestone was in the audience for the session and suggested afterward that we consider assembling an edited volume on the topic. Over the course of the next day, this group—with the addition of André Sorensen and Chris Silver—began to brainstorm both a set of iconic planned communities to be included and possible contributors. We are grateful to everyone for help in shaping the core ideas for this book.

At a meeting of the Society of American City and Regional Planning History (SACRPH), seventeen of our contributors presented working drafts of their chapters in a series of six sessions titled "The Heritage of Iconic Planned Communities." We owe a special debt to SACRPH and the planners and scholars who attended our sessions and generously provided their feedback and enthusiasm for a book that centered on heritage and preservation issues and on the state of these iconic places in the present. After hearing one or more of the sessions, John Reps and Eugenie Birch pushed us to contact Robert Lockhart from the University of Pennsylvania Press about the project, and we are so grateful for their introduction and recommendation. Larry Vale's address at the seventeenth IPHS conference in Delft, The Netherlands, in 2016 provided the inspiration for our revised introduction. Fellow SACRPH members Walter Greason, Angel David Nieves, David Schuyler, Christopher Silver, and Domenic Vitiello supported Mary Corbin Sies's research and editorial work on this project through their inspiring scholarship and friendship.

We would also like to acknowledge the two anonymous reviewers who read the entire manuscript and provided thoughtful critiques that enabled us to sharpen our arguments and provide a more carefully curated set of chapters.

This anthology might not have made it to publication without the diligent and skilled work of Michael Casiano, a former graduate student and now Ph.D. in American studies from the University of Maryland. Mike served as Mary Corbin Sies's editorial assistant throughout the long process of readying the manuscript for submission. Any amount of praise we lavish on Mike's efforts, his eye for detail, his technical skills, and his intelligent handling of the editorial work will not do justice to his role in bringing this volume to fruition.